THE SLAVOPHILE CONTROVERSY

The Slavophile Controversy

*History of a Conservative Utopia in
Nineteenth-Century Russian Thought*

BY

ANDRZEJ WALICKI

TRANSLATED BY

HILDA ANDREWS-RUSIECKA

CLARENDON PRESS·OXFORD
1975

Oxford University Press, Ely House, London, W.1.

GLASGOW   NEW YORK   TORONTO   MELBOURNE   WELLINGTON
CAPE TOWN   IBADAN   NAIROBI   DAR ES SALAAM   LUSAKA   ADDIS ABABA
DELHI   BOMBAY   CALCUTTA   MADRAS   KARACHI   LAHORE   DACCA
KUALA LUMPUR   SINGAPORE   HONG KONG   TOKYO

ISBN 0 19 822507 5

First published in Poland in 1964 under the title:
W Kręgu Konserwatywnej utopii. Struktura i przemiany rosyjskiego słowianofilstwa
© Państwowe Wydawnictwo Naukowe, Warsaw, 1964

*Printed in Great Britain by
Butler & Tanner Ltd, Frome and London*

Acknowledgements

ON the occasion of the publication of the English edition of this work I should like to take the opportunity of thanking all those friends of mine who have helped in one way or another to bring this about. I must express my special gratitude, in the first place, to Sir Isaiah Berlin who, during the course of our first conversation in 1960, encouraged me to undertake the writing of this book. Later he discussed with me various issues raised in it, helped to arrange its publication in England, and also devoted much time and effort to smoothing out numerous difficulties arising out of the translation. I am also most grateful to Mr. Harry Willetts for his considerable share in dealing with such difficulties.

Special thanks are due to the two Oxford colleges (St. Antony's in 1960 and All Souls in 1966/67 and 1973) where visiting Fellowships enabled me to enjoy many fruitful exchanges with scholars in my own and related fields.

Finally, knowing how much effort is involved in making a translation of a specialist work of this kind, I should like to express my warm thanks to the translator, Mrs. Hilda Andrews-Rusiecka.

ANDRZEJ WALICKI

Warsaw,
April 1975.

Contents

Introduction

IN writing this work it was not the author's intention to demonstrate the application of certain methodological premisses, or to prove a preconceived thesis; the main purpose, rather, was to investigate and present a complex of ideas, the study of which is indispensable to a full understanding of nineteenth-century Russian intellectual history, or even nineteenth-century history as a whole. Nevertheless, in order to define the theme and scope of the work, it may be found useful to explain certain methodological principles.

As the chapter headings show, this study is both more and less than a straightforward historical account of Russian Slavophilism. Apart from the Slavophiles themselves, other thinkers who were not Slavophiles, or were even antagonistic towards them, are also dealt with in some detail, while much information has been omitted that could not properly be left out of a traditional monograph. There is no account, for instance, of the minor members and sympathizers of the movement, no analysis of Slavophile journals, and no detailed treatment of actual literary polemics and the like. Even biographical information about the leading Slavophile thinkers has been reduced to a minimum. If stress is thus laid on the different premisses underlying this work, it is not in order to disparage the biographical approach, with its emphasis on the subject's family background, education, reading, private life, and friendships, but rather to avoid possible misunderstanding concerning the author's aims. Moreover, the preliminary discussion of certain methodological premisses and terminological usage will, it is hoped, provide a useful introduction to the main argument of the book. In his formulation of these premisses the author lays no claim to originality—it is only their application to this particular historical material that may be called original.

The basic 'research unit' in this book—which is both the subject and the tool of research—is the 'phenomenon of the collective consciousness' known as *Weltanschauung*, view of the world.[1] The use of this term implies that it is a comprehensive vision of the world, a meaningful structure and system of cognitive, ethical, and aesthetic values that is internally coherent within its own chosen framework. *Weltanschauung* conceived thus differs both from the looser meaning of the word and from philosophical theory, which is always an expression and conceptualization of a particular view of the world, but never identical with it. The same *Weltanschauung* can be expressed in many philosophical theories, while a single philosophical theory can combine elements from different views of the world, since theoretical coherence does not necessarily imply a coherence of the underlying system of values. A particular *Weltanschauung* may, moreover, be expressed in theological, economic, or historical writings, or its principal vehicle may be works of art. Since *Weltanschauungen* are essentially atheoretical, they need not be expressed through concepts, but find a variety of expressions, thus enabling the investigator to use the tool of comparative analysis and to search for the 'common denominator' in many formally different and apparently heterogeneous cultural products.[2] The history of *Weltanschauungen*—today a discipline *in statu nascendi* in which many Marxist and non-Marxist scholars are showing growing interest[3]—would put an end to the largely conventional and old-fashioned 'division of labour' in scholarship and would encourage the reintegration of artificially isolated branches of the humanities.

What distinguishes a *Weltanschauung* conceived as a totality of a certain sort from the concrete and empirical consciousness of different social groups, is its structural unity, an identifiable homogeneity of what might be called its thought-style. Empirical consciousness is always more or less eclectic, particularly

---

[1] Lucien Goldmann defines *Weltanschauung* as a phenomenon of the collective consciousness which attains maximum clarity in the consciousness of the thinker or poet, and, at the same time, as a methodological tool which enables the historian to distinguish between the essential and inessential aspects of a given cultural product.

Cf. Lucien Goldmann, *The Hidden God. A Study of Tragic Vision in the Pensées of Pascal and the Tragedies of Racine*, trans. by Philip Thody (The Humanity Press, New York 1964).

[2] See Karl Mannheim, *Essays on the Sociology of Knowledge* (Oxford University Press, New York 1952), p. 38 ('On the Interpretation of *Weltanschauung*').

[3] Among the pioneers of this discipline in Poland one should mention especially L. Koczakowski and B. Batko.

at times of increased social mobility; in order to separate significant from fortuitous elements, it is necessary to make use of the category of *Weltanschauung* as a comprehensive and coherent structure of meaning whose 'purest' manifestations are normally to be found in cultural 'objects'. As L. Goldmann has aptly put it:

> The sociology of knowledge may study world-views on two different planes, that of the *real* consciousness of the group, as researchers such as Weber and Groethuysen have studied them, for example, or that of their coherent, exceptional expression in great works of philosophy or art, or even in the lives of certain exceptional individuals. (The latter plane corresponds more or less to the maximum of *potential* consciousness.) The two planes complement and mutually support each other. Though it may not seem so at first, it must be said that the second plane is often easier to study than the first, precisely because world-views are expressed there with more clarity and precision.[1]

Slavophile doctrine, I would suggest, is a particularly rewarding subject of research to the historian of *Weltanschauungen*, and particularly intractable to classifications by a traditional specialist in intellectual taxonomy. Like the majority of nineteenth-century Russian thinkers,[2] the Slavophiles did not fit into the traditional schemes which presuppose a ready-made 'intellectual division of labour'; their doctrine included not only philosophical but also theological and historical constructions, in which unity can be discovered only if they are seen in terms of the pattern of a *Weltanschauung*. The many different interpretations of Slavophilism in specialist literature were not only the product of the ideological but also of the professional background of the author, whose treatment varied according to whether he was primarily a philosopher, an economist, a literary historian, or a theologian. The attempt to interpret Slavophilism as a single comprehensive *Weltanschauung* implies the conscious acceptance of certain limitations; I therefore have, for example, refrained from a critique of philosophical conceptions in Slavophile thought, and from

---

[1] Quoted from Lucien Goldmann, *The Human Sciences and Philosophy*, trans. by Hayden V. White and Robert Anchor (Jonathan Cape, London 1969), p. 130.

[2] See Andrzej Walicki, *Osobowość a historia* (Personality and History), *Studia z dziejów literatury i myśli rosyjskiej* (Warsaw 1959), pp. 6–7.

trying to fit their historical works into the context of Russian historiography. The range of a student of *Weltanschauungen* does not synthetize, but cuts across the fields of interests of the specialists in various humane studies; he is concerned with the history of various branches of knowledge and human creativity only in so far as they express a certain view of the world; the purely theoretical or purely aesthetic value of the works that interest him are for him a matter of marginal importance.

A *Weltanschauung* is, of course, social in origin, and research into it cannot therefore be restricted to a purely immanent analysis. In order to define the 'type' of a given *Weltanschauung* and identify the mechanism of its development, one must analyse its sociological content and establish its relation to the historical structures of society. This should not be confused with microgenetic research, which deduces the ideas of a given thinker from a sociological interpretation of biographical factors. Research of this kind, which is based on an over-simplified model of causal relationships, usually gets bogged down in a vulgarized socio-psychological interpretation and is incapable of explaining why social classes have been represented by thinkers and writers who were not born into these classes and were brought up in quite a different milieu.[1] The approach aimed at here is both historical and structural and attempts to explain the views investigated by placing them within the total structure of the society that contained and determined them. This approach does not assume that an individual's ideas are directly dependent on the sum total of his social involvements (which are often quite fortuitous), but

[1] See Marx's apt remarks in *The Eighteenth Brumaire of Louis Bonaparte*:
'Only one must not form the narrow-minded notion that the petty bourgeoisie, on principle, wishes to enforce an egoistic class interest. Rather, it believes that the *special* conditions of its emancipation are the *general* conditions within the frame of which alone modern society can be saved and the class struggle avoided. Just as little must one imagine that the democratic representatives are indeed all shopkeepers or enthusiastic champions of shopkeepers. According to their education and their individual position they may be as far apart as heaven from earth. What makes them representatives of the petty bourgeoisie is the fact that in their minds they do not get beyond the limits which the latter do not get beyond in life, that they are consequently driven, theoretically, to the same problems and solutions to which material interest and social position drive the latter practically. This is, in general, the relationship between the *political* and *literary representatives* of a class and the class they represent.' (Quoted from: K. Marx and F. Engels, *Selected Works in Two Volumes*, London 1950, vol. i, pp. 249–50.)

rather that there is a correlation between structures of thought and imagination on the one hand, and the social structures— and types of human relationships determined by them—on the other. This gives rise to a certain hypothesis which results in- directly, I would suggest, from the basic thesis of historical materialism. This hypothesis, which might be called anthropo- centric, implies that at the core of every view of the world lies a specific philosophy of man and society. This philosophy is not always conscious of course; frequently—in most instances even—basic problems of view of the world appear in disguise as 'crypto-problems' concealed in an area of speculation that is seemingly 'pure metaphysics', 'pure science', or 'pure art'.[1] This does not mean that man's cognitive curiosity is confined to historical and social issues; it is only one of the consequences of the elementary truth that men belong to the world of human kind and in their reasoning reflect one or another of the laws governing this world.

Two other terms that occur frequently in the following pages are 'ideology' and 'utopia'. While the word 'utopia' is used in the wider meaning it has acquired in the sociology of know- ledge, it should be made clear that the terms 'ideology' and 'utopia' in this study do not correspond exactly to the defini- tions given by Karl Mannheim.[2] His distinction between the 'delusive' function of ideology and the 'debunking' function of utopia appears to be somewhat sterile in view of the fact that in almost all concrete situations these two functions are in- separable. As used in this book the terms *Weltanschauung* and utopia both belong to the domain of ideological phenomena, although not every socio-political ideology can be called a utopia or a comprehensive *Weltanschauung*: it is because *Weltanschauungen* and utopias are *comprehensive* that they differ from ideologies.[3] The term *Weltanschauung* implies a view of the *world*, a view of man and society as a totality; ideology

---

[1] See B. Baczko's postscript to H. Kamieński, *Filozofia ekonomii materialnej ludzkiego społeczeństwa* (The Philosophy of the Material Economy of Human Society) (Warsaw 1959), pp. 500–1.

[2] See Karl Mannheim, *Ideology and Utopia* (New York–London 1952).

[3] In *The Human Sciences and Philosophy* (pp. 117–18) Lucien Goldmann makes a similar differentiation, but links it to the questionable thesis that only entire social classes can be carriers of a view of the world (and then only during their period of decline).

(when it is not a view of the world) only implies certain political and social opinions. Specific socio-political ideologies are usually inspired by *Weltanschauungen*, although the correlation is not necessarily direct; ideologies always contain certain elements deriving from *Weltanschauungen*, but need not themselves be comprehensive views of the world. Members of a nationalistic political party, for example, share a common ideology—a set of motivations to justify their party programme —but need not share a common view of the world; at the same time there are certain situations when men who share a view of the world may not have a common ideological platform. It is important not to confuse the totality of a *Weltanschauung* with complete knowledge of what is to be done. A vision of the world can only give a general and indirect answer to practical problems—an answer that is open to different interpretations, depending on pragmatic factors or differences of opinion on specific details.[1] On the other hand, a total programme of action with concrete solutions for all outstanding social and political questions need not be rooted in any comprehensive and integral view of the world.

Utopia—at least according to the definition I should like to propose—is a specific form of *Weltanschauung*.[2] The quality it shares with the latter is its *totality*: large-scale social utopias demonstrate a comprehensive style of thought and enrich our understanding of historical processes. Their distinguishing feature is that they transcend reality, thereby revealing a powerful tension between the ideal and the actual. This tension, it should be added, can become introverted and thus not lead to any activity aimed at changing the world; violent criticism of existing circumstances can sometimes be a form of a defence-mechanism, a rationalization (in the Freudian sense of the

---

[1] J. Szacki in *Ojczyzna, naród, rewolucja* (Fatherland, Nation, Revolution) (Warsaw 1962), p. 202, has aptly noticed that 'political divisions should not be made absolute, since they are not always permanent and, what is more, rarely have their exact counterpart in the domain of *Weltanschauungen*'.

[2] Utopias and utopianism as part of the history of ideas should not, of course, be confused with literary utopias. Utopian thinkers do not necessarily write 'utopias' nor are the authors of various 'utopias' necessarily utopians, since their works can belong to the domain of satire or literary extravaganza. Sir Thomas More's *Utopia* would not cease to be a utopia (in the sense of a specific literary genre) if it could be proved to be a mere joke and not a serious expression of the *Weltanschauung* of its author.

word) of an equivocal and threatened mode of existence. The possibility of this type of situation provides the justification for the use of the term 'conservative utopia' introduced by Mannheim.

To sum up: all socio-political ideologies are rooted in certain views of the world and all views of the world and utopias belong to the domain of ideological phenomena; not all ideologies, however, are comprehensive views of the world and not all views of the world are utopias. Since in colloquial usage the term 'ideology' is often interchangeable with 'view of the world', the term 'comprehensive view of the world' will be used whenever it becomes necessary to emphasize the difference between the two.

In the following pages the term *Weltanschauung* (or view of the world) is also applied to an individual thinker's view of the world; the term 'social *Weltanschauung*' is therefore used whenever the need arises to emphasize that we are dealing with a wider category, a supra-individual thought structure. This study does not attempt (as Goldmann has attempted to do) to reduce the whole wealth of individual *Weltanschauungen* to just a few basic visions of the world. Its aim, which is perhaps less ambitious but more easily attainable in the light of present knowledge, is to explain the *Weltanschauungen* of individual thinkers by placing them within the wider context of certain comprehensive structures (social *Weltanschauungen*), and to explain the latter within the context of the global structure of a given society. Social *Weltanschauungen*, whatever their definition, are instruments that enable us to investigate the *Weltanschauungen* of individual thinkers; the results of such research into individual views of the world in their turn correct and give precision to our knowledge of the social views of the world they express, and so on *ad infinitum*.

Two terms that still remain to be discussed are 'conservatism' and the adjective 'conservative', both of which occur frequently in this work. Generally speaking, an ideology can be described as 'conservative' either because of its function or because of its content: the first definition refers to ideologies which, in a given situation, are hostile to change (in this sense it is possible to talk of conservative liberals or conservative communists) and implies that they fulfil a conservative function in relation to existing reality (although they can fulfil quite different functions in different conditions). The second definition is concerned with ideas from the point of view of their social content, without regard to their actual social function; these definitions in turn may be both unhistorical and historical.[1] In this study the term 'conservatism' is used according to the historical variant of the 'content definition' of conservatism, and a distinction is made between conservative *ideologies* and conservative *views of the world*. This distinction between conservative ideologies and conservatism as a comprehensive view of the world corresponds to some extent to Mannheim's differentiation between 'traditionalism' and 'modern conservatism'—a view of the world which emerged at a time when the existence of feudal society was already threatened and analysed the very foundations of the 'conservative existence' from a conservative standpoint in order to give new validation to everything that had previously been accepted without reflection.

When we speak of conservatism as a specific historical *Weltanschauung*, what we have in mind is a certain thought-style antagonistic to bourgeois liberalism and the rationalistic–individualistic philosophy of the Enlightenment; a style which has emerged as a response to the French Revolution and the Industrial Revolution in England.[2] Different variants of this style are represented by a large group of thinkers that includes

[1] In his 'Conservatism as an Ideology', *American Political Science Review*, ii (1957), S. P. Huntington lists three definitions of conservatism: (1) conservatism as a feudal and aristocratic ideology, (2) the 'autonomous' definition, according to which conservatism is an entirely autonomous and universal system of ideas and values (an illustration of this definition is to be found in R. Kirk, *The Conservative Mind* (Chicago 1953), which attempts to set up a six-point canon of conservatism) and (3) a 'situational' definition. We can say that the first definition is in fact a historical content definition (one of a number of possible definitions), while the 'autonomous' definition would coincide with what I have called the *unhistorical* content definition.

[2] See Karl Mannheim, 'Conservative Thought' in *Essays on Sociology and Social Psychology* (London 1953). Although this work is undoubtedly the most important attempt made so far to formulate a structural analysis of eighteenth- and nineteenth-century conservative thought, it has, in our opinion, two serious shortcomings. In the first place, Mannheim bases his generalizations almost entirely on German material (the French 'traditionalists', for instance, are not considered worthy of equally serious treatment as representatives of conservative thought. Our standpoint on this matter is presented in the chapter on Chaadaev). Secondly, it is difficult to agree with Mannheim's definition of Hegelian philosophy as *sui generis* the culmination of conservative thought (see below, chapter 7).

Burke, Coleridge and Carlyle in England, the theocratic traditionalists in France, and the conservative romanticists in Germany. The classic (albeit not the only) manifestation of this style is conservative romanticism, a richly diversified philosophical, political, and literary trend that was represented in Russia by the Slavophiles, who made their own original contribution to its history.

After these brief introductory remarks, it might be found useful to add a short description of each section, in order to present the subject-matter and approach of the book in somewhat greater detail.

The book consists of four distinctly separate but related parts, each of which represents an attempt to show different aspects of Slavophilism from different point of view and in different 'significant relationships'.

Part One ('The Antecedents of Slavophilism') sets out to determine the place of Slavophilism in the evolution of Russian conservative thought, to examine it from the point of view of its ideological antecedents, and thus to show the emergence of several important constitutive elements of the Slavophile doctrine. The author attempts to trace the transformation of the traditional conservatism of the hereditary nobility into romantic conservatism, to discover how the characteristic antitheses of 'ancient' and 'modern' Russia (Shcherbatov and Karamzin), Russia and Europe (Pogodin), and 'ancient' and 'modern' Europe (Odoevsky) made their appearance and functioned in pre-Slavophile Russian thought, and to show what part was played in this process by the phenomenon of 'Europeanization' or 'Westernization'—the organic integration of Russia's enlightened élite into the Western European cultural orbit. The main purpose of this section, it should perhaps be made clear, was not to trace influences or to make a genetic study of ideas, but rather to present a structural analysis of pre-Slavophile conservative trends in Russian thought and to obtain comparative material indispensable to the understanding and structuralization of the Slavophile view of the world. This is based on the conviction that in order to grasp the regularities which explain the emergence of a given ideology and to determine its structure and historical individuality it is necessary to compare it with other related ideologies and to place it within a specific development continuum.

Chapter 3 ('The Paradox of Chaadaev') occupies a special place in Part One, since it deals with a thinker who ought perhaps to be called an antagonist rather than a precursor of the Slavophiles. However, in contrast to the liberal–democratic Westernizers of the 1840s, Chaadaev was an antagonist who largely shared his opponents' *conservative* system of values. Chaadaev's ideas, and especially his philosophy of Russian history, acted as a catalyst in the crystallization of Slavophile ideology; an analysis of these ideas helps to explain why the conservative romanticism of the nobility was bound to be opposed to Westernism (even to conservative Westernism and the idealization of medieval Europe), and why at the same time it was forced to assume a utopian character, in which the idealized past was contrasted sharply with the criticized present. It is part of the thesis of this chapter that Slavophilism— especially Ivan Kireevsky's philosophy of history—was *sui generis* a 'reply to Chaadaev'.

Part Two ('Classical Slavophilism') attempts at a sociological–structural analysis of Slavophilism and a comparison of its main variants represented by Ivan Kireevsky, Alekseï Khomyakov, and Konstantin Aksakov. The most general conclusion arising from this analysis, namely that Slavophilism was not merely one variety of conservative sociopolitical ideology, but conservatism in the sense of a *comprehensive Weltanschauung* or 'thought-style', also determined the method of interpretation. The Slavophiles' historical, theological, and philosophical conceptions were analysed from the point of view of their function within a larger view of the world, as the projection of a specific comprehensive vision of the world which was largely concerned with problems of personal identity and interpersonal relations, of the role of the individual and his relation to his social bonds. In turn this same view of the world has been interpreted as an expression of tensions within the existing social reality, as the 'raising to the level of consciousness' of an anachronistic mode of existence subjected to the threat of historical change. In view of the valuable sociological insight shown by the Slavophiles—a type of insight that is characteristic of most representatives of conservative thinking—certain statements made by the Slavophiles themselves have been used as a kind of sociological self-analysis, a commentary on their work, and the attempt was made to translate their conceptions into the language of sociology. This part of the present work owes a great debt to the pioneering studies of Ferdinand Tönnies and Max Weber, who introduced certain historical and conceptual categories which are useful tools for analysing the fundamental divergence of *Weltanschauungen* during the first half of the nineteenth century, and the consequent dispute over capitalism (to use a slight over-simplification) in which representatives of all philosophical trends in Germany were engaged either directly or indirectly.

Part Three ('Confrontations') probably requires a more detailed commentary. Its aim was to present the Slavophiles from the point of view of their immediate opponents and, conversely, to look at the opponents from the point of view of the Slavophiles; to trace their intellectual contacts and to show to what extent they were interested in the same problems. This particular approach was determined by the conviction that the structural analysis of every important social ideology requires first of all a precise analysis of the implicit principles, according to which it accepts or rejects other ideologies; consequently, that the significance of any ideological structure can only be understood by reference to its 'negative frame of reference'.[1] This methodological approach is especially fruitful when applied to periods of intense intellectual controversy, when there is general awareness of a historical turning-point or crisis. The classic example is the great controversy which shook Europe from the French Revolution to the revolution of 1848, in which the Russian Slavophiles also had their share. It is not for nothing that Karl Mannheim called the conservative utopia a 'counter-utopia' to the liberal utopia.

The Slavophiles' main opponents were the group of thinkers known as Westernizers (*zapadniki*); it is characteristic that the names by which both movements came to be known were invented in the heat of the argument by the opponents, so that

[1] See Z. Stefanowska's remarks on the 'type of dependence that results from the polemical attitude'. Z. Stefanowska, *Historia i profecja* (History and Prophecy). Studium o 'Księgach narodu i pielgrzymstwa polskiego' Adama Mickiewicza (Warsaw 1962), pp. 17–20, 81.

the terms 'Slavophilism' and 'Westernism' at first had a pejorative tinge. [1]In the history of Russian thought the Slavophile/ Westernizer controversy was a most fertile source of new ideas, a stage whose significance became clearer with the passage of time. Certain historians (Milyukov and Plekhanov, for instance),[2] were inclined to interpret almost the entire history of Russian social thought as the evolution of a complex set of problems which only found fully conscious expression in the dispute between the Slavophiles and the Westernizers. It is not necessary to subscribe to this view to see that its widespread acceptance was in itself symptomatic.

Hegelian philosophy played a decisive role in the intellectual evolution of the leading Westernizers (Belinsky, Herzen, Granovsky, and Kavelin). Chapter 7—a confrontation of Slavophilism and Hegelianism (which the Slavophiles regarded as the last word in 'Western rationalism')—is therefore intended as an introduction to the polemics between the Slavophiles and Westernizers and helps to place them within the context of the famous Hegelian controversy in Germany. Chapter 8 ('The Roots of Westernism') is a continuation of chapter 7 and attempts to trace the specific quality of the Westernizers' search for a philosophy, its socio-psychological content, and a pattern of its successive stages. Its main purpose is to show the relevance of the Slavophile/Westernizer controversy to the processes of individuation and rationalization of the consciousness which deeply affected the Russian intellectual élite in the 1830s and '40s. In literature these processes led to the portrayal of the 'superfluous men' and in social thought to the emphasis on the problem of the cleavage between the intelligentsia and the common people, and the former's alienation and spiritual 'homelessness'. This was the common experience which determined the unity of the generation known as the 'men of the forties', a generation whose two

[1] See chapter 9.

[2] See P. Milyukov, 'Natsionalizm i obshchestvennoe mnenie' in *Ocherki po istorii russkoĭ kulturȳ*, part 3 (St. Petersburg 1901); and G. V. Plekhanov, *Istoriya russkoĭ obshchestvennoĭ mȳsli, Sochineniya*, vols. xx–xxiii (Moscow–Leningrad 1923–6). Like Milyukov, whom he frequently criticized, Plekhanov interpreted Russian history as the struggle of the Eastern (Asiatic) and Western element, of nationalism and 'Europeanism'. He considered Marxism in Russia to be the continuation and final triumph of Westernism.

aspects were Slavophilism and Westernism. Using Mannheim's concept of 'generations', one might say that the Slavophiles and Westernizers represented two antagonistic 'generation units' within the framework of one 'actual generation'.[1] This relationship is not rendered invalid by the fact that the Slavophiles opposed the processes of individuation and proclaimed that 'national principles' and the Orthodox faith protected them against their corrupting influence; as has been aptly pointed out, anti-individualism is also a product of individualism.[2]

Chapter 9 ('Slavophiles and Westernizers') represents an attempt to systematize the Westernizing point of view on all controversial questions of importance, and to construct models of the two mutually antagonistic utopias represented by Slavophilism and Westernism. It does not set out to give a detailed account of discussions in the press, of minor incidents that accompanied them, or of unsuccessful attempts at reconciliation, etc.; all the bitter ramifications of the debate have not been traced in detail, but instead stress is laid on certain matters that did not figure in the public polemics but nevertheless played an essential part in the controversy. In fact, what this chapter attempts to do is to reveal the essential structure of the Slavophile/Westernizer controversy without describing too much of its details of its successive stages. It should be noted that the treatment of Westernism called for a much greater degree of structuralization than that of Slavophilism. The Westernizers were far less homogeneous as a group and were brought together by a common viewpoint of certain problems rather than by a shared view of the world. It was therefore necessary to construct an 'ideal model' of Westernism,[3]

---

[1] See K. Mannheim, 'The Problem of Generations' in *Essays on the Sociology of Knowledge* (London 1952), pp. 302–4.

[2] See A. Hauser, *The Philosophy of Art History* (London 1959), p. 119.

[3] Any 'ideal model' involves, of course, a certain deformation of the empirical reality, which is the necessary prize for obtaining a more clear and comprehensible picture. Cf. L. Kolakowsky's apt remarks on this: 'En d'autres termes, l'histoire ne peut acquérir un sens que si ou la soumet à des déformations dont la diversité est pratiquement infinie dans les limites de la corrrection historique. Le désir d'éliminer tout arbitraire, c'est-à-dire de parvenir à une image universelle, est inefficace, compte tenu de l'objectif que l'on se propose; il peut, par contre, être opératif si l'on veut retirer au tableau ainsi brossé ces contrastes de coluecrs grâce auxquels il peut être lisible en tout que tableau.... Nous proposons donc une méthode que l'on pourrait appeler une *historiographie expressioniste* qui, en organisant les éléments

whereas for the Slavophiles it was enough to note the general conclusions arising out of the analysis of their view of the world.

Part Four ('The Disintegration of Slavophilism. Different Continuations') analyses the changes that took place within Slavophilism and the absorption of various aspects of Slavophile doctrine by other ideological structures. It sets out to show how changed historical circumstances led to the 'de-utopianization' of Slavophilism, how and why this entailed the disintegration of Slavophilism as a comprehensive view of the world, and how it gradually merged into Panslavism or dwindled into an ideological apology for a specific variant of landowning capitalism. In both instances the total vision of the world—the anti-capitalist utopia determined by sociological factors, but seeing beyond immediate egotistical class interests—was superseded by a socio-political ideology seeking to achieve particular and limited aims and tending more and more to subordinate principles to practical considerations. The last four chapters deal with the problem of Slavophile influence on Russian thought in the second half of the nineteenth century. The main purpose of these last chapters was, first, to show Slavophilism from various perspectives, to indicate the many ways in which its influence made itself felt in different fields; and, secondly, to show that it supplies a 'frame of reference' that helps to explain many problems in the history of Russian thought in the second half of the nineteenth century and is indispensable to a fuller understanding of a whole range of political, historical, and philosophical opinions that were frequently mutually hostile and exclusive. This aim was also constantly kept in mind in earlier parts of this study. From this point of view the theme of the work might be summed up as 'Slavophilism and Slavophile themes in nineteenth-century Russian intellectual history'.

One more aspect of this book perhaps needs to be stressed. In any work of this kind a certain degree of modernization is

---

empiriques du monde historique, les subordonne à une idée centrale conférant une sens à chacun des éléments pris à part et se manifestant dans le système des constructions idéales.' (L. Kolakowsky, *Chrétiens sans église. Le conscience religieuse et le lien confessionnel au xviie siècle*, Editions Gallimard, Paris 1969, p. 355.)

clearly unavoidable. While one must be careful not to succumb to the temptation of a superficial updating, the study of historical documents necessarily requires the investigator to establish some kind of relationship between his source material and his own times. As far as the subject-matter of this study is concerned, we are in a privileged position, since the issues debated by the Slavophiles and Westernizers (the individual's relation to society, types of social integration and spiritual culture, the problem of freedom and alienation, the emancipation of personality, and so on) are no less topical today. One might even venture to suggest that, at any rate in some instances, these issues can be placed in a more meaningful context from our twentieth-century perspective, thus making it possible to discover new depths in old nineteenth-century controversies.

PART ONE

THE ANTECEDENTS OF SLAVOPHILISM

THE study of the antecedents of an ideology has two different aspects: it can be conceived as the investigation of the genesis of its constitutive elements, or as a search for frames of reference. In this study the second method has been chosen since it accords with the methodological premisses of the work as a whole. The meticulous dating of first occurrences or the genetic study of various ideas and motifs in Slavophile doctrine cannot be an aim in itself. In this introductory part I have been concerned rather less with tracing 'influences', than with drawing attention to certain clusters of problems in pre-Slavophile Russian thought which help to put Slavophilism into a meaningful context and to determine its place in Russian intellectual history.

This conception called for a far-reaching selection of material and thus made it possible to discuss the problem of the precursors of Slavophilism in terms of the history of three antitheses: (1) that between 'ancient' and 'modern' Russia (i.e. retrospective criticism of the Petrine reforms and the consequent retrospective idealization of 'ancient' Russia); (2) that between Russia and Europe; and (3) that between 'ancient' and 'modern' Europe which emerged in Western European conservative thought as a response to the social changes brought about by the French Revolution. There is a certain analogy between the first and third antitheses, although this is limited in scope: the first emerged in Russia in the eighteenth century, when the foundations of the feudal system were not yet threatened, while the second emerged in Western Europe in reaction to a new (capitalist) type of social formation. One might say that an essential (though not in itself sufficient) prerequisite of Slavophilism was the appearance of an ideological situation in which Russian conservative criticism of the Petrine reforms could merge organically with Western philosophical romanticism and the conservative–romantic criticism of capitalism. A situation of this kind, complicated by the specific local atmosphere and conditions, came about in Russia during the reign of Nicholas I.

I

'Ancient' and 'Modern' Russia in the Eyes of the Conservative Historians

THE views of Prince Mikhail Shcherbatov, the chief ideologist of the aristocratic opposition during the reign of Catherine, did not, and indeed could not, exert a direct influence on the formation of Slavophile thought. His passionate and unpublishable articles were not intended for publication and did not, in fact, appear until the middle of the nineteenth century. In 1858 Herzen published Shcherbatov's most important and at the same time most 'Slavophile' essay *On the Corruption of Morals in Russia* together with Radishchev's *Journey from Saint Petersburg to Moscow*, thus confronting a left-wing and right-wing critique of autocracy. 'Prince Shcherbatov and A. Radishchev', Herzen wrote, 'represent two extreme points of view on the Russia of Catherine II. Like gloomy sentinels guarding two different gates, they gaze, Janus-like, in two opposite directions.' Radishchev looked forward into the future, while Shcherbatov, 'turning his back on the licentious court of his day and gazing at the gateway through which strode Peter I, sees the solemn and boastful Muscovy beyond; to the angry old man the boring and semi-savage existence of our ancestors appeared some sort of lost ideal'.[1] In this juxtaposition of Shcherbatov and Radishchev Herzen saw a certain analogy with the later Slavophiles and Westernizers, whom he also compared to Janus gazing in two different directions.[2] 'Prince Shcherbatov', Herzen wrote, 'reached his Slavophile conclusions by the same path that has led some young men in Moscow today to adopt Slavophile ideas. Seeing no end to tsarist oppression and no way out, they cursed the reign of

[1] A. I. Herzen, *Sobranie sochineniĭ*, 30 vols. (Moscow 1958), xiii. 272.
[2] Cf. Herzen, *My Past and Thoughts*, trans. by Constance Garnett (A. Knopf, New York 1924), ii. 298.

Peter the Great, repudiated it, and—both morally and literally—donned the peasant's homespun coat.'[1]

In his stimulating essay Herzen somewhat exaggerated the analogy between Shcherbatov and the Slavophiles. The aristocratic critic of eighteenth-century morals had no intention of inviting anyone to put on a peasant's coat, in any sense whatever. His standpoint can only be called 'Slavophile' in a very general sense of the word. In spite of—or perhaps even because of this—Shcherbatov's views, which initiate a critical attitude to the Petrine reforms in Russian historical writing, throw a most interesting light on Slavophile thought and are quite indispensable to the accurate understanding of certain aspects of the Slavophile conception of history.

The 'corruption of morals' and the excessive proliferation of wants and luxury at court were a favourite theme of the Enlightenment which was taken up in France by the aristocratic traditionalists and, above all, by such radical thinkers as Rousseau, Morelly, and Mably. In Russia this theme lent itself to extremely eloquent contrasts, since the changes had been more profound (pre- and post-Petrine Russia) and had come about with greater rapidity. Even during Peter's lifetime Ivan Pososhkov, a wealthy peasant and self-taught economist, made some disillusioned comments on the new age which are not without a certain homely realism. 'The holy imitators of the apostles knew not how to live your way', Pososhkov wrote in his *A Father's Testament* (*c.* 1719); 'instead of garments of cloth of gold they wore shirts of sackcloth; instead of lying on soft down they slept on the hard ground; instead of airy chambers they had dark caves; instead of cavorting in French dances they spent all night at prayer; instead of a surfeit of money they had a surfeit of lice; instead of music and merriment, they wept day and night over human sins.'[2] In the reign of Catherine II the talented satirist Nikolai Novikov, who reflected the moods of the 'third estate' in Russia, put the following views into the mouth of a likeable German, who defended 'the great and ancient Russian virtues':

Ah, if only human strength could give back the Russians their former morals . . . they would become a model to the rest of

[1] Herzen, *Sobr. soch.* xiii. 273.

[2] Quoted from P. Milyukov, *Ocherki po istorii russkoĭ kulturȳ* (Paris 1930), iii. 236.

humanity. It seems to me that earlier wise Russian tsars foresaw, as it were, that as a result of the introduction of the arts and sciences into Russia, the Russian people's greatest treasure, their morals, would vanish for ever; that is why they preferred their subjects to be ignorant of many things, but to remain virtuous and faithful to God, the tsar, and the motherland.[1]

Neither Pososhkov nor Novikov wanted a return to pre-Petrine Russia. In the eighteenth century the old Russia was still too near in time, and the benefits of Europeanization were too obvious from the point of view of the general interests of the enlightened classes. The author of *A Father's Testament* condemned a 'worldly life', but at the same time clearly rejected the conservatism of the Old Believers, although he himself grew up among them.[2] To the arguments in defence of 'ancient Russian virtues' Novikov opposed the scathing irony of an anonymous defender of the new age, without himself taking any definite stand on one side or the other.[3] The traditionalist elements in Pososhkov's and Novikov's views of the world were primarily an expression of their dislike of the most thoroughly Westernized upper strata of the nobility, whose spokesman was Shcherbatov. This traditionalism, instinctive rather than conscious and even (especially in Novikov's case) of secondary importance and at odds with other basic components of their views of the world, was inadequate as a starting-point for a profound critical analysis of the history of 'ancient and modern Russia'. The real pioneer in this field was Shcherbatov, the ideological representative of the enlightened aristocracy and a disciple of Montesquieu, who tried to defend in changed circumstances the lost cause of the Old Boyars' opposition to tsarist autocracy.

Shcherbatov's opposition to the Petrine Reforms was tempered by the recognition that they had been essential to give Russia a much-needed impetus and to awaken her from her lethargy. They had accelerated progress by nearly two hundred years, he estimated in one of his articles.[4] Nevertheless, it

---

[1] *Satiricheskie zhurnalȳ N. I. Novikova* (Moscow–Leningrad 1951), p. 488.
[2] See Milyukov, op. cit. iii. 237.
[3] G. V. Plekhanov, *Istoriya russkoĭ obshchestvennoĭ mȳsli, Sochineniya*, xxii. 307.
[4] An essay entitled 'Primernoe vremyaischislitel'noe polozhenie, vo skol'ko let, pri blagopoluchneĭshikh obstoyatel'stvakh moglabȳ Rossiya sama soboĭ, bez samovlastiya Petŕa Velikogo, doĭti do togo sostoyaniya, v kakom ona nȳne est' v

would be mistaken to conclude (as does M. Raeff in his article on Shcherbatov)[1] that his attitude to Peter was one of unalloyed enthusiasm and admiration. In all his comments on Peter admiration was tempered by criticism, which became more outspoken as time passed and culminated in the *Discourse on the Corruption of Morals*. Shcherbatov's criticism was clearly influenced by Montesquieu's emphasis on the importance of uninterrupted historical continuity and his warning that monarchy without aristocracy could lead to despotism: 'No monarch no nobility; no nobility no monarch, but there may be a despotic prince.'[2]

Shcherbatov's evolution as a political thinker was stimulated by the all-Russian Legislative Commission convened by Catherine in 1767. He showed himself to be an excellent orator and an ardent defender of the traditional rights of the ancient nobility that were threatened by Peter's Table of Ranks. Only the monarch should have the right to confer nobility, Shcherbatov argued. Ennoblement as an automatic privilege attached to a given rank or administrative function leads to careerism and servility, and transforms a monarchy into a despotic bureaucracy. Shcherbatov also opposed all concessions to the peasantry (the limitation of serfdom by law) or to merchants (the establishment of merchant manufactories)—anything, in fact, that might help to undermine the traditional privileges of the aristocracy and hereditary nobility who to him were the mainstay of honour and liberty, the only section of society capable of maintaining its independence without recourse to servility or flattery. In his unpublished articles Shcherbatov stated openly that the ruling system in Russia was not monarchy but despotism, the worst form of government, or rather misgovernment, 'a tyranny where there are no laws but the crazy whims of the despot'. Despotism, he wrote, persecutes virtue, for at the sight of it it has pangs of conscience; it persecutes reason, for 'it is detrimental to autocracy that anyone should investigate the nature of the mutual privileges which forge

---

rassuzhdenii prosveshcheniya i slavȳ'. M. M. Shcherbatov, *Sochineniya* (ii, St. Petersburg 1896).

[1] See M. Raeff, 'State and Nobility in the Ideology of M. M. Shcherbatov', *American Slavic and East European Review* (October 1960).

[2] Montesquieu, *The Spirit of Laws*, trans. by Thomas Nugent, Book ii, p. 14.

social ties or should consider his own situation with a reasoning eye'.[1] In this criticism of despotism, which did not hesitate at times to appeal to 'laws of nature', and demanded 'fundamental rights' and the nobility's share in the government, Shcherbatov came close to the views of the Panin brothers and the liberal wing of the aristocratic opposition. The *Discourse on the Disappearance of all Forms of Government in Russia*, Count Nikita Panin's political testament, contains the following passage which might easily have been written by Shcherbatov: 'A state in which the most venerable of the estates, motivated by honour alone, exists in name only, and the right to call himself a member is sold to every scoundrel who plunders his native land; in which nobility—the only goal of noble souls, the just reward for services rendered to one's country from time immemorial—is obscured by backstairs patronage.'[2] This similarity of views is worth stressing, as it throws into relief the political implications of Shcherbatov's ideas: the traditions of the 'aristocratic opposition', and in particular Panin's *Discourse*, played an important part in forming the ideology of the right-wing faction among the Decembrists.[3]

As a historian (he was the author of a seven-volume *History of Russia*, up to the year 1610), Shcherbatov propounded the view that despotism was by no means a traditional and time-honoured form of government in Russia. The former Russian princes and tsars had shared authority with the boyars, and the alliance of tsar and boyars, which was strictly observed by both sides, was the main factor in the uninterrupted growth of Russian power. It was difficult to reconcile this conception with the despotic but politically successful reign of Ivan the Terrible, but Shcherbatov extricated himself from this dilemma

[1] Quoted from Plekhanov, op. cit., p. 214.

[2] The co-author of the *Discourse* was Panin's secretary, the dramatist D. I. Fonvizin. See D. I. Fonvizin, *Sobranie sochineniĭ*, 2 vols. (Moscow–Leningrad 1959), ii. 254–68 (in this publication the *Discourse* is called *Rassuzhdenie o nepremennïkh gosudarstvennïkh zakonakh*).

[3] The *Discourse* was known in the Northern Union of Decembrists thanks to General M. A. Fonvizin and Colonel I. A. Fonvizin, two relatives of D. I. Fonvizin who were members of the Decembrist group. The Decembrist Nikita Murav'ëv rewrote the *Discourse* as a political pamphlet and adapted it to the reign of Alexander I. See K. V. Pigarev, *Tvorchestvo Fonvizina* (Moscow 1954), p. 147. On the connection between the ideology of the Decembrists and the 'Old Boyar' opposition during the reign of Catherine, see D. Blagoĭ, *Sotsiyologiya tvorchestva Pushkina* (Moscow 1931), pp. 28–30.

by dividing Ivan's reign into two periods. The first period was beneficial to Russia, for the tsar still restrained his passions and took the advice of his boyar duma; in the second period he became a bloody tyrant, murdered his advisers, and brought ruin upon his country.[1] Professing impartiality, Shcherbatov formally condemned Kurbsky's treason but justified it at the same time by Ivan's atrocities; other opponents of the tsar among the boyars and church dignitaries he went so far as to call 'holy men'. For many years such an interpretation of this crucial period in Russian history was an unmistakable feature of historical studies written from the point of view of the nobility. Karamzin's similar treatment of Ivan aroused an outburst of enthusiasm among the Decembrists.[2] The Slavophile interpretation and evaluation of Ivan the Terrible's reign were based on related premises and were one of the main issues in their bitter controversy with S. Solov'ëv and his 'etatist' school in Russian historiography.

The reign of Peter the Great was even less suited to the purpose of proving the need for an alliance between the tsar, the boyars, and the hereditary nobility. In spite of his brutal treatment of the boyars, and his introduction of the Table of Ranks, Peter consolidated and greatly increased Russia's strength and turned her into an important European power. Shcherbatov did not deny this, but set out to show that too high a price had been paid for these merely external successes. The reverse side of progress, he suggested, was profound demoralization: children no longer revered or obeyed their parents, parents neglected their children's upbringing, marital love had disappeared and had given way to widespread adultery, dissipation, and divorce. Noble families were no longer bound by ties of solidarity and every man was concerned for himself alone; there was no friendship, for it was only too easy to sacrifice one's friends to one's own advantage; faithful service to one's sovereign and love of one's country had been replaced by the pursuit of rank and rewards and—to crown it all—no one had sufficient strength of character to tell the sovereign the truth or even to oppose the lawless and harmful

---

[1] See N. L. Rubinstein, *Russkaya istoriografiya* (Moscow 1941), p. 133.
[2] See S. S. Volk, *Istoricheskie vzglyadÿ dekabristov* (Moscow—Leningrad 1958), pp. 383–7.

actions of the court favourite.[1] Shcherbatov devoted most of the *Discourse* to an illustration of these themes, using the morality of the court and the newly created court aristocracy as his examples.

For his starting-point Shcherbatov took the contradiction inherent in the idea of progress obtained at the cost of moral regress. In order to prove his thesis he presented an idealized picture of primitive tribal existence and contrasted its simplicity with the temptations of modern civilization.[2] The distinguishing marks of the tribal society described by Shcherbatov are reverence for existing laws and customs—whether good or bad—strong family ties, corporate solidarity, and, arising out of this, an unbending spirit and readiness to bear sacrifices or even to die for the good of the common cause. It is interesting to note that Shcherbatov, the zealous defender of serfdom, praised the primitive egalitarianism of such tribal societies (including the communal division of property), only making the proviso that as the advance of civilization implied social differentiation it was impossible to preserve this feature.

In many respects Shcherbatov's ideas differed considerably from the popular Enlightenment stereotype. In his interpretation tribal life was not a carefree existence in a state of nature—on the contrary, its most noteworthy feature was a strong social cohesion, and it was this rather than 'natural freedom' that he contrasted with the inner laxity, egoism, and moral anarchy typical of the state of civilization. Primitive tribes, he argued, had no conception of 'voluptuousness' (*slastolyubie*), that is the unrestrained urge to satisfy all sensual appetites and the proliferation of sophisticated artificial requirements which go hand in hand with unhealthy ambition and the desire to impress. The originality of his view lies in the fact that Shcherbatov placed this pre-civilization state in the comparatively recent past rather than in remote prehistoric times, which enabled him to equate the opposition between primitive tribes and civilized nations with that of pre- and post-Petrine Russia.

In the olden days, Shcherbatov pointed out, life in Russia

[1] See M. Shcherbatov, *O povrezhdenii nravov v Rossii*, S predisloviem Iskandera (Trübner and Co., London 1858), pp. 1–2.
[2] Ibid., pp. 4–5.

was simple and untouched by excessive luxury. The tsar made do with seven, at most ten rooms, food and drink consisted of simple home-grown products, and silver table-ware was unknown. It was considered a sin to use wax candles for lighting and four tallow candles sufficed to illuminate a large chamber. The tsars rode on horseback and their wives were carried in undecorated carts. A great many servants were kept, it is true, but this only required a small outlay: servants were only given their board and something towards their footwear—otherwise they had to maintain themselves. The only luxury in clothing were the magnificent furs, but these were a native product and in any case they were passed on from father to son. Above all, no one was subject to the whims of fashion; young people wore the same clothes as their grandparents and had no wish to change their traditional costume.

The upbringing of children in ancient Russia was completely subordinated to religion. Although this encouraged a number of irrational and superstitious beliefs, it also induced fearful obedience to God's commandments; a considerable part in the preservation of morals was played by the strict observance of religious ceremonies, particularly fasts and the daily mass celebrated in family chapels. Amongst other factors that encouraged morality, Shcherbatov mentioned boredom: there was no variety of literature written for entertainment, and no regular social life, so that people were induced by sheer boredom to read the Holy Scriptures and thus to retain their belief.[1]

Shcherbatov was particularly concerned to stress that in the olden days nobility was not determined by rank, but rank by nobility.[2] This principle favoured the flowering of civic virtues, for it restrained the personal ambitions of individuals, subordinating them to the interests of family and estate. Even the custom of *mestnichestvo* played a positive role in keeping alive respect for ancient families and family feeling. To illustrate this thesis, Shcherbatov used the extreme example of Prince Simsky Khabarov: condemned to death by Ivan the Terrible for his refusal to cede his place to Malyuta Skuratov, he asked that his two sons be killed as well, since he feared that in view

[1] Ibid., p. 12.
[2] Ibid., pp. 14–15.

of their youth they might bring dishonour upon their family under the influence of terror and persecution.[1]

Shcherbatov's claim that Peter's reforms introduced a formerly unknown 'voluptuousness' into Russian life has a certain authority, since he personally knew many people who still remembered Peter's reign. His comments clearly reveal the great significance of Peter's reforms for the emancipation of the individual from the domination of tradition and religious ritual. Ruthless absolutist power, state centralization, and the bureaucratic regimentation of various spheres of life restricted the individual far less than the rigorous discipline of religious ceremonies, continual fasts, and accepted conventions that had formerly embraced all spheres of life, both public and private. The 'voluptuousness' of the *Discourse* is nothing other than individualism, whose first primitive stirrings are sometimes both repellent and naïve, witness Shcherbatov's long list of examples of demoralization, careerism, and profligacy.

Shcherbatov drew special attention to the individualization of personal relations and, in consequence, to the basic change in the attitude towards women. The custom of allowing bride and bridegroom to get to know each other before the wedding was new in Peter's reign, as were joint 'assemblies' for men and women and a certain care for one's personal appearance and clothing. 'Passionate love, formerly unknown in an age of primitive customs, began to hold sway over sensitive hearts . . . and the female sex, which had been unaware of its beauty, began to recognize its power.'[2] The only hairdresser in Moscow was besieged by her clients—on various feast-days some of them came three days in advance and had to sleep sitting upright for three nights in order not to spoil their *coiffure*. Dandies of both capitals began to vie with each other in luxury and fashionable dress. Peter, Shcherbatov admitted, had no great love of luxury himself, but he encouraged excess in others in order to stimulate industry, handicrafts, and trade.[3]

In Shcherbatov's view the bureaucratic hierarchy established by Peter was another cause of the corruption of morals. By stimulating personal ambition and—in the last resort—subordinating the nobility to the bureaucracy, Peter's Table of Ranks destroyed the last remnants of aristocratic independence

[1] See M. Shcherbatov p. 13.   [2] Ibid., p. 17.   [3] Ibid., p. 18.

on which civic virtues depended, and helped to spread careerism and servility. 'Is it possible', Shcherbatov asked, 'for people who, from early youth tremble at the stick in the hands of their superiors, to preserve virtue and strength of character?'[1] The suddenness of the reforms, which represented a brutal break in historical continuity, also had a negative influence on the morals of the common people. Peter had been too radical in his war on superstition, he had acted like an inexperienced gardener who prunes his trees at the wrong moment. 'There was less superstition, but also less faith; the former servile fear of hell disappeared, but so did love of God and his holy laws.'[2] In spite of this severe criticism of the new way of life, Shcherbatov did not condemn Peter's reforms wholesale and summed up his views in the following carefully moderate terms: 'The reforms were needed, but perhaps carried too far.'[3] In his political programme Shcherbatov did not envisage a return to pre-Petrine Russia, but rather the limitation of autocracy by aristocratic institutions, on the lines of the Swedish monarchy. The 'conditions' presented to the Empress Anne in 1730 by the Princes Golitsȳn and Dolgoruky, members of the Supreme Privy Council, contained similar postulates.[4] It was a programme that drew its inspiration from the Westernization of Russia and harked back only indirectly to the ancient boyar traditions of Muscovy.

In his criticism of Peter's reforms and in his unusually acute and comprehensive treatment of the issue of 'ancient and modern Russia', Shcherbatov was, to some extent, a precursor of the Slavophiles. From such a general point of view Herzen's comments quoted previously can hardly be questioned. It is a characteristic fact that Shcherbatov, like the Slavophiles, was strongly critical of the transfer of the capital from the old boyar stronghold of Moscow to the newly built St. Petersburg, which personified the supremacy of bureaucratic absolutism.

On the other hand the analogy between Shcherbatov and the nineteenth-century Slavophiles is in many respects superficial and even unreliable. Shcherbatov did not contrast

[1] Ibid., p. 38.
[2] Ibid., p. 29.   [3] Ibid., p. 16.
[4] Shcherbatov called the unsuccessful venture of the Moscow aristocracy a 'lofty idea', which had failed because it had been undertaken as a result of personal ambition (ibid., p. 42).

Russia and Europe and his views on juridical questions, social systems, and the significance of political rights were clearly tinged by Western European and Enlightenment influences and far removed from the romanticism of the Slavophiles and their idealization of the common people. Shcherbatov's belief in the role of the aristocracy was equally 'occidental': it was nourished by the process of Westernization, drew its inspiration from books rather than native tradition, and was modelled on the current ideals of the Western European nobility. The Slavophiles, as we shall see later, treated 'aristocratism' as a disease of societies formed as a result of conquest, a sign of disintegration and individualism which they considered to be quite alien to the truly Christian principles of ancient Russia.

A very interesting light is cast on Shcherbatov's social and political ideas by his utopian tale *Journey to the land of Ophir* (1784). In the apt description of a contemporary scholar, this presents an idealized version of the 'orderly police-state'.[1] Had the Slavophiles been able to read this work, they would have been horrified; so would Montesquieu, from whose writings Shcherbatov drew arguments to bolster up his defence of the rights of the nobility and critique of despotism.

The population of Shcherbatov's Ophir is divided into hermetically sealed-off estates and serfs, whom the author quite simply calls 'slaves'. Every inhabitant's daily life is subject to the most detailed control and excessive luxury or the relaxation of morals is severely punished. Strict regulations lay down what clothes each category of citizen may wear, the size of his house, the number of his servants, what utensils he may use, and even what gratuities he may dispense. In his ideal state, the opponent of bureaucracy and despotism carried the despotic and bureaucratic regimentation of life to extremes. To Shcherbatov there was no contradiction inherent in this, for he did not consider the strict state control of morals to be inconsistent with political liberty. In the state of Ophir there were, after all, such guarantees against despotism as 'fundamental rights', representation of the estates, the abolition of the royal household guard, etc., etc. One of the important guarantees of liberty was to be the law forbidding peasants to complain about their masters to the sovereign. Shcherbatov

1 See Raeff, op. cit.

thought that the right to present petitions to the monarch would reinforce the uncouth peasantry's belief in the 'good tsar', while rulers, made aware of the people's support, might become presumptuous and turn into despots. Ophir, according to Shcherbatov, was not a despotic state, but a law-abiding monarchy combining liberty with strict morality, and discipline with law and order.

Some of the features of Shcherbatov's utopia can be traced to his Freemasonry and to the Masonic cult of formalism, hierarchy, and love of outward distinctions. The Masonic influence emerges most strongly in the sections devoted to education and religion.[1] In the state of Ophir education is free and compulsory for every citizen, although its extent differs for the various estates. Religion is reduced to a rationalistic cult of the supreme being and there are no priests who might profit from religious practices. Sacraments, offerings, and all mysteries are discarded, prayers are short and few, communal prayers resemble Masonic ritual. Atheism, however, is forbidden and attendance at church is compulsory, on pain of punishment.

The Masonic provenance of certain elements in the story is not sufficient to explain it altogether. The best key to an understanding of Shcherbatov's tale is probably supplied by an examination of his views on ancient and modern Russia. Raeff has drawn attention to the fact that the detailed bureaucratic system of the state of Ophir reflects certain features of the reformed Russia;[2] however, a comparison between Ophir and the picture of pre-Petrine Russia drawn in the *Discourse* would seem to offer an even more fruitful approach. In both states private life is governed by strict regulations and norms; in one by legal decrees and in the other by time-honoured customs and religious ritual. In both states social stratification, isolation of estates, and especially the exclusive nature of the nobility are guarantees of social cohesion and the flowering of civic virtues. Finally, in both states strict morals and moderate requirements prevent the spread of the insidious voluptuousness. It is important to note that his antithesis of ancient and

[1] See *Istoriya russkoï literaturÿ* (Soviet Academy of Sciences, Moscow–Leningrad 1947), iv. 81–2 (chapter on Masonic literature).
[2] See Raeff, op. cit.

modern Russia had convinced Shcherbatov that the strict control and regimentation of morals had nothing in common with despotism. Ancient Russia, he maintained, had not been a despotic country (apart from certain periods) and that mainly because society remained faithful to a way of life which precluded arbitrary rule by setting out appropriate spheres of activity for everyone, including the tsar. In modern Russia, however, despotism had spawned 'the corruption of morals', which was to become its most faithful ally.

This last view is almost identical with the Slavophiles' favourite thesis that individualism (Shcherbatov's 'voluptuousness') and arbitrary state autocracy (despotism) are essentially two sides of the same coin. Even in this instance, however, the analogy is limited in scope. According to Slavophile criteria, Shcherbatov would have to be considered an extreme abstract rationalist unable to distinguish between the 'organic' regulation of morals by tradition, and mechanical control by government decrees. In this respect Nikolai Karamzin, author of the official history of the Russian state and ideological leader of the conservative opposition during the reign of Alexander I, came closer to Slavophile ideas.

Like Shcherbatov, the young Karamzin was also a Freemason, but what attracted him to the Masonic movement was not the hope of social change but the ideal of the moral perfectibility of the self. The dramatic defence of civic virtues and outright political opposition of a man like Shcherbatov could have no appeal to a writer who rejected the 'world's clamour' in favour of solitary meditation and 'sweet melancholy, the passion of tender souls'. Karamzin's sentimentalism was part of a trend among the smaller landowners, who were eager to benefit from the abolition of compulsory state service and to retire to their country estates in order to enjoy independence, freedom from politics, and a peaceful family life.[1]

In 1789 and 1790 Karamzin made a grand tour of Germany, Switzerland, England, and France, which provided him with material for his famous *Letters of a Russian Traveller*. Although he met many notable persons on his travels and witnessed the

[1] See R. Pipes. *Karamzin's Memoir on Ancient and Modern Russia* (Harvard University Press, Cambridge, Mass. 1959), p. 10.

early months of the French Revolution, the *Letters* are only a 'lyrical pamphlet', an account of subjective impressions rather than of actual men or events. In his final letter Karamzin described his aim in writing them in the following terms: 'They are a mirror of my soul during the last eighteen months. Twenty years from now (if I should live that long) they will still be a delight to me—even if only to me. I shall peruse them and I shall see what kind of person I was, what I thought and what I dreamed. And between ourselves, what is more interesting to man than his own self?'[1]

Karamzin's introspective world was not, however, proof against the impact of historical events. The beginnings of the French Revolution might have awoken some vague idealistic sympathies in him, but the second phase—the guillotining of the king and the Jacobin terror—filled him with horror. 'France has been struck by lightning . . .', he wrote; 'we witnessed the fire from afar and then each of us returned home in order to thank heaven that his roof was still whole, and to become a wiser man.'[2] The cosmopolitan humanism of Karamzin's *Letters* is best summed up in his statement that 'the national [element] is as nothing compared to the human [element]'.[3] Shortly it was to appear that these ideas were not very firmly rooted. When, as Karamzin put it, the 'Revolution clarified our ideas',[4] he became converted to a conservative nationalism and to an idealization of autocratic rule as the only enduring support of the old order.

Karamzin first expressed his new ideas in a short story called *Natalie, The Boyar's Daughter* (1792). This describes the 'virtuous and simple life of our ancestors', when 'Russians were Russians', dressed like Russians, spoke Russian (and not French), and adhered faithfully to the strict customs of old. Even more typical of Karamzin's new outlook is the short story *Marfa, or the Subjugation of Novgorod* (1803). The love plot in it is entirely subordinated to the historical theme, which describes the clash between the 'republican virtue' of the citizens of

---

[1] N. M. Karamzin, *Letters of a Russian Traveller*, trans. by Florence Jonas (Columbia University Press, New York 1957), p. 340.
[2] Quoted from D. Blagoï, *Istoriya russkoï literaturÿ xviii veka* (Moscow 1946), p. 388.
[3] Quoted from Plekhanov, op. cit., p. 194.
[4] Ibid., p. 197.

Novgorod and the historically necessary principle of autocracy. The author praised both sides for their 'civic virtue',
having seemingly forgotten the charms of intimacy, lonely
melancholy, and egotistical self-analysis. Autocracy emerges
victorious since it is 'not freedom, which is often calamitous,
but *order, justice, and safety* that are the three pillars of a happy
society'.[1]

Karamzin was strengthened in his conservative nationalism
by the Napoleonic Wars and Tsar Alexander I's early liberalism. The peace treaty signed at Tilsit was felt to be a disgrace
by the more patriotically minded section of the nobility and
plans to introduce a legal code imitating the Code Napoléon,
named after the man who had humiliated Russia and was not
only an enemy but also a usurper and heir to the French
Revolution, aroused even greater indignation. The fact that
Mikhail Speransky, the man responsible for these plans and
also for an outline of general government reforms, was a
raznochinets, son of a rural priest, only made matters worse. The
Tsar's ambitious sister, the Grand Duchess Catherine, was the
patroness of the growing conservative camp and it was probably
she who prompted Karamzin to write his detailed *Memoir on
Ancient and Modern Russia* with its bold and searching criticism
of the government's policies. The *Memoir*, which was written
in 1811, when Speransky's influence was still at its height,[2] is
one of the most significant documents of Russian social thought
in the reign of Alexander. Its view of Russian history might
be summed up in the sentence: 'The present is a consequence
of the past; to judge the former one must recollect the
latter.'[3]

In the *Memoir* medieval Russia is presented as a state that
was not only strong, but also the most civilized power in the
Europe of its time.[4] Its outstanding feature, according to
Karamzin, was the coexistence of powerful princes (of Norman
origin) with such 'republican' institutions as the native Slavonic
'folkmoots' (*veche*), which even wielded supreme authority in
Novgorod and Pskov. This was not enough, however, to counteract the evils of the European apanage system which weakened

[1] Quoted from D. Blagoĭ, op. cit., p. 401.
[2] Pipes, *Karamzin's Memoir*, pp. 70–5.
[3] Ibid., p. 103.   [4] Ibid., p. 105.

Russia and made her vulnerable to the Tartars. It was only
when the Muscovite state became strong enough to act as a
centralizing force that it was able to free Russia and re-
establish as well as extend her power. Karamzin conceded that
the destruction of the 'exuberant freedom' of Novgorod and
Pskov was perhaps regrettable, but argued that it was necessary
for the sake of the prosperity and strength of the state. Autocracy, he emphasized, had proved to be Russia's only sheet-
anchor during all times of disaster. 'Autocracy', the *Memoir*
concludes, 'is the Palladium of Russia. On its integrity depends
Russia's happiness.'[1]

In spite of this conclusion Karamzin nevertheless attacked
several of Russia's autocratic rulers, especially those who had
undertaken measures against the nobility. Even though he had
autocratic powers, Karamzin argued, the Russian emperor
should refrain from degrading the nobility which was as ancient
as Russia herself and at all times the mainstay of the monarchy.[2]
He was emphatic in his condemnation of Ivan the Terrible's
bloody campaign against the boyars and stressed that Russian
history clearly showed the benefits that flowed from a close
alliance between an autocratic ruler and the nobility; grievous
consequences were to be expected whenever this alliance was
violated by one side or the other. Although this argument suggests that the nobility had the right to oppose despotism when
it threatened its traditional and time-honoured privileges,
Karamzin, unlike Shcherbatov, was categorically opposed to
any active opposition. All attempts to limit or control autocracy were fraught—in his view—with the danger of the 'hydra
of aristocracy', and internal anarchy.[3] The abuse of autocratic
power was to be condemned, but only on a moral plane—
Karamzin advised civic courage but opposed open rebellion
and was inclined to praise the virtue of faithful allegiance at
any price.[4] Ivan the Terrible may have been a worse tyrant

---

[1] Ibid., p. 200.

[2] Ibid., p. 200.

[3] It is interesting to note Karamzin's attitude to the 'conditions' presented to
Anna Ivanovna by the Moscow aristocracy, on which he commented as follows:
'Impudent and dastardly plots. Pygmies contending for the legacy of a giant. The
aristocracy, the oligarchy was ruining the fatherland . . .' (ibid., p. 127). It is
worth comparing this comment with Shcherbatov's (see p. 29, n. 4 above).

[4] Pipes, *Karamzin's Memoir*, p. 113.

than Caligula or Nero, but Kurbsky's flight to Poland was nevertheless an act of treason.[1]

In order to understand this standpoint, one must realize that in Karamzin's interpretation 'autocracy' meant power undivided rather than unlimited.[2] The monarch ruled by himself, and did not share his power, but his authority did not extend to all spheres of life with equal force. The tsar's absolute authority in affairs of state was to be undisputed, but outside the realm of politics Karamzin felt he should take account of tradition and ancient customs, and relinquish the right to arbitrary interference. In this conception it is possible to discern the germs of the Slavophile idea of the alliance of State and Land—an alliance based on the principle of mutual non-interference.

Peter the Great's reign clearly bore little resemblance to Karamzin's ideal. Like Shcherbatov, Karamzin acknowledged Peter as the maker of modern Russia, but at the same time he was outspokenly critical of the 'pernicious side' of his reign and stressed that Peter's role should not be exaggerated. Only foreigners who were not well acquainted with Russian history, he wrote, could maintain that Peter was solely responsible for Russia's might. Even contacts with the West had started before his reign, although they had been of an entirely different order. At the time of the first Romanovs, Karamzin noted with approval, 'we borrowed, but as if unwillingly, adapting the foreign to the native and blending the new with the old'.[3]

Karamzin argued that, unlike his predecessors, Peter failed to understand that the 'national spirit constitutes the moral strength of states', that specific national features reinforce love of one's native land and therefore deserve the full support of a wise statesman.[4] The spread of education had been necessary, he admitted, but 'Russian dress, food and beards did not interfere with the founding of schools.'[5] Customs should change naturally, any forcible control over them was 'an act of violence which is illegal even for an autocratic monarch'.[6] The sudden and overwhelming impact of European ways had weakened

---

[1] See R. Pipes, 'Karamzin's Conception of the Monarchy', in *Russian Thought and Politics*, Harvard Slavic Studies, iv (Mouton and Co., The Hague 1957), p. 43.

[2] Ibid., pp. 44–6; also Pipes, *Karamzin's Memoir*, pp. 62–3.

[3] Pipes, *Karamzin's Memoir*, p. 120.

[4] Ibid., p. 121.   [5] Ibid., pp. 122.   [6] Ibid.

Russia's national pride; it was admirable, Karamzin thought, that formerly Russians had called foreigners 'infidels', and had been convinced that 'holy Russia' ranked above all other nations: 'Let this be called a delusion, but how much it did to strengthen patriotism and the moral fibre of the country.' Peter's reforms, on the other hand, ensured that 'we became citizens of the world, but ceased in certain respects to be citizens of Russia'.[1]

In pointing out the decline of civic virtues in post-Petrine Russia, Karamzin was continuing the central argument of Shcherbatov's *Discourse*. Like his predecessor, he drew attention to the weakening of kinship ties and the authority of the nobility. 'Noble status', he emphasized, 'should not depend on rank, but rank on noble status; that is the attainment of certain ranks should be made unconditionally dependent on the candidate being a gentleman, a practice we have failed to observe from the time of Peter the Great.'[2] Such similarities should not, however, be allowed to obscure the differences between the two thinkers. Karamzin's nationalism would have been entirely alien to Shcherbatov, who thought that Peter's main error was not so much his offence against national pride as his disregard for age-old social conventions and his ruthless disruption of an accepted mode of life. The difference between the two men is best illustrated by Karamzin's comments on the 'national spirit'—a concept that was familiar to Shcherbatov from his reading of Montesquieu but played no role in any of his writings.

Karamzin's criticism of Peter raised a number of points which later became part and parcel of Slavophile doctrine; it is interesting to note, for instance, that he also stressed the harmful effects of the cleavage between the upper and lower strata of society.[3] Karamzin's nationalism, however, had very little in common with the Slavophiles' romanticism. In the

---

[1] Ibid., p. 124.   [2] Ibid., p. 201.

[3] Karamzin wrote: 'Peter confined his reform to the gentry. Until his reign all Russians, from the plough to the throne, had been alike insofar as they shared certain features of external appearance and customs. After Peter, the higher classes separated themselves from the lower ones, and the Russian peasant, burgher and merchant began to treat the Russian gentry as Germans, thus weakening the spirit of brotherly national unity binding the estates of the realm.' (Ibid., p. 122.)

realm of politics he was a disciple of Machiavelli and his praise of specifically Russian national features was due to pragmatic considerations and not to any belief in their profound spiritual significance. Even when he condemned the removal of the capital to St. Petersburg, which he called a town built on 'tears and corpses', he was influenced not by a romantic reverence for tradition but by purely practical motives.[1]

Karamzin's pragmatism is most noticeable in his attitude to religion. Although he ascribed a more important role to Orthodoxy than the deist Shcherbatov, he always considered religion from a purely secular and political point of view. When he accused Peter of humiliating the clergy and lowering the authority of the Church, it was as part of his defence of the true interests of the state:

Where the welfare of the state is involved [he wrote], a wise monarch shall always find a way of reconciling his will with that of the metropolitan or the patriarch. But it is better for this conciliation to appear as an act of free choice and of inner persuasion rather than of obvious humility. An overt complete dependence of spiritual authority on secular authority derives from the assumption that the former is useless, or at any rate, not essential to political stability— an assumption thoroughly disproven by the experience of ancient Russia and of contemporary Spain.[2]

The epoch that seemed to coincide most closely with Karamzin's ideal was the reign of Catherine the Great—the nobility's 'golden age' when it was relieved of many of its duties but benefited from increased privileges and the general extension of civic rights. Karamzin of course blamed Catherine for the dissolute life at court, her favouritism, Francomania, and love of outward forms and superficial splendour, but at the same time he stressed that she had 'cleansed autocracy from the stain of tyranny', had 'raised the moral value of man', and had created institutions which should serve for many years as the basis for the internal organization of the realm, 'Should we compare all the known periods of Russian history,' he concluded, 'virtually all would agree that Catherine's epoch was the happiest for all Russian citizens—virtually all would prefer to have lived then than at any other time.'[3]

---

[1] Ibid., p. 126.   [2] Ibid., p. 126   [3] Ibid., p. 134.

Catherine's principal contribution, according to Karamzin, was that she mitigated the severity of autocracy without diminishing its authority. After her death, however, this achievement was first threatened by Paul's crazy tyranny[1] and later by Alexander's liberal tendencies. Karamzin's analysis of Russian history was intended as a lesson and warning to Alexander. He reminded the Tsar that the slightest formal restriction of autocracy would prove disastrous and that for the Romanov dynasty their election meant that the emperor was not entitled to take steps to restrict his own authority.

If Alexander, inspired by generous hatred for the abuses of autocracy, should lift a pen and prescribe himself laws other than those of God and his conscience, then the true virtuous citizen of Russia would presume to stop his hand to say: 'Sire! You exceed the limits of your authority. Russia, taught by long disasters, vested before the holy altar the power of autocracy in your ancestor, asking him that he rule her supremely, indivisibly. This covenant is the foundation of your authority, you have no other; you may do everything, but you may not limit your authority by law!'[2]

The keynote of Karamzin's detailed and forthright criticism of Alexander's reign is to be found in the following words: 'All novelty in the political order is an evil to which recourse is to be had only of necessity.'[3] Statutes, for him, were sanctioned by antiquity and custom alone. 'Russia', Karamzin complained, 'has been in existence for a thousand years and not as a savage horde but as a great state. Yet we are constantly being told of new institutions and of new laws, as if we had just emerged from the dark American forests.'[4]

In no uncertain terms Karamzin told Alexander that the introduction of the Code Napoléon in Russia would be tantamount to an open confession of thoughtlessness and want of intelligence. Laws could not be simply transposed, they must arise out of a country's own historical experience, out of native concepts and customs.[5] Instead of legislative changes it would be preferable to find fifty competent governors, since 'men, not documents govern'.[6] The best way, in fact, of strengthening

<hr/>

[1] Karamzin considered Paul to be as much of a tyrant as Ivan the Terrible although he did not hold this to justify his assassination (ibid., p. 136).
[2] Ibid., p. 139.   [3] Ibid., pp. 147–8.   [4] Ibid., p. 158.
[5] Ibid., pp. 185, 188–89.   [6] Ibid., p. 194.

Russia would be to enhance the role of the nobility and clergy: 'The gentry and the clergy, the Senate and the Synod, as repositories of law, over all—the sovereign, the only legislator, the autocratic source of authority—this is the foundation of the Russian monarchy.'[1]

Like Shcherbatov (and in contrast to the Slavophiles) Karamzin was a man of the eighteenth century. History to him was a didactic discipline and its most interesting aspects were political events, the evolution of the state, and the story of wars and rulers. If he looked for historical continuity or accented the role of native traditions and customs, he did so without venturing beyond certain ideas put forward by Montesquieu. Stylistically, too, he was a true son of the eighteenth century: he set out to eliminate Old Church Slavonic archaisms from the language and introduced new words—and therefore new concepts—thus arousing the ire of 'archaists' such as Admiral Shishkov. Karamzin's political views, however, were completely at variance with Enlightenment ideas and the programme that called for Russia's Westernization. He may have quoted Montesquieu, but the latter would have found his conclusions quite unacceptable. His contempt for written laws, his conviction that 'men, not documents govern', was at the opposite pole to the Enlightenment cult of the law (Law with a capital letter) as the principal cornerstone of society. The autocratic ideal praised by Karamzin was an open contradiction of Montesquieu's principle of divided authority; Karamzin indeed compared two sources of authority in one country to two dreadful lions in one cage, ready to tear each other apart.[2] 'In Russia', he wrote in his *Memoir*, 'the sovereign is the living law . . ., our government is fatherly, patriarchal. The father of a family judges and punishes without a protocol. The monarch too must in conditions of a different nature follow only his own conscience and nothing else.'[3] These views, which are quite irreconcilable with the eighteenth-century ideal of the rule of law, certainly implied the abandonment of the struggle for 'fundamental rights' demanded by Shcherbatov and the conservative and liberal wings of the aristocratic opposition during the reign of Catherine.

---

[1] Karamzin p. 204. (Karamzin also recommended that the ranks of the nobility be restricted numerically.) [2] Ibid., p. 139 [3] Ibid., p. 197.

Karamzin's ideas were not original, but reflected opinions current among the gentry. He expressed the small landowners' readiness to yield to autocracy and to relinquish the struggle for political rights in return for further guarantees and the consolidation of their social position. Unlike the Slávophiles, Karamzin never questioned the legal validity of serfdom, and reminded the emperor that in affairs of state the laws of nature must yield to civil law. Any emancipation act, he thought, would have to be preceded by careful historical research into the origins of serfdom, by attempts to establish which peasants were the descendants of former prisoners-of-war and which had become serfs as a result of debts, etc. In any case Karamzin was convinced that emancipation was not in the interests of the peasantry itself, since it would inevitably be followed by their expropriation—not for a moment did he question the nobility's inalienable right to ownership of the land.[1]

In justice to Karamzin it should perhaps be stressed that his conservatism cannot be dismissed as reactionary obscurantism. Although he defended serfdom he was also in favour of humanitarian treatment for the peasants; his 'loyal sentiments' had nothing in common with Arakhcheev's servility, nor can his nationalism be compared to the chauvinist xenophobia propagated by S. N. Glinka.[2] In a letter written towards the end of his life, he even admitted that 'at heart I have remained a republican'.[3] Coming from Karamzin this statement might appear inconsistent, unless we realize that he was merely paying tribute to the abstract superiority of the republican system. At the same time he thought that it demanded too great an effort of virtue on the part of its citizens, could never be powerful, and was quite inapplicable in enormous countries such as Russia. Karamzin's Platonic 'republicanism' therefore gave way to reasons of state; in concrete historical circumstances he was, in his own words, 'a faithful subject of the Russian tsar'. This did not prevent a certain over-zealous informer from denouncing him to the authorites (in 1809) on the grounds that his work was full of 'Jacobin poison' and deserved to be burnt.

[1] Ibid., pp. 162–7.

[2] See A. Koyré, *La Philosophie et le problème national en Russie au début du XIX*ᵉ *siècle* (Paris 1929), pp. 18–22.

[3] See his letter to I. I. Dmitriev in 1818 (quoted from Pipes, 'Karamzin's Conception of the Monarchy', p. 35).

The *Memoir*, with its bold and bitter criticism of the emperor, was banned for many years. Karamzin's contemporaries knew his historical conceptions from his twelve-volume *History of the Russian State*, which did not go beyond the beginning of the seventeenth century. The first eight volumes appeared in 1818, at a time when interest in Russian history was greatly stimulated by the victorious conclusion of the Napoleonic Wars, and its vivid and imaginative narrative at once made it enormously popular. For people brought up on the literature and history of Western Europe it became a true school of national pride. Pushkin wrote of it: 'Three thousand copies were sold within a month—something unprecedented in our country. Everyone, even great ladies, began to read the history of their country. It was an absolute revelation. You would have said that Karamzin discovered ancient Russia as Columbus discovered America.'[1]

Pushkin's comment shows how significant was the role of Karamzin's *History*. It is also worth recalling that all the main ideologists of classical Slavophilism were brought up on it. They too rediscovered ancient Russia in its pages and although they tried to see it from the point of view of the 'people' rather than the 'state', this did not lessen their respect for Karamzin as a historian.

In the history of Russian conservatism Karamzin's work can be regarded as a kind of intermediate link between Shcherbatov's enlightened aristocratic conservatism and the romantic people's conservatism of the Slavophiles. In their critique of the Petrine reforms both Shcherbatov and Karamzin developed similar ideas and used similar 'Slavophile' arguments (it was Belinsky who stressed this similarity to Slavophilism).[2] Both writers were, of course, well acquainted with Montesquieu, whom they considered to be the greatest contemporary authority on 'political science', and might have based their arguments on his observations. In the *Spirit of Laws* in the chapter called 'What

---

[1] Quoted from Blagoï, op. cit., p. 390.

[2] In his 'Review of Russian Literature for the Year 1846' Belinsky wrote: 'It is generally known that Karamzin thought more highly of Ivan III than of Peter the Great and preferred the ancient Russia before Peter to the new Russia. Here we have the source of what is known as Slavophilism, which, by the way, we consider for many reasons to be a very important phenomenon. . . .' V. G. Belinsky, *Polnoe sobranie sochineniĭ* (Moscow 1953–9), x. 17.

are the Natural Means of changing the Manners and Customs
of a Nation', Montesquieu wrote as follows:

> Thus when a prince would make great alterations in his kingdom,
> he should reform by law what is established by law, and change by
> custom what is settled by custom; for it is very bad policy to change
> by law, what ought to be changed by custom.

> The law which obliged the Muscovites to cut off their beards,
> and to shorten their clothes, and the rigour with which Peter I made
> them crop, even to their knees, the long cloaks of those who entered
> into the cities, were instances of tyranny. There are means that may
> be made use of to prevent crimes: these are punishments; there are
> those for changing our customs: these are examples.

> The facility and ease with which that nation has been polished,
> plainly shows, that this prince had a worse opinion of his people
> than they deserved; and that they were not brutes, though he was
> pleased to call them so. The violent measures which he employed
> were needless; he would have attained his end as well by milder
> methods.[1]

Unlike Shcherbatov, Montesquieu did not maintain that the
new way of life introduced into Russia by Peter the Great
represented a 'corruption' of the ancient Russian way of life and
like Karamzin, his faithful disciple in this respect, he criticized
the means used rather than the results. In other respects
Shcherbatov was closer to Montesquieu (and thus further from
the Slavophiles) than Karamzin, since he wished to limit
autocracy through 'fundamental statutes' and by sharing
authority between the monarch and elective bodies representing the aristocracy. Karamzin's criticism of 'tyranny', his plea
for restricted entry to the nobility and a greater role for the
Senate seem to continue the programme of the 'aristocratic
opposition', but in his *Memoir* the demand for political freedom
was reduced to the right to address the emperor openly, without flattery or servility. In this respect Karamzin's standpoint
coincided with that of the Slavophiles, who demanded the right
of free speech but allowed the emperor complete freedom of
decision. His remarks had been sincere, Karamzin wrote in the
closing passage of the *Memoir*, but now he was reverting to the
silence of a faithful subject. According to Konstantin Aksakov,
this was the principle that guided the Land Assemblies of

---

[1] Montesquieu, *The Spirit of the Laws*, i. 306.

Muscovy, who told the Tsar: 'Your conduct in this matter depends on you alone. The *decision* is yours, but this is our *opinion*.'[1]

In his emphasis on the role of national tradition, his criticism of the abstract 'juridical world-view', and a number of other matters, Karamzin had more in common with the Slavophiles than with the rationalist Shcherbatov; in essentials, however, he was closer to Shcherbatov. He did not regard Russia as the antithesis to Europe, the carrier of different 'superior' principles; nor did his strictures of bureaucracy imply a criticism of state organization as such. At the same time he in no way foreshadowed the Slavophile idealization of the common people and, although he recognized the importance of the Orthodox clergy, religion had only a minor place in his view of the world. Above all—and this is perhaps the most important difference—Karamzin, like Shcherbatov, was a spokesman for the concrete interests of the nobility and not for idealized forms of traditional social bonds. His conservatism was far more practical than that of the Slavophiles, but also much more superficial—it was a political ideology rather than a Weltanschauung. It would be difficult to find any discussion in his work of the relationship of the individual to society, or of types of culture and corresponding types of personality; moreover, he did not even touch on the problem of capitalism as a cultural formation. Karamzin's ideology—like that of Shcherbatov—undoubtedly has its place in the prehistory of Slavophile ideas and helps to throw light on their origins, but in no way can it be said to anticipate the specific features of Slavophilism.

The *Memoir on Ancient and Modern Russia* was presented to Alexander I at a time when moderately liberal ideas still predominated in the government's home policies. Shortly afterwards the tide turned towards reaction. Its first victim was Speransky, who was deprived of his post and exiled for his alleged support of Napoleon. After Napoleon's final defeat further reactionary measures were introduced and in 1815 Alexander induced his fellow sovereigns—Francis of Austria and Frederick William of Prussia—to create the Holy Alliance.

[1] K. S. Aksakov, 'Zapiska o vnutrennem sostoyanii Rossii', in L. N. Brodsky, *Rannie slavyanofily* (Moscow 1910), p. 82.

The dominant personality in Russia became Count Arakhcheev, an obtuse reactionary with the outlook of a hired mercenary. The ministry of education, which was handed over to the mystical Count A. Golitsȳn, was transformed, in Karamzin's biting description, into a 'ministry of obscurantism'. In court circles a growing role was played by a fanatical monk, the Archimandrite Photius, a man obsessed by his hatred of the 'caves of Satan' and the 'seven-headed hydra of revolution'. The idea began to gain currency that Russia should be completely isolated from Europe. L. M. Magnitsky, a member of the Central Committee for Education, and later Superintendent of the University of Kazan, wrote at this time: 'How happy Russia would be if she could be cut off from Europe, so that none of the turmoil, no news of the terrible events taking place there, might reach her. A far-sighted censorship and the reconstruction of the national educational system on firm foundations of unshaken faith—these alone can stem the tidal wave of atheism and depravity that is pushing Europe into the abyss.'[1]

The efforts of the fanatical supporters of reaction were not able to put a stop to the progressive ferment, but merely brought about a further polarization of standpoints. After 1812 constitutional and liberal–democratic tendencies led to the secret societies of the Decembrists, who were prepared to implement their programme by force of arms. Their unsuccessful uprising in December 1825 appeared to make the final victory of autocracy a foregone conclusion.

Nicholas I, who succeeded to the throne after the Decembrist revolt was suppressed, vowed that revolution should not penetrate Russia as long as he had a breath left in his body. To all appearances, at least, he kept his word: in spite of the continuous action of corrosive processes, tsarist autocracy during his reign remained—on the surface—a monolithic and inflexible force. Although his reign was not perhaps the 'apogee of autocracy'[2] it has been called by some historians, it must be admitted that Nicholas was able to ensure the temporary stability and even a certain consolidation of autocratic rule. Conservative ideology also became 'stabilized' and mystics like Golitsȳn or hysterical obscurantists like Photius were no longer

[1] Quoted from Koyré, *La Philosophie* . . ., p. 51.
[2] See A. Presnyakov, *Apogeĭ samoderzhaviya, Nikolaĭ I* (Leningrad 1925).

numbered among the tsar's close advisers. Nevertheless, a widespread feeling of imminent menace, of dangers that must be actively opposed, continued to persist. The Minister of Education, for instance, Count S. S. Uvarov, once said that he would die in peace if he succeeded in 'defending Russia for even half a century from the fate prepared for her by theories'.[1]

The government's new programme was summed up by Uvarov in the famous words 'Orthodoxy, autocracy, and nationality'. This triune slogan, a conscious antithesis of the revolutionary device of 'liberty, equality, and fraternity', was apparently very close to Karamzin's ideological programme, although at the same time there were certain essental differences. The word *narodnost'*, the third member of the formula, means both nationality and the German *Volkstum*,[2] and was not only intended to convey a certain nationalistic trend, but also reflected the efforts of the autocratic regime to expand its social base, to rely *directly* on the 'people' in the broad sense of the word. Uvarov's slogan thus contrasted with Montesquieu's idea of 'mediation', which had made such an appeal to Karamzin, and represented an implicit rejection of the nobility's claims to mediate between the sovereign and the people.[3] Unlike Karamzin's nationalism, Uvarov's 'nationality' had no anti-bureaucratic overtones; on the contrary, Uvarov considered bureaucracy to be a truly 'popular' system that put social advance within the reach of all and was therefore a safeguard against social revolution. Under Nicholas the official ideology made conservatism into the basis of government policy, but at the same time was careful to purge this conservatism of anything savouring of the ideas of the ancient nobility that might turn into a criticism of absolutism.

[1] A. V. Nikitenko, *Dnevnik* (Leningrad 1955), i. 174.

[2] See Koyré, op. cit., p. 197 and B. P. Hepner, *Bakounine et le panslavisme révolutionnaire* (Paris 1950), p. 72. M. K. Azadovsky maintains that the term *narodnost'* made its first appearance in 1819 in the correspondence of P. A. Vyazemsky and A. Turgenev, where it was used as the equivalent of the Polish word *narodowość*. 'Why not translate *nationalité* as *narodnost'*?', Vyazemsky wrote to Turgenev. 'The Poles after all have used *narodowość*.' M. K. Azadovsky, *Istoriya russkoĭ fol'kloristiki* (Moscow 1958), pp. 191–2. While accepting this explanation, it should be emphasized that from the beginning the term referred not only to the 'nation' but also to the 'people' and in the 1830s and '40s acquired the emotional overtones of the German *Volkstum*.

[3] The 'loyal feelings' of the Russian people were contrasted in the official ideology with the moods of the gentry. See p. 420.

From this point of view it is extremely illuminating to compare the attitudes of three historians who represented three phases, or rather trends, in Russian conservatism during three successive reigns. In the reign of Catherine the aristocrat Shcherbatov openly opposed despotism and demanded that his class be given not only social privileges but also political rights. In Alexander's reign he was followed by Karamzin, a representative of the enlightened gentry, who was an apologist for autocracy but at the same time critical of its abuses and postulated a close alliance between the tsar and the nobility, grounded in the latter's traditional rights and privileges. Finally, in the reign of Nicholas, we have Mikhail Pogodin, son of a serf, 'a strange mixture of democratism and servility',[1] a nationalist supporter of power politics, and defender of autocracy on the grounds that it was a system in which 'a man of the people has access to the highest state office and a university diploma replaces all privileges.'[2] There is a connection between Shcherbatov and Karamzin; there is also an obvious link between Karamzin and Pogodin; but none at all between Pogodin and Shcherbatov.

The doctrine of Official Nationality propagated by Pogodin and his fellow ideologist, the literary historian S. Shevȳrëv, deserves to be examined in some detail in the present work. Its significance in the 'prehistory' of Slavophile ideas is obvious but needs clarification, the more so since it has given rise to a number of misconceptions.

Pogodin (1800–75) was only a few years older than the senior Slavophiles and, like Kireevsky and Koshelëv, was connected in his youth with the society of wisdom-lovers.[3] Even his early university lectures, in the 1820s, already showed the influence of Schelling; he was looking for an organic growth factor in history, for a body of distinctive ideas which he thought must evolve within every nation in accordance with the general design of providence. 'How does the history of Russia differ from the history of other nations, European and Asiatic?' is the kind of philosophical problem he was interested in and he criticized Karamzin's *History* for not supplying any answers to

---

[1] A description of Pogodin in N. F. Shcherbina's epigram entitled 'Who is it?'
[2] M. P. Pogodin, *Istoriko-kriticheskie otrȳvki* (Moscow 1846), p. 8.
[3] See the following chapter.

questions of this type.[1] He himself claimed to have found an
answer to this question in a comparative analysis of *Nestor's
Chronicle* and the historical studies of Guizot and Thierry, which
had led him to the conclusion that unlike the states of Western
Europe, which were founded on armed conquest, the Russian
state had come into being as a result of a 'voluntary invitation
to rule'. This theory, of course, had far-reaching implications.
Pogodin agreed with the French historians who had traced
back the class struggle to the warfare between two tribes—
conquerors and conquered—and therefore argued that in Russia class struggles and revolution had no place and no historical
sanction. His studies did in fact lead him to conclude that there
were essential differences between the history of Russia and
that of Western Europe. The main differences that he listed
were the apanage system, which could hardly be compared to
feudalism,[2] the lack of a native aristocracy and third estate in
Russia, and the status of the Orthodox Church which, in
Russia as in Byzantium, avoided conflict with the secular
authorities and meekly submitted to the head of the state.
Russian history, Pogodin claimed, was truly free of conflicts:
'Slavery, hatred, pride, and struggle'[3] were all quite foreign to
it. In an attempt to formulate his ideas in philosophical terms,
Pogodin suggested that Western Europe and Russia represented
two great qualitatively different world civilizations: Western
European civilization was heir to ancient Rome and Eastern
European civilization was heir to the Eastern Empire.[4]

This was the first time that the thesis of Russia's essential
distinctiveness from Western Europe, of the contrast between
the 'principles' represented by them, found expression in Russian
historical writing. There can be no doubt that here Pogodin
anticipated Slavophile doctrine on the subject, which was not
formulated until more than ten years later.[5] The Slavophiles

---

[1] See N. Barsukov, *Zhizhń i trudÿ M. P. Pogodina*, 2nd edn. (St. Petersburg 1904),
ii. 242.

[2] According to Pogodin, medieval Russia differed from Western Europe primarily because all the Russian princes were members of one family, bound in
allegiance to the eldest. In his *History of the Russian People* (1829–33) N. A. Polevoï
called this 'family feudalism' and sharply disagreed with Karamzin who thought
it was the Russian equivalent of Western European feudal hierarchy.

[3] Pogodin, *Istoriko-kriticheskie otrÿvki*, p. 62.

[4] See Pogodin, *Istoricheskie aforizmÿ* (Moscow 1836), pp. 29–30.

[5] Pogodin's *Historical Aphorisms*, which were written down in broad outline in

themselves admitted this. Samarin, who studied at Moscow University with K. Aksakov (whom he mainly had in mind in the reference to his fellow students), defined Pogodin's role in his intellectual development as follows:

Among the professors, the one who influenced me and many of the other students most strongly was Pogodin. . . . I would find it impossible to say what he taught us, or to reproduce the subject-matter of his lectures; but he showed us that is was possible to look at Russian history and Russian life in general from a completely new angle. Western formulas are not applicable to us; the Russian way of life is an expression of specific principles unknown to other nations; our evolution is subject to its own laws that have not yet been defined by scholarship. Pogodin spoke chaotically, without submitting evidence, but in such a way that we absorbed his convictions. Before Pogodin the prevailing trend was to search Russian history for parallels to the history of the Western nations; Pogodin was the first, as far as I know—at any rate the first for me and my fellow students—to point to the need to interpret Russian history by its own criteria.[1]

Pogodin's emphasis on the qualitative distinctiveness of Russia and also, to some extent, his antithesis between Russia and Europe, undoubtedly anticipated a number of Slavophile ideas. The Slavophiles, too, assumed that 'pure' Russian principles ruled out struggle, sudden upheavals, and revolution. Both Pogodin's conception and Slavophile doctrine were, in this respect, an ideological reaction against the intensification of the class struggles in the capitalist countries of Western Europe. This real coincidence of views, together with a number of other apparent similarities, have led many scholars to draw too close a parallel between the doctrine of Official Nationality and Slavophilism. One of the most emphatic was Plekhanov, who devoted the whole of a lengthy article to showing that there were no essential differences between Slavophilism and views of Pogodin and Shevȳrëv. 'Slavophilism and the theory of Official Nationality', Plekhanov wrote, 'are essentially one and the same

---

1823–6, were first published in the *Moscow Herald* in 1827. A separate edition was published in 1836. See P. Milyukov, *Glavnȳe techeniya russkoi istoricheskoĭ mȳsli*, 3rd edn. (St. Petersburg 1913), p. 282.

[1] Quoted from Barsukov, op. cit. iv. 4–5.

doctrine, equally close to the hearts of certain ideologists representative of two social strata, but understood by them in different ways. . . . The Slavophiles represented the nobility, while Pogodin was a *raznochinets*.'[1] Plekhanov himself thus drew attention to a fundamental difference, although at the same time he did all he could to belittle its significance. All that divided the two sides, he implied, was Pogodin's lack of sophistication, which grated upon the Slavophiles, and the fact that enlightened noblemen in easy circumstances could afford to show greater independence.[2]

In order to prove his thesis Plekhanov referred to Shevȳrëv's article 'A Russian's View of Contemporary European Civilization', published in 1841 in the first issue of the *Muscovite* (*Moskvityanin*). In this article Shevȳrëv argued that all European countries suffered to a greater or lesser degree from the same dreadful spiritual malady which had manifested itself in Germany as the Reformation and in France as the Revolution. As discussions in the Western press had shown, the West was itself aware of its sickness;[3] some thinkers there were even making the attempt to reconcile philosophy and faith, the most important of them being Schelling, who, after exhaustive inquiries, had become conscious of the inadequacy of philosophy and now payed homage to religion. Shevȳrëv called this 'spiritual act' the 'most momentous psychological fact of our century',[4] but pointed out that Schelling was now silent, since he clearly sensed that his new philosophy was alien to the spirit of the age. The malady of the age was in fact incurable: Russians should therefore resist the 'magic spell' still cast upon them by the West, become aware of their 'distinctiveness', and shake off their apathy and lack of self-confidence. Russia was fortunate in her historical youth; her strength lay in her age-old religious beliefs, her instinct of political unity, and her sense of nationality. Perhaps Russia and no other was a providential

---

[1] Plekhanov, *M. P. Pogodin i bor'ba klassov* (1911), Sochineniya, xxiii. 96–7.

[2] Ibid., pp. 97–101.

[3] To prove his thesis Shevȳrëv quoted a lengthy excerpt from P. Chasles's 'Revue de la littérature anglaise', published in the *Revue de deux mondes* on 1 November 1840. See P. Struve, *Zapiski russkogo nauchnogo instituta v Belgrade* (1940), pp. 224–8. In his article Chasles wrote about Europe's approaching 'death' and of the two young countries—the United States and Russia—that would shortly replace her. (See the *Muscovite* (1841), no. 1, pp. 242–5.)

[4] See the *Muscovite* (1841), no. 1, p. 284.

'guardian force' that would be called upon to rescue and preserve in a higher synthesis all that was valuable in Western
civilization.[1] In order to fulfil this mission, however, she must
free herself from the spiritual hold of the West. So far, Shevȳrëv
pointed out, this was still a remote vision; at the moment Russia
was like a young tree that cannot grow in the shadow of a
mighty oak, or a child whose overflowing energy is restrained
by its old nurse. In his enthusiasm Shevȳrëv was so carried
away that he put forward the following extreme proposition,
which aroused the justified anger of all Westernizers:

> Yes, in our frank, friendly, and close relations with the West we
> have failed to notice that it is like a man who carries within himself
> a dreadful contagious disease, who is surrounded by the dangerous
> exhalations of a poisonous miasma. We kiss him, embrace him,
> share with him the banquet of thought, drain the cup of feeling . . .
> and do not perceive the hidden poison in this carefree intercourse,
> and allow the delights of the banquet to mask the odour of decay
> which he already emanates.[2]

None of the leading Slavophiles could have been guilty of
this kind of vulgar and naturalistic comparison. How, therefore,
can this be reconciled with Pogodin's declaration that he occu-
pied a place *half-way* between East and West, with a greater
inclination towards the East—a position, therefore, which he
claimed to be more moderate than that of the Slavophiles?[3]
Although this suggests that Shevȳrëv went further in his negation of the West than Pogodin, it seems more likely that Plekhanov was right when he insisted that Shevȳrëv's article was
programmatic and also expressed the point of view of Pogodin,
the periodical's owner and editor-in-chief. This need not, however, imply, as Plekhanov insisted, that the standpoint of the
Slavophiles on the issue of 'Europeanism' was identical with
that of the ideologists of Official Nationality. The weakness of
Plekhanov's argument is that he overlooked the fact that the
same first issue of the *Muscovite* contained another programmatic
article, Pogodin's essay on Peter the Great,[4] which, moreover,
preceded Shevȳrëv's contribution.

---

[1] This suggestion comes from the closing part of the article; ibid., p. 296.

[2] Ibid., p. 247.

[3] See Barsukov, op. cit. ii. 224. This comment is also quoted by Plekhanov, who
questioned its accuracy. See *Sochineniya*, xxiii. 45.

[4] Attention was drawn to this article and its place in the system of 'Official

The first words of Pogodin's article set the tone of the whole essay: the Russia of today, he writes, that is European Russia, diplomatic, political, military, and commercial Russia, the Russia of manufactures and schools, literary Russia—all are the creation of Peter the Great.[1] When undertaking to describe his reign, the historian cannot but 'tremble and feel disheartened', lack words, or not know where to begin.[2] Everything, literally everything, forces us to think about this man whom Lomonosov compared to the Almighty. We wake up, look at the calendar, and recollect that it was Peter the Great who taught us to count the years from the birth of Christ. We put on our clothes—our official uniforms are cut according to Peter's instructions, from cloth woven in mills founded by Peter. Newspapers are brought in—Peter introduced them; all articles of daily use remind us of Peter, of his role in establishing trade, or in constructing ships, canals, and roads. At dinner we eat potatoes and herring and drink wine—none of these was known in Russia before Peter. After dinner we drive out for a visit and meet ladies there—it was Peter who introduced the 'assemblée' and ordered women to be admitted to masculine company. We enter university—the first secular institution of higher education in Russia was founded by Peter. A rank is bestowed on us—according to Peter's Table of Ranks; the rank gives us gentry status—for Peter decided it should be so. We travel abroad—we are following Peter's example; foreigners treat us with respect—that too we owe to Peter, who made Russia into a powerful European state. Peter is the key to all our feelings, thoughts, and actions.[3]

Pogodin's article is a true panegyric, one of the most enthusiastic appraisals of Peter in Russian historiography. The impression it leaves on the reader is that Peter created Russia from nothing; it was also clearly intended as a polemic against Slavophile critics of Peter.[4] One of the accusations levelled

Nationality' by N. V. Riasanovsky in his article 'Pogodin and Shevÿrëv in Russian Intellectual History', *Harvard Slavic Studies* (Mouton and Co., The Hague 1957), iv. 149–69, and in his book *Nicholas I and the Official Nationality in Russia* (University of California Press, Berkeley and Los Angeles 1959). Riasanovsky does not, however, show the close connection between Pogodin's attitude to Peter the Great and his 'Norman' theory.

[1] *Muscovite* (1841), no. 1, p. 3.   [2] Ibid., p. 4.   [3] Ibid., pp. 9–11.
[4] Several times in his article Pogodin mentioned the 'new critics' of Peter the

against Peter, Pogodin's article continues, is that in bringing
European civilization to Russia he degraded Russian nationality. Even if this is a valid criticism, was there the slightest
chance, Pogodin asks, that Russia might have avoided Europeanization? 'Russia is part of Europe, together they form a
geographical whole, and she must therefore, from sheer physical necessity, share her fate and take part in her development,
like a planet obedient to the laws of the solar system.'[1] In a
number of other rhetorical questions Pogodin drives home this
point. Can we give up our railways, he asks? We cannot, for
we live in Europe: during Peter's reign it would have been
equally futile to renounce the use of gunpowder and the consequent modernization of the army. Was the price paid for
Europeanization too high? Not in the least: the Revolt of the
streltsy had to be put down by force, no matter what their
nationality; the army reforms made it necessary to conscript
recruits, to bring foreigners to Russia, and to impose higher
taxes; the construction of the fleet demanded even greater sacrifices, which were, however, essential. In defiance of those who
would accuse Peter of going to extremes, Pogodin affirmed
decisively that he himself would not dare to criticize any of his
deeds, even the shaving of beards and the introduction of
German dress.[2] All of Peter's reforms were necessary, not only
from the point of view of relations with neighbouring states,
but also—and above all—from the point of view of Russia's
own internal development.[3]

This high praise is by no means irreconcilable with Pogodin's
conception of Russia's qualitative distinctiveness. When he
stated that ancient Russia was part of the East, he had in mind
the European East; to Pogodin Europe alone was the sole cradle
of civilization, a civilization which all non-European nations
would have to accept sooner or later, willingly, or as a result
of colonization.[4] Moreover he invariably insisted that without
Western European civilization Eastern European civilization
was one-sided. He was therefore quite consistent when he held

---

Great, who had appeared after more than a century of 'unbounded and uncompromising' adulation of the reforming emperor (ibid., p. 11). The suggestion
that in over a century there had been no Russian critic of Peter is, of course, not
accurate.
  [1] Ibid., pp. 11–12.   [2] Ibid., p. 17.   [3] Ibid., p. 16.
  [4] See Pogodin, *Istoricheskie aforizmȳ*, pp. 14–15.

Peter's reforms to contain the germs of the future synthesis of Rome and Byzantium, reason and faith, dynamics and statics, eccentric and concentric forces.[1] Finally, he was consistent in a more profound sense reflecting his social position: namely, as the ideologist of an autocracy which could not and would not repudiate its past[2] and as a member of the non-noble intelligentsia, who owed his university chair and indeed his whole career to Peter's Table of Ranks and the Europeanization of Russia.

Pogodin's article in any case also includes a passage which might be said to bridge the gap between his dithyramb in honour of Peter and Shevȳrëv's conservative and nationalistic exhortations published in the same issue of the *Muscovite*. With the death of Alexander I, Pogodin pointed out, the *European* stage of Russian history initiated by Peter had come to an end. 'The reign of the Emperor Nicholas', he concluded, 'has ushered in a new epoch in Russian history, the *national* epoch, which may, at the peak of its development, become renowned as a new age in the history of Europe and of mankind as a whole.'[3]

It is of some interest to note that Pogodin did not consider Peter's reforms to have been in any way unprecedented in Russian history. There had been two earlier periods of radical change, he wrote, which had come about in response to external stimuli and whose influence had been the more profound since it had affected all social strata alike. These two periods were the foundation of the Russian state by the Normans (Varangians) and its transformation into a centralized autocratic monarchy under the impact of the Mongol conquest.[4] It is worth discussing the first part of Pogodin's theory in greater detail, as his entire interpretation of history rests on his view of the 'calling of the Varangians'. The Varangians, he argued, entered Russian not as invaders, but as rulers invited to extend their rule over willing subjects; Russian statehood, in fact was created in its entirety by the Varangians and the

---

[1] See *Muscovite* (1841), no. 1, p. 24, and Pogodin, *Istoriko-kriticheskie otrȳvki*, pp. 357–8.

[2] Nicholas I considered himself to be the heir of Peter the Great and would not countenance any criticism of his reign.

[3] *Muscovite* (1841), no. 1, pp. 25–6.

[4] Ibid., p.18.

common people's contribution was merely willing subordination and obedience to their foreign rulers.

Nations, like individuals, [wrote Pogodin in his *Historical Aphorisms*] contract marriages and these marriages give birth to new nations, new offspring. Thus marriages took place between the Normans and the Slavs, the Franks and the Gauls, the Visigoths and the Spaniards, the Ostrogoths and the Italians, the Magyars and the inhabitants of Pannonia, the Normans and the Sicilians, the Teutonic Knights and the Prussians, and so forth. Although they were few in number, these husbands quite transformed their wives, together with their entire dowry (the Russian Slavs, for instance, received their entire state system from the Normans). In this respect the origins of all European states are alike.[1]

In the context of early nineteenth-century Russian and Polish historical thought the ideological meaning of Pogodin's conception is quite clear. 'Slavonic principles' were interpreted by him as the source of the 'republican' elements which gave rise to the *veche* (folkmoots) system while the Normans were felt to embody the monarchical principle of state centralism. This stereotype was fixed by Karamzin, who may have regretted 'ancient Russian liberty', but considered autocracy to be a safeguard (the 'Palladium of Russia') and came down decisively on the side of the 'Norman' theory. The Polish historians Rakowiecki, Chodakowski, and above all Joachim Lelewel, all attacked this view and evolved a counter-theory postulating the native origins of the Slavonic states and the concept of Slavonic community self-government.[2] Lelewel's 'republican' theory was adopted by the Decembrists while Pogodin, of course, developed Karamzin's conceptions, but took them to extremes. Karamzin, who belonged to the nobility, regarded the political system of Kievan Russia as the embodiment of both Norman and Slavonic elements and treated the final destruction of 'ancient Russian liberty' as a sad necessity. Pogodin, whose father had been a serf, saw the Normans as the *sole* creators of Russian statehood and regarded the Slavs (i.e. the common people) as so much pliant material to be moulded by the state. In 1848, it is worth adding, the Norman theory gained the Emperor's official stamp of approval.[3]

[1] Pogodin, *Istoricheskie aforizmȳ*, pp. 13–14.
[2] See S. S. Volk, op. cit., pp. 314–19.   [3] Ibid., p. 319.

The Slavophiles' standpoint on the Norman question differed radically from Pogodin's. The theory that the Russian state had been created not by armed conquest but by 'voluntary invitation' did not satisfy the Slavophile thinkers, who were primarily concerned to underline its indigenous, Slavonic nature. (The exception was K. Aksakov, although in his inverted version of Pogodin's theory it was the common people, not the state who embodied superior values.)[1] In Ivan Kireevsky's formulation, Russian statehood was something 'born of the peaceful evolution of national life and national consciousness, a statehood in which the religious and social concepts of the people are embodied in social existence and grow, acquire vigour, and fuse in the all-embracing unity of the social organism'.[2] In contrast to Lelewel, the Slavophiles were careful to make a distinction between their idea of 'folk principles' and 'republicanism',[3] although this did not bring them any closer to Pogodin's point of view. They believed the essence of Russian history to be not the state but the people, and Russian greatness to be founded not on material power but on moral principles preserved in the village communes. Their faith in the common people contrasted with the pessimistic view of Pogodin, who was convinced that only force would turn the Russian peasants into human beings,[4] and that as a nation the Russians must be subject to stimuli and control from outside.[5] The Russian people's sole claim to fame, he thought, was that it provided excellent material for autocratic rule and in a moment of frankness he wrote openly: 'The Russian people is magnificent, but still only potentially magnificent. In reality it is hideous, vile, and bestial.'[6]

It is clear, therefore, that the Slavophiles had sufficient cause to treat the Official Nationality theory with considerable reserve. In spite of Pogodin's repeated invitations their contributions to the *Muscovite* were infrequent. The turning-point came early in 1845, when Pogodin, worried by his dwindling readership, decided to gain the more active collaboration of the

---

[1] See chapter 6, pp. 243–4.
[2] I. V. Kireevsky, *Polnoe sobranie sochineniĭ* (Moscow 1911), i. 184.
[3] See p. 143.   [4] See Barsukov, op. cit. ii. 17.
[5] See Barsukov (ed.), *Pis'ma M. P. Pogodina, S. P. Shevȳrëova i M. A. Maksimovicha k knyaz'yu P. A. Vyazenskomu 1825–1847 godov* (n.p., n.d.), p. 58.
[6] Quoted from Barsukov, *Zhizhn*, ii. 17.

Slavophiles at all costs and even agreed to be replaced by Kireevsky as editor. The Slavophiles put forward their own conditions—the exclusion of Pogodin and Shevȳrëv from the paper's management and various other changes among the contributors—but in fact agreed to a compromise. However, the Slavophile *Muscovite* only appeared for three months: ideological differences became even more marked than before and further collaboration turned out to be impossible.[1] The final break was brought about by Petr Kireevsky's polemic with Pogodin over the origins of the Russian state and the national character of the Russian people.

In the first issue of the *Muscovite* in 1845 (that is the first issue edited by I. Kireevsky) Pogodin published an article entitled 'A Parallel as regards Principle between Russian History and the History of Western European States'.[2] In this article Pogodin claimed that the specific nature of Russian history depended solely on the fact that the Russian people was by its very nature as well as climatic influence meek, obedient, and passively indifferent. Russian and Western states differed in their origins, he suggested, because in the West the native populations had fought against the invaders, while in Russia they had submitted without resistance to the 'first newcomers'. In the West the local populations had imposed their civilization on the 'newcomers', while in Russia the 'newcomers' had grafted their 'civilization of citizenship' on to the local population, who were still 'fallow soil untouched by the plough'.[3] Pogodin himself admitted that the 'voluntary invitation to rule' was in fact a disputable point and differed little from conquest, but held that nevertheless this initially minor difference had set Russian history on to a completely different course. Thanks to the Russian people's meekness and obedience society was able to evolve without the clash of mutual antagonisms and conflict, without an independent aristocracy and a third estate struggling for its rights. In this evolution the only creative force was the increasingly powerful state organization.

Having assumed responsibility for the *Muscovite*'s ideological line, the Slavophiles could hardly leave this article unanswered.

---

[1] See *Ocherki po istorii russkoĭ zhurnalistiki i kritiki* (Leningrad 1950), pp. 493–5.
[2] See Pogodin, *Istoriko-kriticheskie otrȳvki*, pp. 55–83.
[3] Ibid., p. 80.

The reply was written by Petr Kireevsky, who yielded only to
Aksakov in his enthusiasm for the 'common people'. His article
'On Ancient Russian History' was approved by the other
Slavophiles and published in the third issue of the periodical.
Pogodin tried to prevent its publication and printed his own
sharp and dogmatic answer in the same issue as the offending
article. Both sides clearly realized that further collaboration
was impossible. 'Friends are worse than enemies', Pogodin
noted angrily in his diary. 'Everyone is leaving the *Muscovite*
and there is really no point in keeping it going any longer',
Khomyakov wrote to Samarin at the same time.[1]

Pogodin's article, Petr Kireevsky wrote in his reply, expressed two contradictory views at the same time. On the one
hand, its author righly emphasized that Russia had not been
subject to armed conquest, on the other he consistently mini-
mized the difference between conquest and the 'voluntary invitation to rule'. If Pogodin's interpretation of the Russian
national character was correct, invitation and conquest must
be regarded as synonymous.[2] Petr Kireevsky also accused
Pogodin of a pessimistic and unfair view of the Russian national
character.

One must admit [he wrote] that a man who allows *mere climatic
factors in his country* to stop him from taking an interest in public
affairs, and a nation which *quietly submits to the first newcomer*, which
accepts *foreign masters* without resistance, whose *distinguishing
feature* is *absolute meekness and indifference*, which is willing to renounce its faith at the first command of its *foreign rulers*, can scarcely
arouse our sympathy. A nation of this kind would be devoid of all
spiritual strength, all human dignity, a nation rejected by God;
a nation like this could never have created anything great.[3]

Fortunately, P. Kireevsky continued, Pogodin's views were
contradicted by the entire course of Russian history. There
were times when the Russian nation fought to the last man,
offering heroic resistance to all *foreign masters*; during the Tartar
invasions not a single Russian town was conquered without a
bitter struggle; it was not with *meekness* and *indifference* that the

[1] See *Ocherki po istorii russkoĭ zhurnalistiki i kritiki*, p. 494.
[2] *Muscovite* (1845), no. 3, p. 13.
[3] Ibid., p. 14.

Russian people welcomed *foreign masters* in 1612 and 1812. Kireevsky's arguments here are of particular interest, as they refute the widely accepted view that the Slavophiles were prone to uncritical idealization of the common people's passivity. Not long after, the Westernizer Vissarion Belinsky was to use similar arguments in his polemic with Pogodin.[1]

In Petr Kireevsky's view, Pogodin's basic mistake was to look at the social organization of the early Slavs from the point of view of the German historians (mainly A. L. Schlözer), who had initiated research into the origins of the Russian state in the previous century. Kireevsky contrasted their one-sided and unjust interpretation with facts brought to light in research undertaken by Slavonic scholars and summed up in Šafářik's *Slavonic Antiquities* and in W. A. Maciejowski's *History of Slavonic Legislation*. These authors had shown that the early Slavs were by no means 'fallow soil untouched by the plough' but had their own patriarchal social system based on common ownership of the land and on folkmoots ranging from a village meeting to the assembly of the whole people attended only by the elders. The Slavonic tribes had their own princes, voivodes, and chiefs, who submitted to the assemblies and the authority of the Grand Prince; the generally accepted ideal was the *mir*, which meant not only community self-government, but also 'universe', and 'harmony' (the Greek *kosmos*), unity, wholeness, and concord.[2] Slavonic statehood, in fact, was not something imposed from outside, but grew organically out of the native clan system. According to Kireevsky, the Norman dynasty of Riurik and his brothers was selected in accordance with the ancient custom of substituting a new dynasty for an existing ruling family that had grown too numerous, in order to avoid quarrels over seniority; in a similar manner the Poles had ousted the Popiel dynasty and placed the peasant Piast upon the throne.[3] The Normans had not founded the Russian state, nor had the election of Riurik brought about any essential changes; the reason why Nestor had not described the political system obtaining in Russia in his *Primary Chronicle* was simply because nothing had

---

[1] In the *Review of Russian Literature for the Year 1846*; V. G. Belinsky, *Polnoe sobranie sochineniĭ*, x. 23–5.

[2] See *Muscovite* (1845), no. 3, pp. 40–1.

[3] Ibid., pp. 30, 47.

changed in this system, everything remained as it was, traditional and self-evident.[1]

Pogodin's reply was concise and emphatic. He would not admit the justice of any of the criticisms levelled against him and even refused to withdraw formulations that were clearly unfortunate. The distinction between conquest and the voluntary submission to foreign rule was a minor one, he argued, and this justified his use of such phrases as 'subjugation' (*pokorenie*) or 'imposing discipline'. In reply to the various points raised by Petr Kireevsky he again claimed that there had been no princes in Russia before Riurik, no unity among the tribes, and that the word *mir* simply signified the absence of war. The experiences of other Slavonic peoples, he insisted, could not be applied to Russia since their history (early Polish history in particular) had absolutely nothing in common with Russian history. In his reply Pogodin assumed the pose of the objective historian who passes on to his readers only facts learnt from chronicles. 'You try to find a confirmation of your hypothesis in history', he admonished his adversary, 'while I learn from history and only relate what she has told me.'[2] Only in one passage did the 'objective scholar' cast aside his objectivity and accuse Kireevsky on directly ideological grounds: 'By robbing us of our patience and humility, the two greatest Christian virtues and the crowning glory of our history, you serve the cause of the West.'[3]

In view of his break with the *Muscovite* Petr Kireevsky did not publish—or even write—the previously announced second part of his polemical article. It seems likely that this sequel would have dealt with later Russian history, above all with the issue of autocracy. In order to complete the picture, it is worth citing Ivan Kireevsky's views on this subject, expressed in a letter he wrote to Pogodin in 1846. Criticizing an article by Pogodin entitled 'A Historian's Laudatory Word in Honour of Karamzin', Kireevsky accused Karamzin of making insufficient distinction between the two concepts of *yedinovlastie* (the rule of one person) and *samovlastie* (in the sense of unlimited power).[4]

In the olden days, [Kireevsky wrote] allegiance was never unconditional. How many princes were banished for not complying

1 See *Muscovite* (1845) p. 35.   2 Ibid., p. 58.   3 Ibid., p. 55.
4 As we have tried to show, Karamzin's conception of autocracy was closer in

with the conditions! The mere suspicion of a crime aroused the whole of Russia against Boris! The failure to respect Russian customs and observances was enough to destroy the false Dmitry. And what about the legal documents in obedience to which all our rulers, from Shuisky to Anna, kissed the cross? On the contrary, it was a characteristic feature of allegiance in the olden days that it was not *unconditional* but restricted by *law*. The very phrase 'unconditionally loyal subject' is out of keeping with the character of earlier centuries and suggests the ferment of modern times. It is a term from the lexicon of Theophan and Yavorsky.[1]

Kireevsky was certainly aware that his criticism of Karamzin was even more applicable to Pogodin. What he referred to as the 'blind spot in Karamzin's clear-sighted intellect', that is his unqualified vindication of absolutism, his belief in the 'education of the simple, ignorant masses by an enlightened government',[2] was in fact the corner-stone of the theory of Official Nationality; Karamzin himself, as I tried to show earlier in this chapter, was not quite so unequivocal in this respect.

It is possible, at this point, to formulate certain conclusions. The essence of the ideology of Official Nationality, the element which determined its structure, was the concept of unrestricted autocracy. The point of view of autocracy determined Pogodin's views on statehood and the common people, on Europeanization and the historical significance of Peter the Great. These views were essentially different from Slavophile theories: in formulating the thesis that the state was the only creative force in Russian history Pogodin came closer to such conservative Westernizers and 'etatists' as Chicherin, and to the 'étatist' school in Russian historical scholarship, which was strongly opposed by the Slavophiles.[3] For Pogodin autocracy represented the quintessence of the Russian 'principle' and since modern

---

meaning to *yedinovlastie* (as Kireevsky understood it) than to *samovlastie*, in the sense of unlimited power, although his choice of terminology does not make this distinction clear. When Kireevsky attributed to Karamzin an absolute apologia for autocracy, he was clearly influenced by the one-sided selection of quotations from his writings made by Pogodin; on the other hand there can be little doubt that Karamzin's attitude to autocracy was closer to Pogodin's than to that of the Slavophiles.

[1] I. Kireevsky, op. cit. ii. 239.
[2] Ibid., p. 241.
[3] See N. L. Rubinstein, *Russkaya istoriografiya*, p. 265

Russia had not ceased to be an autocractic state he was less concerned in his historical studies with the issue of 'ancient and modern Russia', which was of such importance to the Slavophiles. The Petrine reforms, he argued, did not represent an abrupt break in historical continuity, for when Peter created his state without regard for the beliefs and traditions of the meek and passive common people he only acted as the Normans had once done, thus harking back to the oldest and most venerable Russian traditions.

An analysis of Slavophile theory must be postponed to a later chapter. To anticipate later conclusions one might say that Slavophile thought was primarily concerned with the problem of the traditional social bonds preserved in the peasant commune, which were destroyed both by Western capitalism and by the Westernized bureaucratic absolutism of imperial Russia. For Pogodin and Shevȳrëv this was an issue of secondary importance: Pogodin in fact criticized Slavophile views on the village commune in the course of some comments on an article by Khomyakov.[1] When he contrasted Russia and Europe and criticized Western liberalism it was not because of any romantic dislike of capitalism, or belief in a conservative anti-capitalist utopia, but because he was a convinced defender of autocracy. The differences between Slavophilism and the ideology of Official Nationality were underestimated by contemporaries, even by the Slavophiles themselves. There are good reasons why, in the context of contemporary events, these differences should have become blurred, but this ambiguity cannot be justified in a structural analysis of the two ideologies.

Another aspect of the problem deserves some attention. During the 1840s the Westernizers, who were hostile to the Slavophiles, were inclined to belittle the differences between the Slavophiles and Pogodin and Shevȳrëv; they ranked both sides among the anti-Western 'Muscovite party' and often referred to the *Muscovite* as the 'organ of the Slavophiles'. For an elucidation of this fact one must look not at the doctrine of Official Nationality as such, but into certain of its aspects emphasized by the publishers of the *Muscovite*. The government of Nicholas I represented traditional legitimism and only resorted to nationalist slogans with the greatest reluctance;

[1] See Barsukov, op. cit. vii. 320–1.

whenever there was any conflict of interest between 'national-ism' and legitimism the latter always prevailed, as was shown by the emperor's negative attitude to Panslavism, whose first eager propagandist and ideologist on Russian soil was Mikhail Pogodin.[1] In spite of the inclusion of the world 'nationality' in Uvarov's 'triune formula', Nicholas I considered affairs of state in dynastic categories and opposed any far-reaching attempts to introduce a nationalistic element into autocracy. The views of the emperor's Minister of Finance, Count E. Kankrin—who seriously suggested (according to T. Bulgarin, who backed him) that Russia be called 'Petrovia' and Russians 'Petrovians'[2]— can serve as an extreme illustration of this attitude. Unlike Kankrin (and unlike the emperor himself) Pogodin—for all his respect for the monarchy—was inclined to put 'great power' nationalism in first place and considered legitimism to be a traditional superstition which tended to impede expansionist policies (although he was careful to keep these opinions rela-tively quiet). His extreme conservative anti-Westernism and his efforts to make the Russian autocracy and Russian life as a whole more 'national', were features which brought Pogodin closer to the Slavophiles and made him their ally in the ideo-logical struggle, in spite of intrinsic differences between them. In an age which defined ideological divisions in terms of atti-tudes to 'Western values' these surface similarities proved more important than underlying differences.

[1] See M. Boro-Petrovich, *The Emergence of Russian Panslavism* (Columbia University Press, New York 1958), pp. 26–31, and N. V. Riasanovsky, *Nicholas I and the Official Nationality in Russia*, chapter 5.

[2] Riasanovsky, op. cit., p. 139.

2

The Philosophical Romanticism of
the Lovers of Wisdom: V. F. Odoevsky

In the previous chapter I referred to Pogodin's 'Schellingian-ism', his attempt to formulate the concept of Russia's qualitative distinctness in philosophical terms. This 'Schellingianism', however, was really no more than a superficial 'stylization', a tribute paid to fashion and to the prevailing intellectual climate. In his philosophical thought Pogodin was concerned with the traditional problems of autocracy and the Norman genesis of the Russian state—problems to which the philosophical antithesis of East and West as concentric and eccentric forces was related in a purely external and verbalistic fashion. In Shevȳrëv the elements of philosophical romanticism are more authentic, but his contribution was confined to a reinterpretation of the ideas of the Moscow Lovers of Wisdom in the spirit of Uvarov's 'triune formula'.

In the 1820s the most important of the centres where the anti-Enlightenment romantic philosophy was beginning to take shape was the Society of Lovers of Wisdom. The Lovers of Wisdom were the direct precursors of the Slavophiles and their ideas, particularly the philosophical evolution of the society's president, Prince Vladimir Odoevsky, led directly to issues taken up later in Slavophile anthropology and philosophy of history.

The secret Society of Lovers of Wisdom was organized in 1823 by young people employed in the Archives of the Ministry of Foreign Affairs in Moscow, called by Pushkin 'the young men of the archives'.[1] In principle this circle had only five members (V. F. Odoevsky, D. V. Venevitinov, N. M. Rozhalin, and the later Slavophiles I. V. Kireevsky and A. I. Koshelëv).

---

[1] In *Eugene Onegin* (vii. 49) Pushkin wrote:
> Viewed by the archive youth who cluster
> At any gathering or dance . . .
(translation by Babette Deutsch quoted from *Poems, Prose and Plays of Alexander Pushkin* (Random House, New York 1936)).

Their influence was, however, quite considerable, thanks to their close contacts with the literary society of S. E. Raich (members included Pogodin and Shevȳrëv, V. P. Titov, N. A. Mel'gunov, and the poet F. I. Tyutchev),[1] which was allowed to function openly. The Lovers of Wisdom propagated their ideas in the almanac *Mnemosyne* published in 1824 (the Decembrist V. K. Küchelbecker was one of the contributors). For the word 'philosophy' they substituted the mystical, Masonic term *lyubomudrie* (love of Wisdom) in order to establish their independence of the French *philosophers*. 'To this day [Odoevsky wrote in *Mnemosyne*] everyone imagines a philosopher to resemble one of those eighteenth-century French rattles; I wonder whether there are many people capable of understanding the enormous difference between a truly divine philosophy and that of some Voltaire or Helvetius.' This 'truly divine' philosophy the young Lovers of Wisdom sought in Germany. 'Land of ancient Teutons! Land of noble ideas! It is to you I turn my worshipful gaze',[2] was how the society's president expressed his feelings.

In his *Memoirs* Koshelëv described the meetings of the Society:

German philosophy predominated, i.e. Kant, Fichte, Schelling, Oken, Görres, and others. We sometimes read our own philosophical works, but more frequently we discussed the works of the German philosophers we had just read. The chief subject of our discussions was the general principles upon which human knowledge is founded. Christianity seemed to us suitable only for the masses of the people, but not for lovers of wisdom like us. We prized Spinoza particularly highly and put his works far above the New Testament and the rest of the Holy Scripture.[3]

The most eloquent speaker was the Society's secretary, the poet Venevitinov, whose speeches frequently roused his listeners to rapture. Odoevsky's lyrical recollections give some idea of the high pitch of enthusiasm that prevailed in the Society.

. . . While on this path [i.e. the path of Philosophy] [he wrote], our seekers experienced moments of rapture whose sweetness cannot be

---

[1] See A. I. Koshelëv, *Zapiski (1812–83)* (Berlin 1884), pp. 11–12.
[2] *Mnemosyne*, iv. 163, 169. Quoted from P. N. Sakulin, *Iz istorii russkogo idealizma. Knyaź' V. F. Odoevsky* (Moscow 1913), i. 138, 139.
[3] Koshelëv, op. cit., p. 12.

comprehended by those who have never been tormented by spiritual longings, whose parched lips have not clung to the fountain of thought, who have never been intoxicated by its magic waters, nor by those who corrupted the mind by cold calculation before reaching maturity, who put their hearts up for sale while young and squandered their soul's treasures in the market-place.

Oh divinely happy moments! The philosopher's words to the youth come straight from the heart; the youth sees nature as a harmonious whole; you have no desire to doubt—all is clear, all is comprehensible!

Oh happy moments, harbingers of paradise! Why do you pass so soon?[1]

The Lovers of Wisdom were mainly interested in Schelling's philosophy of art and philosophy of nature (in this respect Koshelëv's account was not quite accurate). They saw the world as a living work of art and art as an organic unity of unconscious and conscious creation, of irrational intuition and rational consciousness, which expressed the most profound essence of the world, the primary unity of subject and object, of spirit and matter, of the unconscious and conscious, of blind will and creative reason. The inspired artist, they thought, does not imitate reality, but creates according to divine principles of creation, and therefore truly deserves to be called a divine being. Art is closely related to philosophy and artistic intuition is one of the tools of philosophy. The greatest of the arts therefore is poetry (Venevitinov defined poetry as the 'mother' of sculpture, painting, and music).[2] No wonder that the young Lovers of Wisdom were implacably hostile to all manifestations of classicism and all 'imitations of French models'. Their most important literary inspiration was German romanticism, on which the poet V. A. Zhukovsky modelled himself.

The Society's philosophy of nature was also romantic. Like Schelling and the Schellingian naturalists in Russia, Vellansky and Pavlov,[3] they opposed atomistic and mechanistic physics

---

[1] W. F. Odoevsky, *Russkie nochi* (predislovie k izdaniyu 1844 goda) (Moscow 1913), p. 50.

[2] See D. V. Venevitinov, 'Sculpture, Painting and Music' in *Izbrannoe* (Moscow 1956), pp. 139–44.

[3] One of the thinkers who influenced Odoevsky most was D. N. Vellansky (See Sakulin, op. cit., p. 131). It is worth noting that Vellansky himself owed much to

and regarded nature as a living, spiritual whole containing within it the creation, movement, and struggle of opposites, of concentric and eccentric forces. This led them to interpret the world in terms of polarity, of the attraction and repulsion of opposites such as darkness and light, the male and female element, positive and negative electricity. Their philosophy certainly included some dialectical features, but at the same time represented a retreat from scientific nature-study to medieval mysticism, alchemy, and magic. For the Lovers of Wisdom nature was only the outer garment of the soul whose manifestations all had a secret symbolic meaning. The key to an understanding of these symbols, and therefore also to an interpretation of the secrets of nature and to its mastery, was to be found in speculative philosophy. In his *Russian Nights* Odoevsky described this period as follows:

My youth was spent at a time when metaphysics was as much in the air as the political sciences are now. We believed in the possibility of an absolute theory which would allow us to create (we used the term 'construct') all the phenomena of nature, just as today we believe in the possibility of a social order that would satisfy all human needs. Perhaps both such a theory and such a social order will really be discovered some day, but *ab posse ad esse consequentia non valet*. However that may be, at that time nature and human life seemed quite clear to us, and we tended to look down upon physicists and chemists, utilitarians who soiled themselves by contact with 'vulgar matter'. . . .[1]

Another important feature of the Society's philosophy was romantic nationalism. Many articles in *Mnemosyne* called for a truly national culture and opposed French influences in the name of the genuine national 'distinctiveness' and 'authenticity' (*Eigentümlichkeit* or *Echtheit*) propagated by German idealism. This call for the creation of a 'national' literature seemed to coincide with the literary programme of the Decembrists, which was why Küchelbecker became a close collaborator on the periodical *Mnemosyne*. The philosophical basis of this

the Polish Schellingian J. Gołuchowski, whose book *Die Philosophie in ihren Verhältnissen zum Leben ganzer Völker und einzelner Menschen* (1822) he translated into Russian in 1834. See G. Shpet, *Ocherk razvitiya russkoĭ filosofii* (Petrograd 1922), i. 126.

[1] Odoevsky, *Russkie nochi*, p. 8.

collaboration was, however, very flimsy. For the Lovers of
Wisdom—as for Herder and the German romantics—the
national problem could not be solved through political struggle
for modern forms of national existence, but purely in the
spiritual sphere, through the development of the organic
principle embodied in a nation's history.[1] According to the
rationalistic views of the Enlightenment (which had a considerable influence on the Decembrists), the nation was above
all a 'body politic' subject to laws, and an 'aggregation of
citizens'.[2] The Lovers of Wisdom on the other hand conceived
the nation as a whole transcending its individual parts, a
unique collective individuality evolving historically by its own
'distinctive' principles. This interpretation could give rise to an
idealization of the irrational elements in national existence, to
a condemnation of 'mechanical changes' and revolutions which
interrupt historical continuity. The proposition that universal
human values can only be attained by way of 'nationality', that
history has destined every nation to have its own, quite separate
mission, was likely to clash with the rationalistic universalism
that was one of the main (though not always consciously formulated) premises of Decembrist thought.

A characteristic expression of these views is to be found in
Venevitinov's article 'On the State of Enlightenment in Russia'
(1826).[3] Russian enlightenment was something borrowed,
Venevitinov maintained, but this did not mean that Russians
were incapable of spontaneous spiritual creativity. The lack of
cultural 'distinctiveness' could be ascribed to the hasty assimilation of the outward trappings of European civilization. Russia
had received a ready-made literature before she was able to
express her own inner essence and find appropriate forms for it.
Hence Russian literature could not boast of a single work that
had sprung from genuine enthusiasm. Russian poetry was not
a poetry of ideas but mere verbal jugglery. In order to be

[1] See M. K. Azadovsky, *Istoriya russkoĭ fol'kloristiki*, pp. 217–18.

[2] Of special interest from this point of view are the opinions of the most radical
of the Decembrists, the leader of the Southern Association, P. I. Pestel. In his
Russian Truth Pestel defined the nation as a 'collection of all those people who,
while belonging to one state, form a civic society'. *Izbrannӯe sotsial'no-politicheskie i
filosofskie proizvedeniya dekabristov* (Moscow 1951), ii. 77.

[3] See Venevitinov, op. cit., pp. 209–14. This article has been analysed in detail
by A. Koyré, *La Philosophie . . .*, pp. 149–52.

forced to think creatively Russia must be isolated from other nations, must have demonstrated to her a total view of the evolution of the human spirit grounded in firm philosophical principles; only then would she discover her own distinctive nature and true destiny.[1]

The Decembrists and Lovers of Wisdom, who came from similar well-educated upper-class families, often interconnected by marriage, were not themselves clearly aware of the ideological differences dividing them. To both sides it seemed that they differed not so much in respect of views as of interests and attitudes. The concern with German idealistic philosophy was a retreat from the political commitment of the Decembrists. The Lovers of Wisdom felt that German philosophy enabled them to comprehend the world as a whole and to penetrate the most profound mysteries of existence. From these heights concrete social and political problems—let alone the petty worries of everyday life—became less important, indeed almost imperceptible.

In one of his works Odoevsky gave the following description of a young Lover of Wisdom: 'The petty worries that weigh down weak humanity are alien to him; he does not notice them from the heights to which his spirit has soared; even the destructive rule of time is nothing to him, for his spirit does not age.'[2] What the Decembrists could not accept was the young philosophers' habit of looking at the world *sub specie aeternitatis*, their contempt for 'earth-bound empiricism' and blindness to prevailing social and historical realities. The correspondence of the two Odoevsky cousins casts an interesting light on these differences. The elder cousin Alexander, who was a Decembrist, accused the younger of 'idolatry', of losing himself in abstractions, and of lacking true independence. The younger, Vladimir, accused the elder of a lack of understanding for the higher concerns of spiritual life.[3]

As A. Koyré has aptly pointed out,[4] the differences between the Lovers of Wisdom and the Decembrists reflected not only the gap between generations, but also the difference between

---

[1] While defending national 'distinctiveness', Venevitinov, in contrast to the Slavophiles, stressed that the true carriers of the 'distinctiveness' are the enlightened classes and not the people. See Azadovsky, op. cit., pp. 219–22.

[2] Quoted from Sakulin, op. cit., p. 298.

[3] See Sakulin, pp. 299–305.   [4] See Koyré, op. cit., p. 43.

the two capitals. The philosophy of the Lovers of Wisdom evolved in Moscow, while the main centre of the Decembrists was St. Petersburg. 'For God's sake,' the Decembrist Küchelbecker wrote to Vladimir Odoevsky, 'tear yourself away from the rotten stinking atmosphere of Moscow.'[1] Semi-patriarchal Moscow with its old noble families, the capital of ancient Muscovy and the centre of Russian religious life, was the main stronghold of conservatism, mysticism, and resistance to rationalist, revolutionary, and liberal thought. In the eighteenth century it had been the chief centre of the Rosicrucians, the mystical wing of Freemasonry, and in the nineteenth century it was to give birth to the Slavophile movement.[2] St. Petersburg, on the other hand, was a town without a past, and at that time the only modern European city in Russia; it was the cradle of the progressive non-noble intelligentsia and the main centre of liberal, bourgeois-democratic, and socialist thought.

Taken to their logical conclusion, the views of the Lovers of Wisdom implied condemnation of the political stand taken by the Decembrists. They themselves were not aware of this however. Koshelëv relates how deeply he was impressed when he overheard the conspirators calmly discuss the need 'd'en finir avec ce gouvernement' at a public reception. The reaction of the Lovers of Wisdom, to whom he related the conversation, was not indignation but—on the contrary—a sudden outburst of interest in politics. For a time everyone plunged into a study of the French liberals (Benjamin Constant and Royer-Collard) and German philosophy seemed about to be deposed. When the first news of the uprising of December 1825 reached Moscow from St. Petersburg the Society of the Lovers of Wisdom was disbanded as a precautionary measure, but its members by no means concealed their sympathy for the revolutionaries. In response to widespread rumours that the Second Army Corps would not take its oath of allegiance to Tsar Nicholas and that General Ermolev was marching on Moscow from the Caucasus, they forgot about Schelling and took riding and fencing lessons to prepare for the coming events. During the wave of arrests,

---

[1] Sakulin, op. cit., p. 304.

[2] G. Florovsky advanced the view that Slavophilism could be said to continue the Masonic mysticism of the reign of Catherine II. G. Florovsky, *Puti russkogo bogoslaviya* (Paris 1937), pp. 116, 254. The Masonic conception of the 'inner man' does indeed have something in common with Kireevsky's anthropology.

which affected Moscow as well, the young idealists dreamt of exile and a martyr's crown, and after the hanging of five Decembrists they became prey to horror and despair. Every one of them, it seemed, had lost a father or a brother.[1] These spontaneous reactions, however, cannot disguise the fact that the ideas of the Lovers of Wisdom were influenced by different intellectual trends and were subject to their own objective logical development. This was to become quite clear after the December uprising.

Although their circle was formally disbanded, the Moscow Lovers of Wisdom remained in close touch with one another and published their work in Pogodin's *Moscow Herald* (*Moskovskiĭ Vestnik*).[2] Their interests, however, underwent a gradual and at first seemingly minor shift from nature philosophy and the 'general foundations of knowledge' to philosophy of history and religion. Of particular interest is the philosophical evolution of Prince V. Odoevsky. Sakulin suggests that the early 1830s, when the former philosophical circle finally disintegrated, marked a turning-point in the evolution of Odoevsky's view of the world[3] from the *lyubomudrie* of the 1820s to a 'philosophical and mystical idealism'. He became interested in a mystical philosophy of history and anthropology and devoted more time to reading the works of mystics and theosophists such as Boehme and Pordage, Saint-Martin and Baader. While this is certainly true, it should be emphasized that the 'turning-point 'did not mark a decisive change, let alone a break with Schellingianism. Schelling himself underwent a comparable philosophical evolution at that time: his Munich lectures foreshadowed his later 'philosophy of mythology' and 'philosophy of revelation'.

One of the vital issues that now engaged Odoevsky's attention was the problem of original sin. Man, he wrote, was once a free spirit; his present dependence on nature is the result of the Fall and the flesh is therefore a disease of the spirit.[4]

---

[1] See Koshelëv, op. cit., pp. 13–18.

[2] This periodical was published from 1829 to 1830. The collaboration between the Lovers of Wisdom and Pogodin was not smooth, even though the latter was not yet at that time a spokesman for the 'Official Nationality'.

[3] See Sakulin, op. cit., p. 324.

[4] Ibid., pp. 446–8 (Sakulin's monograph makes extensive use of the Odoevsky archives).

Regeneration is possible, however, through love and art[1]—mankind's aesthetic development has shown that humanity is capable of regaining its lost integrity and spiritual harmony. In spite of Plato's views, poets are essential to the state[2] and the aesthetic element is an important factor in the process of human regeneration. Art must, however, be permeated by religion: when divorced from religion it is an 'egoistic force'. The same is true about science, which brings about a nation's spiritual death when divorced from religion and poetry.[3] Capitalist England, according to Odoevsky, was an example of a morally dead nation, destroyed by industrialization and the division of labour, by the greed for gold which had expanded industry at the cost of turning man into a machine.[4] Odoevsky thought that every philosophical system had its counterpart in some period in the historical evolution of mankind,[5] and argued that there was a close parallel between the English industrial system, which converted society into an aggregation of individuals not bound together by any moral ties, and English empirical philosophy with its scepticism of anything intangible and its one-sided analytical approach.[6] The characteristic conservative–romantic attack on capitalism and its corollary, the romantic critique of rationalism, thus made its first appearance in Russian thought. This theme, which was of little significance for Pogodin's pseudo-romantic conservatism, was later to be taken up and developed by the Slavophiles.[7]

In his reflections on England Odoevsky differed from the Slavophiles in one important respect: for him the repository of national tradition, the only force capable of resisting the destructive tendencies of the industrial age, were the upper classes. In the people he saw only low and selfish passions whose liberation he feared. So far the salvation of England had been her aristocracy, but now the English were about to introduce reforms (the 1832 Reform Bill), which would allow 'John Bull with his red face and gnarled hands to force his way into Par-

---

[1] Odoevsky called music the most superior of the arts: 'the immediate language of the soul'. Sakulin, op. cit., pp. 506–13.

[2] Ibid., p. 510.   [3] Ibid., p. 564.   [4] Ibid., p. 577.

[5] Ibid., p. 328.   [6] Ibid., pp. 578–80.

[7] It was taken up also by Shevȳrëv who, as a literary critic, critized the growing commercialization of literature (the so-called 'commercial and industrial trend' represented by Bulgarin and Senkovsky).

liament'.[1] Odoevsky's romanticism had a distinctly aristocratic flavour: he was far from subscribing to theories about 'learning from the people' and quite failed to notice the peasant village commune which played such an important role in Slavophile social philosophy.

From the point of view of the romantic philosophy of history and the conception of social cohesion Odoevsky's original theory of 'instinct' is of particular importance.[2] The naturalistic terminology should not, of course, be taken seriously. Odoevsky's 'instinct' is not a biological concept but a powerful irrational force making possible direct contact with God—something akin to that 'divine spark' which, according to the mystics, survived in man after the Fall and made possible his future regeneration. In the history of mankind, Odoevsky wrote, periods of instinct and periods of rationalism followed each other in succession. Instinct was older than reason: primitive peoples behaved like sleep-walkers; they possessed enormous instinctive powers which were, however, weakened by the advance of civilization. The final destruction of instinct was brought about by the rationalism of Rome. Christianity had initiated a new age of instinct, on a higher level than before, but at present the wellspring of humanity's instinctive powers was drying up once more. The fact that the same cycle was being repeated was shown by the high esteem in which the eighteenth century had held the classical heritage. Spontaneity had again been replaced by calculation and truths once understood 'instinctively' could now be comprehended only by laborious effort.

Odoevsky did not carry his hostility to rationalism to extremes, but argued that 'reason must be raised to the level of instinct'.[3] He equated this desirable synthesis of reason and instinct with the synthesis of empiricism (rational and analytical knowledge that is incapable of perceiving its object as a living whole) with philosophical speculation (based upon 'innate ideas' springing directly from instinct).[4] Fortunately the healing power of art, which retains part of the primitive energy

---

[1] Sakulin, op. cit., pp. 581–2.
[2] Ibid., pp. 469–80.
[3] Ibid., p. 482.
[4] It seems probable that Odoevsky took this idea from de Maistre who enlarged upon it in his *Les Soirées de Saint-Petersbourg* (1821).

lost by mankind under the impact of rationalism, could help to strengthen the weakened instincts. 'The poetic impulse is the soul's most precious power' and poetic intuition is never mistaken. Knowledge should become poetry, therefore, and poetry knowledge; the highest form of poetry, according to Odoevsky, being prophetic poetry, with its unerring vision of the future.

Poetry should not only permeate knowledge but also the living social tissue of mankind. Like religion, it is a powerful instinctive force that helps to integrate society; a community in which the advance of science has led to the disappearance of religion and poetry is a degenerate organism. Instinct is a creative principle, an organic force without which all human endeavour—works of art, science, and legislation—are lifeless. Without instinct there can be no living social bonds, since rationalism alone can only create a 'mechanical lifeless' society. These are the arguments by which Odoevsky arrived at his theory that every nation is part of the universal whole and at the same time a separate and closed entity, an 'organism composed of elements forged by the ages'.[1] In his enthusiasm for this vision of an organic whole transcending its individual parts, Odoevsky even defended the death penalty as the organism's right to remove its sick cells.[2]

An important aspect of Odoevsky's theory was his conviction that the wealth of instinctive powers lost by the inhabitants of Western Europe had been preserved by Russia, a young country still living in its 'heroic age'. Thanks to Peter's reforms the Russians had assimilated European achievements, had gained the experience of old men without ceasing to be children.[3] Russia had been entrusted with a lofty mission, that of giving Europe new strength, of breathing new life into the old, fossilized culture. In the social sphere, too, Western Europe had much to learn from Russia. Odoevsky's views on society were an extremely naïve idealization of patriarchal relations which made even serfdom seem infinitely superior to bourgeois society. He conceded that the system was capable of improvement: the landowning gentry, for instance, as guardians of the people, would do well to take a special moral and scientific examination.

---

[1] Sakulin, op. cit., p. 485.
[2] Ibid., p. 558.
[3] Ibid., p. 591.

He considered this scheme to be so daring, however, that he did not expect it to be implemented until the beginning of the twentieth century.[1]

The belief in Russia's special mission was becoming widespread at that time and even found supporters abroad. Franz Baader, one of Odoevsky's favourite philosophers, had long centred his hopes and plans on Russia.[2] In 1839 Mel'gunov told Odoevsky that Schelling himself was interested in Russia and especially in Moscow, where he had so many supporters: 'I knew that Schelling, unlike Görres, held Russia in high esteem and expected her to do great things for humanity.'[3] Shortly afterwards Odoevsky was able to check the truth of this statement for himself. In 1848 he went to Berlin to attend Schelling's lectures on the 'philosophy of revelation', and had a long talk with the old philosopher. In the course of their conversation Schelling told him that Russia 'was destined to do something great'. When they were discussing religion, Odoevsky had the impression that, but for his age, Schelling would probably have become converted to Orthodoxy.[4]

Odoevsky's belief in Russia's mission was closely bound up with his critique of the materialistic and industrial civilization of bourgeois society. His views on this subject—and other ideas evolving from them—were further developed in *Russian Nights*, his most important work. As this book represents a 'summing-up', as it were, of Odoevsky's pre-Slavophile ideas, it is worth discussing at greater length.

Russian Nights was the fruit of many years of thought. Although it was not published in its entirety until 1844 (in volume i of Odoevsky's *Collected Works*), its roots reached back to the 1820s, and various sections appeared in print in the 1830s. The book consists of conversations of friends, interspersed with various tales, reminiscent of E. T. A. Hoffmann's *Serapionsbrüder*. Odoevsky was aware of this resemblance and stated, in the preface, that it was due solely to the 'bond of harmony linking people

---

[1] Ibid., pp. 585–6. In the 1850s Odoevsky changed his mind and became a warm supporter of the government's proposed emancipation reform.
[2] See chapter 4, pp. 161–5.
[3] Quoted from Sakulin, op. cit., pp. 339–40.
[4] Ibid., p. 386.

of all ages and all nations'.[1] The choice of form was influenced by the author's attempt to reconcile the narrator's
'subjectivity' with 'objectivity' through the introduction of a
chorus of different voices, as in Plato's dialogues. In this he
was not entirely successful: the various voices are not of equal
importance and are clearly dominated by the author's mouthpiece, Faust. The conversations reproduced in the book have
the value of a historical document as, in Odoevsky's own words,
they represent a 'reasonably accurate picture of the intellectual
activity of young Muscovites in the 1820s and 1830s, about
which hardly any information has come down to us'.[2]

The conversations cover a wide range of subjects, from music
and poetry to political economy and from epistemology to
philosophy of history. Odoevsky's 'encyclopedism' was a conscious rebellion against over-specialization, an attempt to reconstruct the 'vital unity' of the subject studied. To the child's
fresh, unspoilt intellect, he wrote, physics and chemistry, grammar and history were not separate subjects; they had become
separated because of the artificial divisions of intellectual activity, but the nineteenth century strove to reintegrate them.[3] The
pioneer in this field was Schelling, a new Christopher Columbus
who had discovered an unknown continent: the indivisible
human soul which concealed the most profound mysteries of
the universe in its 'living symbols'.

Basic to Odoevsky's thought was the assumption that there
are 'mysterious elements which shape and connect spiritual and
material life'.[4] In a state of ecstasy, his powers of instinct
exerted to the utmost, the poet sees further and more clearly
than other mortals and can penetrate to the heart of these
mysterious connections. The poet is both prophet and judge,
and even his most fantastic visions always contain a grain of
truth. The numerous visionary and didactic tales in *Russian
Nights* represent the judgement of romantic poetry on the
stifling dullness of capitalism. Typical in this respect is the tale
entitled 'Town without a Name', which tells the story of the
rise and fall of the state of Benthamia. For Odoevsky the

[1] See Odoevsky, *Russkie nochi*, p. 13.
[2] Ibid., p. 21.
[3] Ibid., pp. 10–12.
[4] Ibid., pp. 24, 45.

English utilitarian philosopher was a 'symbolic figure', the personification of the calculating selfishness of the industrial age (the English romanticists, and in particular Coleridge, regarded Bentham in a similar light).[1]

It is worth summarizing the story of Benthamia in some detail. It tells of a group of people who emigrated from the Old World, cut themselves off from tradition, and set out to put Bentham's system into practice on a desert island, on the 'bare ground'. Their God was 'self-interest'; 'self-interest' was an immediate cure for all ills. The colony of Benthamites flourished. A huge memorial to Bentham, bearing the inscription 'self-interest', was put up in the main square of the capital. Some of the inhabitants wanted to build a church, but could not decide how a church would benefit them. The plan was justified on the grounds that it was needed to remind people without cease that self-interest was the sole moral principle and the sole law governing human actions. All agreed and the church was built. Some artists suggested that a theatre be built while others considered it superfluous. The theatre was finally built, however, in order to strengthen the belief that self-interest was the source of all virtue, and disinterestedness the cause of all human misfortunes.

The description of the Benthamites' economic activities resembles an exaggerated version of Weber's 'spirit of capitalism' —the rapacious spirit of rationalized economics which subordinated all spheres of the individual's existence to systematic planning and calculation.

The colony flourished, its activity grew at an unbelievable pace. Early in the morning members of all estates hastily jumped out of bed, fearful of wasting the slightest moment. All commenced their daily tasks; some at the factory bench, some at the plough, and others at the money-lender's counter. It was with difficulty that they found time for a meal. In company they conversed on one subject alone: on matters likely to further self-interest. Numerous books were written on the subject—what am I saying? there were no other books at all. Instead of novels, girls read treatises on textile mills and twelve-year-old boys started to collect capital for trade. Unprofitable pleasantries and entertainment disappeared

[1] See R. Kirk, *The Conservative Mind* (Chicago 1953), chapter 4: 'Romantics and Utilitarians'.

from family life, every minute was accounted for, every action weighed up, and nothing was allowed to go to waste. There was not one peaceful moment given over to the enjoyment of the present—life's roundabout rattled on without cease.[1]

In the meantime the neighbouring island had been settled by another colony consisting of simple farmers who had come there to live, and not in order to try out a system. The Benthamites considered this colony to be good material for 'exploitation'. They started with 'economic penetration' and when this had achieved its object, i.e. had ruined the other colony, they asked themselves whether it would not be a matter of self-interest to seize their neighbours' land altogether? An ultimatum was sent and rejected. The Benthamites then invaded their neighbours, after first drawing up a balance-sheet of the profit and loss involved. In this way they gradually conquered all neighbouring countries and Benthamia became a powerful and greatly feared state.

In Benthamia itself, however, there was growing poverty, for the wealth of some entailed the ruin of others. Events took their course according to the principles of 'noble competition' and the 'natural course of affairs'. Motivated by the lofty principle of self-interest, merchants kept back essential commodities in order to increase demand and sell them later at exorbitant prices; in the name of common sense and profit they gambled on the stock-exchange; they took advantage of their unlimited freedom to set up monopolies. Even the phrase 'the general good' began to seem a sentimental day-dream as different strata of society tried to seize power and to rule solely in their own interest. At first the merchants seized power and banking feudalism was triumphant. All spheres of life were subordinated to commercial profits: religion became superfluous, for morality was reduced to the art of balancing accounts; the aim of intellectual activity was to find ways of cheating that would not cause a loss of credit; poetry was replaced by book-keeping and music by the monotonous din of machinery.

A last prophet appeared at that time and threatened the Benthamites with annihilation, calling on them to repent. No

---

[1] Odoevsky, *Russkie nochi*, pp. 154–5.

one listened to him and he was locked up in a madhouse, but his prophecies came true. The dictatorship of merchants was overthrown and a period of struggle for power now commenced. First the artisans, and later the peasants seized power and ruled the country in their own selfish interest. Benthamia was plunged into chaos and ruin and its population converted into a tribe of nomads; driven by hunger, they indulged in debauchery and desperate struggles for food and power. After a time all the buildings in the magnificent capital (now an 'unknown city') were destroyed, and all that remained was the stone on which Bentham's memorial had once stood; the now savage Benthamites knelt before it in superstitious fear, thinking it some ancient pagan god. Hunger, the plague, and wild animals soon completed the work of extermination.

The story of Benthamia illustrates ideas that recur in different contexts in almost every chapter of *Russian Nights*. Odoevsky was the first consistent and unvarying Russian critic of capitalism from a romantic and conservative point of view. His first comments on the subject (on England) date from the early 1830s, that is several years before the emergence of mature Slavophile thought. In *Russian Nights* he called Malthusianism a crime,[1] and the bourgeois parliamentary system 'the most gigantic fraud in the history of mankind'. He dismissed Benjamin Franklin's 'moral preaching' as the quintessence of the hypocritical egoism of industrial philanthropists, ascribed the success of Adam Smith's economic theories to the enthusiasm of shopkeepers who liked being told from a university chair that they could do what they liked and were always right,[2] and described the laws of political economy as the application of the ruthless laws of nature to the sphere of human relations.[3] Several pages of *Russian Nights* are given over to examples of the poverty, degeneration, high death rate, and widespread crime in the industrialized countries, with England, of course,

---

[1] In his *Russian Nights* Odoevsky devotes a separate tale ('The Last Suicide') to a critique of Malthusianism; in the story mankind's unsuccessful fight against population growth is crowned by an act of collective suicide. Faust comments as follows: 'If the theory of Malthus is correct, then mankind really has no other choice than to place gunpowder under itself and allow itself to be blown up, or else to invent some other equally satisfactory means of proving the Malthusian system.' Odoevsky, *Russkie nochi*, pp. 145–6.

[2] *Russkie nochi*, pp. 179–80, 238.

[3] Ibid., p. 237.

figuring most prominently Odoevsky's attitude to contemporary liberal dogma is aptly summed up in the following dialogue:

Victor: The employment of children in factories is essential for the maintenance of a high level of production.
Faust: I cannot see the point of this excessive productivity . . .
Victor: Have mercy! You want to limit the freedom of industry . . .
Faust: I cannot see the point of this unlimited freedom . . .
Victor: But without it there cannot be any competition . . .
Faust: I cannot see the point of this so-called competition.[1]

Odoevsky's belief in Russia's historic mission was closely bound up with his distrust of European capitalism which so far only Russia had avoided.[2] Western Europe was still powerful, he argued, but her decline was inevitable. The young and vigorous Russian people had been selected by providence to bring health and salvation to a dying culture, to realize the dreams of its finest sons, men such as Baader, Ballanche, and Schelling.[3] Peter the Great had grafted certain Western elements on to Russia and, in the final analysis, had thus strengthened her distinctiveness by curing her original one-sidedness; at present another Peter was needed, a Western European Peter, who would inject the fresh sap of the Slavonic East into the ageing West.[4] The West had no need to fear Russia, for the Russian 'life-force' was not destructive; its victory would also be the victory of Europe, the realization of ancient Christian ideals. When the Western nations came to understand this, it would revive their hopes of a *full life*, they would sense the approach of the age of unity—of one teaching and one teacher—and would repeat with delight the forgotten words from an ancient book: 'Man is the harmonious prayer of the earth.'[5]

In his foreword to *Russian Nights* (1844), in the epilogue, and in one of the notes, Odoevsky rightly stressed that these ideas— originally formulated in the early 1830s—anticipated certain aspects of Slavophile thought.[6] There is, in fact, a considerable similarity, particularly striking when Odoevsky's views are compared to the philosophy of history and anthropology of his

---

[1] *Russkie nochi*, pp. 263–4.
[2] Odoevsky did not of course use the term capitalism, but such phrases as the 'commercial age' or the 'industrial era', etc.
[3] *Russkie nochi*, p. 419.   [4] Ibid., pp. 416–18.
[5] Ibid., p. 422.   [6] See ibid., pp. 22, 342, 419.

close friend Ivan Kireevsky, also originally one of the Lovers of Wisdom. Whereas Pogodin identified the specifically Russian 'principle' with autocracy, Odoevsky, like the Slavophiles, thought it was to be found in the pre-capitalist system of social relations and in certain traditional virtues which had been better preserved in Russia than in the Western countries. There are a number of other very close parallels between *Russian Nights* and Kireevsky's ideas. In their critique of rationalism Odoevsky and Kireevsky made use of similar arguments; both thought that rationalism was responsible for the dichotomy between the knower and the object of knowledge and opposed it in the name of the wholeness of the human spirit; both drew a parallel between the rationalism of Roman and capitalist civilizations; both considered Schelling to be the greatest Western thinker and thought that his philosophy of revelation had made manifest a truth that Europe had finally come to understand, but could no longer implement.

These similarities should not, however, blind us to the differences. Odoevsky was not a Slavophile and never became one. One might say that he transplanted on to Russian soil Western aristocratic romanticism—the romanticism of Novalis, Baader, and the brothers Schlegel—without bothering too much about giving it specifically 'national' or 'Slavonic' characteristics. Apart from a very few allusions to Russian Orthodoxy one would look in vain in Odoevsky's work for any idea of the peculiarity of the Russian historical process or any analysis of contemporary Russian realities to underpin his conviction of the Russian people's special mission. His conception of national mission was based solely on Russia's alleged youth and freshness;[1] he drew no arguments from Russian history, dismissed Peter's reforms with generalities, and quite overlooked the existence of the peasant communes. His view of the world was not eclectic; it had its own style, but in this style there was nothing specifically Russian. He was above all a European who sighed for Europe's past and idealized the universal Christian values

[1] There is much to be said for Berdyaev's suggestion that a distinction should be made between 'missionism' and 'messianism'. The belief that a given nation—like other nations before it—is entrusted with a particular historical mission, need not necessarily imply that it is a 'Messiah of the nations'. See N. Berdyaev, *A. S. Khomyakov* (Moscow 1912), p. 209.

that were extolled by the troubadours and served as a justification of the crusades.

On the other hand, there is no doubt that Russian history did
have its own specific qualities and that a love for the European
past might well clash with a love for the Russian past. As a
schismatic country, Russia had not been part of the European
Christian community during the Middle Ages and had had
neither troubadours, nor knights nor crusades; her boyars were
quite unlike Western European aristocrats and her tsars unlike
Western European kings; and finally, as a result of Peter's
reforms, the links with historical tradition appeared to have
been completely broken. From the point of view of a European
conservative all this might be enough to cast doubt on Russia's
providential mission and even to justify an extremely pessimistic view of her future. This pessimism was to find its expression
in Petr Chaadaev's *Philosophical Letters*.

3

The Paradox of Chaadaev

PETR Chaadaev (1794–1856) is without any doubt one of the most striking thinkers in the history of Russian philosophy. Although he appears to be an isolated figure, standing aloof from the main currents of Russian intellectual life, he nevertheless was the first to formulate a number of basic problems which were taken up by such different thinkers as the Slavophiles and Westernizers, Dostoevsky and Chernyshevsky, the Populists and Vladimir Solov'ëv. In Chaadaev's mind these apparently heterogeneous problems form a coherent system. Scholars who try to find answers to quite another set of questions in his work, and evaluate his standpoint according to extraneous and therefore unhistorical criteria, are necessarily forced to the conclusion that he continually 'contradicts himself and betrays inconsistencies at every step'.[1] It may be argued that statements of this kind represent an admission of defeat on the investigator's part and indicate certain methodological inadequacies. Chaadaev—a thinker whose extreme brand of conservative social philosophy led him to dismiss his country's entire past and present history—is certainly a paradoxical figure, on the scale of such great historical paradoxes as those of Pascal and Rousseau; the contradictions inherent in his views cannot be reduced to simple inconsistencies in reasoning.

Chaadaev was a nephew of Prince Mikhail Shcherbatov, the main ideological representative of the aristocratic opposition in the reign of Catherine; it is worth emphasizing this fact, since the aristocratic and French cosmopolitan influences of his upbringing throw an interesting light on some of his later ideas.

At the age of 15 Chaadaev entered Moscow University but left in 1812 before completing his studies in order to join the

[1] See M. M. Grigoryan, 'Chaadaev and his Philosophical System', in a collection of articles (by different authors) entitled *Iz istorii russkoĭ filosofii*, 2nd edn. (Moscow 1958).

army and serve in the Napoleonic campaigns. After the war he became associated with the Decembrist circle and was one of Pushkin's closest friends. Gershenzon, author of the first monograph devoted to Chaadaev, tried to minimize his links with the Decembrists, and called them the results of a 'misunderstanding'.[1] This view hardly deserves to be taken seriously: even V. V. Zenkovsky agrees in his *History of Russian Philosophy* (written from the point of view of Orthodoxy) that these links were 'very deep and essential'.[2] The young Pushkin justly considered Chaadaev to be one of the most outstanding liberals of the 1820s; his well-known verse *To Chaadaev* (1818) ends with the following lines:

> Comrade, believe: joy's star will leap
> Upon our sight, a radiant token;
> Russia will rouse from her long sleep;
> And where autocracy lies, broken,
> Our names shall yet be graven deep.[3]

This is the most optimistic verse in Pushkin's entire poetry. By an ironic twist of fate, the man to whom these lines were addressed was later to conceive a profoundly pessimistic view of Russia.

Early in 1821, at their Moscow congress, the Decembrists entrusted Yakushkin with the task of initiating Chaadaev into their secret society. The invitation came too late, however: at this very time[4] Chaadaev was about to give up his promising army career for reasons which have never been clarified; at the same time he withdrew from society and the salons in order to immerse himself in the works of religious writers. During this period his view of the world underwent a significant evolution. The spiritual crisis he passed through was so intense that it affected his health and he went abroad to recuperate (in 1823). On his travels he saw something of European intellectual life at first hand and became confirmed in his leanings towards Roman Catholicism, which at that time exerted a considerable

[1] See M. Gershenzon, *P. J. Chaadaev. Zhizn' i myshlenie* (St. Petersburg 1908).
[2] See V. V. Zenkovsky, *A History of Russian Philosophy*, trans. by George L. Kline, 2 vols. (Routledge and Kegan Paul, London 1953), i. 153.
[3] Quoted from *The Poems, Prose and Plays of Alexander Pushkin* (Random House, New York 1936).
[4] Chaadaev handed in his resignation in December 1820 and it was accepted in February 1821. See Grigoryan, op. cit., p. 128.

influence on the Russian aristocracy.[1] Upon his return to Russia in 1826 he withdrew into almost complete seclusion in order to devote himself entirely to the task of formulating his new philosophical beliefs. The fruits of this period were the eight *Philosophical Letters* (written in French between 1828 and 1831), of which only the first—devoted to Russia—was published during its author's lifetime, in the journal *Telescope* (*Teleskop*), in 1836.[2] After completing the *Letters*, Chaadaev was again to be seen in Moscow's literary salons. The city's noble families regarded him as an interesting personality—one of the capital's ornaments—and members of various coteries competed for his notice. Although he was not associated with any particular group he was treated with pronounced respect by the intellectual élite and, perhaps most important of all, it was in discussions with him that the later views of both Westernizers and Slavophiles began to take shape.

Herzen, the leading representative of Westernism in Moscow at that time, paid warm tribute to Chaadaev in *My Past and Thoughts*. The following paragraph vividly portrays the atmosphere surrounding him:

Chaadaev's melancholy and original figure stood out sharply like a mournful reproach against the faded and dreary background of Moscow 'high life'. I liked looking at him among the tawdry aristocracy, flighty Senators, grey-headed rascals, and venerable nonentities. However dense the crowd, the eye found him at once. The years did not mar his graceful figure; he was very fastidious in his dress, his pale delicate face was completely motionless when he was silent, as though made of wax or marble—'a head like a bare skull'; his grey-blue eyes were melancholy and at the same time

---

[1] He was influenced to some extent by Mme Sophie Svechina, a Russian woman who had been converted to Roman Catholicism, was an ardent ultramontanist, and corresponded with de Maistre.

[2] Three *Letters* were published for the first time abroad by the Jesuit priest Father I. S. Gagarin (*Oèuvres choisies de Pierre Tschaadaïef*) and reprinted by Gershenzon in 1913 together with a Russian translation. After the remaining *Letters* had been found, it was established that the first French edition consisted of letters I, VI, and VII; the fragment on architecture which Gagarin called the 'Fourth Letter' turned out to be unconnected with the letters. The remaining letters (II, III, IV, V, and VIII) were found and published in 1935 by D. Shakhovskoï in *Literaturnoe nasledstvo*, vols. xxii–xxiv (Moscow 1935). This edition unfortunately published the letters in Russian translation only, without the original French text. The *Letters* were formally addressed to Mme E. D. Panova, a friend of Chaadaev's.

there was something kindly in them, though his thin lips smiled ironically. For ten years he stood with folded arms, by some column, by some tree on the boulevard, in drawing-rooms and theatres, at the club and, an embodied veto, a living protest, gazed at the vortex of faces senselessly twisting and turning about him. He became whimsical and eccentric, held himself aloof from society, yet could not leave it altogether, then uttered his message, quietly concealing it, just as in his features he concealed passion under a layer of ice. Then he was silent again, showed himself whimsical, dissatisfied, irritated; again he was an oppressive influence in Moscow society, and again he could not leave it. Old and young alike were awkward and ill at ease with him; they, God knows why, were abashed by his immobile face, his direct glance, his gloomy mockery, his malignant condescension. What compelled them to invite him . . . still more to visit him? It is a very difficult question.[1]

To this testimony one might add Khomyakov's tribute to Chaadaev: 'At a time when thought seemed buried in a deep and involuntary sleep he was especially dear to all, for he kept watch himself and aroused others to watchfulness. . . . Perhaps no one prized him so highly as those who were considered his enemies.'[2]

Chaadaev's ideas were a challenge that alerted both Slavophiles and Westernizers. Both considered it to be their duty to attack his legacy of pessimism. After his famous diagnosis Russia's future as a European nation ceased to be self-evident and Westernizers could no longer make do without a definite philosophy of history or without critical reflection on the 'distinctiveness' of the historical process in Russia. The founders of Slavophile thought, on the other hand, were stimulated by Chaadaev to try and search Russian history for the moral and religious principles and spiritual essence he had declared missing.

Chaadaev both knew and greatly admired German philosophy and also felt most closely drawn to Schelling, whom he met in 1825 and with whom he later corresponded. It is worth noting, however, that he had also read Kant and even Hegel, something of a rarity in Russia at that time (the late 1820s and early

[1] Alexander Herzen, *My Past and Thoughts*, ii. 264.
[2] A. S. Khomyakov, *Polnoe sobranie sochinenii* (Moscow 1914), vol. iii (obituary notice for Chaadaev).

1830s). The major influence on him, however, was that of French philosophy and philosophy of history (especially de Bonald, Ballanche, and de Maistre, as well as Chateaubriand and the Lamennais of the 'theocratic' period). Chaadaev's *Weltanschauung* is an interesting example of the synthesis of Catholic ideas (or rather the ideas of the French and German romanticists who flirted with Catholicism) and pre-romantic, anti-Enlightenment traditionalism—in fact a synthesis of 'romantic' and 'classical' Catholicism. In spite of the undoubted attraction Roman Catholicism had for him, Chaadaev himself did not break with Orthodoxy—of the various creeds he considered Catholicism to be the best, although not the sole repository of ecumenical truth.

The problem of Russia is undoubtedly the starting-point and central issue of Chaadaev's philosophy.[1] His thought can, however, be arranged in deductive sequence: his ideas on Russia derive formally from the overall premises of his metaphysics, theory of cognition, philosophical anthropology, and philosophy of history. For the sake of greater clarity it would seem desirable to preserve this sequence and to bring out its salient points.

In contrast to the philosophers of the Enlightenment, Chaadaev emphasized that the aspiration to individual freedom is not natural to man. Being is hierarchical in structure, the natural order is based on *dependence*, and man therefore aspires to subordinate himself.[2] Since human actions are directed from outside by a supra-individual force, the power of human reason is in direct proportion to man's obedience, submissiveness, and docility.[3] It follows that mathematics, which, according to Chaadaev, precludes all individual and arbitrary reasoning and completely subordinates the mind to universal truths, must be considered the most superior science.[4] Paraphrasing one of Bacon's aphorisms, Chaadaev cited natural philosophy (and later logical analysis) as examples of the mind's submission to general laws.[5] Intuition—the gift of formulating bold syntheses

---

[1] This was rightly stressed by Grigoryan (op. cit.) who criticizes Zenkovsky's stress on Chaadaev's purely metaphysical and theological conceptions.

[2] See *Literaturnoe nasledstvo*, xxii–xxiv. 31.

[3] Chaadaev quoted Montaigne: 'L'obéir est le propre office d'une âme raisonnable, recognissant un celest supérieur et bienfacteur' (*Literaturnoe nasledstvo*, xxii–xxiv. 30).

[4] Ibid., p. 31.   [5] Ibid., p. 32.

—is not an internal cognitive faculty, he stressed, but the reflection of a higher intelligence: only by submitting wholly to this superior power, which acts through us and yet independently of us, can the truth be comprehended by intuitive insight. To strive after the autonomy of individual reason is absurd, and therefore a source of unhappiness and the main obstacle to our understanding of the truth. The mind of the individual is anchored in the universal mind and draws its nourishment from it. An element of this universal mind—the memory of the divine words spoken to man before the Fall—is still deeply embedded in human consciousness, but men can only come to know these divine truths through the mediation of society. Without society the individual is only a lost molecule, 'an atom that has jumped out of its appointed orbit'.[1] His strong emphasis on sociality led Chaadaev to regard individual reason as something artificial—the reason of man after the Fall. The man who proclaims the autonomy of his limited reason, who seeks to reach by himself for the apple from the tree of knowledge, is guilty, he maintained, of a repetition of original sin. Kant's *Critique of Pure Reason* showed the impotence of the isolated individual's reason; in fact it was essentially a critique of *artificial* reason torn from the source of wisdom.[2] This type of reason—a subjective reason—separates man from the world and makes true understanding impossible. Such true understanding can only be attained through collective knowledge, through participation in a collective consciousness or 'universal mind' that transcends individual minds; this 'superior consciousness' derives from God, who is the supreme principle of the unity of the world.

The moral autonomy of the individual was another concept Chaadaev condemned as absurd: 'moral law', like truth, he suggested, does not lie within us, as Kant believed, but outside us.[3] If man is left to himself his moral decline will become more and more rapid. Only the great divinely inspired heroes of history seem to have been able to conform quite naturally to the precepts of morality;[4] ordinary human beings, whose

[1] Chaadaev, p. 45.
[2] On the title-page of his copy of Kant's *Critique of Pure Reason* Chaadaev wrote: 'Apologete adamitischer Vernunft'.
[3] See *Literaturnoe nasledstvo*, xxii–xxiv. 36.
[4] See ibid., p. 33.

actions are not guided by 'mysterious stimuli', must submit to the strict discipline of inherited traditions. A truly profound psychology, therefore, is one that recognizes the heredity of ideas, the existence of a historical memory transmitted from generation to generation. Chaadaev, it should be noted, was bitterly opposed to 'empirical psychology', which he accused of regarding the human psyche as merely subject to the mechanical play of fortuitous associations.[1]

Man's vocation in life, Chaadaev thought, is to live in complete dependence; true freedom consists in moral harmony, in the conscious subordination of voluntary actions to the influence of a higher power, a universal law. The supreme perfection would be the utter renunciation of individual will. Then, instead of being separated from nature, as he is now, man would fuse with it; every movement of his soul would harmonize with the entire universe; he would be liberated from his own narrow, subjective reason and would feel himself living the life of our first father, Adam, before the expulsion from Paradise. To abdicate one's individuality ('the fatal *self*') would mean to transcend time and space and enter the state of eternity and unlimited duration.[2]

Although Chaadaev expressly rejected pantheism, there is a clearly discernible element of romantic pantheism in this vision. He claimed that his notion of an objective unity entirely external to the reality transmitted by our impressions had 'nothing in common' with pantheism, which he called an erroneous belief although it was professed by the majority of contemporary philosophers.[3] In spite of this declaration it can be argued that Chaadaev's own conception was not entirely devoid of pantheistic overtones, whatever he himself may have thought: one might call it panentheism—an attempt to reconcile pantheistic elements with traditional Christian theism. The *Great All*[4] about which he wrote in the *Letters* has a hierarchical structure consisting of four grades: at the summit of the hierarchy is God; his emanation is the universal mind which Chaadaev identified with the *social sphere*, the supra-individual and universal collective consciousness preserved in tradition. Considerably below this come the empirical individual consciousness, the

[1] See ibid., pp. 33, 44.
[3] Ibid., p. 46.
[2] See ibid., pp. 34–5.
[4] Ibid.

sc—d

consciousness of persons who have lost their grasp on the wholeness of being. The lowest (fourth) grade is nature before man.[1] In this way God is not identified with the universe, as in the pantheistic conception, although he is not separate from it either, as in traditional theism.

Chaadaev's conception of the social sphere and its decisive significance in human life is of particular interest. Knowledge, he maintained, is a form of collective consciousness and arises from the interaction of many people, from the collision of many conscious minds. Without social contacts and the social sphere, which allow traditions to be handed down, human beings would never have emerged from the animal state. Anticipating Durkheim's ideas (like the French traditionalists) Chaadaev suggested that 'inborn ideas' and '*a priori* judgements' are essentially ideas and judgements handed down by tradition and accepted by individuals as self-evident truths not requiring substantiation.[2] Following de Bonald, Chaadaev ascribed special importance to language: 'There can be no doubt,' he wrote, 'that the major factor in shaping the soul is language; without it one cannot conceive of the emergence of consciousness in the individual, or its growth in the human race.'[3] But language alone, he added, cannot explain 'the great phenomenon of universal consciousness', for thoughts can also be conveyed by non-linguistic, non-material means: 'A thousand invisible bonds unite the thoughts of a rational being to those of another; our most intimate thoughts find all sorts of ways of reproducing themselves outside our minds, by answering and crossing one another; they fuse with one another, combine, pass from one mind to another, germinate, fructify, and finally engender collective consciousness.'[4] This collective consciousness cannot be reduced to the sum of its individual parts; it is only through participation in this supra-individual sphere that a human being can come to know God and become a vessel filled with divine truth. The way to God does not lead through individualistic self-cultivation and solitary asceticism; but through the strict observance of the traditional norms and conventions

---

[1] See *Literaturnoe nasledstvo* p. 50.   [2] Ibid., p. 56.   [3] Ibid., p. 49.
[4] Ibid., English text quoted, with minor changes, from *Russian Philosophy*, ed. by James M. Edie, James P. Scanlan and Mary-Barbara Zeldin, with the collaboration of George L. Kline, 3 vols. (Quadrangle Books, Chicago 1956), i. 134.

of social life;[1] the effort to transcend individualism and to 'fuse' with God is essentially identical with the striving after complete sociality. This means that 'man's destiny in this world is solely to strive to annihilate his individual existence and to transform it into a wholly social or non-individual existence'.[2]

In spite of his emphasis on sociality, Chaadaev held a typically aristocratic belief in the élitist theory of knowledge.[3] The common people, he wrote, has nothing to do with Reason ('Was hat das Volk mit der Vernunft zu schaffen?'), nor should the voice of the people be equated with the voice of God, whatever Lamennais may have said.[4] If God were to vouchsafe another Revelation, he would not make use of the common people, but of chosen individuals with special spiritual qualities. Chaadaev criticized Protestantism for its individualistic egalitarianism and because it belittled the role of the Church. His dislike of mystical trends was based on similar premisses. If we assume that the essence of mysticism is to strive after direct individual contact with God and thus to bypass the alienated, institutionalized forms of religious life,[5] we must treat Chaadaev as a determined opponent of mysticism. This is the conclusion reached by T. G. Masaryk, who maintained that Chaadaev could not be called a mystic since he laid stress on the objective and 'social' rather than the subjective aspects of religious life.[6]

In spite of a certain one-sidedness, Masaryk's point of view seems better founded than that of Gershenzon, who wrote that Chaadaev's *Weltanschauung* was 'the outlook of a Decembrist who became a mystic', although he qualified this definition by calling Chaadaev's mysticism 'social mysticism'.[7] Although

[1] Chaadaev also stressed the need to cultivate one's external surroundings (ibid., pp. 18–19) and to adhere strictly to the observance of religious rites which he called the 'soul's regime'. See Chaadaev, *Sochineniya i pis'ma*, 2 vols., ed. M. O. Gershenzon (Moscow 1913–14), i. 76–7.
[2] Chaadaev, *Sochineniya*, i. 121.
[3] See W. Stark, *The Sociology of Knowledge* (London 1958), pp. 41–3.
[4] See Chaadaev, *Sochineniya*, i. 214.
[5] Cf. L. Kołakowski, 'Mistyka i konflikt społeczny' (Mysticism and Social Conflict), *Studia Filozoficzne* (1959), nos. 3/12, and J. Wach, *Socjologia religii* (The Sociology of Religion) (Warsaw 1961), pp. 172, 263.
[6] See T. G. Masaryk, *The Spirit of Russia*, 2 vols. (London–New York 1955), i. 227. The first edition of Masaryk's book appeared in German in 1914.
[7] Gershenzon, op. cit.

Chaadaev adopted certain notions held by the mystics, he was not himself a mystical theosophist and opposed mysticism in so far as it seemed to him to represent anti-ecclesiastical tendencies.[1] Some of his statements in defence of the temporal social and organizational function of religion have the ring of blasphemy: 'What is the good of becoming united in the Saviour, if we are divided amongst ourselves?'[2] We are not yet in heaven, that we may violate the established order with impunity, that we may neglect the 'visible' organizational side of the Church.[3] The papacy, Chaadaev thought, would have been essential even if it had been a merely temporal institution, established by men in order to safeguard their unity, and for the sake of the 'centralization' of Christian thought.[4]

The question of Chaadaev's relation to mysticism is closely connected with another problem of vital importance for an interpretation of the *Philosophical Letters*: namely his relationship to the Catholic traditionalists on the one hand, and to the conservative romanticists on the other.

In the conservative philosophy of the German romanticists the concept of tradition was given an irrational content and set up in opposition—on a par with inspiration, prophetic insight, and other direct gifts of providence—to reason, which represented revolutionary negation. For the French theocratic traditionalists, particularly those of the older generation, whose intellectual roots were in the eighteenth century (a partial exception was de Maistre),[5] the basic opposition was between reason and tradition on the one hand, and uncontrolled irrational forces on the other; it was the latter rather than reason, that they considered to be the mainspring and motive force of revolution. De Bonald demonstrated the identity of reason and

---

[1] The mystical 'Diary' attributed by Gershenzon to the young Chaadaev in fact belonged to D. A. Obleukhov. See Shakhovskoï, 'Yakushkin and Chaadaev' in *Dekabristy̆ i ikh vremya* (Moscow 1925).

[2] Chaadaev, *Sochineniya*, i. 117.

[3] See ibid., p. 118.

[4] See ibid.,pp. 118–19.

[5] De Maistre was closer to the mystics who (especially Saint-Martin) exerted a certain influence on him via Freemasonry, and to the conservative romanticists whose works he knew and appreciated (especially Haller and Baader). However, even de Maistre was not an out-and-out irrationalist; he attacked 'individual reason' in the name of 'universal reason' and combined intuitionism with the praise of syllogism and the rationalism of *a priori* knowledge.

revelation and was emphatic in his assertion that the Catholic faith—unlike Protestantism—was a religion of revelation rather than inspiration;[1] he regarded tradition as the embodiment of reason, not as its opposite, and accused revolutionary doctrines of being dominated by non-rational imagination. Lamennais stressed that the truth was not to be comprehended by the senses or feeling, but solely by reason, which must exercise control even over inspiration.[2] For the traditionalists, reason as well as tradition (the Catholic tradition of course) stood for a universal element—both were agents of universal harmony, in contrast to the destructive force of irrational and particularist aspirations. De Bonald compared Christianity to mathematical laws, while Lamennais compared it to Newton's law of gravitation and the laws of balance, adding that the repudiation of Catholicism was tantamount to a repudiation of reason.[3]

These facts make it possible to establish a considerable degree of similarity between Chaadaev and the traditionalists, especially de Bonald. Unlike the romanticists, Chaadaev selected the scholastic rather than the mystical Christian tradition; he did not reject rationalism, regarded reason as an integrating rather than a destructive force, and highly esteemed the 'Western Syllogism' and 'logical analysis'. Like de Bonald and Lamennais, he compared the universality and compelling force of mathematical laws and the laws of gravitation to the universality of Christianity, opposed the spiritualization of religion, and propounded his own individual brand of sociologism (differing from that of the romanticists) in the theory of knowledge and morality. He did not share the romanticists' (or Slavophiles') faith in the possibility of a total internalization of tradition and pointed out that obedience to tradition is rarely associated with spontaneity but required, above all, conscious submission to specific social forms and conventions.[4] At the same time, however, such traces of romantic influence as his

---

[1] See L. Brunschvicg, *Le Progrès de la conscience dans la philosophie occidentale* (Paris 1953), ii. 490, 497.

[2] See E. Bréhier, *Histoire de la philosophie*, vol. ii: *La Philosophie moderne*, Fascicule 3 (Paris 1957), p. 585; and Brunschvicg, op. cit., p. 489.

[3] See Lamennais, *L'Essai sur l'indifférence en matière de religion* (1817–1923). Copious underlinings in the copy of this work found in Chaadaev's library, show that it was read very carefully; see *Literaturnoe nasledstvo*, xxii–xxiv. 43.

[4] Hence we have Chaadaev's emphasis on etiquette and his stress on the importance of all external forms and social conventions.

cult of outstanding charismatic individuals, his prophetic vein, and romantic historicism clearly distinguish the argument of the *Philosophical Letters* from the static conception of de Bonald. Certain mystical elements are also traceable to the influence of romantic philosophy, particularly that of Schelling and Ballanche. All these features are most clearly discernable in Chaadaev's philosophy of history.

In contrast to Enlightenment historians Chaadaev held that men's voluntary acts play a negligible role in history, that autonomous activity always belongs to the domain of conscious or unconscious egoism (de Bonald's view) and as such cannot contribute to the advancement of mankind.[1] He therefore posited a universal mind—the collective consciousness of mankind—which evolves within the historical process. The creative force of history is thus a superior, supra-individual force: the masses obey it blindly, like 'inanimate atoms', while chosen individuals are conscious instruments in its service.[2] The Christian is able to read the secret of man's destiny in ancient symbols and traditions whose origins are lost in the bosom of the Creator.[3] These traditions were preserved in their purest form among a chosen people, just as the original act of Revelation was somehow renewed in privileged individuals.

If you take away this people [Chaadaev wrote], if you take away these privileged men, you will have to assume that Divine Thought revealed itself equally fully, equally vividly among all peoples, at all times, in the general life of man, and in each individual. This would mean, as you see, the destruction of all personality and of all freedom in the intellectual world. . . . It is evident that there are only as much personality, as much freedom, as there are diversity of intelligence, diversity of moral strength, diversity of knowledge.[4]

In this emphasis on the inequality of nations and individuals as a prerequisite of their individual diversity, Chaadaev, who elsewhere treated individuality as an evil, took up the characteristic theme of romantic pluralism.

The role of the historian, Chaadaev argued, is to search for the meaning of history, to read in it the Creator's design, and not merely to collect and analyse facts. This was an attempt to

---

[1] See *Literaturnoe nasledstvo*, xxii–xxiv. 24.
[2] See Chaadaev, *Sochineniya*, i. 93.   [3] See *Literaturnoe nasledstvo*, xxii–xxiv. 27.
[4] See Chaadaev, *Sochineniya*, i. 95. English text quoted from *Russian Philosophy*, i. 138.

return to a religious interpretation of history, which had been secularized by the Englightenment.[1] Chaadaev ascribed tremendous importance to history and thought that it ought to be the fundamental and central philosophical discipline.

Historical thought [he wrote], is called upon today to rise to a height infinitely greater than that on which it has remained until now; one might say that today the mind feels at ease only in the domain of history; that it does nothing but constantly double back on time past, and seeks to acquire new powers only on the basis of its memories, of the contemplation of the course it has already traversed, of the study of the forces that have directed its progress through the ages.[2]

Since, in Chaadaev's view, the 'narrative' and 'psychological' methods were incapable of solving the problems to be tackled by history, he preferred the providentialist approach of the age 'when the Christian spirit dominated science'. The 'profound though poorly articulated thought' of Providentialism could not, however, make up for the imperfections of historical criticism, as Chaadaev was well aware.[3] Hence he concluded that the 'reason of the age requires a wholly new philosophy of history; a philosophy as little resembling current philosophy as the skilled analyses of present-day astronomy resemble the gnomic observations of Hipparchus and the other astronomers of antiquity'.[4] This new philosophy of history would overthrow the Enlightenment concept of the 'mechanical perfectibility of our nature' and would demonstrate that true progress would have been impossible without the advent of Christianity[5]; it would, 'according to Pascal's colourful expression', perceive that 'the whole succession of men . . . is one man who exists always'.[6] One of its most important contributions would be to make nations aware of their destinies, to teach them to submit to a common goal—the universal reunion of mankind—and, by clarifying the past, enable them in some measure to foresee the future.[7]

[1] See Chaadaev, *Sochineniya*, i. 121.
[2] Ibid., p. 97. *Russian Philosophy*, i. 139.
[3] Chaadaev, *Sochineniya*, i. 98.
[4] Ibid., *Russian Philosophy*, i. 140.
[5] Chaadaev, *Sochineniya*, p. 104.
[6] Ibid., p. 120. *Russian Philosophy*, i. 134.
[7] Ibid., p. 101.

From the theoretical point of view Chaadaev's ideas, which attempted to reconcile the notion of a transcendent Providence with an immanentist philosophy of history (just as his panentheism attempted to reconcile theism with pantheism), have little in common with traditional Providentialism. Central to his thought was the concept of mediation, of a higher supraindividual consciousness which mediates between God and man. On the other hand he had no clear answer to a number of problems that played an important part in the Hegelian controversies of the 1840s, among them the issue of the personal or impersonal nature of God.

The new philosophy of history, Chaadaev wrote, would revise the existing scale of values: the undeserved reputation of individualists and sceptics such as Socrates and Marcus Aurelius would be 'engulfed by nothingness'; the name of Aristotle would be pronounced with disgust, Homer would be recognized as a degrading influence, and the importance ascribed to classical Greece and ancient civilization as a whole would turn out to have been vastly exaggerated. On the other hand, men like Moses, David, or Mohammed, who had felt the flame of history through which 'divine inspiration' makes itself known, would again be duly revered. Future historians would concentrate their attention on the first centuries of the Christian era and on the Middle Ages; they would show that since the time of Christ the substance of history had been Christianity and that the essence of Christianity was realized in the movement of history.

Chaadaev's interpretation of the Middle Ages—his view of the papacy, attitude to the Reformation, and favourable assessment of Islam (which he regarded as one of the Christian sects) clearly betray the influence of de Maistre, coloured by some of Chateaubriand's romantic aestheticism.[1] The papacy, he wrote, was a 'visible symbol of unity' and also a symbol of the world-

---

[1] For a discussion of de Maistre's influence on Chaadaev see M. Stepanov, 'Joseph de Maistre in Russia', in: *Literaturnoe nasledstvo*, xxix–xxx. 618; and Ch. Quénet, *Tchaadaev et les lettres philosophiques. Contribution à l'étude du mouvement des idées en Russie* (Paris 1931), pp. 155–60.

Les Soirées de St. Petersbourg was not published until 1837, but the ideas in it circulated in Russia previously, since de Maistre's stay there as ambassador of the Kingdom of Sardinia. Quénet (op. cit., p. 157) suggests that Chaadaev might have met de Maistre in person.

wide reunion of the future; in the Middle Ages it had helped to weld Europe into one great Christian nation. The Renaissance and Reformation were responsible for mankind's relapse into the social atomization of paganism;[1] the Catholic Church, therefore, must never compromise with the Protestant confessions, as this would be tantamount to sanctioning division.[2] Fortunately, Chaadaev thought, the Reformation had not been able to destroy everything: Christendom had passed through all the phases of corruption that were an inseparable aspect of freedom, but did not—and indeed could not—collapse.[3] Even now some great turning-point was felt to be near; having outlived its political role Christianity was becoming social and mankind was entering the last phase of the establishment of the kingdom of heaven upon earth. In the eighth and last 'Letter' Chaadaev wrote about the coming fusion of souls and of the various moral powers of the world into one single soul and one single power. 'This fusion', he stressed, 'is the whole mission of Christianity. Truth is one: the Kingdom of God, Heaven on earth, all the promises of the Gospels are but the pre-vision of the union of all the thoughts of men into one single thought; and that single thought is God's thought itself, and that is the moral law realized.'[4] With this final act, the mission of humanity would be completed and the time would be ripe 'for the resolution [*dénouement*] of the universe, the great apocalyptic synthesis'.[5]

The language here is no longer that of de Bonald or the other apologists for the classical harmony of Roman Catholicism. Chaadaev's vision is part of the same philosophical orientation as the Joachimism of Schelling and the Polish romantics, as Cieszkowski's Paracletism and the 'palingenetic' views of Ballanche. Together with certain chiliastic elements, the mysticism he had rejected in his ontology and theory of cognition found its way into his philosophy of history. Nevertheless the formal coherence of his system is not, I would suggest, the most important criterion in an assessment of Chaadaev's role. His

---

[1] See Chaadaev, *Sochineniya*, i. 110, 117 (Chaadaev uses the term *désunité*).
[2] See ibid.
[3] See ibid., pp. 113–14. This can be compared to de Maistre's statement that Christian civilization is a civilization *qui n'admette de décadence*.
[4] *Literaturnoe nasledstvo*, xxii–xxiv. 62. *Russian Philosophy*, i. 154.
[5] Ibid.

originality lies in the fact that he attempted a synthesis of de Bonald's classical and partially rationalist traditionalism with romantic charisma and chiliasm—a synthesis, as it were, of the existing Petrine Church with the Johannine Church of the future.[1] His interpretation of tradition coincides with that of de Bonald, but unlike the latter he believed that revelation and reason did not rule out inspiration.

It was from the vantage-point of this philosophy of history that Chaadaev tried to look at Russia, or, more accurately perhaps, it was his view of Russia that led him to adopt this particular philosophy of history. Chaadaev was an aristocrat and a European; it was with pride that he called European civilization 'our civilization'; in Russia he could not perceive the things that he loved and which to him represented universal and absolute values. His philosophy grew out of his attempt to analyse what it was he found lacking in his native country. It is significant that the 'Letter' devoted to Russia was the first of the series and the only one to be published during the author's lifetime.

Russia, Chaadaev argues, was a country that seemed to have been overlooked by Providence. She lay between East and West and belonged to geography rather than to history; she would hardly be noticed if she did not happen to extend from Germany to the Behring Straits. Without the Tatar invasion, which spent itself in Russia and thus spared Europe, no history textbook would find her worth a mention. 'This is the result of our never having walked hand in hand with other nations', Chaadaev wrote; 'we belong to none of the great families of mankind; we are neither of the West nor of the East, and we possess the traditions of neither. Somehow divorced from time and space, the universal education of mankind has not touched us.'[2]

Russia had not experienced the continuity of tradition, that 'wonderful interconnection' of human ideas in the succession of

---

[1] The philosophy of Ballanche represents a similar trend. Chaadaev himself drew attention to the close relationship between his *Letters* and the theories of Ballanche in a letter to A. I. Turgenev; *Sochineniya*, i. 188.

[2] This and subsequent quotation from the *First Letter* are taken from Chaadaev, *Sochineniya*, ii. 74–105; *Russian Philosophy*, i. 106–25.

the centuries; everything in it was fortuitous, fragmentary, and unrepeated. Russians were not attached to anything, nobody had a 'definite sphere of existence, proper habits, and rules', in their own families they felt like strangers, in their own houses they behaved like visitors and, though they lived in cities, they were nomads. The semi-wild nomads were more attached to their steppes and deserts than Russians were to their cities. The Russian nation had never had any inspired heroes, had never passed through a poetic period of passionate unease, of exuberant, seemingly aimless activity; Russian history consisted of successive phases of brutal barbarism and crude superstition, followed by the humiliating yoke of Tartar domination, the spirit of which, Chaadaev suggested, was later inherited by Russia's national rulers. Russia's youth was a period of dull and gloomy existence, lacking in force and energy, with nothing to brighten it but an occasional crime. Her history could offer 'no endearing reminiscence, no venerable memorial to speak to you powerfully of the past and to reproduce it for you in a vivid and colourful manner. We live only in the narrowest of presents, without past and without future, in the midst of a flat calm.' The moral atmosphere of the West—the ideas of duty, justice, right, and order—were unknown, and so was the 'Western syllogism', logic and methodical thinking. Deprived of guiding ideas and the support of history, the Russian found himself lost in the world; he did not hold dear 'the progress of any community of ideas or interests': unable to establish the interconnection between himself and what came before him and what was to follow him, he lost his firm footing and all sense of certainty. On the other hand he was distinguished by a peculiarly carefree nature and at times by a special boldness typical of beings who are indifferent to everything and have nothing to lose. Russia did not belong to the moral sphere: her daily life had not yet attained a firm and definite form, but was in a state of permanent fermentation resembling the original chaos which preceded the present state of our planet.

The Russian people was therefore exceptional among the nations, was the conclusion Chaadaev drew from his analysis. It was a people without history, without its own guiding ideas or 'moral personality', but existing only to teach the world a great lesson. Such a people did not contribute to the evolution

of the universal consciousness and was incapable of real progress; it was a 'homeless foundling' forsaken by God. In the
following paragraph from the 'First Letter' Chaadaev's bitter
analysis reaches its climax:

We Russians, like illegitimate children, come into this world
without patrimony, without any links with people who lived on the
earth before us. We have in our hearts none of those lessons which
have preceded our own existence. Each one of us must himself once
again tie the broken thread of the family. What among other peoples
is a matter of habit, instinct, we can only get into our heads by
hammer strokes. Our memories go no further back than yesterday;
we are, as it were, strangers to ourselves. We walk through time so
singly that as we advance the past escapes us forever. This is a
natural result of a culture based wholly on borrowing and imitation.
There is among us no inward development, no natural progress;
new ideas throw out the old ones because they do not arise from the
latter, but come among us from heaven knows where. Since we
accept only ready-made ideas the ineradicable traces which a progressive movement of ideas engraves on the mind and which gives
ideas their forcefulness makes no furrow on our intellect. We grow,
but we do not mature; we advance, but obliquely, that is in a
direction which does not lead to the goal. . . . Isolated in the world,
we have given nothing to the world, we have taught nothing to the
world; we have contributed nothing to the progress of the human
spirit. And we have disfigured everything we have touched of that
progress. From the very first moment of our social existence, nothing
has emanated from us for the common good of men; not a single
useful thought has sprouted in the sterile soil of our country; not
a single great truth has sprung from our midst . . .

In the last pages of the letter Chaadaev tried to analyse the
reasons for Russia's peculiar fate and suggested that they were
to be found in her isolation, her exclusion from the universal
fellowship, her religious and national separation. These in turn
had their roots in the Schism, in separation from the universal
church; Russians were Christians, Chaadaev conceded, but
then so were the Abyssinians. For many centuries the Russian
people had lived in seclusion and had subordinated Christianity to the nationalist superstition, the worst of the super-
stitions dividing humanity. The nations of Europe held hands
as they traversed the centuries, together they fought to free the
Holy Sepulchre and together they worshipped God in one

language; their voices raised in unison to the Supreme Being formed a marvellous choir, a thousand times more sublime than the most wonderful harmony of the physical world. Chaadaev clearly equated the history of the West with sacred history and even suggested that the kingdom of heaven on earth had already been partially realized in Europe. In order to raise above empirical vegetation to a spiritual life, he concluded, Russia would have to repeat the entire past development of Europe from the beginning.

The fragment on serfdom in the 'Second Letter' is of great interest when taken in conjunction with the argument of the 'First Letter'. Chaadaev regarded serfdom as the central fact in Russian society and the source of its unhealthy atmosphere and paralysis. In the West the church had abolished serfdom, whereas in Russia she had presided over its introduction without a murmur. 'This alone', Chaadaev wrote, 'might make us inclined to question the Orthodox confession of which we are so proud.'[1] It is clear from this that Chaadaev's defence of the Catholic Middle Ages should not be interpreted as an apologia for the specific selfish interests of the aristocracy; it was rather a utopian vision intended as a counterpoise to the wilfulness and usurpations of Russian despotism and to the servility and dead torpor of the Russian Orthodox Church.[2]

The fact that Chaadaev was not alone in this attitude is shown by the example of V. S. Pecherin, a promising young Classics professor at the University of Moscow. In 1836 (the year that the 'First Letter' was published), Pecherin left Russia and resolved not to return. Subsequently he became a Catholic convert and entered the ultra-strict order of the Redemptorists. In his papers Gershenzon found a short verse whose vehement passion far surpassed what Herzen called Chaadaev's 'deliberate curse'.[3]

> How sweet it is to hate one's country
> And eagerly await her destruction.
> And to see in the destruction of one's country
> The dawn of a world reborn.[4]

---

[1] *Literaturnoe nasledstvo*, xxii–xxiv. 23.

[2] Below the first *Philosophical Letter* Chaadaev wrote 'Necropolis 1829, 1 December'.

[3] An expression used by Herzen in *My Past and Thoughts*, ii. 272.

[4] Quoted from M. Gershenzon, *Istoriya molodoĭ Rossii* (Moscow–Petrograd 1923).

Some elements in Chaadaev's view of Russia can be traced back to the writings of the French traditionalists. De Bonald, too, wrote that Russia, situated between Europe and Asia, was still an unformed society, that the Russian people was intrinsically nomadic, and that the houses of the Muscovites were merely Scythian chariots from which the wheels had been removed.[1] De Maistre, who lived in Russia for many years, called her a country ignorant of certain universal truths that were the fruits of an ancient civilization. He too thought that this was the result of the isolation following the religious Schism and would only be remedied if Russia rejoined the Western Catholic community.[2] It seems likely that Chaadaev was acquainted with these views, and that they probably helped to form his own.[3] His ideas, in turn, profoundly influenced another Catholic conservative, the Marquis de Custine, whose well-known book *Russia in the Year 1839* contains a character sketch of Chaadaev, a summary of the 'First Letter', and a description of the outcry that followed its publication.

These similarities suggest the need for another look at the problem of Chaadaev's conservatism. While the term 'conservative' would obviously fit Chaadaev in a European context, it seems less applicable in a Russian context, especially if we consider that he himself pointed out Russia's lack of such basic prerequisites of conservatism as a sense of settled abode, tradition, and historical roots.

If we define conservatism functionally (or 'situationally', as

[1] See de Bonald, *Pensées sur divers sujets* . . . (1812). The passage dealing with 'nomads', which is strikingly similar to Chaadaev's ideas, reads as follows: 'Les Russes sont encore un peuple nomade, au moins d'inclination, et les maisons de Moscou n'étaient que les charriots des Scythes dont on avait ôté les roues. Aussi les Russes ont un singulier penchant à varier la distribution et l'ameublement de leurs maisons; on dirait que, ne pouvant les changer de place, ils y changent tout ce qu'ils peuvent.' Quoted from Quénet, op. cit., p. 162. See also *Europa und Russland. Texte zum Problem des westeuropäischen und russischen Selbstverständnisses*, ed. by D. Tschiževskij and Dieter Groh (Darmstadt 1959), p. 56.

[2] See Quénet, op. cit., pp. 157–9. It must be emphasized that in his practical conclusions de Maistre differed from Chaadaev, who was opposed to serfdom. In his *Quatre chapitres sur la Russie* (1811) de Maistre appealed to Alexander I to protect the nobility's privileges and give up the idea of abolishing serfdom or even any support for the individual emancipation of the peasants. Serfdom was necessary in Russia, de Maistre argued, since Orthodoxy was not capable of fulfilling the social role played by Catholicism in the West.

[3] See Stepanov, op. cit., p. 618.

in S. P. Huntington's terminology),[1] we are forced to conclude that Chaadaev was not a conservative. His ideas did not reinforce the Russian *status quo*, negated the existing reality, and fulfilled a destructive function in relation to it. On the other hand, by applying a 'content' definition of conservatism and viewing Chaadaev's ideas against the general European background, we arrive at a somewhat different conclusion. This kind of systematization leaves no doubts concerning Chaadaev's relation to European conservatism in the widest sense of the term.

In order to understand Chaadaev's standpoint, it must be remembered that his ideas were imbued by a spirit of opposition to the 'Orthodox, autocratic, and national' Russia of Nicholas I. The 'First Letter' was printed at a time when the official ideologists lost no opportunity of proclaiming that while the West was rotten, Russia prospered, that her past, present, and future were entirely enviable, and that she alone was a 'sheet-anchor' for the entire human race. The publication of the 'Letter' caused a violent reaction. At the emperor's personal instigation Chaadaev was declared insane and placed under police and medical supervision; the periodical *Telescope* was closed down and its editor, N. I. Nadezhdin, was exiled to Ust-Sysolsk. These measures were considered by many to be too moderate; even Odoevsky was outraged by the publication of the 'Letter'.[2]

From Herzen's vivid account we know what effect the 'Letter' had on the most radical sections of the young intelligentsia. It was 'a shot that rang out in the dark night; whether it was something foundering that proclaimed its own wreck, whether it was a signal, a cry for help, whether it was news of the dawn or news that there would not be one—it was all the same: one had to wake up.'[3]

Chaadaev probably wrote his 'Philosophical Letter' in about 1829 and several years elapsed before its publication. During

[1] See S. P. Huntington, 'Conservatism as an Ideology', *American Political Science Review*, ii (1957).

[2] See Koyré, *Études sur l'histoire de la pensée philosophique en Russie* (Paris 1950), pp. 29–30. In a letter to Shevȳrëv, Odoevsky wrote: 'I say about Europe what Chaadaev has said about Russia, and *vice versa*.' Quoted from H. Kohn, *The Mind of Modern Russia* (New Brunswick, New Jersey 1955), p. 15.

[3] Herzen, *My Past and Thoughts*, ii. 261.

this time his views gradually changed, so that when it finally appeared it was no longer an accurate reflection of its author's current standpoint.

The July Revolution in France was a shock which undermined Chaadaev's calm and unshaken faith in Europe. The Europe he loved was the old aristocratic Europe where the wounds inflicted by the Revolution were healing over during the Bourbon restoration. 'Not so long ago, only a year ago,' he wrote to Pushkin in 1831, 'the world was utterly tranquil about its present and future fate. . . . Reason was born anew, humanity recovered its memory, conflicting views were reconciled, passion was stifled, anger had nothing to feed on, and human ambitions and vanity were satisfied by splendid undertakings.'[1] Suddenly, because of one man's (Charles X) stupidity, everything had come to naught. 'Tears come to my eyes when I look at the tremendous disaster that has befallen an old society—my society; this all-embracing evil that has so unexpectedly fallen upon my Europe has doubled my personal unhappiness.'[2] Chaadaev's only consolation was his belief in the wisdom of the mysterious decrees of Providence. 'I am not the only one to hope that reason will again become reasonable', he continues his letter. 'But how and when shall we see this return of reason to itself? Will it come about through the actions of some mighty spirit entrusted by Providence with a special mission, or will it be the outcome of a whole series of events sent by Providence to serve as a lesson to humanity? I do not know.'[3]

This admission of ignorance implied that Providence might well make use of entirely new means and new forces. Horrified by the revolutionary events in Europe, Chaadaev began to value his native Russia; influenced by his discussions with the future Slavophiles, above all with Ivan Kireevsky, he began to see Russia as a force reserved by Providence for a special mission and therefore kept apart so far from the great family of nations that had participated in history.

The scandal that accompanied the publication of the first 'Philosophical Letter' induced Chaadaev to redefine his current views of Russia in order to justify himself to the authorities and,

---

[1] Chaadaev, *Sochineniya*, i. 164.
[2] Ibid., i. 164–5.   [3] Ibid. i. 165.

to a lesser extent, to public opinion. The result was the *Apology of a Madman* (*Apologie d'un fou*) written in 1837.

Chaadaev opened his defence by stating that (contrary to the general view) love of his native land was not something alien to him. But while love of one's country is a splendid thing, love of truth, he insisted, is finer still; patriotism divides nations and love of truth forms a bond between them; the Kingdom of Heaven is reached not by way of one's native land but by way of the truth.

Chaadaev admitted that his interpretation of Russian history in the 'Philosophical Letter' was too severe, but adhered to his main theses, although he differed in the conclusions he drew from them. He repeated his assertion that Russia was a country without history and that its past revealed a lack of spontaneous internal development. If she had been a historical nation, he argued, the Petrine reforms would have proved impossible, for ancient and deep-rooted traditions would have offered resistance to the legislator's arbitrary decisions. Russia, however, was only a blank sheet of paper:

> This level plain lies open, waste and white,
> A wide-spread page prepared for God to write.[1]

The Petrine reforms did not represent a sin against historical continuity or against 'historical authenticity' since there had

---

[1] Adam Mickiewicz, 'Forefather's Eve', Part III, 'Digression'. Many parallels between Mickiewicz's 'Digression' and Chaadaev's 'First Philosophical Letter' are discussed in chapter I of W. Lednicki's *Russia, Poland and the West* (Roy Publishers, New York). Lednicki suggests that Mickiewicz might have met Chaadaev during his stay in Russia and that some passages in the 'Digression' echoed their conversations. This hypothesis seems probable, especially in view of the striking similarity of certain passages. Chaadaev wrote: 'Even in our very eyes I find something strangely vague, cold, uncertain, something which resembles to an extent the physiognomie of people at the lowest scale of the social ladder. When I was abroad, particularly in the south where faces are so animated and expressive, I often compared the faces of my compatriots with those of the natives, and I was struck by the mute air of our features.' In Mickiewicz's 'Digression' we have the following passage:

> . . . But every face is like their home, a plain,
> A waste on which no inward light shines forth.
> Their hearts, like underground volcanoes, throw
> Upon the cheeks no flame or fierce desire.
> Their moving lips reflect no ardent glow;
> No wrinkled brows fade with the dying fire
> Seen on men's foreheads in more favored lands.

never been any such thing. In relation to a nation without history, Peter's measures were just and apt. It is worth noting that this statement can be inverted: its concealed aim was to convince Peter's heirs that only the view of Russia as a country without a history could justify the violence of Peter's reforms and, consequently, the legality of his arbitrary and bureaucratic despotism.

'I love my country', Chaadaev wrote, 'as I was taught to do by Peter the Great.'[1] Russia's isolation was not her fault, but the fault of her geographical situation. Russia had no history, but an absence of history could also be regarded as a privilege. Fettered by their own traditions, by their splendid history, the nations of Europe built their future with difficulty in a bitter struggle against the forces of the past; in Russia, on the other hand, the emperor's mighty will was enough to cause all opinions to retreat into the background, all convictions to collapse, and all minds to welcome the new ideas.[2] In constructing its future, the Russian people could make use of the experience of European nations and avoid their mistakes, guided solely by the 'voice of enlightened reason and conscious will'.[3] 'History has already eluded us, to be sure', Chaadaev wrote, 'but science is ours; we cannot undertake the entire work of the human spirit from the beginning, but we can participate in its future work; we cannot control our past, but the future depends on our efforts.'[4] These were the arguments on which Chaadaev based his conviction that Russia was destined to 'solve the majority of problems affecting the social order, to lead to their conclusion the majority of ideas originating among older nations, and to give an answer to the most important questions perplexing humanity'.[5]

O'er which have passed, through many weary years,
Such strong traditions, sorrows, hopes and fears
That in each face a nation's history stands.
And here the eyes of men are large and clear,
Like their unstoried towns; no storm-tossed heart
Makes anguished glances from their pupils dart
Or hopeless sorrow in their depth appear:
Viewed from afar they seem austere and great;
But near of hand, empty and desolate.

(G. R. Noyes, *Poems by Adam Mickiewicz* (New York 1944), p. 339.)
[1] Chaadaev, *Sochineniya*, i. 230.   [2] See ibid., p. 231.
[3] Ibid., p. 232.   [4] Ibid., pp. 231–2.   [5] Ibid., pp. 230–1.

Chaadaev's view of Russia is an exact counterpart of Locke's *tabula rasa* theory of the human mind. In his book *Edmund Burke and the Revolt against the Eighteenth Century* A. Cobban comments on the implications of this doctrine:

If man is given us at birth packed full of innate principles, inexorable instincts, inborn traditions, it is obvious that little fresh can be made of him; he will live and die precisely as his fathers lived and died and any attempt to alter or improve his lot is doomed to disappointment. Sweeping away the whole accepted theory of man at a blow, Locke presents us with an entirely different situation, in which man's mind when he is born is no more than a sheet of blank paper whereon we may write what we will. No more revolutionary doctrine has ever been put forward. For by it most obviously education and environment become lord and master of man, and it is possible to change the whole face of society in a single generation.[1]

The *Apology of a Madman* brings the tragic paradox of Chaadaev into sharp focus. The philosopher who believed that the 'fundamental fact of psychology' was the supra-individual inheritance of ideas, and who was whole-heartedly opposed to Locke's empiricism, was at the same time forced to argue that his own country was a blank sheet of paper, a land without a heritage, and an exception to the general rule. This was tantamount to admitting that none of his views of humanity, society, or history could be applied to his native Russia. What made the paradox even greater, was that Chaadaev, the conservative, accepted the anti-conservative implications of the *tabula rasa* theory, and even saw in them Russia's only chance.

The view of Russia as a country where nothing had yet been done and where everything, therefore, could be accomplished, was by no means a new one; it had been expressed by Leibniz after the Petrine reforms[2] and by Diderot in connection with legislation introduced by Catherine.[3] In the writings of both these philosophers, however, this theory is of minor importance,

[1] A. Cobban, *Edmund Burke and the Revolt against the Eighteenth Century* (London 1929), p. 24.
[2] See *Europa und Russland*, op. cit., pp. 15–17, and L. Richter, *Leibniz und sein Russlandbild* (Berlin 1946).
[3] See Plekhanov, *Sochineniya*, xxii. 144. In his *Essai historique sur la police*, written for Catherine II, Diderot stated that as a young country whose forms of government had not yet become permanently fixed, Russia was particularly malleable.

and not something that flowed from their basic philosophical premisses. It was only for Chaadaev that it became a cornerstone of the ideological position which summed up his whole inner conflict. Thanks to him various versions of the 'blank sheet of paper' theory came to play an important part in the ideology of the revolutionary Populists. Herzen, who took over the idea directly from Chaadaev, expressed it in terms that were almost identical: Russians were unencumbered by the 'burden of history', he wrote, and there was nothing in their past for them to love (with the exception of the peasant commune); they were the proletariat, as it were, of European nations and therefore had nothing to lose and everything to gain in a revolution.[1] Mikhailovsky, who was probably also harking back to Chaadaev, thought that the 'lack of history' was to blame, on the one hand, for the weakness typical of many Russians, and on the other, for the boldness of 'Russian negation',[2] which would stop at nothing. Still another version of the 'blank sheet of paper' theory was developed by Tkachev, who maintained that Russian autocracy was weak and 'suspended in the air', since it was not deeply rooted in history. It was precisely this weakness and lack of spontaneity of the 'historical classes', he thought, that would ensure the 'will to rule' of the revolutionary minority a relatively easy victory.[3]

It is not the aim of this work to evaluate these ideas, or to separate their 'myth-making' content from 'realistic' elements.

---

and suitable material to be worken on by the creative will of a wise legislator: 'How fortunate is the nation in whose land nothing has as yet been done!'

[1] See Herzen, *Sochineniya*, vii. 15–16, pp. 298–9.

[2] In his article 'Proudhon and Belinsky' Mikhailovsky wrote: 'History bestows strength, firmness, a decisive character, but . . . also forges the heavy yoke of tradition which hampers the liberty of the critical spirit. The absence of history induces weakness, moral spinelessness, but, on the other hand, if in such a milieu there is an individual endowed with the instinct for truth, he will be capable of a greater courage and broader horizons than a European; and that just because he is not weighed down by history, not rendered helpless by the pressure of tradition. The courage of Russian negation astonishes Europeans. In their eyes it is a sign of savagery, of barbarism, and they are partly right. In view of his lack of history a Russian has no reason to prize even the multiplication-table, but also has no reason to prize—let us say, the social barriers which in our past have never attained European definition or permanence.' N. K. Mikhailovsky, *Polnoe sobranie sochineniĭ* (St Petersburg 1909), iii. 681, 683–4.

[3] See especially the famous 'Open letter to Mr. F. Engels', P. N. Tkachev, *Izbrannȳe sochineniya*, vol. iii (Moscow 1932).

My reason for quoting them here was to throw into greater relief the paradox of a thinker who glorified history and at the same time denied its existence in his own country; who was a disciple of the French traditionalists and at the same time exerted a seminal influence on the ideologists of the Russian Revolution.

It is difficult to be sure today whether the more optimistic view of Russia's future outlined in the *Apology of a Madman* represented Chaadaev's real opinion; taking into account the specific circumstances under which the essay was written, as well as the entire body of his earlier and later ideas, this would seem doubtful. This is not to accuse Chaadaev of being entirely insincere; it is likely that he really did admit the possibility of a great future for Russia, but he was far from holding this view unreservedly, or from founding all his hopes on it. In any case he could hardly be enthusiastic about a future Russian civilization deprived of its religious basis and founded on purely scientific and anti-historical principles.

However we interpret the *Apology*, the view that the Russian people was incapable of spontaneous historical creativity undoubtedly continued to be central to Chaadaev's thought. In the *Apology* he expressed concern at the appearance of 'fanatical Slavs' who rummaged through libraries and archives in search of documents to refute this view.[1] He regarded the emergence of Slavophilism as a matter of great moment, 'the first act of the liberated national reason'; at the same time he was saddened and disturbed by the conviction that it was 'a passionate reaction against enlightenment, against the ideas of the West that have made us what we are, and to whom they [i.e. the Slavophiles] owe their being'.[2] It is significant that in place of Slavophilism Chaadaev upheld the idea of 'enlightened government', and in a sense even appealed to the government, pointing out that the Slavophile movement represented a threat to the heritage of Peter the Great and could do unforeseen damage.

A letter Chaadaev wrote to Schelling in May 1842 throws a characteristic light on his struggle against Slavophile ideas.[3] The philosophy of revelation expounded by Schelling in Berlin

[1] See Chaadaev, *Sochineniya*, i. 224.
[2] Ibid., p. 227.   [3] See ibid., pp. 244–6.

was welcomed by the Slavophiles as a weighty argument in their disputes with the Westernizers, most of whom belonged to the Hegelian school attacked by Schelling. Chaadaev's role in these quarrels was complicated by the fact that he himself considered Schelling the greatest of the German philosophers, and the philosophy of revelation an important step towards the reconciliation of religion and philosophy. The purpose of his letter, which supplied Schelling with detailed information about the activities of the Slavophiles, was to secure an authoritative statement condemning the movement and supporting his (Chaadaev's) standpoint in the Moscow discussions. The letter, it must be admitted, shows great tactical ability: the author reminds Schelling of their former acquaintance, is sharply critical of Hegel, makes the quite unwarranted charge that the general acceptance of Hegelian philosophy in Russia is to blame for the emergence of Slavophilism, and stresses that the Slavophiles want to found a 'new and exceptional' philosophy which would overthrow all previous systems, including, of course, Schelling's.

In the course of frequent discussions with the Slavophiles Chaadaev made certain concessions to the 'new school' and, in his own words, 'became somewhat slavonified'.[1] The most important of these concessions was a change in his one-sidedly negative approach to Orthodoxy. He was ready to concede that the Orthodox faith was superior to Catholicism as far as purity of dogma was concerned, and came to regard the Eastern Church as representing the development of the ascetic and contemplative side of Christianity, thus supplementing, in a sense, the 'sociality' and 'activity' of the Roman Church.[2] He went so far as to accept the Slavophiles' assertion that pre-Petrine Russia had been 'the product of religious principle', that the 'good and simple-souled' Russian people had accepted the teachings of the Gospels in their original form and had applied them to family life.[3] These concessions were not on matters of principle, however. In an exhaustive letter to the Compte Circourt (1846), Chaadaev drew his attention to the importance of Slavophile ideas and asked him to publish Khomyakov's article 'Foreigners' Views on Russia' in the French

---

[1] See Chaadaev, *Sochineniya*, i. p. 254.
[2] See ibid.   [3] See ibid., pp. 270, 273.

press; at the same time he maintained the position of an implacable Westernizer and bolstered it up with new arguments.[1]

The letter to Circourt is worth examining in some detail. In it Chaadaev took up the Slavophiles' line of reasoning and at times even repeated their arguments, but drew diametrically different conclusions from them. Conceding, for instance, that Orthodoxy was Christianity in its original form, he argued from this that the Russian people had accepted the principles of Christianity before its social character had clearly emerged; hence Christianity permeated family and home life in ancient Russia, but was not able to influence the formation of social and political relations. Chaadaev also inverted the Slavophile thesis of the pernicious influence of Rome on Catholicism by pointing out that since the capital of the Roman Empire before the Schism was Byzantium, the remoteness of Western Christendom from the seat of imperial power helped to consolidate its independence. In the Eastern Empire, on the other hand, the Church was subordinate to the secular authorities, while the clergy inherited Greek submissiveness to the emperors and made no effort either to 'socialize' Christianity or to 'Christianize' the social system. He even succeeded in turning to his own account the Slavophile argument that Russian society, unlike the societies in the West, was not founded on armed conquest. In the West, he suggested, servitude (i.e. serfdom) had come about as the result of conquest, whereas in Russia it had evolved by itself without arousing the anger of the clergy or even of the people. This fact was without historical precedent and helped to prove that from the very beginning everything in Russia was directed towards the subjugation of man and men's minds.

Chaadaev summed up his argument as follows:

We shall not throw off the influence of alien ideas until we have fully understood the path along which we have travelled, until an involuntary confession of all our errors has escaped our lips, until a cry of pain and repentance that will echo throughout the world has burst from our breast. Only then, in the natural course of events, shall we take our place amongst those nations that are destined to act on behalf of humanity, not only as battering-rams or truncheons, but also as bearers of ideas.[2]

---

[1] See ibid., pp. 268–75.
[2] Ibid., p. 274.

The activity of the Slavophiles, Chaadaev thought, would ultimately help to bring this future nearer. Their research into the specific nature of Russian history, for instance, would contribute to a better understanding of the past and lead to unexpected discoveries. 'Even now,' he wrote, 'in this very school that tries to revive the past, more than one enlightened mind and more than one sincere spirit have been forced to acknowledge this or that sin committed by our fathers.'[1]

In a letter he wrote to Khomyakov in 1844 Chaadaev again reverted to the same theme. After thanking Khomyakov for his severe condemnation of Ivan the Terrible, he expressed the hope that further research would convince him that this 'monster was possible only in the particular country in which he made his appearance'. 'After this,' Chaadaev suggested ironically, 'all that remains is to trace his direct derivation from the common people, from that family and communal way of life which makes us superior to the other nations of the world, and which we should be trying hard to restore. In expectation of this conclusion—but not of the said restoration—I thank you once more for your article, which I read with the utmost pleasure . . .'[2]

The events of 1848 were to bring about a further modification in Chaadaev's view of Russia—the final abandonment, in fact, of the hopes expressed in the *Apology of a Madman*. It was the Russian emperor who now became 'the real leader of European reaction', as Mickiewicz put it.[3] This conviction was shared by another romantic poet, Fëdor Tyutchev, albeit from the other side of the barricades. Only two real forces, he wrote, are involved in the present struggle: Russia and revolution. 'For them no compromise, no negotiations are possible; the existence of one means the death of the other.'[4]

In spite of Chaadaev's attachment to conservative values his reaction to the revolutionary events in Europe was very different from Tyutchev's. Evidence of this is a draft proclamation in which he set out to inform the Russian peasantry of the revolu-

---

[1] See Chaadaev, *Sochineniya*, i pp. 274-5.

[2] Ibid., p. 249.

[3] Adam Mickiewicz, *Collected Works* (*Dzieła*, vol. xii, Warsaw 1955), p. 196; from *La Tribune des Peuples*.

[4] F. I. Tyutchev, 'La Russie et le Révolution', in *Polnoe sobranie sochineniĭ*, 8th ed. (Petrograd, n.d.), p. 542.

tionary events in Europe.[1] This curious document, which was addressed to the 'Russian people, Orthodox Christians' and composed in a pseudo-popular idiom, opens with the announcement that the Christian nations have rebelled, have begun to 'rock like the ocean, the sea', have risen against their 'lords, the tsars', against oppression and slavery, and want no other kings beside the King of Heaven. The proclamation was not finished and the circumstances of its composition are still a matter of speculation. While it would be extremely naïve to accept it as evidence that Chaadaev had joined the side of the revolutionary peasants, it seems clear that he did not sympathize with the Tsar's counter-revolutionary campaign and wanted to play his part in defeating it.

This attitude was no doubt reinforced by the dreary years oı reaction, the persecution of all philosophical movements, and the 'censorship terror', that followed in Russia after the 1848 revolutions. Chaadaev's criticism of Russia and particularly of Russian nationalism—both the official and the Slavophile varieties—became still sharper and more vehement. In a note on one of Khomyakov's theological brochures he described tsarist rule as 'Western despotism' and blamed it for the fact that Reformation influences had stopped short at the Russian frontier (unlike the Slavophiles who thought this was due to the specific virtues of Orthodoxy). Protestantisms, he wrote, had come to a halt at the point where the 'realm of ideas' ended and the 'realm of brutal fact and ritual' began.[2] In his 'Letter from an Unknown Man to an Unknown Woman', written at the beginning of the Crimean War (in 1854), Chaadaev suggested that the war had been started by 'pseudo-nationalist reactionaries' who were in the grip of a monomania and influenced the government's foreign policy.[3]

The fact that Chaadaev's *Weltanschauung* underwent a further evolution, in the course of which conservative elements became less pronounced and retreated into the background, is interestingly reflected in his condemnation of the Slavophiles' 'retrospective utopias', which he contrasted with the patriotism of his youth. This is how he described the mood of the time when

[1] See D. Shakhovskoï, 'An Unpublished Proclamation drafted by P. J. Chaadaev in 1848' in *Literaturnoe nasledstvo*, xxii–xxiv. 679–82.
[2] Chaadaev, *Sochineniya*, i. 304–6.   [3] See ibid., p. 309.

many members of his own circle were drawing closer to the Decembrists:

No, a thousand times no! This is not how we loved our country in our youth! We wished her happiness and sound institutions; sometimes we even ventured to wish her more liberty, if that were possible; but we did not consider her to be either the most powerful or the happiest country in the world. It never even occurred to us that Russia was the embodiment of some abstract principle containing within herself the final solution of the social question; or that she was a world apart, the direct and legal heir of the famous Eastern Empire, its equal in all matters as far as laws and reputation are concerned; or that it was her mission to absorb all the Slavonic nations and thus to bring about a renaissance of mankind; and in particular we did not believe that Europe was ready to collapse into barbarism and that we were destined to save her with the crumbs of the very civilization that not long before had led us out of our centuries-long torpor. We looked up to Europe with esteem, even with respect, for we knew that she had taught us many things, our own history among them. If, by chance, we happened to gain a victory over her, as in the case of Peter the Great, we said to the defeated: 'it is to you we owe this victory.'[1]

Nevertheless it was impossible for Chaadaev to return to the patriotism of the 1820s. Towards the end of his life he reverted to the pessimism of the first 'Philosophical Letter' and became confirmed in his conviction (though this was now backed up by different arguments) that Russia was after all 'a world apart'—a world of evil, servitude, and creative impotence. A most illuminating article written during the Crimean War (1854) and intended for (anonymous) publication in the French press was discovered among Chaadaev's papers by the Soviet scholar D. Shakhovskoï.[2] In it Chaadaev went so far as to state that by comparison with Russia everything in Europe—monarchs, governments, and people—was the embodiment of liberty, and that the war between Europe and Russia was the 'natural conflict of light and darkness'. The article concludes with the words:

When Russia is discussed she is often thought to be a country like any other; in fact this is not so. Russia is an entire world apart, sub-

[1] Chaadaev p. 308.
[2] Chaadaev, 'Neopublikovannaya stat'ya', "Zvenya", vols. iii–iv (Moscow–Leningrad 1934), pp. 365–90.

missive to the will, whim, or fancy of one man: whether his name be Peter or Ivan, in every case he is the personification of arbitrary rule. Contrary to all the laws of human coexistence, Russia moves in one direction only—towards her own enslavement and the enslavement of all her neighbours. That is why it would be beneficial —not only in the interest of other nations, but also in her own—to force her to adopt another path.[1]

This unfair but impassioned judgement is likely to arouse mixed feelings in the reader: admiration for its truly Russian 'courage of negation' and at the same time a sense of tragic awe at the writer's complete alienation from his own society. Chaadaev's life concluded with a double defeat: the aristocratic Westernizer was disappointed by an increasingly bourgeoisified Europe and the Russian patriot was estranged from his own country by the depressing realities of Russia under Nicholas I.

Chaadaev's criticism of Slavophilism was often unfair and occasionally even superficial, since it failed to make an adequate analysis of its internal structure. He was convinced, for instance, that Khomyakov's view of Ivan the Terrible represented a concession to Westernism, something that distinguished Khomyakov from the other Slavophiles, whereas in fact it arose from the fundamental premises of Slavophile doctrine. He equated Slavophilism with nationalism and did not distinguish it from the doctrine of Official Nationality; moreover, since he was accustomed to regard the government as an organ of enlightenment and Europeanization, he reproached the Slavophiles for those sins for which he should rather have blamed the government-inspired nationalism. At the same time his criticism failed to take account of such basic aspects of Slavophile philosophy as the problem of personality and social bonds, types of culture, and the role of rationalism.

In the Slavophile/Westernizer controversy Chaadaev held a position that was untypical. His own Westernism did not admit the view that Russia ought to pas through a stage of capitalist development; he considered the Middle Ages to have been the high-water mark of European development, while capitalism (to which he devoted little attention) was to him evidence of the grave crisis of European civilization rather than

[1] Ibid., p. 380.

an essential constituent of 'Europeanism'. The democratic and liberal Westernizers of the 1840s graduated from the Hegelian school and their philosophical evolution was in the direction of materialism and atheism. Chaadaev, on the other hand, like the Slavophiles, founded his hopes on a future religious renaissance and welcomed the anti-Hegelian philosophy of revelation expounded by Schelling. The Westernizers set out to establish a philosophical basis for the autonomy of the individual, expressed in untrammelled and creative activity; Chaadaev, like the Slavophiles, expressly rejected the autonomy of the individual and the creative nature of his own freely willed actions.

This 'untypicality' is, however, especially illuminating: the profound contradictions of Chaadaev's Westernism accentuate *a contrario* the essential correctness of the line of development followed by the mainstream of Westernizing thought.

Chaadaev's attempt to reconcile Westernism and conservatism was bound to fail. No Russian could be satisfied by a defence of a conservative system of values which had the built-in reservation that it could not be applied in underprivileged Russia, where it was most needed. The call for a remaking of the whole of Russian history, from the reversal of the Schism to the repetition of all the evolutionary stages of medieval Europe, was too obviously utopian to serve as a programme for action. The *Apology of a Madman* did, it is true, imply another tempting choice—that of constructing the future without reference to history, by purely rational means; but the admission of this possibility was tantamount to stating that Russia could only develop outside and independently of the conservative system of values.

Chaadaev's conservative convictions were, moreover, contradicted by the course of events in Europe itself. The beloved aristocratic Europe of his dreams was becoming a thing of the past; the leading European states were the scene of acute class struggles—of bourgeois liberal, as well as of radical, democratic, and socialist movements. Russia, on the other hand, turned out to be the mainstay of European conservatism. In this context it was difficult to reconcile conservatism with Westernism, and it is not surprising that in Russia they were bound to part company.

The paradox of Chaadaev also helps to throw light on many

points of Slavophile doctrine. His thesis that Russia was a country without history, without its own deep-rooted national culture (for how else was it possible to explain Peter the Great's violent reforms which took no account of any traditions?), made a profound impression on the Slavophiles. His arguments forced them to give their conservatism a 'popular' character, for it was only among the common people, whom Chaadaev had over-looked, that Russian history retained its continuity; only the common people had not been affected by Europeanization and had remained faithful to the traditions and religion of their fathers. In Russia, the Slavophiles concluded, the only haven of Toryism was the peasant's primitive hut.[1]

The revolutionary events in Europe, which deprived Wes-ternizing conservatism of its foundations, at the same time helped to consolidate the conservatism of the Slavophiles. Under these changed circumstances the Slavophiles were likely to be tempted to reverse Chaadaev's thesis and to show that it was Europe that had always lacked the proper conditions for true conservatism. Their criticism of contemporary Europe and of the entire European past can be interpreted as a reply to Chaadaev's eulogy of European history, while their conserva-tive utopian vision of ancient Orthodox Russia can be regarded as a counterpoise to Chaadaev's idealization of ancient Catho-lic Europe.

[1] See Y. Samarin, *Sochineniya* (Moscow 1877), i. 401-2.

PART TWO

CLASSICIAL SLAVOPHILISM

4

Ivan Kireevsky

IVAN Kireevsky (1806–56), the founder of Slavophile doctrine was born of an old noble family which kept up national traditions and religion without rejecting Western European influences. His father Vasily was a highly cultured man who knew five languages and owned a vast library; he was an enlightened conservative and had been a Freemason in his youth. As an enthusiastic Anglophile he was steeped in eighteenth-century English literature and had turned the grounds of his family manor in the village of Dolbino into an English park. His deepseated dislike of the writings of the French Enlightenment sometimes took an extreme form: he was so violently opposed to the current fashion for Voltaire, that on his visits to Moscow he would buy up the philosopher's works merely in order to destroy them.[1] After his death in 1812, Ivan, who was still very young, was brought up by his mother, one of the best-educated Russian women of her time, and by his stepfather A. A. Elagin, an admirer of Kant and one of the first Russian translators of Schelling. Another relative who played an important part in Kireevsky's upbringing was his mother's uncle, the famous poet Vasily Zhukovsky, translator and popularizer of German romantic literature. As a ten-year-old boy the young Ivan had already read his father's entire collection of French literature and by the age of twelve he had acquired a good command of German. At the same time Zhukovsky also taught him to appreciate Russian literature.

In 1821 the Elagins moved from Dolbino to Moscow. Their new home, known as the 'Elagin salon', soon became one of the main focal points of intellectual life in Moscow and the scene of intense philosophical and literary disputes. Kireevsky graduated from Moscow university, joined the Society of the Lovers of Wisdom, and announced that his aim in life would henceforth be ceaseless self-improvement. He chose literature

---

[1] See Koyré, *Études sur l'histoire de la pensée philosophique en Russie*, p. 2.

as his main field and defined his future plans in the following words: 'We shall render unto true religion what is hers by right, combine the beautiful with morality, awaken love of truth, replace foolish liberalism by respect for law, and prize a pure life more highly than a pure style.'[1] He was acquainted with almost all the outstanding Moscow personalities of the time, including the Polish poet Adam Mickiewicz. When the latter was to leave Moscow in 1826, his friends presented him with a gold cup which had their names engraved on it. In his verse 'To Mickiewicz',[2] written to mark the occasion, Kireevsky says that a talisman hidden in the cup will link the poet's thoughts and dreams with the thoughts and dreams of those who presented him with it, that an 'invisible thread' will transmit to him the 'tremulous heart-beats' of his Russian friends, and inform them, in turn, of the cares and sorrows of the exiled poet:

> By the anxious tremors of their hearts
> They will know of your sorrows;
> When they recollect you from afar,
> Their thoughts will echo yours in distant harmony.

The starting-point, therefore, from which Kireevsky's thought evolved, was the largely conservative variant of Western European philosophical and literary romanticism which was introduced into Russian literature by Zhukovsky and cultivated by the Society of the Lovers of Wisdom. Kireevsky's intellectual biography would not, however, be complete without reference to the tremendous influence of his youngest brother Peter (1808–56), later to become the leading Slavophile folklore specialist. His contemporaries were unanimous in their view that Peter Kireevsky was a living embodiment of the best vanishing patriarchal traditions of the old Russian artistocracy. His character became formed very early and revealed unusual stability; throughout his life he was unwavering in his attachment to national traditions and the Orthodox faith, his love of the Russian people and countryside, and his instinctive

---

[1] I. V. Kireevsky, *Polnoe sobranie sochineniĭ*, ed. M. O. Gershenzon, 2 vols. (Moscow 1911), i. 10.

[2] Kireevsky, ii. 210. On the cup were engraved the names of the two Kireevsky brothers, their stepfather A. A. Elagin, the poet E. Boratÿnsky, N. M. Rozhalin, N. A. Polevoĭ, S. S. Sheṽyrëv, and S. Sobolevsky. All of them were directly or indirectly associated with the Lovers of Wisdom Circle. Mickiewicz's Moscow acquaintances also included A. Khomyakov and M. Pogodin.

aversion to Western culture. Even in the early 1830s Peter Kireevsky was said by Buslaev to be a fanatical opponent of Peter the Great, so much so that he regretted bearing the same name.[1] The strength of his convictions and his inner integrity exerted a profound influence on his brother Ivan, who possessed these qualities to a far lesser degree.

Unlike his brother, Ivan Kireevsky was not by nature born 'fully formed'; his Slavophilism was the outcome of conscious thought and a complicated philosophical evolution. It is worth considering this evolution in some detail, as it helps to reveal the links connecting Slavophilism with the romanticism of the Lovers of Wisdom and Chaadaev's conservative Westernism.

FROM LOVER OF WISDOM TO SLAVOPHILE

It is more than significant that in his first article, entitled 'Random Thoughts about the Character of Pushkin's Poetry' (1828), Kireevsky set out to prove that in Pushkin Russia had finally found her long-awaited great national poet. Kireevsky saw 'national' features even in those works of Pushkin which might seem, at first glance, to be merely modelled on Western writers. Pushkin was a truly 'national' writer, he wrote, a poet of reality, moulded at the core of his nation's life; his works were a spontaneous manifestation of the spiritual essence of the Russian people, expressed for the first time in perfect poetical form. Pushkin was the first poet to remain completely 'national' while at the same time assimilating the cultural traditions of the West. Apart from these ideas, Kireevsky's article contains some characteristic remarks on the old age and decline of European culture; he poured ridicule on the Russian followers of Byron and suggested that in a young and hopeful state such as Russia there could be no place for a disenchanted Byronic hero.

The postulate that literature must be 'national', put forward in the article on Pushkin, was backed up with further arguments in the 'Review of Russian Literature for the Year 1829'. Here Kireevsky emphasized that the way to a truly national culture led through history and philosophy. 'Respect for reality', he wrote, 'is the essence of the stage of intellectual development at which Europe has now halted, and which is characterized by the historical orientation in all spheres of human existence

[1] See M. Gershenzon, *Obrazȳ proshlogo* (Moscow 1912), p. 124.

and spiritual life. In our times history lies at the core of all knowledge, it is the science of sciences, the only factor determining all development; the historical orientation is all-embracing.'[1] History itself, however, ought to become permeated by philosophy—Karamzin's *History* could no longer suffice for contemporary Russia. 'For us philosophy is essential . . . the entire development of our intellectual life calls for it.'[2] The first step towards creating a national philosophy should be the assimilation of Germany's intellectual contribution, hence the 'German orientation' represented by the Lovers of Wisdom favoured the emergence of an independent Russian philosophy, just as the 'German orientation' in literature, represented first by Zhukovsky, had liberated Russian writing from French influences and helped to create an indigenous literature.

Nevertheless [stressed Kireevsky], other people's thoughts are useful only in so far as they serve to fertilize one's own. German philosophy cannot strike root in Russia. Our own philosophy should grow out of our own life, out of our current problems and dominant private and national concerns. When and how this will happen time will show. But the inclination towards German philosophy, which is beginning to become widely known here, already represents an important step in the right direction.[3]

Kireevsky had a clearly defined conception of the mutual relationship between Russia and Western Europe. He greatly admired Western Civilization, but from its very perfection he drew the conclusion that its role must shortly be played out. The unity of European civilization had already disintegrated—individual nations had fulfilled their mission and were living a life of isolation; what Europe needed now was an influx of fresh blood, a new focal point, a nation 'that would rule over the others thanks to her political and intellectual predominance'.[4] Within the sphere of influence of European civilization there were only two nations that were young as well as great: the United States of America and Russia. The former was disqualified, however, by her remoteness and her 'one-sided English civilization'. This left Russia, whose civilization had been moulded by the efforts of all the most important nations

---

[1] Kireevsky, ii. 18–19.   [2] Ibid., p. 27.
[3] Ibid.   [4] Ibid., p. 38.

of Europe; they had given her an all-European, non-exclusive character and had thus prepared the ground for her future influence on the whole of Europe. As the 'youngest sister in a large family' Russia had inherited the achievements and experience of her predecessors, and this would facilitate her mission. Her geographical position and size were another factor in her favour.[1]

The view of Russia and the United States as two youthful vigorous successors of European civilization was to gain ground in Europe after the publication of de Tocqueville's *De la démocratie en Amerique* (1835); it is worth noting, therefore, that Kireevsky wrote his essay five years before de Tocqueville's famous analysis.

Kireevsky's comments on Russia's future historical mission were not in keeping with his views in general. His 'Review of Russian Literature for the Year 1829' is therefore of the utmost interest just because of the characteristic contradictions concealed below the surface of the article. To begin with, the 'Review' is far more 'Western' in character than might appear at first sight. On the one hand Kireevsky called in it for the creation of a truly national philosophy and literature, one that could not be imported from outside, but on the other he maintained that Russian culture and civilization were imported in their entirety and were the fruit of the combined efforts of the leading nations of Europe. Although he stressed the dominant role of historicism in contemporary intellectual life, interpreting historicism as the theory of the organic continuity of national life, his assertion that Russia was a youthful country in fact implied silent recognition of the fact that everything in Russia had begun with Peter's reforms, with a violent break in historical continuity. This contradiction in the young Kireevsky's *Weltanschauung* had its deep sociological roots: on the one hand he was heir to an ancient family, the representative of a section of society that prized tradition and owed its privileges not to Peter's Table of Ranks, but to a long 'organic' historical process; on the other hand he was an educated European intellectual, privileged in the enjoyment of cultural values which he prized highly, and fully aware of the fact that he owed these values to the Europeanization of

[1] Ibid., pp. 38–9.

Russia, to the violent interference and 'Jacobin' methods of the 'revolutionary tsar'.

At the beginning of 1830 Kireevsky left Russia for his first and only visit abroad. In his travels he went no further than Germany, as his projected journey to France was prevented by the July revolution and concern for his family aroused by news of a cholera epidemic in Russia. His impressions of Germany were mixed. In Berlin he attended lectures by Hegel (with whom he discussed Russia), Schleiermacher, and Savigny, and in Munich he heard Schelling. He felt that he was in touch with Europe's greatest intellects, but at the same time was shocked by the philistinism of the students and the narrow middle-class values of German society as a whole. He came to the conclusion that Russians were the only people still capable of being roused to enthusiasm by spiritual issues. 'Like all that is huge,' he wrote in one of his letters, 'it is only from a distance that Russia can be seen in proper perspective.'[1]

As a result of his travels Kireevsky's philosophy of history underwent a certain evolution which, in spite of his very critical attitude to Germany, brought him closer to Westernism. As Koyré has convincingly pointed out, some part in this evolution must be ascribed to the influence of Chaadaev, whom he came to know well on his return to Russia.[2] Kireevsky reformulated his views to include a severer evaluation of Russia and a less pessimistic estimate of the potentialities of Western civilization. Although he had not long since called for the cultivation of national individuality and the rejection of foreign influences, he now began publication of a new periodical significantly called the *European*.

The most interesting piece published in the *European* was Kireevsky's own article, 'The Nineteenth Century' (1832). This aroused the suspicions of the emperor himself and led to the suppression of the journal.[3]

In his new article Kireevsky again returned to the question of

[1] Kireevsky, i. 48.

[2] See Koyré, *La Philosophie et le problème national en Russie au début du 19ème siècle,* chapter 6.

[3] The emperor's main objection seemed to be that Kireevsky's argument concerning the 'synthesizing tendency' characteristic of contemporary Europe was in fact praise of the French constitutional monarchy as a compromise between feudal reaction and revolutionary achievements.

Russia's relations with the West, for which he claimed great practical significance. The most outstanding feature of contemporary Russia, he suggested, was the coexistence of traditional, national features side by side with the elements of European culture that had been grafted on to them. The problem of the mutual relationship of Russia and the West was therefore an issue affecting Russia's *internal* development: whatever solution was arrived at would inevitably determine the direction in which the Russian nation would evolve.

In spite of destructive forces operating within it, Kireevsky argued, European civilization had the organic character that Russia lacked. Although she had been in existence for a thousand years, Russia had not created a true civilization of her own and was still considered a young country. Her culture was borrowed and those elements that were indigenous—if left to themselves in isolation from Europe—lacked the potential for creative development. Like Chaadaev, Kireevsky concluded that so far Russia had contributed nothing to the historical development of mankind.

Following Guizot and Savigny, Kireevsky listed three basic constituents of European civilization and culture:[1]
(1) the Christian religion
(2) the character of the youthful barbarian peoples who had overthrown the Roman empire
(3) the classical heritage.

While the first two constituents—the barbarian peoples and Christianity—were to be found in Russia as well, unfortunately she lacked the third element: the heritage of Classical Antiquity. The specific quality of Russian civilization therefore was not that she represented something different, or possessed some additional feature, but that she lacked an essential element. European culture was rooted in the Graeco-Latin heritage common to all European nations, and this provided the basis for a universal culture. Russian civilization, which lacked this basis, was condemned to isolation and unable to participate in the forward march of the human race.

At this stage Kireevsky still thought that classical antiquity had exerted a beneficial influence on the Catholic Church. Christianity had become strengthened in the ceaseless struggle

[1] Kireevsky used the terms *obrazovannost'* and *prosveshchenie*.

between the pagan and Christian elements, and at the same time had absorbed all that was most valuable in the classical heritage. As the intermediary between antiquity and the barbarians the Church was the main integrating force in Europe and thus helped to make the Middle Ages a wonderful age of spiritual unity.[1] Moreover the powerful ecclesiastical organization provided a counterpoise to feudal particularism so that Europe was able to resist the Arab conquest. In Russia, Kireevsky conceded, the Christian religion might have remained purer, but the influence of the Orthodox Church suffered because of its isolation from the ancient world. Lacking such an essential integrating force, Russia was conquered by the Tartars and her progress was arrested for many centuries.

Since it was deprived of spiritual unity Russia had to strive for material unity and material power. This was responsible, Kireevsky believed, for the origins of autocracy and for Russia's enormous size. A few years earlier he had regarded this same size as a matter for rejoicing, but now, under Chaadaev's influence, he thought it evidence of the soullessness of Russian civilization. This colossus of a state, he complained, absorbed the nation's entire strength, matter gained ground at the expense of spirit, and the gulf dividing Russia from the West grew wider and wider. The West, in the meantime, had turned back to the original source of its civilization during the Renaissance, had assimilated the heritage of classical antiquity, and created a new civilization that could be shared by the whole of mankind. In order to participate in this civilization Russia would have to relive the entire past history of Europe.

Kireevsky was quite aware that it would be impossible to repeat Europe's whole development cycle from the beginning, but did not therefore conclude that it would be impossible to Europeanize Russia. Instead he suggested that the true Europeanization of Russia had begun during the reign of Catherine and not of Peter the Great. Peter, he wrote, wanted to transfer European civilization mechanically, like a ready-made garment, and was therefore only superficially successful. True Europeanization became possible only during the reign of Catherine, in the second half of the eighteenth century, when European

[1] Apart from the undoubted influence of Chaadaev, this also reveals the influence of the famous essay *Die Christenheit oder Europa* by Novalis.

civilization had completed the first important cycle of its development and was just entering a new cycle and the construction of a new and qualitatively different civilization. It was not possible to transplant an old and fully-formed civilization whose growth had been an organic process—hence Peter's reforms were only partially successful. Russia could, however, take part in the construction of the new civilization which originated in the middle of the eighteenth century and developed in the nineteenth—hence Catherine's reforms were crowned with success.

For us European civilization has two aspects [Kireevsky wrote]; there is one civilization before the middle and another after the middle of the eighteenth century. The older European civilization was indissolubly bound up with the whole system of its gradual evolution and in order to share it one would have to relive Europe's entire past. The new civilization is the antithesis of the old and has an autonomous existence. Hence a nation starting out to civilize itself can adopt it in its entirety and assimilate it directly as it stands. That is why it was not until the eighteenth and more especially the nineteenth century, that civilization began to make rapid headway in Russia and America.[1]

The unambiguous conclusion of this argument was that Russia ought to take advantage of the unusual opportunity offered her—the opportunity of participating in the construction of a new European civilization in which she could play an essential and even dominant role.

In his article Kireevsky rejected the slogan of national distinctiveness (*samobytnost'*) which he had propagated himself some years previously. In Europe, he suggested, this slogan would have some meaning, but in Russia the hankering after 'nationality' was equivalent to a hankering after the absence of civilization. What Classical Antiquity had been for Europe, Europe was now for Russia. For the time being it was Russia's duty to assimilate Western culture, a goal she was still far from attaining: 'The hem of our Russian caftan shows below the European frockcoat', he wrote; 'we have shaved our beards, but have not washed our faces.'[2] There was no need to fear the loss of national individuality; this was quite impossible in view of Russia's geographical environment and her separate traditions

---

[1] Kireevsky, i. 107–8.   [2] Ibid. ii. 60.

and religion. So far the Russian national character had been barbaric, isolated, and static; when fused with European elements it would become capable of creative evolution. The article in the *European* was the culmination of the young Kireevsky's Westernism. The influence of Chaadaev is clearly discernible in its hankering after an integral and universal civilization, its condemnation of national isolation, and its conception of the Catholic Church and the social role of religion. Kireevsky's Westernism differed from Chaadaev's, however, on the question of Russia's possible participation in European culture. For Chaadaev Russia could play a truly creative part only if she relived the whole of European history—hence his profound pessimism. Kireevsky suggested that it was enough to participate in the new development cycle that had commenced in the middle of the eighteenth century, something that was incomparably less complicated and already in process of realization. This theory, of course, gave good grounds for optimism.

In this way Kireevsky's new theory skilfully resolved one of the main contradictions inherent in his previous view, namely the contradiction between his positive evaluation of the results of Europeanization and his emphatically negative attitude to violent and abrupt changes—like the Petrine reforms—which broke the thread of historical continuity. Kireevsky contrasted the 'mechanical' and 'superficial' measures introduced by Peter, the enemy of the boyars, with the 'organic' (and therefore effective) methods used during the reign of Catherine, the 'golden age' of the Russian nobility. This is not to imply, of course, that he approved of Catherine the philosopher and correspondent of the French encyclopedists—in this respect he was faithful to his family tradition. His approval was reserved for her legislation after the Pugachev revolt and for Catherine the Anglophile who rejected the Enlightenment's ideas of 'natural law' and for whom the greatest legal authority was no longer Cesare Beccaria but Sir William Blackstone, the conservative English jurist.

In order to resolve one contradiction Kireevsky became guilty of another—one that was less obvious perhaps, but that nevertheless threatens his entire philosophical edifice. As this contradiction is difficult to perceive when a purely immanent method of analysis is used, it was overlooked even by Koyré in his penetrating and detailed discussion of Kireevsky's 'Nineteenth Century'.

His comments on the growth of industry and the decisive role of the French Revolution show that Kireevsky was aware of the fact that the emerging new cultural pattern in Europe was capitalist. By advocating Russia's participation in the construction of the new civilization he in fact anticipated the liberal Westernizers of the 1840s. And yet his Westernism was not consistent. Like Chaadaev, he was in love with Europe's past and his Westernizing views were not part of a liberal ideology, or an unequivocal declaration of support for the new way of life and therefore for capitalism. It is clear that Kireevsky disliked the heroic revolutionary age of the new civilization—at present, he suggested, events were tending towards a synthesis of the achievements of the Enlightenment and Revolution with the conservative ideology of the Holy Alliance. Symptoms of this trend were the 'return to history' and to the Middle Ages, the reconciliation of materialism and spiritualism in Schelling's philosophy of 'identity', the fusion of classical and romantic tendencies in the 'poetry of reality', and, above all, the mutual interpenetration of religion and social life.[1] The new civilization, Kireevsky wrote, would be based on religion—conceived not as outward ritual nor as inner personal conviction but as the chief factor promoting social cohesion, as a kind of national unanimity rooted in tradition and sanctified in social organization.[2]

These ideas, which might be said to contain the germs of Kireevsky's future Slavophilism, clearly have little in common with liberalism as a 'style of thought' and suffer from inconsistencies and internal contradictions. As a Westernizer who believed that it was in Russia's interest to participate in the construction of the new civilization Kireevsky might have been expected to give it his whole-hearted support and to reject any survivals of the old completed evolutionary cycle. In actual fact, however, the young Kireevsky's ideal was a harmonious synthesis of the old and new, a compromise between conservatism and liberalism which would ensure the predominance, in the ideological sphere, of such conservative elements as religion and uninterrupted historical continuity.

[1] See ibid. i. 88–94.   [2] See ibid., pp. 93–4.

Whenever Kireevsky discussed Europe, he tried to emphasize the organic historical relationship between the old and new civilizations. On the other hand, it was one of the implications of his new theory that Russia could only take part in the construction of this new civilization in as much as she was an entirely new organism without historical foundations. This dilemma faced him with a choice between two theories: *either* the new European civilization was organically bound up with the old, in which case Russia could not possibly participate in its construction; *or* else such an organic relationship did not exist, in which case it was hardly possible to claim that events in Europe were tending towards organic synthesis. This did not exclude the possibility of a great Russian future, but only if one accepted the fact that the new civilization (both Russian and European) would be built by purely rational methods, without reliance on the past. This was the conclusion Chaadaev reached a few years later (for Russia at any rate), when he argued that Russia's opportunity depended on the fact that she was a blank page, neither burdened by tradition nor backward-looking, 'History has already eluded us, to be sure,' he wrote, 'but science is ours.'[1]

Kireevsky was not willing to give up either his faith in a great Russian future, or his belief in the organic relationship of past and future. He was therefore bound to try and evolve a new philosophical interpretation of history in which organic development would be typical of Russia rather than Europe; in order to do this he had to revise his judgement of Classical Antiquity, and to transfer the emphasis to 'pure' Christianity, undefiled by contact with a great pagan civilization. In short, he had to give up Westernism and reach the conclusion that Russia was capable of developing by herself, without the help of other European nations and in a different direction.

The fundamental tenets of the Slavophile philosophy of history were formulated by Kireevsky several years after the suppression of the *European*. During this time he is generally supposed to have undergone a complete 'conversion'. Koshelëv attributes a decisive influence to Kireevsky's wife, a deeply religious woman whose favourite reading was the Greek Fathers of the

1 See the quotation on p. 106.

Church.[1] Whenever the couple read Schelling together, she apparently maintained that the philosopher's leading ideas had long been familiar to her from the writings of the Church Fathers. Koshelëv suggests that under his wife's influence Kireevsky then proceeded to study these writings and established contact with ecclesiastical circles in Moscow. Near his country estate was the famous Optina Cloister where he soon became a frequent visitor, helping the monks in work on some of the classical texts of Greek patristics. This represented a turning-point in his life: the secular philosopher who had suggested that his wife read Voltaire became a deeply religious Orthodox Christian.

While this account is accurate enough as far as details are concerned, it is hardly convincing as a whole. It hardly seems possible to talk of the 'conversion' of someone who had always attributed great significance to religion, had evinced the greatest dislike of Voltairean ideas, and had had the example of his brother Peter's unshaken Orthodox faith always before him. On the other hand, it is equally difficult to draw a parallel between Kireevsky's faith and that of a community of Orthodox monks. Vladimir Solov'ëv has suggested quite a different interpretation which casts doubt on the sincerity of Kireevsky's 'conversion'.[2] In evidence he quotes an interesting story told by Herzen, presumably based on Kireevsky's own account:

I once stood at a shrine and gazed at a wonder-working icon of the Mother of God, thinking of the childlike faith of the people praying to it; some women and infirm old men knelt, crossing themselves and bowing down to the earth. With ardent hope I gazed at the holy features, and little by little the secret of their marvellous power began to grow clear to me. Yes, this was not simply a painted board . . . for whole ages it had absorbed these streams of passionate aspiration, the prayers of the afflicted and unhappy; it must have become filled with power that pours from it, that is reflected from it upon believers. It had become a living organism, a meeting-place between the Creator and men. Thinking of this, I looked once more at the old men, at the women and children prostrate in the dust, and at the holy icon—then I myself saw the features of the Mother of

---

[1] Koshelëv's note, entitled 'Istoriya obrashcheniya Ivana Vasil'evicha', was published as an addition to vol. i of Kireevsky's *Polnoe sobranie sochineniï* (cf. i. 285–6).

[2] See V. S. Solov'ëv, *Natsional'nȳ vopros v Rossii* (St. Petersburg 1891), i. 37–9.

God suffused with life; she looked with love and mercy at these simple folk . . . and I sank on my knees and meekly prayed to her.[1]

Solov'ëv suggests that this story reveals Kireevsky's faith to have been far from orthodox. A truly religious man would have believed the icon to be holy and capable of performing miracles by virtue of its supernatural powers, whereas Kireevsky seemed to believe that the real miracle-working power was the people's faith. Whether or not one agrees with Solov'ëv's conclusion that this episode shows Kireevsky in an unfavourable light, depends entirely on one's point of view. The diagnosis, however, can hardly be questioned: Kireevsky's faith was essentially 'philosophical' and cannot be compared to the 'childlike faith' of the people.[2]

The account related by Herzen shows the influence of mysticism, although it is quite obviously social mysticism rather than the solitary mysticism of an anchorite. In this instance, too, religion clearly fascinated Kireevsky as a social phenomenon, something that concerned relations between human beings. Orthodoxy began to interest him when it turned out to be an essential element in his historiosophical constructions. This clearly shows that Kireevsky's Slavophilism was not in fact the outcome of his 'conversion', but grew naturally out of his previous intellectual evolution.

PHILOSOPHY OF HISTORY

Kireevsky formulated the principal tenets of the Slavophile philosophy of history as early as 1839 in his unpublished article 'A Reply to Khomyakov'.

The same scheme which had served him in 1832 as the framework for his Westernizing conception now provided the framework for his new article. As before, Kireevsky listed three constituents of Western civilization (Christianity, plus the young Barbarian races, plus the classical heritage) and as before he considered Russia's exclusion from the classical heritage to be the essential feature distinguishing her from the West. His evalua-

---

[1] Herzen, *My Past and Thoughts*, ii. 289–90.

[2] That Kireevsky was inclined to interpret the articles of faith symbolically is shown by the title of one of his manuscripts: 'An attempt to prove that the so-called paradise is the image of the inner man', Tsentr. Gos. Lit. Archiv, Moscow, fond 236, op. 1, nr 16.

tion of this same classical civilization, however, underwent a complete change.

'The ancient world of classical paganism', he wrote, 'in fact represents the triumph of human reason over the totality of man's inner and outward life; the triumph of naked and pure reason relying on itself alone and recognizing nothing above or outside itself.'[1] The lack of such a heritage should clearly not be considered a deprivation but a true blessing of fate.

Another article, 'On the Character of European Civilization and its Relationship to Russian Civilization', written for the *Moscow Miscellany* (*Moskovskii Sbornik*) in 1852, was Kireevsky's clearest and most systematic exposition of the Slavophile philosophy of history. In it he repeated and developed the chief points from his earlier 'Reply to Khomyakov', while also introducing certain important innovations.

The first of these innovations was that he no longer treated ancient civilization as a uniform whole, but instead emphasized the leading role of Rome in the dissemination of rationalism. It was the ancient Romans, Kireevsky stressed, who had set up logic—the abstract reason of the lone individual—as the sole arbiter of the universe. Since rationalist cognition is not capable of apprehending the inner essence of things but only their external form, the Romans excelled mainly in the realm of law, a sphere characterized by the pernicious rationalization and formalization of vital social bonds. Roman society was nothing but an aggregation of rationally thinking individuals motivated by personal advantage—individuals who were not connected by any community of conviction, faith, or custom. 'The Roman', Kireevsky wrote, 'knew almost no human ties other than the ties of common interest, nor any unity other than the unity of party.'[2] From this it followed that human relations could only be regulated by juridical convention, whose observance was guaranteed solely by the external constraint exercised by the state apparatus. The converse of internal disintegration was an external, institutionalized, and formal integration based on coercion and felt to be coercion. 'Bonds based on coercion chained people together but did not unite them.'[3]

It was not only Roman civilization as a whole that was artificial, Kireevsky thought; even the Latin tongue suffered from

---

[1] Kireevsky, i. 111.　　　　[2] Ibid., p. 187.　　　　[3] Ibid., p. 255.

a certain artificiality, a lack of natural ease and vital spontaneity, for its spirit was constricted by the logicality of its external grammatical structure. Society, too, was an artificial structure: a mechanical aggregation of individuals rather than an organic community.

Kireevsky did not deny that Greek civilization had also been infected by rationalism, but thought the disease had done less damage there. Custom and tradition had retained their authority, patriarchal social bonds had not entirely disappeared, and Christianity had fallen on more fertile ground. It should be noted that Kireevsky's partial rehabilitation of Greece was not intended to apply to the Athens of Pericles, but only to the patriarchal Greece of Homer and to Byzantium as the centre of Byzantine Christianity, contrasted with Roman Christianity. This partial change of attitude can be attributed to Kireevsky's growing religious orthodoxy. Eastern Christianity had its roots in Greece and a total condemnation of Greek civilization might have made it difficult to explain this fact within the framework of the Slavophile philosophy of history.

Kireevsky's second, more significant innovation was his adoption of Pogodin's theory, based on Karamzin, that Russian statehood was not the outcome of invasion but of a 'voluntary invitation to rule'.

Scarcely any European country [he wrote], has attained statehood as a result of the peaceful evolution of national life and national consciousness; the kind of statehood where the religious and social concepts prevalent in the community are embodied in social life and grow naturally, become formed and fuse into a universal harmony whose true reflection is the harmonious homogeneity of the social organism. On the contrary, by some strange quirk of history, the social life of Europe was almost everywhere created by force, out of the life and death struggle of two hostile tribes, out of the lawlessness of conquerors and the resistance of the conquered, and—finally—out of fortuitous treaties which brought the quarrels of hostile elements to an apparent close.[1]

Kireevsky's philosophy of history posited that every culture and civilization owed its character to the religion prevalent in it. For Western Europe this religion was Roman Catholicism, which, he maintained, had become warped by the triumphant

[1] Kireevsky p. 184.

heritage of ancient Rome. In the spirit of classical rationalism—a philosophy incapable of transcending the limitations of isolated individual reason—the Roman Church first identified supra-individual religious consciousness with the consiousness of the hierarchy, even granting the latter the right to introduce illegitimate changes into dogmas hallowed by tradition; and later with the consciousness of the Pope, an elected individual endowed with external authority. The Roman Pope succumbed to the temptation of the Devil and, modelling himself on the Roman emperors, decided to create a universal state on earth. Only Orthodoxy, which never strove for secular power and remembered that the kingdom of Christ was 'not of this world', preserved the teachings of Jesus in all their purity. Thanks to her virgin purity it was humble Russia, deprived of great pagan traditions, that was able to assimilate Christianity fully and preserve it untainted. The humiliating dependence of Orthodoxy on the secular authorities thus became idealized in Kireevsky's interpretation into a sign of truly Christian humility and the capacity to renounce wordly goods.

Kireevsky also contrasted the energetic outside pursuits of the Catholic Church in Western Europe with Orthodoxy's life of prayer and contemplation concentrated in quiet monasteries. Catholicism, he conceded, had achieved great external successes, had created an efficient organization and become the true heir of the riches of classical civilization, but at the same time it had lost its spiritual integrity and degenerated into an instrument of purely external, mechanical social cohesion. Gradually living faith was replaced by an abstract scholasticism which was, in fact, an attempt to rationalize religious faith and to prove dogmas by rationalistic arguments. The rationalization of faith led to the disintegration of the organic Christian community so that the Church became something external and alien to its worshippers. The community of tradition was replaced by relations based on contracts and legal convention, *internal* consolidation was replaced by obedience to hierarchy and authority and *internal* dictates and restraints were replaced by *external* dictates and restraints. The confusion of these two sphere—the sphere of reason and secular authority with the sphere of faith and the Church community—proved harmful to both. Living faith was dismissed as 'mysticism' and science was persecuted for want of understanding of the fact that its progress did not represent a threat to true faith, but could at most overthrow the rationalistic justification of various dogmas. While the Catholic Church was engaged in the fanatical persecution of freedom of conscience the Pope sanctioned the sale of indulgences which enabled the faithful to shift the weight of their own consciences and destroyed every Christian's personal responsibility for his sins before God.

Kireevsky regarded the structure of Western European feudalism as another example of the disintegrating force of rationalism and individualism. 'Private and social life in the West', he wrote as early as 1839, 'are based in their entirety on the concept of an individual and separate independence which presupposes the isolation of the individual in society. Hence the sanctity of external formal relations, the sanctity of private property and all types of legal conventions.'[1] Since feudalism was founded on the conquest of one tribe by another, relations between the lower and higher estates in a given society could not be based on internal solidarity, on a common faith, or on shared customs and traditions; instead they were forced to rely on external constraint or on a rational and formal definition of rights and privileges. Each estate existed in complete isolation from the other. Demoralized by its one-sidedly privileged position, the ruling estate became imbued with the rationalistic and individualistic ideas of classical paganism and disintegrated into a number of isolated entities, each refusing to submit to any authority whatsoever. The most fitting symbol of this medieval individualism, according to Kireevsky, was the robber–baron who locked himself up in his castle, which was cut off from the rest of the community by a high wall and moat. On his own estates he enjoyed absolute freedom, but his relations with his equals were guided not by an inner sense of justice, but by an external and conventional code of honour. 'Each individual member of the aristocracy wished to set himself up as the highest law in relation to other people. The concept of the state or nation as a community could not penetrate to their independent hearts, which were surrounded by an armour of iron and pride. Only rules that they themselves had thought up and laid down to deal with external, formal relations, could to

[1] Kireevsky p. 113.

some extent regulate their lawless pride. Thus the rules of honour, though engendered by the needs of the time as the only possible substitute for law at a time of lawlessness, reveal such far-reaching one-sidedness of social formation, such an extreme external and formal approach to human relations, that even when seen in isolation from the totality of European life they fully reflect the entire evolution of European society.

'Inside his own castle every knight was a separate state', Kireevsky continued. 'Hence relations between knights could only have an external, formal character. In the same way their relations with other estates could only be external and formal.' That is why the development of civil law was in the direction of a formal and external legalism. 'Roman law, which was still alive and in force in certain European cities, further strengthened this trend towards external formalism.'[1]

Since the social organization of European nations was brought about by force it was incapable of gradual organic growth and had to develop mechanically, by means of *coups d'état* and revolutions. The history of Europe was the history of the struggles of various parties: 'Parties representing popes and emperors, towns, churches, and courts, governments and private persons, religious and political views, the bourgeoisie, even metaphysical beliefs, engaged in a ceaseless struggle and tried to adapt the prevailing systems of government to their own particular goals.'[2] Under these circumstances 'European civilization was finally bound to destroy the edifice it had itself constructed.'[3] This destructive phase had been ushered in by the Reformation, which Kireevsky considered to be the natural outcome of Catholicism, the justified revolt of the individual against the external authority of the pope and the church hierarchy. Notions of individual liberty were only an apparent contradiction of the principle of external authority—both, according to Kireevsky, had their roots in the individual's separation from the collective consciousness, in the licence granted to him to make an arbitrary interpretation of revealed truths living on in the collective consciousness of the people. Hence Protestantism was merely a further step on the road to rationalism and individualism; in their extreme form these made their appearance during the French Revolution, which in Europe ushered

[1] Ibid., pp. 191–2.   [2] Ibid., pp. 192–3.   [3] Ibid., p. 193.

in an epoch of complete social atomization. The apparently united medieval Europe fell apart and so did its spiritual unity; all that remained were self-seeking individuals, strangers to one another, endowed with a naked logical reason that enabled them to calculate maximum profit. This atomization, Kireevsky suggested, led logically to the idea of a 'social contract', which provided the only rational social bond linking isolated, autonomous individuals and was clearly not 'the brainchild of the encyclopedists, but a concrete idal that had once been the unconscious and was now the conscious goal of all Western nations'.[1] Organic communities were replaced by associations based on calculation and contracts, and the whole of human energy was redirected to the outside, to feverish and restless activity. This world without God and without a soul was governed by the mechanism of industrial production.

Only one serious thing [Kireevsky wrote] was left to man, and that was industry. For him the reality of being survived only in his physical person. Industry rules the world without faith or poetry. In our time it unites and divides people. It determines one's fatherland, it delineates classes, it lies at the base of state structures, it moves nations, it declares war, makes peace, changes *mores*, gives direction to science, and determines the character of cultures. Men bow down before it and erect temples to it. It is the real deity in which people sincerely believe and to which they submit. Unselfish activity has become inconceivable; it has acquired the same significance in the contemporary world as chivalry had in the time of Cervantes.[2]

The aesthetic motif ('world without poetry') in this condemnation of industrial civilization shows the close connection between Kireevsky's Slavophilism and the romantic *Weltanschauung* of the Lovers of Wisdom. The diatribe against industry is almost a paraphrase of the famous verse written by the romantic poet Evgeny Boratỹnsky, who was connected with the circle of the Lovers of Wisdom.

> The century strides along its iron road.
> Self-interest holds hearts in its grip.
> The multitude dreams only

[1] Kireevsky p. 116.
[2] Ibid., p. 246 (essay on *New Principles in Philosophy*); quoted from *Russian Philosophy*, i. 195; the last sentence has been retranslated.

Ever more shameless dreams of the real and profitable.
Childish dreams of poetry
Have disappeared in the glare of enlightenment;
But that is of no concern
To generations absorbed in industrial labour.[1]

Kireevsky now proceeded to contrast his unflattering sketch of medieval Europe with an idealized view of social development in pre-Petrine Russia. In Russia, he wrote, 'there were neither invaders nor conquered tribes. She knew nothing of the cast-iron division into isolated estates, nor of one-sided privilege and consequent political and moral struggles, mutual contempt, hatred, and envy. Princes and boyars, the clergy and the common people, all classes and sections of the population were permeated by one spirit, by identical convictions, similar concepts, and identical aspirations towards a common goal.' On all essential questions there was complete unanimity. 'Russian society developed spontaneously and naturally, under the influence of a single inner conviction implanted by the Orthodox Church and hallowed by tradition.' According to Kireevsky this society knew neither the extremes of inequality nor abstract egalitarianism; it was 'not a plane but a ladder; however, the rungs of this ladder were not immobile, they grew in a natural fashion, as befits limbs essential to the social organism'.[2]

Ancient Russian law knew nothing of the formal logic and abstract rationalism of Roman law. It was customary law, based on usage, tradition, and custom, and organically rooted in history. In Russia, Kireevsky argued, learned jurists could never have invented laws: 'in a society based on unanimity the power of custom, the sanctity of tradition, and the durability of relations established by usage are so great that they cannot be violated without shaking the foundations of society. Each forcible change based on a logical proposition would be a thrust at the very heart of the social organism.'[3] The logical development of jurisprudence and the planning of social changes according to preconceived ideas were, on the contrary, characteristic of artificial societies founded on formal contracts and

[1] From a poem entitled 'Poslednii poet'.
[2] Kireevsky, i. 206.
[3] Ibid., pp. 207–8.

governed not by *convictions* but by *opinions* which were always volatile and fortuitous, even though widely held.

In his analysis Kireevsky laid particular stress on the absence of the Western European concept of private property in ancient Russia. The notion of the sanctity and inviolability of private property was, he suggested, simply another product of the individualism that pervaded all aspects of European life, and therefore unknown in pre-Petrine Russia. This theory is supported by certain historical facts, namely the widespread common ownership of peasant land and the fact that the ancient nobility had not owned their estates absolutely, but had held them in return for services to the state (in the army or state administration).[1] Kireevsky made use of these facts to idealize ancient Russian society as a cohesive community which recognized that land was owned by the tsar, or in other words by the nation as a whole. The individualistic concept of 'sacred' inviolate and exclusive property rights led, he considered, to the dehumanization and depersonalization of human relations and transformed society into a collection of private properties with people assigned to them (this recalls Marx's analysis of entail, which deprived the landowner of his identity by turning him into 'a property of his own property').[2]

This would not have been possible in ancient Russia, Kireevsky maintained. 'In Russia the social system is based on personality while the right of ownership is merely a *fortuitous* relationship. . . . Society was not composed of private properties with persons assigned to them, but of persons to whom properties were assigned.'[3] In ancient Russia absolute private ownership was exceptional and the enjoyment of property was made dependent on services rendered to society by a given person. The individual's role in society, therefore, was not deter-

---

[1] It should be added that apart from conditional ownership (*pomest'e*—the equivalent of the Western European *beneficium*) there also existed in ancient Russia hereditary ownership of the land (*votchina*—the equivalent of the Western European *senioria*).

[2] Cf. Marx, *Kritik des Hegelschen Staatsrechts*: 'Das Eigentum ist hier nicht mehr, insofern ≪ich meinen Willen darin lege≫, sondern mein Wille ist, ≪insofern er im Eigentum liegt≫. Mein Wille besitzt hier nicht, sondern ist besessen. . . . Das *Majovrat* ist das sich selbst zur *Religion* gewordene, das selbst versunkene, von seiner Selbständigkeit und Herrlichkeit *entzückte Privateigentum*.' (K. Marx, F. Engels, *Werke*, Dietz Verlag, Berlin 1961, i. 306.)

[3] Kireevsky, i. 209–10.

mined by property: on the contrary, the individual's property was determined by his role in society.

Kireevsky portrayed Western European feudal society as a collection of knightly castles, their surroundings settled by the 'base rabble'. 'The knight was a person; the rabble was part of his castle. The bellicose relations between the different castles, their relations with the free cities, the king, and the Church—here you have the entire history of the West.'[1]

The medieval Russian society described by Kireevsky presents a strong contrast. It contained neither castles nor base rabble, neither noble knights nor a king waging war on them. The basic units of the social organism were small peasant communes (the *obshchina*) which were founded on collective land tenure, on harmony, and community of custom, and governed by the *mir*—an assembly of elders which settled controversial matters in accordance with time-honoured tradition and the principle of unanimity. 'The multitude of small communes that made up Russia was covered by a dense network of churches, monasteries, and hermits' cells from which identical notions of the relations governing public and private life radiated ceaselessly in all directions.'[2] Through the Church individual communes merged into larger units functioning according to the same principles and in the same way. The whole of Russia was one large *mir*, a community of land, faith, and custom embracing the entire nation.

Kireevsky's conception, which emphasized the ancient Russian *mir* as the basic social unit and at the same time as a general principle on which the system was founded, was an intentional counterweight to Karamzin's apologia for autocracy and the centralized state. Certain elements in it bear a superficial resemblance to the Decembrists' interpretation of history with its idealization of the 'republican' and 'folkmoot' (*veche*) system of Kievian Russia. For the Decembrists the village communes— called 'small republics' by Kakhovsky[3]—were living survivals of this system. This analogy is, however, somewhat superficial and misleading. Kireevsky did not use the term 'republican' to describe the ancient Russian system of government; on the contrary, for him the republican system was the product of

---

[1] Ibid., pp. 206–7.   [2] Ibid., p. 113.
[3] See Volk, *Istoricheskie vzglyadÿ dekabristov*, p. 203.

Western individualism—an 'artificial' system based on a rationalistic 'social contract'. The republican system was not a community of faith and custom, it had no moral foundations, and so far from being based on unanimity it gave rise to the most violent struggles of particular and party interests. For Kireevsky it was simply government by the 'material majority' in conditions of total social atomization.[1]

Kireevsky's theory was not narrowly nationalistic. He did not ascribe the superiority of ancient Russian civilization to specifically Russian features but only to the fact that Christian principles in Russia had been saved by certain historical circumstances from the distortions suffered by Western Catholicism.

The social organization of ancient Russia [he wrote] must be prized particularly highly for the sake of the traces it bears of pure Christian principles whose influence on the readily submissive Slavonic tribes encountered no obstacles. It is not any inborn advantages of the Slavonic stock that today fill us with hope for its future splendour. Not in the least! Inborn tribal features, like the soil on which the seed is cast, can only accelerate or delay its growth; they can assure it ample or meagre nourishment; provide it with the opportunity of more or less untrammelled development; but the character of the fruit depends not on the soil, but on the seed cast on it.[2]

The greatest difficulty raised by this interpretation of Russian history is to find an explanation for the deep changes effected by Peter the Great. Kireevsky had to explain why this harmonious civilization without internal contradictions yielded to Europeanization imposed from the outside; how it could have produced Peter, the destroyer of national traditions, the uncritical admirer of all that was German.

In accordance with Christian doctrine Kireevsky believed that there could be no punishment without guilt and in his article 'A Reply to Khomyakov' he set out to show that the guilt lay with the Orthodox Church itself. Ancient Russian civilization, he argued, would not have given way before German influence

---

[1] Although Kireevsky did not use the term 'atomization' (he made use of *raz'edinenie* or *razlad*) it exactly reflects his meaning. Already in his article 'The Nineteenth Century' he wrote as follows about the disintegrating corrosion of rationalism and empiricism during the Enlightenment: 'The wholeness of moral existence disintegrated into its component parts, into the elementary [*azbuchnÿe*] material elements of existence.' Kireevsky, i. 88.

[2] Ibid., p. 204.

without the arbitrary measures taken by the hierarchy, in defiance of the fact that the majority of the faithful were Old Believers; Church reforms preceded any prepared the way for state reforms. This explanation was logical and wholly in keeping with the spirit of Slavophile doctrine: the analogy between Slavophiles and Old Believers readily suggested itself to contemporaries.[1]

Kireevsky's favourable comments on the Old Believers were, however, only part of a passing phase. In later years his religious beliefs developed in the direction of greater orthodoxy and his attitude to the sect condemned by the official church hierarchy was therefore bound to change.

In his essay 'On the Character of European Civilization and its Relationship to Russian Civilization' Kireevsky gave a new explanation for the mechanical Europeanization of Russia. The old way of life, he suggested, had been too secluded, too liable to stagnation and the cult of external formalism; it had been guilty of clinging not only to the spirit but also to the letter of tradition and in the Old Believers these features were carried to extremes. The dead hand of traditionalism had weakened the inner spiritual life, and had induced envy of the great though purely external achievements of European nations and a hankering after brilliance, polish, and luxury. It was the upper classes which mainly gave way to temptation and only they were affected by Peter's reforms.

In his warning to Russia of the consequences that would follow if the 'enlightened sections of society' became divorced from the common people, Kireevsky used Poland as an example. Characteristic features of ancient Poland, in his opinion, were inner dissension and the complete divorce of the thoroughly Westernized upper classes from the common people. This allowed the Polish gentry to attain an extremely high level of education: 'Unimpeded by the *mores* and mental outlook of the common people,' Kireevsky wrote, 'the Polish aristocracy was the most brilliant and most highly educated aristocracy in Europe. They could be compared to a team of swift-footed

---

[1] Belinsky already called the Slavophiles 'literary Old Believers'; and in Herzen's writings too we often find parallels drawn between the Old Believers and the Slavophiles; even Grigor'ev, who was closer to them, thought this analogy to be an apt one. See A. A. Grigor'ev, *Materialȳ dlya biografii*, ed. by V. Knyazhnin (Petrograd 1917), p. 185.

horses who had broken loose from a heavy carriage in order to gallop ahead all the more lightly.[1] Their isolation, however, prevented their culture from taking root in the national soil and making an essential contribution to the treasure-house of world civilization.[2] Ultimately the nation's internal dissension brought about its political annihilation.

The Petrine reforms introduced into Russia the dualism that had been typical of the former Polish gentry-state. The ancient Russian way of life had survived among the lower sections of society and was still a vital element in the 'holy Orthodox Church'. Former patriarchal family relations still obtained among the common people, who alone resisted the lure exerted by the concept of absolute private property. Unlike Konstantin Aksakov, however, Kireevsky did not place too much reliance on the people:[3] he emphasized that their attachment to old traditions was unconscious and purely a matter of habit, that one could no longer speak of a national unity of conviction, faith, or culture, and that the rebirth of Russia would only become possible when the enlightened classes also adopted Christian principles. Here it should be noted that Kireevsky never identified 'Christian principles' with 'folk' principles, as did some later Slavophiles.

Unlike the other Slavophiles, Kireevsky was by no means enthusiastic about plans to abolish serfdom. Although he agreed that the institution could not be reconciled with Christian principles, he felt that emancipation would only be beneficial 'when the Western spirit has ceased to dominate Russian life and thought'. It must be admitted that from the point of view of an opponent of capitalism and an apologist for pre-capitalist, patriarchal relations Kireevsky was undeniably right. If the peasants were set free 'prematurely', he foresaw the emergence of an 'extreme antagonism between the estates'; 'it fills one with horror to think what this might lead to'.[4]

In the closing paragraphs of his essay, Kireevsky stressed that he was not calling for a literal 'return' to old pre-Petrine

---

[1] Kireevsky, i. 147.

[2] The only exception acknowledged by Kireevsky was Copernicus.

[3] In his 'Letter to My Moscow Friends' (March/April 1847) Kireevsky stressed the danger of confusing the two concepts *narodnost'* and *prostonarodnost'*. Kireevsky, ii. 247.

[4] Ibid. ii. 252–3.

Russia. If an aspect of the old way of life were to occur to him in a dream, he wrote, the vision would fill him with terror rather than delight:

This kind of transposition of the past into the present would be equivalent to transferring the wheels of one machine to another differing in size and function; ultimately one of the two would have to break—either the wheel or the machine. . . . There is only one thing I desire [he concluded], namely that the principles of conduct preserved in the teachings of the holy Orthodox Church permeate the convictions of all sections of society and all estates. I do not want these higher principles to supplant the European education grafted on to Russia, but to dominate and envelop it fully, to give it a higher meaning and the opportunity of further development, so that the inner integrity of ancient Russia is granted to a new, present, and future Orthodox Russia.[1]

In spite of its obvious conservatism, Kireevsky's article aroused the suspicions of the government. Nicholas I felt himself to be the heir of Peter the Great and wanted to be a European emperor rather than an ancient Russian tsar. In spite of his veneration for Orthodoxy and pure national principles, he had no intention of adapting his state apparatus to the requirements of religion or national traditions. Moreover, he had some grounds for suspecting that the suggestion that law should grow organically out of customs and tradition was an attempt to restrict the despotism of autocracy. The Central Censor's Office struck the right note in its special report to the emperor:

It is not clear what Kireevsky means by the integrity of Orthodox Russia; it is obvious, however, that in his apparently loyal article he fails to do justice to the immortal services of the Great Russian Reformer and his imperial heirs, who were untiring in their efforts to bring Western civilization to their subjects and only by this means were able to raise the power and glory of our Fatherland to their present splendour.[2]

Comments on other articles in the almanac were similar, with predictable results. The *Moscow Miscellany* suffered an even

[1] Ibid. i. 221–2.
[2] Tsentr. Gos. Istorich. Arkhiv SSSR, fond 772, op. 1, ed. khr. 2819, p. 35. The censor commented also on articles by K. Aksakov published in the *Moscow Miscellany* (1852) or intended for the second volume of the *Miscellany* (1853). In

worse fate than the *European*: it was closed down and five of its principal contributors (including Kireevsky) were placed under police surveillance and ordered to obtain special permission from the Central Censor's Office for any future publication. Kireevsky was profoundly disheartened by these harsh measures.

Nicholas I quite rightly discerned the difference between his own conservatism and that of the Slavophiles. The Slavophile conception of ancient Russia embodied the ideals of the boyar opposition to absolutism: it was by no means an oversight that Kireevsky failed to discuss the significance of autocracy, which the official doctrines recognized as the foundation and 'Palladium of Russia'; what is more, his arguments could, strictly speaking, be held to suggest that there had been no autocracy in Russia before Peter the Great.[1] His critique of rationalism was directed not only at bourgeois rationalism—the rationalism of the calculating merchant and manufacturer—but also at the bureaucratic rationalism of absolute monarchy. Konstantin Aksakov left no room for doubt on this question when he contrasted State and Land and called state organization merely an 'external truth', 'the principle of slavery, of external coercion'.

Slavophile ideology had no clear prescription for dealing with the burning social problems of the time. It is worth noting that the Slavophiles themselves were often profoundly pessimistic about the chances of curing Russia. Kireevsky thought that the desired goal could still be attained 'as long as the Russian spirit retains its power, as long as faith is not extinguished, as long as traces of its former integrity still survive'.[2] The insistent repetition of 'as long as' shows that Kireevsky regarded the likelihood of 'saving' his beloved Russia to be a last slender chance which could easily be thrown away for ever.

Kireevsky's underlying pessimism did not conflict with the concept of historicism which was the pivot of his philosophy of

---

the article 'On the Social Organization of the Early Slavs' he suspected propaganda for 'democratic principles' and in the article on folk epics (*bÿlinÿ*) he was disturbed by the description of the intimate and unconstrained relations between the *bÿlinÿ* heroes (members of the royal retinue) and the ruling family.

[1] In this connection it is interesting to note Kireevsky's critical remarks on Pogodin's article 'A Historian's Laudatory Word in Honour of Karamzin', which are quoted on p. 60–1.

[2] Kireevsky, i. 269.

history. From the very beginning of his career he had regarded history as 'the central discipline, the science of sciences', but he nevertheless rejected the view that it was governed by reason or necessity. While admitting the existence of historical regularities, he thought these were a feature of relationship of elements in social structures rather than a necessary and inviolable law of history. 'Nothing is easier', he wrote, 'than to represent real facts as unavoidable results of higher laws of reasonable necessity; but nothing so distorts a genuine understanding of history as these imaginary laws of reasonable necessity which are in fact merely laws of reasonable probability.'[1] In his view it was one of the characteristics of historical regularity that it could be violated— national organisms could and *should* develop historically, like a tree from a seed, but their growth could be disturbed, they could fall sick and die. The laws of development were not a force that could overcome all obstacles by the steam-roller of necessity—they were constantly beset by danger, and a development according to its own inherent laws is a precious gift that must be protected against annihilation.

In his philosophy of history Kireevsky concentrated on investigating the functioning and disintegration of two great civilizational structures—a 'truly Christian' and a 'rationalist' civilization—but failed to formulate *universal* or *general* laws of history which would provide an 'inevitable' and rational explanation for the extinction of every civilization in turn. The disintegration of the 'Christian community' described by him is in fact the story of the inevitable Fall of man after he has transgressed against divine law and desired to 'be like God, knowing good and evil'. In Christian doctrine, however, the Fall is followed by redemption and the coming of the Messiah. If Kireevsky had wanted to construct a universal Christian system embracing the entire past and future 'until the times are fulfilled', he would have been bound to introduce the motif of the Fall and a messianic theme. The issue of messianism is, however, nowhere raised in his writings,[2] which only provide an

---

[1] Ibid., p. 244. *Russian Philosophy*, i. 193.

[2] The belief that every nation has to accomplish a certain historical mission, and even the conviction that such a mission is being or is about to be accomplished by one's own nation, is not enough to be called messianism. Strictly speaking 'messianism' requires faith not in a 'mission' but in a 'Messiah'—that is in a unique chosen people.

interpretation of a specific *segment* of time. He was no doubt deterred from constructing a messianic system by his distrust of speculation—by 'respect for reality'—and his traditionalism on religious questions, which made him suspicious of extravagant mysticism and prophetic revelations. Nicholas Berdyaev, an admirer of Solov'ëv and Cieszkowski, had some grounds for complaining that Slavophile ideology suffered from a lack of 'the prophetic and mystical element'.[1]

PHILOSOPHY OF MAN. RATIONALISM AS A DISINTEGRATING FACTOR

Kireevsky's general philosophical views form an important supplement as well as a frame of reference for his philosophy of history. His most mature and systematic philosophical statement is the essay *On the Necessity and Possibility of New Principles in Philosophy* published posthumously in 1856.

In this essay Kireevsky set out to attack the rationalist view of man and to contrast it with the human psyche uncontaminated by rationalism. The ideal personality portrayed in the essay is an integral structure with a vital core and 'inner focus' that serves to harmonize the separate psychic powers and safeguards the inner unity and 'wholeness' (*tselostnost'*, *tsel'nost'*) of the spirit. As natural reason is only one of these psychic powers, man can only preserve his inner wholeness by subordinating reason to his 'total' psyche. The unifying principle is concealed but can be grasped by means of inner concentration; it is only this 'vital focus hidden from the ordinary condition of the human soul' but accessible to those who seek it[2] that makes the psyche something more than an aggregate of heterogeneous functions. Rationalism, therefore, represents the greatest threat to inner wholeness. Together with the one-sided development of abstract reason man loses the capacity for direct cognition of the truth and that 'inner root of the understanding where all the separate powers fuse into one living and

---

[1] The Slavophiles, Berdyaev wrote, did not examine the problem of 'East and West' on an 'eschatological or apocalyptical basis'. 'Only the intuition of the mystic or artist can grasp the spirit of a nation and the nation's religious vocation depends on prophecies. The Slavophiles, on the other hand, can almost be accused of falling into the error of economic materialism.' Berdyaev, *A. S. Kkomyakov* (Moscow 1912), p. 178.

[2] Kireevsky, i. 250.

whole vision of the mind'.[1] Rationalism breaks up the psyche into a number of separate and unconnected faculties, each of which lays claim to autonomy. This is followed by inner conflict, corresponding to the conflict between different kinds of sectional, party interests in societies founded on rationalistic principles. Inner divisions remain even when reason succeeds in dominating the other faculties: the autocratic rule of reason intensifies the disintegration of the psyche, just as rationally conceived social bonds (Roman legislation and the Catholic principle of external authority) 'chain men together but do not unite them' and thus intensify social atomization.

The inhabitants of Western Europe, Kireevsky thought, had long since lost their inner wholeness, their capacity for inner concentration and grasp on the profound current of spiritual life. 'Western man', he wrote, 'fritters away his life in separate aspirations and although, with the help of reason, he combines them into one comprehensive plan, nevertheless he is a different man at different moments of his life.'[2] Religious feeling, the power of reason, aesthetic sensibility, and the desire for personal advantage were all located in different compartments, separate and not dependent on one another. This was responsible for the amorality of Western civilization, which could continue to advance even when the inner psychic powers had become weakened, when total havoc reigned in the sphere of moral values.[3] At the same time, Kireevsky stressed, Western civilization suffered from a tragic dilemma, from 'the division of life as a whole and that of all the separate spheres of individual and social being'.[4] Western man had lost his living faith since 'faith is not to be found in any of the disconnected cognitive faculties, it is not the prerogative of logical reason alone, nor of the voice of conscience, but embraces man's whole personality and manifests itself only when inner wholeness has been attained and then in proportion to the degree of this wholeness'.[5]

Kireevsky contrasted the tragic inner conflict of rationalism with what he called thought directed by faith, whose essence was the striving 'to concentrate the separate psychic powers

[1] Ibid., p. 249.   [2] Ibid., p. 210.
[3] See ibid., p. 266.   [4] Ibid., p. 218.   [5] Ibid., p. 275.

into one single power, to seek out that inner focus of being
where reason, will, feeling, and conscience, the beautiful and
the true, the wonderful and the desirable, the just and the
merciful—and the whole sweep of the mind—are fused together
into one living unity, thus restoring the essential personality in
all its primary indivisibility'.[1] Thanks to Orthodoxy Russians
were still capable of attaining this kind of inner integration. In
their search for truth they were guided not by natural reason
but by integral reason, which represents the harmonious unity
of all the psychic powers: 'For the Orthodox believer knows
that the wholeness of truth needs the wholeness of reason, and
the quest for this wholeness is his constant preoccupation.'[2]

Kireevsky's standpoint could be described by the term 'integralism', which distinguishes between reason (i.e. natural
reason) and the 'whole' personality—a total spiritual structure
embracing reason but as a non-autonomous and entirely submissive faculty. Kireevsky made a similar distinction between
rational truths, which are fragmentary and partial, and total
truths, to which man is committed as a moral being. Such
truths are not only, or not so much, an attribute of our judgement, but primarily an attribute of human existence. This
standpoint, consistent in its rejection of the autonomy of the
separate spheres of human existence and activity, led Kireevsky
to contrast two diametrically opposed types of civilization
which he called 'inner' and 'external' or 'integral' and 'logico-
technical'.[3] The concept of progress, he stressed, was only appropriate when applied to the latter; the role of the former, on the
other hand, was to preserve and disseminate the act of revelation on which it was based. While both types of civilization
were essential and supplemented each other, the role of the
inner-directed civilization was of fundamental importance since
it formed the convictions of individuals as well as nations. This
theory helped Kireevsky to explain Russian backwardness and
the rapid progress of Western civilization. Western Europe, he
argued, had overtaken ancient Russia in science and technology
because she had chosen the easy path of purely external
development, which did not involve the effort to perfect man

---

[1] See Kireevsky, p. 275.
[2] Ibid., p. 251. *Russian Philosophy*, i. 200.
[3] See Kireevsky, i. 159.

or to intensify and spread the 'inner' civilization. Ancient Russian civilization, unlike its European counterpart, had an integral character based on an established *moral* hierarchy of values. In the olden days Russians would not have understood political economy, for example; they could not have reconciled the existence of a separate profoundly amoral science of wealth that was not subordinated to higher values, with the 'wholeness' of their world outlook.[1]

Certain historians of Russian philosophy have emphasized—as Kireevsky himself did—the direct connection between his 'integralism' and Christian anthropology (the concept of the 'inner man', the myth of the Fall), and the mystical philosophy of the Eastern Fathers of the Church.[2] A connection certainly exists and it has been analysed in great detail by H. Lanz whose conclusions can be summarized as follows: Kireevsky took over the doctrine of 'integrity' (the term used by Lanz) directly from the Greek Church Fathers. From 1852—that is while writing his *New Principles in Philosophy*—he was helping Father Makary of the Optina Cloister to translate various excerpts from the works of St. Isaac of Syria. In his tractate *De Mundi Contemptu* the latter had expounded a theory stating that wisdom (*sapientia*) could be attained by concentrating all one's spiritual powers (*totas vires*), and that its seat was not the intellect but the heart (*cor*), which was the integrating focus of the human psyche; a man lacking wisdom was like a city without walls—he was defenceless against the conflicting aspirations which rent him, deprived him of character, and made him incapable of comprehending higher truths. These ideas were formulated more clearly still by Maximus the Confessor, who argued that reason was only an organ of knowledge, whereas the organ of wisdom was the whole psyche; only when it possessed inner wholeness could the human soul be a vessel of absolute truth. 'Thus,' Lanz writes, 'in contrast to the Scholastic thinkers of the West, the Greek Fathers lay a special emphasis upon the element of personal integrity, of which our rational ego is merely a part.' The over-all conclusion of his argument is that Slavophilism 'is *simply and solely* a modern continuation of a religious tradition that had been dominating Russian life since

---

[1] See ibid., pp. 214–15.
[2] See Zenkovsky, *A History of Russian Philosophy*, i. 214–19.

the time of St. Vladimir and which was temporarily driven into the underworld by the violent reforms of Peter the Great and his successors'.[1]

This argument hardly seems convincing, even if we set aside the circumstance that Kireevsky first formulated his doctrine of 'wholeness' a good many years before 1852. Its greatest weakness is that Lanz ignored the similarity between Kireevsky's ideas and the views of the German romantics (especially their conservative wing), and the fact that Kireevsky's interest in German romantic philosophy long preceded his interest in Eastern patristic writings. If his wife found in Schelling ideas familiar to her from her reading of the Greek Fathers, Kireevsky himself found in the Greek Fathers ideas familiar to him from the writings of the romantic philosophers, and used them to propound a typically romantic philosophy of history.

Friedrich Schlegel's *Philosophy of Life* is an excellent and typical example of the anti-rationalistic 'integralism' of the conservative romantics. In Schlegel's conception the psyche is an integral structure which also possesses a hidden focus (*Mittelpunkt*);[2] this focus is the 'thinking and loving soul'[3] which unites the four main spiritual faculties: understanding (*Verstand*), imagination, reason (*Vernunft*), and will. The development of rationalism destroys the 'primary unity' of the psychic powers, tears, them away from their focus and sets them at odds with one another, so that will conflicts with reason, understanding with imagination, and faith with science; the former unity is replaced by inner conflict and rupture (*Innerliche Wietracht, Zwiespalt*). 'In the intellectual order,' Schlegel wrote, 'thought conflicts with reality and science with faith; in the inner life the infinite conflicts with the finite and the eternal with the temporal. What a painful dichotomy plagues all the spheres of the intellect!'[4] This spiritual chaos was the counterpart of social anarchy; Schlegel compared the 'inner rupture' of the faculties of the human psyche to 'civil war, the struggles of menacing political parties which plague the disordered

---

[1] H. Lanz, 'The Philosophy of Ivan Kireevsky', *The Slavonic Review*, iv/12, March 1925, 603-4.

[2] Schlegel used the expressions *das vollständige Bewusstseyn, die Einheit des Bewus stseyn . . ., die ganze Struktur des Bewusstseyn.*

[3] Fr. von Schlegel, *Philosophie des Lebens* (Vienna 1828), pp. 15, 24-5, 137.

[4] Ibid., p. 135.

state'.[1] The main task of philosophy, therefore, was to rebuild man's 'primary unity' with the help of profound religious faith and to tear the human soul away from the 'autocratic rule of reason'.[2]

Although the similarity with Kireevsky's ideas is quite striking, it is worth noting that Schlegel made far greater use of motifs taken from Christian mysticism and mythology, especially the myth of the Fall and future rebirth of man which forms the structural pivot of his philosophy of history.

The similarities between Schlegel and Kireevsky are not merely a matter of influence. They spring rather from the common desire of both philosophers to combat the 'social atomization' of bourgeois liberal society from a conservative vantage-point, and from their valid recognition of the close relationship between atomistic social theories and atomistic theories of the human psyche.[3]

Kireevsky's 'anthropology' provided the foundations for his theory of cognition. 'Logical thinking, when separated from the other cognitive faculties,' he wrote, 'is a natural attribute of the mind that has lost its own wholeness';[4] rationalism, therefore, acts as a disintegrating force, since it transforms reality into a collection of isolated fragments bound together only by a cobweb of abstract relationships. Reason, according to Kireevsky's definition, is a purely formal cognitive faculty which can only grasp abstract notions and relationships; the substantial, on the other hand, can only be comprehended by a faculty that is itself substantial[5]—in other words by the total psyche. In true understanding, therefore, intuition, feeling, and will, instinct and aesthetic sensibility all act together with reason. This kind of understanding presupposes a vital and *immediate* connection between the knower and the object of knowledge. By isolating the knower from reality and setting him up in opposition to it, rationalism casts doubt upon the reality and objective nature of the universe. For the rationalist, in fact, abstract thought is more real than being. Descartes, Kireevsky wrote scornfully,

[1] Ibid., pp. 271–2.   [2] Ibid., pp. 136–7.
[3] On the close historical relationship between social theories and psychology see A. Cobban, *Edmund Burke and the Revolt against the Eighteenth Century* (London 1929), pp. 15–24.
[4] Kireevsky, i. 276.   [5] See ibid., p. 274.

only believed in his own existence when he had deduced from thought by means of a logical syllogism.[1] True cognition, therefore, cannot be content to define external relationships but must attempt to penetrate to the substantial essence of things, must be a kind of *revelation* or *immediate* cognition. Only *believing reason*, as Kireevsky called it, can achieve direct contact with God, the supreme principle of the unity of the universe.

Since not all individuals possess the capacity for true cognition to the same degree, Kireevsky posited the existence of a spiritual hierarchy, of people who are 'illuminated by a superior light and the power of faith'.[2] The main weakness of Protestantism, he felt, was its attempt to find a common basis of truth 'in that part of human cognition which can be shared by *every* individual'.[3] That is why philosophy inspired by Protestantism had to restrict itself to the domain of logical reason, shared by every man regardless of his moral worth. 'The concentration of all spiritual forces into a single power, the integrity of mind essential for attaining integral truth, could not be within everyone's reach. Only relative, negative, and logical reason could be recognized as a universal authority; it alone could command the general and absolute recognition of its conclusions.'[4]

In this passage Kireevsky incidentally put forward the idea (later accepted and developed in the sociology of knowledge) that there is a connection between rationalism and cognitive egalitarianism, and that the trend towards the formalization and universality of knowledge is conditioned by 'the democratic demand that [these] truths should be the same for everyone'.[5]

---

[1] See Kireevsky, i. 196.   [2] Ibid., p. 278.   [3] Ibid., p. 230.   [4] Ibid.

[5] Mannheim wrote: 'The demand for universal validity had marked consequences for the accompanying theory of knowledge. It followed therefrom that only those forms of knowledge are legitimate which touched and appealed to what is common in all human beings. The elaboration of the notion of a 'consciousness in itself' is no more than a distillation of those traits in the individual human consciousness which we may assume to be the same in all men, be they Negroes or Europeans, medievals or moderns. The primary common foundation of this common consciousness was found first of all in the conceptions of time and space, and in close connection therewith, in the purely formal realm of mathematics. Here, it was felt, a platform had been erected which every man could share. . . . The foremost aim of this mode of thought was a purified body of generally valid knowledge which is knowable by all and communicable to all.

. . . it is easily possible that there are truths or correct intuitions which are accessible only to a certain personal disposition or to a definite orientation of interests of a certain group. The democratic cosmopolitanism of the ascendant

Karl Mannheim has shown the unmistakable connection between this demand and the aspirations of the ascending bourgeoisie as well as the emergence of the capitalist system. Epistemological egalitarianism developed at the same time as the
barriers dividing different estates, local groups, provinces, and
nations were beginning to break down; it reflected and expressed the rapid increase of vertical and horizontal social
mobility and the diminishing importance of tradition as a link
in the chain of interpersonal relations. Epistemological élitism,
which opposed these trends, defended religion and tradition as
examples of 'concrete' knowledge revealed in the course of
direct collective experience and not accessible to outsiders. In
Kireevsky's time this was tantamount to supporting a pre-
capitalistic and pre-industrial model of society.

At first glance this élitist theory of knowledge seems incompatible with the elements of sociologism that are an unmistakable feature of Kireevsky's theory of knowledge (cf. his
statements that 'everything essential in the human soul grows
in it socially'[1] and that true faith—and therefore knowledge—
cannot be experienced by an individual in isolation).[2] It appears
difficult, for instance, to reconcile Kireevsky's aristocratic epistemology with his belief that the development of 'Orthodox
thought' should be 'the joint task of all thinking and believing
human beings' and that 'genius, which necessarily involves
originality', might even prove to be an obstacle in arriving at
the truth.[3] In actual fact there is no real contradiction. At the
apex of his spiritual hierarchy Kireevsky placed not men of
genius but those who were illuminated by a 'superior light' and
unusually strong faith. People of this kind, he wrote, owe their
spiritual superiority to their inner wholeness, which is a function
of the organic ties binding them to the community; they are
conscious organs of the collective and their exceptionally strong
faith springs from their exceptionally close fusion with the
Church as a social organism. Kireevsky's doctrine did not,
therefore, involve that aristocratic contempt for the common

---

bourgeoisie denied the value and the right to existence of these insights. With this,
there was revealed a purely sociological component in the criterion of truth,
namely the democratic demand that these truths should be the same for everyone.'
K. Mannheim, *Ideology and Utopia* (New York–London 1952), p. 149.

[1] Kireevsky, i. 254.   [2] Ibid., p. 277.   [3] Ibid., p. 270.

people which is so characteristic of the views of Odoevsky and Chaadaev.

Out of these ideas grew the concept, later developed by Khomyakov, of 'organic togetherness' (*sobornost'*, from the Russian words *sobirat'*—together, and *sobor*—council. In its application to Church history the term *sobornost'* can be translated as the 'principle of conciliarism'). This concept implies that the truth cannot be comprehended except through participation in the 'community of love'; that those in whom the consciousness of this community is exceptionally strong are, in fact, only its exponents and organs of a *supra-individual consciousness*. This idea—though not always explicitly formulated—lies at the root of everything that Kireevsky wrote in the sphere of philosophy or philosophy of history.[1] For him rationalism was destructive because it was responsible for the separation of individual reason from the supra-individual consciousness, for the fragmentation of every whole into isolated fragments, and for man's 'falling away' from the Creator.

In his remarks on the history of rationalist thought in the *New Principles in Philosophy* (and elsewhere), Kireevsky called Aristotle the first great rationalist and Hegel the last and greatest. Medieval Catholicism, he thought, had been imbued with the destructive influence of Aristotle, while scholasticism, a system which required the justification of faith by logical syllogisms, represented the victory of rationalism. The precious germs of a new anti-rationalist philosophy revealed in Pascal's *Pensées*[2] had been stifled by Descartes and Protestantism. It was French Enlightenment philosophy, however, that represented the most aggressive and primitive embodiment of rationalism. The great German thinkers showed up the worthlessness of this philosophy, but even they did not break with rationalism. The distinction they made between *Verstand* and *Vernunft* represented an attempt to save the essence of rationalism by divesting it of

---

[1] 'The Orthodox Church', Kireevsky wrote, 'does not limit its self-consciousness to any particular epoch, however much this epoch might consider itself wiser than any former. The sum total of all Christians of all ages, past and present, comprises one indivisible, eternal, living assembly of the faithful, held together just as much by the unity of consciousness as through the communion of prayer.' Kireevsky, i. 248; *Russian Philosophy*, i. 197.

[2] Kireevsky, i. 231, ii. 104–8.

its inflexible and primitive features and making it both subtler and more flexible.[1]

Philosophical reason constantly altered its forms. No sooner would its inadequacy be understood than it would evade its critics by appearing in another guise, leaving its earlier form as a mere empty shell in their hands. Thus, in order to avoid charges of inadequacy, it passed from formal-logical proofs to experiential observations on the one hand, and to the inner consciousness of truth on the other, and called its earlier manner of thought 'dry and abstract' [*rassudochnỹ*] and its later 'rational' [*razumnỹ*]. But having also discovered the inadequacy of the new form in the course of its development, philosophical reason referred to it too as dry and abstract and proceeded to *pure reason*. When Jacobi excoriated the narrowness of the theory of pure reason as expressed in the systems of Kant and Fichte, he learned to his surprise at the end of his lengthy polemics, extending over many years, that everything he said about *reason* [*razum*] should be applied to the *intellect* [*rassudok*]. The theory of Kant and Fichte proved to be based on the intellect. The development of reason was to begin only with the system of Schelling and Hegel.[2]

Kireevsky admitted that

reason, as understood by the latest philosophical school, is not to be confused with logical understanding which consists in the formal concatenation of concepts and progresses by syllogistic deductions and proofs. According to the laws of intellectual necessity, reason in its latest aspect derives its knowledge not from abstract notions, but from the very root of self-consciousness where being and thought become absolutely identical. It does not operate logically, by means of abstract speculation, but by means of dialectical development deriving from the essence of the subject.[3]

Hegelian philosophy took cognitive rationalism to its logical conclusion and thereby exhausted its potentialities: the last word of reason enabled reason itself to perceive its own limitations clearly. It became clear that rationalist knowledge—even at its most subtle and flexible—is negative knowledge and only applies to the sphere of probability; it finally leads to the transformation of the whole of reality into a transparent dialectic of thought evolving from itself, and to the acceptance of

---

[1] See Kireevsky, i. 247. [2] Ibid., p. 258. [3] Ibid.

human reason as the self-consciousness of the universe. Philosophical reason was bound to realize its own one-sidedness and indeed did so in the person of the aged Schelling, who evolved his religious philosophy of revelation in opposition to Hegelianism.

Although Kireevsky called Schelling one of those thinkers who are born only once in a thousand years,[1] he nevertheless criticized the philosophy of revelation for confining itself to a merely negative critique of rationalism. The dilemma, as Kireevsky saw it, was that a new, positive philosophy required true religious faith, whereas Western Christianity—both Roman Catholicism and Protestantism—was itself infected by the incurable disease of rationalism. Although Schelling was aware of this and attempted to cleanse Christianity of the deposits of rationalism, it was 'a lamentable task to create a faith for oneself'.[2] The new philosophy, Kireevsky concluded, would have to be based on Orthodoxy, which had preserved the supra-individual Christian consciousness in all its purity. It was Russia's mission, therefore, to create a new Christian philosophy.

It is clear that Kireevsky intended Slavophile philosophy to prepare for and initiate a new philosophical age, to be a turning-point in the history of human thought. The essence of this new 'Russian Orthodox' philosophy was to be the rejection of autonomy in favour of 'wholeness' in all spheres of human life, both individual and social: the autonomy of reason was to be rejected in the name of spiritual wholeness, the autonomy of the individual in the name of the wholeness of both individual and society, and the autonomy of the separate spheres of human activity in the name of cultural wholeness. It was the role of the Orthodox faith to guarantee and safeguard this wholeness.

KIREEVSKY AND THE GERMAN CONSERVATIVE ROMANTICS

Strictly speaking, Kireevsky's philosophical views were not something entirely new, but only an interesting variant of European conservative romanticism. As a result of specific historical circumstances this movement was most strongly repre-

---

[1] See Kireevsky, i. 261.   [2] Ibid., p. 262.

sented in Germany; as Mannheim has aptly observed, 'Germany achieved for the ideology of conservatism what France did for the Enlightenment—she exploited it to the fullest extent of its logical conclusions.'[1]

To the German romanticists Kireevsky owed not only the general orientation of his philosophy—his criticism of rationalism, of social atomization, and of legalistic and naturalistic modes of thought—but also a number of specific concepts. It seems very probable that he made use of Jacobi's notions of 'immediate knowledge' and 'reason vitalized by faith' in his theory of knowledge. In his criticism of rationalist dialectics and his assertion that 'a bare logical concept cannot grasp reality as such' Kireevsky was repeating Schelling's arguments, which he had come across as early as 1830, when attending his lectures in Munich. Friedrich Schlegel was, as I have attempted to show, the leading inspiration of his philosophy of man and probably also of his social philosophy and philosophy of history. The concept that law should grow organically out of custom was clearly influenced by Savigny while the utterly negative historical role Kireevsky ascribed to ancient Rome coincides with the views of Adam Müller, for whom the spirit of Rome—personified by the Roman empire and Roman law—was the primary source of industrialism, capitalism, the French Revolution, and centralized despotism of the 'Napoleonic' type;[2] the criticism of absolute private property, which is strongly emphasized by Kireevsky, also has its exact counterpart in the economic writings of Müller.[3] Finally, the view that medieval scholasticism was the precursor of modern rationalism and that classical German philosophy was only seemingly critical of rationalism while actually helping to consolidate it on new foundations, can also be found in the writings of Friedrich Schlegel.[4]

There are particularly numerous and interesting parallels between Kireevsky and Franz von Baader. Regarding God as the principle of unity and the Devil as the principle of division,

---

[1] See K. Mannheim, *Essays on Sociology and Social Psychology* (London 1953), p. 82.

[2] See ibid., p. 105.

[3] See Z. Kuderowicz, 'Problematyka wolności u Adama Müllera' ('Adam Müller and the problem of freedom'), *Archiwum Historii Filozofii i Myśli Społecznej* (Warsaw 1961), no. 7, pp. 23–4.

[4] See Schlegel, op. cit., pp. 347–8.

Baader deduced the existence of evil from the selfish striving
for autonomy of the part in relation to the whole; he believed
that the principle of autonomy led to the growing fragmentation of reality and turned man into a progressively incomplete
and fragmented being.[1] Baader developed the social implications of this metaphysics of evil in his pamphlet *On the Need for
a New and Closer Relationship between Religion and Politics Caused
by the French Revolution* (1814).[2] Religion and love, he suggested,
are prerequisites of freedom; despotism, on the other hand,
depends on the principle of egoism; there is no difference between aristocratic and democratic despotism—in both cases the
bond of love has been broken and this, in fact, is the essence of
despotism; despotism is authority without love and not any
particular political system. In accordance with this view,
Baader distinguished two types of bond existing both in nature
and in social life: a bond based on love, on the mutual attraction of particles, and a bond based on coercion. The 'atomists'
(supporters of Newton's and Kepler's mechanistic physics)
denied the existence of mutual 'sympathy' between the attracting particles and tended to interpret it as a hidden constraint;
similar arguments were put forward by atomists in the spiritual
sphere, who were supporters of a mechanistic society composed
of isolated individuals submitting to an external authority.
According to Baader the two types of bond stood in inverse
proportion to each other: love made force superfluous and
force in its turn destroyed bonds based on love. One might
risk the assertion that Kireevsky's entire philosophy of history
is, as it were, an illustration of these ideas; in his interpretation
the whole of European history was a process consisting in the
replacement of 'organic' and 'inner' ties by external ties based
on force which exercised an external restraint on the struggle of
selfish, isolated individuals.

It is an interesting fact that this particular pamphlet by
Baader was dedicated to the Russian Minister of Education,
the mystically inclined Prince Alexander Golitsȳn; it was really
intended for the Emperor Alexander, whom Baader considered

---

[1] See E. Susini, *Franz von Baader et le romantisme mystique* (Paris 1942), iii. 269–81

[2] Franz von Baader, *Über das durch die franzö́s. Revolution herbeigeführte Bedürfniss
einer neuen und innigeren Verbindung der Religion mit der Politik. Sämmtliche Werke* (Leipzig 1851–60).

—since the Russian victory over Napoleon—to have been divinely appointed to direct the noble task of re-Christianizing Europe.[1] The pamphlet met the approval of the founder of the Holy Alliance and Baader was entrusted with the somewhat unusual task of writing a textbook of religious instruction for the Russian clergy. For reasons that have never been explained the textbook failed to appear; it seems likely that this was due to the understandable opposition of the Church hierarchy. Nevertheless, through Prince Golitsȳn Baader remained in close touch with the court at St. Petersburg; in 1817 he was appointed to the salaried post of 'literary correspondent', which involved writing regular reports for the Emperor on religious and philosophical trends in Germany.

This appointment, however, failed to satisfy Baader, who wished to exert a more immediate influence on the Emperor's policies. With this in mind, he set out for Russia in the autumn of 1822, accompanied by the Livonian Baron Boris von Yxküll. His first aim was a meeting with Prince Golitsȳn. The mission, however, ended in complete fiasco: after being held up at the frontier, Baader had to wait several months for permission to enter Russia and was finally not only refused, but also relieved of his appointment as correspondent. This reversal of fortune was due to changes in the Emperor's mood as well as in his circle of advisers—Golitsȳn's influence was declining daily, while a fanatical monk, the Archimandrite Photius, a bitter opponent of all mystics, pietists, and illuminists, was gradually gaining ascendancy.

In spite of this set-back to his ambitious plans, Baader continued to be interested in Russia and especially the Orthodox Church. As time went on, he became increasingly hostile to the papacy and convinced that the Orthodox Church was the only Christian Church not yet infected by rationalism. He expounded his views in a number of essays, two of which—*Die römisch-katholische und die griechisch-russische Kirche* and *Der morgenländische und abendländische Katholizismus*—were directly concerned with the Orthodox Church. The essay on 'Eastern and Western

[1] For much information on 'Baader and Russia' the author is indebted to the unpublished master's dissertation by A. Gleason, 'F. Baader and the Holy Alliance. A Study in the Russian Projection of German Thought' (Harvard University 1960).

Catholicism' was written with the help of Shevȳrëv, whom Baader had got to know in 1840.[1] Copies of the essay were sent to the Emperor Nicholas and his Minister of Education, S. S. Uvarov.

Towards the end of his life Baader entered into correspondence with Uvarov. One of his letters was a little essay with the significant title 'The Mission of the Russian Church in View of the Decline of Christianity in the West',[2] which sums up his philosophical reflections over many years. In the opening paragraph of his letter Baader argues that the West was divided—torn between the stagnating dictatorship of Rome and Protestant anarchy and fragmentation. He blamed the papacy for the Reformation and stressed that the same principles, applied in another sphere, had led to the French Revolution. Since the time of Descartes, he pointed out, Western philosophy had degenerated; faith now conflicted with reason and reason with faith, while society and learning had been deprived of their Christian content. Fortunately Providence had preserved the Russian Church from the destructive influence of the West; it had remained faithful to the old Catholicism and had defended it against two enemies—papism and Protestantism; the Russian Church was therefore the only force which could mediate between the Western confessions and help to bring about a European spiritual renaissance. Baader closed his letter with the suggestion that Uvarov should send Russian students to Munich to listen to his lectures and learn how to fight the 'plague of our time'.

The similarity between Baader's ideas and Kireevsky's hardly requires any comment. It seems likely that Kireevsky came across Baader during his stay in Munich and that later he read at least some of his writings. In his *New Principles in Philosophy* Baader is mentioned as one of the precursors of the Schellingian Philosophy of Revelation, as a thinker who protested again the ruinous trend in Western speculation but was unfortunately unable to change the direction of philosophical development.[3]

---

[1] See P. V. Struve, *Zapiski russkogo nauchnogo instituta v Belgrade* (1940), pp. 206, 211–16.

[2] See E. Susini, *Lettres inédites de Franz von Baader* (Paris 1942), pp. 456–61.

[3] See Kireevsky, i. 260.

Baader's views can be better understood in the context of the general interest in Russian affairs which was widespread in Germany at that time. The Russia of Nicholas was the mainstay of the Holy Alliance, a huge empire that exerted a considerable influence on the home and foreign policies of the various fragmented German states, and at the same time a country where the basic elements of a pre-capitalist social system showed an unusual vitality; as such it aroused both sympathy and hatred in Germany. It was only the conservatives, of course, who were favourably disposed towards Russia—some of them shared Schelling's view (expressed in conversation with W. Odoevsky), that 'Russia is destined to do great things.' In his *Philosophy of History* Friedrich Schlegel maintained that the era of modern civilization initiated by Peter's reforms had been introduced suddenly, mechanically, and artificially, but that thanks to this 'artificiality' it had not been able to sink deep roots, so that many good things already lost in Western Europe had in consequence been preserved in Russia.[1] Towards the end of the 1840s the Prussian conservative Baron August von Haxthausen —who was partially under the influence of the Slavophiles— wrote a lengthy book in which he extolled the Russian peasant commune (together with the nobleman's manor, to which it was bound by patriarchal community ties) as a basic socio-economic unit capable of offering resistance to both capitalism and the socialist ideas then circulating in Europe.[2]

The fact that Kireevsky was influenced by the German conservative romantics in no way detracts from the epistemological significance of his ideas. His system of thought was not fortuitous and showed no trace of eclecticism; his ideology, like that of the German romantics, approached the ideal type of conservatism as a 'dynamic, historical structural configuration'.[3] His philosophical interpretation of history was based on his analysis of certain concrete problems in the history of Europe and Russia from a conservative vantage point. All

[1] See Fr. von Schlegel, *Philosophie der Geschichte* (Vienna 1829), pp. 271–2.

[2] See August Freiherr von Haxthausen, *Studien über die innern Zustände, das Volksleben und insbesondere die ländlichen Einrichtungen Russlands*, 3 vols. (Hannover–Berlin 1847–52). During his travels in Russia, which were financed by the Russian government, Haxthausen also met the leading Slavophiles.

[3] See Mannheim, *Conservative Thought*, pp. 96–7.

parallels between Kireevsky and the German conservatives can be explained, I suggest, not only by the immediate influence of the latter, but also—and most of all—by an objective similarity in historical circumstances and in the social relations prevailing in Russia and Germany, particularly Prussia. Neither Russia nor Prussia had a strong progressive bourgeoisie, both had experienced a revolution 'from above' (Peter the Great and Frederick the Great), in both countries the rationalization of social relations had taken the form of 'bureaucratic rationalism', and in both states the organs of state power represented a force that was to some degree independent of and alienated from the historically determined social structure.[1] Both Russia and Germany (though to a different extent) were backward countries faced by the necessity of moving towards a bourgeois system at a time when capitalism had emerged totally victorious in the more economically advanced countries of Europe. This enabled German and Russian thinkers to make a theoretical analysis of the new system while comparing it with the still vital elements of a pre-capitalist social structure surviving in their native countries.

From their particular vantage-point the conservative philosophers were able to perceive phenomena in capitalism that were entirely outside the field of vision of liberal bourgeois thinkers. Many writers have drawn attention to the numerous (though always only partial) similarities between strictures of capitalism from the 'Right' and from the 'Left'. An instructive illustration of this is several startling parallels to be found in the works of Kireevsky and Marx. Kireevsky regarded capitalism as a system that frustrates inner unity and confronts the individual as an external, alien social force; Marx expressed a similar idea when he wrote that only in a bourgeois society did 'different forms of social union confront the individual as a mere means to his private ends, as an outward necessity'.[2]

[1] Cf. Marx–Engels, *The German Ideology* (Lawrence and Wishart, London 1965), p. 78: 'The independence of the State is only found nowadays in those countries where the estates have not yet completely developed into classes, where the estates, done away with in more advanced countries, still have a part to play, and where there exists a mixture; countries, that is to say, in which no one section of the population can achieve dominance over the others. This is the case particularly in Germany.' Of course, it was also the case of Russia.

[2] Karl Marx, *A Contribution to the Critique of Political Economy* (*Introduction*), trans. by N. I. Stone (London 1904), p. 267.

Kireevsky opposed the concept of inviolable, absolute private property and argued with some reason that this led to the depersonalization of human relations, to the domination of things over men—a society founded on this concept of property was merely a sum 'of private properties with persons assigned to them'; Marx made this observation the basis of his theory of economic alienation and even went so far as to accept the argument that *personal* dependence in the Middle Ages prevented the emergence of objectified social relations characteristic of commodity production.[1] The young Marx also developed another favourite theme of Kireevsky's, namely his criticism of the growing autonomy of the different spheres of human activity and the consequent disintegration of the personality. He wrote: 'The nature of alienation implies that each sphere applies a different and contradictory norm, that morality does not apply the same norm as political economy, etc., because each of them is a particular alienation of man; each is concentrated upon a specific area of alienated activity and is itself alienated from the other.'[2]

While these parallels are of some interest, it should be strongly emphasized that they cannot be taken too far. The Marxist ideal of a 'whole man' differs fundamentally from Kireevsky's 'integral personality'; its basic premiss is not the rejection of moral autonomy, nor unreasoning faith; on the contrary, it postulates maximal autonomy, rational awareness, and liberation from all kinds of 'elemental forces'. Only the diagnosis of the disease was common: both thinkers noted a disturbance in the balance between man and the objectified 'externalized' world of his products.

'Consistent conservatives ("positivists")', wrote the young

---

[1] In *Capital* Marx wrote: 'Personal dependence here characterizes the social relations of production just as much as it does the other spheres of life organized on the basis of that production. But for the very reason that personal dependence forms the groundwork of society, there is no necessity for labour and its products to assume a fantastic form different from their reality. They take the shape, in the transactions of society, of services in kind and payments in kind . . . No matter then, what we may think of the parts played by the different classes of people themselves in this society, the social relations between individuals in the performance of their labour appear at all events as their own mutual personal relations, and are not disguised under the shape of social relations between the products of labour.' *Capital*, vol. i (Lawrence and Wishart, London 1954), p. 77.

[2] K. Marx, *Early Writings*, trans. and ed. by T. B. Bottomore (London 1963), p. 173 (from: *Economic and Philosophical Manuscripts*, Third Manuscript).

Bakunin during his Left-Hegelian period, 'are truly to be pitied, since their aspirations are nearly always honest in origin.' When they idealize the past they 'are right in so far as that past was a living totality in itself and as such seems far richer and more vital than our divided present; their great error is that they think they can convert this past, with its by-gone ways, into the present'.[1] This was a tragic mistake which induced the 'positivists', in their longing for 'living fullness', to fight in defence of a dead reality.

This judgement can be fittingly applied to the romantic ideology of the Slavophiles.

TWO TYPES OF SOCIAL BONDS

In order to arrive at a better understanding of the social content of Slavophilism, it must be realized that the characteristic Slavophile confrontation of Russia and Europe was the exact counterpart of the contrast between two types of society, two historical formations, or two types of bond connecting the individual with the collective. When Kireevsky wrote about Russia and Europe, it was frequently not geographical entities that he had in mind; he considered the United States, for instance, to be the purest expression of European principles.[2] What he was primarily interested in was something affecting the internal development of both Russia and Europe—namely the contrast between a Christian society and a society based on rationalism. It was not Europe and Russia that were irreconcilable opposites, but rationalism and pure Christianity:[3] the struggle between Christian principles and rationalism was being waged both in Europe and in Russia, the only difference being that in Russia the scale had not yet inclined to the side of

---

[1] M. Bakunin, *The Reaction in Germany, Deutsche Jahrbücher für Wissenschaft und Kunst*, ed. Arnold Ruge (Leipzig), v, nos. 247–51.

[2] See another comment by Kireevsky: 'As for European principles—in the final guise that they have assumed, taken in isolation from Europe's previous existence, and used as the basis of a new nation's civilization—what can they create apart from a pitiful caricature of civilization, comparable to a poem which has been created solely on the basis of poetic rules? The attempt has already been made. It would seem that being based on such rational principles, and after such a magnificent start, the United States must have a wonderful future before them. But what was the result? Only the external forms of society developed and strangled man by their mechanism.' Kireevsky, i. 153.

[3] See Kireevsky's letter to A. Koshelëv on 11 November 1855. Kireevsky, ii. 287–8.

rationalism, whereas in Europe, owing to specific historical circumstances, the victory of rationalism both in philosophy and in social relations was already assured. Kireevsky's views were not narrowly nationalistic: the pivot on which his philosophy of history hinged was not the struggle of different national 'substances', but that of two contrasting types of social bond. This struggle had once gone on or was still going on within *every* European nation; in contemporary Russia the conflict was between the 'people' (*narod*) and 'society' (*obshchestvo*), between those sections of the community that had remained faithful to old traditions, and the educated strata who were imbued with the ideas of modern European civilization.

The typology adopted by Ferdinand Tönnies in his *Community and Society* can be of great assistance in the clarification and systematization of Slavophile concepts of social cohesion; his contrast between *Gemeinschaft* and *Gesellschaft* corresponds to the Slavophile antithesis of Russia and Europe, of 'people' and 'society' and of Christian and rationalist cultures. The similarity is not fortuitous: Tönnies, like many later German sociologists, was influenced by the conservative philosophers of the first half of the nineteenth century and on occasion even made use of their concepts. A comparison between Kireevsky and Tönnies makes it possible to bring out and emphasize the strong sociological element in Kireevsky's ideas, the skill of his structural formulations, and the great internal cohesion and consistency of his views on social problems as a whole.[1]

1. In Tönnies's interpretation *Gemeinschaft* is a whole composed of individuals endowed with natural will (*Wesenwille*) while *Gesellschaft* is made up of individuals endowed with rational will (*Kürwille*).[2] In the *Gemeinschaft* the past is a living

---

[1] Tönnies's theory can be interpreted in two ways, both as a historical generalization and as a purely formal and unhistorical typology (in the latter instance the concept of *Gemeinschaft* would be almost identical with D. H. Cooley's 'primary group'). R. Aron writes: 'Ces deux concepts avaient une signification à la fois historique et supra-historique, structures fondamentales des sociétés et moments différents du devenir social.' R. Aron, *La Sociologie allemande contemporaine* (Paris 1950), p. 23. In the present comparison of Tönnies and Kireevsky the emphasis is placed on the first, historical aspect of his sociological theory. Cf. A Walicki, 'Personality and Society in the Ideology of Russian Slavophiles: A Study in the Sociology of Knowledge', *California Slavic Studies*, ii (1963), 8–9.

[2] The following extracts from the work of Tönnies are quoted from the most recent American edition. F. Tönnies, *Community and Society* (*Gemeinschaft und*

part of the present, since individuals guided by natural will do not see the future as a certain ideal which should be consciously realized; natural will is the psychological equivalent of vital functions, it is immanent in activity, and contains the future only in embryo or emergent form; hence a community develops organically, like a tree from a seed. Rational will, on the other hand, is subordinated to calculation and is prior to activity; society is concerned with the future, for rational will is concerned with planning future actions.[1] This notion is an improved expression of Kireevsky's antithesis of the whole personality and the personality disintegrated by rationalism. Kireevsky, too, considered 'action according to a preconceived plan'[2] to be one of the essential characteristics of rationalistic behaviour. (Similarities in the two philosophers' interpretation of rationalism also extend to the strictly epistemological sphere: like Kireevsky, Tönnies believed that rational knowledge reduced something living to something inanimate and that 'living', 'organic' reality could not be grasped by rational cognition.)

2. The type of community Tönnies calls *Gemeinschaft* is a living organism founded on mutual understanding and embracing the whole man; *Gesellschaft*, on the other hand, is an artificial product, a mechanical aggregate involving the coexistence of individuals dependent on, but at the same time strangers to, one another. This idea, expressed in the same terminology (organism versus mechanism), is one of the basic concepts developed by Kireevsky throughout his work.

3. *Gemeinschaft* is based on concord (*Eintracht, concordia*), on family feeling, and a community of faith and custom; in *Gesellschaft* there is no community of moral values, but only a temporary community of interests; things rather than values act as the consolidating factor. In *Gesellschaft* organic social bonds are replaced by convention, by a written or unwritten contract; every member pursues his own ends, and outside the sphere of convention a war is waged below the surface where all are against all. These ideas have their exact counterpart in Kireev-

---

Gesellschaft), trans. and ed. by Charles P. Loomis, (The Michigan State University Press, East Lansing 1957). Loomis uses the terms 'natural will' for '*Wesenwille*' and 'rational will' for '*Kürwille*'.

[1] See Tönnies, op. cit., part 2, para. 1, 2, 3, pp. 103–4.
[2] See Kireevsky, i. 208.

sky's praise of the concord and unanimity governing the ancient Russian way of life, his strictures of European individualism, lack of inner moral unity, and the struggle of particular interests, his arguments that industry was the sole god of modern civilization and that the contract was 'once the unconscious and now the conscious goal of all Western nations'.[1]

4. In *Gemeinschaft* the expression of the collective will is religion (from the point of view of the individual, faith), while in *Gesellschaft* it is public opinion (from the point of the individual, theory).[2] This corresponds to Kireevsky's distinction between conviction and opinion:

Opinion and conviction are two different mainsprings of two entirely different social mechanisms. The difference consists not only in the fact that opinion is less stable than conviction, that it is the product of logical reasoning, whereas conviction is the outcome of life as a whole; in the political sense there is one more difference between them: conviction is the instinctive expression of the totality of social relations, while opinion is the expression of an excessive solidarity with that part of society's interests which coincide with the interest of one party, and lends the deceptive appearance of concern for the general welfare to self-seeking exclusivity.[3]

In this interpretation 'conviction' is, in fact, identical with religion, which Kireevsky defined as the expression of a nation's unanimity, evolving out of tradition and sanctified in social organization. In one of his letters to Koshelëv, Kireevsky confirmed this interpretation: 'For you the main element that determines the civilization of a particular state and the direction in which it will develop—in a word, its *spirit*—is *public opinion*, that is to say *majority opinion*. For me the spirit of the state is the *ruling faith of the people*.'[4]

5. In *Gemeinschaft* there is no such thing as absolute private property, nor its corollary, the depersonalization of interhuman relations (Tönnies went so far as to suggest that in *Gemeinschaft* even slavery is something 'human', since a slave treated like a member of the family is a 'morally free' person).[5] Tönnies cited the German *Mark* and the Indian village community as

---

[1] Ibid., p. 116.
[2] See Tönnies, op. cit., part 1, para. 30, p. 218.
[3] Kireevsky, i. 208.   [4] Ibid., ii. 278.
[5] See Tönnies, op. cit., part 1, para. 13, p. 54.

examples of *Gemeinschaft* types of ownership and emphasized that seigniorial property rights did not amount to absolute ownership. In this instance too there are obvious parallels with Kireevsky's idealization of the peasant *commune* and social relations in pre-Petrine Russia.

6. *Gemeinschaft* is ruled by common and family law, growing organically out of tradition and folkways; *Gesellschaft* is based on abstract and theoretical law, modelled on commercial contracts. Rationalistic legislation disrupts the traditional ties of family religion and *mores*, emancipates the individual from all organic bonds, and thereby brings about the victory of egoism, greed, and ambition, the transformation of society into an artificial aggregation of independent human entities equal before the law. Kireevsky expressed identical views in his analysis of Roman law, of the 'logical development of law' in Western Europe and of ancient Russian common law which 'grew out of life and had nothing in common with abstract logical development'.

7. The bearer of the idea of *Gemeinschaft* is the common people. Like the Slavophiles, Tönnies contrasted the simple life of the people with society life, where polite conventions conceal the struggle of ambition, unceasing rivalries, and masked mutual hostilities.[1] The antithesis of 'people' and 'society' is also one of the central motifs of Slavophile thought: Kireevsky wrote that the daily life of the common people was ruled by 'stable customs' and polite society by the 'whims of fashion';[2] that the patriarchal family survived only among the former, whereas in society family ties were gradually being eroded;[3] and that the people had remained faithful to ancient Russian traditions, whereas society was the artificial product of Peter's reforms. According to Tönnies, the *Volk* lost its essential character as soon as it was subjected to capitalist influences;[4] the Slavophiles, who would have agreed with this view, maintained that the *Volk* as such had disappeared in the West, and survived only in the Slavonic countries, especially Russia.

8. In *Gemeinschaft* there is no room for individualism; an organic, inner unity prevents the individual from coming into conflict with the community; social forces are not experienced

---

[1] See Tönnies, op. cit., part 1 para. 25, p. 78.   [2] See Kireevsky, i. 218.
[3] See ibid., pp. 212–13.
[4] See Tönnies, op. cit., part 2, para. 42, p. 169.

as something external or alien. The essence of *Gesellschaft*, on the other hand, is conflict: relations between isolated individuals are invariably strained, and the conventions regulating these relations are felt to be a purely external constraint.[1] 'Arbitrary freedom [of the individual]', Tönnies wrote, 'and arbitrary despotism [of the Caesar or the State] are not mutually exclusive. They are only a dual phenomenon of the same situation. They may struggle with each other more or less, but by nature they are allies.'[2]

As I have tried to show, this is a recurring theme in Kireevsky's writing whenever he discussed ancient Rome and the historical experience of Western Europe.

9. There is a most remarkable correspondence between Kireevsky's and Tönnies's evaluation of ancient Rome and the part played by Roman law in the erosion of 'organic' social ties. According to Tönnies, the decay of *mores* and of the Roman family was an inevitable concomitant of the emergence of a rationalized legal system.[3] Ancient Rome also gave birth to the 'abstract human being', emancipated from all ties binding him to a concrete collective, who 'appears as a ghost in broad daylight'.[4] An analogous process of disintegration recurred—on a larger scale—in Christian Europe. The classical heritage allowed Europe to develop faster, but the price paid for this was the violation of the harmonious structure of *Gemeinschaft*.[5] 'The assimilation of Roman law', Tönnies wrote, 'has served and still serves to further the development of *Gesellschaft* in a large part of the Christian–German world.'[6]

Tönnies's argument clearly implies the existence of three essential elements in European civilization (Christianity, plus the Germanic tribes, plus the classical heritage) corresponding exactly to Kireevsky's categories (Christianity, plus the young barbarian peoples, plus the classical heritage). Both thinkers agreed that while the first two elements fused organically into a harmonious whole, the third element, the classical heritage (represented chiefly by Roman law), acted as a disintegrating factor. Tönnies did not, it is true, regard Roman law as the 'ultimate cause' of the disintegration of *Gemeinschaft*, but only

---

[1] See ibid., part 1, para. 19, p. 65.   [2] Ibid., part 3, para. 19, p. 203.
[3] See ibid., part 3, para. 19, p. 202.   [4] Ibid., part 3, para. 18, p. 202.
[5] See ibid., part 3, para. 20, p. 203.   [6] Ibid.

as a 'ready tool';[1] he ascribed greater importance to the development of trade and trade routes and of industrial civilization. Kireevsky was inclined to emphasize the role of the spiritual factor, but admitted that the rational civilization of the Romans only gave way before the pressure of Christianity because it had no 'railways, no electric telegraph, and none of those discoveries which now force the world to submit to the authority of heartless calculation'.[2]

It is worth noting that this view of the role of Roman law in European history has been brilliantly analysed and corroborated by Max Weber. 'The tremendous after-effect of Roman Law, as transformed by the late Roman bureaucratic state,' Weber wrote, 'stands out in nothing more clearly than in the fact that everywhere the evolution of political management in the direction of the evolving rational state has been borne by trained jurists.'[3] 'It has been the work of *jurists* to give birth to the modern Occidental state as well as to the Occidental churches.'[4] This evolution, according to Weber, was 'peculiar to the Occident' and had no analogy anywhere else in the world.[5] Kireevsky would have subscribed whole-heartedly to this statement.

If I have pointed out certain similarities in the ideas of Kireevsky and Tönnies, it was not in order to suggest that the former anticipated an incomparably more complex and internally coherent contribution to sociological theory; in any case, the present study is *not primarily* concerned to evaluate the ideas of either Tönnies or Kireevsky from the point of view of their contribution to scholarship. The fact remains that the typology of Ferdinand Tönnies provides conceptual tools which make it easier to understand the sociological element in Kireevsky's thought, and facilitate the systematization of a certain type of social ideology in philosophical and sociological categories.

German conservatism of the first half of the nineteenth century, wrote Karl Mannheim in his work on *Conservative Thought*,

---

[1] See Tönnies op. cit., part 3, para. 20, p. 203.
[2] Kireevsky, i. 238.
[3] Quoted from Max Weber, 'Politics as a Vocation', *Essays on Sociology*, ed. by H. H. Gerth and C. Wright Mills (New York 1958), p. 93.
[4] Ibid., p. 94.
[5] Ibid., p. 299 ('Die Wirtschaftsethik der Weltreligionen').

was an ideological defence of *Gemeinschaft* against *Gesellschaft.*[1]
This passing comment is perhaps even truer when applied to
Kireevsky. One might go even further and suggest that Kireevsky's theories (and Slavophile doctrines as a whole) provide a
more consistent defence of *Gemeinschaft* than those of the conservative German romantics. Most of the latter, for instance,
were deeply imbued by aristocratic and feudal ideas. Schlegel's
defence of aristocratic privilege even included a vindication of
the Hindu caste system, while Haller denied the possibility
that a moral ideal could be common to all members of a given
society; each estate, he maintained, represents a distinct system
of values and therefore must be allowed the right to separate
development. This defence of the medieval social hierarchy was
linked to the conservative aestheticizing concept of the 'great
chain of being',[2] which placed loving emphasis on social
'diversity', on the unique flavour of every corporate individuality, and postulated that every link in the chain was irreplaceable and should be preserved in all its distinctive individuality.
These elements are not to be found in Kireevsky, whose description of ancient Russia emphasized the *uniformity* of customs
and *mores* linking all social estates. He considered the 'diversity'
of Western Europe in the Middle Ages to be an evil, the result
of conquest and the distortion of Christianity by the classical
heritage, and was sharply critical of Western feudalism, aristocratism, the isolation of the privileged sections of society from
the common people, and the inflexible barriers between estates.
This position was closer to the ideal of *Gemeinschaft* than that of
Haller, Schlegel, or the other apologists for feudalism in the
narrow, juridical sense of the word. The *Gemeinschaft* type of
social bond—like the natural economy on which it depends—
cannot be equated with feudalism as a legal and political
system; it can survive feudalism and can also disintegrate while
the feudal system is at its peak. Tönnies pointed out that in
Western Europe the disintegration of the patriarchal community was a process that took place *within* the feudal system and
that seigniorial property rights were already becoming transformed into individual, private ownership in medieval times.

---

[1] See Mannheim, *Conservative Thought*, p. 89.
[2] See A. O. Lovejoy, *The Great Chain of Being* (Harber and Brothers, New York),
chapter 9.

The historical sociology of Max Weber can, I think, be of considerable help in an understanding of the Slavophile criticism of Western feudalism. In developing and enriching Tönnies's ideas, Weber distinguished types of authority and modes of human activity corresponding to the basic division of social ties into emotional community ties, characteristic of a pre-capitalist economy, and rationalized ties, which reflect the growth of capitalism in the economic sphere and of bureaucracy in the juridico-political sphere (*Vergemeinschaftung* and *Vergesellschaftung*). The general typology of Slavophilism within this framework presents no difficulty: in Weberian categories it was a system of thought that idealized traditional community ties, actions determined by internalized traditions, and authority sanctioned by custom. In order to make this rather too general definition more precise, we must have recourse to the distinction between feudalism and patrimonialism as two basic variants of traditional authority. This distinction gives rise to important ideological implications, which Professor Reinhard Bendix in his book on Weber has formulated as follows:

Feudalism is domination by the few who are skilled in war; patrimonialism is domination by one who requires officials for the exercise of his authority. A patrimonial ruler is in some measure dependent upon the good will of his subjects (unless his domination is based on military occupation); feudalism can dispense with such good will. Patrimonialism appeals to the masses against the privileged status groups; not the warrior-hero but the 'good King', the 'father of his people', is its prevailing ideal. That the patrimonial ruler sees to the welfare of his subjects is the basis on which he legitimates his rule in his own and their eyes. The 'welfare state' is the legend of patrimonialism, in contrast to the feudal image of a free cameraderie of warriors pledged in loyalty to their leader.[1]

Weber suggested that the difference between feudalism and patrimonialism is of great significance for the sociology of the state in the pre-bureaucratic epoch. It should be added that he regarded patrimonialism as a closer approximation to the 'ideal' type of traditional authority than feudalism. Patrimonial rule, he wrote, tends to be personal and patriarchal whereas feudalism, in spite of personalized conventions, always involves a

---

[1] R. Bendix, *Max Weber. An Intellectual Portrait* (New York 1960), p. 362.

contractual relationship and tends to be impersonal and legalistic.[1] Moreover feudalism was far more limited in range and with the exception of Japan was found only in Western Europe.

An analysis of Kireevsky's ideas in these categories might produce the conclusion that the real purpose of his overdrawn contrast between ancient Russia and medieval Europe was to express this difference between two basic variants of traditional authority. The 'ancient boyar' element in Kireevsky's thought was still within the framework of the patrimonial ideal, unlike the Western European aristocratic ideals of Prince Shcherbatov. Kireevsky condemned autocratic absolutism ('sultanism' in Weber's terminology) and, unlike Karamzin, even allowed that it was permissible to oppose an authority that violated traditional laws. He was more concerned, however, to condemn aristocratic licence and to emphasize the fact that in ancient Russia social position had depended on service to the state rather than on birth or ownership of the land. These ideas, which were by no means new in Russian social philosophy, helped to consolidate the popular ideal of a 'people's monarchy' —an ideal that was anti-aristocratic and anti-bureaucratic at the same time.

Both the ideal of a *Gemeinschaft* type of community and the 'people's', 'patriarchal' ideal of patrimonial rule can be defended from the standpoint of various classes, including the gentry, the peasantry, or the petty bourgeoisie. When analysing different conservative anti-capitalist ideologies it is essential to see what interest they primarily set out to represent: whether that of one particular class (the gentry, for instance), or that of the pre-capitalist social structure as a whole. I would suggest that Slavophilism is an example of the latter type of ideology, although I would by no means wish to deny the strong ties connecting the Slavophile thinkers with the ancient nobility or to represent them as philosophers who broke with their own class. Slavophilism was the ideology of the hereditary Russian nobility who were reluctant to stand up on their own behalf as a privileged group defending its own selfish interests, and therefore attempted to sublimate and universalize traditional values and to create an ideological platform that would unite all classes

[1] See ibid., pp. 362, 379.

and social strata representing 'ancient Russia' This, I believe, sums up the essence of classical Slavophilism and at the same time explains its Utopianism and rapid disintegration at the very moment that historical events made it possible to proceed from ideas to action.

5

Alekseĭ Khomyakov

THERE has never been any unanimity among Russian—or Western—scholars on whether Kireevsky or Khomyakov should be considered the founder and leader of the Slavophile movement. M. O. Gershenzon, one of the best historians of ideas in pre-revolutionary Russia, claimed priority for Kireevsky, whose works he called the 'common source of Russian truth and Russian untruth'.[1] During the same period Nicholas Berdyaev lent his support to the view of the younger generation of Slavophile epigones, for whom Alekseĭ Khomyakov was the central figure of Slavophilism and the man ultimately responsible for its ideological foundations.[2] The argument was later perpetuated in Western literature on the subject.[3]

Although this difference of opinion might appear of little importance, the interpretation of Slavophile doctrine is largely determined by the attitude taken in this controversy. This becomes quite clear when we examine the arguments used by that supporters of Khomyakov. Although Berdyaev wrote 'Slavophilism was not and could not be created by an individual. It was the fruit of a united effort, a community of

---

[1] Kireevsky, i, p. v. In his *Istoricheskie zapiski* (Moscow 1910), p. 36, Gershenzon wrote: 'The whole of Slavophile metaphysics and philosophy of history is only a further development of ideas formulated by Kireevsky.'

[2] See N. Berdyaev, *Alexeĭ Stepanovich Khomyakov* (Moscow 1912). Berdyaev suggested that Gershenzon's Jewish origins prevented him from understanding the Orthodox faith.

[3] Gershenzon was supported by Masaryk, who wrote: 'To Kireevskii we owe the most profound and the most general formulation of slavophilism as a philosophic doctrine, and Homjakov was more influenced by Kireevskii than Kireevskii by Homjakov. As a matter of mere chronology Kireevskii was the philosophic founder of slavophilism.' T. G. Masaryk, *The Spirit of Russia*, i. 238. In France Gershenzon's standpoint was upheld by Koyré in *Études sur l'histoire de la pensée philosophique en Russie* and Berdyaev's by Father A. Gratieux in *A. S. Khomiakov et le mouvement slavophile*, 2 vols. (Paris 1939). N. V. Riasanovsky in *Russia and the West in the Teaching of the Slavophiles*, and P. K. Christoff in *An Introduction to Nineteenth Century Russian Slavophilism*, vol. i, *A. S. Xomjakov* (Mouton and Co., The Hague 1961), are inclined to see Khomyakov as the central figure in Slavophilism, but ascribe secondary importance to this problem.

consciousness and creativity',[1] he nevertheless considered that the central, pivotal role in this collective, supra-individual philosophical task belonged to Khomyakov. His argument runs as follows:

Khomyakov was the strongest, most all-round, and most active member of the school, and the Slavophile best endowed with the capacity for dialectical argument. He contributed to Slavophile theology and Slavophile philosophy, Slavophile history and Slavophile philology, Slavophile journalism and Slavophile poetry. Ivan Kireevsky was the romanticist of the movement, a contemplative personality, withdrawn and inclined to mysticism; he was neither belligerent nor very productive. Khomyakov, on the other hand, was the most realistic of the Slavophiles and at the same time the most aggressive and belligerent, a strong dialectician and born publicist. Each complemented the other. *If it is agreed, however, that the soul of Slavophilism is Christianity,* then priority must be given to Khomyakov. Throughout his entire life Khomyakov retained unshaken faith in the Church [*tsterkovnoe soznanie*], a Christian faith as firm as a rock: he was never subject to temptation, never hesitated, never experienced a spiritual crisis. Ivan Kireevsky became a Christian relatively late in life, not until the 1840s; in ecclesiastical and religious matters he followed Khomyakov, was under his influence. Khomyakov was the cornerstone, the granite rock of Slavophilism. Although he wrote poems, he was the poet of Slavophilism to a far lesser degree than Kireevsky.

He was a human monolith, without inner flaws, or a sense of the tragic. 'He was always a dogmatist. Dogmatic obstinacy pervades his entire personality.' Berdyaev concludes his portrait with the significant comment: 'For many Kireevsky must appear the more attractive personality, closer to our age than Khomyakov. It is Khomyakov, however, of whom we are more in need.'[2]

Although Berdyaev's description suffers from a number of inaccuracies and a certain obtrusive stylization, it is not entirely without foundation. From the 'Christian' point of view Khomyakov must certainly stand in the foreground and overshadow the other Slavophile thinkers. The literature devoted to Khomyakov—far ampler than the few works on Kireevsky—

---

[1] In the original: *sobornost' soznaniya* and *sobornost' tvorchestva*.
[2] Berdyaev, op. cit., pp. 25–39 (italics by A.W.).

was largely written by the epigones of Slavophilism[1] or by 'lay theologians' who propagated a return to religion and took an active part in trying to shape an Orthodox Russian culture. They were at the height of theirinfluence in the years of reaction after 1905 and continued to be active in *émigré* circles after the Revolution. They were responsible for a downright cult of Khomyakov as the 'crystal-clear' representative of the spirit of Orthodoxy and the collective soul of the Russian nation. The works this cult gave rise to are unmatched examples of cheap and superficial hagiography.[2]

In view of the express aim of the present study, it must be made quite clear that to the issues with which we are most closely concerned it was Kireevsky and not Khomyakov who made the first and decisive contribution. It is to Kireevsky, for instance, that we owe the Slavophile conception of integral personality and its close concomitant, the ideal of social bonds. It could even be argued that in the sphere of philosophy and philosophy of history Khomyakov merely continued Kireevsky's ideas and considered himself the latter's disciple. Moreover, the fact that Kireevsky experienced a period of intense philosophical inquiry before adopting Orthodox religious beliefs makes his views of particular interest to the historian of social thought.

It would be erroneous to conclude from this that Khomyakov is therefore of minor interest and lesser importance. He was doubtless a powerful individuality and his view of the world is an important part of Russian intellectual history. As a thinker he was perhaps less profound and creative than Kireevsky, but he was also more versatile and dynamic. In spite of his indolence, typical of the Russian landed gentry, he had the temperament of a leader, organizer, and popularizer—from this point of view he was certainly the main figure in the Slavophile *movement*. He was not responsible for the ideological foundations of the movement, but nevertheless his contribution was essential and cannot be disregarded.

Alexeĭ Stepanovich Khomyakov (1804–60) came from the same kind of family background as Kireevsky. His parents belonged

[1] A typical example is the 1500-page-long monograph by V. Zavitnevich, *A. S. Khomyakov*, 2 vols. (Kiev 1902).

[2] See the pamphlet by E. Skobtseva, *A. Khomyakov* (Paris 1929).

to the old hereditary gentry who lived on their country estates and remained faithful to national and religious traditions. His mother was a strong-minded woman and firm believer in the old virtues, whereas his father, who gambled and lost a good deal of money at cards, seemed to be an example of the evil results of the superficial adoption of European ways. The mother was the real head of the household and set the tone of Khomyakov's early life; in her children she inculcated a dogmatic traditionalism which went hand in hand with an obscure fear of a threatening environment and the need for a constant defensive vigilance. When the young Alexeï visited St. Petersburg for the first time he felt that he had come to a pagan town and determined to suffer tortures rather than let himself be forced to abandon his faith.

An important aspect of the traditions cultivated by the Khomyakov family was their paternal attitude to the peasants. This paternalism had its own 'ideology' and was conceived as the landowner's moral responsibility for the fate of his peasants —implying both the right to exert paternal authority over them and the duty to show them paternal care, to help them in case of need and to make a just settlement of controversial questions. The Khomyakovs treated their serfs as persons entrusted to their care rather than as their property; they regarded themselves and their peasants as members of one community, almost of one family. Of course, this was only 'ideology', but it was held with equal sincerity by both sides which made it possible in many instances to tone down conflicts between landowner and serfs.

It is worth quoting a characteristic account of the way in which Khomyakov's forefathers became owners of their estates. In the middle of the eighteenth century these estates belonged to another branch of the family whose last representative, having no heir, told his peasants on his death-bed to choose a master among his numerous distant relatives. The peasants did in fact send emissaries to all the Khomyakovs dispersed throughout Russia, collected information about them, held a council, and decided unanimously that the estates be handed over to a poor sergeant of the guard, Fëdor Stepanovich Khomyakov. The elected owner did not betray their trust and was long remembered as a just master and thrifty manager.

Alexeï Khomyakov tried to emulate his ancestor; the story

of the latter's succession to the estates strengthened his trust in the collective decisions of the *mir* and the conviction that the land was not merely the purely private and 'absolute' property of the nobility. Samarin relates how the peasants wept at his grave and exclaimed that they would never find another master like him. This was, however, only one side of the coin; the obverse side of Khomyakov's traditional patriarchal care was his ancient Russian severity to the peasants, and his entirely modern ability to calculate profit and loss. As V. Semévsky's detailed investigations have shown, the standard of living of the peasants on Khomyakov's estates was far below the average in the same province.[1] This does not seem to have escaped the notice of contemporaries: in a verse pamphlet entitled *A Moscow Madhouse* (1858) the Countess Rostopchina wrote thus about Khomyakov:

> Watch-dog of Orthodoxy among the people,
> He strictly observes all fasts,
> Writes lengthily about freedom
> And protests against all foolish errors.
> His clarion-calls against Russia's misdeeds
> Resound in the four corners of the earth.
> They say, however, that this prophet
> Treats his peasants with a heavy hand.[2]

In keeping with the boyar traditions of the hereditary nobility, who were anxious to emphasize their difference from the civil service nobility, Khomyakov held no state office; military service alone, he maintained, did not disgrace a gentleman. At the age of 17 he tried to run away from home in order to fight for the freedom of Orthodox Greece. A year later (1822) he enlisted in a Guards regiment, but seems to have remained quite immune from Decembrist ideas, which were very influential in officer circles. He is said to have told Rӯleev that of all kinds of revolution, a military revolution was the greatest outrage against justice.[3]

Khomyakov's burning wish to take part in a real war was

---

[1] See V. I. Semévsky, *Krestyanskiĭ vopros v Rossii v XVIII i pervoĭ polovine XIX veka* (St. Petersburg 1888), ii. 397–9.

[2] Quoted from Semévsky, op. cit., p. 400. See also Herzen's letter to his Moscow friends dated 30 January 1848 (*Sobr. soch.* xxiii. 58).

[3] See Zavitnevich, op. cit. i. 93.

granted a year later, in 1828, during the Russo–Turkish campaign in the Balkans. He was an excellent cavalryman, but his methods of fighting had more in common with medieval combat than with post-Napoleonic military techniques. Wearing his cuirass and brandishing his sword, he was always in the front ranks looking for an individual adversary; the battles he preferred were the kind where the outcome was decided by personal bravery rather than superior manpower or strategy. He had no interest in the fashionable army pastimes of gambling and revelry and in fact astonished his brother officers by the Spartan strictness of his morals. In spite of his natural liveliness and good humour he retained a dogmatic belief in ritual and carefully observed all fasts as well as the solemn promise—made to his mother—that he would abstain from pre-marital sexual relations.

Khomyakov's belligerence and good swordsmanship were useful assets during philosophical disputes. In his memoirs Herzen described him in action:

Gifted with a powerful and mobile intelligence, a good memory and the power of rapid reflection, rich in resources and indiscriminate in the use of them, he spent his whole life in heated and inexhaustible argument. An unwearying and unresting fighter, he cut and thrust, attacked and pursued, pelted with witticisms and quotations, frightened his opponents and drove them into an enchanted forest from which there was no escape without a prayer—in short, if he attacked a conviction, the conviction was lost, if he attacked a man's logic, the logic was lost.

Khomyakov was really a dangerous opponent; a hardened old duellist of dialectics, he took advantage of the slightest inadvertance, the slightest concession. An extraordinarily gifted man, with formidable stores of erudition at his disposal, he was like the medieval knights who guarded the Madonna and slept fully armed. At any hour of the day or night he was ready for the most intricate argument, and to secure the triumph of his Slavophile views turned everything in the world to use, from the casuistry of Byzantine theologians to the subleties of a tricky lawyer. His refutations, often only apparent, always dazzled and confounded his opponent.[1]

All who knew Khomyakov were astounded by his versatile talents and interests. Pogodin even called him the Russian Pico

---

[1] Herzen, *My Past and Thoughts*, i. 284–5.

della Mirandola.[1] He was a poet and philosopher who also enjoyed field-sports; he wrote theological treatises and undertook homoeopathic cures; he invented new steam-engines and an improved type of gun.[2] He studied Scandinavian mythology and Buddhist cosmogony, investigated the relationship between Russian and Sanskrit, and at the sime time proved an admirable manager of his estates, sparing time to work out plans for agricultural credit banks and for the emancipation of the peasants. Whatever he was engaged in, he always remained himself, among his peasants, in the salons of the Moscow nobility, and even in the drawing-rooms of the English aristocracy.

Clearly a man of Khomyakov's powerful personality exercised a tremendous fascination and influence on many members of his circle. On the other hand it must be emphasized that there was another side to his character. Herzen, with his extreme sensitivity to moral nuances, treated Khomyakov with greater reserve than the other Slavophiles, whose personal integrity he never questioned.[3] The passage from his memoirs quoted above reflects a somewhat moderated version of his ambivalent attitude to Khomyakov. Herzen describes Khomyakov's shrewdness, his unscrupulous methods and Byzantine cunning, which emphatically ran counter to the Slavophile ideal of spontaneity and simplicity. A striking example of his lack of scruple in forcing through his ideas was his attempt to publish his treatise *The Church is One* in Greek, with a foreword stating that it was a newly discovered manuscript reflecting the standpoint of the Orthodox Church.[4] This attempted hoax (which was not carried out) was kept secret even from his closest collaborators and shows that in spite of his professed views he was not in practice averse to Jesuitical lack of scruples. No doubt this was another aspect of his 'realism'.

Khomyakov was a practical and sober thinker: he was not a

[1] See Zavitnevich, op. cit. i. 100–1.

[2] Khomyakov sent one of his inventions—a steam-engine he christened 'Moskovka'—to the Great Exhibition in London in 1851. A detailed description and plan of this engine is included in the third volume of his collected works. See A. S. Khomyakov, *Polnoe sobranie sochinenii*, 4th edn. (Moscow 1914), vol. iii.

[3] See Herzen's comment on the 'soulless Khomyakov' made in his Diary on 17 December 1844. Herzen, *Sob. soch.* ii. 397.

[4] See S. Bolshakoff, *The Doctrine of the Unity of the Church in the Works of Khomyakov and Moehler* (London 1946), p. 127.

mystic, in spite of his mystical conception of the Church, and was more realistic in his judgement of Russia than either Kireevsky or Aksakov. It would be difficult to find a severer estimate of Muscovite Russia than his article 'On the Old and the New'. It may be doubted, however, whether this sober level-headedness greatly redounds to Khomyakov's credit as a man. It is probably another sign of his excessive adaptability, of his readiness to accept the divergence between ideal and reality. Herzen thought this was a deliberate method: the method of 'treacherous agreement' by which one disarmed one's opponent without making any concessions oneself. In spite of his critical attitude to Russian's past and present, Khomyakov was far more of a nationalist than Kireevsky or Aksakov, the 'romanticists of Slavophilism'. He was in fact a chauvinist and given to enthusiastic visions of military victories and Russian power. These ideals, to which he gave naïve expression in his youthful dramas *Yermak* and *The False Dmitry* were not modified in any essential way by the anti-state and anti-political elements in Slavophile ideology.

Khomyakov's poem 'To Russia', written in March 1854, just before the outbreak of the Crimean War, is usually quoted as a sign of his severely critical attitude to Russia, his patriotic suffering, and moral indignation. The poem is a moral indictment of Russia as a country unworthy of her great mission, a land of black injustice, slavery, and shameful apathy:

> Smeared with dark injustice in the law courts,
> And branded with the mark of slavery:
> Full of godless flattery, foul lies,
> Of deadly apathy and vice,
> And every other known depravity!

The poem aroused the indignation of government circles and 'patriotic public opinion'; Moscow's Governor-General asked Khomyakov for a written guarantee that he would not distribute his poems without submitting them to the St. Petersburg censor for approval. It is clear, however, that 'patriotic public opinion' failed to understand the real meaning of the poem. In spite of her sins, Khomyakov in fact suggested, Russia was a chosen country; God himself had summoned her to a holy war and victory would therefore be hers.

Oh unworthy to be chosen,
Yet you were chosen. Cleanse yourself swiftly
In the waters of repentance,
Lest a twofold punishment
Should fall like a thunderbolt upon your head.

Your soul in meek obedience,
Your head covered with ashes,
Devote yourself to humble prayer
And bathe the wounds of a depraved conscience
In the holy balm of tears.

Then arise, faithful to your mission,
And hurl yourself into the thick of bloody battles!
Fight with cunning for your brethren,
Bear aloft God's banner with firm grasp,
And smite with the sword—God's sword.[1]

The superficial interpretation was that Khomyakov called on Russia to atone, to wash herself clean with tears of pain and contrition. For the reactionary 'patriots' this was too much of a stumbling-block whereas for Khomyakov's apologists it was ground for praise. A legend grew up around Khomyakov's attitude to the Crimean War. According to Samarin he rejoiced over Russia's defeats: when asked why he was smiling when all were in tears, he replied that he had been weeping alone for thirty years and was now entitled to rejoice at the sight of the universal lament from which Russia would arise reborn.[2] While not questioning the truth of this account, it should be pointed out that Khomyakov only adopted this attitude when Russia's military defeat was quite inevitable. Before the war broke out he did not reflect on the beneficial effects of defeat but joined in the general enthusiasm. This is clearly shown by his 'Letter to a Foreign Friend Written before the Outbreak of the Eastern War' (1854), which was intended for publication in a foreign journal. In this letter Khomyakov wrote that Russia was undertaking a 'holy war', a war it would be profanation to compare to the crusades. Russia was the bearer of tremendous new principles, and was appointed to regenerate the world. The Western

---

[1] Khomyakov, *Stikhotvoreniya*, ed. by V. A. Frantsev (Prague 1934), pp. 118–19. The first strophe is quoted from P. K. Christoff, op. cit., p. 106.
[2] See Samarin's foreword to the first Russian edition of Khomyakov's theological writings; Khomyakov, ii, p. xiv.

powers should be thanked for bringing about the war and thus contributing to the victory of these great principles. 'Therefore let the banners fly and the trumpets sound! Flottez, pavillons! Sonnez, trompettes de la bataille! Nations, ruez-vous au combat! Dieu fait marcher l'Humanité!'[1]

The 'Letter to a Foreign Friend' written at the same time as the poem 'To Russia' suggests that the latter, too, was intended as a clarion-call to the 'holy war'. The opening and closing lines of the poem make its intentions quite clear: in spite of her sins, Russia was a 'divine tool', appointed to overcome 'blind, raging, and savage forces', by wielding 'God's sword'. The poem's stern reproaches did not conflict with the author's conviction that Russia represented infinitely higher moral principles than did her opponents.

It should perhaps be emphasized that Khomyakov's chauvinism was not specifically Slavophile. On the contrary, it anticipated the later Panslavist movement which dressed up certain chauvinistic slogans in terminology borrowed from Slavophilism. Khomyakov's belief, that the principles represented by Russia could triumph through the war clearly contradicted the Slavophile utopia, which held that Russia, unlike the West, based itself on moral strength and had no need to take recourse to force.

ECCLESIOLOGY

The most significant and at the same time most 'Slavophile' part of Khomyakov's writings was his theological works. These were mainly concerned with ecclesiology (the role of the church) and far less with matters of strict dogma. The content and history of dogmas interested Khomyakov only in so far as he thought them a symbolic expression of the essence of the Church, which for him was above all an ideal social organism, an antidote to the social atomization and spiritual disintegration of the contemporary world.[2]

The essay *The Church is One* was Khomyakov's only consistent attempt to systematize his views. Apart from this essay his

---

[1] Khomyakov (1914), iii. 195.
[2] See G. Florovsky, *Puti russkogo bogosloviya* (Paris 1937), pp. 250–1.

arguments are scattered in pamphlets polemicizing with Catholics and Protestants, and proselytizing letters to various people including the Jansenist Bishop Looss and the Protestant theologian Bunsen. The most important of these letters are the series addressed to the Anglican theologian William Palmer, a Fellow of Magdalen College and member of the Oxford Movement. Although his correspondence with Palmer helped Khomyakov to clarify some of his own theological opinions, it is an exaggeration to claim that his ecclesiology is therefore a 'by-product of the Oxford Movement'.[1] Khomyakov's theology was not directly influenced by Tractarianism, but on the other hand his general aims were very similar; he, too, was motivated by an anti-intellectual conception of faith, by distrust of individualism and isolationism, and by the quest for a pure and undefiled church tradition.

Khomyakov's influence on Palmer is a most instructive episode in the latter's intellectual biography. In the course of his historical and theological studies Palmer came to the conclusion that the Catholic, Orthodox, and Anglican Churches were three branches of one and the same Church, separated merely by chance. Anglicans who happened to be in Russia were entitled to the Sacraments of the Orthodox Church, while Orthodox and Catholic Christians could celebrate communion in an Anglican church. Palmer was most favourably disposed towards Orthodoxy and was anxious to prove his theories by actually taking communion in an Orthodox church. Unfortunately neither the Russian nor the Greek ecclesiastical authorities would take his claims to membership seriously. Palmer was persistent—he visited Russia three times (in 1841, 1842, and 1843) and even agreed to take a special examination in Orthodox theology in which, however, he was failed. Even so Orthodoxy retained his sympathy and under the influence of further studies and his contacts and correspondence with Khomyakov, he even came to the conclusion that in the dispute with Rome right was on the side of the Eastern Church. Under Khomyakov's eager proselytizing Palmer came very close to conversion, but again the attitude of the hierarchy, which demanded a second baptism, proved a stumbling-block. Khomyakov tried to intervene, but without success. Palmer

---

[1] See S. Bolshakoff, op. cit., p. 77.

finally became converted to Catholicism, although he stipulated the right to retain his own private views on the Schism. To the end of his life he kept up his interest in Orthodoxy and Russia, published an account of his travels there (with a foreword by Cardinal Newman),[1] and wrote a lengthy monograph on the Patriarch Nikon; however, he was not prepared to regard Orthodoxy as the sole and exclusive repository of ecumenical truth. In Palmer's case the Catholic Church, accused by Khomyakov of formalism, narrow separatism, intolerance, and a 'magical' attitude to the sacraments and liturgy, proved that these strictures applied to an even greater degree to the 'inwardly free' Orthodox Church. Khomyakov was quite aware of this and in one of his earliest letters warned Palmer not to confuse the ideal 'principles' of the Church with their implementation in practice: 'There is only one thing we can ask and one thing we may demand, namely that the faith we profess be not judged according to our [the Orthodox Church's] acts.'[2] This request is an excellent commentary on Khomyakov's conception of Orthodoxy and his methods of defence.

Khomyakov's ecclesiology took as its starting-point Kireevsky's criticism of Catholicism and Protestantism—the two Western confessions. For Khomyakov the essence of early Christianity was the 'identity of unity and freedom which manifests itself in the law of spiritual love'.[3] When Rome wilfully changed the symbol of faith (the *filioque*) by enshrining the private opinions of the Western bishops as a dogma, she broke the law of love and thereby condemned herself to rationalism— to justification by reasoning which is divorced from love and cannot supply the vital bond that would unite the faithful within the Church. From that moment unity and freedom became mutually exclusive concepts. The Church of Rome chose unity without freedom—a purely external and material unity symbolized in the person of the pope. Catholicism therefore stood for the blind subordination of the individual to the external authority of pope and hierarchy, for the substitution of utilitarianism for love, of subjection for brotherhood, and of a

---

[1] See W. Palmer, *Notes of a Visit to the Russian Church*. Selected and arranged by Cardinal Newman (London 1882).
[2] Khomyakov (1914), ii. 351.
[3] See Khomyakov (1878), i. 151.

purely external institutionalized 'political' unity for the freedom of inner bonds. Even the mass was something external and alien to the celebrants: in a Catholic church the congregation were lonely strangers to one another who took no part in the service, could not understand the language, and were merely fulfilling a duty on which their personal salvation depended.[1] Khomyakov gives an amusing account of the 'materialistic' conception of man's relationship to God as revealed in the Catholic system of indulgences. With the ledger of his good and evil deeds in his hand, he writes, the individual proceeds to argue his case before God. It is not difficult to secure a favourable outcome: if the defendant is a good citizen of the church-state, an obedient servant of his superiors, a modicum of good intentions and deeds is all that is needed to increase the association of shareholders in paradise by one member. An excess of good deeds can be converted into floating capital; any shortcomings can be eked out by a loan from wealthier capitalists. Nothing matters as long as the total balance-sheet is correct.[2]

Khomyakov called the Reformation part of a justified reaction against Catholic 'materialism', the individual's protest against the Catholic authoritarianism which frustrated his freedom. This protest, however, was purely negative, and restricted to the narrow sphere of rationalism, which was the tragic consequence of the Schism, the falling away from the true church. For materialistic rationalism, the Protestants substituted idealistic rationalism;[3] in their over-spiritualization of religion they abolished all visible signs of the religious bond and thus intensified the sense of loneliness. Freedom conceived rationally only resulted in a purely external freedom, without unity, which led to total internal and external social atomization. In its later phases Protestantism became converted into philosophical idealism and this, in turn, became atheism and materialism.[4] Western European feudalism, according to Khomyakov, was also a product of Catholicism, while the spiritual teaching of Protestantism was responsible for the whole of modern civilization: 'The entire modern history of Europe', he wrote 'belongs to Protestantism, even in countries which

---

[1] See Khomyakov (1914), ii. 117–19.
[2] See ibid., p. 125.
[3] See ibid., p. 76.
[4] See ibid. i. 150–1.

formally are Catholic.' Now 'Protestantism has departed from the sphere of dogmatic religion and moved to the misty regions of philosophical thought, i.e. to philosophical scepticism; in the social domain it has passed into a state of endless ferment which is shaking the Western world.'[1] This world was looking for a new unifying principle, but all attempts to find or create such principles resulted in disaster, since a true inner unifying principle could not be invented or created artificially. Khomyakov regarded socialist and communist utopian systems as unsuccessful attempts to stem psychological and social atomization: 'All these systems which appear to have been conjured up by the concrete symptoms of society's sickness, and are apparently aimed at curing them, have in actual fact arisen from an internal sickness of the spirit and have tried to fill the void caused by the decline of faith and the illusion of faith that had existed before.'[2]

Khomyakov suggested that the secret of the harmonious reconciliation of freedom and unity lost by the West was preserved in Orthodoxy, which had remained faithful to the early Christian tradition. This secret was that of a free and inner unity, illuminated by the divine Grace of the Holy Spirit. Khomyakov used the term *sobornost'* to describe the essence of this voluntary and organic fellowship. This word, frequently found in Old Church Slavonic, was, he maintained, the exact equivalent of the original Greek meaning of 'Catholicism'.[3] The *sobor* or council was the organ of the Holy Spirit and therefore expressed the unity of all, that is *unity in multiplicity*.[4] Khomyakov probably formulated this definition under the influence of J. A. Moehler, a leading Catholic romanticist theologian from Tübingen, whose interpretation of Catholicism was in turn influenced by a conservative social philosophy. In his early book *Die Einheit der Kirche oder das Prinzip des Katholizismus* (1825) Moehler contrasted the 'ecclesiastical egoism' of heretics and Protestants, who represent 'multiplicity without unity' (*die Vielheit ohne Einheit*), with the Catholic principle of 'unity in multiplicity' (*die Einheit in her Vielheit*), which ensures the harmonious reconciliation of individual diversity with communal togetherness.

---

[1] See Khomyakov (1914), p. 149.   [2] Ibid., p. 150.
[3] See ibid. ii. 321; in keeping with this interpretation of the word 'Catholic', Khomyakov refused to apply the term to the Roman Catholic Church and instead used such words as 'Romanism' or 'Latinism'.
[4] Khomyakov (1914), ii. 326.

The similarity with Khomyakov's *sobornost'* is obvious. There are a number of other interesting parallels between the two thinkers: both, for instance, were eager to revive the 'pure' traditions of early Christianity.[1]

The concept of *sobornost'* determined Khomyakov's highly 'Pneumatic' view of the church,[2] with its emphasis on the 'invisible' church as an embodiment of the Holy Spirit rather than an 'institution or doctrine'. Khomyakov emphasized that this ecclesiastical consciousness was a gift of divine Grace. In a letter to Palmer he even upheld the extreme view that if all Anglicans were persuaded by theological studies to adopt dogmas and symbols identical with those of Orthodoxy, their faith would still be Protestant, the product of reasoning and not of a state of divine Grace.[3] To Khomyakov the subjective act of *believing* only became true *faith* under divine inspiration, from which isolated individuals were excluded; it was a gift that could only be bestowed by the apostolic 'conciliar' Eastern Church.[4]

This theory also determined Khomyakov's extreme immanentism, his conviction that inner ecclesiastical consciousness was the only criterion of truth and his rejection of the notion of authority. 'The church is not an authority,' he wrote, 'for God is not an authority, nor is Jesus Christ an authority, for authority is something external.'[5] The cognizance of divine truths, Khomyakov argued, is a function of mutual Christian love and this love is its only guarantee; anyone for whom hope and faith are not enough and who looks for other, external

[1] On Möhler's influence on Khomyakov see Fr. A. Pawłowski, *Idea Kościoła w ujeciu rosyjskiej szkoły teologii i historiozofii* (The Idea of the Church in Russian Theology and Philosophy of History), part 2 (Warsaw 1935); Fr. S. Tyszkiewicz, 'La Théologie moehlerienne de l'unité et les théologiens pravoslaves' in *L'Eglise est Une* (Paris 1939), ed. Fr. P. Chaillet; G. Florovsky, op. cit., pp. 278–9, and S. Bolshakoff, op. cit. There are certain interesting analogies between Khomyakov and the theological writings of the young Hegel which were not published until 1909. In the critique of Catholicism which forms part of the discussion of a 'people's religion' Hegel uses arguments similar to those used by Khomyakov (the alienation of the church organization, its juridical character, and therefore its 'external' relation to the individual, the dictatorship of the clergy as the obverse of social atomization). See *Christentum und Volksreligion Hegels theologische Jugendschriften* (Tübingen 1907).
[2] See Fr. A. Pawłowski, op. cit., p. 41.
[3] See Khomyakov (1914), ii. 375.
[4] See ibid., p. 209.   [5] Ibid., p. 54.

pledges for the spirit of love is already a rationalist. The church does not ask what Biblical texts are true, where to look for the true traditions, which decisions of the synod should have validity and which actions are pleasing in the eyes of God—it does not ask since it possesses inner immediate knowledge, and knows itself as a living organic expression of truth and love.[1] This divinely inspired 'self-consciousness' of the church finds its fullest expression in the continuity of church traditions. *Internalized tradition* is more important than the Catholic belief in the authority of the pope and hierarchy and the Protestant appeal to the authority of the Scriptures (both of which were rejected by Khomyakov). The Scriptures are immanent in relation to the universal consciousness of the church, for words are incapable of conveying the divine truth. Controversies on the authorship or authenticity of various Biblical texts are therefore of no importance, since the Scriptures are the work of the church as a whole and textual authenticity depends entirely on their acceptance by the collective consciousness of the church community.

Christianity [wrote Khomyakov] is nothing other than freedom in Christ. . . . I consider the church to have greater freedom than the Protestants. For Protestantism holds the Scriptures to be an infallible and at the same time *external* authority, while to the church the Scriptures are evidence of herself; she regards them as an inner fact of her own existence. It is therefore quite erroneous to suppose that the church demands enforced unity or enforced obedience; on the contrary, the church abhors both the former and the latter, for in matters of faith enforced unity is falsehood and enforced obedience is death.[2]

Khomyakov's ecclesiological immanentism influenced his view of ritual and liturgy. He called ritual 'free poetic symbolism'[3] and thought that clinging to ancient rituals and ascribing magical power to them was typical of Catholic 'materialism'. At the same time he was by no means in sympathy with the 'Protestant' tendency to emphasize the spiritual content of religion at the expense of ritual; church rites, he maintained, were an important element of tradition and all liturgical changes should be introduced slowly and 'organically', and with the approval of all the people of the church, clergy as well

---

[1] See Khomyakov (1914), ii. 8.   [2] Ibid., pp. 198–9.   [3] Ibid., p. 183.

as laity. Though the Patriarch Nikon had been right to try and change 'the old ritual', his high-handed measures had only aroused opposition. The Old Believers represented the 'materialistic' (Catholic) attitude to ritual, while the *molokane* represented its opposite pole, the tendency to deny its importance. True Orthodox Christianity, which combined the traditional wealth of ritual with spiritual contemplation, was a synthesis of these two conflicting trends.[1]

As a logical consequence of his denial of external authority Khomyakov argued that infallibility was vested in the entire body of the church. He was confirmed in his view by the Eastern Patriarchs' reply in 1848 to the encyclical of Pope Pius IX *In suprema Petri Apostolica Sede*. Khomyakov regarded this reply as a most important landmark in the history of the church, and in particular stressed the significance of the paragraph stating that in Orthodoxy neither Patriarchs nor ecumenical councils are entitled to introduce changes, since the church as a whole community is the guardian of the true faith.[2] In Khomyakov's interpretation this meant that even the decisions of the synod require the approval of all believers—a universal approval expressed through the assimilation of such changes, so that they become an organic part of tradition. In a further extension of this notion Khomyakov maintained that Orthodoxy, unlike Catholicism or Protestantism, absolutely rejects the division of the church into teachers and taught. The church in its totality is the teacher,[3] and although it is the hierarchy's special duty to teach, it is not its exclusive prerogative; the repository of truth is the body of believers as a whole. Within the church no one has authority: the head of the church is Jesus Christ and she recognizes no other authority above her.[4]

The most serious argument against this interpretation was the charge of 'caesaro-papism' frequently levelled against the Orthodox Church. Khomyakov answered this charge by stressing that in Orthodoxy the people were led by the secular ruler only in matters affecting the material, temporal role of the church.[5] While he did not admit this to his Catholic polemicists, Khomyakov regretted the humiliating dependence of the Russian Orthodox Church on the secular authorities, although he

[1] See ibid. iii. 448–50. [2] See ibid. ii. 61.
[3] See ibid., pp. 61–2. [4] See ibid., p. 34. [5] See ibid., pp. 35–6.

maintained that this was primarily an external dependence and therefore of no fundamental importance. The Eastern Church, he argued, had never aspired to political freedom, but instead had preserved her inner independence. The correct relationship between church and state was one of mutual recognition and non-interference; an ideal that was often violated, Khomyakov admitted, in the interests of the secular arm. Ideally, however, the church should submit to the emperor in all political matters, and the emperor to the church in all spiritual matters. Khomyakov regarded the acquisition of material wealth and all 'external' activity on the part of the church as a sign of 'Romanism'. Like Kireevsky he was following the traditions of the 'trans-Volga elders' who believed that the essence of Orthodox Christianity was to vanquish the temporal world through inner integration and spiritual contemplation. The most outstanding Russian ecclesiastics—Iosif Volotsky, who had sought to increase the material power of the church against the opposition of the elders, and the Patriarch Nikon, who had tried to 'raise the church to the level of an independent state within the state'—were therefore, according to Khomyakov, representative of Western Catholic tendency within the Eastern Orthodoxy.[1]

In his interesting work *The Idea of the Church as interpreted in Russian Theology and Philosophy of History*, Fr. A. Pawłowski made a detailed analysis of Khomyakov's conception from an orthodox Catholic point of view. His conclusion was that Khomyakov's opinions were an extreme expression of 'liberalism' and 'ecclesiological democracy', comparable in many respects to progressive tendencies in contemporary Catholic modernism. Khomyakov's views, Fr. Pawłowski wrote,

clearly reveal a revolutionary tendency. In the first place he rejects (not without some hesitation) the idea of religious authority *per se*, eliminates the difference between the teacher and the taught, and argues that the duty or moral right to teach is vested not only in the hierarchy but also in the entire body of believers, thus dismissing the authority of instruction bestowed on the hierarchy by the will of our Lord. He believes that the guarantee of infallibility, by which

[1] An interesting appraisal of various trends in the history of Orthodoxy is to be found in Samarin's master's thesis 'Stepan Yavorsky and Theophan Prokopovich', which was written under Khomyakov's influence (see chapter 7).

he does not mean preservation from the possibility of error in matters of faith and morality but the full and perfect comprehension of the truth, is to be sought directly, without any intermediary, in mutual love or the altruistic fellowship of the faithful; and acknowledges the Holy Spirit alone as the only intermediary and source of the infallibility of the church. For polemical reasons and in order to prove the originality of Russian Orthodox Christianity, Khomyakov thus attempted to set the principle of the totality of the faithful against the institution of primacy and the conception of ecumenical truth against that of papal infallibility.[1]

Fr. Pawłowski's interesting view nevertheless requires some comment to bring Khomyakov's meaning into more precise focus. When speaking of his 'liberalism' or 'democracy' one must bear in mind that for Khomyakov the concept of 'the church as a whole' by no means meant the total sum of formal adherents of Orthodoxy; *sobornost'* was not a synonym for 'parliamentarianism', nor should the always infallible standpoint of the 'entire church' be interpreted as the sum of the private opinions of its individual members. In order to understand Khomyakov's ecclesiology properly, we must realize that what he had in mind when he spoke of the freedom of the church was not the personal 'Protestant' freedom of individual believers, but the freedom of the church as a supra-individual organic whole.

Slavophile ecclesiology cannot be discussed in isolation from Slavophile social philosophy—there are in fact very close analogies between the Slavophiles' reflections on the church and their conception of the secular norms governing social life. The relationship of church and state corresponds exactly to the relationship of State and Land.[2] In both instances Slavophile philosophy posited the principle of mutual non-intervention, that is absolute freedom of political decisions for the state and the right to total 'inner freedom' for church and Land. In the church the divine grace of the Holy Spirit played the same integrating role as did the irrational 'elemental force of history' in society; the principle of unanimity applied equally to the church and to the village commune, which Samarin called 'the secular and historical embodiment of the church', and which therefore,

---

[1] Pawłowski, op. cit., pp. 238–9.
[2] See below, pp. 245–55.

like the church, ensured the harmonious reconciliation of unity and freedom. The harm done by the loosening of social bonds, rootlessness, and cosmopolitanism resembled the ill effects of loss of faith: both transformed the personality into a mechanical aggregate of isolated autonomous functions and reduced the consciousness to a sum of compartmentalized unrelated fragments.

As these striking analogies show, Khomyakov regarded the church as some kind of ideal model of a specific type of social bonds. An excellent illustration of the meaning of the word *sobornost'* in relation to social life is to be found, I would suggest, in the following comments on the ancient Russian 'ritual art of living' made by a modern follower of Khomyakov:

The ritual art of living was expressed in solemn nation-wide festivals, in which the Tsar, clergy and people took part, but its manifestations were no less devoutly observed in every Russian home. It controlled the behaviour of the individual as much as it did all the official functions of Church and State.

The birth of a child, marriages or funerals, all the happy and unhappy events of human life, the visit of a guest, the start of a journey, all were the occasion for some rite. Food, clothing, manners, meals, the way they greeted each other and expressed their sorrows or joy, all were made part of the great dramatic theme, of which the source of inspiration was the story of the incarnation. . . .

The idea of such a divine drama was borrowed by the Russians from the Byzantine Empire, but they introduced so many novel elements into it that they transformed it into their own original creation. The main Russian achievement was to make the rhythm of the movement so perfect that the whole nation could act as one body with the others and yet spontaneously and freely. This was the Russian ideal expressed by the word *sobornost'*—the togetherness or oneness of life, unrestricted by any legal or intellectual barriers, but obeying the guidance of the Holy Spirit, and therefore enjoying unity in complete freedom.[1]

Quite apart from the accuracy of its depiction of ancient Russia, this quotation very aptly grasps the essence of Khomyakov's conception of freedom and the specific elements of the Slavophile notion of social cohesion related to it. According to this conception freedom is not a function of the individual but of

[1] N. Zernov, *Three Russian Prophets. Khomyakov, Dostoevsky, Solov'ëv* (London 1944), pp. 37–8.

the collective; the individual is free only in his social aspirations and this freedom depends essentially on complete identification with the group. Unhampered individual activity cannot be called freedom; on the contrary, it brings about a situation in which arbitrary external conventions become the only cohesive force in society. Since man is altogether a social being, he has freedom of action only when his activities are guided by ideally assimilated social dictates and norms that are not felt to be constraints. This harmony is not achieved by external factors such as social organization or division of labour, but by the common consciousness, or what Emile Durkheim has called the 'harmony of collective representations'. This 'free unity' is symbolized by the traditional tribal dance performed without a leader.[1] The freedom allowed by this type of unity is therefore a freedom prior to the stage of individuation: not freedom of the individual, but of the social collective.

Khomyakov was quite right to stress the contrast between the principle of *sobornost'* and the democratic and liberal ideas nourished by Protestant individualism. The main weakness of his conception was its utter impracticability, characteristic of the Slavophile movement. The Orthodox church leaders, who did not share Khomyakov's opposition to the hierarchical structure of the church or to its division into teachers and taught, had every right to doubt the vitality of the 'conciliar spirit' of their congregation or the efficacy of spontaneous unanimity as the sole pledge of the unity of faith. This resulted in the ironical situation that the theological works of the 'knight of Orthodox Christianity' had to be printed abroad (mainly in French) and were strictly prohibited in Russia. Their publication was not sanctioned by the Holy Synod until 1879, and even then the Russian edition had to be prefaced by a statement to the effect that 'the vagueness and want of precision of certain expressions are due to their author's lack of specific theological training [*sic!*].'[2]

In spite of this dubious recommendation, Khomyakov's writings exerted a great and decisive influence on Russian theology. The first posthumous Russian edition of his theological works

[1] See St. Ossowski, *O osobliwościach nauk społecznych* (On the Peculiarities of the Social Sciences) (Warsaw 1962), chapter 2.
[2] See Khomyakov (1914), first unnumbered page after the title-page of vol. ii.

was published with a preface by Samarin, in which he called Khomyakov a 'Doctor of the Church'[1] who had made an epoch-making contribution to the history of Russian Orthodoxy. That this was not an isolated opinion is shown by similar claims made later by other 'lay theologians' (including Bulgakov, Berdyaev, L. Karsavin, and S. Frank) and even by professional theologians (who were, however, more moderate in their praise). Khomyakov's ecclesiology turned out to be the most lasting part of Slavophile doctrine: it might be said, without exaggeration, that in the twentieth century it became the main source of inspiration for Orthodox religious thought.

Nevertheless, even when his theological influence was at its height, Khomyakov was accused of excessive 'concessions to Protestantism and of anticipating certain modernistic trends'. These accusations are contained in a brochure written by the Orthodox theologian Fr. Pavel Florensky and published in 1916 by the Sergeevskaya Lavra.[2] In this brochure Fr. Florensky put forward all the criticisms later repeated by Fr. Pawłowski from a Catholic point of view. He called Khomyakov's version of Orthodoxy a 'perfected, improved Protestantism', accused him of tearing out the 'wheat of Orthodoxy' together with the 'tares of Catholicism', and of rejecting ecclesiastical authority, obligatory canons, and the 'principle of fear'; he even questioned Khomyakov's political loyalty and suggested that he subscribed to the democratic principle of popular sovereignty. Florensky undoubtedly represented the point of view of a large section of the higher clergy, who only refrained from attacking Khomyakov's ideas because they recognized their usefulness in attracting to Orthodoxy the growing number of Russian intellectuals. A typical illustration of this is Florensky's caustic remark: 'It is not fitting to mention all this [i.e. Khomyakov's heterodoxy] in print, although similar views were expressed frequently in friendly conversations.'[3]

[1] Khomyakov ii, p. xxxvi. Samarin wrote: 'In using this title we know very well that some will consider our words to be an arrogant challenge and others an expression of the blind partiality of the disciple towards his master; the former will be indignant and the latter derisive. We know all this is advance, but we also know that future generations will not be surprised that in 1867 someone dared to express this thought in print and sign it with his name, but rather that there was a time when to express this thought required even a particle of courage and firmness.'

[2] See P. Florensky, *Okolo Khomyakova* (Sergev Posad 1916).

[3] Ibid., p. 22.

EPISTEMOLOGY

Of the leading Slavophiles, Ivan Kireevsky and Khomyakov showed the greatest interest in pure philosophical speculation. Khomyakov consciously continued Kireevsky's ideas in this field—his first 'strictly philosophical' essay for instance was headed 'Comments on Fragments found in I. V. Kireevsky's Papers'. This does not mean that Khomyakov's own ideas lack originality; on the contrary, his contribution to the theory of knowledge is highly individual, but it is questionable whether it can be treated as a representative part of Slavophile doctrine as a whole, particularly when we consider his characteristic voluntarism (not found in Kireevsky), which is difficult to reconcile, at first sight, with his conservative social philosophy.

In working out his epistemological views, Khomyakov took as his point of departure the critique of Western European rationalism or, strictly speaking, German idealist philosophy. Following Kireevsky, Khomyakov accused the idealists of attributing autonomy and absoluteness to the intellect (*Verstand*) and of identifying it erroneously with 'integral reason', the product of all the cognitive faculties. Although German idealism claimed to be a philosophy of dialectical reason (*Vernunft*), in actual fact, he argued, it could not transcend the cramping fetters of bare intellect. It was an essentially reflective, anti-ontological cognitive system which put up a barrier between man and the experienced reality; its effect, therefore, was to transform 'living knowledge' into a system of abstract concepts, to reduce the object of knowledge to a series of phenomena and to the logical structure of their mutual relationships. This type of cognition was purely external and therefore impoverished and inadequate: 'To comprehend the truth, the mind itself must conform to all the laws of the spiritual world not only by its logical structure, but also by the totality of its vital inner forces and talents.'[1] Khomyakov compared the results of rational cognition to the knowledge of colours of a blind student of optics (a comparison to be found already in Locke; Khomyakov probably borrowed it from de Maistre):[2]

A blind man acquires knowledge from birth; among all the other sciences he comes across optics, studies it, gets to know its laws,

[1] Khomyakov (1814), i. 281.
[2] See A. Gratieux, *A. S. Khomiakov et le mouvement slavophile*, ii. 230.

aptly defines certain phenomena (for instance by comparing bright red to the notes of a trumpet) and perhaps even contributes some new ideas to the subject; but the blind student's guardian can see. Which of them knows more about light? The student knows its laws, but these laws may coincide with the laws of other forces; there might even be a force that is governed by the most characteristic of all laws, the law of interference; but whoever can claim to know something that is similar to light itself? The guardian who sees it, knows it; the blind student has not the slightest idea of it, what is more, everything that he knows of its laws he knows only on the basis of data learnt from the man who can see.[1]

This proved that the purely rational knowedge of the student of optics had nothing in common with a true 'understanding' of phenomena, for 'understanding' meant the reconstruction, or 'transformation of the understandable into a fact of our inner life'.[2]

In Khomyakov's interpretation, therefore, rational cognition, while being part of 'integral reason', is not its organic root, which is free *will* and *faith*. Will and faith must precede and provide material for logical cognition since without them men cannot distinguish actual reality from its subjective representation. Both free will and faith are 'immediate' faculties: will is immediate consciousness at the pre-objective stage—the creative energy of integral reason—while faith is the 'sight of reason', the cognitive faculty which apprehends the vital essence of the object and makes it available for analysis by the intellect.[3] Rationalism is the product of the separation of the intellect from faith and free will and therefore replaces immediate knowledge about pre-objective reality by reflective knowledge about the subjective appearance of objects. Since the sphere of the intellect is governed by necessity—which precludes free will— rational cognition cannot comprehend the will nor can it understand objective noumenal reality, for this requires faith, immediate living knowledge.

What kind of knowledge is this knowledge that is not based on rational comprehension [Khomyakov asked]? It does not exist independently from the experienced reality, but is permeated by it and grasps the relationship of this reality to the as-yet-unmanifested

[1] Khomyakov (1914), i. 279–80.
[2] Ibid., p. 330.					[3] See ibid., p. 327.

first principle; it beats with every pulse of life, accepting all of life's multiplicity and penetrating it with its own meaning; it does not require proof for itself and its laws; it does not and cannot doubt itself. . . . It does not usurp the province of the intellect, but itself furnishes the intellect with all the data for independent activity, and in turn is enriched by the latter's wealth; it is a knowledge which is in the highest degree living and in the highest degree irresistible. It is not yet integral reason, for the wholeness of reason also embraces the entire realm of the intellect; it is what German philosophy has often called by the vague term immediate knowledge [*das un-mittelbare Wissen*], something that might be called internal know-ledge, but which in view of the pre-eminent role of the whole sphere ought to be called faith.

Khomyakov summed up his argument as follows: 'Reason lives in the perception of phenomena by faith and then, in abstract-ing, it acts upon itself in rationality; the vital essence of what is experienced is reflected in the life of faith, and the logic of its laws is reflected in the sphere of the intellect.'[1]

The word 'faith' occurs in two different meanings in Khom-yakov's philosophical writings. On the one hand, as in the quotation above, he used it to denote the living immediate knowledge that is the root of all knowledge; on the other he also used it as a synonym for the highest possible stage of integral reason (Kireevsky's 'concentration of all the cognitive powers into a single power') which, he wrote, is able to achieve a kind of 'clairvoyance', the power of penetrating into the 'profound mysteries of things divine and human'.[2] Having attained this state, reason becomes conscious of its identity with the phenomena of the objective world and at the same time learns to distinguish between those phenomena which derive from itself and those independent of it. The ability to make this kind of distinction is a function of the will, whereas the ability to perceive objects is a function of faith (in the sense of imme-diate living knowledge); the logical structure of phenomena, on the other hand, is perceived by the intellect, which is an analytical faculty. Faith in the sense of 'clairvoyance' is a synthesis of all these cognitive faculties, attainable only through a high degree of inner integration. This requires the renun-ciation of all individualism, for the supreme truth is 'only

[1] Ibid., pp. 278–9.   [2] Ibid., p. 282.

accessible to a reason which is harmoniously organized internally and in full moral accord with the omnipresent reason'; a reason which 'conforms to all the laws of the spiritual world'.[1]

In consequence of earthly imperfection, Khomyakov argued, no single individual can attain the highest stage of integral reason. 'The isolated individual represents absolute impotence and unalleviated inner schism.'[2] An individual can comprehend the truth only in so far as he becomes an organ of the supra-individual social consciousness and is bound in love to other people. Or, as Khomyakov put it,

of all the general laws of reason endowed with free will—or free will endowed with reason (for this is the definition of the spirit itself)— the primary, supreme, and most perfect law for the uncorrupted soul is the law of love. To exist in harmony with this law means to sharpen the perceptions of the mind to the utmost and to enlarge its horizons; we should submit to it therefore and allow its harmony to help us to overcome the obstinate discord of our intellectual faculties.

Love, on the other hand, he added,

cannot be aspired to in isolation; it demands, finds, and produces responses and mutual relationships, and itself grows, becomes stronger and perfected in such responses and mutual relationships. Hence the community of love is not only useful, but absolutely essential to the attainment of the truth—the conquest of truth depends on it and is impossible without it. The truth which is inaccessible to separate individuals is accessible only to a community of individuals bound together by love. This is what clearly distinguishes Orthodox teaching from all other religions; from Romanism, which is based on external authority and from Protestantism which turns man into an isolated individual and permits him to enjoy freedom in a vacuum of rational abstractions. Whatever has been said about this supreme truth also applies to philosophy. Seemingly accessible to only a few, it is in fact created and shared by all.[3]

To Kireevsky's conception of 'inner wholeness' and its corollary, the ideal of the wholeness of truth, Khomyakov added the proposition that every attempt to comprehend the truth is

---

[1] Khomyakov (1914), i. p 282.
[2] Ibid.,p. 161.
[3] Ibid., p. 283.

an act of 'organic togetherness', an unforced loving fusion with the supra-individual community. This conception formed a bridge between Khomyakov's epistemology and his theory of the church as a 'living organism of truth and love'. Since the whole truth is entrusted only to the church as a whole, it is only through active participation in the life of the church that its individual members develop their cognitive faculties fully.

Khomyakov's irrationalism—like Kireevsky's—reflected a general trend in European romanticism. His conception of faith as the 'sight of reason' is closely related to similar ideas put forward by Jacobi and Baader[1] and also coincides, as Samarin pointed out, with the idea of 'spiritual sight' (intuition) expounded by Mickiewicz in his Paris lectures on Slavonic literature, with which Khomyakov must have been familiar.[2] This irrationalism was not so much the product of an independent theory of cognition, as a protest against the effects of 'rationalism' in social life; in fact it represented an attempt to defend immediate, emotional social bonds, which were threatened with destruction in an age of capitalist rationalization of production, motivation of individual behaviour, and social organization. The holistic nature of Slavophile irrationalism reflected an attitude typical of the conservative romanticists, who set the absolute primacy of the social organism as a whole against bourgeois individualism. Khomyakov himself was fully aware of the close relationship between his theory of cognition and his social ideals and lost no opportunity of stressing their interdependence.

A characteristic aspect of Khomyakov's thought was his stress on the will as an active and independent creative principle of reason—something that led Berdyaev to compare him to Bergson and the Pragmatists.[3] In his philosophical system necessity was reduced to a *manifestation of alien will* and materialism and idealism were conceived as two aspects of 'necessitarianism',[4] an outlook that eliminates freedom in favour of natural or logical determinism. This voluntaristic aspect of Khomyakov's thought is particularly striking when it is

---

[1] See E. Susini, *Franz von Baader et le romantisme mystique* (Paris 1942), iii. 114–33.

[2] See Samarin, *Sochineniya* (Moscow 1911), xii. 175–6.

[3] Berdyaev, op. cit., p. 126. Gratieux too compares Khomyakov to Bergson (op. cit., ii. 263.

[4] See Khomyakov (1914), i. 312.

compared to the equally conservative and romantic *Weltan-schauung* of Chaadaev, who posited the absolute elimination of individual will and argued that all great moral and intellectual attainments spring from the acceptance of the principle of submission.

This difference cannot be explained by merely repeating Berdyaev's opinion that Khomyakov's theories express the 'genius of freedom' that was supposedly typical of Slavophilism and the antithesis of the specifically Catholic 'genius of author-ity'.[1] For Chaadaev the principle of 'submission' was a weapon against rationalist subjectivism, against the claims of reason to participate consciously in the shaping of social relations. His-tory has its own higher reason, he argued, and the intervention of subjective human reason can only lead to disastrous conse-quences. This argument, produced here in a very much simpli-fied outline, was intended as a counterweight to the ideas of the Enlightenment, responsible for the 'anti-historical' events of the French Revolution. Khomyakov's motivation, on the other hand, was rather different: in his philosophical writings he discussed problems that had interested conservative thinkers before Hegel, but he did so in the *post-Hegelian* era, when it was not Enlightenment thought but Hegelian panlogism that was considered to be the highest stage of rationalism. It was difficult to level the accusation of subjectivism at Hegel's rationalism. In Hegelian philosophy the rationalization of social relations was justified by the idea of 'necessity', by the irrever-sibility of the historical process; it was the 'anti-historical' romanticists, on the contrary, who were now shown to be guilty of 'arbitrary' conclusions. In consequence the romantic philo-sophers were forced to concentrate their attacks on Hegel's 'panlogism' and 'fatalism', to which they opposed an irra-tionalistic 'philosophy of freedom'.[2]

It seems worthwhile pointing out in this connection certain analogies between Khomyakov's views and those of the Polish romantic messianists. Like Cieszkowski, Khomyakov maintained that thought was not capable of creative acts, that Hegelian

[1] See Berdyaev, op. cit., p. 124. Berdyaev compared Khomyakov not to Chaadaev but to the French traditionalists, de Maistre and de Bonald.

[2] See T. Kroński, 'Messianic and Catholic philosophy in Poland in the middle of the nineteenth century', in *Rozważania wokół Hegla* (Thoughts about Hegel) (Warsaw 1960).

rationalism had abolished will as an independent and active element of the human spirit; like Cieszkowski and Libelt, he fought the 'despotism of reason' and agreed with the latter that 'before reason all materiality [in Khomyakov the 'substratum'] turns into dust,' that the sphere of reason only contains 'existence *in potentia*, but not life, not existence *in actu*'.[1] It is true that Khomyakov made no attempt to develop a 'philosophy of action', but nevertheless the voluntaristic element in his view of the world flowed from the same source as did the voluntarism of the Polish 'national philosophers'; it is even quite possible that some of his ideas were a distant echo of August Cieszkowski's German philosophical writings.[2]

In order to understand Khomyakov's voluntarism we must realize that when he wrote of the independence and activity of the free will it was not *individual* will that he had in mind. For Khomyakov free will and faith, on which he thought cognition was based, were shaped by the collective and drew their energy from it. This aspect of his thought was later developed by Samarin, who anticipated to a certain extent—and in a highly mystical guise—the fundamental theses of the sociology of knowledge. The individual's thought processes, Samarin wrote, are determined by a 'layer of congealed concepts and images' created in the consciousness by will and faith. 'Every man has his faith, but while one man is conscious of this, another who declares his faith in word and deed is not consciously aware of it and believes that he takes nothing "on faith".'[3]

This passage expresses a conviction, not always explicitly stressed by Khomyakov but implicit in all his epistemological views, that philosophical doctrines—those expounded as well as those criticized by him—were primarily manifestations of a definite emotional and volitional structure. This conviction, together with his attempt to distinguish between two fundamental types of collective faith and will, formed the basis of Khomyakov's philosophy of history.

---

[1] K. Libelt, *Filozofia i krytyka* (Poznań 1874), i. 15–18.

[2] In the 1840s Khomyakov carefully followed philosophical trends in Germany and it therefore seems unlikely that he would overlook a work as characteristic as *Gott und Palingenesie* (1842); Cieszkowski's earlier work, *Prolegomena zur Historiosophie*, might have been brought to his attention by Herzen who was greatly impressed by it (see pp. 379–82).

[3] Samarin, *Sochineniya*, i. 114–15.

PHILOSOPHY OF HISTORY

Khomyakov's chief contribution to the Slavophile philosophy of history is contained in the three posthumously published volumes of his *Notes on Universal History*. This compilation of largely unorganized and unfinished drafts nevertheless contains a number of original formulations which throw an important light on Khomyakov's ideas and his special position among Slavophile thinkers.

Unlike Kireevsky, who was preoccupied with the distinction between Russia and Europe, and constructed his theories on the contrast between classical civilization and Christianity, Khomyakov was fired by the ambition to work out a philosophical synthesis of world history. The basic premiss of his theory was that the historical process could be explained by isolating its 'primary elements', whose pure substance was most apparent at the dawn of history although in later ages it continued to manifest itself in different combinations.[1] The goal Khomyakov set himself was to make a 'reasonable'[2] interpretation of history which would illuminate the historical process 'from within' by pinpointing the activity of the primary spiritual forces that shaped the character of nations and individuals. 'It is not individual acts nor the fates of nations, but the fate, existence, and universal concerns of mankind that are the true material of history', he wrote in his *Notes*. 'In abstract terms let us say that I, a tiny fragment of humanity, can trace the evolution of my soul, my inner spiritual life, in the outward existence of millions of people dispersed all over the globe.'[3]

In his *Notes* Khomyakov divided mankind into three subdivisions based on categories of race, state, and religion. Of these three categories the least important was the second and the most important was the third, the category of faith. 'The people's religious belief is the first and chief factor to which historians should pay attention. . . . The degree of education, its character, and source are determined by the force, character, and source of religion. . . . The religion of the primitive races determined their historical fate; history became transformed into historical myth and has come down to us in that form only.'[4] The stress on religion as the main factor determining

---

[1] See Khomyakov (1904), v. 68.   [2] See ibid., p. 79.
[3] Ibid., pp. 29–30.   [4] Ibid., p. 131.

the history of nations was, of course, one of the fundamental axioms of Slavophile doctrine. It is interesting to note, however, that Khomyakov was not entirely consistent in the conclusions he drew from this: on occasions he even reversed the argument by suggesting that the ruling religion did not so much shape the nation's history as reflect it. Therefore religions that originated at times of peace were humanitarian and mild, while fanaticism and human sacrifice were signs that a particular nation had passed through a stage of bloody religious or tribal warfare. In view of this and other statements it is difficult to avoid the conclusion that Khomyakov considered religion to have quite mundane origins. 'Every mythology's heaven', he wrote, 'is, as we have already stated, a reflection of the earth, and the anger of men is expressed as the anger of the gods.'[1] A comparison with similar well-known comments made by Feuerbach or the young Marx, readily springs to mind.[2] In order to absolve Khomyakov from the charge of glaring inconsistency, we must remember that he did not apply his argument to Christianity, the only true 'revealed' faith; but in spite of this formal exemption, Berdyaev was surely justified in saying that Khomyakov's *Notes* had no room for 'historical mysticism', eschatology, or prophetic elements.[3] In fact some of Khomyakov's reflections on the leading role of religion in human existence suggest that he was merely concerned to stress that religion, though not the only integrating force in history, was of greater significance than belonging to a particular state or race.

The task of interpreting Khomyakov's views is complicated by his voluntaristic metaphysics. The character of a particular religion was not, he argued, determined by its ritual or the number of its gods; it could not be defined in intellectual categories, but solely in terms of the will, whose basic categories are freedom and necessity. 'Freedom and necessity are the mysterious underlying principle around which are concentrated, in various ways, all the thoughts of man. In the language of religion, which transposes into the invisible heavens the laws that govern the visible world and man, its visible ruler, freedom expresses itself in creation and necessity in birth.'[4] The religions of freedom Khomyakov called Iranian and the religions of

[1] Ibid., p. 200.   [2] See Marx, Fourth thesis on Feuerbach.
[3] See Berdyaev, op. cit., pp. 154, 185.   [4] See Khomyakov, v. 217.

necessity Kushite; his philosophy of history was an attempt to reconstruct and follow the struggle of the Iranian and Kushite principles throughout the course of history.

As the Iranian religions were spiritual, their god was always a personal deity, the creator of the world; Kushitism, on the other hand, always resulted in pantheism, which was either 'nihilistic' (Buddhism) or materialistic (Shivaism);[1] the so-called system of 'emanation' (in which the Kushite element predominated) represented an unsuccessful attempt at compromise.[2] The Iranian gods (e.g. Brahma) created freely, while the Kushite gods (e.g. Shiva) gave birth under the constraint of necessity. The favourite symbol of the Kushite religions was the serpent, while the Iranian principle was always inimical to serpents (Hercules and the hydra, Apollo and the python, Vishnu-Krishna and the dragon, etc.).[3] The Kushites expressed themselves in the visual arts, especially in architecture, and the Iranians in words, since the human soul only required poetry when it became conscious of the value of free thought. Hence in India—a country that was half-Iranian and half-Kushite—Shivaism produced no poetry, whereas under the religion of Brahma and Vishnu poetry flourished.[4] Kushitism (with the exception of Buddhism) led to a religious materialism in which faith resembled a kind of 'transcendental physics', prayer a magical incantation, and ritual a talisman. The symbol of the Kushite cult was a rich proliferation of outward forms expressed in the magnificent flowering of art and architecture. The distinguishing mark of the Iranian religions, on the other hand, was that they conceived tradition as a common spiritual heritage. In abstract thought the Iranian principle represented synthesis while the Kushite principle stood for analysis and a rationalist orientation (logic being within the sphere of necessity);[5] in social life Iranianism safeguarded the natural community based on free association while Kushitism created the state, a conventional and artificial social organization. Iranianism was always renewed through the effort of great minds, while Kushitism drew its strength from the inertia and apathy of the masses. This explained the relative weakness of Iranian civilizations, which required unceasing moral vigilance, and the

---

[1] See Khomyakov, v. 225–9.   [2] See ibid., p. 253.
[3] See ibid., p. 220.   [4] See ibid., p. 332.   [5] Khomyakov, vi. 59.

strength of Kushitism, which could not decay since it was itself the expression of profound human decadence.[1]

It was with this conceptual equipment that Khomyakov set out to write a universal history. Without attempting to reproduce his argument in detail, I should like to draw attention to some of its most important elements. In the *Notes* the races inhabiting the earth were also divided into Iranians and Kushites.[2] The cradle of the Iranian races was Iran, while the Kushite races came from Ethiopia. Khomyakov stressed that religion and education were not invariably linked to colour or other anthropological features, but that these nevertheless played an important part.[3] The white races of Europe and Asia, who were noted for their nobility and spiritual purity, had a natural affinity for the Iranian principle,[4] while the black races of Africa were examples of Kushitism in its most degenerate form: their indolent passivity, Khomyakov wrote, showed that they had almost entirely lost their creative spiritual energy.[5]

The ancient centres of Kushite civilization were Babylon, Egypt, China, southern India, and Kashmir. Among these, India and China were deserving of relatively high esteem. Khomyakov even called Buddhism the greatest event before Christianity in the spiritual history of mankind. 'The magnificent purity of an ascetic faith taken together with the fiery proclamation of the truth, heroic suffering, and, finally, the sublimity of a proud spirit seeking freedom in self-annihilation —all these fuse into a matchless whole, unequalled in vainglorious Europe or in the rest of the world.'[6] Buddhism was nevertheless a Kushite religion, although it differed from the passionate and sensual Shivaism; it sought freedom in nonbeing precisely because there seemed to be no room for it in reality.

[1] See Khomyakov, v. 329.

[2] A. F. Hilferding, the editor of the *Notes on Universal History*, maintains that Khomyakov's categories in fact coincide with the division into Aryan and none Aryan tribes, since Iran is only the later name for Aryana, i.e. the land of the Aryans (see Khomyakov, v. 390, footnote). This is contradicted by the fact that Khomyakov considered the Israelites to be the purest Iranian stock.

[3] Khomyakov, v. 358.

[4] See ibid.

[5] See ibid., pp. 359, 518.

[6] Khomyakov, vi. 174.

Within the limits of Kushitism China represented a spiritual principle at the opposite end of the scale, for her faith was a thoroughly worldly 'religion of the state'. She could be compared to ancient Rome, although Khomyakov made one important reservation in her favour: the Roman empire was based on the principle of self-interest, while China was inspired by moral principles. Like all manifestations of Kushitism Chinese morality was merely formalistic and conventional, but nevertheless the 'great effort to carry out a great task was not wasted'.[1]

In the pre-Christian world only Israel had remained faithful to pure Iranian principles.[2] Her social organization was not in the least conventional or artificial and showed no signs of 'state' unity: 'A great man draws his fellow men after him and is recognized by them as their leader, without any established rites or contracts.'[3] The religion of the Israelites—the first monotheistic faith—was a pure expression of the inspired spirit of freedom.

Khomyakov's judgement of ancient Greece and Rome (particularly the latter) was much more critical in tone. He accused both Greeks and Romans of an absolute lack of genius in the religious sphere and called their beliefs examples of a 'senseless syncretism, a disorderly amalgam of Iranian and Kushite elements'.[4] Although their substance was largely Iranian, the Kushite element had the ascendancy, for spiritual freedom must be absolute—the slightest concession to necessity entailed its destruction.[5]

Khomyakov cited the Prometheus myth as a symbolic rendering of the struggle between Iranian and Kushite principles. 'Prometheus is the symbol of eternal human liberty, of moral law enslaved by the world of elemental forces.'[6] He had been chained to the rock by three Kushite deities—Zeus (fate), Mercury (earth-bound wisdom), and Vulcan (fire)—but the day would come when the northern god Heracles would tear apart his chains. In daily life, however—both private and social—the Greeks did not take the liberation of Prometheus seriously and did not rebel against their inwardly corrupt gods.

---

[1] Khomyakov, vi. 93. 	[2] Khomyakov, v. 341.
[3] Khomyakov, vi. 153. 	[4] Khomyakov, v. 250 and see vi. 124.
[5] See Khomyakov, v. 322. 	[6] Ibid., p. 251.

Khomyakov suggested that religion in Greece had never embraced the totality of spiritual life and that this explained both the flowering of Greek philosophy[1] and Greek individualism, which ushered in a new era—the 'age of man'. In Hellenism man was, in fact, the supreme and sole deity, just as the only true faith was faith in human worth.[2] Knowing Khomyakov's own convictions we may be sure that this belief too represented the victorious Kushite principle. The arguments he used to lead up to this conclusion are, however, neither clear nor consistent and rely chiefly on an attempt to prove that what the Greeks worshipped in man was not his freedom, but his external 'plastic' beauty, another sign of Kushite materialism.[3]

Khomyakov did not present his views of Greece at all clearly, especially by comparison with Kireevsky's schematic but lucid treatment of the same subject. In the *Notes* he conceded reluctantly that Greece 'holds one of the first places in the history of mankind' and even attributed this to 'her untrammelled development, universality, and the special clarity of her spiritual life'.[4] Like the liberal historians he praised Athens and condemned Sparta's one-sided military development, her 'monstrous immorality against which man's soul revolts.'[5] His comments on Greek art were equally ambivalent: on the one hand he called it a magnificent synthesis of the visual genius of the Kushites with the poetic genius of the Iranians[6] and on the other condemned it as an expression of the cult of material, external beauty—a typical sign of Kushite idolatry.

Khomyakov's far more severe strictures on ancient Rome were more in keeping with orthodox Slavophile views. Rome he argued, had been founded by exiles from Latium and was therefore a town without ancestors or tradition, 'a mature man, an egoist without ancestry among a multitude of tribes in the stage of childhood'.[7] Roman civilization was an illustration of Kushite conventionality and artificiality. Its religion was an external truth, the lifeless and formal cult of legality; religion was a state institution and the state itself was an embodiment

---

[1] Khomyakov, vi. 250.
[2] See ibid., pp. 237–9.
[3] See ibid., p. 253.
[4] Ibid., p. 247.
[5] Ibid., pp. 241–2.
[6] See ibid., p. 248.
[7] Khomyakov, vi. 79–80.

of the principle of self-interest and the prototype, as it were, of the bourgeois states of modern Europe.[1] It was Rome who had given birth to the modern utilitarian and individualistic personality and to the concept of 'the social contract elevated to the rank of an absolute truth not requiring any additional sanction'.[2] Because of this Khomyakov utterly rejected the messianic conception of Moscow as a 'third Rome': the comparison with 'the iron severity' of Rome was, he felt, an insult to the Christian nations.[3]

It will be readily apparent that Khomyakov's strictures on Rome were simply a repetition of Kireevsky's. It is interesting to note, however, that unlike the latter he did not regard Rome —on indeed Greece—as either the source of all evil or the most influential factor in the history of European civilization. From the point of view of the eternal struggle between the Iranian and Kushite principles classical civilization could no longer be regarded as a turning-point in the history of mankind.

To a certain extent this is also true of Khomyakov's interpretation of the role of Christianity. In his *Notes* he suggested that Christianity was not so much a revelation of entirely new truths, as a 'return to a forgotten teaching',[4] the triumph of ancient Iranian teaching (based on tradition), and its peak achievement.[5] 'That is why', he wrote, 'up to our era Christianity (whether accepted or rejected) is the law for all enlightened humanity; only ignoramuses, however, can fail to distinguish between the church, i.e. the strict and logical development of the Christian principle, and societies who may profess Christianity but do not live according to its principles.'[6]

This reservation is significant, since it shows exactly where Khomyakov's philosophy of history diverged from his ecclesiology. Christianity was the peak achievement of the Iranian principle in the spiritual sphere, but not in the historical arena where its coming had not affected the eternal struggle of the Iranian and Kushite elements.

Although Christianity was largely responsible for the downfall of the Roman Empire, the early Christians were taught by their long-drawn-out struggle against the authorities to regard

[1] See Khomyakov, vi. 79.   [2] Khomyakov, vi. 401.
[3] Khomyakov, v. 79.   [4] Ibid., p. 344.
[5] Khomyakov, vi. 409.   [6] Ibid., p. 412.

the state as an institution alien to the Christian spirit. Hence they made no move to found a state of their own but submitted to the old laws, in return demanding only respect and the recognition of their faith. According to Khomyakov, this was the main source of the weakness of Christian Rome: 'The state-building force of Christianity', he wrote, 'could only come to the fore in young, uncivilized peoples.'[1]

To discuss Khomyakov's views on Catholicism and Orthodoxy and on the causes of the Schism, would entail the unnecessary repetition of matters discussed earlier. This does not mean, of course, that the *Notes on Universal History* add nothing new to Khomyakov's theological works. They contain a number of stimulating ideas including, for instance, an interesting distinction between the Western and Byzantine ecumenical councils (corresponding to the Slavophile antithesis between European parliaments and the Russian Land Assemblies),[2] a comparison between the papacy and the caliphate, and the intriguing hypothesis that Roman Catholic expansionism owed its impetus to its contacts and struggles with Islam.[3] These ideas, however, are only of marginal importance; what is undoubtedly of far greater significance is that in his *Notes* Khomyakov attempted to fit Christianity as a whole into the Iranian–Kushite matrix. To do this he had to endow Western Christianity with such typical Kushite features as a conventional state organization, the conception of prayer as a magical incantation, and a talismanic attitude to liturgy.[4] This left Eastern Christianity, faithful to tradition and spiritual freedom, as the upholder of the pure Iranian principle.

According to Khomyakov the Germanic tribes, who became the leading force in Europe after the fall of the Roman Empire, also belonged to the Iranian race (like the Slavs) and were therefore superior to the Latin peoples who had been profoundly contaminated by Kushitism; however, their victory

[1] See ibid., p. 458.
[2] Khomyakov, vii. 199. In the East the ecumenical councils *expressed* the universal consciousness of the Church, and their decisions became binding only when they were accepted by the entire Church community; in the West ecumenical councils were a kind of *governing* body, and their decisions were legally binding. 'In the East the word of the councils was a testimony and in the West it was a verdict.'
[3] See Khomyakov, vii. 77.
[4] See ibid., p. 450.

over Rome only denoted a partial victory of the Iranian spirit.[1] There were certain elements in their character and tribal structure which rendered them particularly liable to Kushite influences as expressed in Roman law and its principle of 'logical necessity'. Needless to say, they differed from the Slavonic nations in this respect. After many centuries the seed of Kushitism sown in the Germanic soul came to fruition in idealist philosophy—primarily in Hegelianism—which was strictly comparable to Buddhism.[2] According to Khomyakov, to define freedom as the 'free recognition of necessity' was merely 'a miserable logical subterfuge derived by the persistent effort of German philosophy from the logical, that is necessary, laws of the material-intellectual world'[3] Defining freedom in such a way was tantamount, in fact, to acknowledging the victory of Kushitism.

The essential difference between the Germanic and Slavonic peoples was that the former lived by conquest and the latter by agriculture. According to Khomyakov even the German word *Volk* expressed the German military spirit; the Slavonic word *narod*, he argued, comes from *rodit'* (to give birth) and thus illustrates the natural origins of the common people; the German *Volk*, on the other hand, is derived from *füllen* (to fill) or *voll* (full) and is therefore the equivalent of the Slavonic term for regiment (*polk*, from *polnit'*).[4] Although both the village commune and the principle of collective responsibility or accountability (the Slavonic *krugovaya poruka*) were known among the Germans; the German commune differed from its Slavonic counterpart in being based on the conventional fraternity of the warrior team.[5] The military organization of the Germanic tribes gave rise to European feudalism, a system that was quite foreign to the true spirit of Slavdom. The fact that the German states were based on conquest ruled out any hope of fraternal fellowship between rulers and subjects, sowed the seed of future conflicts and civil war, and thus prepared the ground for the inevitable and steady growth of the 'arbitrariness' and juridical conventionality of social life. Other factors that facilitated Kushite influence were the fatal process of 'Latinization', which was enouraged by Germany's membership of the Holy Roman Empire, and

---

[1] See Khomyakov, vii. 42–3.
[3] Ibid. v. 225.   [4] See ibid. vii. 17.
[2] See Khomyakov, vi. 175.
[5] See ibid., pp. 15–16.

the assimilation of Roman law and distortion of Christianity
by the Church of Rome. In the end the commune disappeared
and the common people became transformed into a body of
slaves without rights. The towns had more freedom, but they
were alien and hostile to the countryside; their population
could not be regarded as part of the people, since the latter
was an alien concept to Roman law, which recognized nothing
but the individual and the state.[1] Inner cohesion was replaced
by external bonds and fraternal fellowship by an aristocratic
individualism that valued the individual (as Greek individualism had once done) not as a human being, but for his external
attributes of power, authority, and beauty.[2]

It is a curious aspect of Khomyakov's theories that he
specifically excepted England from these harmful influences.
The true Iranian qualities of the ancient Teutons had, he suggested, been far better preserved in Britain than elsewhere.[3]
England did not adopt Roman institutions,[4] and was converted
to a brand of Christianity that was not yet defiled by 'Romanism' and on the whole preserved its original character in later
ages, in spite of the 'historical provincialism' which divided it
from the true church (i.e. Orthodoxy).[5] The commune persisted
longer in England than elsewhere in Europe and the English
aristocracy—unlike its Continental counterpart—sought an alliance with the people and helped them to gain their rights. This
was made possible by the 'artificial' origins of English feudalism
which was transplanted fully grown from the Continent by
William the Conqueror; this 'artificiality' was reflected in the
weakness of the aristocracy and forced the latter to seek an
alliance with the people against the king.[6] The Anglo-Saxons,
of course, represented the Iranian principle, and the Normans
the Latin-Kushite element.

In keeping with the law of creativity mentioned earlier, the
Normans produced great architecture while the Anglo-Saxons

[1] Ibid., p. 267.
[2] See ibid., p. 264.
[3] See ibid., p. 412.
[4] See ibid. iii. 234-5.
[5] In his theological writings Khomyakov emphasized that there were no essential dogmatic differences between Anglicanism and Orthodoxy (thus agreeing
with Palmer), and that only their 'historical provincionalism' kept the Anglicans
away from the true Church. See Khomyakov, ii. 221.
[6] See Khomyakov, vii. 402-5.

expressed themselves in songs and poems.¹ This dualism was also reflected in medieval English literature:

Everything conventional related to the life of society, everything created artifically (and especially everything elegant) had a name derived from Latin. Everything that was alive, rustic, spritual, natural—divine one might say—had a Germanic source, and these two trends can be observed throughout the entire history of the English language. The character of a given author or a given epoch can be determined by ascertaining which of these two elements— the Germanic or the Latin—predominates in their language.²

For all the corruption introduced by the Normans, England remained 'a country that was more reasonable and better integrated than the rest of Europe'.³ Khomyakov went so far in his liking for England as to suggest that Slavs must have played a considerable role in British history; he claimed to have found traces of their influence in the religion of the Saxons and even in the name 'Angle' which he thought was a variant of the tribal name of the Uglichi.⁴ The crowning proof of Slavonic influence was the principle of the unanimous jury, which the Slavophiles considered to be a specifically Slavonic institution and one that the rest of the world completely failed to understand.⁵

Khomyakov did not continue his *Notes on Universal History* beyond the beginning of the Middle Ages, when the first Slavonic states had just emerged from obscurity. The *Notes* nevertheless contain many references to the Slavs, most of them attempting to prove that as representatives of the pure Iranian spirit the future was in their hands. In view of the basic importance of this conception for Slavophile doctrine, it is worth undertaking the difficult task of collecting and systematizing these scattered comments on the nature of the Slavonic tribes and their past role in the history of mankind.

Khomyakov laid stress on the fact that in contrast to the Germanic tribes the Slavs had always been purely agricultural peoples. The importance of this distinction is readily understood if we take into account Khomyakov's known view that agricultural peoples were closer to 'universally human' principles than warrior races.⁶ Unlike the latter they had no sense

---

¹ See Khomyakov, vii. 409.   ² Ibid., p. 399.   ³ Ibid., p. 410.
⁴ See ibid., pp. 338–42.   ⁵ See ibid., p. 344.   ⁶ See ibid. v. 106, 108, 118.

of aristocractic superiority and their behaviour to other races contrasted srikingly with that of the Dutch or English in their colonies. A Russian in Siberia frequently spoke the dialect of the Yakuts or Buryats, a Cossack would marry a Chechen woman, and a peasant would take a Tartar or Mordva wife. In fact, Khomyakov pointed out, the whole of Russia 'declared that its pride and joy was the great-grandson of the Negro Hannibal [i.e. Pushkin], to whom these freedom-loving men who talk of equality in America would deny the privilege of citizenship or even the right to marry the white daughter of a German washerwoman or an English butcher'.[1] The Slavonic ideal—personified by the *bylina* hero Ilya Muromets—was not the homeless and restless knight enamoured of his own strength and will, but the meek and gentle strength that defends the weak and defenceless against licence and lawlessness.[2] To illustrate his contention that the Slavs were a more 'social' people than the Germans, Khomyakov contrasted the individualistic Anglo-Saxon pioneers who had colonized the empty plains of the Mississippi with the Russian settlers who had moved to Siberia in whole villages.[3] He stressed, however, that their very gentleness, sociability, and receptivity to all that was human made the Slavs an easy prey to foreign conquest; since they could not endure a self-sufficient and hermetically sealed existence, they were liable to lose their national character in an alien environment.[4] Although highly talented, they lacked energy and resilience; they inspired other peoples and awoke the dormant elements within them, while themselves remaining without glory, 'but steeped in some kind of half-yearning which attains no goal, in a half-life which resembles a dream'.[5] In spite of this veritable 'Oblomovism', Khomyakov insisted that the Slavs personified the pure Iranian element and called them the rare example of a tribe which could be said to have gone forth to meet Christianity instead of merely waiting for it.[6]

Khomyakov's belief in the mission of Slavdom led him to put forward some fantastic hypotheses intended to vindicate the Slavonic contribution to world history which, he claimed, prejudiced German historians had done their best to overlook.

---

[1] Ibid., p. 107.
[2] See ibid., p. 505.
[3] See ibid., pp. 509–10.
[4] See ibid.
[5] See ibid., p. 307.
[6] See ibid., p. 319.

Thus he suggested that the anthropomorphism of the proto-Slavonic religion had exerted a great influence on the religious beliefs of the Greeks and indirectly on their art;[1] that the depiction of Trojan family life in the *Iliad* proved that Troy had been a Slavonic colony;[2] and that the conquered Slavs had not only laboured for the savage Teutons, but had also been their teachers.[3] The Huns, Khomyakov suggested, were in fact the Cossacks of Eastern Slavdom; by driving out the German invaders Attila had made possible the emergence of Poland, Kievian Russia, and other Slavonic states.[4] He even compiled a 'Comparison of Russian and Sanskrit Words',[5] a survey of over 1000 words intended to illustrate the relationship—or even 'complete identity'—of the 'Slavonic tongue' with Sanskrit,[6] and indirectly the purely Iranian origin of the Slav races.

It was axiomatic to Khomyakov that the spirit of Slavdom (and therefore of Iranianism) was expressed in its purest form in the Russian people. The very numerical superiority of the Russians was proof of the fact that they were imbued more deeply than the other Slaves by the spirit of fraternity, sociality, and love. The overwhelming might of the Russian state, its territorial expansion, and growing significance in world affairs were not the product of chance, for Russia's external power was a sign of her inner strength.[7]

It will come as no surprise to the reader to learn that in his *Notes* Khomyakov placed the Poles at the opposite end of the Slavonic scale; like the other Slavophiles, he would have been in full agreement with Tyutchev's well-known verse branding Poland as the 'Judas of Slavdom'.[8] Poland's recorded history, he argued, began with an act of fratricide, when she helped the Germans to exterminate the Baltic Wends in the tenth century.[9] Only in Poland had Catholicism become deeply

[1] See Khomyakov, v. 306–7.   [2] See ibid. vi. 110.

[3] See ibid. v. 435.

[4] See ibid. vi. 463. Khomyakov adopted this theory from the Bulgarian Slavic scholar J. Venelin.

[5] See ibid. v. 421. Khomyakov often spoke of the Slavs as one nation using one language.

[6] See ibid., pp. 535–87.

[7] See ibid., p. 529.

[8] Tyutchev's *Slavyanam* written on the occasion of the Slavonic Congress in Moscow in 1867.

[9] See Khomyakov, v. 186.

rooted; among the other Western Slavs the adoption of Catholicism or Protestantism was a historical accident which did not succeed in destroying their at least potential spiritual readiness for Orthodoxy (the Hussite movement being an example of such a potentially Orthodox trend).[1] By asking the pope for his blessing and petitioning the German emperor for a royal title, Boleslav the Brave, the first Polish King, gave symbolic sanction to Poland's dependence on the West. Only superficial historians, maintained Khomyakov, could dismiss as unimportant such apparently trivial matters as a papal blessing or the assumption of vassal status; submission to force, though not without its consequences, was frequently a matter of chance, whereas voluntary dependence originated in a moral decision and left permanent traces.[2]

From various scattered comments in reviews and articles it is possible to reconstruct—at least in general outline—Khomyakov's view of later Polish history. Poland's dependence on the West was aggravated, he believed, by the growing gulf which divided the Latinized aristocracy from the common people. The alien product of this was an aristocratic civilization 'as soft as silk and as tough as iron', which worshipped individuality and force, scorned the family and the fellowship of the community, and by its military strength and seductive charms represented a threat to every country where the family and communal life still survived.[3] This 'Polish Gentry-state' was in fact the antithesis of Russia. The decisive trial of strength came in 1612, when Russia emerged victorious, thanks to the active help of the whole people, thus demonstrating the moral superiority of the Russian principle.

There is little point in speculating on how Khomyakov would have developed his theme in subsequent volumes of his *History*. His general standpoint and basic thesis are quite clear as it is, and are perhaps best expressed in his own words: 'At least the potentiality of rebirth, if not its fully formed embryo, has been preserved for humanity by the Slavs';[4] and since the leading force and greatest hope of Slavdom was Russia, 'the

---

[1] See ibid. iii. 138. This was accepted by the ideologists of Panslavism.

[2] See Khomyakov, vii. 308.

[3] Ibid. iii. 99–101; a comparison of Poles and Russians in an enthusiastic review of Glinka's opera *A Life for the Tsar* (*Ivan Susanin*).

[4] Ibid., p. 140.

interests of Muscovy coincide with the over-all interests of mankind'.[1] 'From every point of view', Khomyakov concluded, 'the Russian question is undoubtedly the only universal issue of our time.'[2]

As Nicholas Riasanovsky has convincingly demonstrated, the central motif of Khomyakov's *Notes on Universal History* was probably influenced by Friedrich Schlegel.[3] In his *Philosophy of History* Schlegel distinguished between two basic types of will, each of which determined a different path of historical development: natural, carnal will directed towards material objects and enslaved to nature, and divine will, conforming to a higher destiny and directed to spiritual goals. In Schlegel's work these two types of will were represented by the descendants of two primitive races, the Cainites and the Sethites. Unlike Khomyakov, Schlegel did not try to reduce the entire course of history to a struggle between these two races, although he too believed that 'distant echoes' of this struggle could be discerned even in the modern world.

It seems clear, therefore, that Khomyakov's philosophy oi history, like Ivan Kireevsky's, was mainly inspired by conservative German romanticism. Nevertheless, as the systems constructed by the two leading Slavophile thinkers differ on a number of essential points it is pertinent to ask which of them was a better expression of the essence of classical Slavophilism or, to put it more concretely, which of them provided a more efficient underpinning for the Slavophile conception of personality and social cohesion. We are justified in posing this question since Slavophile ideology has a definite 'internal structure' with its own set of rules; although the Slavophile thinkers themselves differed as to their awareness of this structure, it is clearly discernible in the light of modern sociological and historical research and is open to scholarly analysis.

It is obvious, even at first glance, that the fundamental antithesis between Russia and Europe, which forms the structural pivot of Slavophile doctrine, has become blurred in Khomyakov's *Notes*. Not only are the Orthodox religion and Russia deprived of all their exclusiveness, but—what is more

[1] Khomyakov, viii. 58. [2] Ibid., p. 247.
[3] See Riasanovsky, op. cit., pp. 215–16.

important—the former is reduced to being only one of a number of Iranian religions, while the latter is merely presented as the bearer of principles previously embodied in such perfect representatives as the Israelites. This extended interpretation of the first member of the opposition could, of course, be reconciled with the spirit of Slavophile ideology; even Kireevsky realized that the contrast between Russia and Europe stood for a much deeper opposition between types of personality and social bonds which the Russia/Europe antithesis—or even the Christian and pre-Christian antithesis—was inadequate to express. It is, however, Khomyakov's interpretation of the second member of the opposition that is most open to doubt. In the light of structural analysis it is clear that the most widely applicable negative frame of reference for Slavophile doctrine was 'rationalism'—i.e. the rationalist interpretation of the personality and of inter-personal relations, which in the nineteenth century was associated primarily with the capitalist rationalization of production processes. From a historical point of view the Slavophiles were therefore fully justified in regarding capitalist Western Europe as the negative pole of their antithesis. Khomyakov, too, subscribed to this view, but there is little evidence of this in his philosophy of history. According to his conception of the struggle between Iranianism and Kushitism, the antithesis of the principles represented by Orthodox Russia would have to be sought in Africa or Asia rather than in Western Europe, since European civilization (like Classical Antiquity) was, in spite of all, a fusion of Iranian and Kushite elements (with the former predominating, though contaminated by the latter). This conception gave rise to contradictions which became obvious when Khomyakov tried to apply the categories of Iranianism and Kushitism to modern history. In one of his digressions he referred to contemporary Europe as the 'ripe embryo' of fatal Kushite influence in the womb of Iranianism,[1] while in another he commented enthusiastically on the greatness and triumph of Iran (in this instance the white races), ranking Russia alongside the colonizing nations of Western Europe: 'Spirit has triumphed over matter and the Iranian race has conquered the world. Centuries have gone by, but its rule has not weakened, the future

[1] See Khomyakov, vii. 43.

of mankind is in its hands. The descendants are harvesting the fruit of the merits of their ancestors.'[1] The optimistic nature of this and similar pronouncements contrasts strikingly with the pessimistic—almost catastrophic—diagnosis made by Ivan Kireevsky and Konstantin Aksakov, who were convinced that the contemporary world represented the victory of alien and hostile principles and that the only hope of salvation lay in a spiritual revolution which would turn back the course of history.

Khomyakov's views on Russia's past and present were also quite out of step with orthodox Slavophile doctrine, especially where his evaluation of modern Russian statehood and, by inference, his attitude to the Petrine reforms were concerned. Like the other Slavophiles, Khomyakov regarded the state as a rationalistic organization and therefore both conventional and artificial; however, he went much further in stressing its necessary functions and even spoke of the 'state-building force of Christianity'.[2] For Kireevsky and Aksakov the rapid growth of Russian power after the reforms was a purely external achievement and actually represented a fatal threat to their ideals; for Khomyakov it was testimony to Russia's greatness and represented the triumph of the pure Iranian spirit embodied in her.[3] Khomyakov's dissident point of view found clearest expression in his unpublished article 'On the Old and the New' (1839) intended as a polemic against Kireevsky's opinions. In ancient Russia, Khomyakov maintained in his article, there had been neither education, nor law and order, nor justice, nor government loved by the people, nor an enlightened and free church; Peter the Great had made many errors, but future generations would always remember him with gratitude, for he deserved credit for awakening Russia's strength and her awareness of her strength.[4] Under Kireevsky's influence Khomyakov later modified his view of ancient Russia (although he always preserved a greater measure of critical distance), but this in no way affected his estimate of Peter the Great and the political successes of the reformed empire. Khomyakov's truly 'imperial' nationalism was closely related to his interest in the other Slavonic nations and to his

[1] See Khomyakov, v. 529. [2] See ibid. vi. 548, vii. 161–2.
[3] See ibid. v. 529. [4] See ibid. i. 366–75.

dream of uniting them under Russia's aegis. It is worth noting that Kireevsky was totally uninterested in the idea of Slavdom and that for Konstantin Aksakov it played at most a secondary role; in this respect Khomyakov's standpoint represents an intermediate link between the classical Slavophilism of the 1840s and '50s and the later Panslavism of Ivan Aksakov, Pogodin, and Danilevsky (this will be discussed in a later chapter).

It is significant that neither Herzen, who held long discussions with Khomyakov, nor the Slavophiles themselves, who did all they could to encourage him to continue his *Notes*, showed much interest in his historical theories. In their expositions of Slavophilism none of its adherents ever mentioned the Iranian/Kushite struggle; this conception was largely irrelevant to the ideological discussions of the 1840s, although it might have served as a historical underpinning for Panslavism. Even its basic philosophical assumptions did not entirely harmonize with the spirit of classical Slavophilism, which required the rejection of the Hegelian conception of necessity and the irreversibility of historical processes, but not the construction of an entire *Weltanschauung* on the negation of all necessity. It would have been enough, for instance, to distinguish between outward and inward necessity, between rational will and 'organic' will. From the Slavophile standpoint Khomyakov could be charged with overlooking the principle of *sobornost'* in his philosophy of history and of failing to make a clear enough distinction between his own conception of freedom and the liberal–individualistic point of view (in his evaluation of Athens, for example, or the Promethean myth). Khomyakov's view of the role of the masses in history was closer to Granovsky's[1] than to Kireevsky's or Aksakov's: the masses, he suggested in the *Notes*, were steeped in a pure life of the instinct, in 'material' passions, and therefore tended to forget about human dignity and were a constant prey to Kushitism; Iranianism, on the other hand, was guarded only by great men, by divinely inspired individuals.[2] It is obviously difficult to reconcile this view with the Slavophile thesis that in Russia the common people alone had remained faithful to her moral ideals and 'inner truth'.

[1] See chapter 9. [2] See Khomyakov, v. 327–9.

Closer analysis thus reveals why the *Notes on Universal History* —which was after all Khomyakov's main work—made no essential contribution to Slavophile ideology. In this respect his publicistic writings of the 1840s, particularly his 'Letter on England', 'A Foreigner's View of Russians', and 'A Russian's View of Foreigners', were of far greater importance. While perhaps less ambitious than the *Notes*, these articles were more intimately in touch with problems of close concern to the Slavophiles and the intellectual life of the epoch, and should not be overlooked in a general survey of Khomyakov's work and his contribution to Slavophilism.

The most interesting general theoretical statements are to be found in the 'Letter on England', written just after a visit to England in 1847. Khomyakov was confirmed in his Slavophilism by what he saw on his visit and was so delighted with Oxford that in one of his letters he even compared it to his beloved Moscow.[1] The qualities that attracted him were England's conservatism, her attachment to traditions, and talent for striking a happy mean between the 'old' and the 'new'. He was impressed by the conservative nature of English progress which seemed to develop naturally without the intervention of the 'surgeon's knife', and without severing the organic links with the past. Khomyakov was of course aware of England's position as the most advanced capitalist country, a country with a proletariat, whose emergence he was anxious to prevent in Russia at all costs. If, in spite of this, his impressions were favourable rather than otherwise, this seems to suggest that his attitude to capitalism was not entirely hostile. As we shall see later, this was a distinguishing mark of Khomyakov's practical 'realism'. In the 'Letter on England', however, this tendency remained in the background and the main body of the article was taken up by reflections on historical continuity which would have been entirely acceptable to Kireevsky and Aksakov.

The secret of undisturbed social evolution, argued Khomyakov, was the harmonious collaboration of two forces:

One of them—the fundamental, innate force that is characteristic of the system as a whole, of the entire past history of a given society— is the force of life, developing independently from its own principles,

---

[1] See Khomyakov, vii. 172.

from its organic foundations; the second—the rational force of individuals—is founded on the first, which lends it vitality; it is incapable of creating anything by itself nor does it strive to create; it only participates in the general development and prevents it from ending up in the blind alley of dead instinct or in unsound one-sidedness. Both forces are necessary, but the second—the force of consciousness and intellect—ought to be bound to the first force—the force of life and creativity—by a vital and all-embracing love. Dissension and struggle result whenever the unity of faith and love is broken.[1]

An inner division of this kind had occurred in England, Khomyakov wrote, and was reflected in the struggle of Whigs and Tories. The Tories embodied the 'elemental force of history', a vital, organic, and 'historical' force nourished by local tradition, religion, and custom; Toryism was 'all joy of life', an elemental force opposed to all restrictions, artificial conventions, or rationalization. 'In England Toryism is every ancient oak with its long branches, every old belfry looming on the horizon';[2] Toryism was the poetry of life, spontaneity, freedom. Whiggism, on the other hand, was the 'rational force of individuals' divorced from social energy, an 'analytical (force) that does not believe in the past'. Its distinguishing marks were inner aridity, and creative barrenness: 'At its roots there is scepticism, a rationalism that neither loves nor believes in history, an individualistic egoism that does not recognize the validity of natural, simple feelings when they are without logical foundations, and which finally leads to disintegration.' Whiggism tried to replace natural social bonds by 'bonds that are seemingly not so strict, but in fact not so free, just because they are conventional; it likes to replace simplicity of conscience and spirit by a sophisticated police of forms.'[3]

According to Khomyakov the split between Tories and Whigs in England was not complete—every Englishman, even a Whig, had some traces of Toryism in his make-up. The common people were profoundly attached to the past and the English aristocracy was not alienated from society; it was 'not an institution but a product of its native soil and history; a part of Toryism and not an independent and separate force'. By comparison France, where the 'elemental force of history' had

[1] Ibid., pp. 127–8.   [2] Ibid., p. 130.   [3] Ibid., p. 129.

almost dried up, was in a far worse position:[1] 'A shallow and
poverty-stricken spiritual life has long been a distinguishing
feature of this country which has neither true art (with the
exception of its medieval architecture), nor true poetry; but it
became still more poverty-stricken when it tore itself away from
its past in the bloody revolution at the end of last century.'[2]
The French Revolution resulted in the complete atomization
of French society and the utter aridity of her spiritual life;
deprived of its source, poetry became transformed into rhetoric
and the pursuit of form and external effects.

Khomyakov's analysis of the struggle between Whigs and
Tories included Russia, where he saw a similar cleavage
between enlightened society and the common people, the most
disastrous consequence of the Petrine reforms. His attempt to
analyse the results of this cleavage led him to put forward a
number of interesting ideas (to be dealt with in a later chapter)
on the alienation and inner disintegration of the 'Russian
Europeans' who had become a 'colonial' class in their own
country. He pointed out that in Russia the contrast between
Whigs and Tories was even sharper than in England, for
Russian Whiggism—unlike its English counterpart—had been
imported from outside. Russian Whigs were therefore more
alienated from their own people than the English Whigs, but,
on the other hand, Russian Toryism was all the purer.

If you wish to find Tory principles outside England [Khomyakov
wrote], look around you; you will find them in a form all the more
perfect for not bearing the stigma of individualism. Here you have
the majestic golden domes of the Kremlin; there, in the south, are
the Kiev Cave Monastery and in the north the Solovetsky Monastery,
a centre of homely virtues and above all a centre of independent,
unyielding Orthodoxy. Look again: here you have the force which
once called Kuzma Minin the representative of the Land of Russia,
which armed Pozharsky and crowned its enterprise by electing
Michael and the entire Romanov dynasty to the throne; here, at
last, you have the village commune with its principle of unanimity
and its trials based on conscience, custom, and inner truth.[3]

The contrast between Whigs and Tories did not altogether
correspond to the distinction between Kushites and Iranians

---

[1] Khomyakov, v. 50–1.   [2] Ibid.
[3] Ibid., pp. 137–8.

(the difference can be seen most clearly in a comparison of Whigs and Kushites) but helped to express the essence of Slavophile doctrine far more clearly. Above all it threw into relief the points of similarity between the struggle of the Slavophiles and Westernizers and that of the conservatives and liberals in Western Europe. Samarin developed this idea in a most interesting marginal comment on de Tocqueville's *L'Ancien Régime et la révolution*.

> Tocqueville, Montalembert, Riehl, Stein [he wrote] are the Western Slavophiles. As far as their opinions and final postulates are concerned they are all closer to us than to our Westernizers. . . . But there is a difference as well: when Tocqueville, Montalembert, Riehl, and the others defend freedom of life and tradition their warmest sympathy is with the aristocracy, for in the historical conditions of Western Europe the aristocracy implements practical real-life Toryism better than any other party . . . We, on the contrary, appeal to the common people, although our motives are the same as those that induce them to sympathize with the aristocracy; for here it is the people that cultivates the capacity for self-sacrifice, untrammelled moral instinct, and respect for tradition. In Russia the only haven of Toryism is the peasant's hut.[1]

When he wrote this passage, Samarin did not realize that he was in fact pinpointing the main reason for the disintegration of Slavophilism, namely the need to gain the support of the people in circumstances which made this quite impossible. In view of the equation of 'Toryism' with the common people, the most desirable solution to the peasant problem, which certainly brooked no delay, would appear to have been one that assured the peasantry the greatest amount of independence (including economic independence) from the 'Whig' nobility and bureaucracy. As we shall see, only Konstantin Aksakov, the most fanatical and least practical of the Slavophiles, was prepared to accept something approaching this point of view. Ivan Kireevsky thought that all changes should be put off until the upper classes had become converted to Slavophile ideals—a view that was both consistent and in its own way faithful to the spirit of the more conservative aspects of Slavophilism. Khomyakov—like Koshelëv and Samarin—chose the intermediate

---

[1] Y. F. Samarin, *Sochineniya* (Moscow 1877), i. 401–2.

and less consistent but more 'realistic' solution of sacrificing the Slavophile utopia to the immediate interests of his class.

THE PEASANT QUESTION

Khomyakov's pronouncements on the peasant question fall under two heads, depending on whether they date from the 1840s or from the second half of the 1850s, when preparations for the emanicpation act of 1861 were already under way. In both groups utopian ideals are found side by side with sober and practical calculation, but in the later period references to utopian solutions become proportionately fewer.

Khomyakov was always a decided opponent of serfdom. In his article 'On the Old and the New' he called it 'a shameless violation of all rights' and in a letter to the Countess Bludova in 1848 he even accused the whole of 'enlightened society' in Russia of being unconscious enemies of their country: 'We are [Russia's] enemies because we have become foreigners, because we are the masters and our own countrymen are our serfs, because we stupefy the people and deprive ourselves of the opportunity of a true culture, etc.'[1]

However, Khomyakov qualified his condemnation of serfdom with the disingenuous argument that it was an essentially Western institution which had not succeeded in destroying fraternal relations and moral fellowship between master and man: 'In Russia serfdom is only a brutal police measure which was invented to meet the needs of the state, but has not destroyed human brotherhood, whereas in the German coastal regions [i.e. Courland and Livonia] it was an indigenous evil springing from conquest and tribal violence. In Russia it was only the fruit of ignorance, but there it was the result of a crime.'[2]

There are no grounds for supposing, however, that in the 1840s Khomyakov actually considered emancipation at all. In his two articles 'On Rural Conditions', published in the *Muscovite* in 1842, he maintained, with other practical advice, that the agricultural question could be solved if the landlords would only have recourse to two ancient Russian institutions in their dealings with the peasants; namely the *polovnichestvo* (sharecropping) and the village commune.

---

[1] Khomyakov, vii. 391.
[2] Quoted from Semëvsky, op. cit., p. 390.

A modification in the *polovnichestvo* suggested by Khomyakov was that the system of taking half the peasant's produce could be brought up to date by taking half the peasant's labour instead, and by separating the manor lands from the communal holdings. This improvement would supposedly allow the landlord greater room for manœuvre 'without restricting the peasant in any way'.[1] The gist of the advice was that labour dues should be regulated and should not exceed the statutory three days a week. When he came to discuss the village commune Khomyakov did not merely praise it as an ideal social unit and panacea against proletarianization, but also emphasized its practical advantages to the gentry. Although the censorship prevented him from speaking quite plainly, he tried to convince his readers that serfdom was unnecessary, since the commune bound the peasant to the land and the system of collective responsibility for all types of taxes and dues was enough to guarantee the performance of all feudal duties.[2]

By comparison with other Slavophile writings of the 1840s, in which the village commune was usually discussed theoretically, as an essential element in the Slavophile utopia, Khomyakov's articles were exceptional in that they analysed the commune from the point of view of concrete class interests and its practical bearing on the agrarian question. It is an interesting sidelight on his attitude that it met with a certain amount of disapproval inside the Slavophile camp. In 1840 Alexander Koshelëv, a close friend of the leading Slavophiles and, apart from Khomyakov, their chief expert on agricultural questions, wrote a long critical letter to his friend in which he accused him of falling into two serious errors. Koshelëv argued that periodic redistribution of the communal holdings would prevent the necessary intense cultivation of the land, and accused Khomyakov of being inconsistent in propagating the principle of communally held land for the peasants but not for the landowners, since this would, in fact, perpetuate the division into estates and therefore the dualism of Russian life criticized by the Slavophiles.[3]

---

[1] Khomyakov, iii. 77.
[2] See ibid., p. 71.
[3] See N. P. Kolupanov, *Biografiya A. I. Koshelëva* (Moscow 1889–92), ii. 103–5 (Appendix). Koshelëv's arguments are discussed at greater length on pp. 478–82.

In an unpublished article entitled 'On the Village Commune. A Reply to a Friend', Khomyakov retorted by arguing that agricultural progress did not depend on private ownership of the land. In Western Europe agriculture was least advanced in France, although the peasants owned their land, and most highly developed in England, although English farmers were mainly tenants on a twenty-five-year lease. In Russia the frequency with which communal holdings were redistributed varied, and it was therefore quite feasible to try and ensure that in future redistribution would only be undertaken every twenty or thirty years. In England high agricultural productivity went hand in hand with the proletarianization of the masses, the heightening of social antagonisms, and the danger of revolution; the French system prevented the emergence of a proletariat[1] but acted as a brake on agriculture and—above all—had a deleterious effect on minds and morals by encouraging selfish property instincts and restricting the peasant's intellectual horizon. The Russian village commune, Khomyakov concluded, avoided the defects of the English and French systems by preventing both proletarianization and the egoism of the small property-owner. Khomyakov thought that the experience of Europe—the bitter struggle of labour and capital and the anti-social individualism of workers and manufacturers—showed that the communal principle ought to be applied to industry as well. Industrial artels, co-operatively run mills, and rural manufactories set up by merchants were evidence that the 'industrial commune, the phalanstery, one might say', already existed in Russia in embryo. 'All this', Khomyakov wrote, 'is not yet fully developed, but our industry as a whole is not developed. . . . When our social system is founded on simpler principles [i.e. after emancipation] all these beginnings will grow, and the commercial, or rather industrial, commune will take shape by itself.'[2]

To the accusation that he was perpetuating dualism and social divisions, Khomyakov replied that as far as ownership of the land was concerned this dualism was an eternal indigenous feature of Russian society, and that he had no intention of re-

---

[1] This statement shows that Khomyakov was quite unaware of the potential problem represented by the emergence of rich individual farmers.

[2] Khomyakov, iii. 468.

stricting the privilege of private ownership of the land to the nobility alone. 'Granting the peasants the right to own property,' he wrote, 'in no way affects the village commune. Individual activity and enterprise ought to have their rights and their sphere of action; it is enough for them to retain a foothold in the commune, and that in it or through it they can become socialized and will never become lost in selfish isolation.' This conception, which formally, at least, has much in common with the plan put forward by P. S. Pestel[1] in his *Russian Truth*, treated the communal ownership of land as a means of providing social security and, at the same time, as a social safety mechanism that would put a brake on unrestrained development in order to reduce conflict to a minimum. It is clear, however, that even if Khomyakov's plan allowed the peasants to own their land, manor lands were still to remain in the hands of the landowners who would thus be exempted from the 'communal principle' upheld by Khomyakov and the other Slavophiles as a precious heritage of the ancient Russian way of life.

It was Samarin who showed Khomyakov a way out of this dilemma. In the frequently quoted letter he wrote to Samarin in 1848 Khomyakov announced joyfully that he had found a way out of the 'juridical antinomy'.[2] In fact his solution added little that was new to the ideas developed by Kireevsky in the late 1830s. Briefly his argument ran as follows: all ownership was in fact a form of use and therefore something relative; the peasant used the communal land, and while the landlord might

---

[1] Pestel's plan provided for the division of the land into two equal parts: the first—to be owned by the community—was to provide everyone with a minimum living, while the second—to be owned privately—was to be used to produce a surplus. Everyone would have the right to obtain from his commune a plot large enough to keep a family of five people; if the commune had more land under social ownership several such plots could be asked for. In this way every citizen would have the opportunity to become wealthy and display initiative on his private land, while at the same time his welfare would be secured by the plot in his native commune. Pestel thought this plan would ensure absolute economic freedom while at the same time preventing proletarianization. He uses the existence of the village commune in Russia as an argument for the ease with which it would be possible to implement his plan.

There are interesting expositions of Pestel's plan in F. Venturi, *Roots of Revolution* (Il populismo russo) (London 1960), pp. 4–6, and *Istoriya russkoĭ ekonomicheskoĭ mȳsli* (Moscow 1958), ii. 141–60.

[2] See Semëvsky, op. cit., pp. 391–2.

be the owner in relation to the peasants and other landowners, his ownership was only a *use* of state lands. The existing situation was complicated by the fact that the communal land legally belonged to the landlord, but in future (i.e. after emancipation) the difference between the 'owners' (i.e. the nobility) and the 'users' (the peasants) would only be one of degree; the peasants would be owner-users of the communal land and the landlords owner-users of the 'land of the great commune', i.e. state land. On closer examination it is clear that from the point of view of the communal principle this solution, which still allowed the nobility the right to bequeath or divide their land as they wished, was a solution in name only. In this respect the Slavophile historical utopia, in which boyars and nobles held their land in return for services to the state, was far more consistent. Khomyakov was not, however, in the least inclined to draw any practical conclusion from such historical reflections and, like the other Slavophiles, had no desire to burden his class by the reintroduction of compulsory state service.

This inconsistency (inconsistency, that is, from the point of view of the Slavophile utopia) becomes even more striking when we examine Khomyakov's reaction to various concrete issues that demanded attention during the preparations for the emancipation act. He was not directly involved in the practical work that preceded the reforms, but tried to influence them through other Slavophiles (Samarin, Koshelëv, and Prince Vladimir Cherkassky), who were members of Drafting Commissions or provincial committees; he also took the opportunity of stating his views to the chairman of the Drafting Commissions, Ya. I. Rostovtsev. His statement 'On the abolition of Serfdom in Russia. A Letter to Ya. I. Rostovtsev' (1859) is a fascinating document which clearly reveals the class bias of his proposed agrarian solution.

Khomyakov justified the proposal to give land to the emancipated serfs as a measure to prevent a 'blood-bath in the near or at least not so distant future', which might be expected from the rapid 'proletarianization' of the countryside. Unlike Samarin and Koshelëv, however, who thought that the peasants should receive all the communal land, Khomyakov suggested they should be given about two desyatinas per person, which would have meant a reduction by more than one-third of the average peasant holding. He also urged the preservation of the village commune on the grounds of its convenience to the landlords, who would find it easier to conclude collective agreements through the *mir* (self-government of the commune), where the principle of collective responsibility would safeguard the landowners' interests. Moreover, the *mir* would help to reinforce law and order, share the burden of administration with the landlord and government, and help to collect the successive instalments of compensation. Khomyakov thought that the total amount of compensation should be settled by the government to prevent the social antagonism that might arise if the gentry had to bargain directly with the peasants, for 'driving a bargain is always accompanied by a hidden sense of hostility', especially where the transaction was not voluntary and neither side trusted the other.[1] Khomyakov also recommended that the landlords should receive the entire compensation money from the government in one payment, in order to acquire capital for investment and that the annual repayments should be demanded with the greatest severity. 'I consider it my duty to add', he wrote to Rostovtsev, 'that the annual compensation instalments should be enforced through the *mir* and with the greatest severity, through the sale of livestock, property, etc. In instances of extreme negligence it should be possible to expel whole villages to Siberia and to confiscate their land; but cases of this kind will almost certainly not occur. In this matter inexorable and seemingly cruel severity is true mercy.'[2]

The letter to Rostovtsev is an interesting commentary on Khomyakov's avowal that 'where the peasant question is concerned, he did not like utopians.'[3] In fact Khomyakov's 'practical' and 'realistic' projects were a striking contradiction of the fundamental anti-capitalist spirit of the Slavophile utopia. So far from discussing the prevention of capitalism in Russia, he showed that in practice he was merely concerned to alleviate its disadvantages to the landowning nobility; he did not consider either the possibility of applying the communal principle to the nobility, or a return to the ancient Russian system of land tenure in payment for state service; in fact he

[1] See Khomyakov, iii. 304.   [2] Ibid., p. 314.
[3] See Semëvsky, op. cit., p. 400.

had no difficulty in dismissing the interests of the idealized peasantry whenever they seemed likely to conflict with those of the nobility. A similar standpoint was adopted by the Slavophiles who served on the Drafting Commissions prior to the emancipation act. It was this that prompted the Soviet economic historian N. A. Tsagolov to suggest that the Slavophiles were primarily concerned to find peaceful forms of bourgeois development and 'were not critical of capitalism as such, but only of its Western variant'.[1]

By using the vague phrase 'Western variant', Tsagolov appears to overlook the fact that European capitalism was 'classical' capitalism and had developed in many different 'variants'. He thereby exposes the weakness of his argument which is, in fact, essentially an involuntary concession to the traditional view according to which Slavophilism was defined in terms of 'Western' and 'Russian' evolutionary paths. Although S. S. Dmitriev's interesting analogy between the Slavophiles and the 'feudal socialists'—prompted by Khomyakov's proposal for industrial artels—was criticized by Tsagolov, it is, I believe, nearer the truth.[2] The political and economic practice of the Slavophiles in no way invalidates this comparison; as the following passage from the *Communist Manifesto* shows, Marx, who had introduced the term 'feudal socialism', stressed that both the contradiction between theory and practice and the search for peaceful solutions were distinguishing features of 'feudal socialism':

What they upbraid the bourgeoisie with is not so much that it creates a proletariat, as that it creates a *revolutionary* proletariat. In political practice, therefore, they join in all the coercive measures against the working class; and in ordinary life, despite their high-falutin phrases, they stoop to pick up the golden apples dropped from the tree of industry, and to barter truth, love and honour for traffic in wool, beetroot-sugar and potato-spirits.[3]

In spite of the contradiction between their anti-capitalist theory and their practice of adapting themselves to the new

---

[1] N. A. Tsagolov, *Ocherki russkoĭ ekonomicheskoĭ mÿsli perioda padeniya krepostnogo prava* (Moscow 1956), p. 234.

[2] See S. S. Dmitriev, 'Slavyanofilÿ i Slavyanofil'stvo' in *Istorik-marksist* (1941), no. 1/89, pp. 94–5.

[3] K. Marx and F. Engels, *Selected Works* (Moscow 1969), i. 128–9.

circumstances Marx did not question the anti-capitalist views of the 'feudal socialists'. Nor are there any grounds for questioning the anti-capitalist nature of classical Slavophilism, which in this respect had a great deal in common with 'feudal socialism' in the West. The difference between the two trends was not so much a matter of ideology as of a different balance of class forces. In countries where the bourgeoisie was the ruling class, the 'feudal socialists' were able to appeal to its immediate antagonist—the proletariat—and could 'wave the proletarian alms-bag in order to rally the people to them'.[1] In backward peasant Russia, where the proletariat hardly existed, and the bourgeoisie was not a force to be reckoned with, the political balance was quite different. On the one hand the Russian 'people' (i.e. the peasantry) was still unaffected by capitalist civilization and could thus be idealized as the defender of ancient traditions barring the way to poisonous Western influences—this explains the emphasis on the 'people' in the earlier Slavophile anti-capitalist utopia. On the other hand, the ideologists of the landowning class in Russia could hardly appeal to the people (in other words the serfs), since the latter's interests, unlike those of the European proletariat, were opposed to those of the nobility. In Russia bourgeois exploitation was still an abstraction, whereas feudal exploitation was the hated reality; to shake the 'peasant's alms-bag' under these circumstances would have been tantamount to opposing the nobility as a class. This explains why the emancipation reforms (when theory became practice) forced the leading Slavophiles to choose between the betrayal of their peasant utopia or their class interests. They chose the former alternative. This is a historical fact which may have blunted the anti-capitalist edge of Slavophile doctrine but does not entitle us to question the anti-capitalist character of their *Weltanschauung* as expressed in the Slavophile utopia. It is precisely this utopian *Weltanschauung* which is the most original aspect of Slavophilism and ensures it a place in the history of ideas. It was not an accident, moreover, that the betrayal of the Slavophile utopia initiated— as we shall see—the disintegration of Slavophilism, and that *classical* Slavophilism disappeared in Russia after the reforms.

[1] Ibid., p. 128.

6

Konstantin Aksakov

KONSTANTIN Aksakov (1817–60) was certainly the most
extreme and fanatical of the Slavophiles. He wore peasant
dress and a beard in order to draw closer to the 'people'
(although, according to Chaadaev, this only led the people to
mistake him for a Persian),[1] and once made the extravagant
claim that 'Russian history is the Confession of the Universe;
to read it is like reading the Lives of the Saints.'[2] Because of his
earnest single-mindedness Aksakov has sometimes been called
the Slavophile Belinsky, although this is not, in fact, a very
discerning comment on his character. For all his 'furious consistency', Belinsky never lost contact with reality, whereas
Aksakov was a utopian idealist always ready to deny an obvious
truth in the name of 'principle'. Even in his own home, apart
from the Elagin salon, the main meeting-place of the Moscow
Slavophiles, his extravagant idealism aroused mixed feelings.
His younger brother Ivan, who was also a Slavophile, once
wrote about the difference between them: 'Unlike Konstantin
I cannot find consolation in slogans like "only the principle
matters, all the rest is just incidental." '[3]

Konstantin's father Sergeï Aksakov, author of the *Chronicle
of a Russian Family* and a Slavophile sympathizer, treated his
son with tolerant indulgence and once said about him: 'It
would be a fine thing, no doubt, if he could spend his entire life
in his present agreeable state of error, for he could hardly be
undeceived without profound and bitter disappointment; he
had better go on believing in the perfection of ancient Russia.'[4]

This is not to suggest that Aksakov's Slavophile utopia was
merely the arbitrary creation of his own fancy. Its raw material
consisted of concrete historical elements, and Aksakov's

---

[1] Herzen, *My Past and Thoughts*, ii. 273.
[2] K. S. Aksakov, *Polnoe sobranie sochineniĭ*, 3 vols. (Moscow 1861–80), i. 625.
[3] *I. S. Aksakov v yego pis'makh* (Moscow 1888), vol. ii, part 1, pp. 300–3.
[4] Quoted from V. D. Smirnov, *Aksakovÿ, ikh zhizhn' i literaturnaya deyatel'nost'*
(St. Petersburg 1895), p. 67.

attempts to paint a portrait using only elements of which he approved, and excluding everything that might throw doubt on his ideal vision, enhances rather than detracts from the value of his work for the student of the Slavophile *Weltanschauung*.

The reality that the Slavophile idealist knew best was his family, which, like those of the other Slavophiles, was steeped in old manorial traditions. In his memoirs I. I. Panaev wrote that Aksakov 'spent his whole life under his own roof and clung to it like an oyster to its shell; he could not conceive an independent life without his family background'.[1] Aksakov did not, in fact, long survive his father's death, which affected him so profoundly that he went abroad for his health and died shortly afterwards on one of the Aegean Islands. The Greek Orthodox priest who attended his death-bed is said to have been impressed by his 'saintliness'; it is true that Aksakov led a singularly quiet and virtuous life apparently immune to temptation; no woman's name, for instance, was ever connected with his.

In a certain rather broad sense of the word 'Slavophilism' was a family tradition among the Aksakovs. In his youth his father, Sergeĭ, had been a friend of Admiral A. S. Shishkov, leader of the literary 'archaists' who attacked Karamzin and other 'innovators' and modernizers of literary Russian. Shishkov and his society of 'Lovers of the Russian Word' were conservative nationalists who angrily defended the 'old style' and called for an 'indigenous and popular' literature.[2] Their rearguard action on behalf of Church Slavonic was part of a wider struggle against the secularization of social life; what had started as a dislike of gallicisms ended as an entirely political Francophobia. Belinsky called Shishkov and his followers precursors of the Slavophiles;[3] the latter did not repudiate the connection, although the admiral's main claim to fame were some linguistic monstrosities invented to cleanse Russian of non-Slavonic elements. Khomyakov wrote about him: 'We are not ashamed of Shishkov and his Slavophilism. Although his

---

[1] I. I. Panaev, *Literaturnȳe vospominaniya* (Leningrad 1950), p. 151.

[2] This 'popular' character had little in common with the romantic emphasis on 'folk' qualities. Shishkov and his followers considered Krȳlov's fables to be the most perfect realization of what they were aiming at.

[3] See Belinsky, *Poln. sob. soch.* ix. 681.

views were still vague and although his efforts were confined
to a very narrow sphere, he did a great deal of good and sowed
many healthy seeds.'[1] Sergeï Aksakov always remembered
Shishkov with gratitude and even attributed to him the virtues
of his own autobiographical trilogy written towards the end of
his life, during the flowering of Russian realism.

The statement that Konstantin Aksakov 'clung' to his home
should not be interpreted too literally. He cannot be accused of
withdrawing into family life and ignoring anything outside his
own narrow circle. Panaev's comment is only interesting in so
far as it illuminates Aksakov's characteristic way of digesting
and evaluating reality. His vision of the world was that of a
dualistic Manichean conflict of good and evil: on the one hand
there was the familiar background where one could feel 'at
home', and on the other the alien and hostile world outside.
Home included the family, the village commune, which was a
kind of extended family, and Moscow, the capital of the old
patriarchal Russia. Outside was represented primarily by St.
Petersburg, the incarnation of everything evil that had come
to peaceful Russia from the West. It is a mistake, in my opinion,
to dismiss this opposition as nothing but nationalistic xenophobia; for Aksakov the supreme value was not 'Russianness'
as such, but a community life based on a sense of emotional
fellowship. When he criticized European civilization it was on
the assumption that not only Russians but native Europeans
also felt alienated within it.

Although Aksakov's adoption of Slavophilism was influenced
and to a certain extent even determined by family traditions it
was not an entirely straightforward process. Like Kireevsky,
Aksakov went through a stage of enthusiasm for Hegelianism—
the philosophy that was to provide the groundwork for Westernism. The contribution made to Kireevsky's intellectual development by the Lovers of Wisdom was supplied, in Aksakov's case,
by the Stankevich Circle. His membership of this circle is less
surprising when we consider that he joined it at a time when it
was dominated by the thoroughgoing romantic and anti-
Enlightenment interpretation of Hegelianism from which
Bakunin and Belinsky derived their 'reconciliation' with
reality. As Aksakov had never been at odds with reality, the

[1] Khomyakov, iii. 207.

word 'reconciliation' would have meant little to him—hence Bakunin counted him among the 'aesthetes' who had not yet passed through the wearisome stage of 'reflection'.[1] Nevertheless Aksakov and the other members of the Stankevich Circle had many points of contact: Bakunin's and Belinsky's intense *Franzosenfresserei* coincided, superficially at least, with the Aksakov family's traditional Francophobia, while the passionate philosophical enthusiasm of the Moscow Hegelians and their romantic cult of friendship (which Belinsky struggled against even then, but never managed to overcome entirely) appealed to Aksakov's own unworldly nature.

In the early 1840s, when the Stankevich Circle fell apart and most of its former members went over to the Hegelian Left, Aksakov drew closer to Kireevsky and Khomyakov. Although at first he tried to combine Slavophilism with Hegelian philosophy, and to maintain friendly relations with his former associates, this proved to be impossible. The break with his Hegelian friends was soon followed by a complete break with Hegelian philosophy. The sacrifice of friendship which this profound change of outlook rendered necessary was painful to both sides.

> In 1844 [Herzen recalled later], when our differences had reached such a point that neither the Slavophiles nor we cared to go on meeting, I was walking along the street one day when I saw Konstantin Aksakov in a sledge. I bowed to him in a friendly way. He was on the point of driving by, but he suddenly stopped the coachman, got out of his sledge and came towards me.
> 'It hurts me too much', he said, 'to pass you and not say good-bye. You understand that after all that has happened between your friends and mine I am not coming to see you; I am sorry, very sorry, but there is no help for it. I wanted to shake you by the hand and say good-bye.' He went rapidly towards his sledge, but suddenly turned round. I was standing in the same place, and I was sad; he rushed up to me, threw his arms around me and kissed me warmly. I had tears in my eyes. How I loved him at that moment of strife![2]

---

[1] Ivan Aksakov relates that Bakunin 'sorted' his friends into various 'development stages' according to Hegel's *Phenomenology*: Konstantin Aksakov was at the lowest stage of *Schönseeligkeit*, Bakunin himself was at the highest stage, the 'embodiment of the spirit', and the rest of the members of the circle were at the stage of 'reflection'. See D. I. Chizhevsky, *Gegiel' v Rossii* (Paris 1939).

[2] Herzen, *My Past and Thoughts*, ii. 294.

Aksakov's farewell to Granovsky, related by Annenkov in his memoirs, was even more dramatic. Aksakov drove to Granovsky's rooms at night, 'woke him up, flung his arms around him and holding him in a close embrace announced that he had come to perform a most painful and bitter duty—to break off relations with him and bid him farewell as to a lost friend, in spite of the deep respect and love he felt for his character and personality'. Granovsky tried to convince Aksakov that there was no need to end their friendship, but his 'resolve was unshaken and he departed greatly moved and in tears'.[1]

Aksakov's opinions in the early 1840s, when he tried to reconcile Hegelian philosophy with Kireevsky's and Khomyakov's ideas, were worked out most fully in his master's thesis on *Lomonosov in the History of Russian Language and Literature* (1846). As this chapter is mainly concerned with Aksakov's mature views rather than with his evolution as a thinker, this thesis will be discussed later in chapter 7,[2] which deals with the interesting phenomenon of 'Orthodox–Christian Hegelianism'.

PHILOSOPHY OF HISTORY

The final stage of Aksakov's evolution towards Slavophilism came at the end of the 1840s. Although many of his earlier ideas had a distinctly Slavophile flavour, as was to be expected of a thinker who might be called a 'born' Slavophile, they were scattered comments rather than part of a homogeneous theory. It was only some years after his final abandonment of Hegelianism that Aksakov attempted to outline his historical views in some detail.

In an article published in 1850 Aksakov took up the theme of Russia's 'uniqueness' (*samobytnost*). 'Russia', he wrote, 'is an absolutely distinct country, not in the least comparable to the states and lands of Europe.' The differences dividing Russia from Europe had been obvious from the very beginning; unlike the European states, the Russian state had been formed not by conquest but by voluntary invitation to rule. The European states were founded on mutual hostility and authority had appeared there as a hostile force, an armed warrior band

---

[1] P. V. Annenkov, *The Extraordinary Decade*, trans. by Irwin R. Titunik (Ann Arbor, University of Michigan, 1968), p. 94.
[2] See pp. 289–300.

conquering an alien people. Therefore, Aksakov concluded, 'Western states were built on *force, slavery,* and *enmity.* The Russian state was built on *voluntary consent, freedom,* and *peace.*' This fundamental difference determined the later fate of Russia and the West.

The West [according to Aksakov], having passed from a state of servitude to a state of revolt, takes revolt for freedom, glories in it and sees servitude in Russia. Russia, on the other hand, steadfastly protects the government acknowledged by her, protects it willingly, *freely,* and therefore regards the rebel as only another incarnation of the slave who today grovels before the idol of rebellion as formerly he grovelled before the idol of authority; for only a slave rebels, but not a man who is free.

Like the other leading Slavophiles, Aksakov regarded the Schism as another factor that had influenced the divergent development of Russia and Europe. 'It seems presumptuous to put forward one's views on such an issue, but I hardly think we are mistaken to suggest that both the true and the false way of Faith fell to the lot of the country that deserved it: the former to Russia and the latter to the West.'[1] Although Aksakov's sincerity and his deep attachment to Orthodoxy cannot be doubted, it seems clear that what distinguished Russia from the West in his eyes was primarily her different origins as a state rather than her faith. In this respect Aksakov's conception differs from Kireevsky's and Khomyakov's and is perhaps closer to that of Pogodin, who identified the search for the 'idea' or 'historical principle' of a given nation with research into its beginnings and especially into the origins of its state organization. The difference between Aksakov and the older Slavophiles was not only one of emphasis, for unlike the Kireevsky brothers Aksakov accepted Pogodin's 'Norman theory' and emphasized the non-native origins of Russian statehood. On the other hand, a closer reading shows that despite this superficial similarity the two thinkers differed radically in their evaluation of the role of statehood as such. For Pogodin the state was the main creative force in Russian history, whereas the common people's role was merely one of passive obedience; for Aksakov

[1] All these quotations come from Aksakov's article 'On the Same Subject' published in 1860 (the title refers to an earlier essay entitled 'Fundamental Principles of Russian History'). Aksakov, i. 7–17.

the real creative force was the people, whose way of life he called a 'holy shrine' to be guarded by the state against external dangers. For Pogodin the essence of Russia's 'uniqueness' was a strong state apparatus, whereas for Aksakov state organization as such was something typical of the West, accepted by the Russian people merely as a necessary evil. The 'Norman theory' appealed to Aksakov just because he was far more suspicious of the state as an institution than Kireevsky and Khomyakov, and considered its non-native origins in Russia to prove that the Russian people was essentially non-political, and had sent for rulers from overseas since it was neither able nor willing to produce any itself.

Fundamental to Aksakov's conception was the distinction between what he called 'inner' and 'external' truth. The former represented 'freedom' and 'good', and the latter 'servitude' and 'evil'. For individuals, inner truth is the voice of conscience, while for society it is the sum total of values embodied in religion, tradition, and customs—in a word everything that helps to forge inner bonds based on shared moral convictions. External truth, on the other hand, is represented by the state apparatus and juridical system, by everything that constrains people through the imposition of 'external' and artificial norms. This was, of course, a repetition of Kireevsky's and Khomyakov's criticism of institutions based on rationalized and formal bonds, with the one difference that Aksakov failed to make any distinction between rational ('theoretical') and historical ('positive') law, between the rational and the organic state, or between a modern and a patrimonial bureaucracy. Rationality—that is the acceptance of conventional norms and contracts—was considered by Aksakov to be an inevitable concomitant of legal and political organization in all countries and at all times. In his view Russia differed from the West not because her state apparatus developed along other lines, but because the state system itself was not the 'principle' or chief factor in Russian social organization. When defective human nature and the requirements of defence made it necessary to introduce some kind of state organization, the Russians 'invited' their new rulers from outside in order to avoid a betrayal of the 'inner truth' by forming their own state. The tsar was granted absolute autocratic power so that the people might shun all contact with the 'external truth' or affairs of state. 'The Slavs', Aksakov wrote, 'realized that the state is a necessary evil and called it into being without confusing it with the community, with the inner moral element, the life principle that they preserved within themselves. That is why the State never fascinated our common people, and never figured in popular aspirations; that is why our people was never anxious to assume state power (the republic), but selected a monarch and handed over power to the man appointed to wield it.'[1]

In the West history took the opposite course; in view of the lack of moral concord and the enmity dividing the invaders from the tribes they had conquered the external truth inevitably became the sole authority in social relations. The peoples of Western Europe relinquished the 'inner, free, and moral social principle' and turned instead to the ideal of 'state, office (institution), centralization, and external authority'. Fascinated by the idea of the state, they themselves finally aspired too statehood—'hence revolutions, unrest, and *coups d'état*, hence the choice of the external path based on force towards an external order based on force'.

The republic, [Aksakov wrote] represents the common people's attempt to replace the monarch, to assume statehood itself; in other words, it is an attempt to abandon the path of morality and freedom, the path of inner truth, and to take the external road of state organization. The most extreme form of such aspirations can be observed in the United States; there, in a country without natural ties of kinship, without shared recollections or traditions, lacking a common faith, these fatal ambitions can find an outlet. Instead of a living people you have a state machine constructed of human beings. Human contacts assume a political character and peace and order are based not on love, but on mutual advantage.[2]

Since the 'calling of the Varangians', the main impetus in Russian history had been provided by two forces which tried to hamper each other as little as possible. These forces were the 'Land' (*zemlya*) (or, in other words, the people that lived by the light of the inner truth) and the State, which protected it and was entrusted with absolute authority in the political sphere, but in return refrained from interfering in social matters. Relations between Land and State were based

[1] Aksakov, i. 57. [2] Ibid., pp. 57–8.

on agreement and trust, and on the principle of mutual non-interference. Of its own free will the State consulted the people, who presented its point of view at the Land Assemblies (*zemskiĭ sobor*) but left the final decision in the monarch's hands. The people could be sure of complete freedom to live and think as it pleased, while the monarch had complete freedom of action in the political sphere. This mutual relationship was not guaranteed by any legal norms.

A guarantee is not required! [Aksakov insisted]. A guarantee is an evil. Where it is necessary, good is absent; and life where good is absent had better disintegrate than continue with the aid of evil. The whole power is in the idea. What good are conditions and contracts when the inner authority is missing? No contract can restrain men where there is no inner inclination. The whole power depends on moral conviction. That is the treasure possessed by Russia, for she has always believed in it and has never taken recourse to contracts.[1]

In ancient Russia, according to Aksakov, the division into Land and State, into 'people of the land' and 'state servitors' had not been a permanent one. Since the barriers between the estates were fluid and ultimately depended on service, it was always possible to pass from one category to the other. Moreover, Russia had known neither unrestricted private ownership of property nor a Western-type aristocracy. The boyars' enjoyment of their estates and their peasants' labour was merely a form of payment for state service; boyars who were not actually engaged in any official duties could be called up at any moment and were not entitled to refuse: 'they were on indefinite leave, as it were, and did not enjoy their estates for nothing'. Therefore, concluded Aksakov, 'there was not a single man in Russia who enjoyed his property for nothing (or even less as a legal privilege)'[2]—an idyllic view of medieval property relations that might well have irritated even some of his Slavophile friends.

Although in theory the principles represented by Land and State were diametrically opposed, in practice, Aksakov suggested, this opposition was mitigated by the common faith and way of life shared by both.

To the people every official, from the boyar downwards, was like one of themselves . . . Thanks to life and faith the State became as one

[1] Aksakov, i. 9–10.   [2] Ibid., p. 14.

with the Land. At times of external danger—in 1612 for instance—the Land identified its cause with that of the State. At times of peace the Land was ready to serve the State with its council, not as a legal privilege but as a social duty. Since the monarchs had no reason to fear the people, they themselves asked for this advice; they listened to the opinion of the merchants, encouraged the boyars to find out what the peasants were thinking, and in matters of special importance convened the Land Assembly at which the 'state servitors' deliberated together with the 'people of the land' and the clergy, who mediated between Land and State and helped to hold them together. As long as the Land Assembly was sitting, the State "disappeared, as it were, and the monarch then became the leader of the Land.

Moments of this kind were, of course, exceptional and if too greatly prolonged would have endangered the normal life of the Land; that is why, when 'the discussions drew to a close, the common people returned to their fields and other duties and the State again guarded the Land unaided'.[1]

These idyllic relations described by Aksakov were twice seriously disturbed; each time the culprit was the State and yet the loyalty of the betrayed Land remained unshaken. The first traitor to true Russian principles was Ivan the Terrible, whose completely unfounded suspicions of the Land turned him into a bloodthirsty persecutor of the people; in order to erect an unsurmountable barrier between State and Land he introduced the institution of the *oprichnina* (from *oprich* meaning separately, apart), an association of men in no way connected with the traditional life of the Land whose devotion to the Tsar, their sole benefactor, was boundless. Ivan himself abolished this institution a few years later, when he became convinced of the people's absolute loyalty. During the Time of Troubles which followed his death the cause of State and Land became united once again, even more firmly than before. When the enemy was driven out the history of the 'calling of the Varangians' repeated itself: as confiding as ever Russia offered the throne to Michael Romanov, entrusting him with unlimited power without demanding any guarantee in return.

To Aksakov the eighteenth century, when the boyars' Duma gained in importance and the Land Assemblies were convened

[1] Ibid., p. 15.

relatively often, represented the high-water mark of Russian glory. The Romanovs, he pointed out, were anxious to make up for the backwardness caused by the Tartar yoke and encouraged education and contacts with the West, but gradually, without betraying native Russian principles. Unfortunately this policy was soon discontinued: in the person of Peter the Great the State again betrayed the Land, introduced revolutionary changes in Russia, and from a 'necessary evil' became a *principle* that tried to force the people into brutal submission. Peter's violent reforms were far more disastrous than Ivan's bloody reign because they 'attacked the very roots of the native tree' and pushed Russia into the orbit of the West, into the path of 'external truth'. Only the common people had kept faith with the inner truth; if they too abandoned it and became imbued by the ambition to rule the State themselves, the inner truth would perish and the source of spiritual freedom dry up. However, Aksakov saw hope in the fact that 'society', the very people, that is, who had once turned their backs on native principles, had lately given birth to a new movement which proclaimed that 'Russians should be Russians, should take the Russian path, the path of faith, meekness, and the inner life; that a way of life based on these principles should be reintroduced in all its details'.[1] This new movement was struggling with its main antagonist, the pro-Western party, for dominance over the hearts and minds of the enlightened classes, was trying to call them to repentance and a return to the bosom of the common people. The outcome of this struggle would decide the future fate of the land of Russia.

This view of Russian history was established in general outline by the end of the 1840s, although in later years Aksakov developed some of its aspects in greater detail. In 1855, for instance, he applied his philosophical conceptions of Russian history to an analysis of contemporary affairs and set out a programme of political action in his detailed memorial *On the Internal Affairs of Russia* submitted to the new emperor, Alexander II, on his accession to the throne. As the first Slavophile attempt to influence government policy, this memorial is worth discussing in greater detail.

* * *

[1] Aksakov, i. 24.

In the opening pages of his memorial Aksakov set out to convince the emperor that there were no grounds for fearing a possible revolution in Russia, and that, like medicine given to a healthy man, preventive measures taken by the government were merely harmful. This fear of 'Western phantoms', he argued, sprang from a lack of knowledge of the Russian nation, which was not tempted by visions of political power. Russian history had not a single example to offer of an uprising against a legitimate ruler for the sake of political rights—any uprisings that had taken place were directed against real or imagined usurpers, in the name of the legitimate ruler. Novgorod, for instance, had ceased to rebel as soon as it recognized the authority of the Tsar; the boyars' oligarchic pretensions had failed to gain the support of the common people; and the persecuted Old Believers had sought refuge in flight or even martyrdom, but never in rebellion. Without this national spirit, Aksakov pointed out, a constitution would have been adopted long since. This was not a legalistic or servile spirit, as might be supposed by those who tried to apply the Western categories of liberalism and conservatism to Russia. Revolution and conservatism (i.e. legitimism) were both equally foreign to the Russian nation, which had absolutely no interest in politics. The common people of Russia—perhaps the only truly Christian people in the world—remembered the words of our Lord: 'Render unto Caesar the things which are Caesar's' and 'my Kingdom is not of this world'; that is why it had chosen the path of inner truth which our Saviour had pointed out when he said 'the Kingdom of God is within you.' This was the reason for its boundless obedience to authority, and why revolution was impossible in Russia.[1]

Although these quotations from the Gospels might give the impression that the Russian people was devoted to a rich contemplative and spiritual life, and had turned its back on the 'things of this world', Aksakov's 'inner truth' in fact encompassed such entirely mundane activities and virtues as agricultural labour, crafts, trade, and family life. It was not so much a spiritualization of the sacred as the elevation of the entire non-political content of social life to the level of a sacred rite—

---

[1] Quotations from the memorial are taken from L. N. Brodsky, *Rannie slavyanofily* (Moscow 1910), pp. 69–97.

a 'religious service' or 'social prayer' as Aksakov called it. When he wrote about the 'external truth', what he had in mind was something external to the community and not to the individual; tradition, for instance, was not an alien or external agency but one of the organic forces that cement society. Only the sphere of political and juridical relations was inevitably 'external' and could not be 'internalized', since it was based on convention and artificial norms.

There has been a tendency among some scholars to suggest, quite mistakenly, that Aksakov's insistence on the non-political nature of the Russian people meant that he himself shared the indifference to 'political forms' typical of many utopian socialists, anarchists, and Populists.[1] In fact Aksakov repeatedly emphasized that the choice of 'political form' was not a matter of indifference, and that the best form of government ('the least evil' rather) was an absolute monarchy. All other forms— whether democratic or aristocratic—allowed the people to participate in the government to a greater or lesser degree and therefore helped to warp its character by encouraging it to abandon the path of the inner truth. 'Political liberty cannot be called freedom', Aksakov wrote. 'Only where the people have nothing to do with the government, only where there is an absolute and unrestricted monarchy which safeguards the people's freedom in the moral sphere, only then can you speak of true freedom on earth.' True freedom, he added, is the breath of the Holy Ghost.

Aksakov did his best to persuade the new emperor to share his belief that the State was not an end in itself but existed for the people and must know what the people wanted; that freedom of speech, therefore, was not a political privilege but one of the inalienable rights of man. In pre-Petrine Russia, he maintained, this right had been fully respected; the monarch had complete liberty of action, but the Land was assured of unrestricted freedom of speech and thought. The 'people of the Land' did not impose their views on the government and regarded attendance at the Land Assemblies as an onerous duty rather than a desirable privilege. On the other hand, when the tsars sounded public opinion, it was not as a reluctant con-

---

[1] Brodsky repeats the claim that the Slavophiles were 'entirely indifferent' to all forms of government (op. cit., p. liv).

cession to popular pressure, but as a means of safeguarding the moral ties binding together State and Land. In practice, Aksakov admitted, these rules of conduct had not always been strictly adhered to, but the rules themselves were perfect, or at least the best possible. It was only in Peter's reign 'that the evil arose that is also the evil of our own times'.

In Peter's reign the State invaded the people's moral freedom, tradition, and customs. A cleavage came about between the 'people of the land' and the 'State servitors'; the upper strata of society became divorced from the people, adopted foreign dress, and even ceased to use the vernacular. The Tsar no longer needed ancient Moscow and built a new capital, St. Petersburg, which he populated with government officials who were either completely alienated from their own nation or simply foreigners; even the soil on which St. Petersburg was built was foreign soil. The Land could now be compared to conquered territory and the State to an occupying power; the emperor became a despot and the freely submissive people became slaves on their native soil. The sections of society divorced from the people—especially the nobility—became affected by political ambitions and this gave rise to a series of palace revolutions culminating in the Decembrist uprising, which represented the logical outcome of the pernicious influences coming from the West.

The genuine common people, Aksakov argued, that is the merchants, townsfolk, and above all the peasants, did not revolt, despite these drastic changes, and thus proved that loyalty was deeply ingrained in them—the thesis he had put forward in the opening sections of the memorial. Any apparent exceptions were only isolated examples of rowdyism (the Revolt of the Strettsy) or were even proof of the anti-revolutionary nature of the Russian people like the Pugachev uprising which was staged on behalf of the legitimate emperor, Peter III. After these reassuring conclusions Aksakov suddenly launched into a series of warnings and ominous prophecies. The danger of the Petrine system, he wrote, was that if the people was converted into a body of slaves one day, it might revolt the next. If it was deprived of inner freedom it was forced to aspire to external (or in other words political) freedom. The longer the system remained in force, the more terrible would be the tide of revolution which would end by engulfing Russia when she ceased to be herself. 'Russia has only endured thus long', he concluded, 'because her age-old strength has not yet given out, because she still preserves part of pre-Petrine Russia.'

In the remaining pages of the memorial Aksakov painted a very bleak picture of contemporary Russia.

The present state of the country [he told the emperor] is one of internal cleavage concealed under a shameless lie. . . . This division has provided fertile soil for the riotous weed of flattery; under the pretence that nothing is amiss it has turned respect for the emperor into blind worship and even idolatry. . . . Mutual sincerity and trust have everywhere given way to falsehood and deceit. In spite of its unlimited powers the government cannot cajole people into truth and honesty; that is impossible without a free public opinion. All men lie to one another; they are aware of it themselves, but go on lying and no one knows where it will end. Widespread demoralization and the weakening of the moral fibre of society have assumed huge proportions. Bribery and organized official plunder are terrifying. They have become so much part of the general atmosphere that not only dishonest people but men who are decent, good, and in their own way honest are often thieves too; there are few exceptions. It is no longer a personal but a social sin; a sin that illustrates the immorality of the social situation itself, of the entire system.

This desperate situation, Aksakov suggested, was the direct result of the deification of the state and its violation of the moral freedom of speech and conscience: 'If this system were to be entirely successful, it would transform man into an obedient unthinking and unprincipled animal.' The idolatrous worship of external truth deprived men of everything that made them into moral beings. The emperor alone was the only conscience and fatherland to his subjects, whose duty it was to obey him in slavish submission. As the head of the Church, the emperor was even his subjects' faith. The emperor 'is even your God, he is God on earth', was Aksakov's bitter conclusion.

In spite of this very pessimistic view Aksakov was confident that everything could easily be put right; the remedy was to understand Russia and to revert to her spiritual heritage. If the State granted the Land freedom of thought and speech, the Land would repay it with her confidence and strength. The only valid role of censorship, Aksakov thought, was to protect personal reputation. In time there should be complete freedom of speech, for in a free exchange of views the truth would prevail; to doubt this was almost impious, since God and truth were one. On the other hand, Aksakov felt it was still too early to convene a Land Assembly, since there was no unanimity among the estates. The nobility had become separated from the people, the merchants represented a curious mixture of traditional Russian and Western elements and the peasants, who had been prevented for so many years from taking an active part in the country's affairs, could have little to say after so long a period of passive silence. For the time being therefore, he suggested, the government should do no more than consult representatives of the various estates. Like the future Land Assemblies, these consultations should not be binding or regular; the government was to sound opinion and convene Assemblies whenever it thought fit.

The concluding paragraph of the memorial underlines Aksakov's main thesis: 'To the government the unlimited freedom to *rule*, which is its exclusive prerogative; to the people full freedom in their *inner and outward life* to be safeguarded by the government. *To the government the right to act* and consequently, legislative authority; *To the people the right to hold opinions* and consequently, freedom of speech.'

In a special appendix, which summarized the main points of the memorial, Aksakov repeated his conclusion but took up a more clear-cut attitude on the question of the Land Assembly; while freedom of speech was necessary right away, he wrote, the Land Assembly was required shortly; freedom of speech was essential, the Assembly was necessary and useful.

Because of several ambiguities, the textual interpretation of Aksakov's memorial presents certain difficulties. Soloviev called the Slavophiles 'archaic liberals' who were persecuted by the government for their liberalism and by the liberals for their 'archaism'.[1] This definition, which does not entirely fit Kireevsky, aptly sums up Aksakov's views, or at least the difficulties involved in their interpretation. His memorial to

---

[1] Solov'ëv used the phrase 'archeological liberals', but it is obvious that the adjective 'archeological' was intended to suggest 'archaism' and not 'archeology' in the contemporary meaning of the word; V. S. Solov'ëv, *Natsional'ÿ vopros v Rossii*, 2nd edn. (St. Petersburg 1891), p. 30.

Alexander II can be discussed both as part of the history of Russian conservatism, or of Russian liberalism, and its interpretation will differ accordingly.

If we compare Aksakov's memorial with Karamzin's classical manifesto *On Ancient and Modern Russia* we find several striking parallels between the two writers' conception of autocracy. When they wrote about 'unlimited monarchy', both meant that political power was indivisible rather than unlimited in scope; both, in effect, restricted the ruler's freedom of action to the domain of politics, which they tried to consider apart from social life as a whole; both criticized the Petrine reforms in almost identical terms (although Karamzin drew attention to their positive role in the consolidation of the Russian state); finally, both writers preached moral independence and set a personal example of courage by telling 'the truth without sycophancy or cant'.

These similarities should not, however, obscure the essential difference that while Karamzin was a conservative defending the *status quo*, Aksakov was anxious to convince the emperor of the need for change and conjured up an idyllic version of the past in order to throw a severely critical light on his own day. Where Karamzin made his appeal in the name of the landed gentry and its class interests, Aksakov spoke on behalf of the 'people' and accused the nobility of betraying 'people's principles'.

The differences become most apparent when we pass from general conceptions of 'ancient' and 'modern' Russia to concrete criticisms of the government. Apart from its general thesis, discussed in chapter 1, Karamzin's memorial contained very detailed and concrete strictures of Russia's foreign policy, legislation, and financial position. Aksakov, on the other hand, confined himself to criticism based on general principles and backed up by broad moral and historiosophical generalizations. It is clear that the first memorial was written by a realist and practical statesman, and the second by a romanticist and utopian. This would help to explain the paradoxical fact that Aksakov completely ignored the land reform issue. Unlike Karamzin he was an ardent opponent of serfdom, which he considered to be alien to the spirit of ancient Russia, though only part of the broader issue of the mutual relationship of Land and State. Although tactical considerations may have played their part in Aksakov's choice of emphasis, he was no doubt mainly influenced by his utopian faith in the possibility of rapid and radical moral rebirth once the State refrained from oppressing the Land and allowed it to live by the light of the inner truth.

Aksakov's antithesis between Land (society) and State was essentially inspired by conservative philosophy and sprang from the dislike, shared by all Slavophiles, of rationalized and therefore 'external' forms of social relations. Similar views were expounded in Germany by several historians of civilization, including W. H. Riehl, whom Samarin called one of the 'Western Slavophiles'.[1] Ivan Aksakov drew attention to this similarity and compared his brother's comments on the non-political nature of the Russian people with Riehl's statement 'Das deutsche Volk ist kein politisches Volk, sondern ein soziales.'[2] On the other hand, of course, there were also liberals of various trends who distinguished between the socio-economic and politico-juridical sphere and were in favour of reducing state intervention in social life as much as possible. This otherwise trivial circumstance explains the superficial similarity between Aksakov's definition of the state as 'watchdog of the land' and Lassalle's well-known aphorism comparing the liberal state to a night-watchman. Although the liberals' conception of society had nothing in common with the 'organic' theories of the conservatives, this did not prevent conservatives who were disturbed by the proliferation of bureaucracy from making use of liberal arguments against state interference. Liberals, on the other hand, were not averse to using conservative criticism of state centralism or to searching the past for earlier models of modern representative institutions.[3] All this serves to explain the premises of 'archaic liberalism' and suggests that there was a basis for Slavophile influence on Right-wing liberals in Russia. As will be seen later, this is not just a matter of conjecture: some of the moderate liberals active in the local self-government institutions (*zemstvos*) established in 1864 were profoundly influenced by Slavophile ideas.

[1] Samarin, *Sochineniya* (Moscow 1877), i. 401.
[2] Quoted from I. S. Aksakov, *Sochineniya* (Moscow 1886), ii. 513.
[3] The call for a parliament of the estates to act as an advisory body was an essential part of the political platform of the German conservatives in the 1830s and '40s.

I would even venture to suggest that the establishment of the *zemstvos*, one of Alexander's important liberal reforms, was partly the result of consistent Slavophile agitation.

Despite these links it is necessary to make an important reservation: Slavophile ideology (or rather certain aspects of it) may have exerted a rather limited influence on the political aims of the liberals, but it was not capable of spanning the gap between the conservative and liberal views of the world. Aksakov's 'archaic liberalism' can only be called liberal in a very general sense of the word; it had nothing in common with liberalism as a bourgeois *Weltanschauung*. This is shown by an analysis of Aksakov's ideal of social bonds, which throws an additional light on the views he expounded—not always with sufficient clarity—in his memorial.

THE IDEAL OF SOCIAL BONDS

For Aksakov the village commune represented an ideal model of social bonds. Of all the Slavophiles he was certainly the most ardent and uncritical admirer of the rural *mir*; when reading his writings one has the impression that he felt the commune was even more important than the Orthodox faith, that true Christianity, indeed, could hardly exist outside it. This curious point of view can perhaps be explained by the fact that for Aksakov the commune was not merely a historically determined form of social organization in rural Russia, but also—and perhaps even primarily—an ideal community based on the principle of genuine fellowship. Anticipating later conclusions, one might say that Aksakov's notion of the village commune corresponds to Tönnies's *Gemeinschaft*, and is therefore a theoretical and structural rather than a concrete historical category (although Aksakov himself would not have been aware of the difference). In his writings the term *obshchina* is universalized to such an extent, that in many contexts it is used to denote 'community' rather than 'village community' or commune. It is not surprising, of course, that the two terms are interchangeable, since to Aksakov the concrete Russian village commune was the most perfect incarnation of the 'community' principle as a universal norm of human relations.

The commune [Aksakov wrote] is that supreme principle which will find nothing superior to itself, but can only evolve, develop, purify, and elevate itself . . . The commune is an association of people who have renounced their personal egoism, their individuality, and express common accord: this is an act of love, a noble Christian act which expresses itself more or less clearly in its various other manifestations. Thus the commune is a moral choir and just as each individual voice in the chorus is not lost but only subordinated to the over-all harmony, and can be heard together with all the other voices—so too in the commune the individual is not lost but merely renounces his exclusivity in the name of general accord and finds himself on a higher and purer level, in mutual harmony with other individuals motivated by similar self-abnegation; just as every voice contributes to the vocal harmony, so in the spiritual harmony of the commune every personality makes itself heard, not in isolation but as part of the group—and thus you have the noble phenomenon of the harmonious coexistence of rational beings (consciousnesses): you have fellowship, the commune—the triumph of the human spirit.[1]

The nearest approach to this ideal was the Russian village commune, which, Aksakov asserted, had always been a 'rational' rather than a 'biological' association of human beings. This claim, which Aksakov justified with much erudition and inventiveness in his historical writings, was a deliberate challenge of the view, held by the Westernizing historians K. Kavelin and S. Solov'ëv, that the *obshchina* was a survival of primitive kinship relations. To Aksakov this was an attempt to minimize the *moral* role of the commune and to deny its universal significance. Mindful of his own early Hegelian training, he was unwilling to see his social ideal ranked with the 'immediately natural' half-brutish sphere of existence and was anxious to convince his opponents that the commune was governed by 'reason' and 'consciousness'. This gave rise to numerous misunderstandings: Solov'ëv, for instance, was even under the impression that Aksakov wanted to prove that the Russian village commune was based not on kinship but on contract. The latter of course protested violently against such an interpretation of his views; the Russian commune, he told Solov'ëv, 'is a manifestation of the people's thought, an expression of the national spirit, a living and not an artificial expression'; it followed from this that it was based not on contract but on 'living custom'.[2] By this Aksakov meant that

---

[1] K. S. Aksakov, i. 292.   [2] Ibid., p. 202.

the commune was not the creation of individual but of collective thought, that it was not 'invented' but arose spontaneously like every free manifestation of the human spirit. By contrast with associations based only on rational and egotistical motives, the Russian village commune looked after its members, put a brake on random and uncontrolled development, and settled controversial matters at communal councils (village meetings, folkmoots, or Land Assemblies) by word and persuasion not by force, as became beings endowed by God with reason and consciousness. This was what Aksakov meant when he spoke of the 'consciousness' of the commune, which was a quality that had nothing in common with the Western rationalism condemned by the Slavophiles. The 'rationality' of the commune was part of its moral nature, a quality which Aksakov denied to Western societies based on the 'external truth'.

Opposition to the 'kinship theory' was a new element in Slavophilism. The 'senior' Slavophiles had seen nothing wrong in tracing back the village commune to primitive kinship or tribal organization. In his *Notes on Universal History* Khomyakov had even claimed that the ties of kinship and 'natural fraternity' of the Slavonic commune were what made it superior to the 'conventional' Teutonic warrior band community.[1] In his polemic with Pogodin, Petr Kireevsky put forward a detailed and carefully argued theory of a proto-Slavonic 'kinship way of life' which he regarded as proof of the native origins of Russian statehood.[2] It was Aksakov, however, who was the most prolific publicist among the Slavophiles; hence Slavophilism came to be regarded as a doctrine whole-heartedly opposed to the 'kinship theory' although apart from Aksakov's somewhat eccentric point of view there is little evidence to justify this conclusion.

At the end of the 1850s Khomyakov was converted to Aksakov's point of view on the characteristic grounds that he had come to regard the clan organization as the embryo of the Western European aristocracy. In one of his works Riehl had related that North German and Scandinavian peasants possessed something like a coat of arms—an emblem that was associated with their homes and changed after every move. To

---

[1] Khomyakov, vii. 17.
[2] See chapter 1, pp. 58–60.

Solov'ëv this proved that the peasants were guided by material considerations (their homes) since a true coat of arms was related to a man's personal honour. Khomyakov countered by arguing that the coat of arms was only the insignia of a family, that is of a purely material blood relationship, whereas the house symbolized the family as a moral community and social unit.[1]

The fact that the decisions of the village self-government were based not on written laws but on 'conscience' enhanced the value of the village commune still further in Aksakov's eyes. His point of view was perhaps an extreme example of the romantic dislike of formalized legal codes and legislation; he accepted the law merely as a necessary evil, as an aspect of the external truth which had no place in a genuine 'community'.

The path of external truth, Aksakov wrote, is both comfortable and straightforward; 'Man's inner nature is externalized',[2] the dictates of conscience are codified, human relations become depersonalized, and free moral bonds are replaced by constraints. This path is tempting, for the human spirit is inclined to moral indolence and the law allows him to treat his duties as a purely mechanical formality.

Formal or rather external law requires an *act* to be moral within the meaning of the law, but cares not in the least whether the man himself is moral or what motives inspire the act. On the contrary, the law aspires to a perfection that would in fact make it unnecessary for a man to be moral provided he acts morally or in accordance with legality. Its aim is to establish a system perfect enough to render the soul superfluous, so that even without it men could act morally and be decent human beings.[3]

That is why 'the domination of external law in society undermines man's moral worth and teaches him to act without an inner moral impulse.' This was true of the state as well: 'The more elaborate the state apparatus, the more rapidly is man's inner world superseded by institutions and the more powerful are the fetters restricting society, even though the State appears to satisfy all its needs.'[4]

As will be readily perceived, this passage represents an attempt to come to grips with the problem of alienation which

[1] See Khomyakov, iii. 342.   [2] Aksakov, i. 249.
[3] Ibid., p. 52.   [4] Ibid., p. 249.

had engaged the other Slavophiles. The 'external truth',
Aksakov was pointing out, is an alienated truth and the process
of alienation is accompanied by increasing frustration. What
distinguished the Slavophile concept of alienation, however,
was that it concerned not individuals but the community;
according to Slavophile doctrine alienation was by definition
out of the question in a community—provided it was a genuine
one. The voice of conscience which Aksakov defended was not
individualized, but belonged to the community as a whole.
The adversaries of Slavophilism could easily have riposted by
arguing that it was total identification of the individual with
the community that led by a 'straightforward path' to 'moral
indolence'.

It would be unjust to equate Aksakov's anti-individualism
with the anti-individualism of the traditionalists and extreme
conservative romanticists, who refused to allow the individual
any natural rights. Like Fichte, Aksakov conceded to the individual the very important right to secede from a community
whose moral views he found entirely distasteful. His view of
the world could perhaps best be described as a kind of conservative anarchism: since the inner truth could not be reconciled with any external constraint, the most the ideal community
could do was to remove the dissenting individual if he himself
refused to leave voluntarily. According to Aksakov, this was
what the communes had done in ancient Russia. (He later
developed this idea in his reflections on the *izgoi*—people who
had been expelled from their commune and lacked the support
of any other community.) On the other hand Aksakov firmly
believed that individuals who wished to remain in their community ought to give up all claims to moral autonomy and even
recommended that no peasant should have the right to sue
his commune.

The peasant [he wrote] is a living particle of his commune, and as
long as he is part of it he thereby recognizes its full authority and the
irrevocable nature of its decisions. It is possible to permit an individual to leave the commune if he so wish, but so long as he remains
a member, so long does the commune represent the supreme
authority and its word the irrevocable truth. The council of the
commune (*mir*) is in effect a little *sobor*, the supreme authority which
no one can judge. It is possible to transgress its wishes by force, to

distort or reject them, but by force alone; it cannot be done on a legal basis. That is the meaning of the commune, its essence—without it it would not be a commune. The common people understand the meaning of the commune aright and express it in the saying: no one can judge the commune; God alone is its judge.[1]

This quotation tells us a good deal about Aksakov's conception of the mutual relationship of Land and State. It is clear that he considered the autonomy of the community and the autonomy of the individual to be mutually exclusive concepts. In his memorial he demanded the right of 'moral liberty' for one but not for the other; freedom was to be a function of the peasant commune as a whole and not of concrete individuals who, if they wished to enjoy individual freedom of conscience, were forced to join the despised outcasts (*izgoi*) who lived in voluntary exile, rejected by society.

This peculiar view of the relationship between individual and society explains Aksakov's dislike of decisions based on a majority vote. Indeed the principle of unanimity, which he considered characteristic of village self-government, was one of the most cherished aspects of his model society. As long as society was a spiritual community, a moral unit, as it were, then all matters affecting it ought to be settled unanimously; to accept the principle of a majority vote was to sanction discord, and therefore the destruction of the community. In practice it would have meant accepting the view that society was no more than the sum of its individual parts or that spiritual community could be reduced to a mere sum of individual views. The following quotation is a good illustration of how important the principle of unanimity was to Aksakov.

Unanimity is a complicated issue; however, it is always difficult to attain the heights of moral achievement, and most difficult of all to be a Christian; and yet this does not mean that men should give up reaching for moral heights or renounce Christianity. Moreover the common people, whose way of life is based on the principle of community and unanimity, will find it far easier to achieve this goal than those who consider a majority verdict to be legally binding or equate it with the law itself. This is not the right place for recalling how from earliest times the Slavs tried to preserve the cherished

[1] K. S. Aksakov, *Zamechaniya na novoe administrativnoe ustroĭstvo krest'yan v Rossii* (Leipzig 1861), p. 107.

principle of unanimity; how, when unable to reach agreement, they preferred rather to do battle, to inflict punishment upon themselves, as it were, for their imperfection; how in order to wrest agreement from a few they had recourse to violence, and all this in order to avoid recognizing majority decisions as legally valid, as a principle; in order not to destroy the principle of universal concord on which rested a unity of a higher order—the unity of the commune. When they could no longer agree, and discord became an established fact, they allowed it to be expressed as a fact—in enmity, battle, and agreement enforced by violence; for they never considered the possibility of accepting disagreement as a principle, nor did they confer on disagreement the status of a principle by accepting it as something normal and allowing the majority to lord it over the minority.[1]

When he wrote these words, Aksakov was not aware that the principle of unanimity was not peculiar to Slavonic communities. Khomyakov's mental horizon was perhaps less restricted, but even he attributed the English jury system with its unanimous verdict to Slavonic influence. In fact the unanimity which was binding on the Russian village self-government was only one of the survivals of the medieval *unanimitas*, an archaic form of corporate will which was gradually, though not without a lengthy struggle, superseded in Europe by the principle of majority decisions.[2] The fact that the Polish *liberum veto* was also based on the old *unanimitas* was recognized by Mickiewicz when he compared it to the unanimous vote of the cardinals' conclave or the English jury. In his *Cours de la littérature slave* Mickiewicz comments as follows on the anecdote about the ancient Slavs, which Aksakov had taken from Dietmar's *Chronicle*:

The veto was not an invention of the Poles but goes back to the beginning of Slavonic history. The right of veto existed in all Slavonic communities, where property, the law, and duties were common to all; every man benefited from a particle of the supreme laws. The

[1] K. S. Aksakov, i. 292–3.

[2] See W. Konopczyński, *Le Liberum veto. Étude sur le développement du principe majoritaire* (Paris 1930, Polish edition Cracow 1918). This work analyses in detail the process of the transition from unanimity to the majority vote in Western Europe and in Poland, but regrettably does not touch on analogous processes in Russia. See also K. Grzybowski *Teorie reprezentacji w Polsce Odrodzenia* (Representational Theories in Poland during the Renaissance) (Warsaw 1959).

communities, however, safeguarded themselves against the veto by force, coercing opponents with sticks to vote in line with majority opinion. The veto also existed in Russian and Bohemian communities.[1]

This juxtaposition of two types of 'unanimity'—that of the village commune and of the Polish gentry-state—provides an interesting illustration of the fact that this principle is capable of interpretation from different points of view. The Polish romantic poet Juliusz Slowacki praised the *liberum veto* (the converse of unanimity) as an expression of Polish individualism. To Aksakov, on the contrary, unanimity implied the individual's physical and moral submission to the community, his renunciation of the right to a separate point of view in the name of general harmony. Many other similar protests against the majority principle are to be found in early nineteenth-century romantic philosophy, and a comparison with these views will, perhaps, help to clarify the specific nature of Aksakov's ideas. However, in view of the lack of any comparative study of this kind, I must restrict myself to a few general remarks.

Opposition to the majority principle was characteristic of the conservative romanticists and was largely conditioned by their fear of the 'despotic' application of this principle during the French Revolution. In his *Appeal from the New to the Old Whigs* Edmund Burke argued that the unanimity of the English jury and the former Polish parliament was far juster than the French 'despotism of the majority'. From a defence of the rights of the minority, Burke passed to a defence of its privileges and concluded that a country should be governed by *virtute majores* rather than *numero plures*.[2] The protest of the German romantic historians (Adam Müller, Karl Ludwig Haller, and Friedrich Schlegel) against a 'mechanical majority' was part of their unconcealed apology for feudalism and defence of feudal social hierarchy. True representation, they argued, could only be through the estates; decisions based on a count of votes were always fortuitous and could not express the organic wholeness of popular aspirations. Schlegel called such

---

[1] Mickiewicz, *Literatura słowiańska*, 2nd course, lecture 5, *Dzieła* (Warsaw 1955), x. 66.

[2] E. Burke, *An Appeal from the New to the Old Whigs* (London 1791), pp. 125–9. See also L. Konopczyński, op. cit., pp. 143–7.

elections a 'lottery' and maintained that when voting the people acted merely as a sum total of abstractly equal individuals and could not therefore manifest itself as a historical personality.[1] Haller, a thinker who defended medieval particularism, criticized the centralized bureaucratic state for destroying the historically determined distinctiveness and independence of small territorial units; the majority, he argued, could not lay down laws binding on everyone, for such laws could only be the outcome of unanimous agreement.

On several points these views differ considerably from Aksakov's ideas. So far from defending aristocratic privileges, Aksakov was definitely opposed to them; although he also thought of the future Land Assembly as a body representing the estates, he hardly attached much importance to this point, since he was not primarily concerned to maintain the traditional estate barriers. When he criticized the majority principle it was not on behalf of a social hierarchy, but in the name of the fraternal unanimity of the whole land of Russia. On the other hand, there are several important similarities between Aksakov's attacks on the majority vote and those of the German conservative romanticists, and these are perhaps of greater significance. Aksakov too was definitely opposed to the principle of 'one man, one vote', since this, he thought, would be tantamount to restricting the freedom of the commune, which ought not to be bound by formalities or the opinions of stupid or immoral individuals.[2] In his attacks on election procedure he quoted a conversation with a 'certain peasant'—a kind of home-grown Schlegel—who compared elections to 'drawing lots by means of balls' and said he could not respect their outcome, which was the result of chance, not the truth.[3] For Aksakov, as for the conservative romanticists, criticism of majority verdicts was essentially criticism of bourgeois 'social fragmentation' and of 'mechanical' forms of social integration. It therefore seems reasonable to conclude that on the whole Aksakov's world-view did not go beyond the limits of conservatism; what gave it its distinctive flavour was that it was a 'people's' conservatism which based itself on archaic layers of

---

[1] See Schlegel, *Philosophie des Lebens* (Wien 1928), p. 395.
[2] See K. S. Aksakov, *Zamechaniya* . . ., p. 10.
[3] K. S. Aksakov, i. 293.

the consciousness to be found (in Samarin's phrase) in the 'peasant's hut'.[1]

Aksakov's idealization of 'unanimity' shows in a new light the numerous appeals for freedom of speech to be found in his memorial. It is clear that far from accepting pluralism in the sphere of moral beliefs, he regarded freedom of speech—freedom of argument it would perhaps be more accurate to say— as only a means of arriving at unanimous agreement. This conviction can be accounted for by the structure of the Slavophile *Weltanschauung* which idealized social bonds based on a collective consciousness—a consciousness that had not yet been exposed to processes of individuation or rationalization.

In a previous chapter an attempt was made to analyse certain aspects of Kireevsky's philosophy of history by comparing them with the sociological concepts of Friedrich Tönnies and Max Weber. An analysis of Aksakov's views makes it possible to expand this comparison by several interesting points.

In his writings Aksakov introduced a new pair of antithetical concepts—Land (or people) and State—corresponding exactly to the contradistinction Tönnies makes between *Volkstum* and *Staatstum* (the people being a natural and organic community and the state an artificial, mechanical, and external structure). Kireevsky, like the majority of the conservative romantics, thought that a state could be organic (ancient Russia for example) and therefore did not share Aksakov's approval of the 'Norman' theory; Tönnies reserved the term 'state' for the modern bureaucratic apparatus associated with the evolution of *Gesellschaft*; Aksakov universalized the characteristic features of the modern state and transferred them to statehood as such, not excluding the earliest stage of its historical development.

Another specific feature of Aksakov's conception was his stress on the tremendous role played in the community by the living word; by discussion as a means of arriving at mutual understanding and unanimous agreement. Here too there is a similarity with Tönnies who described language as 'the living understanding both in its content and in its form'[2] and wrote that mutual understanding (*consensus*), community of thought

---

[1] Samarin, *Sochineniya*, i. 401–2.

[2] F. Tönnies, *Community and Society*, part 1, para. 9.

and feeling, and *concord* (*Eintracht*) were the basis of *Gemeinschaft*.

Both Aksakov and Tönnies laid stress on speech as an organ of 'living understanding' and contrasted it with the method of settling disputes by an appeal to written statutes. For Tönnies state legislation was a form of corporate will typical of *Gesellschaft*, which tended to drive out tradition, common law, and folkways. Aksakov equated state legislation with the law as such, and opposed it as part of the external truth, which appealed to abstract regulations rather than the 'living understanding' represented by tradition, custom, and the family.

When applied to the juridical sphere, Aksakov's antithesis between the inner and external truth corresponds to Weber's differentiation between 'substantially rational' justice (the 'Khadi-justice') and 'formally rational' justice.[1] The former is judgement according to conscience and backed by ethical and religious norms, while the latter implies a rational judicial system based on a strict and universally valid legal code. It is characteristic of pre-rational communal societies (Weber's *Vergemeinschaftung*) that they dispense justice according to 'substantially rational' principles, of which the jury system is a survival. As will be seen from this brief comparison, Aksakov's theories can be interpreted (in Weberian categories) as a consistent criticism of bureaucratic legalism from a conservative standpoint, combined with a romantic idealization of archaic institutions and old, pre-rational forms of social consciousness.

THE PEOPLE'S UTOPIA

The only authority which Aksakov cited in support of his communal ideal was that of timeless morality, and his defence of Christianity was along similar lines. When he argued against the Hegelian concept of historical necessity (in a polemic with S. Solov'ëv) he did so in the name of 'eternal truth', rather than any new interpretation of the historical process. 'Istina ne vremenshchik i ot vremeni ne zavisit' ('Truth is not a time server and does not depend on time'), he wrote in an apt aphorism.[2] Kireevsky and Khomyakov had also laid stress on the supra-historical and timeless virtues of ancient Russian

---

[1] See R. Bendix, *Max Weber. An Intellectual Portrait* (Garden City, New York 1960), pp. 387–411. [2] K. S. Aksakov, i. 174–5.

principles, and argued against Hegelian 'necessitarianism', but in Aksakov's approach there is a subtle shift of emphasis perhaps hardly noticeable at a casual reading. Whereas in the writings of the 'senior' Slavophiles utopian motifs were carefully subordinated to an over-all conservative historicism, Aksakov, for all his enthusiasm for historical studies, gave precedence to a sentimental and moralizing utopia which he set up in opposition to 'history' as a truly Christian and eternal 'inner truth'—the 'kingdom not of this world' of the Gospels. This was recognized by G. Florovsky when he wrote that the tragedy of Slavophilism was that it attempted to 'find a way out of history', to take refuge in the village commune from the hurly-burly of politics.[1] Although this comment is not perhaps an entirely fair description of Slavophilism as a whole, it aptly sums up one of the most characteristic aspects of Aksakov's *Weltanschauung*, in which classical (i.e. anti-historical) utopianism played an essential role.

Aksakov's utopianism was, I believe, closely related to his fanatical 'folk-mania', which set him apart even from the other Slavophiles. Ivan Kireevsky was no doubt thinking of Aksakov when he wrote his lengthy epistle 'To my Moscow Friends' (1847), in which he expressed his concern at the habit of identifying the 'common people' with the entire nation.[2] Koshel'ëv even went so far as to attack the cult of the common people, who, he argued, had no claim to universal significance in Russia apart from its role as a carrier of Orthodoxy.[3] While Slavophilism as an ideology attempted to bridge the gap between the conservatism of the ancient landed nobility and that of the peasantry, within the movement there was room for different shades of opinion. One might say that Ivan Kireevsky still had both feet firmly planted on the nobility's side of the bridge, while Aksakov came closest to the peasantry's side.

In his historical writings Aksakov's 'folk-mania' expressed itself in violent attacks on the 'étatist' school, which identified the history of Russia with that of the Russian state and upper

---

[1] See Florovsky, *Puti russkogo bogosloviya*, pp. 251–2.

[2] Kireevsky, ii. 217.

[3] This statement was formulated by Koshelëv as a reproach against Ivan Aksakov (see A. G. Dement'ev, *Ocherki po istorii russkoĭ zhurnalistiki 1840–1840 godov*, p. 396). Koshelëv, it is worth noting, thought Ivan Aksakov inspired greater confidence than his brother Konstantin.

classes. He justly accused S. Solov'ëv of overlooking the common people in Russian history,[1] and demanded that research
be undertaken into the history of the peasantry (a demand he
himself partially met); he also vindicated the role of oral
traditions as an important source of historical information, and
was as great an enthusiast of folklore as Peter Kireevsky.
Aksakov's views influenced such professional Slavophile
historians as A. N. Popov and in particular I. D. Belyaev,
author of a valuable pioneering study, *The Peasants in Russia*.[2]
It might seem, therefore, that his theories added a new dimen-
sion to historical writing; this was the conclusion arrived at by
N. Rubinstein, who wrote that the historical views of the
Slavophiles (which he analysed largely on the basis of Aksakov's
writings) represented a 'healthy reaction' against the 'étatist'
school and that allowing for a certain modernization of their
terminology, it was possible to see a parallel between their view
of the law and the Marxist interpretation of the juridical system
as part of the 'superstructure'.[3]

There is certainly a good deal to be said for this point of
view, but only as far as the 'senior' Slavophiles are concerned.
As another N. Rubinstein has shown in his interesting study of
Russian historiography[4] quoted in a previous chapter, Aksakov's
work presents a peculiar paradox: although he opposed the
'étatist' school, he based his own historical writings on an
extremely simplified version of the political history taught by
Karamzin and Pogodin. This was the inevitable outcome of his
abstract distinction between Land and State as inner and
external truth. By positing that the moral greatness of the
Russian people lay in its refusal to take part in politics, he was
forced to eliminate the people from political history (except
at times of national danger, as in the year 1612). The common
people therefore existed outside history, as it were, and the *mir*
(a word that means both the 'village commune' and the
'world') represented its entire universe. Having accepted this
point of view, Aksakov voluntarily restricted his intellectual

[1] K. S. Aksakov, i. 253–4.

[2] I. D. Belaev, *Krest'yane na Rusi* (Moscow 1860).

[3] N. Rubinstein, 'The Historical Theory of the Slavophiles and its Class Roots'
in *Russkaya istoricheskaya literatura v klassovom osveshchenii*, ed. by M. N. Pokrovsky
(Moscow 1927), pp. 74–5.

[4] N. L. Rubinstein, *Russkaya istoriografiya*, pp. 278–9.

horizon by confining his attention to the *mir*. Since the closed
and autarkic peasant commune could hardly be the basis of a
new interpretation of Russian history, it provided instead the
raw material for a retrospective, Christian people's utopia—a
timeless moral ideal by which concrete historical reality was
to be judged. It is along these lines that we must interpret
Aksakov's statement (made in his polemic against S. Solov'ëv),
that 'It is not the sequence of phenomena and historical forms
that should be the basis for an understanding of history but
rather, on the one hand, the ideal of an all-embracing truth,
since all historical manifestations must be defined by their
relationship to this truth, and, on the other, the people's principle by which history is imbued.[1] Aksakov expressed this idea
even more forcefully in his arguments against the concept of
historical progress; true progress, he maintained, could only
be progress towards the *truth* and not mere forward movement
which did not take into account the path taken; a historical
path could be false, for it was not the path that should determine the ideal, but the ideal the path.[2]

One of the most extreme examples of Aksakov's 'folk-mania'
is his play *Prince Lupovitsky, or a Visit to the Country*, written in
1851. For all its *naïveté* and clumsiness, this play is worth discussing as an extreme example of the anti-aristocratic implications of Slavophile ideology.

When the play opens Prince Lupovitsky is travelling from
Paris to his family estates in order to devote himself to the welfare of his peasants. He hopes to Europeanize them, to spread
'enlightenment', inspired by the humanitarian belief that not
only Europeans but Russian peasants too are 'human beings,
so to speak'. He is full of goodwill and rejects the advice of the
Westernizer Salutin, who first questions the sense of the whole
enterprise and then advises him to 'enlighten' his peasants with
an 'iron hand', like Peter the Great. On arrival the Prince
delivers an absurd speech, telling his peasants that he intends
to share with them the 'moral treasures' and fruitful ideas he
himself has acquired in the West. As it happens, the roles are
reversed: in conversations with the wise commune *starosta*
(headman), Anton, the self-styled teacher comes to realize that

---

[1] K. S. Aksakov, i. 174.
[2] See Brodsky, *Rannie slavyanofily*, pp. 111–12.

he has much to learn from the people and is forced to exclaim: 'Je suis battu, complètement battu.'

In his first conversation with Anton, Prince Lupovitsky admonishes him on the need for religious piety, although it appears that he himself has no real understanding of either faith or liturgy. Later the prince advises the *starosta* to organize a popular festival and procession and to use the proceeds for the relief of the poor. Anton's reply is as follows: 'Then a man, dear master, is to give alms to the poor not for the Lord's sake, but for his own pleasure? What merit is there in that? How does the soul benefit by it?'[1]

The prince, very much taken aback, replies that there are certain benefits involved; Anton rejects the benefits, since they entail harm to the soul. The peasants, he informs his master, think of charity as something holy, and make the sign of the cross when they give alms; the poor, too, prize the goodwill of the giver, his compassionate 'sigh from the soul', more highly than the alms themselves; therefore good should be good and should not be confused with noise and dancing. Since the prince can produce no counter-arguments he has to concede once more: 'Je suis battu, tout à fait.'[2]

The climax in this confrontation of two contrasting worlds is the following scene (quoted in its entirety) in which the prince tries to give Anton a lesson in personal hygiene.

Prince: Just look how dirty your hands are; what a difference when you compare them to mine. You should be ashamed of yourself.

Anton: Who should be ashamed of himself, dear master?

Prince: You of course.

Anton: Oh no. We have to grub in the dung, so what do you expect. Your delicate hands, dear master, are white, because ours are black—and I wish you joy of it.[3]

The prince has several further suggestions to make: for instance that the peasant women ought to change their stockings every time they get wet and that their husbands should put on European dress. Each time Anton emerges victorious from the

[1] K. S. Aksakov, *Knyaz' Lupovitsky ili priezd v derevnyu* (Leipzig 1857), p. 57.
[2] Ibid., p. 69.
[3] Ibid., p. 62.

argument. The unfortunate 'enlightener's' final summing up is: 'il a toujours raison'.

Apart from conversations of this kind, which make up the bulk of the play, there is also a subsidiary love interest involving the orphan Andreï and Anton's daughter Parasha. Andreï hesitates to declare his love, since he expects to be conscripted into the army. He is saved by the decision of the village commune, for according to ancient custom the *mir* cannot 'wrong an orphan'. However, another peasant must be found as a substitute for Andreï, and tradition says that the choice should fall on Anton's household, where there are the largest number of sons. The peasants are sorry for the good old man and in the end the commune decides to collect money in order to redeem the recruit. The prince is enchanted by this generosity and exclaims: 'Mais c'est sublime, c'est beau, ca!... Quel peuple!'[1] The play ends happily: the prince, who knows about Andreï's love for Parasha (his valet Jerôme was beaten by Andreï for attempting to press his attentions on her) plays matchmaker and unites the happy couple. In his last monologue he calls out: 'When I leave here it will be with greater esteem for the people! Je vous estime, monsieur le people!'[2]

Aksakov's article 'The Public and the People', published in 1857 in the Slavophile periodical *Hearsay* (*Molva*), covers the same ground as *Prince Lupovitsky* and provides an excellent commentary to the play.

The public [Aksakov wrote] imports thoughts and feelings, Mazurkas and Polkas, from overseas; the people draws its ideas from a native spring. The public speaks French, and the people speaks Russian. The public wears German dress and the people Russian dress. The public follows Parisian fashions and the people observes its Russian customs. The public (or at least the majority) eats meat on fast-days, whereas the people keeps the fast. The public sleeps, when the people has long since risen to start work. The public works (it shuffles its feet across the dance floor), while the people sleeps or is already rising in order to work once more. The public despises the people; the people forgives the public. The public is a bare hundred and fifty years old, but no one can tell the people's age. The public is a passing phenomenon, the people is eternal. Both among the public and the people you will find gold and mud; but

[1] Ibid., p. 83.   [2] Ibid., p. 87.

among the public there is mud even in the gold, whereas among
the people there is gold even in the mud. The public leads a
worldly life (society, balls, etc.); the people, on the other hand,
has its *mir* (village assembly). Both public and people have their
epithets: we call the public *honoured*, the people, on the other hand,
is known as *Orthodox*.[1]

Aksakov's essay caused a tremendous outcry in government
circles. The Minister of Education, A. S. Norov, wrote:
'Epithets like this can only help to stir up hostility between the
various social estates. To present the lower orders as a pattern
of all possible virtues and the upper classes as an example of all
possible deficiencies and moral weaknesses is harmful, and
pseudo-intellectual paradoxes of this kind are likely to have
fatal consequences. Particularly at the present time. . . .'
Count N. Grabbe was even more emphatic and called the
article 'a burning fuse thrown into a cellar full of gunpowder;
in our uneasy times that is more than a mistake'.[2]

These comments, which now strike us as a historical curiosity,
reflect the genuine fear of Slavophilism among higher tsarist
officials. This uneasiness, which is difficult to understand today,
was inherited from the previous reign and disappeared completely when a number of Slavophiles (Koshelëv and Samarin
among them) became active in the Drafting Commissions. At
the beginning of Alexander's reign suspicion of Slavophile
intentions was still strong enough, however, to lead to re-
pressions: since the emperor agreed with Norov's point of view,
the publishers of *Hearsay* were cautioned and the periodical was
shortly afterwards closed down.

In his *Memoirs* Koshelëv describes an entertaining incident
to round off this story. When the Minister of Education, Norov,
met Aksakov in person for the first time, he hastened to inform
Koshelëv 'with a feeling of special satisfaction': 'I have met
K. Aksakov. I expected to find a bear, or even a tiger, but he
turned out to be very affable and even good-natured, I should
say.'[3]

Aksakov's *Comments* on the land reforms, published posthumously in Leipzig in 1861, form an interesting and original

---

[1] L. N. Brodsky, op. cit., pp. 121–2.   [2] Ibid., pp. 104–5.
[3] A. I. Koshelëv, *Zapiski* (Berlin 1884), p. 87.

supplement to his views on the commune. According to the publisher's introduction, these *Comments* were written in 1859, that is before the proclamation of the Emancipation Act on 19 February 1861, but as the draft proposals attacked by Aksakov were almost all included in the final version of the decree his criticism could still be considered topical.[1]

Judging by a letter written to Khomyakov towards the end of 1857, Aksakov regarded the proposed emancipation of the serfs with mixed feelings.

The nobility [he wrote] will be relieved of its function as gaoler—I congratulate them with all my heart—but the peasants will not be discharged from their prison; they will go from one prison to another; will it at least be a better one? The only good thing is that this time it will be a prison shared by all. But I doubt if life in it will be any better. On many estates, especially those farmed by tenants, the authority of the landowner was like a glass dome which allowed the peasants to continue their independent and free way of life without fear of the police and above all without the oppressive guardianship of the government, which the state and apanage peasants know so well. The ancient Russian social system has been preserved in its entirety in many tenant estates, where frequently men have not set eyes on a landowner for a hundred years. Your own estate in Vologda is the best example of this. Now all these glass domes will be taken off and the peasants will feel the full weight of state institutions and state tutelage.[2]

Aksakov devoted his *Comments* largely, or rather entirely, to a defence of the village commune as a self-governing unit secure from the interference of both state and nobility. Purely economic matters were of lesser importance, he wrote with disarming candour; 'When the issue of larger or smaller allotments of land, or the value of estates is under discussion, then, to begin with, I know very little about such matters and furthermore, they are not all that important. But where the Russian people's soul is concerned, its vital principle—the village communal principle, the *mir*, the village assembly—where those are concerned I am something of an expert and cannot remain silent.'[3] Since he was as ready to overlook the economic interests of the nobility as those of the peasantry, this comment

---

[1] See K. S. Aksakov, *Zamechaniya* . . ., p. v.
[2] Ibid., p. 2.
[3] Ibid., p. 7.

can hardly be dismissed as insincere. (V. Semëvsky, who was always very quick to sense any discrepancy between public declarations and private actions on the peasant question, apparently had good grounds for thinking that Aksakov, unlike the other Slavophiles, was in favour of emancipation without compensation.)[1] It is worth stressing the point that Aksakov's *Comments* were an angry protest against plans to transform the commune into a useful administrative tool for the administration and large landowners, and that his criticism of the government proposals also applied to the Slavophiles on the Drafting Commissions, who were in full agreement with the official line.

The administration's proposals, Aksakov wrote, destroyed the independence of the commune and 'shackled it hand and foot'.[2] They attempted to decide when a commune was a commune, introduced the alien principle of majority decisions, and transformed the village assembly into a pitiful imitation of gentry elections. A commune presided over by a *starosta*, counting votes and taking majority decisions, was not a *mir*—this kind of *mir* could be found in any club, the English Club for instance or the Gentry Club;[3] the fear that the decisions of the commune might not be legally valid was nonsense. 'Don't worry', Aksakov pointed out ironically. 'The commune has a long history; we have had self-styled tsars, but we have never yet had a self-styled *mir*.'[4] The mania for regulating and introducing 'order' at every step was fatal to everything vital, for life itself was 'disorder' from the bureaucratic point of view.[5] Every commune should administer its own justice; no matter whether the court was run by an elected judge or by the elders, there ought to be no outside interference.[6] 'Give people a chance to do something by themselves', Aksakov pleaded. 'You are not dealing with cattle, after all, but with the people, who have a much better understanding of social matters than you, members of the honourable gentry assembly.' He pointed out that although the government agreed in theory that the landowner could not be placed in authority over the commune, and ought not to interfere in its affairs, in practice it hedged about

---

[1] V. I. Semëvsky, *Krest'yanskiĭ vopros v Rossii v XVIII i v pervoĭ polovine XIX veka* (St. Petersburg 1888), p. 418.

[2] K. S. Aksakov, *Zamechaniya . . .*, p. 101.

[3] See ibid., p. 13.   [4] Ibid., p. 14.

[5] Ibid., p. 42.   [6] Ibid., p. 108.

this principle with a large number of reservations and turned the landowner into 'a kind of supervisor and teacher of the village'.[1] To Aksakov all these steps represented a crime against the people, a death blow to the vitality of the Russian way of life, and the annihilation of the last stronghold of Russian liberty.

Aksakov's own proposals in the *Comments* included the establishment of *okrugi*—self-governing units composed of several communes which were to act as buffers between the peasants and the State. The government would make its wishes and requirements known to the officials of the *okrugi* and the latter would pass them on to the individual communes. How the government's wishes were to be carried out, was to be left entirely to the peasants: the State decided *what* was to be done and the peasants decided *how* it was to be done.[2] Aksakov insisted that the *okrugi* had no authority over the communes, but were only empowered to act as intermediaries and to take decisions affecting all their members, such as the erection of churches (on the whole the boundaries of the *okrugi* were to coincide with parish boundaries). In all matters affecting a particular village the supreme authority and sovereign power was to be vested in the commune, whose decisions were to be final.[3]

Aksakov found a certain difficulty in dealing with the problem of corporal punishment. Although in principle he opposed it as a relic of Tartar rule and therefore alien to the Russian spirit, he could hardly agree to its statutory abolition, as this would violate the commune's right to self-government.[4] The commune, he argued, was a moral organism, unlike the State, whose mechanical structure made the external interference of the law both acceptable and natural; its evolution ought therefore to be gradual and autonomous, and the abolition of corporal punishment should be the outcome of an 'inner process', of moral evolution without coercion.[5] It is worth adding that in this particular instance Aksakov's anxiety was unfounded, as the authorities had no intention of restricting the freedom of action of the commune in this domain. As a gesture of respect for common law peasants were not to benefit

---

[1] Ibid., pp. 10, 114. [2] See ibid., p. 36.
[3] See ibid., pp. 106–7. [4] See ibid., pp. 81–5. [5] See ibid., p. 85.

from the provisions of the new act and continued to be liable to corporal punishment until the revolution.

It is a characteristic fact that scholars who have studied the Slavophiles' attitude to the emancipation reforms have almost invariably overlooked Aksakov's *Comments*.[1] The reason for this is to be sought, no doubt, in the complex nature of the problem. Aksakov's views cannot be dismissed with the generalization that he defended the commune as an institution facilitating the collection of taxes or preventing the exodus of peasants from the countryside, thus ensuring a source of cheap labour for the large landowners. Nor can they be neatly filed under the heading of aristocratic conservatism or one of the versions of the 'Prussian' road to capitalism. It is only by comparison with the conservative elements in Populism that Aksakov's place in the history of Russian social thought can be seen in perspective. Unfortunately Marxist scholars have tended to overlook this link on the erroneous assumption that there could be no points of contact between Slavophilism, the ideology of the gentry, and Populism, a peasant ideology (or an expression of the point of view of the *raznochintsy̆*, which reflected the interests of the peasants). It may therefore be found fruitful to compare Aksakov's views with those of the historian A. P. Shchapov, an enthusiastic admirer of ancient Russia, whose theories of Russia's historical development were—to quote a Marxist point of view—'the best historical justification of Russian Populism'.[2]

Afanassy Prokof'evich Shchapov, son of a Siberian Orthodox deacon and a Buryat peasant woman, led a very different life from that of the Slavophile thinker. His student days at an Irkutsk seminary, where he was constantly hungry, eaten by lice, beaten, and humiliated, cannot be compared to the comfortable existence of Aksakov, who spent his formative years in a highly cultured 'nest of gentle folk'. And yet both these men were united later by their fanatical love of the Russian countryside which became sublimated in Shchapov's memory by contrast with the wretched reality of his seminary. Like Aksakov,

[1] See N. A. Tsagolov, for instance, *Ocherki russkoĭ ekonomicheskoĭ mȳsli perioda padeniya krepostnogo prava* (Moscow 1956); or *Istoriya russkoĭ ekonomicheskoĭ mȳsli* (Moscow 1958), vol. i, part 2.

[2] See A. Sidorov's discussion of Shchapov in *Russkaya istoricheskaya literatura v klassovom osveshchenii*, p. 312.

Shchapov created an idyllic picture of an ancient Russia betrayed by the upper classes and preserved in flawless perfection in the peasant commune. As a student at the Kazan Theological Academy he spent seventeen hours daily at his narrow desk eagerly absorbing the spirit of 'communal freedom' and 'communal socialism' from ancient documents and chronicles. He was also an ardent reader of Slavophile periodicals and 'keenly kept track of everything that was produced by their adherents'.[1]

Like Aksakov, Shchapov based his interpretation on the distinction between Land and State as two historical forms of Russian national life. The State was the embodiment of a dry and abstract idea, while the people was a living organism whose basic cells were the communes. In his article 'The Village Community' (1862) Shchapov wrote:

The age-old, immortal, and everlasting peasant commune, the mainstay of the Russian world, is the ancient warp and original model of our self-development. In former bygone times of free historical creativity our people, by its own united and unaided effort and legendary strength, built the rural assembly system on the popular and communal foundations of people's councils and people's self-government. In those days the people was brought up in the spirit of the *mir*: the communal spirit became second nature to it, transfused its whole being, became a living and fertile principle, the creative strength of our entire self-development. That is why the *commune* has so much vitality and is so enduring. The *mir*, which is the core, warp, and architectural foundation of unhampered, popular self-government of the Land based on assemblies, survived untouched by all the stormy epochs in our history. The municipal acts of Peter the Great and the municipal statutes of Catherine II distorted, marred, and broke up the municipal commune and transformed the towns into guild and administrative corporations. But the core of the free and popular rural assembly system created by the people itself survived in the mighty peasant *mir*, and found its mainstay in the village commune.[2]

This quotation—one of many—sums up Shchapov's entire philosophy of Russian history. The examples he used to illustrate his interpretation were taken mainly from the story of the

[1] N. Y. Aristov, *Afanasy Prokof'evich Shchapov* (*Zhizn' i sochineniya*) (St. Petersburg 1883), p. 30.
[2] A. P. Shchapov, *Sochineniya* (St. Petersburg 1906), i. 762.

popular movement of land settlement in the new territories and the history of the Old Believers, whom he considered to have preserved the most genuine and popular form of Orthodoxy, uncorrupted by state influence. Shchapov also paid special attention to the Land Assemblies and frequently used the term *sobornost'* to describe the principle of 'people's self-government on the land'. His ideas bear a strikingly close relationship to Slavophilism or, more accurately, to the historical theories and 'people's utopia' of Konstantin Aksakov.

Shchapov himself was aware of this resemblance and once he had gained recognition in progressive circles did his best to ward off any suspicions of Slavophile sympathies. In liberal circles Slavophile ideas were dismissed at best with indulgent irony, as a sign of intellectual backwardness.[1] Nevertheless Slavophile ideas seeped into Populist ideology, both directly and indirectly; anarchist elements, as well as what Lenin called the Populists' characteristic 'economic romanticism',[2] contributed a specific flavour to the Populist idealization of the self-governing commune. Another striking example of the influence of Slavophile thought on Populism is the publicist G. Z. Eliseev,[3] who stressed the 'distinctiveness' of Russian statehood and civilization and, like Kireevsky and Khomyakov, attributed this primarily to Russia's isolation from the classical tradition and above all from Roman juridical thought. He painted an idealized picture of the 'rural' and 'folk' system obtaining in ancient Russia which had escaped the ill effects of individualism, the Roman concept of private property, Western feudalism, and aristocracy. The difference between Shchapov and Eliseev was mainly one of emphasis: Shchapov, whose chief works were published in the late 1850s and early '60s, set up his retrospective utopias in opposition to state centralism and serfdom; for Eliseev, whose articles appeared in the first three decades following the Great Reforms, the chief enemy

---

[1] Shchapov's biographer writes: 'Although Afanasy Prokof'evich shared and indeed constantly propagated the views and convictions of the Slavophiles, he did not consider himself to be a member of their movement or a supporter of their original doctrine; sometimes he even seemed to be afraid lest he be called a Slavophile.' N. Y. Aristov, op. cit., p. 44.

[2] See Lenin, *A Characterization of Economic Romanticism* (1897).

[3] See B. P. Koz'min, *Iz istorii revolyutsionnoĭ mȳsli v Rossii* (Moscow 1961), pp. 68–9.

was capitalism, and he therefore contrasted 'ancient Russian principles' with the 'moloch of plutocracy' and liberal economic doctrines.

During his Populist period Plekhanov was strongly influenced by Shchapov's ideas and himself wrote that 'if they were not the basis of Populism, they at least represented an important contribution to its theories'.[1] In 1880, in an article expounding the programme of the *Cherny Peredel* (Black Soil Redistribution) party, Plekhanov summed up the history of Russia as a 'tragic story of the life-and-death struggle of two diametrically opposed principles of social organization: the popular-communal and the state-individualistic principles'.[2] When he wrote these words he can hardly have been aware that one of the sources of this interpretation of Russian history, which he had borrowed from Shchapov, was the distinction between two opposing 'principles' made in ths 1840s by a utopian thinker who was certainly hostile to anything smacking of revolution.[3]

In this discussion of Aksakov's 'Populism' and the elements in his thinking that distinguish him from the other Slavophiles, it may be found interesting to confront his 'people's utopia' with the Christian anarchist utopia of Count Leo Tolstoy. Like Tolstoy, Aksakov tried to span the gap between the ideology of the conservative landed gentry and that of the patriarchal peasantry, but unlike Tolstoy he was unable to break with the old manorial civilization and official religion. His views might perhaps be called an intermediate link between two ideologies defending patriarchal Russia: between the conservative and Orthodox Christian romanticism of Kireevsky and the moralizing and anarchistic Christian Populism of Tolstoy.

When we compare the anarchistic elements in Aksakov's and Tolstoy's doctrines, we find certain striking similarities; in contrast to Kireevsky, both writers dismissed all forms of statehood as 'the principle of evil, of eternal coercion' (Aksakov); in contrast to Bakunin and the Revolutionary Populists, both

[1] Plekhanov, *Sochineniya*, 2nd edn. (Moscow–Petrograd, n.d.), ii. 10.

[2] Ibid., i. 111.

[3] Several years later, when Plekhanov had moved towards Marxism, the connection between Shchapov's ideas and those of the Slavophiles appeared quite obvious to him. See his article on Shchapov written in 1883; *Sochineniya*, ii. 10–20.

preached a 'Christian' and anti-revolutionary anarchism which restricted itself to moral opposition to the dictates of the State and even appealed to the consciences of government leaders.[1] Aksakov, however, could not bring himself to criticize the state as an instrument of social oppression; his 'anarchism' was pale and abstract compared with Tolstoy's violent and radical, almost 'nihilistic', criticism of the state apparatus in his day.

In the religious sphere the similarity between Aksakov and Tolstoy is perhaps less obvious, but should not be overshadowed by the fact (important though it is) that Aksakov idealized Orthodoxy, whereas Tolstoy was the last great heretic, a passionate and unswerving denouncer of the official Church. For both writers religion was primarily evangelical and moralistic, and, unlike the conservative romanticists, both thought that the primitive peasant commune came closer to being a true model of Christianity than the Church as a historical force. This was linked to a moralizing anti-historicism which Tolstoy had adopted as a conscious programme and which also emerges clearly in Aksakov's writings, even though their author was not always fully aware of it. Both thinkers were absolutists in ethics and epistemology, and both rehabilitated *postulative* thinking (like the Populist 'subjective sociologists') and judged history according to a moral ideal rather than the ideal by historical standards. This point of view entailed not only the negation of Hegelian historicism and the evolutionary theory of progress (a point on which Aksakov and Tolstoy were in full agreement), but also the negation of the conservative historicism of the romanticists. As might have been expected, Aksakov could not be consistent on this last point: unlike Tolstoy he rejected the 'organic' nature of history, but postulated 'organicity' as an essential constituent of his social ideal.

Another aspect of Aksakov's and Tolstoy's moralism was their common dislike of aestheticism.[2] According to Aksakov the view of aesthetic values as autonomous was a pagan ten-

---

[1] On Tolstoy's 'Christian anarchism' see V. F. Asmus, *Mirovozzrenie Tolstogo, Literaturnoe nasledstvo* (Moscow 1961), vol. lxix, part 1.

[2] An extreme example of Aksakov's anti-aestheticism is his description of Ivan the Terrible as an 'artistic nature', a man who was under the spell of external beauty, which might be called amoral since it does not always coincide with goodness. Ivan's conduct was not influenced by moral dictates but by the aesthetic ideal of a powerful ruler (Aksakov, i. 167–8).

dency characteristic of the West but quite alien to ancient Russia, which valued simplicity and 'inner beauty' and rejected the temptation of outward splendour. This belief was reinforced by a certain universalistic egalitarianism—an element in Aksakov's ideology which clearly distinguishes him from the German conservative romanticists and brings him closer to Tolstoy's philosophy. Both thinkers were sworn enemies of the aesthetic cult of diversity and uniqueness which served as a justification of social barriers. What distinguished the common people from the privileged sections of society in Aksakov's eyes was that it had no distinct features, no separate character; a man of the people was simply called a 'man' or a 'Christian' (*kristianin*), for he had no other titles or distinctions. 'Oh, how rich is that poverty!', Aksakov wrote. 'The people, that is known by no other name than *man* or *Christian*, is the ideal of a human and Christian society'; the upper classes, he concluded, would also merge with the people when they forgot the differences dividing them from other men, when they became conscious of nothing but their humanity and Christianity.[1] It is, of course, still a far cry from these ideas (which coexisted uneasily with Aksakov's undoubted nationalism) to Tolstoy's condemnation of all barriers dividing human beings. Aksakov's views, after all, did not obviously contradict those of the 'senior' Slavophiles, who also regarded social homogeneity as an asset. However, in his *Weltanschauung* these elements were more deeply rooted and were reinforced by a total rejection of an élitist theory of knowledge (as preached by Kireevsky and Khomyakov among others) and to some extent by a mild and tentative tendency towards an egalitarian view of social relations. In his model society Kireevsky clearly accepted social hierarchy (though one less rigid than in medieval Europe) and the leading role of the nobility. Aksakov's 'people's utopia' (though he may not have been aware of it) gives the impression that the peasants could exist quite well without the nobility, and thus anticipated Tolstoy's view of the 'upper classes' as an unnecessary and artificial growth on the body of the people. In fact, Aksakov fully agreed with Tolstoy's argument that the 'educated classes' should learn from peasants and not try to teach them.

[1] Quoted from Brodsky, *Rannie slavyanofily*, pp. 114–15.

To conclude our confrontation, I should like to draw attention to the fact that both thinkers shared the view that 'evil should not be opposed by force'. Aksakov expounded this view in an article called 'A Few Comments on the Mutual Relationship of Good and Evil' which was to have appeared (posthumously) in the newspaper *Day* on 31 October 1861. The article was confiscated by the censor and as the text was probably lost it has never been published. The censor wrote the following report of its contents:

This article is a concise and logical exposition of a number of abstract ideas on the struggle of good and evil, on the lack of sincerity in our inclination towards good and dislike of evil, on the confusion between the principles of good and evil; *it shows the moral character of this struggle and most emphatically opposes the use of force as a method borrowed from evil and therefore a concession to evil and a compromise with evil*; it points out that the method of free persuasion is the only one worthy of good and the truth. In conclusion the author expresses his disagreement with the view that means sanctify the end.[1]

As will be seen from this account (and other fragments not quoted here), Aksakov's standpoint was still far removed from Tolstoy's radicalism. He made no direct condemnation of wars, the police, prisons, and executions, and the censor himself admitted that the author 'in no way relates his conclusions to Russia or in fact to the State'. The article was no doubt intended as an argument in favour of freedom of speech and did not even hint indirectly at the possibility of opposing absolutely all forms of state coercion. It is significant, nevertheless, in that it suggests an interesting evolution in Aksakov's ethical views; while he had always considered force to be an instrument of external truth, he had never previously formulated any theory of not opposing evil by force and during the early days of the Crimean War had even succumbed to the chauvinistic slogans of the war party.[2] It is of additional interest that this evolution took place at a time when the other Slavo-

---

[1] Tsentr. Gos. Istorich. Arkhiv. SSSR (Leningrad), fond 772, op. 1, Ed. khr. 5840.

[2] This is shown by Aksakov's article 'O vostochnom voprose' (dated 6 February 1854). Tsentr. Gos. Lit. Arkhiv. (Moscow), fond 10, op. 1. Ed. khr. 219. This article is discussed in chapter 12, pp. 496–7.

philes were moving in an entirely different direction, becoming active campaigners on behalf of the government, defenders of the class interests of the nobility, or downright chauvinists.

It is most instructive to look back at the three representatives of classical Slavophilism—Ivan Kireevsky, Alexeï Khomyakov, and Konstantin Aksakov—from the vantage-point of the period of the Great Reforms of the 1860s. Khomyakov, who propounded Slavophile ecclesiology and the theory of *sobornost'*, betrayed his anti-capitalist conservative utopia in favour of a 'practical' policy whose ultimate goal was a capitalist economy suited to the needs of large landowners. Kireevsky died on the eve of the new era, convinced that the proposed reforms were premature, and faithful to the conservative romantic utopia with its nostalgia for the old manorial civilization. Aksakov, the most uncompromising of the utopians, attempted to redress the balance by eliminating the aristocratic features of classical Slavophilism and transforming the Slavophile utopia into a kind of Christian Populism, thus bringing it closer to the archaic *Weltanschauung* of the patriarchal peasantry. The remaining Slavophiles—for all the differences dividing them— followed in Khomyakov's footsteps, which is, no doubt, one of the reasons why the latter is considered the central figure in Slavophilism as a political movement. For the historian of conservative utopias, however, Aksakov's uncompromising folk utopianism, for all its half-measures, represents an aspect of Slavophilism that is perhaps more interesting and hardly less important for an understanding of the various trends within this movement.

PART THREE

CONFRONTATIONS

7

Slavophilism and Hegelian Philosophy

'PHILOSOPHICAL notions', wrote Ivan Kireevsky in 1845, 'have become quite commonplace here now. There is scarcely a person who does not use philosophical terminology, nor any young man who is not steeped in reflections on Hegel; there is scarcely a book or an article that does not betray the influence of German thought and ten-year-old boys discourse on concrete objectivity.'[1] Herzen, too, wrote about the prevalent enthusiasm for Hegel.

They discussed these subjects incessantly; there was not a paragraph in the three parts of the *Logic*, in the two of the *Aesthetic*, the *Encyclopaedia*, and so on, which had not been the subject of desperate disputes for several nights altogether. People who loved each other avoided each other for weeks at a time because they disagreed about the definition of 'all-embracing spirit', or had taken as a personal insult an opinion on the 'absolute personality and its existence in itself'. Every insignificant pamphlet published in Berlin or other provincial or district town of German philosophy was ordered and read to tatters and smudges, and the leaves fell out in a few days, if only there was a mention of Hegel in it.[2]

In view of ample further testimony of this kind, one is fully justified in speaking of the 'Hegelian atmosphere of the 1840s'.[3] The impact of Hegelian philosophy in Russia and Poland cannot be compared to that of any other Western thinker: its influence was both widespread and profound; it reached to distant provincial centres and even left its mark on Russian literature. In one way or another Hegelianism can certainly be said to have provided a 'frame of reference' for almost all philosophical and historiosophical ideas that emerged in Russia between 1837 and 1845. A confrontation of Slavophilism and Hegelianism is therefore doubly useful, since it allows us to examine Slavophilism in the context of wider philosophical

[1] Kireevsky, ii. 133.   [2] Herzen, *My Past and Thoughts*, ii. 115.
[3] See D. I. Chizhevsky, *Gegel' v Rossii* (Paris 1939).

disputes (the Hegelian controversies in Germany) and at the same time helps us to understand the philosophical position of the Slavophiles' immediate antagonists—the Russian Westernizers—who were profoundly influenced by Hegel's thought.

The extent of Hegel's influence was a matter of great concern in government circles. As early as 1841, in an article entitled 'Is German Philosophy possible in Russia?', I. I. Davidov, who was acting as the mouthpiece of the Minister of Education, S. S. Uvarov, answered the question posed in the title of the article with a decisive 'no'. 'As we are a youthful nation,' he wrote, 'we need not adopt a philosophy which another nation has evolved in its senile old age.[1]' The events of 1848 brought matters to a head. After the dismissal of the over 'liberal' Uvarov, the new Minister of Education, Prince Shirinsky-Shakhmatov, closed down philosophy departments at all Russian universities; lectures on philosophy and logic were entrusted to Orthodox theologians, and new censorship regulations prohibited any reference to Hegel or his work. This met the demand of the extreme obscurantist wing, who had long proclaimed that all philosophy was hostile to religion and that the 'sophistries of Western philosophers are but as sounding brass or a tinkling cymbal'.[2]

It would be a crying historical injustice to equate Slavophilism with obscurantism. However, it would be an even greater error to ignore (as Chizhevsky does) the obvious fact that in the 1840s the Slavophiles were the most serious and also most consistent opponents of Hegelianism in Russia.

Chizhevsky's argument is straightforward: Slavophilism, he suggests, essentially represented an attempt to justify the special historical mission of the Russian people, while Hegelianism provided an excellent ideological groundwork for all 'messianic' motifs. In a conversation with Baron Boris von Yxküll Hegel had himself suggested the possibility that Russia might be regarded as the heir of the European nations, who had already, to a greater or lesser extent, attained their evolutionary goal.[3] The 'junior' Slavophiles—Konstantin Aksakov and Yurii

[1] D. I. Chizhevsky, *Gegel' v Rossii* (Paris 1939). p. 230.
[2] An open letter from M. N. Zagoskin to the publisher of the *Mayak* (*Lighthouse*). Quoted from A. Grigor'ev, *Sochineniya* (St. Petersburg 1876), i. 534.
[3] See Chizhevsky, op. cit., p. 164.

Samarin—converted Hegel's 'possibility' into a definite doc-trine. They passed through 'the school of Hegelian philo-sophy, were Slavophiles and Hegelians for several years, and though they later transcended their Hegelianism this was a dialectical transcendence [*Aufhebung*] which cannot be equated with a simple "negation".'[1] The early Hegelianism of Aksakov and Samarin, Chizhevsky points out, was not questioned by their contemporaries. Herzen called them 'Orthodox-Christian Hegelians' and Ivan Aksakov maintained that they had attempted to construct on Hegelian principles 'a whole view of the world . . . a kind of phenomenology of the mind of the Russian nation, together with its history, customs, and even its Orthodox religion'.[2]

It is a pity that historians of Russian thought have paid insufficient attention to the interesting intellectual phenomenon of Orthodox-Christian Hegelianism to which Chizhevsky was the first to draw attention. A closer look at this curious amalgam of ideas does not, however, confirm his thesis that 'Hegelian philosophy was in an excellent position to serve as the ground-work of Slavophilism.'[3] The Orthodox-Christian Hegelians were not yet Slavophiles. Though for a time Hegelianism co-existed with Slavophile tendencies in their view of the world, it cannot be said to have underpinned these tendencies, or to have evolved from them. Aksakov's and Samarin's final full acceptance of Slavophilism meant the conscious and consistent abandonment of their Hegelian position.

'THE ORTHODOX-CHRISTIAN HEGELIANS'

The first document of Orthodox-Christian Hegelianism was Aksakov's pamphlet *A Few Words on Gogol's Poem 'Chichikov's Fortunes or Dead Souls'*. In it the young critic, until recently a member of the Stankevich Circle, proclaimed that *Dead Souls* heralded the renaissance of the Homeric epic. Since Homer's day, Aksakov wrote, the history of literature had merely chronicled its own gradual decline, until the emergence of the novel, a literary genre thot harked back to the epic of ancient times. The novel was however a degenerate form of the epic; unable to express 'the spirit of wholeness' it concentrated on the fortuitous actions of individuals in a purely private and isolated

[1] Ibid., p. 165.   [2] Ibid., p. 166.   [3] Ibid., p. 164.

sphere of life. And yet, Aksakov claimed, amidst this general decline the Homeric epic was reborn in Gogol's 'poem'. Gogol showed 'the whole world, where rivers splash and murmur once more as in Homer, where the sun rises, nature glows in all her beauty, and man is alive; a world which is whole, which reveals to us the profound inner content of our ordinary lives, in which one spirit connects all phenomena'.[1] Since Aksakov could not have been entirely unaware that the subject of *Dead Souls*, primarily a satirical novel, did not comply with the canons of the epic, he put the emphasis on Gogol's 'creative act' which, he maintained, placed him above Pushkin and all other contemporary writers. The subject of the 'poem', he suggested, would be developed more extensively and with even greater brilliance in the parts to follow. This was foreshadowed by the poetic digressions, in which Gogol caught the 'eternal, substantial content of Russian life'. Aksakov's prognosis was in line with Gogol's own declaration that '. . . perhaps in this very novel [i.e. in later volumes] some chords hitherto unstruck may be discerned, the wealth of the Russian soul may be set forth. . . .'[2]

According to Aksakov the Homeric character of Gogol's 'creative act' was to be found in his frequent elaborate epic similes. It is clear, of course, that the 'Homeric' similes in *Dead Souls* have a mock-heroic function and are merely one of the satiric tools used to underline the contrast between the novel's prosaic content and its exalted epic form. In his polemic with Aksakov Belinsky pointed out quite rightly that while the ancient epic was an affirmation of the world, *Dead Souls* represented a 'negation' of the reality depicted.[3]

In his reflections on the ancient epic Aksakov repeated appropriate extracts from Hegel's *Aesthetics*, although Hegel was quite clearly not interested in any revival of the patriarchal 'heroic age'.[4] Aksakov's Slavophile leanings are revealed by his nostalgia

[1] A. S. Aksakov, *Neskol'ko slov o poeme Gogolya*, '*Pokhozhdeniya Chichikova ili mërtvye dushi*' (Moscow 1842).

[2] Gogol, *Dead Souls*, trans. by Constance Garnett (Alfred Knopf, New York 1923), ii. 43.

[3] See V. G. Belinsky, *Polnoe sobranie sochinenii*, 12 vols. (Soviet Academy of Sciences, Moscow 1953–9), vi. 255.

[4] Hegel associated the 'heroic' epoch with a low level of economic development and, especially, with a primitive division of labour.

for 'naïve' poetry, for a literature that would be a spontaneous expression of the 'substance' of the whole people. In Gogol he looked for the qualities which he later claimed—with far greater justification—to have found in the Russian folk epics (*bÿlinÿ*). Aksakov was by no means isolated in his attempts to bring contemporary writing closer to the Homeric ideals of simplicity and *'naïveté'*. Kireevsky, for instance, stressed the 'Slavophile' character of such a literary programme in a letter to V. Zhukovsky, after the latter's publication of his translation of the *Odyssey* (1845).

Your *Odyssey* [Kireevsky wrote] ought to bring about a radical change in our literature, to turn it back from the path of artifice, and direct it towards immediate experience. This artless candour in poetry is the very thing we lack, and I think we are better able to prize it than those older nations who lack candour and who contemplate their image in the polished mirrors of their mannered writers. This living expression of the spirit of the Greek people will make it easier to understand our own national character, which survives but weakly in our disappearing folk epics.[1]

Aksakov's pamphlet, which attempted to ascribe 'Homeric simplicity' to a writer who was essentially a master of subtle and bitter irony, must be dismissed as an interesting historical curiosity. His master's thesis on *Lomonosov in the History of Russian Language and Literature*, published in 1846, reveals far greater intellectual maturity. This work, which has, until recently, been undeservedly overlooked by critics and historians of Russian philosophy, has been described by the Soviet scholar M. Azadovsky as 'one of the outstanding documents of Russian Hegelianism in the philological sciences'. 'Aksakov's dissertation', Azadovsky wrote, 'is of considerable historical significance. The title of the work is too narrow a description of its real content, which in fact represents an attempt to perceive the evolution of the Russian nation and Russian culture in terms of a comprehensive structure.'[2]

By the time this monograph was published, Aksakov was no longer a Hegelian. This probably accounts for the inclusion in

---

[1] Kireevsky, ii. 237.
[2] M. K. Azadovsky, *Istoriya russkoĭ fol'kloristiki* (Moscow 1958), pp. 380–1.

the preface of the following paragraph, which clearly distorts the ideas expounded in the work:

Before Peter the Great [Aksakov wrote], we were inseparably bound to our native Russia, we loved her; our love was not free, however, it erred in being one-sided, it was fearful of anything foreign; ignorance and isolation were the only means we knew of protecting our national character; our love therefore had its dark side, which allowed feelings to become unbalanced. This is in fact what happened. Peter drew out into the light of day what had been lurking in the shadows: he discovered the one-sidedness, dealt it a blow, and thus became a turning-point. The post-Petrine age represents a new one-sidedness; no nation could go to greater extremes: we even went so far as to renounce our history, our literature, and our very language. Our capital was established in a city with a foreign name, on a foreign shore, not bound to Russia by any historical memories. . . . Now, however, a new age is dawning: today our relationship with our native land and our love for her are without that one-sidedness which might have weakened them; it is not in isolation from other countries or in fear that they seek support, we have, after all, absorbed Western enlightenment and not in vain either. . . . After shaking off the alienation of the previous epoch, the epoch of negation, we return imbued by a reasonable love for our native land and bound to her by bonds that no one will ever be able to break.[1]

In spite of appearances to the contrary, this passage cnnot be said to recapitulate the main argument of the thesis. Nor was Chicherin right when he commented that Aksakov had grown a beard according to Hegelian dialectics: 'In ancient Russia there were beards, in modern Russia they were shaved off, therefore in future they ought to make a come-back.'[2] It has unfortunately become common to interpret Aksakov's dissertation by a mechanical application of the Hegelian dialectical triad, with pre-Petrine Russia being the thesis, St. Petersburg Russia the antithesis, and the future Slavophile Russia the synthesis. This interpretation was even repeated by Chizhevsky, which suggests that his reading of the dissertation itself was not sufficiently close.[3] In the dialectical triad which forms the struc-

---

[1] Aksakov, *Lomonosov v istorii russkoĭ literaturȳ i russkogo yazȳka* (Moscow 1846), pp. 6–7.

[2] Quoted from Chizhevsky, op. cit., p. 169.

[3] A. Koryé follows Chizhevsky in this erroneous interpretation in his *Hegel en Russie. Études sur l'histoire de la pensée philosophique en Russie*, pp. 166–7.

tural pivot of Aksakov's work pre-Petrine Russia represents not the thesis but the antithesis, the negation of the universal idea of humanity, whereas post-Petrine Russia represents the synthesis, the return to the lost universality. His argument therefore took the 'universal' and not the particularism of ancient patriarchal Russia as its starting-point.

Aksakov's argument can be outlined as follows: The universal as universal cannot exist in reality; it is merely being in the abstract. In order to exist, the universal must negate itself: this gives rise to the non-universal (antithesis), or in other words, the 'particular' (*Besonderheit*), which is the negation of the universal as universal. The 'particular' in turn is negated (the negation of the negation), and universality finds itself again in 'singularity' (*Einzelnheit*). Now however this universality has become concrete thanks to negation and is no longer abstract but real. The return to universality is not a retrograde step—the restored universality has passed through negation and thanks to this has acquired 'reality'.

This scheme served as the foundation of Aksakov's philosophy of history. Since universal man and the idea of humanity are mere abstractions they must be negated by the 'particular', that is by a nation locked up in its exclusive national existence. The 'negation of the negation' is the individual who has liberated himself from purely national determinations and has thus restored universal human values. The liberated individual does not however cease to be a member of one particular nation; through the individual the nation shakes off its exclusivity and becomes elevated to universality, while universality becomes concrete and is transformed into reality.

Pre-Petrine Russia was an isolated nation and therefore represented the stage of 'particularity', the negation of the 'universal'. Christianity at this time expressed universal values, but the Russian people was not yet ready to assimilate them. The 'universal' in the Christian religion was given to the people as a treasure-house that must remain locked until the people became worthy of it and fully able to understand and assimilate the values it contained. The end of the Riurik dynasty ushered in the third stage, that is the overcoming of national isolation. Support for the False Dmitry, the Revolt of the *Streltsy*, and the Old Believers was evidence of the people's reluctance to give up

its 'national exclusivity'; they 'expressed the fear of nationality,
the vague premonition that its time was nearly over'.[1] A new
need now made itself felt in Russia, a higher need which
required the individual within the nation to be set free. The
individual in this case was the gigantic figure of Peter the
Great; with him 'the exclusive national character of Russia
disappeared for ever in a terrible bloody struggle and a new
epoch was born'.[2] In this epoch it was the role of the 'universal'
to transcend nationality but at the same time preserve it—
purged of its 'exclusivity'—as a necessary 'moment' of historical
development.

Historical movement, Aksakov argued, did not mean the
direct transition from one stage or 'moment' to the next. The
new stage was always 'one-sided', but this was a necessary one-
sidedness which provided the motive force of history. Peter's
attempt to annihilate national character altogether was an
essential but temporary one-sidedness of this kind. The need
for this self-negation sprang from within the nation itself: 'No
nation has ever had the courage to undertake such a decisive,
comprehensive, and consistent negation of its own national
character and hence no nation can have such universal world-
historical significance as the Russian nation', Aksakov wrote.[3]
All material aspects of national character were destroyed in the
fire of negation; the only thing that remained was the abstract
national substance represented by the common people, silent
and cut off from political life. It was now time to overcome the
one-sidedness that had been a symptom of the initial stage of the
new epoch. The time was ripe for a return to Russia's own
substance, for a reasoning love of one's native land whose
exclusivity had been overcome but was preserved at the same
time through its elevation to the universal. 'The way to this
higher sphere', Aksakov concluded, 'was shown by Peter the
Great.'[4]

Aksakov believed that the historical development of Russian
language and literature was governed by the same general rules.
He was an outspoken opponent of the view that language was
a set of conventional signs and conceived it instead as 'thought
made flesh', as a supra-individual sphere of consciousness 'irra-

---

[1] Aksakov, *Lomonosov* . . ., p. 53.   [2] Ibid., p. 55.
[3] Ibid., p. 51.   [4] Ibid.

diated' by the spirit and objectivizing its development. The pages dealing with the history of language are amongst the most interesting parts of Aksakov's thesis and, like his works on grammar, represent a valuable contribution to Russian linguistics. A. Koyré wrote that 'Aksakov's philosophy of language must undoubtedly be considered one of the most brilliant achievements of Russian Hegelianism.'[1] As a detailed discussion of Aksakov's linguistic theories lies outside the scope of the present work, I shall confine myself to summarizing them briefly only in so far as they are relevant to his philosophy of history.

Aksakov called oral folk compositions an immediate expression of the national substance representing the 'particular' stage in literature, since their content is neither universally human nor individual. As the creation of the nation as a whole rather than any individual poet, folk songs are always perfect in form, and their subject-matter is always necessary and real since the people is always 'true to itself'. In ancient Russia, Aksakov wrote, folk ballads summing up the meaning of national existence were sung everywhere. In these ballads there was no room for individual treatment: 'a bride weeps, but not because a particular bride is unhappy; it is the common fate, the lot of brides among the people'.[2]

Apart from folk songs and ballads, ancient Russia also had its religious literature, written in Church Slavonic. This literature housed the universal element in Christianity, which the people was not yet ready to assimilate. Church Slavonic was particularly well suited to expressing the universal: 'To plunge into Church Slavonic,' Aksakov commented, 'which is as far removed from all haphazardness as heaven is from earth, is to be transported into another world where all is timeless as in a temple, hallowed by the presence of infinity and the divine.'[3] Aksakov expanded these ideas in his contrastive analysis of the language of Church literature and traditional oral literature. This led him to conclude that the 'universal' in language was expressed through the 'organic sentence' which combines highly

---

[1] Koyré, *Hegel en Russie*, p. 167. See also V. Vinogradov, 'Russkaya nauka o russkom literaturnom yazyke', *Uchenye zapiski*, vol. iii/1 (Moscow 1946).
[2] Aksakov, *Lomonosov* . . ., p. 37.
[3] Ibid., p. 41.

developed inflection with a strong syntactical structure. Ancient Russian literature lacked this 'universal' element; even when the language of oral traditions infiltrated into written literature it preserved its colloquial and idiomatic character; the lack of definite syntactical rules and the 'primitive clumsiness' of its inflections resulted in an 'inorganic' sentence structure. Nevertheless the 'clumsy' inflections and stiff, unchanging forms hinted at the presence of powerful forces slumbering within the language. Aksakov was anxious that this 'immobility' which, he maintained, contained the powerful germ of life, should not be confused with the senile immobility of languages (like English) that had completed their development cycle and lost their inflections.[1] Syntax (i.e. the 'universal') only developed in the abstract language of Church Slavonic, but the element of the 'universal' was urgently needed in the living language of the people. A harbinger of the approaching new 'development stage' was the linguistic patchwork characteristic of the seventeenth century with its eclectic mingling of two linguistic spheres—the absorption of vulgarisms and colloquialisms into the written language and borrowings from foreign languages. To Aksakov this was evidence that 'the sphere of nationality together with the universal and its language, which soars above it in abstract form, has already become shaken'.[2]

The role of Lomonosov was to be the Peter the Great of Russian literature. 'Lomonosov's importance', Aksakov concluded, 'is the importance of the individual, of personality in poetry, or, in other words, the significance of the individual poetic nature which was previously absorbed by an integral and exclusively national existence.'[3] Lomonosov was responsible for transferring the universal element from the abstract 'holy' language to the living language, and for encouraging literature to deal with individual and therefore universally human content. As literary creation was no longer a collective act, it was now possible for bad and unsuccessful works to be written and this necessitated the strict division into literary genres and forms. Lomonosov's 'theory of three styles' introduced order into the linguistic patchwork inherited from the seventeenth century.

[1] See Aksakov, *Lomonosov* . . ., p. 86.   [2] Ibid., p. 274.
[3] See the 'theses' appended at the end of Aksakov's book on unnumbered pages (thesis 5).

Most important, however, was the appearance of the 'organic sentence' with its strong syntactical construction and supple inflection. This type of sentence, Aksakov stressed, could only make its appearance after the emancipation of the individual: the language of a pre-individualized people is always an 'inorganic' spoken language—only the individual contemplating his thoughts, which already contain the 'universal' element, and endeavouring to put them down on paper, can liberate the 'universal' element in language.[1]

Although Lomonosov initiated a new 'moment' in the evolution of Russian language and literature, his approach, like that of Peter the Great, was one-sided. His immediate successors carried this one-sidedness to extremes, so that the 'bookish' language, with its heavy Germanic syntax, began to drive out the living vernacular. This imbalance could only be overcome by restoring the rights of the spoken language without disturbing the organic structure of the sentence, which was governed by the laws of the 'universal'. Karamzin defended the rights of the spoken language, while his opponent, Admiral Shishkov, was a champion of 'organic structure'. It was Pushkin, however, who turned out to be Lomonosov's true heir and successor: his creative genius transcended Lomonosov's one-sidedness and represented a true synthesis of the national and the 'universal', of the spoken language of the people and the 'organic structure' of the written language.

An analysis of Aksakov's dissertation provides powerful arguments against the view that it was possible to achieve a harmonious reconciliation of Slavophilism and Hegelianism. Whatever Aksakov may have thought, Khomyakov and Kireevsky could hardly consider his work to be a contribution to Slavophilism. His evaluation of Peter the Great, his conception of the 'particular' and the 'universal', and his assumption that by setting free the 'universal' element in the nation Peter the Great had paved the way to the full understanding and assimilation of Christianity, were all at variance with the basic premises of Slavophile doctrine. On the other hand, Aksakov's historiosophical framework could clearly provide an excellent underpinning for a Westernizing interpretation of Russian history. Similar ideas were put forward by Belinsky, who always

[1] Aksakov, *Lomonosov* . . ., p. 258.

stressed the need for a synthesis of the national and universal elements and considered the Petrine reforms to have been of tremendous significance in this respect. The idea that Lomonosov was the Peter the Great of Russian literature can be found in Belinsky's article *Literary Reveries* as early as 1834. The critic was even inclined to agree that it was time to overcome the 'one-sidedness' of Peter's reforms. 'Russia', he wrote in 1847, 'has made full use of the period of transformation, has drained it to the last drop; the reforms have done their part and it is now time for her to develop independently and unaided.'[1]

Even more revealing is a comparison of Aksakov's thesis with Kavelin's dissertation *A Brief Survey of Juridical Relations in Ancient Russia* (1847). This work, which was greeted with indignation by the Slavophiles and considered by Belinsky and Herzen to express the point of view of all Westernizers,[2] was essentially a repetition of the young Aksakov's Hegelian ideas. The Russian historical process, according to Kavelin, consisted in the gradual emancipation of the individual, who had formerly been wholly subordinated to the patriarchal community. This was accompanied by the disintegration of isolated 'physical' nationality (nationality as a set of external and congealed traditions) and the emergence of a 'spiritual nationality permeated by the universally human element, of nationality as an aspect of the nation's moral character and not merely an external, physical attribute'. The Petrine reforms represented the culmination of this process. 'In the person of Peter,' wrote Kavelin, 'individuality came into its absolute rights in Russia, escaped from the grip of immediate, innate, and exclusively national determinations, transcended them, and subordinated them to herself. The whole of Peter's private life and political activity represent the first phase in the self-realization of the principle of individuality in Russian history.'[3] The victory of individuality was interpreted by Kavelin as the victory of true Christianity, of a religion that cherished the ideal of the absolute value of the human personality.

Although Kavelin and Aksakov wrote their theses at almost the same time, they did so quite independently of each other. Any similarities can be explained by the fact that the ideas

---

[1] Belinsky, x. 19.   [2] See chapter 9, pp. 404–8.
[3] K. D. Kavelin, *Sobranie sochinenii* (St. Petersburg 1887), i. 58.

they expounded flowed naturally from a current interpretation of Hegelianism. It is worth recalling that Kavelin's article, which was printed in *The Contemporary (Sovremennik)* a few months after the publication of Aksakov's dissertation, caused quite an uproar in Slavophile circles. Samarin, acting as spokesman for the entire Slavophile movement,[1] indignantly rejected Kavelin's assumption that individuality had only emerged at the time of the Petrine reforms. Samarin's criticism of Kavelin naturally applied to the young Aksakov as well. In spite of his avowed intentions, Aksakov's thesis supported the standpoint of the Westernizers. Aksakov himself realized this, which was partly why he thought it necessary to make such a firm and unmistakable repudiation of Hegelianism.

Aksakov relinquished his favourable estimation of the 'liberated individual' without much difficulty. 'Individuality as a principle', he later said, 'is the greatest of evils and the most unbridled profligacy.'[2] The notion that there were universal values shared by the whole of humanity proved to be far more deeply embedded in his consciousness. The former Hegelian was reluctant to admit to himself that he was betraying these values and was not convinced by Khomyakov's argument that 'the notion of a universal spirit of a collective humanity' was nothing but mysticism and an 'impalpable abstraction'.[3] Aksakov extricated himself from this difficulty by the simple and radical expedient of converting his original Hegelian conception into its opposite.

In this new interpretation, pre-Petrine Russia was not a land of 'exclusive nationality' unripe for Christianity, but the only true Christian people in the world, the exponent of the universal human values betrayed by all the other nations. The same was of course true of the 'common people' of modern Russia, which had remained faithful to the old ideals in spite of Peter's reforms. 'The Russian nation', Aksakov wrote, 'is not a nation; it is humanity. It is a nation only by virtue of being surrounded by other nations locked in their own exclusive nationality.'[4] Peter's reforms did not set free the 'universal' element in the Russian nation—on the contrary, they signified the victory of 'exclusive nationality', though not Russia's own

---

[1] See chapter 9, pp. 408–11.   [2] Aksakov, *Zamechaniya* . . ., p. 72.
[3] Khomyakov, i. 36.   [4] Aksakov, i. 630.

but that of a foreign nationality imposed from outside. The struggle to return to true native principles was therefore at the same time a struggle for universal values.

The artificiality of this historiosophical construction exemplifies the difficulties of reconciling conservative nationalism with the universalist ideal of *humanitas*.

Aksakov's closest friend in the early 1840s was Yuriĭ Samarin. Together they studied at Moscow University and together they started to write their master's dissertations in 1840. Through Aksakov, Samarin came under the influence of German philosophical ideas emanating from the Stankevich Circle, which he described in the late 1830s as 'a circle of young men with whose ideas on philosophy and literature I am in whole-hearted agreement'.[1] In the 1840s, after the Stankevich Circle had broken up, and Slavophile philosophy had fully matured, Samarin and Aksakov represented a separate standpoint in Moscow literary salons, where they continued to try and reconcile Slavophile ideas with Hegelian philosophy, which was the target of impassioned attacks by Kireevsky and Khomyakov.

The public discussion of Samarin's dissertation *Stepan Yavorsky and Theophan Prokopovich* caused a sensation in Moscow literary circles. Chaadaev was 'moved to tears' by this triumph of scholarship in 'quiet god-fearing Moscow', although he disagreed with most of Samarin's propositions. 'I am convinced', he wrote, 'that since our universities have been in existence no young man, especially one so recently still a student, has tackled such important problems in so masterly a fashion.'[2] Although Chaadaev was not alone in his enthusiasm, Samarin was also criticized for his temerity in considering the Orthodox religion a fit subject for 'individual philosophizing'. The university was influenced by these arguments and only agreed to publish the third and least interesting part of Samarin's work, entitled *Stepan Javorsky and Theophan Prokopovich as Preachers*.[3]

---

[1] Dm. Samarin, 'Dannÿe dlya biografii Y. F. Samarina za 1840–1845 g.g.', in Y. F. Samarin, *Stepan Yavorsky i Theophan Prokopovich, Sochineniya* (Moscow 1880), vol. v, p. xxxvi

[2] P. I. Chaadaev, *Sochineniya i pis'ma*, i. 250.

[3] The government's mistrust of the Slavophile circle is clearly shown by the fact that the censor considered even Aksakov's thesis on Lomonosov to contain 'sharp and improper' expressions about Peter the Great (i.e. Aksakov's discussion of the

The views of the two leading theologians in the reign of Peter the Great served Samarin as a spring-board for reflections on the essence of Orthodoxy, Catholicism, and Protestantism. By pointing out the relationship between Catholicism and Protestantism on the one hand and the two theological trends represented by Yavorsky and Prokopovich on the other, Samarin made an important and original contribution to scholarship.[1] He himself was of course more interested in outlining a philosophy of religion than in compiling historical facts.

The essence of the Church, Samarin argued, is the 'inner unity of life in Grace', which transforms a congregation of worshippers into a 'living, organic whole'. The individual is only entitled to be called a member of the Church when he has 'subjugated his individuality, has ceased to serve and exist for himself, and has thus become a living vessel of Grace'.[2] The spirit of God dwells in the organic unity of all Christians and not in any chosen individual or isolated individuals existing as separate fragments. The sole organ of this spiritual wholeness, according to Samarin, is the ecumenical council.

Catholicism and Protestantism, Samarin suggested, are two deviations from this truly Christian conception of the Church. Under the influence of classical Rome Catholicism adopted an abstract conception of unity symbolized in the person of the pope. Unity conceived in this way is a purely external quality: the faithful are not gathered *within* the Church but *under* the Church, as subjects and not as members of a community. Protestantism represented an attempt to overcome this alienation, to attain the 'immediate reconciliation of each isolated individual with God';[3] this attempt, however, only brought about the total destruction of unity. According to Protestant doctrine the divine spirit dwells in every separate individual, hence every individual is a Church unto himself. Samarin regarded this doctrine as an expression of Teutonic individualism exemplified

'one-sidedness' of Peter's reforms). As a result Minister Uvarov forbade further sales of the book and the appearance of any articles or reviews on the subject. (Tsentr. Gos. Istorich. Arkhiv. SSSR, Leningrad, fond 735, op. 10, yed. khr. 190.)

[1] In his history of Russian theology (*Puti russkogo bogosloviya*) G. Florovsky made use of Samarin's conclusions.

[2] Y. F. Samarin, *S. Javorsky i T. Prokopovich*, p. 452.

[3] Ibid., p. 455.

in feudal particularism and aristocratic licence. 'Protestantism', he wrote, 'is religious feudalism . . .; knight and Protestant are two incarnations of the same man in different spheres.'[1]

This basic antithesis—between the 'Roman' and the 'Teutonic' element and between Catholic 'unity' and Protestant 'plurality'—gave rise to a number of other contrasts. For Catholicism, Samarin suggested, the way to salvation was through 'deeds' alone, moreover deeds conceived as something purely external, as a kind of magic. Protestantism, on the other hand, subjectivized religion and opposed 'deeds' by individual 'faith'. Catholicism struggled for political power, while Protestantism was content with servile dependence on the secular authorities. Catholicism attempted to subjugate science, whereas Protestantism ultimately tried to turn religion itself into a scientific system. In early eighteenth-century Russia the Catholic tendency was represented by Stepan Yavorsky and the conservative wing of the clergy, who tried to oppose Peter's reforms and the consequent secularization of public life the Protestant tendency found a spokesman in Theophan Prokopovich, an enthusiastic and energetic supporter of Peter's policies.

Samarin pointed out that although Yavorsky and Prokopovich created mutually contradictory theological systems, neither was officially condemned by the Orthodox Church. In accepting two contradictory systems, the Church therefore showed that she was without a theological system of her own. Surprisingly, this led Samarin to the significant conclusion that the poverty of Orthodox theological thought was evidence of the superiority of Orthodoxy over the Western confessions.

The theologians' attempt to fit 'living faith' into a system, Samarin argued, stems from rationalism, which is incompatible with religion. Rationalized and codified systems of faith make their appearance when there is no longer any genuine conviction; theological theory is only needed as an integrating factor where there is no living, organic unity, and its contribution is merely to reinforce existing alienation and disintegration. A truly Christian Church admits rational arguments only in disputes, as a defensive weapon against outside attack. This is what happened in the case of Yavorsky and Prokopovich.

[1] Y. F. Samarin, *S. Javorsky i T. Prokopovich*, p. 455

In Russia [Samarin wrote] the influence of Catholicism and Protestantism in church doctrine was apparent in two systems, each concerned with refuting everything essential in the other. One of these systems was borrowed from the Catholics and the other from the Protestants. The first was a one-sided attempt to counteract the influence of the Reformation and the other an equally one-sided attempt to counteract the Jesuit school. Orthodoxy tolerates both by acknowledging their negative role—both guard her frontiers from opposing positions.

Nevertheless, the Church has not considered either system worthy of adoption as her own, but neither has she condemned them. It follows that the Church rejects as alien and unacceptable the common concept on which both are founded—the concept of a theological system. We are entitled to say that the Orthodox Church is without a system of its own and ought to remain without one.[1]

So far from revealing any specifically Hegelian element, the general plan of Samarin's dissertation outlined here rather anticipated the main points of Khomyakov's theological theories. The influence of Hegelianism in Samarin's work can be traced only in his aesthetic notions (in the chapter on Yavorsky and Prokopovich as preachers) and in his extremely tentative proposition on the *evolution* of the Church. Samarin defended this proposition (which recalls Newman's similar conception)[2] in eager discussions with Khomyakov and Kireevsky, and with his friend and correspondent A. N. Popov. It was not the *life* of the Church that evolved, he argued, but only her *consciousness*;[3] this evolution consisted in the change from 'being in itself' to 'being for itself'. As historical evidence for his point of view he quoted the reforms of the Patriarch Nikon. While the Catholic Church was static and living elements broke away from it, in Russia the entire Orthodox Church moved forward and the Old Believers, representatives of an obstinate and petrified conservatism, broke away from it.[4] Samarin's argument encountered energetic opposition: Samarin's evolution, asserted Popov, was not really an evolution but merely the development of the individual's understanding of Christianity. Kireevsky, on the other hand, argued that Nikon's reforms were a mere local phenomenon, evidence of the progress of the Church in Russia,

[1] Ibid., p. 163.   [2] See Koyré, op. cit., p. 170.

[3] See Dm. Samarin, 'Dannye dlya biografi Y. F. Samarina', p. xli.

[4] See Y. F. Samarin, *S. Yavorsky i T. Prokopovich*, p. 16.

but having nothing in common with the growth of the consciousness of the Universal Church.[1]

It should be stressed that Samarin did not intend his thesis
concerning the evolution of the Church to be the structural
pivot of his dissertation. There is, in fact, no evidence for
Koyré's claim that Samarin presented this evolution in terms
of the dialectal triad of thesis (Catholicism), antithesis (Protestantism), and synthesis (Orthodoxy).[2] In Samarin's interpretation Orthodoxy represented the stage preceding Catholicism
and Protestantism, and was already illuminated by the full
and ultimate truth. Orthodoxy could be presented as the synthesis of Catholicism and Protestantism only by making a
distinction between 'historical' and 'logical' categories. Samarin,
however, made no such distinction; he conceived Orthodoxy as
a synthesis of unity and multiplicity, but without any suggestion
that it was the product of a certain evolution. In fact, like
Khomyakov, he was not so much influenced by Hegelian logic
as by the theological writings of J. A. Möhler.[3]

Hegelian influence on Samarin can be seen most clearly in his
discussion of the relationship between religion and philosophy
and the role of religion as a stage in the evolution of the
Absolute. For Samarin this problem marked the onset of a true
crisis of conscience. Herzen, who witnessed the struggle, was
hopeful that as a result of this inner crisis Samarin would
finally come down on the side of 'science' (i.e. philosophy),
abandoning Slavophile views in the process.

'Our age is the age of science', Samarin wrote to Popov in
December 1843. 'You know that by science I mean philosophy
and that when I speak of philosophy, I mean Hegel. Only by
taking over this science from Germany, which is incapable of
continuing it (since this science posits a kind of existence that
cannot be realized in Western Europe); only in this way will
there come about a reconciliation of consciousness and being
that will mark the triumph of Russia over the West.'[4] After this
opening remark, Samarin made a confession which Kireevsky

[1] See D. Samarin, op. cit., pp. xliii, l.
[2] See Koyré, op. cit., p. 169.
[3] In his thesis Samarin referred to Möhler's 'symbolism' and called him a
Catholic theologian who had 'liberated himself from his former narrow concepts'.
Y. F. Samarin, op. cit., p. 23, footnote.
[4] Quoted from D. Samarin, op. cit., p. liii.

and Khomyakov must surely have regarded as blasphemous: 'Research into the Orthodox faith . . .', he wrote, 'has led me to the conclusion that it will neither realize its potential nor triumph, until it has gained the sanction of science; that the issue of the Church involves the philosophical issue and that the fate of Orthodoxy is inseparably bound up with Hegel. I am quite clear about this and that is why I have consciously put my theological studies aside and am taking up philosophy.'[1]

B. Nolde believes this passage to show that Samarin had after all become convinced that Orthodoxy should create its own theological system, basing itself on Hegelian philosophy.[2] This interpretation, I would suggest, is quite unfounded. While pursuing his studies of Catholicism, Samarin had come to the conclusion that there were no essential differences between Catholicism and Orthodoxy in the realm of dogma and that the latter's only claim to originality was that it had no 'system' (i.e. no theology) and was not concerned with creating its own 'science'. If, however, the Orthodox Church was right to exclude science from its sphere of interest, this was tantamount to admitting that science represented a separate autonomous sphere. 'If science [i.e. philosophy] exists as a distinct spiritual sphere,' Samarin argued in a letter to Khomyakov, 'apart from art and religion, then it ought to be the highest sphere, the final stage in the development of ideas.' For the mind, by 'conceiving the need for the inconceivable (i.e. the church), establishes its superiority over it. And that is just what the mind has achieved in its last phase.'[3] (A recapitulation of Hegel's argument that while philosophy understood religion the converse was not true.)

This argument faced the young philosopher with a difficult dilemma: if religion was the highest spiritual sphere, then Orthodoxy, which had not attempted to create its own 'system', was in all respects inferior to the Western confessions; this meant that the superiority of Orthodoxy could only be established if religion was accepted as an irreducible but inferior spiritual sphere. By recognizing religion as an essential but inferior, pre-philosophical stage of spiritual development,

[1] Ibid., p. liv.
[2] See B. E. Nolde, *Yuriĭ Samarin i ego vremya* (Paris 1926), p. 29.
[3] Quoted from D. Samarin, op. cit., pp. lviii–lix.

Hegelian philosophy appeared to Samarin to 'sanction' Russian Orthodoxy, while at the same time condemning the rationalistic [i.e. philosophical] pretensions of the Western confessions. What Samarin hoped to find in Hegelianism was not a philosophical basis for a theological system, but, on the contrary, support for the view that, being a sphere of the imagination, religion betrayed its own essence when it was tempted to create a conceptual system. Though 'transcended', by philosophy, the Orthodox faith would survive as an 'ever present moment of spiritual development'.[1]

From the Slavophile point of view this solution was more illusory than real. The Orthodox Hegelian position was, in fact, self-contradictory: as Slavophiles, Aksakov and Samarin had to defend Orthodoxy and ancient Russia, but as Hegelians they were forced to regard them as 'moments' which had been transcended and which could only survive as 'a necessary development stage', according to the law of 'dialectical transcendence'. Samarin himself admitted to Herzen that he could not 'logically develop the idea of the immanent coexistence of religion and science, the idea that *das Aufheben* by science did not infringe the reality of the Church.'[2] Herzen aptly described Samarin's conflict as the 'inner dichotomy of a man whose intellect destroys what his heart and imagination absorb, and who then puts his reason to sleep and again gives his imagination full reign'.[3] Samarin had to make his choice between Orthodoxy and Hegelianism. 'His noble intellect', Herzen wrote, 'does not permit him to remain content with this formal, external coexistence or rather with the *juxta positio*'.[4]

Herzen's hopes were disappointed, for Samarin did finally go over to the Slavophile camp. He was profoundly influenced in his choice by Khomyakov, whose role he described as follows: 'For those who retained the sensitivity of unalloyed religious feelings but were entangled in contradictions and rent in two, Khomyakov was a kind of liberating force; he led them out into boundless space, into God's universe, and gave them back wholeness of religious feeling.'[5]

---

[1] Quoted from D. Samarin, op. cit., p. lx.   [2] Herzen, ii. 250.
[3] Ibid.
[4] Ibid., p. 327.
[5] Samarin's introduction to the second volume of Khomyakov's *Collected Works* (Moscow 1886).

Both this comment and Samarin's article 'On Popular Education' (1856) suggest the kind of arguments that led him away from Orthodox-Christian Hegelianism. The most important of them was perhaps the Slavophile concept of inner *wholeness*, a quality which depends on faith and is threatened by autonomy. The Slavophiles taught that the autonomy of individuals is a disintegrating force in society, while the autonomy of reason or any particular psychic faculty 'fragments' the personality of individual man. Samarin came to regard the Hegelian concept of different stages of spiritual development as the philosophical expression of the disintegration of Western man whose soul is divided into 'compartments' and who—in Kireevsky's words—'is a different man at the different moments of his life'.[1]

As a philosophical structure Slavophile Hegelianism did not stand the test of time. But for that very reason it is a most instructive chapter in the history of Russian thought.

THE SLAVOPHILE CRITIQUE OF HEGELIANISM

It is characteristic of intellectual trends in Russia in the 1840s that the controversy between Samarin and Herzen was not so much concerned with the relationship between Europe and Russia, as with the abstract problem of the relationship between philosophy and religion. This once again illustrates the point that the quarrel between the Slavophiles and Westernizers was about issues of more than local significance and should be examined against the background of similar disputes sparked off in German philosophical circles by Hegelianism. The adoption of a rationalist or irrationalist philosophical system was at that time the touchstone of a man's allegiance to the philosophical Left or Right. From this point of view the Slavophiles represented the extreme philosophical Right and were more consistent in their criticism of rationalism than like-minded philosophers in Germany.

The analogy between the Slavophiles and the post-Hegelian philosophical Right in Germany cannot, however, be taken too far. The latter trend included philosophers who opposed Hegelianism or tried to deduce from it the idea of an otherworldly personal God as an essential objective basis for human

[1] Kireevsky, i. 210.

individuality; they therefore grouped not only the extreme
Right Hegelians (Göschel and Schaller), but also the 'speculative theists' who flirted with Hegelianism (the younger Fichte
and Weisse) and the anti-Hegelians (the later Schelling, Leo,
the followers of Schleiermacher, and other 'Christian philosophers'). For the Slavophiles the problem of the other-
worldliness or personality of God did not play so important a
role and certainly did not form the pivot of their critique of
Hegelianism, although the young Samarin was undoubtedly
disturbed by the fact that it was not possible to pray to an
impersonal Hegelian God. In discussions with Herzen, Khomyakov pointed out that one could not logically deduce the
'Persönlichkeit Gottes, *die Transcendenz*' from Hegelian principles, since these inevitably led to '*Immanenz* and life—*inneres
Gähren* realized in the idea'.[1] In Khomyakov's eyes this was an
obvious absurdity, evidence of the bankruptcy of Western
philosophy. It is worth emphasizing, however, that Khomyakov
did not, in fact, have a precise and considered point of view
of his own on the issue of the other-worldliness of God. This
did not escape Herzen, who described in his *Diary* the following
discussion he once had with the leading Slavophile:

After a long conversation I finally asked him to tell me his own
conception, the underlying idea, since this kind of negation [the
negation of a Hegelian solution] is still no kind of proposition.
However, he avoided giving me an answer. At first he used the
expression *being is God*, then he said *God is outside the world*. What do
you mean—I asked—being apart from existence? Obviously not
apart—he answered, but he did not continue this train of thought
and, what is more, did not continue it along Christian lines. In any
case it was already late. However, I suspect that he had no ready
answer.[2]

Herzen wrote this account in 1842, but even later Khomyakov failed to work out any conception of the relationship of
God to the universe. The issue of the this-worldliness or other-
worldliness of God did not hold an important place in Slavophile thought and therefore did not require a precisely formulated solution. This was because the Slavophiles, unlike the
post-Hegelian Right in Germany, did not take Hegelian concepts as the point of departure for their philosophical specula-

---

[1] Herzen, ii. 250.   [2] Ibid., p. 252.

tion. Instead they harked back to intellectual problems that had interested the *pre-Hegelian* conservative romanticists— problems that focused not on Hegelianism but on the role of the French Revolution and the philosophical heritage of the Enlightenment. However, although it was an ideology influenced by conservative romanticism, Slavophile doctrine belonged to a later period and came to maturity in the *post-Hegelian* era. To the Slavophiles, therefore, it was not Enlightenment philosophy but Hegelianism that seemed the personification of European rationalism and thus became the 'frame of reference' (though not the starting-point) for their own theories. 'Hegel', Khomyakov wrote, 'is the most complete and, I shall venture to say, the only rationalist in the world.'[1] The Slavophiles were forced to concentrate on criticism of Hegelianism because of its enormous popularity in Russia, and also because the ideas of their main opponents (especially Belinsky and Herzen) were formed in the early 1840s under the influence of Left Hegelianism; that, incidentally, is why Herzen asked Khomyakov to comment on a problem of immediate interest to the Hegelian Right. The Slavophiles therefore felt bound to demonstrate that the conservative romantic critique of Enlightenment rationalism was also applicable to Hegel's dialectical rationalism; that Hegel's reason (*Vernunft*) was merely the most perfect and highest embodiment of the same rationalism that had earlier been represented by the less sophisticated Enlightenment philosophy of the intellect (*Verstand*).[2] In their attempts to prove the essential identity of all forms of rationalism, the Slavophiles emphasized their common 'pagan' origins. According to Kireevsky, Hegel's views were basically identical with those of Aristotle while dialectics were first formulated by Heraclitus and the Eleatic school: 'Hegel took a different path, which was outside Aristotle's system, but he agreed with him both in his final conclusions and in his view of the relationship between mind and truth. He constructed a new system, but as Aristotle himself would have done if he had been reborn in our times. . . .'[3]

[1] Khomyakov, i. 293.
[2] See Kireevsky, i. 247.
[3] Ibid., p. 234. See Marcuse's statement that Hegel's philosophy was in fact a reinterpretation of Aristotle's ontology. H. Marcuse, *Reason and Revolution. Hegel and the Rise of Social Theory* (New York 1954), p. 42.

Although the Slavophiles' critique of Hegelianism was part of their critique of rationalism as such, both in philosophy and social relations, it nevertheless deserves separate treatment. The aim is not to make a systematic compilation of all Slavophile comments on Hegel, but rather to show, by a comparative analysis of the two systems, that Hegel was by no means a neutral figure in the doctrinal dispute between the Slavophiles and Westernizers. Only comparable elements, of course, lend themselves to comparison. These comparable elements would seem to fall under five main heads.

1. The theoretical basis of rationalism.
2. The rationalization of the motivation of human actions.
3. The rationalization of social bonds.
4. The rationalization of the historical process.
5. The historical necessity of rationalization.

In Slavophile doctrine these problems were closely related (as indeed they were in Hegelian philosophy). Like Hegel, the Slavophile philosophers regarded philosophy as a reflection of the historical principles governing social life, and social life itself as 'the outward, historical development of an underlying philosophical system'.[1]

1. For Kireevsky the original sin of rationalism was an attitude that might be summed up in the phrase 'epistemological anti-ontologism';[2] an attitude which assumes the isolation of the knower from reality, turns cognition into a purely conceptual process and fails to grasp the reality and objectivity of the universe. The extreme version of this attitude was the Cartesian 'cogito ergo sum' which posited the primacy of thought over being and deduced being from thought instead of the other way round.[3]

It was from this starting-point that Khomyakov developed his systematic critique of classical German philosophy. Its founder, Kant, argued Khomyakov, went no further than saying that being—the thing-in-itself—was unknowable; Hegel, who took rationalism to its utmost limits, announced that the world of things had no objective existence, that the 'thing-in-itself' existed only in knowledge (the concept).[4] With this

---

[1] Khomyakov, iii. 240–1.
[2] See V. V. Zenkovsky, *A History of Russian Philosophy* (London 1953), i. 219.
[3] See Kireevsky, i. 196.   [4] See Khomyakov, i. 293.

statement, which brought the development of rationalism to its logical final end, the German school broke up. This break-up Khomyakov regarded as the school's triumph:

The decline [he wrote] did not come about because its representatives, formidable to the end, grew tired, and not because there was less interest shown in it by the public, who followed its development with unwavering, ,almost superstitious attention, and not because of petty schisms arising out of the uncertainty or obscurity of statements delivered by the great masters; nor was it driven out by some new and powerful doctrine. It collapsed because of all philosophical schools it was the only one to follow its path to the end, consistent to the last conclusion. Faced by an impossible task—the reconstruction of being from an abstract law—it came to a stop and collapsed. It undoubtedly deserves eternal glory in the history of learning. It defined and closed the circle of abstract thought based on pure intellect and established its laws clearly and unambiguously for the whole of mankind and for all times.[1]

The collapse of the school was a warning against the temptations of rationalism, which aimed to subjugate the entire spiritual sphere: 'By adopting the concept as the sole basis of all thought, we destroy the world, for the concept turns every actuality belonging to it into a pure, abstract possibility.'[2] One of the destructive results of this process was the development of post-Hegelian philosophy in Germany.

According to Khomyakov, the theoretical error in Hegelian philosophy was that it made no distinction between the real fact and its conceptual formula and that it confused two methods of achieving knowledge: analysis, which passes from the 'universal' to the concrete, and synthesis, which leads from the concrete to the universal.

Common to the entire school is an error which is not yet obvious in the founder, Kant, but is absolutely typical of Hegel and which consists in the repeated identification of the development of concepts in the individual consciousness with the movement of reality itself. It is true that the way of the concept and the way of reality are indeed identical, but they are identical as a ladder is the same for him who climbs up and for him who comes down: the way is the same, but the movement is diametrically opposed.[3]

[1] Ibid., p. 273.
[2] Ibid., pp. 299–300, quoted according to *Russian Philosophy*, i. 232.
[3] Khomyakov, i. 144–5.

Khomyakov illustrated this idea (which recalls Marx's critique of Hegel in the *Introduction to a Critique of Political Economy*)[1] with the example of a man looking at the dome of St. Peter's: from the fact that he sees the dome the man concludes that the dome exists, for if it did not exist he could not in fact see it; this does not mean, however, that the dome only exists because this particular man can see it. In order to avoid this nonsensical but inevitable conclusion it was necessary to introduce the collective genius of mankind; that is

a living and real being, set apart from the individuals that make up the human race, developing according to the strict laws of logical necessity, and transforming all particular individuals into hieroglyphs, symbols or puppets through whom it elucidates the mysteries of its inner meaning. The individuals who have been converted into puppets are now blindly obedient to the external law; no longer does history know, or want to know, the logic of their internal development, although this internal logic alone is of real significance. This is the second absurdity, introduced in order to avoid the first, but not, of course, introduced unambiguously, but by means of skilful phrases that are half-precise and half-metaphor.[2]

Because it identified the dialectics of concepts with real movement, Hegelian philosophy became transformed into a 'mystical-rationalistic teleology'.[3] Hegel 'understood history in reverse, having set out the present and the result as something significant and necessary, the inevitable product of the past';[4] the logical formula of historical development for him became the cause of actual development. When we study historical reality, Khomyakov pointed out, we pass from results to causes, and the causes are therefore conditioned by their results. This is only true of cognition however; where reality is concerned, the converse is true: 'The present anticipates the future for it contains the future as the seed contains the fruit; however, it would be absurd to maintain that the future fruit conditions the growth of the seed, or that the result conditions the cause;

---

[1] See K. Marx, *A Contribution to the Critique of Political Economy*, trans. by N. I. Stone, London 1904, pp. 293–4: '. . . the method of advancing from the abstract to the concrete is but a way of thinking by which the concrete is grasped and is reproduced in our mind as a concrete. It is by no means, however, the process which itself generates the concrete.'

[2] Khomyakov, i. 144.

[3] Ibid., iii. 344.   [4] Ibid. i. 36.

and yet this is how the entire Hegelian school interprets history.'[1] These arguments have a surprising affinity with the young Marx's comments on the speculative interpretation of history, which became possible when a teleological order was substituted for the causal order. The relationship between the present and the past, Marx wrote in the *German Ideology*,

can be speculatively distorted so that later history is made the goal of earlier history, e.g. the goal ascribed to the discovery of America is to further the eruption of the French Revolution. Thereby history receives its own special aims and becomes a 'person ranking with other persons' . . . while what is designated with the words 'destiny', 'goal', 'germ', or 'idea', of earlier history is nothing more than an abstraction formed from later history, from the active influence which earlier history exercises on later history.[2]

These points of agreement between Khomyakov and Marx are an interesting illustration of the fact that critics of Hegel from the Right and from the Left had certain assumptions in common.[3] One aspect of Hegel's philosophy which drew the fire of both sides (in polemics which used similar arguments although the ultimate aims were very different) was his panlogism and instrumentalism. Both Right and Left regarded panlogism as the 'annihilation of the personality', but whereas the Right sought the necessary metaphysical basis of personality in the theistic conception of a personal God,[4] the Left, or at least its most consistent representatives, thought the 'affirmation of the individual' depended on the 'negation of God' (Feuerbach) and on materialism, which set the individual free both from the patriarchal personal God and from Hegel's impersonal spirit. Opposing Hegel, both the Right and the Left rehabilitated the value of immediacy, though what the philosophers of the Right had in mind was the immediacy of the bonds linking the individual with an irrational supra-individual whole, whereas Feuerbach and Stirner[5] were concerned with the

---

[1] Ibid. vii. 446.

[2] K. Marx and F. Engels, *The German Ideology* (Lawrence and Wishart, London 1965), p. 59.

[3] The terms 'Right' and 'Left' are here used in their strictly historical meaning and should therefore not be taken to have universal significance.

[4] See Kroński, op. cit., pp. 157–228.

[5] See Z. Kuderowicz, 'Misja filozofii i jej przemiany', *Archiwum Historii Filozofii i Myśli Społecznej*, vol. vii (Warsaw 1962).

immediacy of the individual as a physical being endowed not merely with an intellect, but with feelings and senses.[1] When conservatives took up the cudgels against Hegel's historiosophical instrumentalism, it was either in order to defend the Christian conception of the individual being endowed with an immortal soul, and absolute criteria of good and evil (the Right-wing Hegelians); or else in order to protest against the tyranny of historical Reason and to assert the right of irrational collective individualities (nations) to live according to principles of their own impervious to reason and to refuse to submit to allegedly universal laws (the conservative romanticists, in Russia especially Apollon Grigoryev). The left (Feuerbach, and Belinsky and Herzen in Russia) also criticized instrumentalism, but did so as part of the individual's revolt against the tyranny of the Universal and the Hegelian Absolute; to them the antithesis of historical Reason was not irrationalism, but the autonomy of individual reason.[2] When Khomyakov criticized Hegel's teleology for its reduction of the individual's role to that of a puppet, he was not—in contrast to Marx and the philosophical Left—concerned to defend concrete human beings as the sole makers of history. His aim rather was to show that the historical process was not directed by reason but by the mysterious decrees of Providence;[3] that what individuals should obey was not the dictates of universal reason moving within the historical process (which, according to Khomyakov, would have meant obedience to something 'external'), but the dictates of an internalized tradition accepted without reflection, which constitutes man's 'spiritual substance'.

In this context a comparision between Khomyakov's standpoint and Herzen's critique of the 'Buddhist' interpretation of Hegelianism proves extremely illuminating.[4] 'Buddhism' was the charge that Herzen laid at the door of the 'formalist' Hegelians, although he admitted that Hegel himself was partially responsible for the 'Buddhist' interpretation of his philosophy. Khomyakov also called Hegelianism the philosophical counterpart of Buddhism[5] and suggested that the evolution of

---

[1] See chapter 8, p. 382.   [2] See ibid., pp. 389–92.

[3] See Khomyakov, vii. 446.

[4] The reference is to Herzen's article 'Buddhism in Science' (1843), the last part of his cycle *Dilettantism in Science*.

[5] See Khomyakov, vi. 175.

the Buddhist doctrine reflected the various conceptions held by different exponents of Hegelianism. He regarded nihilism, the self-annihilating striving after Nirvana, to be a feature shared by both Buddhism and Hegelianism,[1] and suggested that in Hegel it stemmed from his anti-ontological rationalism, which attempted to create a 'world without a substratum'. Consistent rationalism, according to Khomyakov, was a philosophy that totally eliminated will as an autonomous creative attribute of the personality, having precedence over the sphere of cognition. Herzen used a similar argument when he opposed the Nirvana of conceptual abstraction, which annihilates the personality, and protested against panlogism on the ground that apart from logical thought processes man 'is also endowed with will, which might be called positive reason, creative reason'.[2]

Where Herzen attempted to formulate a theory of his own, in *Buddhism in Science*, the analogy with Khomyakov ceases to be valid. Herzen needed 'will as creative reason' in order to 'activate philosophy' (*odeĭstvorenie filosofii*), and to create the foundations for a 'philosophy of action', which would undertake the conscious transformation of the world in the direction of greater rationalization. Like Feuerbach, Herzen defended himself against the danger of Buddhist self-destruction by turning towards materialism, a system which guaranteed the 'substantiality' of the individual, reaffirmed the real physical existence of man and nature, and thereby opposed the despotism of the spirit. Herzen's own example therefore illustrates—partially at least—Khomyakov's thesis that the natural outcome of the break-up of the Hegelian school was materialism. Since the problem of how to 'create a world without a substratum' turned out to be insoluble, it became necessary to find some kind of substratum at all costs.

And thus Hegelianism [Khomyakov ironically pointed out], the most abstract of human abstractions, simply seized hold of matter and passed to the purest and crudest materialism. Matter becomes the substratum, but otherwise Hegel's system is retained; i.e. the terminology, most of the definitions, the transitions of thought, logical tricks, etc. all are retained—in a word, everything that can

---

[1] See ibid. i. 94.
[2] Herzen, iii. 76.

be called the manufacturing process of Hegel's mind. The great thinker did not live long enough to suffer this humiliation, but perhaps his disciples would not have dared so to humiliate their teacher if the grave had not concealed his terrifying countenance.[1]

The Slavophile standpoint was expressed by Khomyakov in his notion of integral reason, which he intended as an antidote to Hegelianism (Kireevsky preferred the expression 'integral personality'). Khomyakov's integral reason included conceptual cognition but based itself on *will*, its active faculty, and *faith*, a perceptive faculty which can grasp the 'living reality' of the object perceived: 'In this sphere, which precedes logical cognition and which is filled with a vital consciousness that does not need demonstrations or arguments, man becomes capable of distinguishing between the creations of his mind and the external world. Here, by the touchstone of his free will, man perceives what in his objective world is the product of his creative (subjective) activity and what exists independently of it.'[2] Both *will* and *faith* are granted to man *directly*; *faith* is internal, *immediate* knowledge. When defining the nature of this fundamental cognitive faculty, Khomyakov used the term *das unmittelbare Wissen* borrowed from Jacobi.[3] His perception that Hegelianism in this respect represented a diametrically opposed standpoint was not unfounded: 'Immediacy in man', wrote Hegel, 'is something undesirable, something that should be overcome.'[4] Immediacy as such, he argued, played no part whatsoever in cognition and the phenomenon known as immediate knowledge, so far from precluding mediation in the cognitive process, was always its outcome.[5]

In many ways the Slavophile critique of Hegelianism recalls Schelling's views. After a long conversation K. L. Michelet once told the young Kireevsky: 'Jowohl! Sie können vielleicht Recht haben, aber diese Meinung gehört vielmehr zu dem Schellingischen, als zu dem Hegelischen System.'[6] A few years later (1830) Kireevsky listened eagerly to Schellings's Munich lectures, in which the ageing philosopher accused Hegel of

[1] Khomyakov, i. 302.   [2] Ibid., p. 327.
[3] See ibid., p. 279.
[4] Hegel, 'Lectures on the Philosophy of Religion', *Sämmtliche Werke* (Leipzig 1929), vol. ix, part 3, p. 106.
[5] See M. F. Ovsyannikov, *Filosofia Gegela* (Moscow 1959), p. 93.
[6] Kireevsky, i. 36.

reducing reality to a 'lifeless schematism' and argued that the 'logical concept is empty and does not comprehend reality as such'.[1] In the later Slavophile period of his philosophical development Kireevsky considered Schelling to have been the first Western European philosopher to realize the bankruptcy of rationalism; Hegel, on the other hand, he called the greatest European rationalist, a thinker utterly satisfied with the 'immaterial world of concepts'.

However, neither Schelling nor any other theoretical critic of rationalism satisfied the Slavophile philosophers; the guarantee and essential prerequisite of true faith, they insisted, was a life guided by tradition and participation in a supra-individual community—the type of community that had disintegrated in Western Europe. Social disintegration, in their view, could only lead to rationalism or else to a theoretical, purely negative critique of rationalism born of nostalgia for a lost tradition. Thus, only their own social philosophy, in fact, which claimed to have found in Orthodoxy and the communal traditions of the Russian people the values irrevocably lost in Europe, was capable of providing a positive critique of rationalism (and therefore also of Hegelianism).

2. The rational basis of the motivation of human actions interested Hegel in connection with the issue of freedom with which his philosophy of history was ultimately concerned. Hegel distinguished two concepts of freedom: 'substantial' and 'subjective' freedom.

Substantial freedom [he wrote] is the abstract undeveloped reason implicit in volition, proceeding to develop itself in the state. But in this phase of reason there is still wanting personal insight and will, that is subjective freedom, which is realized only in the individual and which constitutes the reflection of the individual in his own conscience. Where there is merely substantial freedom commands and laws are regarded as something fixed and abstract to which the subject holds himself in absolute servitude. These laws need not concur with the desire of the individual, and the subjects are consequently like children, who obey their parents without will or insight of their own.[2]

---

[1] See Kuno Fischer, *F. W. J. Schelling, Geschichte der neuern Philosophie* (Heidelberg 1872), vol. vi.

[2] Hegel, *The Philosophy of History*, trans. by J. Sibtree, Revised edn. (Willey Book Co., New York 1944), p. 98.

The process of rationalization, which forms the meaningful content of history, leads to the appearance of subjective freedom. The latter is an inseparable element of rationalization, for the process of the emancipation of reason (the 'Universal') is accompanied by the emancipation of the individual 'who comprehends himself as a *person*, that is recognizes himself in his single existence as possessing universality—as capable of abstraction from and surrendering all speciality; and therefore, as inherently infinite'.[1] 'Pure universal thought, since its nature is universality, is apt to bring the special and spontaneous—belief, trust, customary morality—to reflect upon itself, and its primitive simplicity'; it becomes necessary to establish the rational motivation of actions, that is 'insight derived from rational grounds and the requirement of such grounds'.[2]

Hegel was far from idealizing subjective freedom; he stressed that its immediate consequence was 'the isolation of individuals from each other and from the whole . . .; their aggressive selfishness and vanity; their seeking personal advantage and consulting this at the expense of the state at large'.[3] Rational freedom, on the other hand, he called 'the principle of thought, perception, reasoning, insight derived from rational grounds'.[4] He defined 'rationality' as the unity of objective (substantial) and subjective freedom,[5] but emphasized that it was subjective freedom which formed a turning-point in history, a gulf separating ancient and modern times.[6] When Christianity made its appearance 'unreflective ethics could not continue to hold its ground against the principle of subjective freedom'.[7] The conduct of modern man, Hegel wrote in his *Philosophy of Law*, is governed by the consciously taken decision 'I will' and this principle must be respected by the state.[8]

Even the most superficial examination of Slavophile ideology shows that although the Slavophiles did not use Hegelian terminology, they stood for substantial freedom and regarded

[1] Hegel, *The Philosophy of History*, p. 70.
[2] Ibid., pp. 76–7.
[3] Ibid.   [4] Ibid., p. 77.
[5] See Hegel, *Grundlinien der Philosophie des Rechts*, § 258.
[6] See ibid., § 124.
[7] Hegel, *The Philosophy of History*, p. 334.
[8] See Hegel, *Grundlinien* . . ., § 274.

subjective freedom as 'the greatest of evils and the most unbridled profligacy in the world' (in the words of Aksakov,
quoted earlier in this chapter). The Slavophiles thought that
freedom was a function of the collective rather than the individual human being; Aksakov maintained that the word
svoboda was derived from *svoĭ bȳt* (one's own being), that is
conduct according to internalized norms accepted in the collective recognized as one's own.[1] Individual actions need not be
rationalized since the collective is guided by its own supra-
individual reason. Aksakov wrote, 'the peasant reasons with
"folk" reason . . . the people's mode of life precludes individual
stupidity.'[2] Folk reason in fact is the unthinking assimilation of
tradition, belief, and customs. The Slavophiles quite agreed
with Hegel that obedience to tradition could be compared to
children's obedience to their parents, but they differed radically
in their evaluation of such parental care: in their eyes Hegel's
subjective freedom tore man away from his 'natural family
bonds and the fellowship of the natural community', and
instead gave him the 'complete freedom of homeless orphanhood'.[3]

This was not the only profound difference between the
Hegelian and Slavophile conception of freedom. For Hegel freedom meant the *freedom of reason*, liberation from any kind of
irrational 'spontaneity'; the Slavophiles, on the other hand,
interpreted freedom as irrational spontaneity or as *freedom from
reason*. The Hegelian will was always conscious will directed
towards definite goals, otherwise it was instinct;[4] for the Slavophiles will preceded cognition and therefore could not be conscious. Hegel posited that man felt 'at home' only in the
process of thinking whereas for the Slavophiles ratiocination
induced alienation, stifled spontaneity, and brought about a
painful inner duality of personality. In order to avoid this,
human beings should not be guided by rational motivation but
by tradition. As Khomyakov put it:

In intellectual speculation and convictions founded upon it there is
neither completeness nor life. Faith and the fullness of religious life

[1] Aksakov, *Zamechaniya* . . ., p. 3.
[2] Aksakov, i. 632.
[3] Aksakov, iii. 99.
[4] See Hegel, *Grundlinien* . . ., § 4.

are inseparable from tradition, which encompasses and unites thought and conditions of being, feeling, and reasoning. Men cannot create tradition and therefore reforms, even when they improve an old doctrine, restrict the sphere of spiritual activity and destroy the unity of inward and outward existence.

The weakness of the reformer is inner conflict; the strength of the carrier of tradition is peace of mind and inner calm. Both the conflict and the peace of mind are handed down to their disciples and the centuries cannot obliterate them. Within the confines of tradition there is freedom, for the outward forms of life are ready for the spirit within. . . .[1]

The Slavophile ideal was thus inner harmony founded on the complete consonance of man's inward and outward existence. This notion was quite foreign to Hegel, to whom absolute harmony was the equivalent of absolute stagnation. The Slavophiles and the Hegelians differed primarily in the values they attached to certain concepts. Like the Slavophiles, Hegel regarded 'subjectivity' as a source of anxiety and pain, but added that man's dualism and inner division (*Zweiheit* and *Zerissenheit*)[2] are bound up with his spiritual nature and that only an animal lives in harmony with itself and the world around it. 'Subjectivity' opened the way to evil, but at the same time turned men into God-like beings. In his *Philosophy of Law* Hegel referred to the myth of the Fall and argued that it was possible to concur with the view that man resembles God in his knowledge of good and evil if one thought of man not as a child, but as an independent human being, and of good as the knowledge of it.[3] Although it might appear that Hegel (unlike the Slavophiles) had overlooked the fact that in the Bible Eve is condemned for plucking the apple from the Tree of Knowledge, he had merely placed the myth within the context of a peculiar dialectical theodicy. He did not think that the destruction of paradisiacal harmony was something good as such; in contradistinction to the Slavophiles, however, he saw in the Biblical Fall a prerequisite of progress, a necessary 'moment' in the dialectical 'Odyssey of the Spirit'.

Like the Slavophiles, Hegel asserted that 'the principle of

[1] Khomyakov, v. 328.
[2] Hegel, *Ästhetik* (Berlin 1955), p. 134.
[3] Hegel, *Grundlinien* . . ., § 139.

infinite subjective freedom' was a Western principle.[1] That was why the Western nations were carriers of progress ('historical nations') and why no true Hegelian could be a Slavophile and no Slavophile a Hegelian.

3. The problem of the rational basis of individual actions was closely bound up with the whole issue of the rational basis of historical acts, of the validation of conscious decisions affecting whole nations and states. In the specific context of German post-feudal particularism this issue turned into a dispute between the supporters of 'theoretical' (rational) law, who aimed at a reform of the existing system and state centralization 'from above', and those who defended 'historical' ('positive') law as an organic whole that had evolved out of customs and traditions and could not be changed mechanically to suit the arbitrary will of the legislator.

There can be little doubt as to where Slavophile sympathies lay. In their eyes only social phenomena that were deeply rooted in the past and grew from the soil, independently of rationality and subjective individual will, had history's stamp of approval. In societies where the 'bond of faith and love' had not yet snapped, the individual's power of reasoning was subordinated to tradition and 'by itself creates nothing and does not aspire to create anything'.[2] For the Slavophiles the domination of a rational juridical system was typical of the West and one of the main differences distinguishing it from ancient Russia.

Roman and Western legislation [Kireevsky wrote] deduces logical propositions from every legal convention by abstract reasoning and asserts that form *is* the law; it then attempts to combine all forms into a rational system in which every part could be correctly deduced from the whole, in accordance with abstract and rational necessity, while the whole would not only be reasonable, but *reason itself in written form*. Common law, on the other hand, as it existed in Russia, grew out of life and its evolution had nothing to do with abstract logic. In Russia the law was not drawn up in advance by learned jurists: it was not the subject of profound and eloquent discussions in any legislative assembly and did not later fall like snow on the heads of the surprised public, breaking up some established arrangement

---

[1] Hegel, *The Philosophy of History*, p. 393.
[2] Khomyakov, i. 127.

in social relations. In Russia the law was not drawn up but was in fact only written down on paper when it had taken shape by itself in the minds of the people, had become accepted as custom and part of folkways. The logical development of law is only possible where society itself is based on artificial conventions.[1]

The Slavophiles were amongst the most consistent opponents of 'rational' legislation; in pointing out the rational nature of Roman law and its role in European history they went further than Savigny and the 'Romanist' wing of the historical school of jurisprudence, who maintained that the Roman law assimilated by Germans was in fact 'positive' law.

Arguments put forward by the historical school against 'theoretical' law were often employed by the Slavophiles (especially by Aksakov) to attack juridical systems as such. In the specific historical context this is understandable: the legislation introduced by Russia's absolute rulers, in particular that of Peter the Great, which was still in force in the nineteenth century, took absolutely no account of national traditions or customs, and was far more 'theoretical' than the legislation of Frederick II. This explains why the antithesis between 'historical' custom and 'theoretical' (rational) law assumed such an extreme form in Slavophile thought.

At the opposite pole to the point of view of the conservative romanticists was the 'juridical view of the world' (Engels) of the Enlightenment, with its faith in the omnipotence of rational legislation deduced from the abstract axioms of 'natural law'. Hegel's position in the dispute on the nature of the legislative system was complicated by the fact that, like the historical school, he was sharply critical of the anti-historical approach of Enlightenment thinkers. Hegel's dialectical rationalism, however, had nothing in common with the romanticists' idealization of historical evolution as an irrational elemental force. There is sufficient evidence of this in the *Philosophy of Right*, which was devoted to polemics with the historical school and in the political essays, especially the *Württemberg Estates* (1817) and the *English Reform Bill* (1831).[2]

---

[1] Kireevsky, i. 208.

[2] The following pages owe much to the analysis of Hegel's political works contained in the unpublished doctoral thesis by Z. Pełczyński, 'Hegel's Minor Political Works' (Faculty of Social Studies of the University of Oxford, July 1956).

'The fundamental error in the position adopted by the Württemberg Estates', Hegel wrote, 'lies in this, that they start from *positive* law'; that

they demanded rights on the sole ground that they had been possessed of them before. They acted like a merchant who proposed to ply his trade just the same on a ship in which his capital was sunk, even though it had gone to the bottom, and to expect others to advance the same credit to him on the strength of it as before. . . . One might say of the Württemberg Estates what has been said of the returned French émigrés: they have forgotten nothing and learnt nothing. They seem to have slept through the last twenty-five years, possibly the richest that world history has had, and for us the most instructive, because it is to them that our world and our ideas belong.[1]

According to Hegel, the 'positivity' of law was not an argument in its favour; only the 'rationality' of law mattered, although he had in mind rationality in a definite historical context, rather than any abstract quality. This latter reservation did not bring Hegel any closer to the historical school, since the dispute between them was not about historicism but about whether changes in legislation could be the result of conscious and rationally motivated decisions. Here Hegel took up a clear and unambiguous standpoint: without in the least condemning *a priori* all traditional institutions, he definitely rejected the traditionalist approach to law. In Hegel's eyes the English legislative system, which was idealized by the conservatives, was an extreme example of a non-rational approach. In his essay on the Reform Bill he expressed the hope that thanks to the methods used to prepare for them, the electoral reforms now being undertaken (in 1831) would usher in the age of 'political rationality' in England. The conservative romanticists on the other hand, stressed the 'organic' nature of 'positive' law, organic being anything that had its roots in the remote past and 'grew' spontaneously, without the intervention of rational reflection (the British constitution, for instance, but not the Code Napoléon).

In fact Britain was often quoted by the Slavophiles as the

[1] *Hegel's Political Writings*, trans. by T. M. Knox, with an Introductory Essay by Z. A. Pełczyński (Oxford 1964), pp. 281, 283.

European country where the 'organic principles of life' had been best preserved.[1] It is interesting to note that for Hegel the term 'organic' had an entirely different meaning. This emerges clearly from his comparison between the British 'constitution' and the 'constitution' of the former German Empire:[2] both, according to him, were the creation of chance, force, and whim; both were 'positive' and irrational and formed an aggregate rather than a system. It was wrong to apply the term 'organic' to the British constitution, which recalled an old house with a multitude of irregular additions; what was truly organic, was the modern notion of the state as a rationally organized and systematic entity.[3] Only the full unfolding of an idea could be called organic, and 'organicity' was therefore an attribute of organized, internally coherent, and purposeful systems. Rationality was not the antithesis but rather a prerequisite of organic development. It is clear that Hegel, in contrast to the Slavophiles, regarded 'organicity' as a product of the systematizing activity of historical reason.

4. Hegel considered the state to be the most organic and therefore the most rational form of social organization. The Hegelian state, which was derived from the rationalist traditions of Protestantism and the Enlightenment, was the direct antithesis of the patriarchal 'Christian state' idealized by the Catholic romantics. It was a bureaucratic and legalistic state, a rationalized and depersonalized structure, founded on the authority of reason rather than irrational tradition; in which inter-personal relations were regulated according to a tidy system of clearly formulated and published edicts. To the Hegelians the Kingdom of Prussia seemed to correspond most closely to their ideal: they considered the bureaucratic centralized state to be the most important factor in the rationalization of social relations, and a powerful support in the struggle against the forces of reaction which went under the general name of 'romanticism'.[4] The attitude of the Hegelians to Frederick the Great recalls the Russian Westernizers' characteristic cult of Peter the Great, while the attacks of the German

---

[1] See Khomyakov's 'Letter about England' in vol. i of his *Collected Works*.
[2] *Hegel's Political Writings*, pp. 299–300.
[3] See ibid., pp. 247–9.
[4] See Cornu, *Karl Marx und Friedrich Engels. Leben und Werke* (Berlin 1954), vol. i, chapter III.

romantics on the philosopher-king' recalled the Slavophiles' attacks on the 'revolutionary tsar'.

In all essentials the Slavophile conception of the state was analogous to Hegel's, except that where Hegel approved, the Slavophiles disapproved. The Slavophile thinkers agreed with Hegel that the essence of the state was rationalism, and this confirmed them in their belief that the state was in itself an evil, perhaps essential in view of human imperfection, but merely in the narrow and strictly separate realm of politics. The 'state principle', they argued, was only an 'external truth' and as such ought not to interfere in the people's way of life, where 'truly Christian' and unrationalized forms of social bonds still prevailed.

In Slavophile theory the exponent of the organic principle was the common people, while the state was a soulless mechanism; according to Hegelian theory the people (nation) only became organic when it assumed the guise of a state; when not organized in a state the common people was merely an 'inorganic multitude', and 'formless mass' whose actions were 'elemental, irrational, barbarous, and frightful'.[1] Hegel criticized the British Tories for their opposition to a rational unification of the law, whereas the Slavophiles praised them for their defence of the multicentricity of social life, which sprang from the 'organic evolution of history'.[2] According to the Slavophiles the path of 'external truth' (of state and law) led to the depersonalization of human relations and to the substitution of alienated institutionalized forms of social relations for mutual trust and unanimity. With certain reservations, Hegel regarded depersonalization as a sign of progress, and argued that authority was purely personal only among barbarians: in civilized nations the impersonal and all-embracing authority of the law stood between the ruler and his subjects.[3] For Hegel attitudes to the law were a fundamental criterion for judging the 'false brothers and friends of the so-called people'.[4] The cornerstone of the Slavophile conception of organic togetherness (*sobornost'*) was the 'principle of love', which was the antithesis of individualism and external authority. For Hegel 'love'

---

[1] Hegel, *Grundlinien* . . ., § 303. [2] See Khomyakov, i. 123–9.
[3] See Hegel, *Schriften zur Politik und Rechtsphilosophie* (Die Philosophische Bibliothek) (1923), pp. 70–1. [4] Foreword to the *Philosophy of Right*.

was only a sentiment, an immediate spontaneous feeling which ranked below the rationality and universality of the 'concept'. Love was an entirely legitimate sentiment within the family, but in the state, Hegel wrote, 'feeling disappears. . . . There the content must be rational and known to us'.[1] It was because the Slavophiles agreed with this definition that they proclaimed the superiority of the family and wanted political relations to approximate as closely as possible to patriarchal family relations.

I have deliberately overemphasized the points of difference between these two conceptions: in fact Hegel fully realized that the process of rationalization could not embrace all spheres of life and was himself critical of abstract rationality and its social consequences. He also allowed a place for the non-rationalized social bonds idealized by the Slavophiles, but only as a subordinate element within an essentially rational construction that was evolving towards ever greater rationality. The Slavophiles, in their turn, were willing to grant the value of Hegelian reason, but only as an element subordinate to 'integral wholeness'. Hegelian reason, Kireevsky wrote, contradicts 'Orthodox thinking' only in so far as it sets itself up as the highest cognitive faculty;[2] Khomyakov was even prepared to accept the relative usefulness of the 'rational force of individuals' in society, but stressed that tradition—'a fundamental innate force, developing according to its own distinct laws from its principles, its organic roots'—must always be superior.[3] In fact the Slavophiles and Hegel differed not so much in their interpretation of historical details, as in their conception of the historical process as a whole.

It is worth illustrating this difference by a concrete example. For Hegel as well as for the Slavophiles ancient Rome, where the state had become a pure abstraction and was transformed into an autonomous goal, represented the 'realm of abstract universality'. The Slavophile conception of ancient Rome, which declared the abstract universality of the law to be the reverse side of the process of internal atomization, had its counterpart to a large extent in Hegel's philosophy of history; both Hegel and the Slavophiles, for instance, treated Rome as a

[1] Hegel, *Grundlinien* . . ., § 158.
[2] See Kireevsky, i. 257.   [3] See Khomyakov, i. 127.

kind of archetype of bourgeois society.[1] In the Hegelian system, however, Rome represented humanity's manhood, that is *a step forward* in relation to the 'unreflective ethics' of the Greeks: individuals were subordinated to the universal, but in return acquired their own 'universality or in other words, individuality',[2] and this paved the way for the future national reconciliation of the particular and the universal. To the Slavophiles on the other hand Rome represented the death of the spirit, the *conclusion* of an entire historical cycle which was later repeated in Western Europe and led to the same symptoms of decline.

It is clear therefore that unless we isolate the problem from its historiosophical context the similarity between Hegel's view of Rome and that of the Slavophiles is more apparent than real. The same is true of similarities between Hegelian and romantic criticism of the 'abstractness' of Enlightenment rationalism and the 'atomism' of its social philosophy. The romantic critics of the Enlightenment refuted rationalism in principle, whereas Hegel sought to establish it on new dialectical and historical foundations. Friedrich Schlegel defined the difference when he wrote that the philosophy of these professed opponents of the Enlightenment was only a more subtle and flexible and therefore more dangerous form of rationalism;[3] Khomyakov made an identical observation when he called Hegelian reason Enlightenment reason in dialectical guise.

In the 1830s and '40s, when there was a radical polarization of political attitudes among German philosophers, it became more and more obvious that though Hegelian philosophy was critical of eighteenth-century thought it actually stood for the same basic values as those defended by Enlightenment philosophy. The most outspoken expression of this view was K. Köppen's pamphlet *Frederick the Great and his Opponents* (published in 1840 and dedicated to Karl Marx), which called on the traditional Hegelians to renounce their criticism of the Enlightenment and to admit openly that they were its heirs.

It is high time [Köppen wrote] to desist from shallow declamations against the eighteenth-century philosophers and to recognize even the German representatives of the Enlightenment, though they may

[1] See Ovsynnikov, op. cit., pp. 72, 240–1.
[2] Hegel, *The Philosophy of History*, p. 100.
[3] See Schlegel, *Philosophie des Lebens* (Vienna 1928), lecture 1.

be bores. In reality, we owe them a great deal, as much as to Luther and the leaders of the Reformation and perhaps even more. . . . It [the Enlightenment] was a Prometheus who descended to earth with the gift of heavenly light in order to enlighten the blind, the common people and the laity, and to liberate them from superstition and error. . . . This should be taken into consideration by the apostles of the new salvation who are so willing to condemn the abstract reason of the eighteenth century without realizing that they are attacking their own cause.[1]

As will be seen later, the philosophical Left in Russia passed through a similar evolution, from passionate Francophobia to an equally passionate vindication of the French Enlightenment.

5. The Slavophiles were in complete agreement with Hegel that the real content of Western European history was the gradual advance of rationalization; however, they were not prepared to accept this proposition as a necessary and universal law. In the Russian context the Hegelian conception of historical laws was a weapon in the hands of the Westernizers, since it justified the historical inevitability and irreversibility of Europeanization and exposed the utopian character of Slavophile doctrine. Belinsky called the Slavophiles men 'who do not recognize the rational necessity of great historical events'.[2] The Slavophiles took up the challenge; they dismissed the idea of historical necessity as theoretically unsound and morally offensive, since it sanctioned all evil (e.g. the excesses of Ivan the Terrible) by identifying success with legal validity. It is interesting to recall that Belinsky used similar arguments during his period of revolt against the 'Moloch of the Universal', another example of the superficial resemblance between criticism of Hegel from the Right and from the Left.

The reproach of 'historical immoralism' was to some extent justified in the case of the 'étatist' school (S. Solov'ëv and B. Chicherin) whose interpretation of Hegel stressed the need for centralization and the creative role of the state in Russian history. It is all the more interesting to note the sharp reaction in Slavophile circles to Solov'ëv's article 'Schlözer and the Anti-historical Orientation in Historiography' (1857). In this

---

[1] Quoted from Cornu, op. cit., p. 163. The young Marx too tried to 'rehabilitate' the Enlightenment but, unlike Köppen, did not therefore become an apologist for 'enlightened absolutism'.

[2] Belinsky, x. 14.

article Solov'ëv accused the Slavophiles of falling into the basic error of anti-historicism.

The phrase

'anti-historical orientation' is hardly apt . . . [Aksakov wrote in his reply to Solov'ëv], but the word has not been uttered in vain. The followers of this orientation, in Mr. Solov'ëv's sense of the term, understand history in a most curious and one-sided manner. It believes that the chronological order of historical events presupposes the inevitable progress from the good to the better, so that today always represents the truth and yesterday is fit for condemnation. This is not a cult of history but a cult of time.[1]

Khomyakov's comments were identical. In what sense, he asked, do the Slavophiles represent an anti-historical orientation? Do they negate the past? Do they reject historical knowledge? Do they wish to remould the past according to a model of their own? By no means; the real point at issue was that the trend criticized by Solov'ëv

does not enthuse over every historical period. It knows that the history of a nation, like the evolution of man, can be temporarily deflected from the norm (sometimes for a long time) . . . that an epoch is not always better because it comes later and that the present does not always keep faith with the inner law which is the pattern of correct development; finally it knows that it is often necessary to search in the past for those rational principles which, though momentarily suppressed and debarred from an active role, should still (to use Mr. Samarin's happy expression) grow from the past into the future.[2]

These words provide the most concise summing-up of the Slavophile conception of historicism. It is worth analysing them in some detail in the context of other Slavophile comments.

The Slavophiles reacted with sincere and unfeigned indignation to the reproach of being anti-historical. In their ideology historicity had an entirely positive value: it was in the name of historicity that they rejected rationalism which 'negates the past', and criticized the Petrine reforms, which they regarded as a violation of history, the 'rational individual's' arbitrary infringement of the 'elemental force of history'. They were

---

[1] Aksakov, i. 173–4.
[2] Khomyakov, iii. 283.

prepared for a defence of the reforms from a rationalist standpoint, but what shocked and outraged them was that the
Westernizing historians dared to speak in the name of *history*, to
claim that the term 'history' sanctioned everything which
(from the Slavophile standpoint) was in fact a brutal contradiction of genuine historicity. Herzen commented as follows:
'While being supporters of the historical principle they [the
Slavophiles] constantly forgot that everything accomplished
after Peter I was also history, and that no living power, let
alone the spectres of the past, is capable of blotting out accomplished facts or preventing their consequences.'[1]

Herzen was mistaken when he claimed to discern a contradiction or 'error' in the Slavophile standpoint, which in fact
only expressed their conviction that not all 'accomplished facts'
deserved to be called 'historical' and that by no means all
existing societies could lay claim to 'historicity'. Hegel himself
maintained that not everything which exists, is by the same
token 'historical'. For the Hegelians, however, the essential
criterion of the 'historical' character of a given fact was its
necessity and rationality, while for the Slavophiles, who in this
instance too represented a specific variant of European conservative romanticism, 'historicity' was an attribute which
stood in inverse proportion to Hegelian necessity and rationality.

How then was it possible to distinguish between 'historical'
and 'non-historical' reality? According to the conservative
romantics' conception of historicity, the rationalist is incapable of answering this question since he lacks the quality of
intuition or historical instinct. Nevertheless, one may try to
point out at least certain constituents of this 'historicity'.

The term 'historical' was applied by the Slavophiles to everything that preserved the uninterrupted continuity of tradition
and bore the unmistakable stamp of truly national heritage
and national character. National character, they maintained,
is formed by historical (and even geographical) circumstances
but is also a 'moral individuality' which, once formed, must be
treated as an objective and immutable factor in the historical
process. The most important national tradition is religion. The
term 'historicity' should therefore be applied to everything that
is permanent rather than variable. In this definition the empha-

[1] Herzen, vii. 234.

sis was placed not on the dynamics of historical processes, but on their continuity, conceived as 'organic growth' without internal disturbances or catastrophes. Historical reality could show conformity to certain rules (cf. Khomyakov's 'inner law' which forms the groundwork of progress), but these were more in the nature of internal norms than necessary or universal laws of history. To the Slavophiles 'historicity' had nothing in common with necessity; it was an internal and organic quality, while necessity was always something external and rational. The laws of necessity applied only in logic and the realm of the intellect; if they made their appearance in social life this was a symptom of the disease and approaching death of the social organism.

'Nothing is easier', wrote Kireevsky, 'than to represent every fact of reality as an inevitable consequence of the supreme laws of rational necessity, but nothing would so distort our actual understanding of history as these imaginary laws of rational necessity, which are actually only laws of rational possibility.'[1] Khomyakov regarded Hegelianism as the philosophical embodiment of the basic principles of Kushitism, the worship of necessity; since he thought that materialism was founded on the same principles, he regarded attempts to combine materialism and Hegelianism as something supremely natural. 'Pure rationalism and materialism', he wrote, 'are nothing but two sides of the same system, which I cannot call anything but the system of *necessitarianism* or unfreedom.'[2] The term unfreedom in this context signified the elimination of free will—the sphere of emotion and desires—in favour of reason or its corollary, the negation of freedom, which had no place in the rational realm of the laws of necessity.

For the Slavophiles, therefore, 'historicity' was not an inevitable feature of historical development, making its way by the force of necessity and crushing everything that stood in its way. Its position was constantly threatened and had to be carefully guarded; although its violation was fraught with terrible consequences (the disintegration of society), it could be violated, as the examples of the Petrine Reforms, the French Revolution, and the whole history of Western Europe had shown. 'Historicity' was therefore not a 'necessary' phenomenon, since the

[1] Kireevsky, i. 244.   [2] Khomyakov, i. 312.

laws of necessity governed only those societies whose fundamental principles had been poisoned by rationalism. Western European capitalism for instance, was the *necessary* by-product of the entire development of Europe hitherto and yet at the same time it represented the contradiction of all historicity.

For the Slavophiles regularity in the sense of development according to certain rules meant something quite different from regularity in the normative sense—a value judgement, which contrasts regular (natural) development with irregular (artificial) development. Every development is regular (in the former meaning of the word), otherwise it cannot be called development, Khomyakov wrote, adding however that 'the regular development of falsehood does not transform it into truth'.[1] This standpoint implies the total rejection of the concept of progress as a necessary law of history, so that whether a development can be called progressive in fact depends entirely on the principles in which it is rooted. Hence Aksakov suggested that the slogan 'forward' should be replaced by that of 'forward towards the truth', on the grounds that 'movement *forward towards the truth* cannot be equated with movement *forward* along one path, since the path itself can be false.'[2]

In rejecting the theory of progress as a law of history the Slavophiles made clear their opposition both to the evolutionist and to the dialectical approach to history. Although their theories were not fully worked out, they were clearly tending to a cyclical interpretation of history.[3] This is shown by their adoption of the then popular theory comparing historical development to the growth of the organism (the ages of 'childhood' and 'manhood'), and by their opposition to universalist theories of the 'history of mankind'.

In Hegel's dialectical approach to the philosophy of history, the categories of 'youth', 'maturity', etc. were applied to the history of individual nations—but also, and perhaps primarily, to the history of mankind as a whole. To Hegel the proper material of history was mankind, while individual nations (and civilizations) were only 'moments' in the historical process. In Hegelian terms the ancient East represented the childhood of

---

[1] Khomyakov, p. 140   [2] Brodsky, *Rannie slavyanofily*, p. 111.
[3] For a discussion of dialectic, evolutionary, and cyclical theories of history see H. Meyerhoff, *Time in Literature* (Berkeley and Los Angeles 1960).

man, Greece its youth, Rome its manhood, and Germany its old age, a period not of weakness but of full spiritual ripeness.[1] In the Slavophile philosophy of history such categories as childhood and old age etc. were applied solely to the history of individual nations or civilizations (cf. the concept 'European civilization'). The history of mankind was not the history of a collective human being evolving within the historical process, but merely the history of individual civilizations which passed through the same stages (from childhood to old age) and perished in order to yield their place to others.

In their criticism of the Hegelian universalism the Slavophiles were sometimes very close to Herder. Like Herder, they attacked the hidden Europocentric premiss of all conceptions of a unilinear, teleological development of history. However, they did not share Herder's tendency to create another universalism—universalism as a principle of plenitude, sanctifying cultural differences, explaining them as irreducible to each other but equally important for the elaboration of the all-embracing pluralist idea of mankind. The Slavophiles saw in this the danger of aesthetic relativism to which they were decidedly opposed. This is, perhaps, the reason why they were so strangely cold towards Herder, in spite of his high and deserved reputation among the western and southern Slavs. They were not satisfied with destroying the Europocentric universalism and replacing it with a pluralist universalism to which every nation could bring its unique and irreplaceable contribution. They wanted a type of universalism which would ascribe universal value to their own, 'truly Christian' (i.e. 'truly Russian') principles. They rejected all kinds of cultural relativism because they believed in absolute truth and identified it with their own truth. Thus the Russian people, as the carrier of 'truly Christian' principles, became the only incarnation of a true universalism.

This rather curious universalism had, of course, nothing in common with the belief that mankind as a whole was the collective subject of history. Khomyakov in fact rejected the foundations of the Hegelian philosophy of history because of its 'mystical concept of a collective spirit of a collective mankind'.[2] What is more, in their Orthodox universalism the Slavophiles

[1] See Hegel, *The Philosophy of History*, p. 101.
[2] Khomyakov, i. 36.

quite definitely rejected rationalist universalism and the idea of universal and all-embracing laws of history. Only reason is everywhere the same, Khomyakov wrote; the organism is everywhere different.[1] To the universality of reason the Slavophiles opposed the universality of the Church; they rejected the Hegelian philosophy of history in the name of a romantic 'organicity' which refused to yield to the necessary and universal laws of history.

In order to avoid a one-sided interpretation of the relationship between Slavophile ideology and Hegelianism it should be emphasized that unlike the obscurantists the Slavophiles treated Hegel with respect and played their part in propagating his works in Russia. The closing words of Kireevsky's 'New Principles in Philosophy' (his last article) are that German philosophy, taken in conjunction with Schelling's philosophy of revelation, could serve as the most convenient point of departure for an independent Russian philosophy based on the basic principles of ancient Russian culture.[2] Khomyakov called the Germans 'Europe's great adversary' and regretted that 'France and England unfortunately were too little acquainted with the development of learning in Germany'.[3] He was convinced that German philosophy could only be defeated with its own weapons and that the Orthodox faith should be given a philosophical 'slant' (not, of course, by turning it into a rational system, but by demonstrating its superiority over philosophy in philosophical terms); otherwise it faced the threat of being replaced by learning borrowed from outside (*obrazovanie*). Kireevsky called philosophy an intermediary link between learning and faith which only appeared when faith had become displaced in favour of 'external education'. It could therefore do one of two things: either it could force out faith in favour of learning, or else it could transcend learning and give a new meaning to 'external education' by imbuing it with the spirit and principles of faith.[4] The Slavophile thinkers wished to create a philosophy capable of performing this latter function: but first they had to undertake the critical transcending of

[1] See Khomyakov, vii. 325.   [2] See Kireevsky, i. 264.
[3] Khomyakov, vi. 532.
[4] See Kireevsky, i. 253.

German philosophy by depriving it of its dangerous cutting-edge—rationalism.

In their social philosophy the Slavophiles were largely concerned with problems which formed the groundwork of Hegel's philosophy of history and in many instances they even made use of Hegelian terminology (i.e. the categories of 'immediacy' and 'reflection'). They even borrowed such Hegelian propositions as the characterization of ancient Rome and the conception of the state as the most purely rational social structure, etc. The Slavophile critique of rationalism can safely be interpreted as a 'reply' to Hegel and even to German philosophy as a whole. Slavophile thought can therefore only be fully understood in the context of German intellectual life in the first half of the nineteenth century. Since Slavophile thinkers were probably at least partially aware of this, they were understandably keen to promote the study of German philosophy and regarded the decline of its influence in Russia (in the 1860s) as a symptom of a general decline in intellectual and cultural life.

8

The Roots of Westernism

THE confrontation of Slavophilism and Hegelian philosophy in the previous chapter was intended as an introduction to the fundamental ideological debate of the 1840s—a debate in which the terms 'Slavophile' and 'Westernizer' were invented by each side as a convenient label for the other. The Slavophile/ Westernizer controversy, however, had certain distinctive features of its own. If I may be allowed to anticipate later conclusions, the quarrel between the conservative romantics (including the Slavophiles) and the Hegelians might be called essentially a dispute over rationalism, whereas the conflict between the Slavophiles and Westernizers was largely about the concept of personality, with rationalism playing an important but secondary role. The Westernizers had their Hegelian phase in the 1840s, transcended it in true Hegelian fashion, and ended up by opposing the Hegelian *Weltgeist* in the name of the autonomous individual and his moral postulates. This inevitably brought them into conflict with the Slavophiles, who were not merely concerned to restrict the autonomy of the individual (as Hegel had been), but denied its very foundations.

The idea that there was a connection between the Westernism of the 1840s and the concept of the independent, autonomous personality is not a new one and was first formulated by Herzen in his *On the Development of Revolutionary Ideas in Russia*, published in 1850.

What Belinsky and his friends [wrote Herzen] had to offer in place of Slavophilism was not any kind of doctrine or closed system, but only vital sympathy for anything that concerns contemporary man; unbounded love for freedom of thought and hatred for everything that restricts it: for authority, brute force, and religion. They looked at the Russian and European question from a point of view utterly opposed to Slavophilism.

It seemed to them that one of the most important reasons for Russia's abject enslavement was the lack of personal independence;

this was the source of the government's complete disregard of the rights of individuals and the latter's lack of protest; hence the authorities' cynicism and the people's excessive patience. Russia's future will be fraught with great danger for Europe, and many misfortunes for herself, if the ferment of emancipation does not first enter the realm of individual rights.[1]

The nature of Herzen's book and the public for whom it was intended are responsible for the emphasis on the political aspect of Westernism in this passage. As I shall try to show, this aspect by no means exhausts the complex ideological content of the Westernizers' conception of 'personality', but shows only one of the conclusions to which they were led by the complicated dialectic underlying this conception. The aim of this chapter is to show to what extent this 'personalism' meshes with and organizes the entire body of philosophical views held by Belinsky and his circle; how arduous philosophical speculation, originally not in the least concerned with the problem of Russia and Europe, gave rise to a system of values that was diametrically opposed to Slavophilism.

An aim formulated in this particular way makes it necessary to inquire into the socio-psychological processes which determined this particular line of philosophical investigation rather than any other. I should like to suggest that the key to an understanding of the Westernizing view of the individual, its genesis and ideological function, is to be found in Turgenev's 'superfluous man'—a historically determined phenomenon specific to Russia in the reign of Nicholas I.[2] This phenomenon does not belong to the domain of literary criticism alone, but is surely an integral part of the history of social philosophy in Russia.

THE SLAVOPHILES AND THE 'SUPERFLUOUS MEN'

In any discussion of the 'superfluous men'—and especially their relationship to Russian *philosophy*—Chaadaev deserves a special place. In his 'Philosophical Letter' he was not only the first to express in moving terms the 'homesickness' of the man who suffers from a sense of alienation, but also the first to attempt a

[1] Herzen, vii. 109.
[2] 'Superfluous men' as a literary type are discussed in A. Lavretsky, *Lishnie lyudi, Literaturnaya entsiklopediya* (Moscow 1932), vi. 514–40.

historiosophical explanation of its underlying causes. It was the lot of every Russian to be superfluous, Chaadaev argued, because Russia herself was a superfluous country, forgotten by Providence and with no part in the historical progress of mankind. His later modification of this idea (in the *Apology of a Madman*) and his attempts to justify the hope that in future Russia would fulfil an important historical mission, could not detract from the tragic eloquence of the first Letter. Russians were unwanted 'illegitimate children', without a past and lacking the support of any kind of community transcending its individual members, Chaadaev argued; in their heads 'there is absolutely nothing general, everything in them is individual, and everything is transitory and incomplete'.[1] These words contain the leitmotiv of Chaadaev's later tragic reflections on 'superfluousness': the pain of individuality felt as alienation, as isolation from the universal' and 'real'. 'We are destroyed by the emptiness and chaos of our past, and in the present we feel the lack of general purposes of whatever kind'.[2] Herzen wrote in his *Diary* in 1842. 'We are men without a country, even worse than without a country', wrote Belinsky in 1841; 'we are men whose country is a spectre; can you wonder that we ourselves are spectres, that our friendship, our love, our strivings, our activity are all spectres?'[3]

The series of 'superfluous men' portrayed in Russian literature was foreshadowed in Pushkin's 'Byronic' poems, but the first fully fledged representative of the species was his Eugene Onegin. In this context it is worth calling attention to Chaadaev's 'Byronism' and to the fact that Pushkin himself considered Chaadaev to be a connoisseur of Romantic *ennui* and world-weariness in the style of Byron and Chateaubriand.[4] Milyukov, for instance, suggests that the lines in the 'Caucasian Prisoner', beginning with the words 'He probed the uncharted depths of man and world' were intended to refer to Chaadaev.[5] It is even more likely that Chaadaev served Pushkin as the model for his portrait of Onegin (his study, dress, and made of

---

[1] All quotations from Chaadaev's 'First Philosophical Letter' are taken from volume i of *Russian Philosophy*, i. 106–25 (trans. by Mary-Barbara Zeldin).
[2] Herzen, ii. 227.
[3] Belinsky, xii. 67.
[4] See Charles Quénet, *Tchaadaev et les lettres philosophiques* (Paris 1931), p. 40.
[5] See ibid.

life). His Byronic spleen attracted the attention of his Decembrist friends: 'Do let me have some news of Peter Chaadaev', S. I. Murav'ëv-Apostol wrote to Yakushkin (16/28 May 1825).

Have the clear skies of Italy driven away that boredom from which he suffered so dreadfully in Petersburg, before he went abroad? Byron did great harm when he introduced the fashion for that artificial disenchantment which spares no one capable of surrendering to reflection. Some imagine that this boredom is a sign of profundity. Perhaps that is so in England, but here, where there is so much to be done, where even someone living in the country can always busy himself with improving the lot of the poor peasants, let them first try some practical activity and only later philosophize about boredom.[1]

The young Kireevsky criticized the Byronic fashion in similar terms: fortunately characters like Childe Harold were an unnatural phenomenon in Russia, he wrote in 1828 in an article on Pushkin's poetry; Russia was, after all, a young country, still full of hope and providing extensive opportunities for creative action. 'What is there to be done here by a disenchanted Childe Harold?'[2]

In his 'Philosophical Letter' Chaadaev showed that it was possible to invert this argument. There were better and more valid grounds for a sense of emptiness and boredom in Russia than in the West, he argued, since the former was a country without history, a barren desert. In the West men were supported by continuity of tradition, by an atmosphere imbued by such ideas as duty, right, and order; in Russia they were deprived of this support. 'It is a trait of human nature that a man gets lost when he can find no means to bind himself with what has come before him and what will follow upon him. Then all consistency, all certainty escapes him. Lacking the guiding sense of continuous duration, he finds himself lost in the world. There are lost souls in every country; but in ours it is a general characteristic.' A sense of the futility of life was natural in a country existing without a purpose, a country that would not even be noticed if it did not stretch from the Bering Strait to the Oder. Russia's alleged youth was no answer; Russia never had a genuine youth, 'none of that period of exuberant activity, of the fervent turmoil of the moral forces of

[1] Ibid., p. 85.   [2] Kireevsky, ii. 10.

nations'; her existence was always 'dull and gloomy'. Chaadaev's 'Philosophical Letter' contains an indirect answer, as it
were, to the optimism of the Lovers of Wisdom and Murav'ëv-
Apostol's advice: what activity, he asked, can be undertaken
in a 'society which wavers about without convictions and without rules even for daily life, and where that life is still completely lacking in order'? In this argument Chaadaev anticipated a recurrent philosophical motif characteristic of the
'superfluous men', namely the renunciation of political action,
the sense of impotence in face of an all-powerful rational or
irrational fate.

Chaadaev's most valuable insight into this problem, however,
is the magnificent passage in which he described Russian
spiritual homelessness. Russians were freer than Europeans, he
wrote, for Providence had refused to interfere in their concerns.
But for that very reason they were homeless wanderers, 'alone
in the world', deprived of helm and anchor, condemned to
stray without aim or direction:

Look about you. Don't you think that we are very restless? We all
resemble travellers. Nobody has a definite sphere of existence, we
have no proper habits, there are no rules, there is no domestic life,
there is nothing to which we could be attached, nothing that would
awaken our sympathy or affection—nothing durable, nothing
lasting; everything flows, everything passes, leaving no traces either
outside or within us. In our own houses we seem to be guests, in our
families we look like strangers, in our cities we look like nomads,
even more than the nomads who drive their herds in our steppes,
for they are more attached to their deserts than we to our cities.

These words exactly sum up the state of mind of the 'superfluous men' of the 1830s and '40s. 'Our generation are Jews
wandering aimlessly in the desert', wrote Belinsky in 1840. 'Our
souls are like houses built with crooked beams—they are full of
cracks.'[1] The young Turgenev also compared his generation to
nomads in temporary dwellings.[2] 'A wanderer in Europe, a
stranger at home, and a stranger abroad',[3] is how Herzen
described the hero of his novel, and Ogarëv echoed this with his

---

[1] Belinsky, xi. 526, 528.
[2] In a verse called 'Confession'; I. S. Turgenev, *Sobranie sochineniĭ*, 12 vols.
(Moscow 1953–8), x. 67–8.
[3] Herzen, iv. 122.

'*Ich bin ein Fremdling überall*—a homeless wanderer from country to country.'[1] The motif of homelessness, incapacity for 'nest-building' or finding one's niche in life recurs in the biographies of all the 'superfluous men' in Turgenev's novels.

Although a comparison between these quotations and Chaadaev's 'Letter' is valid, it cannot be taken too far. Belinsky, Ogarëv, and Herzen did not suggest that homelessness or alienation was the inevitable lot of all Russians; on the contrary they believed them to be typical rather of their own cultural milieu and their own generation, which had come to maturity during an 'age of transition'. 'We straddle two epochs', Herzen wrote, 'and that is why thinking men find life so particularly tough and complicated. Old convictions and the entire former view of the world are rocking on their foundations, but they are still held dear. New convictions, all-embracing and lofty, have not yet born fruit; the early leaves and buds suggest that the trees will bear superb blossom, but the blossom has not yet appeared and has no appeal to us.'[2] The superfluous men of the 1840s did not consider alienation and homelessness as necessarily bad, but regarded them somewhat in the light of painful birth-pangs ushering in a new and better world. Homelessness, they hoped, only meant abandoning a cramped old dwelling in order to participate actively in the construction of a new and free society. 'Life at home is impossible!', Ogarëv wrote to Herzen in 1845. 'Just think of it; it is out of the question, I'm convinced. A man who is a stranger at home ought to sever relations with his family. He should tell them that he is a stranger to them. And even if we were strangers to the whole world, we should say so. . . . It is our sacred duty to be free. I am sick of carrying all this locked up within me, what I need is action. Yes, I the weak, indecisive, unpractical dreamer (*der Grübelnde*) —I need action!'[3]

Nevertheless these quotations show that the 'men of the 1840s' could—and did—find in Chaadaev's 'Letter' a classical description of their own state of alienation. With this important

---

[1] In a poem called 'Humour'; N. I. Ogarëv, *Izbrannie proizvedeniya* (Moscow 1956), ii. 29.

[2] Herzen, iii. 7.

[3] 'Iz perepiski nedavnikh deyateleĭ', *Russkaya Mȳsl'* (1892), nr. 2. Quoted from Ch. Vetrinsky (V. E. Cheshikhin), *T. N. Granovsky i yego vremya*, 2nd edn. (St. Petersburg 1905), p. 278.

difference, that they realized their spiritual exile was due not to their national character but to their specific intellectual make-up and was even to some extent a fate they had chosen themselves. Chaadaev's 'Letter' gave a superb description of the malady, but failed to grasp its essence. Nevertheless, he was the first to formulate the problem, and give it due importance, and thus inspired later attempts to diagnose the phenomenon in a more concrete historical context. One of these attempts is to be found in Slavophile doctrine.

It is no exaggeration to say that Chaadaev's 'Philosophical Letter' provided a frame of reference, as it were, for almost all Slavophiles whenever they attempted to consider the 'rootlessness' and alienation (from folkways) of the Russian intelligentsia. They agreed that the state of spiritual malaise described in the 'Letter' was entirely real and of great significance, but in their diagnosis they suggested that the malady only affected Europeanized 'polite society'—the artificial product of the Petrine reforms—and not the common people. The malady was purely European in origin, and had been brought to Russia from outside; however, in view of the greater gulf between 'the native foundations' and the 'abstract non-national civilization' represented by 'society' the symptoms were more acute in Russia than elsewhere. From this point of view Chaadaev's pessimism and profound disillusionment were the inevitable consequence of his isolation from the common people and were to be welcomed as evidence that alienation was a painful state and not something accepted as normal.

Our spiritual malady [Khomyakov wrote] flowed from the cleavage between enlightened society and the people. Its symptom was society's profound loss of faith in itself and in the people from whom it had torn itself away. This loss of faith was valid and rational, for having become separated from the people the enlightened classes lost their immediate sense of the latter's historical significance, but their consciousness was not sufficiently developed for them to grasp this significance rationally. As always, the finest among us suffered most from the disease.[1]

The cleavage which Peter introduced into Russian society had an adverse effect on both sides: learning represented by the

[1] Khomyakov, iii. 425.

educated classes lost its vitality and Europeanized Russians became 'colonizers in their own country'; on the other hand, as the intelligentsia became more alienated, the 'mental activity of the lower classes declined'.[1] Khomyakov agreed with Chaadaev that Russian learning had made no contribution to the general progress of mankind, but believed that the cause was to be sought elsewhere: not in Russia's isolation, in her exclusion from universality, but on the contrary, in the separation of Russian learning from its national fountain-head, in its cosmopolitanism, eclecticism, and lack of 'wholeness'.[2] These were also to blame for society's lack of 'wholeness' and for the inner fragmentation of individuals separated from the common people.

Our isolation from real life, from past and present [wrote Khomyakov] has almost succeeded in depriving us of our fatherland; those in whom this alienation (*otchuzhdenie*) is particularly strong deserve compassion rather than blame. Such men are to be pitied, like anyone else without a fatherland, like a Jew or a gipsy; perhaps even more so, for a Jew finds a substitute for his fatherland in his religious exclusiveness and a gipsy in his tribal exclusiveness. Such men are victims of spurious development.[3]

This passage can be regarded as Khomyakov's reply to Chaadaev's 'Philosophical Letter'. It is true, he implies, that Russians have no history and no traditions, that nothing connects them with bygone generations, that in their heads 'everything is individual', that they are without support and live like gipsies or nomads—but all this only concerns those sections of society that are uprooted and have lost their links with the people. It is not in Europe, therefore, that salvation lies, but in a return to the people and the ancestral religion, in a reconstruction of the former traditional community life weakened by Europeanization. The alienated upper classes, Khomyakov thought, must make an effort to know the people's way of life, its lore, and customs.

By tearing ourselves away from the past [he wrote] we educated people have thrown away our history, gaining instead an artificial lack of ancestry (*bezrodstvo*) and the melancholy privilege of a cold heart. But the form and content of historical documents, folk songs,

---

[1] Khomyakov, i. 22. Simone Weil argues along exactly the same lines in her *Enracinement*. She writes of the propagators of a rootless civilization that theirs is a colonial mentality with a difference of degree only.

[2] See Khomyakov, iii. 224; i. 45; iii. 167.   [3] Ibid. i. 45.

and tales awaken the stifled forces within us; they illuminate our understanding and expand our intellect; they lead us out of our orphaned state and show us a past in which we can find consolation and a present which can inspire us with affection.[1]

It is interesting to note that the Slavophile conception can be said to invert Chaadaev's views without changing his basic scale of values or the over-all relations of cause and effect. In both conceptions spiritual homelessness was seen to be an evil springing from a lack of tradition (or its rejection) and both condemned individualism and looked for a remedy in a supra-individual community and the integration of society through religion. Both reactions are, in fact, typical of the nineteenth-century conservative romantics' response to the processes of alienation that accompanied the disintegration of traditional social bonds. The Slavophile interpretation was both more profound and set in a firmer historical context than that of Chaadaev, who, apart from his views on the social role of religion, showed little interest in the sociological analysis of pre-capitalist social structures. By relating the state of 'homelessness' to 'orphanhood' and the disintegration of patriarchal family ties (both literally and metaphorically—i.e. the disintegration of communal traditions in social life as a whole) the Slavophile thinkers anticipated a theory put forward later by many nineteenth-century sociologists (Le Play, Tönnies, and Durkheim) as well as by contemporary scholars.[2]

The diagnosis of the disease must not be confused with the remedies proposed which, for both Chaadaev and the Slavophiles, were conservative utopias—visions of a land whose inhabitants knew neither alienation nor homelessness. For Chaadaev this land was Europe before the French Revolution, while for the Slavophiles it was Russia before the Petrine reforms.

Just as the Society of the Lovers of Wisdom had played a formative role in the evolution of Slavophile doctrine, so the Stan-

[1] See Khomyakov, iii. 167.

[2] 'The familistic relationship', wrote P. A. Sorokin in *Society, Culture and Personality*, 'eliminates or reduces to a minimum the feeling of being a stranger or outsider. . . . The ideal familistic relationship is the opposite pole of the "stranger" the "outsider", and the "private" as a sociological category.' P. A. Sorokin, *Society, Culture and Personality. Their Structure and Dynamics* (New York–London 1947), pp. 101–2.

kevich Circle, which was active in Moscow in the 1830s, might be called a laboratory that helped to form the theoretical self-awareness of the 'superfluous men'.

Nikolai Stankevich (1813–40) was in many ways thoroughly representative of the younger progressive intelligentsia of gentry origin. In Annenkov's words, he 'personified the *youthfulness* of one of the stages of our development; he united all the best and noblest characteristics, aspirations, and hopes of his companions.'[1] The Stankevich Circle counted among its members the radical democrat Belinsky, the liberals Granovsky and Botkin, the anarchist Bakunin, and even the Slavophile Konstantin Aksakov; Herzen and Ogarëv, the founders of 'Russian socialism', were closely associated with the circle. Ivan Turgenev, whose books are both an indictment of and a literary monument to the superfluous men of the 1840s, wrote that his association with Stankevich marked the 'beginning of my spiritual development'. 'How eagerly I listened to him, I who was destined to be the last of his companions, whom he taught to serve the Truth by his own example, by the poetry of his life and words. . . . Stankevich! It is to you I owe my rebirth, you held out your hand and showed me my goal.'[2]

For all these very different men Stankevich personified the 'philosophical stage' in their intellectual development; a period when they still believed that they would be able to define their relationship to reality on a purely philosophical plane and that philosophy—above all German philosophy—would solve all the outstanding problems tormenting them. This conviction was expressed by Stankevich himself when he wrote: 'The fetters that trammelled my soul fell away when I understood that there is no knowledge beyond one all-embracing idea, that life is the self-intoxication of love, that all else is delusion.'[3] For the young Bakunin philosophy was a matter of life and death, of 'redemption' or 'fall'; he was justified in writing about himself that the 'boundless desire for knowledge is the kernel, the inner essence of my entire spiritual being'.[4] 'Devil take the French!',

---

[1] N. V. Stankevich, *Perepiska ego i biografiya napisannaya P. V. Annenkovȳm* (Moscow 1857), pp. 236–7.

[2] Turgenev, *Sobr. soch.* (Moscow 1958), xii. 19–20.

[3] Stankevich, *Perepiska . . .*, p. 197.

[4] Quoted from A. A. Kornilov, *Molodȳe godȳ M. A. Bakunina (Iz istorii russkogo romantizma)* (Moscow 1915), p. 624.

Belinsky wrote in 1837; 'Germany, that is the Jersualem for the modern generation and that is where they should turn their eyes filled with hope and expectation; thence a new Christ will come, but not a persecuted saviour bearing wounds and a martyr's crown, but one surrounded by a halo of glory.'[1]

In his memoirs Apollon Grigor'ev, the 'last romantic', sketched a fascinating picture of the eager intellectual ferment at that time:

How could you sit there, you a young man, with all your physical powers and aspirations still unimpaired, on an enchanting, stimulating, sunny spring morning, while Moscow's Easter bells were pealing, and yet be wholly absorbed in the work of one of those crazy seekers or demonstrators of the tail of the Absolute. . . . There you would sit, with your heart bursting in your breast and your head inflamed—not by the intoxicating breath of spring wafting in through the window, but by the breath of those enormous worlds bound together into a single whole by the power of organic thought; or else, in the sweat of your brow, you would drag up doubts capable of bringing down the entire edifice of time-honoured convictions and morality . . . and all the time you suffered and grew thin and sallow. . . . Ah, how sickeningly sweet was that torment and suffering! Ah, those sleepless nights, when with a sob we fell on our knees in a longing for prayer, and at the same time destroyed our capacity for prayer by analytical reflection; nights of intellectual frenzy that lasted until dawn or the sound of matins—into what lofty regions they transported our souls.[2]

The tone of these recollections as well as the content of endless epistles in which even the most commonplace matters were given a philosophical slant; the dramatic stories of philosophical conversions, of successes and failures in the 'translation of philosophy into life'—all these suggest that the intellectual ferment of those years was a symptom of something more than a mere passion for pure inquiry. 'In philosophy', Turgenev wrote in his memoirs, 'we sought everything other than pure thought.'[3] Nevertheless, the widespread view that the real object of these intellectual searchings was to bridge the gap between theory and social practice, is something of an over-

---

[1] Belinsky, xi. 152.
[2] 'Moi literaturnÿe i nravstvennÿe skital'chestva', in A. Grigoriev, *Vospominaniya* (*i vospominaniya o něm*) (Academiya, Moscow–Leningrad, 1930), pp. 88–9.
[3] Turgenev, *Sobr. soch.* x. 280.

simplification. The interest in practical activity came later, when belief in the efficacy of philosophy had cooled off and the passions and illusions aroused by it came to be examined in a critical light.

The key to an understanding of the philosophical passions aroused in the young Grigor'ev and the members of the Stankevich Circle is to be found in a socio-psychological process that contemporary scholars writing on historical psychology have called *individuation* and *rationalization*.[1] This process, which involved the emergence of the individual rationalized self-consciousness from the uncritically accepted cocoon of homogeneous traditional norms and collective impressions, had begun much earlier, but gained great impetus in Europe after the French Revolution, with the final disintegration of the old system of values. Although man now ceased to be the mere plaything of economic and political processes and assumed a relatively independent role, the victorious political system which had cut the fetters of tradition at the same time brought into play new and powerful mechanisms of social conformity which threatened the individual's hard-won autonomy.

Although it might be asked why autocratic and Orthodox Russia, so different from Europe in its economic, social, and political development, should be agitated by a similar—and even more intense—process of intellectual ferment, this question would betray unawareness of the extent to which early nineteenth-century Russia was an organic part of the European cultural scene. During the reign of Nicholas westernization proceeded at a rapid pace, in spite of attempts to halt the spread of the 'infection'; although political democracy was unknown in Russia and capitalist production still in its infancy, there did exist a common cultural heritage shared by all educated people—a *European* heritage born of the 'free competition of ideas'. It is even possible to speak of a 'free exchange of ideas' in Russia itself, in spite of the efforts of the censor and the official ideologists whose role it was to ensure intellectual conformity. In Herzen's words, it was an 'age of external constraint and inner liberation'.[2] Literature and philosophy, which involved an intimate acquaintance with the outlook of other

[1] See Zevedei Barbu, *Problems of Historical Psychology* (London 1961).
[2] Herzen, xiv. 157.

historical periods, nations, and societies, became a powerful stimulus enlarging narrow intellectual horizons and liberating the individual from the pressure of received truths 'imbibed at the breast' and accepted unquestioningly. The struggle for the emancipation of the personality, which could not be played out on the political arena, became 'interiorized'[1] and found an outlet in philosophical exaltation and the superfluous men's cult of introspection.[2] Total interiorization proved impossible, however: after 'inner' liberation was bound to come the demand for 'outward' liberation, for exteriorization, and the 'translation of philosophy into action'.

Another aspect of this problem is closely related to the specific role then played by Russian literature. 'Our literature', Belinsky wrote, '. . . initiated the inner *rapprochement* of the different estates, shaped a specific kind of public opinion, and created a specific social class which differed from the usual "third estate" in that it included not only members of the merchant and urban middle class, but men of all social groups united by education, which in Russia has expressed itself almost exclusively in love of literature.'[3] In this remark Belinsky showed his awareness of an important phenomenon—the sociological role of education.[4] Participation in a common universal cultural heritage created a new social group—the

---

[1] The term 'interiorization' is used in a sense different from 'internalization'. By 'internalization' I mean such a far-reaching assimilation of social norms of behaviour that the individual ceases to regard them as something 'external' or 'alien' (this was the sense in which the phrase 'internalized tradition' was used in the discussion of Khomyakov's notion of *sobornost'*). By 'interiorization', on the other hand, I mean the transferring of the realization of specific values from the external (social) world to the sphere of the personality and the experiencing of tensions and conflicts connected with them not in action (social or political) but only in 'thought'.

[2] The flowering of German philosophy in the first half of the nineteenth century was conditioned by similar factors. Marx wrote: 'Just as the nations of the ancient world lived their prehistory in the imagination, in mythology, so we Germans have lived our post-history in thought, *in philosophy*. We are *philosophical* contemporaries of the present day without being its *historical* contemporaries.' (K. Marx, *Early Writings*, trans. and ed. by T. B. Bottomore, London 1963, p. 49.) There is an interesting discussion of these questions in M. Malia, *Alexander Herzen and the Birth of Russian Socialism* (Harvard University Press 1961), chapter 5.

[3] Belinsky, ix. 432.

[4] Mannheim has written: 'Participation in a common educational heritage tends to suppress differences of birth, status, profession, and wealth, and to unite the individual educated people on the basis of the education they have received.' K. Mannheim, *Ideology and Utopia* (New York–London 1952), p. 138.

intelligentsia—which, because of Russia's general backwardness, was more alienated from society as a whole and more independent in relation to the privileged classes than intellectuals in the advanced countries of Europe. Interpreted in terms of historical psychology, the problem of the superfluous men was one of individuation, whereas in terms of historical sociology it reflected the birth-pangs of the Russian intelligentsia, the painful severance of the umbilical cord connecting it to the old world.[1]

These questions figured largely in Slavophile doctrine. In their analysis of the cleavage between 'society' and the people (in the broad sense of the word), and of the alienating influence of a 'cosompolitan' education, the Slavophiles dealt with an essential and very real aspect of the problem—one of which members of the Stankevich Circle were also aware .

In order to arrive at a better understanding of the specific phenomenon of the first 'superfluous men', and of the emotional climate and intellectual aura surrounding them, two points should be borne in mind: (1) Most of the superfluous men came from the educated nobility which was beginning to decline as a class just as its culture was attaining new heights of self-conscious refinement and subtlety; and (2) European romantic literature exerted a profound influence in Russia, which must be understood if certain features characteristic of the reception of classical German philosophy are to be seen in true perspective.

The philosophical problems discussed in romantic literature that aroused the greatest interest were certain aesthetic formulations expressed in the characteristic antithesis of 'naïve' and 'sentimental' poetry (Schiller), or 'immediacy' and 'reflection' (or 'consciousness'). The state of 'immediacy' presupposed an 'instinctive' and 'unconscious' existence according to laws and principles that were not open to doubt or rational interpretation. 'Reflection', on the other hand, was the name given to the acute individual intellect which exercised merciless control over everything (itself included) ; and to 'consciousness', which intensified suffering but at the same time was ground for pride.[2]

[1] See Mannheim, 'The Problem of the Intelligentsia. An Inquiry into Its Past and Present Role' in *Essays on the Sociology of Culture* (London 1956).
[2] Belinsky, xi. 526.

That is why the myth of the 'lost paradise' and of Satan, the first creature who dared to seek knowledge and freedom, enjoyed such great popularity (cf. Goethe's *Faust* and Byron's *Cain*). The tempting words of the serpent, 'Be as the gods', could have served as the motto for romantic iconoclasm. The literature of the period tried to analyse the relationship between individuality and suffering, freedom and evil. As Byron put it:

> Sorrow is knowledge:
> They who know the most
> Must mourn the deepest
> O'er the fatal truth.
> The tree of Knowledge
> Is not that of Life.

All these problems can be found in Stankevich's letters and poetry.[1] In his poem 'The Prophet's Secret' (clearly influenced by Schiller's ballad 'Cassandra') Stankevich suggested that the burden of individual self-consciousness was so heavy that it had better be cast off, lest it should disturb humanity's 'soothing sleep'. Of course, this was impossible: once awake, man was condemned to carry the lonely burden of individuality and freedom; for him there was no well-trodden path—what his forefathers considered 'normal' and commonplace he must think out anew and this filled him with a painful and indefinable *Weltschmerz*. Interestingly enough, Stankevich also attempted to give these problems artistic utterance in an immature but very characteristic short story entitled *A Few Moments in the Life of Count Z*.

The hero of the story 'like all young men in the grip of enthusiasms, was at first utterly absorbed by metaphysis; later he turned eagerly to the study of history, religion, and art . . . but still his soul was a yawning emptiness and the worm of melancholy gnawed at his heart'. He longed for holy action, but came to realize that he was incapable of it; he tore himself away from the earth, but failed to reach heaven. The harmonious universe of his childhood had been shattered. This is how Stankevich described the 'lost paradise':

[1] These problems are discussed in greater detail in Janina and Andrzej Walicki, 'U Zródeł problematyki "zbędnego człowieka" w twórczości Turgieneva' (The Source of the Problem of the 'Superfluous Man' in Turgenev's Work), *Slavia Orientalis* (1957), vol. vi.

A tranquil day rises over the blessed homestead of his father, the sun's first rays illuminate the road, and the honest rustics greet their young master with a smile. Now he walks along the field— from afar he can hear a drawn-out melody, scythe rings against stone, mowers and harvesters are absorbed in their work; in the far distance the dark woods tremble in their misty shroud and all around are animated by the smile of the early morning sun . . . mounting joy fills all souls . . . breasts swell in a deeper and freer breath . . . the spark of love glows brightly and is about to encompass the whole of nature.[1]

For Count Z. there is no return to this patriarchal idyll of the good master and his honest peasants for his soul is in the grip of hellish discord. This inner confusion is symbolized by his performance on the piano: as he begins to play there is a peaceful ripple of harmonious sounds, but this soon turns into a series of strident discords until at last he strikes the keys with particular force, and the strings of the instrument snap with a groan. The count's existence, too, is compared to a snapped string—even love cannot resolve its dissonance into harmony, and it is only after death that his soul finds consolation in the presence of God

The fact that *Count Z.* is an early work is shown not only by the date of composition (1834) but also by the sentimental haze surrounding its hero. Count Z. embodies the emotions and mentality of the men of the 1830s, before the advent of Hegelianism. 'In my opinion', Herzen wrote in his autobiography, 'a man who has not lived through Hegel's phenomenology . . . who has not passed through that furnace and been tempered by it, is not complete, not modern.'[2] The enthusiastic martyrs of philosophy could find a classic diagnosis of their sufferings in Hegel's concept of the 'unhappy consciousness'—of a subjectivism aware of its own inadequacy, a divided consciousness reflecting its own image and pained to perceive its total separation from life.[3] Hegelianism to them was a dazzling discovery of real life, a key to the understanding of their own weakness, inner division, and incapacity for action. Philosophy seemed to

---

[1] Stankevich, *Perepiska* . . ., pp. 386–7.

[2] Herzen, *My Past and Thoughts*, ii. 121.

[3] See J. Hyppolite, *Genèse et structure de la phénoménologie de l'esprit de Hegel* (Paris 1946), vol. i, chapter 3; and J. Wahl, *Le Malheur de la conscience dans la philosophie de Hegel* (Paris 1930).

show them the way to reintegration into reality, but since they were debarred from following it their isolation, 'abstractness', and 'spectral' nature beame an even heavier burden.[1] They felt that they were the victims of their own 'subjectivism'; the knowledge that though their consciousness had already lost touch with 'immediacy', it was unable to realize the Hegelian goal of becoming rational consciousness, of taking its place in reality, overcoming painful alienation and internal dissonance, and achieving the harmonious reconciliation of the supra-individual substance with individual 'self-consciousness'. Even when he fully accepted the philosophy of the Absolute, with its implication that all contradictions are resolved on a higher plane, Stankevich still continued to complain that he was a prey to reflection and *Schönseeligkeit*, while Belinsky wrote bitterly: 'We are all spectres'; 'for spectres there is no salvation, even on a desert island'; 'our favourite (and rational) dream was to raise our whole life to the level of reality. . . . But the dream was only a dream and a dream it will remain.'[2] These words could serve as an illustration of Hegel's remarks on the *Schöne Seele* which lacked *die Kraft der Entäusserung* and was therefore forced to objectivize its intentions in the verbal sphere alone.[3]

Hegelian philosophy allowed the 'superfluous men' to regard their inner division as a transitional stage in the 'Odyssey of the Spirit'. It enabled them to realize there could be no return to 'immediate harmony' and that 'abstraction' and 'reflection' were necessary stages on the way to the fulfilment of man's mission. Most important of all, it inspired them with the belief that the split personality could again be reintegrated. In his *Letters on the Study of Nature* Herzen wrote:

The dual nature of man consists in the very fact that apart from his positive existence he cannot avoid the negation of being; he is not only separated from nature, but also divided within himself: this division torments him and the torment impels him forward. . . .

[1] The term 'spectre' (German *Spuk*) in the philosophical terminology of the time meant a man confined within the magic circle of particular concerns, someone unable—in spite of his efforts—to rise to participation in the supra-individual 'objective' sphere. It is worth noting that Gustav in Mickiewicz's *Forefather's Eve* is a 'spectre' in this sense of the word; he realizes his own 'spectrality' and sets out to warn others.

[2] Belinsky, xi. 527, xii. 66.

[3] Hegel, *Phänomenologie des Geistes* (Leipzig 1949), p. 462; see also B. Baczko, *Hegel a Rousseau*, part 2, *Studia Filozoficzne* (1959), no. 1, pp. 146–9.

Like a wedge, the division between man and nature gradually divides everything into opposing parts, even man's soul itself; this is the *divide et impera* of logic—the way to a true and eternal fusion of all that was split in two . . .[1]

Since attempts to overcome this 'dualism' were painful and tiring, it is hardly surprising that the process was accompanied by doubts and often masochistic self-criticism. One of the accusations most frequently heard was that of 'Hamletism', for Hamlet seemed to be the embodiment of such hated weaknesses as incapacity for action and atrophy of the will brought about by too much reflection. 'I too was a prey to reflection, I too felt the lack of all spontaneity', says the hero of one of Turgenev's short stories which is even called *The Hamlet of Shchigrovsk*.[2] 'Hamlet! There you have me, the pure essence!', the young Ogarëv wrote to his bride. 'A man capable of spitting into his own face because of his spiritual weakness, but incapable of overcoming this weakness or of doing anything at all.'[3]

Excessive reflection, *Grübeleien*, perpetual self-analysis—these are the unvarying theme of the complaints and bitter self-accusations that fill the pages of the correspondence of Stankevich, Belinsky, and Bakunin, Herzen and Ogarëv; even the letters of the more reticent and level-headed Timofeĭ Nikolaevich Granovsky are not free of them. Turgenev's writings contain a vertitable anatomy of reflection. In *A Month in the Country* he compares incessant self-analysis to lace-making in a stuffy room and concludes: 'Lace is a fine thing, but a drink of fresh water on a hot day is much better.'[4] To see one's consciousness reflected in an endless series of mirrors merely induced disgust: 'I am sick of my own face, I am like a man condemned to spend his whole life in a room surrounded by mirrors',[5] complains the hero of Turgenev's short story *Correspondence*, who might have been the author himself. Reflection meant entangling oneself in an ingenious cobweb: 'I was my own spider', is

---

[1] Herzen, iii. 132, 134.

[2] Turgenev, *A Sportsman's Sketches*, trans. by Constance Garnett, *Works*, 14 vols. (Heinemann, London 1894–8).

[3] Quoted from M. Gershenzon, 'Lyubov' Ogarëva' in *Obrazÿ proshlogo* (Moscow 1912), p. 422.

[4] Turgenev, *A Month in the Country*, *Three Plays*, trans. by Constance Garnett (Cassell and Co. 1934), pp. 13–14.

[5] Turgenev, 'Perepiska', *Sobr. soch.* (Moscow 1953), vi. 91.

how Turgenev put it in another short story.[1] Reflection was responsible for a state of eternal indecision which even stood in the way of love and family happiness. This incapacity which, as Chernyshevsky rightly observed,[2] was characteristic of almost all the 'superfluous men' in the literature of the time, was not a mere literary convention but reflected the actual state of affairs. As early as 1841 Belinsky wrote in his *Letters to Botkin*: 'Botkin, you were in love and your love came to nothing. The story of my love was similar. Stankevich was of a higher calibre than either of us, but he suffered the same fate. No, we were not made for love, to be husbands and fathers of families.'[3]

There is a classic definition of reflection in Belinsky's article on Lermontov.

In the state of reflection [he wrote] you are split into two men, of whom one lives while the other observes and judges him. In a state of reflection no emotion, no thought, and no act can be complete: as soon as feeling, intention, or the desire for action is conceived, the enemy concealed within examines the embryo, analyses it, and tries to determine whether the thought is just and true, the emotion real, or the intention valid, what their aim is, and whither they are tending; then the fragrant bud of feeling droops without blooming, thought fractures into infinitesimal particles, like a sunbeam reflected in crystal, the hand raised to action is turned to stone in the attempt and fails to strike . . .

> Thus conscience does make cowards of us all;
> And thus the native hue of resolution
> Is sicklied o'er with the pale cast of thought;
> And enterprises of great pith and moment,
> With this regard, their currents turned awry,
> And lose the name of action.

—says Shakespeare's Hamlet, the poetic apotheosis of reflection.[4]

In the light of this quotation, the Slavophiles' concept of personality acquires special significance. Reflection to them was clearly nothing other than the general 'spiritual and intellectual dualism' which, they felt, was the inevitable concomitant of Western European rationalism and individualism. To the

[1] Turgenev, 'Perepiska', *Sobr. soch.* (Moscow 1953), vi. 91.
[2] In the article 'Russkiĭ chelovek na rendez-vous' (1858).
[3] Belinsky, xii. 67.
[4] Belinsky, iv. 253.

divided and doubt-ridden personality of the superfluous men they opposed their ideal of a personality integrated by faith, inner concentration, and a spiritual focus, by the 'profound quiet and peace of the inner self-consciousness'. To the Slavophiles individuality and autonomy were certainly not prerequisites of personality, but the source of its disintegration; in their view strength of character was proportionate to the individual's 'wholeness', harmony, inner certainty and peace, rooted in untroubled faith. Theirs was in fact a consistent defence of the ideal of the human personality before the onset of individuation.

It was one of the fundamental premises of Slavophile philosophy that there was a correlation between social structure and the structure of the human personality; Kireevsky's entire history of philosophy rested on the notion that types of social integration and types of personal integration (or disintegration) are strictly interdependent, a belief which forms the link between the Slavophiles' criticism of the superfluous men and their doctrine as a whole. According to this, the inner division of the personality was one aspect of the dualism pervading all spheres of life in Europe which was introduced into Russia with the Petrine reforms. The source of this dualism was the dichotomy between Christian and rationalist principles inherited from classical Roman civilization; this dichotomy lay at the roots of European civilization and found expression in religion, legislation, and culture, as well as in the inner division and fragmentation of Western man. When the 'superfluous men' complained of the painful cleavage between feeling and thought, will and reason, 'spontaneity' and 'consciousness', the Slavophiles felt confirmed in their diagnosis. Their return to the past —to Orthodoxy and old communal traditions—was part of their nostalgia for the 'wholeness' (*tselnost*) of spirit, lost as a result of Europeanization. According to the Slavophile diagnosis, what the superfluous men called 'reflection' and the inner dualism this produced, were the inevitable result of the 'wrong turning' taken by Russia during the reign of Peter; this false turning, they warned, would lead to 'dualism of the spirit, dualism of the intellect, dualism of scholarship, dualism of the estates, dualism of society, dualism of legislation and family obligations, dualism of morality and feeling, dualism throughout the whole range of human existence and all the different types of existence in the public and private sphere'.[1]

By pointing to the relationship between the phenomenon of the 'superfluous men' and the process of Europeanization the Slavophiles drew attention to a problem that was to be restated by later Russian thinkers. In the controversy between the Slavophiles and Westernizers the 'superfluous men' (unless they ceased to be themselves) could only belong to the latter camp; any attempts to combine Slavophile ideas with the poetry of reflection and moral disquiet (cf. Grigor'ev) flowed from a longing for a synthesis of Slavophilism and Westernism which was in fact unattainable. Without the historical context of Slavophile doctrine the problem of the 'superfluous men' loses its specific character and sharpness of focus. It is of little importance that relatively few Slavophile comments touch directly on the problem. What does matter is that Slavophile philosophy as a whole was concerned with issues that had a close though indirect bearing on the subject. Slavophile theology and the concept of 'organic togetherness' postulated a supra-individual collective consciousness which precluded the isolation of individual human beings and their 'superfluousness'; the Slavophile notion of 'immediate' integral knowledge (faith) was directed against the rational 'reflection' to which the 'superfluous men' were a prey; the Slavophile theory of an integrated harmonious personality—a pre-individuation ideal—was the antithesis of the divided, anxiety-ridden personality of the superfluous men; their philosophy of history represented an attempt to explain the chain of events which—in the West as well as in Russia—had produced rationalism, individualism, the disintegration of traditional communities, and the alienation and 'orphanhood' of the individual that accompanied them. The Slavophiles examined the question of 'superfluousness' in depth, but—unlike other thinkers—believed that the process of individuation could be prevented, that 'dualism' was only a 'diseased state and not a necessary precondition of development',[2] and that the way was still open to a return to an ideally *internalized* tradition accepted without reflection.

[1] Kireevsky, i. 210.
[2] Excerpt from a letter by Kireevsky, addressee unknown. Tsentr. Gos. Lit. Arkhiv. Moscow, fond 236–Kireevskie, op. 1, ?478.

A return of this kind, assuming that it was possible, would have been tantamount to the end of Slavophilism. The Slavophile philosophy set out to analyse social phenomena which, by its own criteria, were not susceptible of rational analysis. It seems relevant to ask whether the Slavophiles would have attempted to study old communal traditions if they themselves had still been firmly rooted in these traditions. In his history of Russian theology G. Florovsky gives the following answer:

The least valid view of Slavophilism is to regard it as something like an immediate and organic manifestation of the 'folk' element (as Gershenson did). Berdayev is mistaken when he writes that Slavophilism was 'the psychology and philosophy of the country house, of warm and comfortable nests' . . . at any rate, its voice was certainly not the voice of the people but the voice of the intelligentsia— the voice of the new educated strata of society who had passed through the temptations and experiences of Europeanism. Slavophilism was an act of reflection and not a manifestation of the primitive . . . hence you have the dramatic 'return to the past', and the constant tension of contrasts (a characteristic feature of romanticism as a *Weltanschauung*). Apollon Grigor'ev once wrote: 'the Slavophiles believed blindly, fanatically in the essence of folkways of which they knew nothing, and this faith of theirs was considered a virtue.' . . . This formulation is perhaps exaggerated, but the exaggeration contains a good deal of truth. . . . Slavophilism is part of the history of Russian thought, not of Russian instinct. . . . In fact it is part of the history of European influence in Russia.[1]

This view provides a necessary counterweight to oversimplified interpretations of Slavophilism, but itself suffers from a certain one-sidedness. The truth would seem to lie somewhere between the two extremes. Slavophile philosophy is interesting precisely because of its ability to look at tradition from the 'inside' as well as from the 'outside'. Thanks to their specific position the Slavophiles—like the German conservatives[2]— contributed more to our understanding of pre-rational forms of social bonds and the pre-individuation type of personality than did any of their contemporaries. The Slavophile movement is perhaps another example of the truth of Hegel's aphorism that Minerva's owl takes flight most readily at dusk.

[1] Florovsky, *Puti russkogo bogosloviya*, p. 253.
[2] See Mannheim, 'Conservative Thought', in *Essays on Sociology and Social Psychology*, pp. 121–2.

One of the signals heralding the twilight of the way of life idealized by the Slavophiles was, in fact, the appearance of 'superfluous men' in the comfortable country-houses of the nobility.

Criticism of Western individualism—more primitive than that of the Slavophiles but founded on similar premisses—was a cornerstone of all conservative doctrines during the reign of Nicholas. It is understandable that the conservative press was hostile to and highly suspicious of all literary attempts to show the complicated problems of the 'superfluous men' from the 'inside'. Particular hostility—downright hatred at times—was shown to Lermontov, whose work was felt to embody individualism in its most arrogant and challenging form. The conservative critic S. Burachok launched a furious attack on the 'bacillus of self' embodied in Lermontov's *A Hero of our Time*, and on the 'spiritual pride' demonstrated in the 'abuses to which the notions of individual freedom and reason have led in France and Germany'.[1] According to Stepan Shavȳrëv, Lermontov's Pechorin was quite out of touch with real life: 'Pechyerin is only a phantom projected by the West, the shadow of a disease flickering in the imagination of our poets. . . . There he is the hero of a world existing in reality, here he is only a product of the mind.' The real world which gave birth to Pechorin was 'an age symbolized by the philosophical pride that wanted to plumb all the mysteries of the universe through the agency of the human spirit alone, and through the trivial exertions of an industry that pandered to all the whims of an organism debilitated by sensual indulgence'.[2] Conservative critics contrasted Pechyerin with another character from Lermontov's work—the simple, kind-hearted Captain Maxim Maximich, who was not given to 'speculation'. It is interesting to note that this preference was shared by the Emperor himself.

The captain's character [Nicholas wrote] was sketched in masterly fashion . . . when I began reading this novel I was delighted and hopeful that he would turn out to be the hero of our time . . . but the captain's appearance in this work is like a hope unfulfilled. Mr.

---

[1] Quoted from E. Mikhailova, *Proza Lermontova* (Moscow 1957), p. 345.
[2] Quoted from *Ocherki po istorii russkoĭ zhurnalistiki i kritiki* (Leningrad 1950), p. 503.

Lermontov demonstrated that he was incapable of developing fully this noble and simple character and instead showed us a number of very unattractive and pitiable individuals who, if they do indeed exist, ought to be kept in the background lest they should exasperate the reader.[1]

This reaction on the part of conservative ideologists was not unjustified: Lermontov's rebellious work, full of dramatic irony, was a powerful factor in the 'negation' of Russian reality, which was so far removed from the postulates of the autonomous personality and independent reason. During the period of Belinsky's self-enforced 'reconciliation with reality' it was Lermontov who was responsible for his inner conflict;[2] he scoffed at the tempting possibility of regaining peace of mind by renouncing the 'subjective individuality and recognizing it as a counterfeit, a spectre'.[3] After Belinsky had rejected reconciliation, Lermontov's influence can be seen in his statement that 'individuality has become a subject which will, I fear, lead me to madness'.[4]

Another illuminating episode is the story of the unsuccessful attempts at a rapprochement made by Turgenev and the Aksakov family.

Turgenev did not possess Lermontov's courage; he felt the burden of his own individualism and was tempted by the charms of lost spontaneity and 'immediate harmony'; his work represents both the ceaseless self-flagellation of a Russian Hamlet and the effort to find balm for his tormented soul. Turgenev's *Sportsman's Sketches* could be called an 'attempt to make use of the virgin soil of folkways which have not yet been exposed to the disintegrating poison of reflection, and thereby to inject new life and healthy sap into a declining literature'.[5] The *Sketches* show a Rousseauesque idealization of nature and the common people, of a world not yet disfigured by the excrescences of a disharmonious and sick civilization. Any discord in this world is discord brought in from outside, by landowners and serfdom;

[1] Quoted from Mikhailova, op. cit., pp. 344–5.
[2] 'Lermontov had the effect of drawing Belinsky into a struggle with himself, a struggle which took place before our eyes.' P. V. Annenkov, *The Extraordinary Decade*, p. 49.
[3] Belinsky, iii. 340. [4] Belinsky, xii. 52.
[5] Turgenev's own words, from an article on Auerbach (written in 1868). Turgenev, *Sobr. soch.* (1958), xi. 349.

where the squire or bailiff cannot interfere, people live in harmony with nature, able to preserve peace of mind and wise humility in the face of destiny. Nature teaches the peasants Stoicism, but not dull indifference—they may not know 'chaos of the soul', but they are not strangers to subtle feelings or a tender heart. For the peasant, rebellion against the laws of nature is something incomprehensible, just as he cannot understand panic-stricken fear of death which he regards as commonplace and absolutely natural; the Russian peasant 'dies as if taking part in a ceremony: peacefully and simply'.[1]

While writing *A Sportsman's Sketches*, Turgenev undoubtedly had in mind Schiller's essay *Über naive und sentimentalische Dichtung*. Like Schiller, Turgenev regarded *naïveté* as the source of 'realism' and mental health—the antithesis of the 'half-sentimental and half-ironic preoccupation with one's own personality'.[2] The Russian people were examples of this Greek *naïveté*; in 1850 Turgenev wrote to Pauline Viardot: 'The childhood of all nations is similar and my (peasant) singers remind me of Homer.'[3]

In the light of this and similar statements, Turgenev's interest in the philosophy of Feuerbach can be readily understood.[4] He regarded Feuerbach as an ally in the struggle against unhealthy subjectivism, was confirmed by him in his belief in the objectivity of nature and the validity of the 'naïve' realistic view of the world. He was attracted by the Spinozan, pantheistic element in Feuerbach, by his belief that 'Nature is God.'

A similar dislike of egotism and reflection, respect for 'the authenticity of the people', love of nature and country life—all these were factors which attracted Turgenev to the Aksakovs. Konstantin Aksakov was overjoyed that Turgenev had at last stopped writing 'à la Lermontoff'.[5] 'Now you see what it means to come into contact with the soil and the common people—you gain vigour at once!',[6] he wrote about the first story in the *Sketches*. Two other stories, *Mumu* and *The Inn*, aroused even greater enthusiasm among the Slavophiles, who considered

---

[1] Turgenev, *A Sportsman's Sketches*. [2] Turgenev, *Sobr. soch.* xii. 163.
[3] Ibid., p. 97. [4] See ibid., p. 49.
[5] 'Pis'ma S. T., K. S. i I. S. Aksakovȳkh k I. S. Turgenevu', *Russkoe obozrenie* (August 1894), pp. 481–2.
[6] *Moskovskiĭ sbornik*, 1847. Quoted from D. N. Ovsyaniko-Kulikovsky, *Etyudȳ o tvorchestve I. S. Turgeneva* (St. Petersburg 1904), p. 251.

them to be an apotheosis of the Russian peasant's humility and simplicity, his complete lack of affectation and deep Christian morality—patriarchal virtues which were incomprehensible to the West. The young Aksakovs believed that Turgenev had almost reached the point of embracing their 'faith'.[1]

In actual fact Turgenev had only come half-way, at the very most. He was closer to the elder Aksakov, Sergeï, who was far from being an Orthodox Slavophile and who supported Turgenev in his polemics with his son Konstantin. Turgenev was an enthusiastic admirer of Sergeï Aksakov's *Notes of a Huntsman in the Orenburg District* and *An Angler's Sketches*, which seemed to him to express his own belief in the healing power of nature:

Together with the fragrant, free, and refreshing air, you breathe in peace of mind, gentle feelings, tolerance towards others, and even towards yourself. Slowly and imperceptibly you cast off self-doubt and contemptuous lack of faith in your own powers, will, and pure intention—that black impotence of the spirit, the epidemic of our time which is foreign to the healthy nature of the Russians but has made its appearance here too as a punishment for our sins.[2]

It is only in this respect that Turgenev—temporarily at least —saw eye to eye with his Slavophile friends. His attitude to the Russian people, on the other hand, was quite devoid of Slavophile overtones. Country life interested him because of its proximity to nature and not because of the survivals of patriarchal social relations. He was quite unmoved by the notion of primitive communal self-government and protested strongly against the Slavophile idealization of the village commune. Konstantin Aksakov's views on the latter he called a 'negation of the rights of the individual', 'for which he had fought so far and for which he intended to fight until the end'.[3] Neither was he interested in Orthodoxy nor indeed in any kind of religious belief, although in his own way he admired people of deep faith. The religious 'self-annihilation of all human dignity in face of divine ordinance' he called a 'triumph of human reason, for a being who has the courage to recognize its own nothingness thereby raises itself to the level of that fantastic godhead

[1] See *Russkoe obozrenie* ii. (1894), 30.
[2] S. T. Aksakov, *Sobr. soch.* (Moscow 1956), iv. 11.
[3] Turgenev, *Sobr. soch.* xii. 204.

whose plaything it believes itself to be. And this godhead, too, is its own creation.' (Clearly a Feuerbachian view.) But, in spite of this, he declared: 'However, I prefer Prometheus, Satan, the embodiment of revolt and individuality. Let me be an atom, but my own master: I do not want salvation but truth, and I expect it from reason and not from Grace.'[1]

As these quotations show, Turgenev was not in the least inclined to reject individualism in so far as this meant the defence of the individual's moral and intellectual autonomy, even at the stage of his development when he was most critical of 'egotism' and subjectivist reflection. It was not the social philosophy of the conservative romanticists, but Rousseau, Schiller, and Feuerbach who helped to shape his view of nature and the common people. In Feuerbachian philosophy he found a doctrine which reconciled pantheistic tendencies with an unequivocal affirmation of the individual.

In later years Turgenev's view of nature as an earth mother, to whom man should return like a prodigal son, was replaced by the notion that nature was a brute force alien to humanity. Nevertheless, the vision of nature as a harmonious realm still occurred in his novels; in *A House of Gentlefolk*, for instance, in Lavretsky's reflections on returning to his neglected country estate:

'Here I am at the very bottom of the river', thought Lavretsky again. 'And always at all times life here is quiet, unhurried', he thought; 'whoever comes within its circle must submit; here there is nothing to agitate, nothing to harass; one can only get on here by making one's way slowly, as the ploughman cuts the furrow with his plough. And what vigour, what health abound in this inactive place! Here under the window the sturdy burdock creeps out of the thick grass; above it the lovage trails its juicy stalks, and the Virgin's tears fling still higher their pink tendrils; and yonder further in the fields is the silky rye, and the oats are already in ear, and every leaf on every tree, every grass on its stalk is spread to its fullest width.'[2]

It is significant that Turgenev put these reflections into the mouth of a character whom he himself called a 'Slavophile'.[3]

[1] Turgenev, *Sobr. soch.* pp. 55–6.
[2] Turgenev, *A Nest of Gentlefolk*, trans. by Constance Garnett, *Collected Works* (Heinemann, London 1894–8), p. 120.
[3] See D. N. Ovsyaniko-Kulikovsky, *Istoriya russkoĭ intelligentsyii*, part i, *Sobr. soch.* (St. Petersburg 1914), vii. 150–1.

The reason for this seems incomprehensible at first, but becomes clear when examined in its historical context: for Turgenev— a typical representative of the 'unhappy consciousness' of the generation of the 1840s—Slavophile philosophy meant any attempt to escape from the tragic dilemma of reflection into the soporific harmony of 'immediate being'.[1]

HEGEL, FEUERBACH, AND THE RUSSIAN 'PHILOSOPHICAL LEFT'

In his brilliant essay *Hamlet and Don Quixote* (1860), in which he defended the 'superfluous men' against the attacks of Cherny-shevsky and Dobrolyubov, Turgenev attempted to show that the disease of 'reflection' was the product of natural laws rather than historical causes and therefore not a transitory stage in the 'phenomenology of mind', but the inevitable fate of every thinking being. This conception, which was most probably derived from Schopenhauer, enabled Turgenev to combine severe criticism of 'Hamletism' with its justification and absolution.[2] This metaphysical-naturalistic interpretation was the intelligent and subtle self-defence of a writer who, in spite of all his efforts, was unable to vanquish the 'Russian Hamlet' within himself.

Herzen and the 'superfluous men' of the Stankevich Circle were by no means concerned to find a justification for Hamletism 'in perpetuity'. On the contrary, the main driving force of their eager philosophical strivings was the desire to overcome their own 'spectral character', self-centred 'reflection', and inner dualism, to find a philosophical formula which would enable them to achieve inner integration and become 'real' people. As a rule their philosophical evolution included two consecutive stages: 'reconciliation with reality' followed by a 'philosophy of action'. Reconciliation meant relinquishing the postulates of 'individual self' and overcoming alienation and inner dualism through reintegration into reality, through *adapting* oneself to the requirements of reality which was largely

[1] The problem of the 'superfluous men', the discussions around this problem in the 1860s, and Turgenev's standpoint are dealt with at greater length in my article 'Slawianofile a "zbędni ludzie" na tle prądów ideowych lat trzydziestych-sześćdziesiątych', *Slavia Orientalis* (1961), x. nr. 4.

[2] See Walicki, 'Turgenev and Schopenhauer', *Oxford Slavonic Papers*, vol. x (1962).

identified with immediate and existing actuality. The 'philosophy of action', in its turn, aimed at overcoming 'reflection' through exteriorization, through the struggle to *change* reality and to *realize* the autonomy of the individual in free and creative activity. 'Activity,' Herzen wrote, 'that is what personality means.'[1]

The fundamental stages of this ideological evolution can be traced in the pronouncements of Stankevich. Stankevich was primarily concerned to overcome subjective *Schönseeligkeit*, to liberate himself from the 'oppressiveness of the particular, from individual passions,[2] and to find support in the sphere of the universal'. At first he saw this as a question of religious identification with God and with a pantheistically conceived nature. Under the influence of Hegel his conception of the problem changed almost imperceptibly into one concerned with the relationship between personality and history, between the subjective aspirations of the individual and historical inevitability.

Stankevich never went through a period of 'reconciliation' with reality and Belinsky's violent attacks on Schiller's 'abstract idealism' surprised and shocked him. However, this was rather because he disliked extremes than because of any fundamental difference of outlook. It is not difficult to find in Stankevich the main elements of the philosophy of reconciliation, namely a belief in the need to submit to the 'universal', the 'soothing' idea that the world is governed by reason, and faith in the efficacy of immersion in 'real life' as an aid to overcoming *Schöneseeligkeit* and 'reflection'.

Stankevich's contribution, however, was more important than this. Frequently his constantly developing ideas anticipated the mental evolution of other thinkers of the Russian philosophical Left. He realized sooner than the other members of his circle that *Allgemeinheit* in Hegel did not mean the annihilation of individuality and that in the *Phenomenology of Mind* individuality emerged victorious.[3] In the last year of his life he even became interested in the early works of Feuerbach. In a

---

[1] Herzen, iii. 69.

[2] Stankevich, *Perepiska ego i biografiya* . . ., p. 255.

[3] See 'Ob otnoshenii filosofii k iskusstvu', in Stankevich, *Perepiska ego i biografiya* . . ., pp. 369–70.

letter to Bakunin he wrote: 'For all his imperfections he is a joy to read. There is a pleasing element of life in him. *Es ist Etwas vom alten Schelling in ihm, aber ohne Fantasterei.*'

In the same letter there are some interesting comments on the Polish philosopher August Cieszkowski who, as we shall see, helped to inspire Herzen's 'philosophy of action'.

An idea perforce becomes an *act*, is conscious of it and takes delight in it. There is a pamphlet by Cieszkowski, *Prolegomena zur Historio-sophie*, where he divides history into three phases: *Kunst, Wissenschaft* (we are at the end of this phase), and *Tat*. The division is not a good one, because it is not based on the idea of history, but the last thought—that learning should turn into action and be submerged in it—is correct. Today it is obvious that the tendency of the age is to reunite the disconnected categories with the life of the heart, to remould philosophy into a single feeling so as not to have it in the head, but in the blood, in the body, in the whole being. I like this valid postulate . . . It can be realized at present, since Hegel's genius has at last liberated sensual imagery and thoughts. Before him it would have been impossible, the outcome would have been *Fantasterei*. In addition to my work on the philosophy of history, I intend to do something in this field.[1]

In spite of his cursory style and imprecise formulations, understandable in a private letter, Stankevich's intention is clear; like Belinsky and Herzen he declared himself in favour of transforming philosophy into action and linked this postulate with Feuerbach's rehabilitation of feeling and sensuality, with the concept of a man of flesh and blood—not a thinking being merely but one who lives a full life. It was typical of Stankevich that he avoided any criticism of Hegel and was concerned to stress that the 'translation of philosophy into action' and even the 'liberation of sensual imagery' was made possible by Hegel's philosophy. Death prevented him from carrying out the plans mentioned in the letter, but any full account of the philosophical evolution of Belinsky, Bakunin, and Ogarëv should note the part played by Stankevich in pointing out the way shortly to be followed by his friends.

After Stankevich went abroad in 1837 the leadership of his circle was taken over by Mikhail Bakunin. Bakunin's devotion to philosophy, which verged upon a fanatical intolerance of

---

[1] Stankevich, *Perepiska* (ed. by A. Stankevich, Moscow 1914), pp. 672–3.

views he did not share, and his enthusiastic proselytism, became almost legendary. For the young Bakunin philosophy was the way to 'salvation' and a substitute for religion; the desired trip to Berlin in 1840 was to him a journey to the 'new Jerusalem'.

At first Bakunin's interpretation of Hegel was coloured by the mystical influence of German romanticism. He was mainly interested in the traditional problem of mysticism: man's separation from God and the search for ways of achieving identification with the Divine Being. Salvation could be achieved, he thought, by killing the 'individual self' and liberating the element of infinity locked within it. The way to salvation led through total reconciliation with reality. Reality, being the will of God, was rational; everything in it was good and nothing evil, for the differentiation between good and evil (the moral standpoint) was caused by the 'falling away' from God: 'whoever hates reality, hates God and does not know him'.[1]

Bakunin's *Foreword to Hegel's School Addresses*, published in 1838 and generally accepted as the first manifesto of Russian Hegelianism, proclaimed the 'reconciliation of reality in all respects and in all spheres of life'. This was to be the remedy for 'reflection' and the 'endless torment and endless disappointment' connected with it. In the *Foreword* Bakunin argued that abstract individualistic rationalism turns man into a 'spectre', into a being torn apart and fragmented at the core. Such a man does not know that the 'real world is greater than his pitiful and powerless self; he does not know that the source of the malady and the evil are within him, in his own abstraction; he is blind to the harmony of God's universe and unable to grasp the truth and happiness inherent in real life'. The original source of this 'spiritual malady' was the Reformation, while French Enlightenment philosophy, Schiller's *Schönseeligkeit*, the philosophical subjectivism of Kant and Fichte, and Byron's bitter, rebellious poetry were further stages of the disease. After the French Revolution, the nadir of 'man's intellectual decline', France was still sick; incurably sick, for she rejected 'religion, divine revelation, and Christianity'. Therefore the first task of the age was to bring about reconciliation and to bridge the gap between the self and the divine world of objective reality;

[1] Quoted from A. A. Kornilov, *Molodye gody M. Bakunina*, p. 398.

'Hegel and Goethe are the leaders in this process of reconciliation, in the return from the state of death to life.'[1]

The discrepancy between these ideas and what Hegel really wrote is obvious. Bakunin's interpretation was in fact highly irrational and mystical and frequently attributed to Hegel ideas current amongst the conservative romantics sympathetic to Catholicism, to whom Hegel was opposed.

Nevertheless, in spite of appearances, the views of the young Bakunin did not spring from social conservatism. Even in the 1830s Bakunin was already a 'nihilist', contemptuous of established traditions and authorities. His mysticism represented an attempt to replace official religion by an extra-ecclesiastical inner religiosity, and was thus a step towards the emancipation of the personality. His Hegelian mysticism was in fact a move away from mysticism towards philosophy. Bakunin was a typical representative of the socially displaced intelligentsia— members of the gentry who had become alienated from their own class and were therefore able to adopt views associated with a different social background.

Bakunin's later philosophical evolution provides telling testimony of this. In Germany (the 'holy land'), his ideas began to develop with such rapidity that they give the impression of sudden leaps from one extreme to another. This was reflected in his choice of friends and acquaintances who included the Right-wing Hegelian Werder and Bettina von Arnim, as well as Arnold Ruge, Herwegh, and Weitling.

The inner logic of Bakunin's thought led him to a gradual affirmation of the active element in personality and a refutation of contemplativeness. Paradoxically, even his temporary recognition of the personality of God and the immortality of the soul was a step in this direction; it was a metaphysical guarantee of the preservation of individuality, an affirmation of the autonomy and activity of the self. In any case, Bakunin's new conception of God lent support to revolutionary negation and the 'philosophy of action' rather than to 'reconciliation with reality': 'Gott [ist] selbst nichts anderes als das wunderthätige Thun seiner selbst . . .—ein Thun das um wirklich begriffen und

---

[1] See Bakunin's article on Hegel's School Speeches, reprinted in: S. A. Vengerov (ed.), *Polnoe sobranie sochineniĭ V. G. Belinskogo*, vol. iv (St. Petersburg 1901), pp. 484–92.

ergriffen zu werden immer neu begriffen werden muss—und das ist die Natur der That, beständig Gott innerhalb seiner selbst zu bethätigen.'[1]

The notion of 'action' was not new in Bakunin's world-view. However, in the 1830s, when he was under the influence of Fichte and before he had read Hegel, he was interested only in 'spiritual acts'. He criticized Belinsky for his 'Robespierrian' interpretation of Fichte and for taking the postulate of 'action' literally. Now, in 1842, Bakunin understood 'action' as active participation in the revolutionary transformation of reality: 'Nur die That is ja Leben,—und die wirkliche That ist nur beim wirklichen Widerspruch, nur bei wirklichen Hindernissen möglich.'[2]

Bakunin's famous article 'The Reaction in Germany' published in *Deutsche Jahrbücher für Wissenschaft und Kunst* (1842)[3] elaborates further the theoretical foundations of the revolutionary 'philosophy of action' and the 'active principle of negation'. The publication of the article coincided with Bakunin's decision not to return to Russia, to abandon philosophy for action, and to devote himself to revolutionary activity. The article dealt with the political situation in Germany, and was directed against the *Juste-milieu*, the eclectic 'compromisers' who, like a good mother, strove for the 'reconciliation of opposing sides'. It was also one of the first serious attempts to make a radical 'Left-wing' interpretation of Hegelianism and to demonstrate what Herzen called 'the algebra of revolution' through the Hegelian dialectic. Bakunin considered Hegel's greatest contribution to be his concept of the contradiction of opposites; in the article he argued that the essence of contradiction is not equilibrium, but the 'preponderance of the negative', whose role is decisive. As the element determining the existence of the positive, the negative alone includes within itself the totality of the contradiction and so it alone has absolute validity. This led Bakunin to place his faith in the eternal spirit who demolishes and destroys as the inexhaustible and eternally creative source of all life: 'Die Lust der Zerstörung is auch eine schaffende Lust.'[4]

---

[1] M. Bakunin, *Sobranie sochinenĭ i pisem* (Moscow 1934–6), iii. 111–12 (original in German).   [2] Ibid., p. 105 (original in German).
[3] *Deutsche Jahrbücher*, Nr. 247–261, 1842.   [4] Ibid.

Bakunin wrote his article under the French pseudonym Jules Elysard. This had a symbolical significance and was meant to show that he now rejected his quite recent Francophobia (*Französenfresserei*). In the eyes of his contemporaries France was, after all, the land of 'action' and revolution; many thinkers (not only German) were attracted by the possibility of a future fusion of the German and French elements, of philosophy with action and politics.[1] Herzen, still unaware of the real authorship of the article, wrote in his diary that Jules Elysard was the first Frenchman to understand Hegel and German philosophy. 'The whole article is perfect from beginning to end. When the French, having grasped German teachings, begin to generalize and popularize them, that will mark the beginning of a great phase of *Betätigung*. The Germans are not yet ready for it. Perhaps we too shall contribute our little mite.'[2]

Arnold Ruge, the editor of the *Deutsche Jahrbücher* and the leader of the Left-wing Hegelians, commented in similar vein.

Other countries [he wrote in a short introductory note] are wresting the wreath of theory from our grasp. We should like to be confident that this new fact, i.e. a Frenchman who understands German philosophy and corrects it—the Right-wing, the moderate, and the Left-wing variety—will induce certain sluggards to rise from their bed of laurels. M. Jules Elysard may be right in predicting a great practical future for us. But more likely he is mistaken, for his example is not enough to make us give up theoretical boastfulness in the realm of theory, to resign our positions of superiority, and—*horribile dictu*—to become Frenchmen.[3]

The chief personality among the philosophical Left in the 1830s and '40s was undoubtedly Vissarion Belinsky. The young Bakunin's Hegelianism only affected a dozen or so of his closest friends, whereas Belinsky's intellectual evolution was to influence an entire generation. In view of the lack of political freedom and the Emperor's deep distrust of all philosophy, literature and literary criticism were at that time the only tolerated outlet for ideological polemics. Belinsky's critical

[1] The first to put forward this idea was probably Heinrich Heine in his *Religion and Philosophy in Germany* (1834).

[2] Herzen, ii. 257.

[3] Quoted from A. A. Kornilov, *Godÿ stranstviĭ Mikhaila Bakunina* (Moscow–Leningrad 1925), p. 178.

essays yielded an enormous influence, unprecedented and unparalleled in nineteenth-century European literature, both on other writers and on the wider reading public. Belinsky's humble social origins and personal experiences made him more fervent than Stankevich and Bakunin in his hatred of serfdom and more determined to find ways of changing social realities.[1] He was looking for a philosophy which would help him to define his attitude towards reality and would justify his protest and struggle. His individuality as a thinker emerged clearly for the first time in 1836, in his interpretation of Fichte, to whom he was introduced by Bakunin. This turned out to be a kind of prologue to his fascinating ideological drama.[2]

Marx wrote that Fichte's subjective idealism was undoubtedly the kind of idealism that 'developed the active side'.[3] In the active, normative character of Fichtean philosophy, in the concept of an all-powerful ego which nothing can crush once it has accepted its vocation, Belinsky saw a sanction of rebellion, even solitary rebellion, as he himself put it, in the new theory he 'smelt blood'. However, his profoundly realistic outlook made him suspect that heroic voluntarism was only an illusory solution and that an 'abstract ideal taken in isolation from geographical and historical conditions of development'[4] was doomed to be shattered when it came into contact with the stern laws of reality.

Towards the end of 1832 Belinsky came across a formulation

---

[1] Unlike his friends, Belinsky, who was the son of a provincial doctor, had to support himself entirely by his own work and was often in straitened circumstances. His childhood was not happy; he attended Moscow University as a government student wearing a uniform and subject to barrack-like discipline in a students' hostel. So far from being awarded a medal for his studies, as Herzen was, he was sent down from the university ostensibly on the grounds of 'ill health and mediocre capability' but really because of his play *Dmitry Kalinin*, a Schillerian tragedy attacking serfdom, which he was naïve enough to submit to the university censorship committee. Belinsky's strong sense of personal dignity was formed early and had nothing aristocratic about it; it evolved as a protest against surrounding reality, against the primitive corporal punishment used in school, brutal family relations, an oppressive society with all its accompanying humiliations, and—last but not least—it was formed under the influence of the glaring contrast between literature, Belinsky's greatest passion from childhood, and his environment as a whole.

[2] The early stage of Belinsky's intellectual evolution is discussed in my book *Osobowość a historia* (Warsaw 1959), chapter 3, 'Belinsky and Romanticism'.

[3] Marx, first thesis on Feuerbach.

[4] Belinsky, xi. 385.

of the problem tormenting him in Hegel's famous thesis that 'the real is rational and the rational is real'. According to this thesis the 'reason' of social reality is a law governing the development of an objective spirit, a law that is entirely unaffected by the subjective claims of individuals. The revolt of the individual against historical reason is always based on particularist grounds—grounds that are only apparent, subjective, and therefore irrational. Belinsky interpreted this as exemption from the moral duty to protest and struggle. 'Force is law and law is force', he wrote in a letter to Stankevich. 'No, I cannot describe the feeling of relief with which I heard these words: it was a liberation.'[1] After paying homage to Historical Reason and admitting that 'freedom is not licence but acting in accordance with the laws of necessity',[2] Belinsky, like Bakunin, affirmed his 'reconciliation with reality'.

Stankevich, who was abroad at the time, was surprised and disturbed by 'furious Vissarion's' extremism, and especially by his attacks on Schiller's 'shallow idealism'. Bakunin, who was himself preaching reconciliation with reality at that time, complained that Belinsky reduced 'reality' to an over-literal and trivial concept. In fact his conversion was an act of tragic self-denial. The enthusiastic glorification of Russian reality to be found in his articles at that time did not adequately reflect his state of mind. This is clear from his private letters, where he spoke his mind more openly and revealed the painful wounds troubling his spirit. To quote his own words, Belinsky 'forced' himself into reconciliation and did so against his own nature, having first pushed aside his own 'subjectivity'. When he proclaimed the idea that the 'annihilation of the particular in the interests of the Universal is a general law',[3] he believed himself to be an example of the particular that was doomed to annihilation or to submission to the severe laws of an alleged necessity.

Even today the best Marxist analysis of Belinsky's period of 'reconciliation' is to be found in the writings of Plekhanov.[4] Later scholars frequently obscured the issue by trying to prove that reconciliation was only a short-lived and unimportant episode in Belinsky's evolution. This view is, I think, quite

---

[1] Ibid., p. 386.   [2] Ibid., p. 219.   [3] Ibid., p. 526.
[4] In particular his 'Belinsky i razumnaya deĭstvitel'nost' ', *Sochineniya*, vol. x 1897).

erroneous; the period marks a crucial stage in Belinsky's development, indispensable to an understanding of his later, more mature views. Belinsky himself maintained that his 'conscious inner life' began precisely at that time.

The value of Plekhanov's work lies in his recognition that 'reconciliation' was an essential stage in Belinsky's development, 'an element which reflected the greatest credit on him'.[1] Plekhanov suggests that it helped Belinsky to overcome his subjectivism and taught him to take into account the objective laws of history. What Belinsky actually 'reconciled' himself to was not so much Russian reality as the 'sad fate of his abstract ideal'. It was his misfortune, Plekhanov argues, that he could not overcome the utopian element in his ideals without an understanding of the objective laws of historical development which only scientific Marxism could have taught him.

In spite of its many insights, Plekhanov's interpretation suffers from a certain oversimplification and requires at least partial revision. Belinsky's inner conflict cannot be reduced to the difficulty of solving a specific theoretical problem. His private correspondence offers convincing proof that he was less preoccupied with the laws governing historical progress than with overcoming the painful problems of his personal alienation. He sought reintegration into the mainstream of national life, which was unaffected by the 'airy and abstract' ideals of the Europeanized intelligentsia. From his own helplessness Belinsky drew the conclusion that existing realities appeared to have the superior sanction of history; he did not give up the idea of action, but pinned his hopes 'not (merely) on escaping into thought, but on life, which offers a greater or smaller share in reality—a share which is not contemplative but active'.[2] He concluded that it was necessary to fight against subjectivism, and that instead of attempting to force reality to conform to one's postulates, one must change oneself by adjusting actively to the requirements of reality.

Plekhanov rightly observed that for Belinsky the issue of 'rational reality' helped to bring into focus a number of other intellectual problems such as the relationship between freedom and necessity, subjectivism and objectivism, the particular and

[1] *Sochineniya*, vol. x (1897). pp. 242–3.
[2] Belinsky, xi. 317.

the universal. However, Plekhanov's interpretation fails to take into account the fact that there are two aspects of 'rational reality'. On the one hand there is the notion of rational socio-historical reality, with its implication that rational postulates must be deduced from the historical development of society rather than from abstract axioms, that active participation in society must be in keeping with the 'rational' and progressive development trends operating within this society. On the other hand there is the notion of *'rational reality' as an attribute of personality*, which means the inner integration of the psyche, the resolution of painful inner conflict, and the achievement of 'real and rational' existence. Since Plekhanov examined Belinsky's intellectual evolution from the vantage point of the 1890s, when he was under the influence of the theoretical polemics waged by Russian Marxists against the 'subjective sociology' of the Popu-lists, he was only concerned with the first aspect of 'rational reality'. His interpretation was one-sided in its emphasis, there-fore, and incomplete although it cannot be dismissed as erro-neous. Not till the 1840s did Belinsky start to ponder seriously on possible ways forward for Russia. In the 'reconciliation' period he was a true member of the 'superfluous generation' and like them was absorbed by the painful problems of 'spectral existence' and 'abstraction' and the effort to become 'real' at all costs.

To Belinsky the notion 'real man' meant something rather different from what it did to Bakunin. In his outlook a thoroughly romantic opposition to *Verstand*, and a cult of 'im-mediacy' and of irrational elements in the national tradition were paradoxically interwoven with a belief in the virtue of sober common sense and of prosaic, commonplace, 'kitchen-sink' reality. For Bakunin a prerequisite of true 'reconciliation' with reality was the mystical identification of the self with the divine essence of the universe. Belinsky's was not so exacting: he was content to adopt the role of a man who did not indulge in sophistries but had both his feet firmly planted on the ground. 'Let the devil take all dreams!', he wrote. 'What is good is what is under your nose, within reach of your hand.'[1] Comments of this kind aroused Bakunin to a state of holy indignation; he considered them proof of 'complete submission

[1] Ibid., p. 258.

to the impulses of vulgar sensuality'.[1] The controversy between Bakunin and Belinsky revealed the fundamental difference in their personal experiences and social background. From the heights of 'absolute' being, Bakunin showed a lordly contempt for 'empirical day-to-day existence' and its tiresome concern with how to live and on what. Belinsky, on the other hand, never lost sight of 'reality, not in its absolute and general sense, but as it appears in human relations'.[2] His vindication of the 'ordinary', of 'simplicity and normality' expressed his desire to break away from the stifling atmosphere of a milieu which he compared to a desert island.[3] The ideal of 'real life' was intended as an antidote to the vicious circle of 'reflection', to the interminable epistolary confessions and the endless analysis of one's own and other people's psyches. Any useful participation in society, however limited in scope, was better, Belinsky felt, than 'rotten reflection pretending to be idealism'.[4]

Belinsky seems to have abandoned 'reconciliation' precisely because it did not—in fact could not—give him what he had expected from it. So far from providing him with a sense of reintegration, it even increased his feeling of alienation. Having reached the conclusion that for him personally the 'rational reality' was something unattainable, Belinsky consoled himself for a time with belief in the 'rationality' of the historical process as a whole, and in an over-all harmony in which even 'dissonances' have their place. However, these 'philosophical consolations' could not arrest the inflow of new ideas. In the years 1840–1841 he underwent a profound process of inner liberation. His personality, which had been formed in the torments of 'reflection', now demanded recognition of the right to express itself in free, autonomous action. In January 1841 Belinsky wrote to Botkin: 'it is time now for the human personality—which is miserable enough as it is—to throw off the degrading fetters of an irrational reality—the opinions of the crowd and the tradition of centuries of barbarism. . . . I understand myself thoroughly now, and have comprehended my nature: both can be fully expressed by the word *Tat*.'[5]

[1] Bakunin, *Sobr. soch. i pisem*, ii. 240. See H. Temkinowa, 'Bakunin a problemy filozofii historii' (Bakunin and the Problems of the Philosophy of History) in the volume *Historia i wolność* (History and Freedom), *Archiwum Historii Filozofii i Myśli Społecznej* (1961), no. 7, p. 187.
[2] Belinsky, xi. 314.   [3] Ibid., p. 527.   [4] Ibid., p. 480.   [5] Ibid., xii. 13.

The struggle for the rights of the individual and for the vindication of *active* participation in history was eventually bound to lead to a radical reassessment of all those aspects of Hegelian philosophy which had provided Belinsky with arguments to justify his 'reconciliation with reality'. With characteristic fervour, he now directed all his energies against Hegel's 'instrumentalism', against a philosophy of history which condemned out of hand the subjectivism of individuals who dared to oppose the inevitable and rational progress of the *Weltgeist*. In March 1842 he wrote to Botkin:

You may laugh if you like, but I still maintain that the fate of the subject, the fate of the individual is more important than the fate of the whole world and the health of the Chinese Emperor [i.e. Hegel's *Allgemeinheit*] . . . I thank you most humbly, Egor Fedorovich (Hegel), I acknowledge your philosophical prowess, but with all due respect to your philosophical cap and gown, I have the honour to inform you that if I should succeed in climbing to the highest rung of the ladder of progress, even then I would ask you to render me an account of all the victims of life and history, of all the victims of chance, superstition, the inquisition, Philip II, and so forth. Otherwise I should hurl myself head foremost from that very top rung. I do not want happiness, even as a gift, if I cannot be easy about the fate of all my brethren, my own flesh and blood. They say that there can be no harmony without dissonance; that may be all very pleasant and proper for music lovers, but certainly not for those who have been picked out to express the idea of dissonance by their fate. . . . What good is it to me to know that reason will ultimately be victorious and that the future will be beautiful, if I was forced by fate to witness the triumph of chance, irrationality, and brute force?[1]

I have quoted this passage at length, since it expresses Belinsky's moral rebellion with unusual force. This was not simply a polemic against Hegel, but a genuine act of rebellion comparable to Ivan Karamazov's refusal to accept a 'harmony' bought by the sufferings of the innocent.[2] It was not by philosophical arguments, but by a moral stand and by the strong conviction that he would not be satisfied with the role of 'means for the momentary expression of the universal' that

[1] Ibid. xii. 22–3.
[2] See Walicki, *Osobowość a historia*, chapter 5 ('Dostoevsky and the Concept of Freedom'); and V. Kirpotin, *Dostoevsky i Belinsky* (Moscow 1960), chapter 13.

Belinsky expressed his protest against Hegel. He was ready to allow that the Absolute Spirit might really exist, but emphasized nevertheless that it could not influence his choice of values.

Of course Belinsky also attempted to work out his objections to the 'philosophy of reconciliation' on a purely theoretical level; in fact the intellectual revision which accompanied his moral rebellion showed great self-discipline and maturity. In spite of his change of emotional attitude to Hegel, he was careful to point out that it was not Hegelian philosophy but its one-sided and therefore false interpretation that had provided the theoretical groundwork for 'reconciliation'. 'The idea of negation should have been developed as a law of history, without which the history of mankind would become a foul and stagnant mire.'[1]

This was an important discovery. In the 1840s it enabled Belinsky to oppose the conservative romantic historicism with a dialectical historicism which was not burdened by a cult of tradition and stressed the process of dialectical change rather than historical continuity. The notion of 'rational reality' became charged with a new content: in Belinsky's mature interpretation not everything that was universal was necessarily rational; the only truly rational aspect was the dynamic side of social reality, the forward-moving trend which contained the negation of existing but outdated forms. This meant that in a conflict between the individual and society right was not always on the side of the latter; frequently—or even as a rule— it was precisely individual protest that expressed the true meaning of history and paved the way for the 'rational reality'. In this way the lot of the individual again became part of history and in a sense was subordinated to it, but no longer on the basis of a fatalistic submission to the alleged inevitability of the *status quo*. Belinsky's new moral imperative and 'principle of subordination' was conceived of as identification with progress, and progress itself was conceived of as a process of liberation of the individual, as the emancipation of reason, and the gradual rationalization of all forms of social existence.

The rejection of 'degrading reconciliation' meant that the objects of love and hate had to be transposed. Belinsky now

[1] Belinsky, xi. 576.

rehabilitated Schiller and Fichte[1] and was pained to recall how he had 'foamed at the mouth' while repeating 'rubbish' against the French, that vanguard of humanity *au drapeau tricolore*.[2] He was ready to value the Enlightenment and his new 'heroes' now included mainly 'destroyers of the old', among them 'Voltaire, the Encyclopedists, and the Terrorists';[3] to writers he recommended 'subjectivity', i.e. an active, critical, and normative attitude to reality.[4]

All this did not imply a radical break with Hcgclianism. Belinsky stressed that he did not base his views purely on abstract reason (*rassudok*), that he did not negate history, but saw in it the 'inevitable and rational unfolding of the idea'.[5] In fact, he moved over to the standpoint of the Left-wing Hegelians who tried to reconcile German philosophy with French revolutionary thought, to bring out more strongly Hegel's links with the rationalist heritage of the Enlightenment, and to combine German 'thought' with French 'action'.

Hegel turned philosophy into a science [Belinsky wrote in a passage which paraphrased certain ideas first put forward by Engels]. His method of speculative thought is the greatest contribution made by the greatest thinker the modern world has known. This method is so unfailing and superior that it alone can serve as a tool for demolishing those propositions of his own philosophy which are now inadequate or erroneous. Hegel only erred in his work when he departed from his own method. In Hegel philosophy is at its zenith, although at the same time, as esoteric knowledge estranged from real life, it has reached a crisis. Now strong and mature, philosophy returns to the noisy life which it was once forced to abandon in order to get to know itself in solitude and silence. Today's Left-wing Hegelians initiated this felicitous reconciliation of philosophy and practical life.[6]

The 'philosophy of action' received most thorough treatment in the writings of Alexander Herzen, who also did most to develop its theoretical foundations. As the beloved, although illegiti-

---

[1] See ibid. xii. 38. [2] Ibid. xi. 576. [3] Ibid. xii. 70.
[4] See Walicki, *Osobowość a historia*, pp. 258–63.
[5] Belinsky, xii, 71.
[6] Ibid. vii. 49–50. These words clearly betray the influence of the young Engels's *Schelling and Revelation*. Belinsky knew about it through an article by Botkin on German literature (*Otechestvennÿe zapiski*, 1843) which repeated almost literally whole passages from Engels's pamphlet.

mate, son of Ivan Jakovlev, a rich and cultured nobleman who was also an admirer of Voltaire, the young Herzen received a typical aristocratic education; he was taught at home, partly by foreign tutors, and graduated from Moscow University with distinction. Nevertheless, although he started out in life with the benefit of an excellent education and financial security, he was always 'unorthodox' and was destined to suffer early for his opinions: in 1834, when he was 22, he was exiled for several years to Perm, Vyatka, and Vladimir, for propagating Saint-Simonism. His compulsory service as a clerk in a provincial town gave him first-hand knowledge of the venal and servile world of bureaucratic and petty serfowners. The drastic contrast between his own conception of human dignity and the grim reality of Russia under Nicholas I proved to be his most formative personal and social experience.

There is a widespread misconception that unlike the other progressive thinkers of his day Herzen was from the outset interested in French socialism and political action rather than in German philosophy.[1] This theory does not, however, bear closer examination. What interested the young Herzen in Saint-Simonism was not so much its political aspect as its philosophy of history and its revelation of a new religion, a new 'organic epoch'. In his view of the world ideas taken from Saint-Simon, Buchez, and Pierre Leroux coexisted happily with other equally influential ideas taken from Schelling and German romantic literature and philosophy. Herzen's intellectual outlook was formed—especially during his exile—under the influence of the reaction against the Enlightenment and of romantic

---

[1] According to this interpretation the circle formed by the young Herzen and Ogarëv was an almost complete contrast to the Stankevich Circle. This view was encouraged by Herzen's comment, written many years later (*My Past and Thoughts*, ii. 114) that he and his friends were considered to be purely political Frondists and Frenchmen, while he thought of Stankevich's followers as abstract sentimentalists and Germans. In reality this retrospective stylization is far removed from the truth. Herzen's almost 'purely political' standpoint must be taken with a grain of salt, for his circle was hardly less prone to abstraction and exalted sentimentalism than that of Stankevich. His so-called 'French' orientation and dislike of Germany must be considered a legend. The best commentary on it is Herzen's letter to Ogarëv on 31 August 1833, in which he writes that France had seen the full flowering of the 'critical age', the 'age of analysis and destruction', but that it was not the French who would be called upon to do the work of construction; the future renaissance, the age of synthesis, would come from Germany, from 'the land of pure Teutons' whose device was 'Alle für einen, einer für alle!' (Herzen, xxi. 26).

criticism of rationalism, materialism, and atheism; a vague sympathy for utopian socialism went hand in hand with a belief in a universal religious regeneration deriving from Ballanche's 'palingenetic' theories.

The young Herzen's ideal was a reconciliation of individual autonomy with a sense of 'belonging' to some supra-individual whole that would give support and meaning to individual existence;[1] he looked for ways of realizing this ideal in the 'social' religion of the Saint-Simonians, in the visions of the romanticists, and even (in exile) in the Gospels and mysticism. This religious phase was partly the outcome of his correspondence with his extremely devout cousin, Natalia Zakhar'ina, whom he married secretly in 1838, under highly romantic circumstances. His religious fervour gradually declined on his return from exile, when he became preoccupied with Hegelian philosophy.

Some part in Herzen's philosophical evolution was played by the Polish Hegelian August Cieszkowski, whose *Prolegomena zur Historiosophie* he read before he began his study of Hegel.[2] Cieszkowski's ideas fitted in with Herzen's desire for action and his hopeful belief in the future. Cieszkowski, like Herzen combined the German idealist philosophy of history with certain motifs taken from the French utopian socialists; he advocated the 'translation of philosophy into life' and suggested that the age of 'feeling' and the age of 'thought' would be followed by the age of 'conscious action' which would be 'organic', 'synthetic', and 'social'. His book, which harmonized with Herzen's romanticism and his 'palingenetic' expectations, also contained certain motifs which were instrumental in turning him from the beginning towards the radical trend of Left-wing Hegelianism (the postulate of a philosophy of action). Cieszkowski's ideals made a great impression on Herzen, for he found in them a corroboration of his own thoughts. In one of his letters he wrote: 'It is surprising to what extent I am in agreement with the author [i.e. Cieszkowski] on all major points. That means that my ideas are correct and I shall therefore work on them

[1] See M. Malia, op. cit., chapter 5.

[2] Cieszkowski's role in Herzen's intellectual evolution is strongly emphasized in G. Shpet, *Filosofskoe mirovozzrenie Gertsena* (Petrograd 1921); see also R. Labry, *A. I. Herzen: Essai sur la formation et le développement de ses idées* (Paris 1928), pp. 202–6; M. Malia, op. cit., pp. 197–9.

with all the more determination.'[1] On the other hand, Herzen's ideas did not in any way fit in with the philosophy of reconciliation then preached by members of the Stankevich Circle. His meeting (in 1840) with Belinsky, who was at that time 'reconciled with reality' was a real shock to him. 'Do you know', he asked Belinsky, 'that from your standpoint you can prove that the monstrous tyranny under which we live is rational and ought to exist?'[2] The reply—'there is no doubt about it'—was quite unacceptable to a man who had just returned from several years of exile.

Nevertheless, since the philosophy of reconciliation claimed to have the authority of Hegel, the last word in 'science', behind it, Herzen was sufficiently interested to undertake a deep and systematic study of Hegelian philosophy. In the course of his work, he came to the conclusion that Bakunin's and Belinsky's interpretation was erroneous, since the 'philosophy of reconciliation' was in fact a 'philosophy of stagnation', while Hegelianism was an 'algebra of revolution which liberates man in a most extraordinary way and leaves not a stone standing of the edifice of Christianity or of the world of legends which have outlived their time'. At the same time, however, Herzen perceived elements in Hegelianism which—if interpreted formalistically—could give rise to an absolutization of History and a cult of historical Reason understood as an impersonal, supra-human, and cruel force alien to man. Herzen therefore felt that it was necessary to fight on two fronts: on the one hand for Hegel and for such an interpretation of his philosophy as would vindicate all the rights of the free and creative individuality, and on the other against the Hegelian 'formalists' who demanded that the individual make a 'servile admission of his own nothingness'. In this struggle Herzen was not alone; Bakunin and Belinsky soon rejected reconciliation with reality and began to throw doubt on its theoretical foundations.

It would hardly be an exaggeration to say that most of Herzen's writings during the 1840s dealt with problems of the self. Now it was not the exotic romantic personality inclined to mysticism and flights into the *Jenseits*, but personality identified

[1] Herzen, xxii. 38.
[2] Herzen, *My Past and Thoughts*, ii. 120.

with autonomy of thought and action, that became the highest value for Herzen and the cornerstone of his thought. From this point of view his most interesting essay is 'Buddhism in Science' (1843), where these problems were linked directly with the postulate of a 'philosophy of action'.

Following Cieszkowski, Herzen divided history into three great epochs corresponding to the three stages in the evolution of the mind: the age of natural immediacy, the age of thought, and the age of action. In the first epoch individuals live in a world of particular interests and cannot attain universality; their existence is individual but unconscious and at the mercy of blind forces. Thought, or science, represents the negation of 'natural immediacy'; this is quite impersonal for 'the self must renounce itself to become a vessel of truth'. Thanks to science, individuality is enabled to attain the sphere of the universal, and to acquire rational consciousness. Nevertheless, individuality does not disappear in the impersonal realm of reason: 'to perish in the state of natural immediacy is to rise again in the spirit and not to perish in the infinity of nothingness as the Buddhists do.' The abstract impersonality of science is in turn negated by conscious action; having transcended its immediacy, the personality realizes itself in action by participating consciously in the historical process and contributing rationality and freedom to history. 'The whole greatness of the reborn personality consists in the fact that two worlds have been preserved in it, that it is both genus and individual, that it has *become* what it was born—or rather what it was born for—a conscious link between both worlds; it has understood its universality while preserving its individuality.' 'He that loses his soul shall find it', Herzen quoted Saint Matthew: the personality must be renounced before it can be recovered; individuality must be permeated by the universal, and 'particular' reason negated by impersonal reason, because this is the only way in which the free and conscious personality can emerge. In Herzen's argument, therefore, personality was not merely a means to progress but its ultimate goal. 'The formalists', those 'Buddhists in science', were content to have raised individuality to the sphere of the supra-individual; having annihilated the personality they were not interested in its rebirth—or in raising it to a higher level through an active participation in history.

Herzen admitted that this was not merely a matter of misinterpretation and that Hegel himself was largely responsible for such a 'Buddhist' reading of his philosophy. Hegelianism, he pointed out, was the highest attainment of abstract 'science', but now science should be negated by action. Hegel was a child of his age—the age of thought—and was absorbed in the sphere of the 'universal' (the sphere of logic); he had forgotten the concrete human philosophy, but the 'personality forgotten by science now demands its rights, demands a full and passionate life, which can only be attained through freely creative action. After negation in the sphere of thought, it now desires negation in other spheres; personality has shown itself to be indispensible.'

It should be stressed that Herzen's attacks were not directed against Hegel's historicism, but against his 'panlogism', i.e. his identification of the laws of history with those of logic. In this he was critical not only of the 'formalists' but of Hegel himself. Apart from the capacity for logical reasoning, Herzen argued, man has will, which 'may be called positive, creative reason'. This Fichtean emphasis on the will was clearly taken over from Cieszkowski, who contrasted Hegelian thought with the 'entirely practical sphere of the will'.[1] In Herzen's view, the future 'age of action' and not the 'age of thought' embodied in Hegel's philosophy was to be the era of true history. Nature was the equivalent of 'natural immediacy' for in nature 'everything is particular, individual, and exists separately' whereas Hegel's logic was the 'moment' of thought which negates all 'immediacy'. The 'moment of action', which would in its turn overcome 'logic', was to be expressed in history, which 'overcomes nature and logic, and then recreates them afresh'. It is worth noting that in terms of the Hegelian triad 'action' represented a dialectical return to 'immediacy'. This was important to Herzen who, like Feuerbach and under Feuerbach's influence, proposed something like a rehabilitation of nature and 'natural immediacy' and implied that as part of nature man is not only a thinking being, but one capable of feeling, passion, and sensuality.[2]

In later years, Herzen's revolt against Hegel's philosophy of history led him to break completely with Hegelianism (cf. *From*

---

[1] A. Cieszkowski, *Prolegomena zur Historiosophie* (Berlin 1838).
[2] This is discussed at length in the preface to Herzen's *Pisma filozoficzne* (Philosophical Writings), ed. by A. Walicki (Warsaw 1969).

the Other Shore), but the article 'Buddhism in Science' (like the *Letters on the Study of Nature*) was still within the Hegelian sphere of influence. Herzen did not repudiate Hegelianism in it, but gave it a highly personalist and activist slant; he critized 'pan-logism', opposed all 'reconciliation' with existing reality in any form, but did not abandon his faith in the rationality of the history of mankind as a whole. While concerned to stress that individuals and nations were not merely the tools of the *Weltgeist* but ends in themselves, he did not deny that human history had an over-all goal and maintained an optimistic belief in rational historical progress. This optimistic note is struck in the closing words of the article: 'When the time comes, the lightning-flash of history will tear apart the clouds, consume all obstacles and then the future, like Pallas Athene, will spring forth in full armour. Faith in the future is our inalienable right, our highest value; faith in the future fills us with love for the present. In moments of trial this faith will save us from despair; and this love will live in noble acts.'[1]

Herzen's philosophy of action was in tune with ideas current among the Left-wing Hegelians in Germany and Poland (E. Dembowski, H. Kamienski). As early as 1840 Arnold Ruge informed readers of his *Hallische Jahrbücher* that the revolutionary *Philosophie der Tat* had got the better of 'contemplative-ness'. Some of Ruge's formulations recall Herzen's essay, even to such characteristic details as the comparison between the philosophy of contemplation and the wisdom of India. Certain ideas put forward by Moses Hess in his article *Die Philosophie der Tat* (1843) came even closer to Herzen's views, as they linked the philosophy of action to the problem of the full flowering and realization of the personality.[2] There is no reason to suppose that either Ruge or Hess exerted any direct influence on Herzen, but it does seem possible—though not particularly significant—that Herzen was influenced to a certain extent by his conversations with Ogarëv, who studied in Germany from 1841 to 1846 and met his friend in 1842, during a brief visit to Russia. The following passage from one of

[1] All the quotations from 'Buddhism in Science' are from Herzen, iii. 64–88.
[2] See A. Cornu, *Karl Marx und Friedrich Engels. Leben und Werke* (Berlin 1954), vol. i. chapter III.

Ogarëv's letters throws an interesting light on his ideas at that time (1841). 'No, messieurs, not all that is real is rational, but all that is rational should become real. *Die Philosophie der Tat* is at present the best orientation in German philosophy. I have found (in it) a reaction against Hegel.' To Ogarëv, as to Herzen, 'action' was closely linked to the problem of the self. 'What we need is acts', Ogarëv wrote in a letter in 1844. 'Somehow I now find the difference between individual and universal existence quite incomprehensible. Everything is individual existence. Even *Das Allgemeine* has become something personal to me, like all the rest. My personal world is formed to the same extent by love for a woman and by love for humanity.' As 'acts' could only be implemented in the real world, Ogarëv's aim was to 'leave behind the sphere of the indefinable, become clear in my inner being, and look for reality in the world, rather than for fantastic delusions. *Mehr praktisch, mehr praktisch sein*— that seems to me to be tantamount to understanding the method by which non-rational reality becomes rational. *Die Praxis ist die Geschichte.* We have to study our past and create our own life and personal history.'[1]

The need for a philosophy of action is a leitmotiv that recurs in the writings of almost all Russian Hegelians associated with Herzen and Stankevich. Herzen was its most articulate exponent and only Bakunin's 'Reaction in Germany' can be compared to 'Buddhism in Science' from this point of view. Moreover, Herzen's notions are extremely instructive, since they reveal with unusual clarity an aspect of the philosophy of action which was especially characteristic of the Philosophical Left in Russia.

To the Young Hegelians in Germany *Die Philosophie der Tat* meant above all a politically committed philosophy which would allow German philosophy to enjoy the political significance that French philosophy had had in the eighteenth century. In their view, Hegel had gone too far in his fight against 'abstraction' and 'subjectivism'. His almost fanatical anti-utopianism had led philosophy to abandon its normative role and to lend its authority to the *Bestehende*. When radicals like Arnold Ruge wrote about the need to 'overcome contem-

[1] Quoted from P. Sakulin, *Russkaya literatura i sotsializm*, 2nd edn. (Moscow 1924), i. 156–9.

plation' what they had in mind was simply the need to make philosophy political. Bakunin made this quite clear in his article in the *Deutsche Jahrbücher*, which was a cross between an abstract treatise on dialectical contradictions and a programme of action for a revolutionary party.

In Herzen's writings too these motifs occur. He wrote about 'transferring negation from the sphere of thought to other spheres', discussed the contribution of the Enlightenment as if he had only just discovered it, and even argued in favour of the antithesis of ideal and reality (strongly condemned by Hegel), on the grounds that 'all upheavals have their beginnings in ideals, dreams, utopias, and abstractions'.[1] Nevertheless, it is clear that he was primarily concerned with another aspect of the problem: in his interpretation 'action' corresponds to the final stage in the flowering of the personality, which strives to express itself creatively and whose ultimate goal is exteriorization and self-realization in the external, objective world. The stages in the evolution of personality enumerated by Herzen correspond to eras of historical development; his conception is therefore a variation on the theme of the *Phenomenology of Mind*, which clearly fascinated him.

It is significant that while demanding 'action', Herzen also indulged in complaints—typical of the 'superfluous men'—of excessive reflection and *Grübeleien*, of the inner paralysis that prevented decisive and effective action. This is illustrated by the following passage from an article written about the same time as the essay on 'Buddhism in Science':

Grübeln is the distinguishing mark of our age. We are reluctant to take a step without understanding it; like Hamlet we are constantly coming to a halt, and thinking, thinking. . . . We have no time for action; ceaselessly we relive the past and present, everything that has happened here and elsewhere; we search for justification, explanations, try to find ideas and truths. Everything that surrounds us has been submitted to the searching eye of criticism. This is a disease that affects all ages of transition. Formerly it was otherwise: all relationships, whether close or distant, family or social, were clearly defined—just or unjust, they were defined. Hence there was no place for lengthy meditation; to have an easy conscience it was enough to conform to positive law. The whole existing order then

[1] Herzen, ii. 173.

seemed natural, like the circulatory and digestive systems whose origins and operation are hidden from our consciousness, although they function according to specific laws and need be neither watched nor understood. For every case there was a ready-made solution; there was nothing better than to live in conformity with an established pattern.[1]

Herzen's argument reveals the close connection between the postulates of the philosophy of action and the moral issues troubling the 'superfluous men'. The victory of thought over 'natural immediacy' corresponded—in this context—to the victory of reflection over instinctive and 'immediate' traditionalism. Herzen's historiosophical framework explained the source of Russian 'Hamletism' and showed how it might be overcome. Reflection, he was in fact saying, was a by-product of the 'age of thought' which deprived man of 'natural immediacy' and ready-made patterns of behaviour, which rationalized consciousness and universalized thought. If nothing were to follow reflection, man would be doomed to 'Buddhist' inactivity. Fortunately, Herzen argued, reflection was not the ultimate stage in the evolution of the personality, but only a 'moment' from which the way led to a life that was no longer natural and immediate, but conscious and free.

By postulating that logic and abstract thought were also subject to dialectical change and therefore to a return—on a higher level—to 'nature' and 'natural immediacy', Herzen's philosophy of action undoubtedly curtailed the 'panlogical' pretensions of Hegelian rationalism. There was nothing in this, however, to please the Slavophiles; in Herzen's conception a return to nature did not mean a return to traditionalism, to the 'immediacy' of the patriarchal village commune idealized by the Slavophiles. Herzen carried on his polemic against Hegelian philosophy in the name of individual autonomy, and therefore in defence of values opposed by the Slavophiles no less violently than rationalism, and like the latter condemned by them as a fruit of the 'wrong turning' taken by Western civilization. In his struggle for the rights of the personality, Herzen formulated ideas which must have filled the Slavophile philosophers with profound disquiet. 'Is not egoism', he asked, 'identical with

1 Herzen, ii. pp. 49–50.

individualization, with that concentration and separation to which all living beings tend, as to their final goal?' He charged moralists who preached against egoism with trying to annihilate '*die feste Burg* of human dignity'.—'If it were possible to tear egoism from the human breast, this would be tantamount to taking away man's vital element, his fertile ferment, the core of his personality.'[1] Fear of egoism was usually a cloak for fear of moral autonomy, of the burden of freedom.

In every man [Herzen wrote] you will find a kind of pocket idolatry, some savage ideas inherited from his childhood nanny, that coexist happily for thirty years alongside opinions that are by no means derived from nannies; you will find some kind of authority, be it ever so tiny, without which the man would perish miserably, without which he would feel an utter orphan. The Votyaks tremble before a stick with a goat's beard tied to it, for that is their medicine-man. The Germans tremble before the terrible spectre of their science. Naturally, the crude, uncivilized Votyak medicine-man is a long way removed from the medicine-man of German philosophy, but it is not difficult to discover common characteristics in them.[2]

At first glance it might appear that these ideas are identical with notions put forward by Max Stirner in his book *The Ego and His Own* published in 1845. There we have the same struggle with 'spectres' and 'bogeys', the same rejection of any kind of heteronomy, the same (apparently) extreme individualism and defence of egoism. In fact there are also important differences. In his apotheosis of egoism Stirner rejected any type of rationalism and equated the emancipation of the individual with the refusal to submit to any kind of imperative, even one deriving from the nature of reason and humanity itself. For Stirner individuality was the antithesis of reason and the abstraction proper to it; the 'ego' must oppose the rational sphere of universal laws if only in the name of its own un-matched 'uniqueness'. Although Herzen occasionally used arguments similar to Stirner's in his polemics with 'panlogism', he nevertheless believed that 'raising itself to the level of the universality of reason' was a necessary prerequisite of individuality. This gave rise to conclusions which were as un-favourable to Stirner's individualistic irrationalism as to the anti-individualistic irrationalism of the Slavophiles. Herzen

[1] Ibid., p. 96.   [2] Ibid., p. 92.

argued that the personality was formed in the struggle of 'consciousness against habit', of 'logic against tradition', and 'thought against fact';[1] in order to unfold, it needed a Socrates to negate the traditions of Athens in the name of universal truth and a Peter the Great who did the same in relation to ancient Russia.[2]

Herzen's conception of personality demanded activity directed towards the realization of supra-personal values. This activity was not something at variance with personality; on the contrary, it was the very element that constituted personality. The individual who was absorbed in purely personal issues frittered himself away for the sake of minor, fortuitous matters: 'The more a man concentrates on personal concerns, the more places he leaves open to the blows of chance. He has only himself to blame, for the human personality is not something closed—it has wide gates which make it possible to go beyond it.'[3] The egoism of a rational human being showed 'the way into the sphere of the universal' and became fused with 'love of science, art, one's fellow men, a life of broad horizons', in a word, with a 'superior kind of humanitarianism'.[4] Materialism (i.e. naturalistic materialism, which Herzen identified with empiricism) could not satisfy Herzen, since he regarded it as the philosophical justification of the 'egoism of nature'—of the analytical, individualizing, and atomizing force. The synthesis of materialism and idealism (rationalism) postulated by Herzen in the *Letters on the Study of Nature* (1845–6) was to be achieved not only for the benefit of science, but also—and even above all —for the sake of the human personality. Materialism was to guard the personality against the tyranny of 'logic' and the hypostatization of universals, while idealism—which represented the 'universal', i.e. the synthetizing and universalizing tendency—was to defend the personality against disintegration (Hume's 'bundle of impressions'),[5] to organize the surrounding

---

[1] Herzen, ii. pp. 89–90.

[2] See ibid. iii. 167. The unexpected juxtaposition of Socrates and Peter the Great in a lecture on ancient philosophy (the third of the *Letters on the Study of Nature*) is an additional illustration of the correspondence between Herzen's philosophical interests and his controversy with the Slavophiles.

[3] Herzen, ii. 63.   [4] Ibid., pp. 96, 97.

[5] In Herzen's view Hume represented the culminating point of materialism (empiricism): '*Consommatum est!* The role of materialism as a logical moment has

world into a rational structure, and to prevent a situation where there were 'atoms, phenomena, a mass of fortuitous facts, but no harmony, no wholeness, and no ordered universe'.[1]

In the 1840s Belinsky, then the recognized leader of the St. Petersburg Westernizers, held similar ethical views. There is interesting evidence of this in his reaction to Stirner's book, which we know from Annenkov's detailed account. The book apparently made a deep impression on Belinsky, who agreed with Stirner (and Herzen) that it would be ridiculous to abhor the word 'egoism', but maintained that the author of *The Ego* had failed to make clear the underlying difference between primitive animal egoism and an egoism imbued by moral principle. 'And egoism will become a moral principle only when every individual is able to fuse the needs of other people, of his country and civilization as a whole, with his own personal needs and regard them as one and the same concern.' Belinsky held that egoism was something natural, an essential prerequisite of individuality, but one that should be linked to a sense of solidarity for the human race as a whole.[2]

Another important element in the intellectual evolution of both Herzen and Belinsky was the philosophy of Ludwig Feuerbach—this becomes clear after a careful analysis of the *ethical function* of Feuerbach's anthropologism. In the sphere of theory Feuerbach was said—by Marx—to represent '*materialism which now coincides with humanism*'.[3] His humanism was a defence of man as a concrete individual being (but not opposed to humanity as a whole, as in Stirner's conception) against such theological and idealistic hypostases as God, Reason, or the Absolute. To Feuerbach the negation of God, Reason, and the spirit meant the affirmation of a man of flesh and blood, an individual and sensual human being. His protest against

---

ended; in the sphere of theory it was not possible to advance further. The world disintegrated into an infinite multiplicity of individual phenomena, our ego disintegrated into an infinite multiplicity of individual sensations' (Herzen, iii. 307). A similar interpretation of Hume's philosophy—from the point of view of its applicability to the theory of personality—may be found in Hans Meyerhoff, *Time in Literature* (Univ. of California Press 1966), pp. 31–4.

[1] Herzen, iii. 304.

[2] Annenkov, *The Extraordinary Decade*, p. 212.

[3] Karl Marx and Friedrich Engels, *The Holy Family or Critique of Critical Critique* (Lawrence and Wishart, London 1956), p. 169.

religious alienation and idealism ('whose mystery is deeply embedded in theology') clearly derived from the same source as Belinsky's and Herzen's struggle against the 'Moloch of the universal'.

There are a number of striking similarities between Feuerbach's philosophy and the writings of Belinsky and Herzen—as their detailed enumeration would go beyond the scope of this book, I shall confine myself to one aspect which is, I believe, of particular interest.[1]

The passage normally cited as proof of Belinsky's materialism is the well-known fragment from the 'Review of Russian Literature for the Year 1846', where he emphasized the close connection between the mind and its material, bodily base, and the former's dependence on the latter. Most scholars quite correctly connect Belinsky's materialism with the direct or indirect influence of Feuerbach, but none, as far as I know, has pointed out the most characteristic aspects of this materialism. They overlooked the problem central to Feuerbach's 'anthropologism' and one that was strongly stressed by Belinsky—namely the close connection between materialism and the problem of personality. In the passage mentioned above Belinsky wrote:

The world is full of people who are sensitive and responsive, but each man has his own specific kind of sensibility. However many reasonable people there are, each one of them has his own reason. This does not mean that human minds differ—if that were so, people could not communicate with one another, but it does mean that every mind has its own individual character. That is why the mind is limited, why the mind of the greatest genius will always be much inferior to the mind of humanity as a whole. But that is also why it is real and concrete. A mind without a body, a mind without a face, a mind that does not work on the blood and is not affected by it, is mere phantasy, a lifeless abstraction. A mind is a man with a body, or rather a man who is a man thanks to his body, in short— a *personality*. That is why there are as many minds as there are people in the world and why only mankind has one reason. . . . The influence of moral qualities on love cannot be denied, but when one loves someone one loves the whole man—not as an idea but as a living being; and in particular one loves something that cannot be either named or defined.[2]

[1] Cf. A. Walicki, 'Hegel, Feuerbach and the Russian Philosophical Left', *Annali dell'Istituto Giangiacomo Feltrinelli*, vol. vi (Milano 1963).
[2] Belinsky, x. 27.

Belinsky's argument here is a precise reflection of Feuerbach's favourite notion that personality is inseparable from its bodily substance. In his *Essence of Christianity* Feuerbach wrote: 'The body alone is that negating, limiting, concentrating, and circumscribing force without which personality is inconceivable. Take away from thy personality its body, and thou takest away that which holds its together. The body is the basis, the subject of personality. Only by the body is a real personality distinguished from the imaginary one of a spectre.'[1] The conclusions to be drawn from this in regard to human reason and emotions coincide with Belinsky's conclusion in the passage quoted. Feuerbach maintained that the new philosophy was not based on 'nameless reason devoid of substance and colour', but on 'reason saturated with blood';[2] it defended the concrete sensual individuality of which man had been deprived by theology and idealism, and based itself on 'true feelings'; since the heart 'does not need abstract, metaphysical, and theological objects, it needs real, sensual objects and persons'.[3] 'Love is materialism; immaterial love is a chimera. In the longing for a distant object the abstract idealist involuntarily confirms the truth of sensuousness.'[4]

In spite of these analogies, which are concrete evidence in support of the view that Belinsky's materialism was inspired by Feuerbach, it is important not to exaggerate the extent of this influence. In fact Belinsky's intellectual evolution was an autonomous process with its own inner laws and not the mere product of external influences. Feuerbach's ideas fell on fertile ground: Belinsky, like Herzen, found in them a reflection of his own problems, confirmation or modification of his own ideas, and answers to questions he had already begun to pose much earlier, while at the height of his enthusiasm for idealist philosophy. Even during his 'reconciliation' period Belinsky had argued that true love 'is love for an individual and not for the values (universals) embodied in him; for the particular and not for an abstract universality'.[5] Even then he longed to be a

---

[1] L. Feuerbach, *The Essence of Christianity*, trans. by H. Evans (London 1854), p. 90.
[2] Feuerbach, *Grundstätze der Philosophie der Zukunft*, § 50.
[3] Ibid., § 34.
[4] Feuerbach, *The Essence of Christianity*, p. 79.
[5] Belinsky, xi. 341.

Confrontations

man of flesh and blood—along Feuerbachian lines. 'Your blood is hot and alive,' he wrote to Bakunin, 'but it flows in your spirit rather than in your veins (if I may make such a comparison); as for me, my spirit resides in my blood, which is hot and violent, and it affects me only when my blood is boiling.'[1]

It is time to return to the passage quoted from the 'Review of Russian Literature for the year 1846'. Certain inconsistencies in Belinsky's argument are immediately obvious: on the one hand he suggests that there are as many minds as there are people, but on the other he does not deny that 'humanity has one reason', and even cites Hegel's argument (from the *Phenomenology of Mind*) that if this were not so, people could not communicate with one another. It seems to me that this inconsistency, like Herzen's reluctance to give unequivocal support to materialism, can be explained by both men's fear of the one-sided supremacy of the 'individualizing and atomizing principle' they considered materialism to represent. While opposing idealism, Belinsky and Herzen tried not to break with dialectical historicism—they had recourse to materialism (which they identified with naturalistic materialism) because it supplied them with arguments against the hypostatization of the 'universal', but rejected it in their analyses of sociological and historical questions. It is characteristic, for instance, that in his 'Review of Russian Literature' Belinsky first discussed the relationship between psychology and physiology and the bodily substance of personality, and then proceeded to formulate an overtly idealist theory which defined nations as the 'personalities of mankind'.

Elements of materialism fulfilled the same function in Belinsky's view of the world as they did in Herzen's—they sprang from the same emotional premises and led to the same ethical postulates. To simplify, one might say that the leading Russian Left-wing Hegelians felt the need for an element that would curtail the excessive 'panlogical' pretensions of Hegelian rationalism and found what they were looking for in Feuerbach's 'anthropological' materialism. For a time, at least, idealist dialectics and 'anthropocentric' materialism played mutually complementary roles in their *Weltanschauung*. This is especially clear in Herzen's philosophy, in which idealism stood for the

---

[1] Belinsky, xi. p. 346.

rationalization of actions, while it was the function of materialism to stress that personality could not be reduced to the universality of impersonal reason. Within the framework of the philosophy of action rationalism represented the 'universal' while materialism defended the rights of the individual self; idealism had the task of defining the individual's place in society and history, while materialism was concerned with his reintegration into the world of nature and with the rehabilitation of man's 'natural side'.

Materialism and rationalist idealism do not, of course, have the same ideological function in every situation and in every period; on the contrary, I should like to emphasize most strongly that my analysis only concerns the specific meaning which these philosophical trends had for the most outstanding and boldest representatives of the Russian Philosophical Left— the two men who were regarded by the Slavophiles as the leading ideologists of Russian Westernism. This chapter is therefore a contribution to an understanding of a conception of personality which—by combining 'Western' rationalism with an equally 'Western' individualism and materialism—must have seemed the quintessence of 'European error' to Slavophile thinkers. In the following chapter I shall try to show how this conception functioned in the Westernizers' pronouncements on historical and social questions.

9

Slavophiles and Westernizers

IT was in 1842 that the ideologists of the Russian Philosophical Left first engaged in polemics with the Slavophiles, thereby making a formal declaration of adherence to 'Westernism'. Their moral and intellectual struggles with the Right-wing 'formalist' interpretation of Hegelianism were then already a thing of the past, while the postulate of 'practice' was directing their attention to historical and social questions. In the foreground, of course, was the issue of Russia's future course and together with it a whole cluster of problems formulated and given detailed consideration in Slavophile writings. Slavophilism provided a mental stimulus and at the same time aroused active opposition by its questioning of the personalist concepts which were central to the philosophy of the Left-wing Hegelians in Russia. Moreover, in the early 1840s the Slavophiles had already contributed an original philosophical interpretation of Russian history. The Westernizers, as Herzen later admitted, were increasingly aware of the need to 'master the themes and issues put into circulation by the Slavophiles'.[1] To the Left, Slavophile conceptions became a kind of negative frame of reference which largely determined their own historiosophical constructs and even their reading (under Khomyakov's influence Herzen immersed himself in reading the voluminous histories of Neander and Gfrörer, paying particular attention to the history of the Ecumenical Councils).[2] There is no reason to suppose that this was due purely to tactical considerations: in the previous chapter an attempt was made to show that it was rather the logical outcome of the search for a coherent *Weltanschauung*. Adapting Herzen's well-known simile, one might say that the Slavophilism and Westernism of the 1840s were, like the two faces of Janus, firmly attached to each other[3]—hence an

---

[1] See Annenkov, *The Extraordinary Decade*, p. 160.
[2] Ibid., p. 98.
[3] See Herzen, *My Past and Thoughts*, ii. 303.

analysis of Westernism is surely an essential step towards a full understanding of the structure and content of Slavophile thought.

As has already been mentioned, the terms 'Slavs', 'Slavophiles', 'our Europeans', 'Europeanists', or 'Westerners' were initially intended as gibes. The word 'Westerner' or 'Westernizer' (*zapadnik*) suggested some kind of national apostasy, while the term 'Slavophile' was intended to epitomize a certain narrow tribal particularism. Many of those who took part in the great ideological controversy of the 1840s—in particular the Slavophiles—frequently stressed that the terms used to describe their particular orientation fell far short of adequacy. In his memoirs Koshelëv wrote: 'All of us, and particularly Khomyakov and Aksakov, were nicknamed Slavophiles, but this term absolutely fails to express the essential nature of our philosophical orientation.'[1] During his short arrest in 1849 Ivan Aksakov made the following explanatory statement to the police:

Men who were devoted to Russia with all their might and all the power of their soul, who humbly studied the treasures of spiritual wealth of the people, who piously revered the basic principle of their way of life, inseparable from Orthodoxy—these men were dubbed, God knows why, Slavophiles, even though in their relation to the Western Slavs there was only a sincere compassion for the position of their brethren by blood and faith.[2]

The fact remains that both nicknames were capable of a positive interpretation and were finally accepted by the ideologists of both sides as something in the nature of a challenge. On behalf of the Slavophiles this decisive step was taken by Khomyakov, who wrote in the Slavophile *Moscow Miscellany*: 'Certain journals jeeringly call us Slavophiles—a name which is linguistically alien and whose Russian equivalent would be the word "Slav-lover" [*Slavyanolyubets*]. I personally am ready to accept this appellation and proudly admit to my affection for the Slavs.'[3]

An attempt to explain why terms of whose inadequacy both

[1] A. Koshelëv, *Zapiski (1812–1883)* (Berlin 1884), p. 76.

[2] Quoted from M. Boro-Petrovich, *The Emergence of Russian Panslavism* (Columbia Univ. Press, New York 1958), pp. 40–1.

[3] Khomyakov, i. 96–7

sides were fully aware nevertheless gained their silent or open approval, was made many years later by the Westernizer P. W. Annenkov. 'The names', he writes, 'by which the two parties mutually called each other—the *Moscow* party and the *Petersburg* party, or *Slavophiles* and *Westernizers*—were not very precise, but we shall retain them because they have become the ones generally used and for lack of better ones. Inaccuracies of this sort are inevitable in all instances where a controversy is not conducted in the manner or in the terms and with the arguments that were really required.'[1]

Although Annenkov was deliberately vague in order to evade the censor, it is clear that he attributed the use of the terms Slavophile and Westernizer to the absence of free discussion and the impossibility of transferring the controversy to the political arena. There is certainly some truth in this explanation, although it, too, suffers from oversimplification. The relative political neutrality of the terms was not their *only* advantage and was not the decisive factor in their adoption.

The terms 'Slavophilism' and 'Westernism' implied a conflict between two types of civilization, and in so far as this suggested a contradiction between the Slavonic and European principles as such this was perhaps a disadvantage. On the other hand, the quarrel between the Slavophiles and Westernizers was essentially a controversy about types of civilization, about the choice of an all-embracing national social system. Moreover, both names expressed, in a sufficiently veiled way to deceive the censor, the fact that the two ideologies took up positions outside the existing social realities, thus emphasizing their common alienation and at least potential opposition to the Russia of Nicholas I, which was neither 'purely Slavonic' nor 'European' (in the sense in which the two antagonistic sides used these terms).

The kernel of the Westernizing system of values was the 'idea of personality' first worked out by the thinkers of the Philosophical Left in the late 1830s and early '40s and later developed through confrontation with the philosophy of Feuerbach. However, the actual dispute between Slavophiles and Westernizers was not so much over the issue of personality (though this was directly or indirectly involved in all the pro-

[1] Annenkov, *The Extraordinary Decade*, p. 83.

nouncements of both sides), as over the role of 'nation' and 'folk', the national and 'folk' character of literature, and the philosophical meaning of Russian history. Contemporary commentators were unanimous in ascribing the main role in this debate to Belinsky, whom Turgenev, with some reason, called a 'central nature'.[1] Herzen, who was absorbed by his attempts to work out a philosophy of personality as well as by the ideological and political battles in Western Europe, confined himself to private discussions with the Slavophiles in Moscow literary salons and to various reflections dispersed throughout his articles and (in particular) his *Diary*; his contribution to Westernism was enormous, but depended mainly on the philosophical speculations discussed in the previous chapter.

ANCIENT AND MODERN RUSSIA IN THE EYES OF
THE WESTERNIZERS

In his philosophical interpretation of Russian history Belinsky was concerned with the same questions that interested the Slavophiles, namely the differences between ancient and modern Russia, the significance of the concept 'nation', and the mutual relationship between the intelligentsia (the 'educated élite' or 'society') and the common people. In order to understand the fundamental differences between the two interpretations it is necessary to analyse the concepts of 'immediacy' and 'consciousness', which frequently occur in Belinsky's writings.

According to Belinsky's definition immediacy is an attribute of human activity whenever 'our nature acts for us, as it were, without waiting for the mediation of thought or consciousness', when we 'act instinctively' in a situation in which it would 'seem impossible to act without conscious deliberation'. The will and consciousness can and should be involved in 'immediate' acts, but not as the source of the creative impulse or the dominating and controlling factor. History, according to Belinsky, 'is an infinite series of immediately rational and rationally immediate acts'; '(free) volition and consciousness in themselves, as separate elements of the human spirit, can never pass into action, and do not come to fruition in the highest sphere of actuality where they represent forces hostile

---

[1] See Turgenev, 'Vospominaniya o Belinskom', *Sobr. soch.* x. 281–2.

to immediacy, which contains the vital creative force. Immediacy is responsible for the origin and evolution of nature; all the phenomena of history and art have come about *immediately.*'[1]

This conception calls to mind Khomyakov's ideas concerning the role played in history by the supra-individual 'elemental force of history' to which the rational, analytical thoughts of individuals are subordinated. The fact that Belinsky's 'immediacy' can almost be identified with Odoevsky's 'instinct', Chaadaev's 'history', and the Slavophiles' 'elemental force of history', is hardly surprising, since these quotations date from the period of 'reconciliation with reality', when Belinsky's interpretation of Hegelian historicism was coloured by his conservative–romantic approach. His break with reconciliation brought with it a thoroughgoing revision of his attitude to immediacy. 'Intellect [*rassudok*]', he wrote to Botkin in 1841, 'now stands higher with me than reason (immediate reason, of course) and that is why I now prefer the blasphemies of Voltaire to the authority of religion, society, anyone!'[2] Although this might seem a paradox, his rehabilitation of the French Enlightenment helped Belinsky to a more profound understanding of Hegelian philosophy, on which he based his new interpretation of the role of immediacy in the historical process.

It was consciousness that now became the 'goal of every nation and the whole of mankind'. 'In the immediate life of mankind', Belinsky wrote, 'we see the aspirations to a rational consciousness, the aspiration to make all that is immediate at the same time conscious, for the full triumph of rationality depends on the harmonious reconciliation of the immediate and conscious elements.'[3] As will readily be seen, this is one of the variants of the triadic interpretation of the development of the spirit in which 'immediacy' is followed by 'reflection' and the two are reconciled in the 'rational reality'. Another variant of this conception is Herzen's ideas (discussed in the previous chapter) on 'natural immediacy' and 'universality', 'nature', and 'logic', and their future synthesis in rational historical action. It was Belinsky, however, who first applied this scheme to Russian history and used it to construct a philosophical

---

[1] Belinsky, iv. 595.   [2] Ibid. xii. 70.
[3] Ibid. viii. 278, 279.

interpretation of the Petrine period which he put forward in his arguments with the Slavophiles.

'Every nation', he wrote, 'lives through two great epochs: the epoch of natural immediacy, in other words the age of child-hood, and the epoch of conscious existence.'[1] This formula was clearly ready-made to fit Russian history: the turning-point dividing the two epochs—a turning-point obvious to all—was the reign of Peter the Great.

Belinsky developed this idea in detail as early as 1841, in his long essay entitled 'The Deeds of Peter the Great', several passages in which were clearly aimed against the recently formed Slavophile interpretation of history. 'There is a differ-ence', Belinsky wrote, 'between a nation in its natural, imme-diate and patriarchal state and this same nation in the rational movement of its historical development.'[2] In the first state, he maintained, it cannot properly be called a nation (*natsiya*) but only a people (*narod*). This choice of terms was not fortuitous: during the reign of Nicholas the word *narodnost'* used—or rather misused—by the exponents of Official Nationality had a decidedly conservative flavour; *natsional'nost'*, on the other hand, thanks to its foreign derivation, evoked the French Revolution and progressive, bourgeois democratic national movements.

The distinction between *narod* and *natsiya*, *narodnost'* and *natsional'nost'* became the cornerstone of Belinsky's interpreta-tion of Russian history. Moreover, in this interpretation the terms *narod* and *narodnost'* acquired a specific meaning: they were labels appled to a patriarchal, internally non-differen-tiated society (or one just beginning to become differentiated) entirely homogeneous in faith and customs and thus having nothing in common not only with the modern bourgeois nations but also with the peak period of feudal development. Belinsky's model for this stage (the nation in the age of 'natural imme-diacy') was pre-Petrine Russia, or rather its somewhat over-simplified picture which is surprisingly like the Slavophile version. Although their conclusions were quite different the similarities between Belinsky's interpretation of Russian history and that of the Slavophiles is quite striking. Like the Slavo-philes he suggested that there was a fundamental difference

[1] Ibid. v. 308. [2] Ibid., p. 135.

between the Middle Ages in Russia and in Western Europe:
Russia had known neither feudalism nor knighthood, nor an
aristocracy in the sense of a 'privileged estate which stands at
the head of the state and mediates between the people and the
ruler; which through its life and activities gives rise to ideal
concepts of personal honour and the inviolability of its rights,
and hands down a superior culture and elegant way of life
from generation to generation'.[1] In his essay 'On the Historical
Evolution of the Notion of Honour', Herzen, too, praised the
ideal of chivalry as a milestone towards the realization of the
autonomy of the personality and the absolute value of the
individual. 'The proud demand for the recognition of the rights
of the knight was the soil on which grew the consciousness of
the rights and dignity of mankind as a whole.'[2] It is most
instructive to compare these views with Kireevsky's interpretation of the Middle Ages. Like Belinsky and Herzen, the Slavophile philosopher regarded aristocratic concepts of honour as
an important stage in the formation of the modern, 'Western'
ideal of an independent autonomous personality, but unlike the
Westernizers he dismissed this ideal as the 'disintegrating principle of egoism' and human wilfulness. The same view of history
thus served different aims and justified entirely different scales
of values.

    To return to Belinsky, however:

The absolute predominance of *narodnost'* [he wrote in his essay on
Peter the Great] must assume a state of natural immediacy in the
country, a patriarchal society in which the social strata are not even
distinguished by different customs but only by certain fine shades
of behaviour, there being no essential difference between them.
This is what Russia was like until the reign of Peter the Great. . . .
The peasant had no difficulty in understanding his master and made
not the least attempt to raise himself to his level, while the master
understood his peasant without having to lower himself in the very
least. . . . And suddenly, by Peter's volition, everything changed:
the man of the people, who did not understand such words as
victory, *rank*, *army*, *general*, *admiral*, or *marshal*, now also failed to
understand the language and actions not only of his Emperor or
lords, but even of the merest infantry officer with his *honour*, *minuet*,
and *Reithosen*. The upper strata continued to understand the lower,

---

[1] Belinsky, iv. p. 138.   [2] Herzen, ii. 163.

but the lower no longer understood the upper. A gulf opened up between the people and their masters, between the soldiers and their officers. But as far as statehood was concerned, the people had ceased to exist—it had now become a nation.[1]

Belinsky showed considerable dialectical skill in dealing with the phenomenon which so disturbed the Slavophiles—namely the growing cleavage between the upper and lower strata of society. He regarded this as confirmation of a certain general rule applying to the formation of modern nation states. 'In the modern world,' he wrote, 'all the elements within society operate in isolation, each one separately and independently . . . in order to develop all the more fully and perfectly . . . and to become fused once more into a new and homogeneous whole on a higher level than the original undifferentiated homogeneity.'[2] In his later polemics with the Slavophiles Belinsky argued that 'the gulf between society and the people will disappear in the course of time, as the progress of civilization transforms the people into society'; he emphasized that this meant 'raising the people to the level of society' and not 'forcing society back to the level of the people'.[3] The Petrine reforms, which had brought about this social cleavage, were also in Belinsky's view, the first and decisive step towards the emergence of modern Russia. 'Before Peter the Great Russia was merely a people [*narod*]; she became a nation [*natsiya*] thanks to the changes initiated by the reformer.'[4]

The aspect of Peter's reforms that Belinsky admired most was their rational, conscious, and purposeful character, their break with traditionalism and unreflective immediacy. However, he did not demand the complete elimination of immediacy from personal relations: since the social organism required 'an internal, immediate, and organic bond'[5] he posited, in line with the conception developed by Herzen in his 'Buddhism in Science', that the negation of immediacy would be followed by the negation of the negation, that is the partial rehabilitation of immediacy after its permeation by the 'universal'. The Petrine reforms represented the negation of immediate particularism in the name of universal European values; in

---

[1] Belinsky, v. 122–3.   [2] Ibid. v. 630.
[3] *Belinsky, Stat'i i materialy* (Leningrad 1949), izd. LGU, p. 24.
[4] Belinsky, v. 124.   [5] Ibid. x. 29.

accordance with the dialectics of growth, however, the universal content had to assume national form and the negation of immediate instinctive nationality had to lead to the emergence of a new conscious sense of nationality. This, in fact, is what happened in Russia. The catalyst which helped to form the modern Russian national consciousness was, in Belinsky's view, the Napoleonic campaign of 1812. 'The ill-fated year 1812,' he wrote, 'which passed over Russia like a terrible hurricane and forced the country to exert all its strength, not only failed to weaken Russia, but even strengthened her and became the immediate cause of her new and greater prosperity, for it uncovered new sources of national wealth and raised the level of industry, trade, and education.'[1] In his article 'About Eugene Onegin' he wrote: 'It is no exaggeration to say that from 1812 to the present day Russia lived through more and took a greater step forward than during the entire preceding period from the reign of Peter to the year 1812.'[2] The year 1812 'kindled national consciousness and national pride' and helped to bring about the birth of public opinion in Russia. 'In the twenties of the present century Russian literature passed from imitation to independent creation and Pushkin appeared on the scene.'[3] In *Eugene Onegin* he became the 'representative of the first waking moments of the emerging social consciousness'.[4]

The conclusion suggested by these quotations is that in spite of their former decisive role, Peter's reforms were now a closed chapter. In his 'Review of Russian Literature in 1846' Belinsky in fact expressly affirmed this view and even conceded that the Slavophiles deserved credit for their criticism of Russia's aping of Europe: 'The Slavophiles have many just comments to make on this subject, and we must go at least half-way towards agreeing with them.'[5] It is characteristic that Belinsky was struck most forcibly by Slavophile criticism of the 'cleavage in Russian life', the lack of 'moral homogeneity' and of a 'clearly delineated national character'—in other words by their criticism of the abstractness and unreal lives of the 'superfluous men', and of 'society forcibly torn away from its immediacy'.[6]

Belinsky, who had his own painful experience in mind,

---

[1] Belinsky, v. 135.   [2] Ibid. vii. 446.
[3] Ibid. xxx. 447.   [4] Ibid., p. 432.
[5] Ibid. x. 17.   [6] Ibid. xi. 526.

agreed with the Slavophiles that separation from immediacy led to alienation from one's own nation and condemned the uprooted individual to an illusory existence; but he did not believe that it was necessary to return to earlier traditions in order to overcome this alienation. 'Were the Slavophiles in fact right,' he asked, 'and did Peter's reforms merely strip us of our national character and turn us into men from nowhere? . . . No, the truth is quite different: Russia has now completed the stage of transformations and has exhausted all its possibilities; the reforms have fulfilled their task, played out their role, done all they could and should do, and it is now time for Russia to develop independently and unaided.'[1] In terms of the Hegelian dialectic, Belinsky pointed out the utopian character of the Slavophiles' positive programme: the Petrine reforms, he argued, together with the symptoms of disease affecting the Westernized élite, were a necessary stage in the development of the Russian nation, just as 'reflection' was a necessary stage in the transition from 'natural' to 'rational' immediacy. The Slavophiles' conception of national 'originality' and 'distinctiveness' (*samobȳtnost'*) was entirely erroneous:

To bypass the period of reforms, to leap over it, as it were, and to return to the preceding stage—is that what they call distinctive development? A truly ridiculous idea, if only because it cannot be done, just as one cannot change the order of the seasons or force winter to come after spring, or autumn to precede summer. To accept this would mean that we must regard the achievements of Peter the Great, his reforms, and later events (perhaps even up to the year 1812, when Russia entered upon a new life) as the products of chance, an unpleasant nightmare that will disappear and vanish as soon as the sleeper awakes and opens his eyes. No, only Manilovs find it appropriate to think along such lines.[2]

Although Belinsky argued that the period of reforms had run its course he by no means ceased to admire the type of historical leader represented by Peter—on the contrary, he continued to look on him as the personification of the idea of rational and conscious activity and therefore a symbol of the values postulated

---

[1] Ibid. x. 19.
[2] Ibid. Manilov—a character from Gogol's *Dead Souls* typifying indolence combined with an inclination towards empty daydreamings.

by the philosophy of action. In 1847 he wrote to Kavelin:
'Peter is my philosophy, my religion, my revelation in everything that concerns Russia. He is an example to great and small,
to all who want to achieve something, to be in any way useful.
Without the immediate element everything is rotten, abstract,
and lifeless, but where there is nothing but immediacy everything is wild and nonsensical.'[1]

This quotation, about which certain scholars have kept an
embarrassed silence, should not be interpreted as a declaration
of faith in enlightened Absolutism as a political programme; it
simply expressed Belinsky's conviction that energetic and conscious activity—activity not in the abstract, but in a concrete
historical setting—fused immediacy and rationality in a higher
synthesis and was therefore a living embodiment of the *Philosophie der Tat*. The Petrine reforms, which tore Russia (strictly
speaking Russian 'society') from immediacy, paved the way for
the 'rotten reflection' of the Russian 'Europeans'; Peter himself, however, could not be accused of 'abstraction' or 'un-
reality'. As a national leader he was the incarnation of action
unhampered by the fetters of tradition or the hesitations of
abstract reflection, firmly rooted in history and consciously
changing historical reality.

Contemporary Westernizers as well as Slavophiles were agreed
that the most complex and systematic contribution to the
Westernizing philosophy of history was made by the young
Moscow historian Konstantin Kavelin, friend and—in a sense—
disciple of Belinsky and Granovsky. His treatise entitled 'A
Brief Survey of Juridical Relations in Ancient Russia' was published in 1847 in the first issue of *Contemporary* (*Sovremennik*) and
fully deserved to be known as the true manifesto of the 'Western
party'. Belinsky was greatly impressed by it and even called it
the first philosophical interpretation of Russian history, under-
valuing his own work in the field. 'Kavelin's article', he wrote
to Herzen, 'is an epoch-making event in the history of Russian
historical writing.'[2]

In his dissertation Kavelin put forward the thesis that the
historical process in Russia consisted in the gradual replacement
of community relations founded on kinship and custom by a

---

[1] Belinsky, xii. 433.   [2] Ibid., p. 267.

system based on political and juridical organization, which furthered the gradual emancipation of the individual from traditional bonds. This process involved the dissolution of 'natural' and 'immediate' nationality and the gradual emergence of a 'spiritual' nationality—nationality as a moral attribute of national existence and not a mere matter of external physical features. To Kavelin this was the 'law governing the development of Russian social life': 'The stages in the evolution of the principle of personality and the corresponding stages in the decline of a purely patriarchal way of life mark the division of Russian history into various periods and ages.'[1]

Like Belinsky's, Kavelin's views of medieval Russia resembled in many respects those of the Slavophiles. The picture he drew of ancient Russia was that of an entirely self-sufficient world, divided from Western Europe by fundamental differences. Outsiders had no influence on the way of life on the Slavonic tribes, nor did alien invaders (the Tartars) settle among the Russians or make any attempt to impose their customs on them. Unlike Western Europe, Russia had no clearly distinct estates, such as a knightage or an aristocracy; her way of life was patriarchal, based on extensive kinship relations, traces of which survived in linguistic usage, for instance in the peasantry's use of such words as 'father' (applied to every superior), 'uncle', 'grandfather', 'brother', 'sister', etc. Apanage Russia bore the same relationship to feudal Europe as the family does to an association.[2] The European Middle Ages represented the apogee of the one-sided interpretation of the principle of personality, of unbridled ancient Teutonic individualism;[3] in Russia individualism did not exist and the individual human being was completely merged in the community. Different starting-points and different paths nevertheless led to the same final result; this result, the regulating mechanism, as it were, of modern history, was the idea of man, in other words the idea of personality 'free from immediate national determinations', and raised to a universal level. In Europe a straight line led from ancient Teutonic individualism to the idea of 'man';

[1] K. D. Kavelin, *Sobr. soch.* (St. Petersburg 1897), i. 18.
[2] See ibid., p. 16.
[3] This theory, which was popularized by Guizot, was developed in Russia by Herzen in his 'Remarks on the Evolution of the Notion of Honour' and in his *Letters on the Study of Nature.*

Russia had not experienced any form of individualism in the past, but the idea of personality in its universal form nevertheless made its appearance at the same time; this meant that in the eighteenth century Russia was able to take the same course as the nations of Europe. Although an external stimulus was needed, the ground for its reception was prepared by the entire course of Russian history.

The turning-point in the emancipation of the individual in Russia was the emergence of the centralized Muscovite state, for which Ivan the Terrible was mainly responsible. This apparently paradoxical view was in fact a logical consequence of the intepretation of Muscovite autocracy in terms of the Hegelian state. The emancipation of personality, reasoned Kavelin, depends upon the rationalization of social relationships, and the emergence of the centralized state is a necessary stage in this process. 'The emergence of the state', he wrote, 'at the same time meant the liberation from a purely patriarchal way of life, the beginning of the independent activity of the individual, and, by implication, the emergence of a civic and juridical social organization based on moral ideas and concerns and not only on kinship.'[1] In his attempt to rehabilitate Ivan the Terrible Kavelin went so far as to defend such utterly compromised innovations as the *oprychnina*,[2] which he tried to present as a consistent attempt to replace hereditary privileges (based on kinship) by personal merit, and therefore to some extent an anticipation of Peter the Great's Table of Ranks. It was Kavelin's thesis that Ivan's innovations in certain respects anticipated Peter's reforms, but were premature and therefore only partially successful. Ivan gave way under the pressure of his 'dull, stupid semi-patriarchal society', lost faith in the possibility of realizing his great plans, life became a torment to him, and he himself turned into 'a sanctimonious hypocrite, tyrant, and coward'.[3]

In Kavelin's scheme the eighteenth century was a period of transition. Although Ivan's measures were not crowned by success, the period saw the beginning of the emancipation of the individual and the decay of the rule of custom, which was gradually replaced by the rule of law. By the end of the century the liberation of leading individuals from the tyranny of tradi-

[1] Kavelin, *Sobr. soch.* i. 45.   [2] See p. 247   [3] Ibid., p. 47.

tion was almost completed. The newly emerged personality was however merely an empty vessel; the ingredient which would infuse life into it had to come from outside. It was at this very historical moment that Peter made his appearance.

In the person of Peter the Great [Kavelin wrote] individuality in Russia entered upon its absolute rights, after throwing off the shackles of immediate, natural, and exclusively national determinations and subordinating them to itself. Both in his private life and in his political measures Peter represented the completion of the first phase in the realization of the principle of personality in Russian history.[1]

It was only at the beginning of the eighteenth century that Russians 'began to live on an intellectual and moral plane.'[2]

Towards the end of his essay Kavelin dealt with Slavophile criticism of the Petrine reforms. He denied that the reforms had interrupted historical continuity and pointed out that the measures were the outcome of processes that had started much earlier. Peter himself was not aware of the difference between ancient and modern Russia—this antithesis was the product of later abstract historical thought. Those responsible for the reforms and their continuation conceived their task on a purely practical level and had no intention of destroying the Russian national character or of tearing the people away from their past. They were simply Russians who 'listened to the voice of sound common sense and refused to be shackled by historical traditions'.[3] The eighteenth century in Russia was a dynamic epoch of strong characters—people without will and character (i.e. the 'superfluous men') only made their appearance later, when the reforms had exhausted their creative momentum. A period of critical reassessment naturally followed, doubts and indecision paralysed the intellect and will to action, but these were not so much due to Peter's reforms as warning signs of a new period of transition, a 'necessary prelude' to the new, emerging social pattern. Educated Russians became aware of an inner emptiness and action gave way to inactivity; it was then, Kavelin wrote, that we first heard of the

antithesis between the Russian and European principles and of the desire to think, act, and feel 'nationally', like the 'people', or at all

[1] Ibid., p. 58. [2] Ibid., p. 59. [3] Ibid., p. 61.

costs like a European. The aspiration towards distinct and independent development and the aspiration towards improvement, which were represented by the two extreme factions, had once been two parts of a whole, but were now divided and mutually hostile. Between the two extremes there was only mental inaction and apathy. The true meaning of the age of reforms was thus lost and forgotten. At present this cleavage, symptom of a newly emerging intellectual and moral life, is about to disappear and become a thing of the past. It is being replaced by the idea of *Man* and his postulates.[1]

Kavelin's article, like Belinsky's 'Review of Russian Literature for the Year 1846' in the same issue of the *Contemporary*, thus concluded with a conciliatory gesture aimed at the Slavophiles. Belinsky even called Slavophilism a 'momentous and significant phenomenon' 'deserving our respect' which deals with 'the most vital and fundamental issues' in Russian society.[2] Both he and Kavelin proclaimed that the age of reforms had outlived its creative momentum and that bureaucratic absolutism no longer fulfilled a progressive role (something they implied, since it could hardly be said outright); both saw in Slavophilism a one-sided but historically justified and necessary expression of the new transitional period and both agreed with many Slavophile criticisms of Westernization. This would suggest that a common standpoint had been agreed on before publication, and that the editors of the new periodical, while critical of Slavophilism, were also anxious to explore the possibility of collaborating with the Slavophiles in the struggle for the realization of new goals. In view of the censorship, it was impossible to state more clearly what these goals were: Kavelin therefore wrote about the 'postulates of *Man*', and Belinsky of 'issues long since solved in Europe'.[3]

The Slavophiles, however, rejected these overtures of friendship; Samarin's article in the *Muscovite* entitled 'On the Historical and Literary Views of the *Contemporary*' was uniformly hostile. Belinsky was dismissed with contemptuous scorn as a writer who was 'always influenced by the views of others', who constantly adopted new ideas and carried them to extremes, thus making it impossible to understand the opinions of one's

---

[1] Kavelin *Sobr. soch.* i. 64.
[2] Belinsky, x. 17. [3] Ibid., p. 32.

adversary.[1] Samarin's reply to Kavelin is far more interesting and deserves more detailed analysis.

Samarin accused Kavelin of confusing two different concepts: 'Personality in the sense of an exclusive individualism which sets itself up to be the measure of all things', and 'personality as an organ of consciousness', whose role it is to integrate man's divided spiritual forces.[2] It was true, he wrote, that personality in the former sense of the word had not existed in ancient Russia, but that was exactly why the other kind of personality came to full fruition there, as exemplified by the spiritual wholeness and strength of ancient Russian monks, princes, and heroes of folk epics.[3] Samarin agreed that Christianity's contribution to history was the idea of the absolute value of man, but stipulated that this only applied to men willing to renounce their selfish 'exclusive' individuality and to submit entirely 'to the community'.[4] The concepts 'man' and 'people' were really identical,[5] he maintained, but they were not the natural outcome of the evolution of the principle of personality (as the Westernizers conceived it) but rather its diametrical opposite: 'left to its own devices Teutonic individuality leads to a blind alley; the idea of man, that is the principle of the absolute unity and submission of individuals to the highest law, is not reached by a logical path leading through successive historical forms of personality, for the analytical process can never by itself become a synthesis'.[6]

The second error of which Samarin accused Kavelin was his emphasis on the kinship principle as the basis of patriarchal social organization. In fact, Samarin argued, kinship ties were only the lowest rung in the community system which, far from decaying, had actually evolved further under the impact of Christianity: 'The Slavonic village commune opened up, as it were, and absorbed the principles of spiritual life, thus becoming the secular and historical embodiment of the church.'[7] The community principle, which had been preserved in Russia thanks to the common people's adherence to tradition, was at present attracting the attention of more and more thinkers in

---

[1] Samarin, *Sochineniya* (Moscow 1877), i. 80.
[2] Ibid., p. 42.   [3] See ibid., p. 56.
[4] See ibid., pp. 34–5.   [5] See ibid., p. 64.
[6] Ibid., pp. 63–4.   [7] Ibid.

the West, who had become aware of the 'weakness of the individual human being and the helplessness of so-called individualism'.[1] The point of contact between Russian history and
the history of the West was that the latter—through its most
far-sighted thinkers—was now expounding an ideal already
realized in the social organization of the Russian people. To
prove this point, Samarin drew attention to the interest in
things Slavonic, which had been greatly stimulated by Mickiewicz's Paris lectures. 'In response to Mickiewicz's eloquent
appeal many eyes, those of George Sand among them, have
turned towards the Slavonic world, conceived as a world based
on the community principle; they have turned to us not from
mere curiosity, but with a certain sympathy and expectation.'[2]

Samarin's real indignation was aroused by Kavelin's rehabilitation of Ivan the Terrible and his statement that Russians only
after Peter's reforms 'began to live on the intellectual and moral
plane'. He dismissed the suggestion that extenuating circumstances might be found to justify Ivan's crimes, as a 'thought
insulting to the moral dignity of man'.[3] In conclusion he rejected
Kavelin's view of Russia's intellectual and moral development
as something not requiring comment: 'one-sidedness carried to
such extremes becomes harmless'.[4]

Among the Westernizers Samarin's article was interpreted,
quite rightly, as a rejection of the proposed cessation of hostilities. Both Belinsky and Kavelin wrote lengthy replies, but while
the former's was sharply polemical in tone, Kavelin's article was
considered too moderate by his friends. 'The Slavophiles
should be dealt with without further ado,' Belinsky wrote to
Kavelin. '. . . Let God be your judge for allowing one of them
to escape scot-free when you had him under your heel. Please
believe me, when you succeed in stepping on a reptile you
should crush it underfoot, absolutely crush it.'[5] Herzen also
thought that Kavelin had treated his opponent too seriously
when he 'ought to have stung him with caustic comments'.[6]
Several years later, however, Herzen himself was to treat the
Slavophiles with great seriousness and to refer to the contro-

---

[1] Samarin, *Sochineniya* (Moscow 1877), i. 38.
[2] Ibid., p. 39.   [3] Ibid., p. 61.
[4] Ibid., p. 62.   [5] Belinsky, xii. 457.
[6] Herzen, xxiii. 58.

versy between Kavelin and Samarin as a conflict of ideas of exceptional significance.[1] A few words remain to be said about the extent to which Belinsky's and Kavelin's arguments coincide and how far they can be regarded as the common standpoint of both Right-wing and Left-wing Westernizers. It seems to me (although certain Soviet scholars would disagree)[2] that there was no essential difference between Kavelin's and Belinsky's points of view. Kavelin's thesis that nations evolve from 'immediate' to 'spiritual' nationality reiterated an idea frequently discussed by Belinsky, while his reinterpretation of Ivan the Terrible was also directly influenced by Belinsky's views,[3] which had so shocked the Slavophiles and had led them to accuse him of 'centralism'.[4] It is true that Kavelin's conception of the evolution of the juridical system in Russia was his own original contribution, but it was entirely in keeping with Belinsky's views on the role of law and legality in political relations, his attitude to social bonds based on traditional customs and to all types of 'immediate' patriarchal relationships. As far as the role of personality was concerned Belinsky was—as I have tried to show—in complete agreement with Kavelin and like him believed that for nations the 'age of consciousness' was the counterpart of the individual's emancipation from 'immediate national determinations'. The concept of personality was at the roots of all Westernizing thought in the 1840s, and there is surely no justification for interpreting Belinsky's comment about personality in Russia being 'only at the embryonic stage' as a sign of his disagreement with Kavelin.[5] Both thinkers believed that

---

[1] See the chapter 'Moscow Panslavism and Russian Europeanism' in the pamphlet *Du développement des idées révolutionnaires en Russie.*

[2] See, for example, E. I. Kiiko, 'Belinsky' v 'Sovremennike', *Uchenye Zapiski LGU* (1954), nr. 171.

[3] See N. Mordovchenko, 'Ivan Grozny v otsenkakh Belinskogo', *Zvezda* (1945), nos 10–11, p. 191; and E. I. Kiiko, op. cit., p. 77.

[4] Annenkov comments as follows on these accusations: 'Because of his impassioned defence of Peter I and of his avowed sympathies with Petersburg, they declared him a petty and scarcely altogether unself-seeking centralist and bureaucrat. He indeed was a centralist, but not in the sense his enemies maintained.' Annenkov, *The Extraordinary Decade*, p. 111.

[5] In a letter to Kavelin on 22 November 1847 (Belinsky, xii. 433), he wrote as follows: 'You accuse me of Slavophilism. This is not entirely groundless, but I believe that in this respect there are no differences between us. Like you, I love the Russian man and have faith in Russia's great future. But, like you, I build no

the Russian historical process consisted in the gradual emancipation of the individual through the rationalization of social relationships; both thought that in spite of its apparent slowness this process had already begun in Russia.

Although Belinsky and Kavelin saw eye to eye on basic issues, it is true that Kavelin's essay contains the germs of certain ideas which were later adopted by the conservative 'étatist' wing among Russian liberals. The most important of these was the interpretation of sixteenth-century Muscovite autocracy in terms of the rationalized Hegelian state. This served as the foundation for Boris Chicherin's glorification of the state as a veritable 'demiurge' in Russian history—the main creative force responsible for the emergence of the nation and the only active and rational force in the Russian historical process. A more detailed exposition of Chicherin's views, which were first formulated in the late 1850s, do not, however, fall within the scope of this work.[1]

---

hopes on this faith and love, nor do I treat them as incontrovertible evidence. After all, it was you who gave currency to the idea that at the heart of the Russian nation's history is the evolution of the personality principle. You and I will not live all that much longer, but Russia will live for centuries and perhaps even millennia. We want everything to be in hurry, but she has no reason to be in hurry. Here at home the personality is only at the embryonic stage and hence types à la Gogol are *so far* most characteristic of Russia. This is as understandable and clear as that two times two makes four. But however impatient we are, and however slowly we feel everything is ripening, in actual fact everything is moving forward at a tremendous pace.' (Belinsky, xii. 433.)

E. Kiĭko (op. cit., pp. 79–80) quotes the middle of this passage (without the first four and last two sentences) and appends the following commentary: 'As the above comment shows, Belinsky by no means considered Russia's past to have been dependent on the evolution of the 'personality principle' since he emphasized that Kavelin's generalizations are too hasty and that, in spite of his theory, personality was only just emerging from the embryonic stage.' In this fashion Belinsky's declaration of agreement with Kavelin is turned into criticism of his thesis! The true meaning of Belinsky's statement is as follows. In reply to the accusation of exaggerated optimism concerning the future of the Russian nation (his 'Slavophilism'), Belinsky maintains that in this respect he does not differ from his correspondent who *also* believes in the future of the Russian nation, as is shown by his theory of the evolution of the personality principle. Belinsky thus does not criticize Kavelin's thesis, but uses it to support the thesis that there are no essential differences between them. The phrase about 'excessive hurry' does not refer to Kavelin's theoretical generalizations but to his understandable 'impatience', which is shared by Belinsky, that the evolution of the nation should make itself felt more clearly within the lifetime of the individual.

[1] See N. L. Rubinstein, *Russkaya istoriografiya* (Moscow 1941), chapter 18.

NARODNOST' AND NATSIONAL'NOST' IN LITERATURE

Although the dispute between Slavophiles and Westernizers did a great deal to stimulate Russian historical thought, history played a lesser role in the evolution of progressive ideas than did literature or literary criticism. It is no exaggeration to say that philosophical and literary theories reached the reading public almost entirely through articles on literature. Herzen's philosophical work was too abstract for the general reader, but Belinsky's literary criticism found its way everywhere, even to the most distant provincial centres, introducing new ideas and dethroning old authorities. Pogodin compared it to water wearing out a stone by its constant dripping.

Belinsky's historical antithesis of ancient and modern Russia naturally had its counterpart in the sphere of aesthetics and literary criticism. In fact it was a two-way process, since his interpretation of Russian history was already implicit in his views on Russian literature, some of which were formulated as early as the 1830s. An analysis of these opinions—especially those concerned with the national character of literature and the relationship between literature and folklore (both typical of Westernism)—reveals Belinsky's uncompromising hostility to all trends that glorified 'primitive folk cultures' (Annenkov's expression) and set them against the 'consciously elaborated principles of European thought'.[1]

In his article 'Literary Reveries' (1834), which marked his début as a critic, Belinsky maintained outright that Russia was still without a literature of her own. What was known as Russian literature, he wrote, was in fact a mere imitation of European models, but the gulf between society and the common people prevented it from being an 'expression or symbol of the nation's inner life'.[2] Belinsky conceded that there were great individual talents such as Derzhavin, Pushkin, Krylov, or Griboedov, but these were mere freaks: there could be no literature without continuity or *samobȳtnost'* and these were at present lacking in Russia. The country was going through its pupilage and what it now needed was education and not literature; this would emerge by itself, without special effort: 'The time will come when the broad stream of education will

[1] Annenkov, *The Extraordinary Decade*, p. 110.
[2] Belinsky, i. 29.

flood the whole of Russia and the nation's intellectual image will become clearly defined; then our artists and writers will stamp all their works with the imprint of the Russian spirit. But now we must learn, learn, and learn!'[1]

A few years later Belinsky abandoned this extreme position and admitted that the 'existence of a Russian literature is a fact that cannot be denied'.[2] To the end of his life, however, he would only recognize European-influenced writing, founded, according to him, by Lomonosov—the 'Peter the Great of Russian literature'. Occasionally he would even give a precise date for the first appearance of a Russian literary work, namely the year 1739, when Lomonosov sent his famous 'Ode on the Conquest of Khotin' from Germany.[3] As far as early Russian writing was concerned, Belinsky did in fact stick to the view expressed—with a certain youthful swagger—in his 'Literary Reveries': 'Is it still necessary to prove that the "Lay of the Host of Igor", the "Legend of the Don Battlefield", "Vassian's Mission to John III", and other literary relics, folk songs, and scholastic church oratory have about as much in common with our literature as the relics of antediluvian writing (if found) would have with Sanskrit, Greek, or Latin literature?'[4]

His sense of the tremendous gulf between ancient and modern Russia prevented Belinsky from seeing early Russian writing as capable of evoking anything other than antiquarian interest. He was willing to make a partial exception for folk poetry, which was being widely collected in the 1830s and inspired the outstanding poets of the time, including Pushkin and Lermontov. Compared with the Slavophiles' enthusiasm, Belinsky's reaction was ambivalent. On the whole his dislike of all kinds of 'folk-mania' was uppermost, but he was ready to concede that folk poetry had its merits as a reminder of the 'childhood of mankind', 'the age of oneness with nature which abounded in naïve and innocent love, the age of natural immediacy when all was clear, and no oppressive thoughts or uneasy questions disturbed us'.[5] At the same time he actively opposed the cult of folk poetry and stressed the fundamental difference between the unsophisticated popular character of literature (*prostonarodnost'*) and its national individuality; in the heat of

---

[1] Belinsky, i. 102.   [2] Ibid. v. 648.   [3] Ibid. x. 8.
[4] Ibid. i. 65 (footnote).   [5] Ibid. v. 309.

the argument he went so far as to claim that 'one short verse by a sophisticated artist is of incomparably greater value than the entire body of folk verse'.[1]

Belinsky's articles on folk poetry, written largely in 1841 and 1842, contain many formulations which recall Aksakov's Hegelian master's dissertation. Anonymous folk poetry, he wrote, is the poetry of the age of immediacy and expresses the limited, particularism of tribal existence. Without the 'Universal', the universally human idea, there can be no true nationality and therefore only those nations who have entered the stage of consciousness can claim to be truly 'national'. Like all 'natural', 'immediate' art Russian folk poetry lacked a universal content; it was 'dumb and useless to the people of other nations and had meaning only for the nation that gave birth to it'.[2] Belinsky called nations individualizations of mankind and thought that the overcoming of tribal particularism—or universalization— was a necessary precondition of nationality and would be brought about by great men—'God's elect'.[3] Peter the Great was one of these elect and his reforms, which represented a radical break with immediacy and brought Russia nearer to the historical nations of Western Europe, were not 'anti-national', but on the contrary, laid the foundations for a truly national culture, universal in content and national in form.[4]

The Hegelian notion of 'historical nations' had an important place in Belinsky's literary criticism. He frequently stressed his faith in the great potentiality of the Russian 'substance', but at the same time emphasized that these potentialities could not be realized without 'historical soil'; that the Russian nation 'was still at the very early stage of its evolution' and could not claim to have world-historical significance in the intellectual life of mankind.[5] When he contrasted ancient Russia with medieval Europe his tone was reminiscent of Chaadaev's. He suggested that Western feudalism, unlike Russian patriarchal society, contained a specific 'universal' idea 'evolving from within itself'; the 'Lay of the Host of Igor', for all its poetic beauty, was entirely lacking in universal values, was nothing but 'childish babble', and could not stand comparison with the medieval epics of chivalry.[6] Although after Peter the Great the Russian

---

[1] Ibid.   [2] Ibid., p. 329.   [3] Ibid., p. 315.
[4] See ibid., pp. 305–6.   [5] See ibid., p. 649.   [6] See ibid., pp. 344–5.

empire had acquired political significance on a world scale, this did not mean that the Russian *nation* and its culture had acquired historical significance. In fact Belinsky denied universal significance to all contemporary and earlier Russian writers, including his own favourites, whom he considered to have made a leading contribution to the formation of Russian national culture. This occasionally led him to make generalizations which—taken out of context—strike us as strange and even baffling: in a polemic with Konstantin Aksakov, for instance, he maintained that as far as content was concerned, Gogol's work was 'of absolutely no importance for world literature' and could not even be compared to the work of such writers of universal historical significance as Fenimore Cooper or George Sand (let alone to the work of Homer or Shakespeare, to whom Aksakov had compared him).[1] This surprising comment should be seen as flowing directly from Belinsky's philosophical thesis that 'Russian literature never had any universally human significance nor can it have any at present.'[2]

The Hegelian distinction between 'historical' and 'unhistorical' nations helped Belinsky to interpret imitation as a necessary stage in the evolution of Russian literature. Nations deprived of 'universally human significance' could not develop without outside stimulus and for them the 'artificial negation— imposed by force—of their own nationality and their own historical development in favour of the civilization of nations representing mankind' was the price they were required to pay for admittance to the world arena.[3] Oral folklore (*slovestnost'*) could not give rise to sophisticated poetry, since it was the 'exclusive domain of the common people, while the enlightened classes create an imitative literature which will remain dominant until national and foreign elements intermingle to form an original indigenous literature'.[4] Prompted by his disagreement with the 'abstract humanists' whom he accused of dividing universal content from national form, Belinsky modified this standpoint some years later. 'The human element does not come from outside', he then wrote, 'but arises within the nation itself' and 'the progress of the nation is national even when it is based on borrowings from other nations.'[5] This

---

[1] See Belinsky, vi. 256.   [2] Ibid., v. 649.   [3] Ibid., p. 553.
[4] Ibid., p. 534.   [5] Ibid. x. 29.

modification, however, did not change his basic view on the relationship between folk culture and national culture. In answer to the hypothetical question of 'what would have happened if Lomonosov had based a new Russian literature on folk elements?', Belinsky replied:

Nothing would have come of it. The monotonous form of our modest folk poetry sufficed to express the limited content of the tribal, natural, immediate, and semi-patriarchal existence of ancient Russia; but the new content was not suitable to it, had no room in it; it also required new forms. What we needed then was not nationality but Europeanization; what we had to do, for our own good, was not to stifle, not to destroy our national character (which would have proved impossible, or, if possible, then fatal), but to hold up (*suspendre*)—as it were—its course and development in order to graft new elements on to it.[1]

The return to folk poetry was regarded by Belinsky as a justified reaction to the imitation of foreign models, but also as a relatively unimportant transitional stage. During the formative period of an independent national literature, he wrote, 'folk poetry captures the interest of the enlightened classes and is imitated even by true artists; shortly, however, it becomes clear to all that it has but little to offer, and it is assigned a modest place in the history of the native language, separate from and unrelated to the history of literature in the strict sense of the word'.[2] Sophisticated attempts to imitate the folk style rarely met with Belinsky's approval; exceptions were Pushkin's ballad 'The Bridegroom' and Lermontov's 'Song of the Merchant Kalashnikov', although he had his reservations about these too. About 'The Bridegroom' he wrote:

In all Russian folk songs taken together there is not more of the folk essence than in this one ballad! It is not works like this, however, that should be regarded as models of poetic creation imbued by the national spirit, and it is hardly surprising that the public have not shown particular interest in this charming ballad. The world it reflects in such picturesque and faithful detail is so strikingly different that it is all too easily accessible to anyone of talent. Moreover, it is such a narrow, small, and uncomplicated world that no true talent will devote too much time to it lest it should result in works that are one-sided, monotonous, boring, and even trivial, in

---

[1] Ibid., p. 14.   [2] Ibid. v. 634.

spite of all their merit . . . Lermontov's 'Song of the Merchant Kalashnikov', which is formally not superior to Pushkin's 'The Bridegroom', is greatly superior to it as far as content is concerned. Compared to this poem all the heroic lays collected by Kirsha Danilov fade into insignificance. For Lermontov however it was only a literary exercise, and there can be no doubt that he would never have written anything else in this genre . . . The feelings and emotions of the inhabitants of this world [the world of folk poetry] are so monotonous in their expression, social relationships in it are so straightforward and uncomplicated, that one work of great talent easily exhausts all its potentialities.[1]

It is hardly surprising that this passage—interpreted as a slight on the people and oral traditions—aroused the Slavophiles to real indignation. In one of his articles Khomyakov referred to it as a characteristic symptom, evidence not only of its author's 'own narrow-mindedness and lack of taste' but also of the profound sickness of Russian civilization as a whole.[2]

While he might have been in two minds about folk songs and ballads, there was no doubt about Belinsky's violent hostility to 'pseudo-romantic imitation folk style' which identified nationality with external attributes of popular traditions (the 'clothes and kitchen-sink' school) and demanded that literature reproduce the life and language of the most backward sections of society. 'Nationality', Belinsky wrote, 'is not a homespun coat, bast slippers, cheap vodka, or sour cabbage.'[3] 'If the national character of poetry is one of its greatest values, then truly national works should undoubtedly be sought among those depicting the life of the social groups that emerged after the reforms of Peter the Great and adopted a civilized way of life.'[4] Belinsky dismissed as unfounded and harmful the notion that the real core of the Russian national character could only be found in 'works on themes taken from the life of the lower uneducated sections of society'.

As a result of this strange notion, all that is best and most educated in Russia is called 'un-Russian'; as a result of this kitchen-sink notion any coarse farce about comic rustics is both Russian and

[1] Belinsky, vii. 434.
[2] See Khomyakov, i. 58–9 ('Mnenie russkikh ob inostrantsakh').
[3] Belinsky, vii. 435.
[4] Ibid.

national, while Griboedov's *Woe from Wit* is only Russian, but not national; any vulgar story like 'The Rollicking Revels of the Young Merchants in St. Mary's Wood' is national and Russian though palpably bad, while *A Hero of our Time* is both excellent and Russian, but not national. . . . No, no, and a thousand times no! It is high time we summoned up all our sound common sense, all the energy of inexorable logic, to help us fight this notion.[1]

In his uncompromising opposition to these 'homespun-slippery notions' Belinsky represented an extreme form of Westernism which occasionally worried even some of his closest friends. Herzen, for example, considered some of his statements rash, smacking of contempt for people in homespun coats and bast slippers, and once told Annenkov that there were times when he found it difficult to defend Belinsky against Khomyakov's attacks.[2] Reservations of this kind (shared also by Granovsky),[3] reflected the psychological make-up of the progressive intelligentsia among the gentry, who were afraid of seeming to parade their 'superiority'. Thanks to his plebeian origins—which Khomyakov was spiteful enough to remind him of—Belinsky suffered from no such over-sensitive scruples. He knew that it was not the common people he despised, but the state-propagated doctrine of nationality. When such works as *Anton the Unfortunate* by Grigorovich and Turgenev's *Sportsman's Sketches* began to appear in the second half of the 1840s—books which did not idealize native backwardness—Belinsky greeted them enthusiastically and defended them ardently against pseudo-aristocratic readers who complained of the 'invasion of peasants in literature'.[4]

In the 1830s and '40s the 'pseudo-romantic folkstyle' ridiculed by Belinsky was in fact an officially inspired literary programme embraced with enthusiasm by all sorts of reactionary writers and journalists. Its representatives were men like M. N. Zagoskin, whose work combined naturalism with a naïve and superficial romanticism, and V. V. Kukolnik, founder of the 'pseudo-grandiose school', as Turgenev called it.[5] The ideologists of Official Nationality appealed to the conservative

---

[1] Ibid., pp. 438–9.
[2] See Annenkov, *The Extraordinary Decade*, p. 93.
[3] Vetrinsky (Cheshikhin) *T. N. Granovsky i ego vremya*, pp. 262–72.
[4] Belinsky, x. 300–1.
[5] 'Lozhnovelichavaya shkola', Turgenev, *Sobr. soch.* x. 289.

strain in the peasantry and to this end widely exploited folk poetry, while the authorities carefully fostered 'naïve peasant talents' such as Slepushkin and Alipanov, who specialized in servile flattery of the Tsar. At the same time, the *Lighthouse* (*Mayak*), a journal that made no attempt to disguise its obscurantism and claimed to represent the 'good peasants', attacked 'Western sophistries' through the mouths of various shady 'wise men of the people' who sang the praises of *Orthodoxy, Autocracy, and Nationality*.[1] Fears of Decembrist influences were still alive and the 'faithful allegiance' of the Russian common people was contrasted with the oppositional mood of the educated gentry. There was a distinct political intention behind the production of such plays as Zagoskin's *The Unsatisfied*, a comedy attacking the progressive gentry, behind Bulgarin's demagogic attacks on Pushkin's 'aristocraticism',[2] and behind the refusal to admit the national character of *Eugene Onegin*, while various 'coarse farces about comic rustics' were held up as a pattern of *narodnost'*. Hence Belinsky's struggle against the 'pseudo-romantic' conception of nationality must be seen as an important political gesture in defence of the educated classes.

It would be an oversimplification, however, to regard Belinsky's views on nationality as the direct outcome of a concrete political situation. As I have tried to show, they had their place in the total structure of his thought (and that of the other Westernizers), and sprang directly from his emphasis on the importance of the emancipated personality and consciousness— the dialectical negation of 'natural immediacy'. The ideological background to Belinsky's thinking was not something specifically and exclusively Russian; it had its almost exact counterpart in Germany, where attitudes to the people (as the carrier of irrational traditions), to *Volkstum*, and folklore were the main issues dividing Hegel from the conservative romanticists.[3] Hence also each side in this conflict found such apt and willing disciples in Russia.

The pseudo-romantic conception of nationality cannot be

---

[1] See Dement'ev, *Ocherki po istorii russkoï zhurnalistiki 1840–1850 gg*, pp. 86–91.
[2] See ibid., pp. 387–91.
[3] See Kroński, *Rozważania wokół Hegla* (Reflections on Hegel) (Warsaw 1960), pp. 112–18.

identified with Slavophilism; it drew its inspiration from official doctrines rather than Slavophilism and its intended public was not the hereditary nobility but the petty provincial gentry and officials, whose vulgarity and xenophobia were matched only by their coarse servility. However, in order to understand the ideological situation of the 1840s, it is important to realize that for the Westernizers the Slavophiles were not clearly distinguishable from the nationalistic fraction among the proponents of Official Nationality. Herzen, who frequently met the leading Slavophiles in Moscow's aristocratic literary salons, was perhaps most conscious of the difference, but even he considered Khomyakov and Kireevsky on the one hand and Pogodin and Shevȳrëv on the other, to represent two wings of one anti-Western 'Muscovite party'.[1] For Belinsky the problem was quite simple: he dismissed Pogodin's *Muscovite* as the organ of the Slavophiles and called the obscurantist *Lighthouse* the 'most extreme and most conservative' expression of Slavophile doctrine.

The *Lighthouse* [he once wrote in a polemic against Samarin] refused to concede an iota of truth to anything that contradicted its fundamental convictions; if it proclaimed that the most outstanding representatives of Russian literature, from Lomonosov and Derzhavin to Pushkin, were infected by the Western heresy, and therefore harmful and a threat to the moral purity of Russian society, then it did so for the sole reason that this was absolutely consistent and strictly in keeping with its doctrinal principles. It was all cast in the same mould: its language, stylistic mannerisms, the literary merit of its poetry and prose, all were quite in keeping with its orientation and aims. It was more Slavophile than the *Muscovite* and was therefore entitled to regard the latter as an inconsistent and contradictory organ of a doctrine that the *Lighthouse* alone represented in all its purity.

The Slavophiles, of course, Belinsky claimed, avoided all mention of the *Lighthouse* and preferred not to acknowledge it, since it did them a very great disservice: 'There are matters which need only be shown in their true colours to be discredited,

---

[1] See Herzen's comment in *My Past and Thoughts*, ii. 294. 'The *Moskvityanin*, however, was pre-eminently the organ of the university doctrinaire set of the Slavophiles. This set might be described not merely as the university, but to some extent as the *government* party.' Herzen used the term 'university' as both Pogodin and Shevȳrëv were professors.

although this is frequently done with the opposite aim in view, namely to raise them in the public esteem.'[1]

Although this may be a somewhat sweeping oversimplification there is more than a grain of truth in it. In the heat of the ideological struggle it is difficult to do justice to one's opponents, but the demarcation lines reflected in the consciousness of the opposing sides always correspond to certain objective differences. While cultured conservatism has little in common with reactionary obscurantism, and the defence of autocracy cannot be equated with the defence of traditional social bonds, it is nevertheless true that processes of individuation and rationalization and the adoption of a system of values generally known as 'Western' represented as much of a threat to the Slavophiles as to the publishers of the *Muscovite* and *Lighthouse*. Little wonder, therefore, that to the Westernizers this was the decisive factor determining their attitudes.

THE INDIVIDUAL AND THE PEOPLE

The Westernizers' conception of the roles of the individual and the masses in history was determined by their view of the people as a carrier of the 'natural immediacy' from which the individual must free himself in order to become a rational and active personality. In order to understand this essential aspect of Westernism it is necessary to devote some space to two more of its representatives—Timofeï Granovsky and Valerian Maïkov.

Granovsky[2] had been one of the leading members of the Stankevich Circle, but in many respects represented a complete contrast to Belinsky. In place of the latter's fearless and sometimes even brutal rejection of compromise solutions, he had what Herzen described as 'a feminine delicacy, a softness of expression and . . . reconciling power'.[3] 'Like Stankevich, Bakunin, and Turgenev, Granovsky went to Germany to study, but his chosen subject was history and he did not go through a stage of 'enthusiasm' for philosophy. His intellectual development in many respects paralleled that of his friends: he too

---

[1] Belinsky, x. 225–6.
[2] 1813–1855; from 1839 he was professor of general history at the University of Moscow.
[3] Herzen, *My Past and Thoughts*, ii. 240.

complained of the pernicious habit of self-analysis and reflection, protested against the idolization of ideas, which he compared to the Indian idols drawn in processions that crushed the worshippers under their wheels,[1] and defended the autonomy and activity of the individual against the fatalist school of French Restoration historians. His dislike of all extremism is shown in Annenkov's story of a split that occurred within the group of Moscow Westernizers who spent a holiday together in Sokolovo in 1846. Granovsky told Herzen that he could never become reconciled to the 'dry and cold idea of the unity of body and soul, for with it the immortality of the soul disappears'.[2] According to Annenkov's account, Herzen quoted Feuerbach's *Essence of Christianity* in support of his viewpoint and was backed up by Ogarëv and later by Belinsky, who was not present at the original discussion.[3] This was the first time that a clearly controversial note had disturbed the apparent harmony of the group of friends; to Herzen it seemed as if a piece of his heart had been torn out.

Granovsky's ideas made their impact chiefly through his lectures; his most important contribution to Westernism was an enormously popular course of public lectures on the Middle Ages held at Moscow University in 1842. 'Granovsky', wrote Herzen, 'turned the lecture-hall into a drawing-room, a meeting-place of the beau monde.'[4] The end of the first lecture was greeted by a spontaneous ovation, ladies and 'young people with flushed cheeks' wept; there were enthusiastic shouts and requests for the lecturer's likeness.[5] The Slavophiles too attended Granovsky's lectures and felt their appeal: many years later Konstantin Aksakov wrote that Granovsky had inspired noble feelings and educated Russian youth.[6]

The content of Granovsky's lectures was decidedly anti-Slavophile; this did not escape the notice of the 'Moscow Party' who therefore hastened to counter them with a course of public lectures on Ancient Russian literature given by Shevÿrëv. The ideological thrust of Granovsky's lectures was contained in his value judgements, in the criteria on which he based his

[1] See Vetrinsky (Cheshikhin), op. cit., p. 104.
[2] Herzen, *My Past and Thoughts*, ii. 349.
[3] Annenkov, *The Extraordinary Decade*, pp. 142–3.
[4] Herzen, *My Past and Thoughts*, ii. 245.
[5] Ibid. [6] See Vetrinsky (Cheshikhin), op. cit., p. 169.

assessment of certain historical phenomena, the following comment on medieval scholasticism is a good illustration of this:

This term, which is in fact our name for medieval scholarship, is not too highly esteemed nowadays. We have become used to thinking of scholasticism as a collection of dialectical formulas devoid of real meaning. This was not true, however, of scholasticism in its early stage, when its intellectual challenge was as bold and spirited as the society which gave birth to it. Its most valuable contribution was, in fact, its youthful fervour. Though lacking objective knowledge, it believed in the power of human reason and was confident that truth could be conquered in battle like a feudal castle. There was no problem that was capable of daunting it, no task too great to be tackled. Of course, scholasticism was incapable of dealing with issues which formed the fatal frontier to our cognitive curiosity, but is helped to shape the noble intellectual penetration and logical force which are characteristic features of European scholarship and lie at the root of all its triumphs.[1]

It is interesting to compare this statement with the view of scholasticism expressed in Kireevsky's essays. Like Granovsky, Kireevsky emphasized the rationalist side of scholasticism, which, however, for that very reason he condemned as a fatal quest for rationalization of religious belief, leading to the disintegration of personality and of society.

Granovsky's historical studies—starting with his master's dissertation, which set out to prove that the legendary Slavonic town of Vieneta ('the Slavonic Venice') had never in fact existed—are full of such anti-Slavophile ideas. In the course of time his attitude to the Slavophiles, which had at first been conciliatory, became more and more openly hostile. Three days before his death, in a letter to Kavelin (2 October 1855) Granovsky wrote as follows: 'I find these people as hateful as graves, they give out an odour of decay. Not a single enlightened thought, not one noble idea. Their opposition is barren since it is based solely on a negation of everything we have achieved during the last hundred and fifty years of our history.'

This letter also includes the following significant passage: 'What we need now is not only another Peter the Great, but also his stick to teach the Russian dunderheads reason.'[2]

---

[1] T. N. Granovsky, *Sochineniya*, 4th edn. (Moscow 1900), p. 266.
[2] Quoted from Vetrinsky (Cheshikhin), op. cit., pp. 364–5.

In his polemics with the Slavophiles Granovsky, like Belinsky, concentrated on a critique of the Slavophile idealization of the people and of popular customs and folklore. 'A large party', he wrote, 'has raised up the standard of popular traditions in our time, exalting it as an expression of infallible collective reason.'[1] This trend, inspired by the German romantics, is hostile to all progress in science as well as in social relations.

The masses, like nature or the Scandinavian god Thor, are thoughtlessly cruel or thoughtlessly good-natured. They become apathetic under the burden of historical and natural determinations, which only the thinking individual can throw off. This individualization of the masses through thought is the essence of historical progress. The goal of history is the moral, enlightened individual, emancipated from fatalistic determining factors, and a society founded on his postulates.[2]

With its emphasis on the autonomous personality and emancipation from 'the determinations of immediacy' this quotation surely expresses the quintessence of the Westernizing philosophy of history as expounded by Belinsky, Kavelin, and Herzen. At the same time it is a good illustration of a potential weakness of Westernism—the fact that it was open to a vulgarized interpretation which overlooked the role of the masses and suggested that history was made only by enlightened and critical minds.

Granovsky himself avoided this kind of oversimplification; he stressed that when outstanding individuals break out of the stagnation of popular tradition they also express the 'collective mind and collective will of the people'. 'Such individuals clothe in living words what had been hidden in the soul of the people, they convert into clear deeds the vague aspirations and desires of their countrymen or their contemporaries.'[3] Nevertheless, Granovsky's conception was not entirely free from ambiguity, if only because the word *narod* itself has a double meaning (people and nation). Evidence could be found in support of the view that when Granovsky wrote about the people whose 'collective will' was expressed in the activity of outstanding individuals, what he had in mind was not the simple 'folk', but only the active part of the nation, the classes who participated in the making of history. An interpretation along these lines, dividing

---

[1] Granovsky, *Sochineniya*, p. 445.
[2] Ibid.   [3] Ibid., pp. 241–2.

the nation into a passive majority and an active minority and absolutizing this division, was put forward in the second half of the 1840s by Valerian Maïkov, a gifted young contributor to the *Annals of the Fatherland*.

Maïkov[1] the first Russian positivist, and a follower of Comte, was neither a member of the superfluous generation nor under the spell of German dialectical idealism. In his intellectual development the place of the Stankevich Circle and Hegelianism was taken by the Petrashevsky Circle, whose members studied French political, economic, and social thought. It should be added that unlike the other members of the circle he did not espouse the utopian theories of Fourier, but was rather a disciple of Feuerbach, Comte, and Mill and a believer in scientific progress. Although he was not an uncritical admirer of Western European capitalism (partly under the influence of V. A. Milyutin)[2] he believed that its further evolution would remove social contradictions and lead to the victory of humanitarian ideals. For Maïkov, Belinsky was a semi-romantic, not trained in sober, logical reasoning. In particular he thought him guilty of an inconsistent and illogical attitude to the problem of nationality. Maïkov held that the ideal of the autonomous personality imbued by universally human values was incompatible with national features. His long article on the poetry of A. V. Kol'tsov is in fact a hidden polemic against Belinsky on the issue of nationality. Belinsky had called Kol'tsov a typical representative of Russian nationality, whereas Maïkov (who also praised Kol'tsov) wrote: 'For my part, I am convinced that a man who can be called a typical representative of any nation whatsoever cannot possibly be a great man, or even someone out of the ordinary.'[3]

---

[1] Valerian Nikolaevich Maïkov (1823–47) was, after Belinsky's departure to the *Contemporary* (i.e. after 1846) the chief literary critic of the *Annals of the Fatherland*. He was a member of the Petrashevsky Circle (with which he broke in 1846) and co-author, with Petrashevsky, of a *Pocket Dictionary of Foreign Terms* (1845), which was, in fact, a compact and popular encyclopedia of the ideas current in the circle.

[2] V. A. Milyutin (1826–55), eminent economist, younger brother of the emancipation reformer, N. A. Milyutin, and the future minister of war, D. A. Milyutin; also a friend of Maïkov. In 1847 he published a number of theoretical articles in the *Annals of the Fatherland* and the *Contemporary*: 'The Proletariat and Pauperization in England and France', 'Malthus and his Opponents', and 'A Sketch concerning National Wealth, or about the Principles of Political Economy'.

[3] V. N. Maïkov, *Sochineniya* (Kiev 1901), i. 54.

Maĭkov agreed with Belinsky that the process of individuation consists in the emancipation of the universally human element from the pressure of immediate and natural determinations; at the same time, however, he accused Belinsky of accepting the 'principle of social determinism' which leads to the conclusion that outstanding individuals are the product of their nation. In Maĭkov's view this was a glaring contradiction in terms: since nationality implies subordination to the community, whose character is determined by external factors, it is incompatible with the autonomy of the individual. Great individuals have to emancipate themselves from nationality rather than express it; the liberation of the personality leads to the creation of a universal civilization accompanied by the total elimination of distinctive national features. 'There is only one true civilization, just as there is only one truth and one good; therefore the more advanced a nation is, the fewer distinctive features its civiliation will show.'[1]

Maĭkov must have been aware of the danger of drawing such a contrast between great individuals and society as a whole, as this opposition fails to explain how the ideas of great men become diffused among the masses and push them forward towards the ideal goal of mankind. He tried to remove this difficulty by formulating the following general law: 'Every nation has two faces, each diametrically opposed to the other: one belongs to the majority, the other to the minority. The national majority always represents a mechanical submission to the influences of climate, environment, tribe, and fate; the minority, on the other hand, goes to the other extreme of denying the importance of these influences.'[2] The minority is the social medium that absorbs and puts into effect the ideas of great individuals, thus influencing the majority and leading it along the path of progress.

Participants in the great ideological discussion of the 1840s presumably had no difficulty in identifying Maĭkov's majority as another version of the common people idealized by the Slavophiles and his 'minority' as the social élite (*obshchestvo*) divorced from the people by the Petrine reforms. Maĭkov's law was therefore essentially a universalization of the Westernizers'

[1] Maĭkov, *Kriticheskie opȳtȳ* (St. Petersburg 1891), p. 389.
[2] Maĭkov, *Sochineniya*, i. 59–60.

view on the role of this élite in Russian history. Unlike Belinsky, Granovsky, and Kavelin, however, Maïkov was unable to see this national division as a result of dialectical process—he made it absolute and identified the transcending of immediate national particularism with the elimination of nationality as such.

Belinsky reacted sharply to Maïkov's article. In the 'Review of Russian Literature for the year 1846' he made it clear that he disagreed utterly with the views put forward by the 'humanist cosmopolitans' (Maïkov was not mentioned by name).

Nationalities [he wrote] are the individualities of mankind. Without nations mankind would be a lifeless abstraction, a word without content, a sound without meaning. In this respect I would rather go over to the Slavophiles than stay with the humanist cosmopolitans, because the former are human beings, even if they are mistaken, while the latter make even the truth sound like the embodiment of some abstract logic . . . Fortunately however, I trust I may stay where I am, without going over to anyone's side.[1]

Belinsky's sharp response alarmed some of his friends who suspected him—quite without cause—of succumbing to Slavophile influences.[2] In his polemic against Maïkov Belinsky was simply defending views he had formulated in the early 1840s in both his articles on folk poetry, where he had made clear his opposition to the 'nationalists' who stood for form without content and to the 'supporters of undifferentiated universality' who wanted to divorce the universally human content from its national form.

The minority [his argument against Maïkov ran] is always a reflection of the majority, both in the positive and the negative sense. . . . A great man is always the child of his country, the son of his nation, for he is great in as much as he is a representative of his nation. The struggle between the individual genius and the people is not a struggle between the universal element and nationality, but simply a struggle between the new and the old, between the idea and empiricism, between reason and superstition. Folkways are founded on habit; the masses accept as reasonable, just, and useful whatever they have become accustomed to and fervently defend those *old* things which a century or not so long before they opposed

---

[1] Belinsky, x. 29.
[2] Annenkov, *The Extraordinary Decade*, p. 163.

equally fervently as something *new*. Their resistance to genius is a necessary factor; it is a form of trial to which they subject him: if he triumphs over all obstacles he is a true genius, that is a legislator and himself a source of the law that entitled him to sway the fate of his native land.[1]

An analysis of this argument suggests that Belinsky and Maïkov were at least in agreement on one vital issue dividing Westernizers and Slavophiles: both regarded the people as a conservative force and believed that progress (of which they took an optimistic view) was always accomplished by individuals. In a review of Prince Vladimir Odoevsky's *Rural Reader*, published a year later, Belinsky reformulated this idea in the following terms: 'The people is the soil that protects the vital sap of progress; the individual is the flower and fruit of this soil. Whenever and wherever any progress was accomplished, it was through the agency of individuals; that is why history always resembles a collection of biographies of great men.'[2]

A comparison of Belinsky's standpoint at the beginning of 1847 with the opinions expressed in the review of the *Rural Reader* written shortly before his death a year later, reveals a certain shift of emphasis. In his polemic against Maïkov Belinsky criticized the 'law of the inevitable division within the nation', whereas in the later article he himself suggested that among all nations (with the exception of the stagnating peoples of Asia) progress was founded on the 'division of national life into people and society', and emphasized that whatever 'mystical philosophers' [i.e. the Slavophiles] might say to the contrary, the common people are 'always children, always immature'[3] and must therefore learn from the educated élite. It is clear that this shift of emphasis was a tactical response to the changing balance of forces in the ideological struggle. In 1848 Maïkov was dead, whereas the conflict with the Slavophiles had reached its climax (in connection with Samarin's article 'On the Opinions of the *Contemporary*'). All the same, it is important to establish to what extent this new emphasis represented an actual change in Belinsky's point of view.

In Belinsky's conception the relationship between the people and individuals (that is emancipated individuals, free from

[1] Belinsky, x. 31.
[2] Ibid., pp. 368–9. [3] Ibid.

'natural determinations') corresponds to the relationship between 'immediacy' and 'consciousness'. This scheme, which was
accepted by Granovsky, Kavelin, and Herzen, allowed the
Westernizers to criticize not only the Slavophiles but also
Maïkov, who absolutized the 'antithesis' stage of the dialectical
triad at the expense of the 'synthesis'. The goal of history,
according to Belinsky, is the emancipated personality in whom
immediacy has been negated by consciousness while being preserved as a 'moment', in order to prevent the individual from
falling prey to the impotence and artificial existence of 'spectral
man'; the people is a conservative force, the carrier of un-
reflecting tradition—only the individual contributes critical
reasoning to history; apart from short periods of spontaneous
and violent activity, the people represents the static element in
history, whereas individuals represent the dynamic element.
This scheme, which underpinned the Westernizing philosophy
of history, can be traced both in the 'Review of Russian Literature for the Year 1846' and in the piece on the *Rural Reader*.
In both articles the common people was compared to the soil
as a reservoir of vital forces and the prerequisite of all development; in both Belinsky rejected 'humanist cosmopolitanism' as
well as Slavophile 'folk-mania'. The only essential difference is
to be found in the attitude to the 'division within the nation'. In
his polemic against Maïkov Belinsky suggested that this division
was by no means an *essential precondition* of progress, whereas a
year later he maintained the very reverse. Belinsky's apparent
change of mind was not so much a concession to Maïkov (who
conceived the essential division quite differently) as a return to
his former interpretation of the mutual relationship of people
and 'society', which had been only temporarily modified as a
result of the polemic with the 'humanist cosmopolitans'.

The evolution in Belinsky's point of view becomes clearer in
the light of his correspondence. In a letter to Annenkov dated
15 February 1848, he wrote that the Slavophiles and Bakunin
(at that time balancing between revolutionary Panslavism and
an anarchical and utopian socialism) had helped him to get rid
of his 'mystical faith in the people'.[1] The analysis of Belinsky's
views presented so far does not provide a satisfactory explanation for this statement, which seems quite inconsistent with his

---

[1] Belinsky, xii. 467.

well-known opposition to all signs of 'folk-mania'. In order to find out what Belinsky meant by this 'mystical faith' and why he only got rid of it in the last months of his life it is necessary to devote some space to a discussion which recapitulated the abstract arguments about 'immediacy and consciousness' in far more concrete form. This was the discussion about Western European capitalism, which divided the Westernizers in the late 1840s.

THE DISPUTE OVER CAPITALISM

In critical studies of Belinsky one frequently meets the statement that after rejecting 'reconciliation with reality' he became a convinced utopian socialist. The main argument in support of this assertion is the following passage in one of his letters to Botkin (8 September 1841): '. . . the idea of socialism has become for me the idea of ideas, the essence of being, the question of questions, the alpha and omega of belief and knowledge'.[1]

In order to see this statement in proper perspective it is necessary, I think, to place it within the context of other pronouncements made by Belinsky at that time. In other letters he defined his central idea as the 'idea of personality' or the 'idea of action'; a little earlier, in December 1840, he wrote in similar terms about liberalism. 'From now on *liberal* and *human being* are synonymous for me, just as I make no distinction between a supporter of absolutism and a supporter of flogging. The idea of liberalism is both rational and Christian to a high degree, for it is the role of liberalism to restore man's personal rights, to reinstate human dignity; the Saviour himself descended to earth and suffered for man on the cross.'[2]

In Western Europe utopian socialism was antagonistic to liberal ideas. In France the term 'socialism' was first introduced in 1834 in Pierre Leroux's famous article 'On Individualism and Socialism', and meant the reverse of individualism,[3] which was equated with the egoism of the economic man of *laissez-faire* economics. Socialism in this very broad sense of the word did not imply the socialization of the means of production and was sometimes extended to cover all kinds of democratic

1 Ibid., p. 318.   2 Ibid. xi. 577.
3 See J. B. Duroselle, *Les Débuts du catholicisme social en France* (Paris 1951), p. 16.

criticism of bourgeois society. As far as Belinsky was concerned, his use of the word 'socialism' was even less precise and there is no evidence to show that in 1841 or 1842 the word had any conscious anti-bourgeois implications for him. In both the letters quoted above he was concerned to rehabilitate the values of the Enlightenment and the French Revolution; in both he inveighed passionately against reconciliation with reality, against the Hegelian *Allgemeinheit* which demanded the suffering of individuals. On closer examination his usage of the word 'socialism' suggests that he regarded it as a synonym for *sotsial'nost'*. When he put forward the slogan 'social solidarity, social solidarity or death!',[1] he was protesting against the social alienation characteristic of the Stankevich Circle, against the ideal of individual perfectability through art and philosophy while the 'crowd was weltering in mud', against the egocentric introspection that cut off the 'superfluous men' from objective issues and matters of wider social concern.[2] The terms socialism and *sotsial'nost'* were clearly used as synonyms for 'socialization', 'social commitment', or 'service to society' rather than with any specific political meaning.

It would be a mistake to conclude from this that Belinsky was totally uninterested in utopian socialism. Although he was less fascinated by it than Herzen, he referred to it often in his correspondence of the 1840s. It is true that he completely ignored the economic aspect of socialist doctrines, but he was impressed by Saint-Simonian ideas on the further liberation of the personality and especially on the emancipation of women. His own vision of 'a new heaven and a new earth' (described in the letter to Botkin quoted above) was concerned with the realization of personal values above all—with the full liberation of the individual from 'senseless forms and rites', from 'contracts and conditions binding the feelings'.[3] Nevertheless, utopian socialism did play a part in Belinsky's intellectual development in one important respect—socialist criticism of bourgeois society opened his eyes to the fact that the promises of the Enlightenment and the French Revolution had not in fact been fulfilled.

This awareness can be seen most clearly in an interesting article on Eugene Sue's *Mystères de Paris*, in which Belinsky

[1] Belinsky, xii. 69.   [2] Ibid., pp. 67–8.   [3] Ibid., p. 70.

wrote of the bourgeoisie's shameful deception of the people in the July Revolution, and criticized the formal equality before the law which allowed the capitalist 'to treat the worker in his smock and wooden clogs as the planter treats his Negroes'. The future of France, he felt, was in the hands of the common people: 'The people is like a child; but this child is growing rapidly and will soon become a man in full possession of his physical and mental powers. Misfortune has taught it sense and has shown up the trashy constitution in its proper light. . . . The people is still weak, but is the only force in France to have preserved the flame of national life and the fresh enthusiasm of convictions which has been extinguished in the educated classes.'[1]

This quotation reveals clearly what Belinsky meant by the 'mystical belief in the people' which he rejected in the last year of his life. The fact that this faith concerned the French people whereas his disillusionment was brought about—among other factors—by the Slavophile idealization of the Russian peasantry, is, I would suggest, a very characteristic feature of the *Weltanschauung* of the democratic Westernizers. For Belinsky the term *narod* had to make do both for the French proletariat and the Russian peasantry still 'browbeaten and inert'. When he wrote and thought about Russia, the term people became a synonym for the nation's conservative childhood in the stage of natural immediacy, while the educated classes seemed the representatives of enlightenment and European values and therefore the prime movers of progress. In the case of France, this scheme had to be reversed: the educated bourgeoisie appeared to be a set of vulgar and greedy shopkeepers, while the people were clearly a progressive force, representatives of the ideals of *liberté*, *égalité*, and *fraternité*.

In his political views Belinsky (unlike Herzen) remained firmly within the bourgeois democratic tradition and was not essentially influenced by socialist ideas. It was not unusual at that time to find a belief in bourgeois democracy combined with disillusionment in the bourgeoisie itself as a ruling class; in Russia, however, the situation was complicated by the fact that belief in the people was monopolized by the Slavophiles and therefore incompatible with Westernism. As we shall see, this

[1] Ibid. viii. 173.

contradiction was the main factor responsible for Belinsky's hesitations in the dispute over capitalism and the historical significance of the bourgeoisie, which in 1847 brought about the final parting of the ways of the leading Westernizers.

Belinsky was aware that his criticism of the bourgeoisie could be exploited by the Slavophiles; in order to avoid this danger, he had to construct a historiosophical system in which European values would not be identical with bourgeois values. From this point of view it is most instructive to examine his comments on Prince Vladmir Odoevsky's *Russian Nights* (1844). While conceding that Odoevsky's criticism of the social and moral consequences of capitalism was justified, he pointed out the danger of drawing false conclusions:

Must we really agree with Faust [a personage from *Russian Nights*] that Europe is about to pass away at any moment while we Slavs shall fry pancakes for the whole world and hold a funeral feast over the corpse? . . . Europe is sick, true enough, but have no fear, she is not going to die; her sickness is due to an excess of health, an excess of vitality; it is a passing malady, an internal crisis, the subterranean struggle of old and new; it is part of the effort of freeing herself from the medieval social order and replacing it by a system based on reason and human nature.[1]

The class struggle—or 'sickness'—tearing Europe apart was therefore diagnosed by Belinsky as the struggle of the medieval social order with a new system based on 'reason and human nature'. There would seem to be no doubt that what he had in mind was the bourgeoisie's struggle against feudal survivals; Belinsky, however, produced a surprising twist: among these survivals he included bourgeois exploitation, pauperism, and other aspects of capitalism criticized by Odoevsky from a conservative–romantic point of view.

That this was not some chance misconception becomes clear when we compare Belinsky's views with those of Herzen, who made this proposition into one of the basic premisses of his philosophy of history. In the contemporary world, Herzen argued, a struggle was going on between the old feudal and Christian social order and the new future order symbolized by such values as 'individuality', 'reason', and 'activity'. Feudalism had been negated twice: the first negation was the Reformation and the second—more far-reaching negation—was the French Revolution; these negations had not, however, been fully implemented.

Feudalism [Herzen wrote in his *Letters on the Study of Nature*] survived the Reformation; it penetrated all aspects of Europe's new existence; those that arose in opposition to it are deeply imbued by its spirit; it is true that feudalism has changed, and it is even truer that something really vital and powerful is growing up beside it; but while waiting to come of age this new life remains under the tutelage of feudalism, which is still alive, in spite of Luther's Reformation and the reformation of the last years of the past century [i.e. the French Revolution].[1]

In his private *Diary* Herzen even arrived at the paradoxical conclusion that America represented the apex of feudal development: 'Whatever might be said to the contrary, middle-class rule really meant the continuation of the feudal social order; it achieved its culmination in America, which has been arrested in a state of one-sided development. North America is the *ne plus ultra* of feudalism in the form it had to take in the post-Reformation world.'[2]

It is clear that the paradoxical aspect of Belinsky's and Herzen's ideological position was the fact that their conception of personality and the philosophy of action were essentially concerned with rehabilitating Enlightenment, or, in other words, bourgeois democratic values. At the same time these values had undergone a process of sublimation—had become 'super-bourgeois' to use Arnold Hauser's term) and could now be directed against the bourgeoisie as an existing social force.[3] This ideological process was characteristic of an age when there was general disillusionment with the concrete social results of the French Revolution. This was widespread among the socially displaced intellectuals in backward countries who had not yet passed through a bourgeois revolution but could already observe the new social contradictions in the advanced capitalist

[1] Herzen, iii. 243.
[2] Ibid. ii. 287. The opinion that capitalism was only a continuation of feudalism was also propounded by one of Herzen's favourite authors, Pierre Leroux.
[3] See A. Hauser, *The Social History of Art* (Routledge and Kegan Paul, London 1952), iii. 91–2.

countries. A classic example of this attitude was Schiller—a writer who exerted a good deal of influence on the two main representatives of Westernism in Russia.[1]

Although they shared a dislike of bourgeois society, there are certain important differences in Belinsky's and Herzen's attitude to the bourgeois West. Belinsky's disappointment was derived from the unfulfilled promises of the Enlightenment, whereas Herzen's criticism was tinged by certain aristocratic leanings. In the 1840s the ideological evolution and range of interests of the two friends also began to diverge. The more realistic Belinsky became aware that it was premature to discuss specifically Russian problems in terms of European socialist theories,[2] whereas Herzen, from his European vantage-point, regarded the socialists as the only consistent opponents of 'feudalism' and devoted himself to studying the works of Proudhon, Considérant, and Louis Blanc. Certain similarities in the opinions held by the utopian socialists and the Slavophiles (especially their attitude to the people) were an argument against the socialists for Belinsky and an argument in favour of the Slavophiles for Herzen. The latter was more diligent in his study of Schiller's aesthetic writings and was much impressed by the Slavophiles' (and Haxthausen's) analysis of the role of the village commune.[3] Annenkov was probably right when he wrote in his memoirs that the Slavophiles' criticism of bourgeois Europe had left its mark on Herzen's 'mind and heart'.[4] Herzen clearly felt that Belinsky's attitude to the Slavophiles was too hostile. On 17 May 1844 he wrote in his *Diary*:

Belinsky says: 'I am a Jew by nature and cannot sup at one table with the Philistines'; he suffers, and because of his suffering he wants to hate and revile the Philistines who have done nothing to deserve it. For Belinsky the Slavophiles are the Philistines: I do not agree with them myself, but Belinsky refuses to accept the truth in the *fatras* of their nonsense. He cannot understand the Slavonic world;

---

[1] See M. Malia, 'Schiller and the Early Russian Left' in the volume *Russian Thought and Politics*, *Harvard Slavic Studies*, vol. iv (Mouton and Co., The Hague 1957).

[2] See his comments in the 'Review of Russian Literature for the Year 1846'; Belinsky, x. 31–2.

[3] Herzen met and talked with Haxthausen during the latter's stay in Russia (see footnote in Herzen's *Diary* on 13 May 1843).

[4] Annenkov, *The Extraordinary Decade*, p. 99.

he looks at it with despair and is not right; he has no *presentiment of the life of the coming century.* And yet this premonition is the beginning of the future. To despair is to kill the embryo in the mother's womb. . . . A strange situation, a kind of involuntary *juste milieu* on the Slavophile issue: in their eyes [i.e. the Slavophiles'] I am a man of the West and in the eyes of their enemies a man of the East. This means that such one-sided labels have already become obsolete.[1]

This entry in Herzen's diary should perhaps be treated with a pinch of salt: in 1844 Herzen and Belinsky had not yet drifted apart quite so far as these comments suggest. On other issues, for instance on the question of atheism, the moral acceptance of revolutionary methods of struggle, etc., Belinsky was closer to Herzen than to such moderate liberals as Granovsky. Nevertheless, differences grew rather than diminished as time went on and became obvious by 1847 when the two friends visited Western Europe for the first time.

The first to leave—after strenuous efforts—was Herzen. The age when Russian idealists went to pay homage in Berlin was now over and the new Jerusalem was Paris, the capital of 'political and social' Europe. For Herzen, brought up under the influence of French culture from his earliest years, the moment of arrival meant the fulfilment of a dream: 'And so I was really in Paris, not in a dream but in reality: this was the Vendôme column, and the Rue de la Paix. *In Paris*—the word meant scarcely less to me than the word 'Moscow'. Of that minute I had been dreaming since my childhood.,[2]

Disillusionment set in quickly, although it would be difficult to distinguish between fresh disappointment and the confirmation of previous doubts. When he left Russia Herzen had no illusions about the France of Louis Philippe which he regarded as a bourgeois incarnation of feudalism, and, like Proudhon and Louis Blanc, he held the bourgeoisie responsible for this degeneration. Even in his first letter to his Moscow friends (addressed to the actor M. S. Shchepkin) Herzen revealed that his aesthetic sensibilities were shocked by the middle-class vulgarity of the Paris theatre.[3] This aesthetic revulsion, which was not without

---

[1] Herzen, ii. 354.   [2] Herzen, *My Past and Thoughts,* iii. 20.
[3] See Herzen, *Sobr. soch.* xxiii. 19–23.

a certain aristocratic tinge, was accompanied by an equally deep moral revulsion. Herzen could see no common ground between his ideal of the autonomous individual, whose first historical embodiment was the medieval knight ready to die in defence of his honour, and the economic individualism of the bourgeoisie, who subjugated the personality to the cash nexus. In his *Letters from the Avenue Marigny*, published in the *Contemporary* in 1847, Herzen thus defined the social role of the bourgeoisie:

The bourgeoisie has no great past and no future. It was good only for a moment, as a negation, as a transition . . . The aristocracy had its own social religion; it is impossible to replace the dogmas of patriotism, the tradition of courage, the shrine of honour by the rules of political economy. Although it is true that there is a religion which is the opposite of feudalism, the bourgeoisie is placed between these two religions.[1]

By the religion which is the opposite of feudalism, Herzen of course meant socialism, the only worthy adversary of the social religion of the nobility. In Herzen's eyes the bourgeoisie was a class of vulgar upstarts, totally unable to create its own religion and therefore attempting to replace it by a 'morality based on arithmetic and the power of money'. By comparison with the nobility it was utterly without moral backbone:

Heir to aristocratic splendour and plebeian crudeness, the bourgeois combines the most glaring faults of both but has lost their virtues. He is as wealthy as a lord and as miserly as a shopkeeper. He has the mentality of a freedman. The end of the French aristocracy was beautiful and noble; like that of a powerful gladiator, who, seeing that death is inevitable, desires a glorious end; 4 August 1789 is a memorial to this heroism; whatever one might say, there is something sublime in this voluntary renunciation of feudal rights.[2]

Among Herzen's friends in Moscow and St. Petersburg the *Letters from the Avenue Marigny* caused understandable consternation. Granovsky and Kavelin accused Herzen of playing into the hands of the reaction and even Ogarëv, his closest friend, asked him to be more moderate in his judgements. 'It seems to me', he wrote, 'that you have paid too little attention to *der Staat in seiner politiko-eokonomischen Entwicklung*. I am afraid that

[1] See Herzen, *Sobr. soch.* v. 34. [2] Ibid.

your theoretical dissatisfaction has prevented you from seeing *die Gesammtheit* of facts and the development trend as a whole.'[1] The most outright opposition came from Botkin, whose standpoint seemed extreme even to such moderate liberals as Annenkov who did not support Herzen but thought it wrong to go too far in the opposite direction. In reply to Annenkov's objections Botkin wrote: 'You rebuke me for defending the bourgeoisie. How, in God's name, can I not defend it when our friends, copying the socialists, present this bourgeoisie as some sort of villainous, disgusting, and destructive monster devouring all that is beautiful in mankind? I can understand this kind of hyperbole in the mouth of a French worker, but when it comes from our wise friend Herzen it only strikes me as funny.'[2] In another letter to Annenkov Botkin put his case even more forcefully:

It seems to me that Herzen has no clear conception of the significance of the old aristocracy about which he is so enthusiastic, or of the bourgeoisie which he so despises. What else is there left? The worker. And what about the peasant? Does Herzen think that extending the franchise will alter the situation of the bourgeoisie? I don't think so. I am no means an admirer of the bourgeoisie; its crudeness, its prosaic vulgarity offend me as much as anyone else; but for me it is facts that count. I am a sceptic—since I can see as much sense as nonsense on both sides I cannot join either, though my whole sympathy is undoubtedly on the side of the workers, as the downtrodden class. And yet I cannot help adding— God grant us such a bourgeoisie![3]

Although Botkin disavowed any special feeling for the bourgeoisie, as the son of a merchant and himself a merchant after his father's death,[4] he sympathized far more warmly with the French bourgeoisie than with the workers and had his own theories on the role of capitalism. The chief Legal Marxist, Peter Struve, was to describe him later as the first Russian intellectual to be a conscious advocate of capitalist development

---

[1] In a letter to Herzen on 7–19 June 1847; *Literaturnoe nasledstvo* (Moscow 1953), lxi. 208.
[2] Quoted from *P. V. Annenkov i ego druz'ya* (St. Petersburg 1892), p. 542.
[3] Ibid., p. 551.
[4] See Vetrinsky (Cheshikhin), *V sorokovуkh godakh* (Moscow 1899); chapter on Botkin.

in Russia.[1] In the 1840s Botkin worked out his own practical philosophy, substituting the 'iron law of political economy' for the Hegelian *Weltgeist*. 'The important thing is not to attack the existing state of affairs,' he wrote in 1840, 'but to find out what causes it, in a word, to discover the laws governing the world of industry.'[2] Botkin too had his utopia—he idealized the role of education and placed his faith in the Westernized educated gentry. The Moscow merchant class, with their determined adherence to tradition, were more likely, he felt, to give credence to Slavophile ideas;[3] but when the situation changed (i.e. after the abolition of serfdom) the gentry, he hoped, would take up trade and industry, not 'like lords' but 'soberly' and with 'adequate knowledge'.[4] In view of the slender basis for this confidence, it is hardly surprising that towards the end of his life Botkin completely abandoned his former ideals and became almost a symbol of the open and cynical betrayal of the progressive ideals of the 'men of the 1840s'.

The extreme divergence between Herzen's and Botkin's views on the bourgeoisie illustrates the dilemma facing the Russian Westernizers as they gained first-hand knowledge of the social realities of Western Europe. The last of Herzen's *Letters from France and Italy*, written not quite a year after the publication of the *Letters from the Avenue Marigny*, show how far behind he had already left Westernism. In his antithesis between Europe and Russia he contrasted the bourgeoisified West with the Russian people, who were uncontaminated by the middle-class virus, uncorrupted by Roman property rights, faithful guardians of the communal system, and had nothing to lose and everything to gain in a future revolution. Botkin's standpoint, on the other hand, led him to an extremely shallow interpretation of Westernism in which a universal ideal was reduced to the level of the bourgeois 'rules of political economy' so despised by Herzen. How difficult the choice was between these two alternatives is shown by the example of Belinsky.

Belinsky went abroad for medical reasons shortly after Herzen, in May 1847. In a letter he sent to Botkin from Salzbrunn

---

[1] As Struve himself confessed, he was not aware of his debt to Botkin when he formulated the slogan 'Let us admit our lack of civilization and learn from capitalism.' Struve, *Na razniye temy* (St. Petersburg 1902), pp. 113–14.

[2] *P. V. Annenkov i ego druz'ya*, p. 525.

[3] See ibid., pp. 539–40.   [4] Ibid., p. 523.

in Lower Silesia he confessed that he now understood for the first time 'the terrible meaning of the words "pauperization" and "proletariat".[1] At the same time he was critical of the French utopian socialists and especially of Louis Blanc, whose *History of the French Revolution* he was then reading. In July 1847 he wrote to Botkin: 'For Blanc the bourgeoisie has been the enemy of mankind and has conspired against its happiness since before the creation; and yet his own work proves that without the *bourgeoisie* we would not have had the revolution he is so enthusiastic about and that all the successes of that class were the fruit of its own labour. What a fool—one loses one's patience with him!'[2]

Although he accused Blanc of an unhistorical assessment of the role of the bourgeoisie in the past, this did not mean that Belinsky himself was ready to evaluate its present and future role positively. In fact there is little doubt that in mid-1847 he was still convinced that the future of France was in the hands of the French people who would learn from history, come to maturity, throw off the bourgeois yoke, and become masters of their own fate. The celebrated *Letter to Gogol*, also written in Salzbrunn, suggests that at this time Belinsky was even inclined to transfer some of this optimistic belief to the Russian people. In his stinging reply to Gogol's *Selected Passages from a Correspondence with Friends*, Belinsky described the Russian people as 'by nature profoundly atheistic', endowed with 'common sense, a sense of reality, and a sound mind,' traits which perhaps foreshadow 'the vastness of its historical destinies in the future'.[3] Apart from the polemic against Maïkov, this was Belinsky's furthest departure from the generally accepted Westernizing view of the people as a conservative and inert force.

Belinsky arrived in Paris in July 1847, when the discussion on the role of the bourgeoisie was at its height. Herzen's ally in the controversy was Bakunin, who launched the slogan 'God save Russia from the bourgeoisie'; on the other side were Sazonov and Annenkov. At first Belinsky supported Herzen but on his return to Russia he tried to take a middle-of-the-road position; later still, in a letter written in February 1848, he was to agree with Annenkov. It is of some interest to analyse his hesitations and to see what exactly made him change his mind.

---

[1] Belinsky, xii. 383.   [2] Ibid., p. 385.   [3] Ibid. x. 215.

s c—p

Unfortunately we have no detailed account of Belinsky's standpoint in the Paris discussions, but from his later correspondence it seems clear that his reaction to the France of Louis Philippe, with its scandals and trials for corruption, was in many respects similar to Herzen's. He regarded the bourgeoisie as the embodiment of particularism, incapable of representing society as a whole. 'Woe to the country that finds itself in the hands of the capitalists', he wrote to Botkin in December 1847: 'they are men without patriotism and devoid of all noble sentiments. To them war or peace only means lesser or greater profits; apart from that they see nothing. The shopkeeper is by nature a trivial, low, and miserable being who deserves our contempt.'[1] He might be admirable as a shopkeeper, but was otherwise unlikeable. Indeed Belinsky confessed to preferring 'spendthrifts, *viveurs*, revellers, and libertines' who stood for the reverse of bourgeois calculation.[2] He was even inclined to share Herzen's pro-aristocratic sentiments! 'In England the middle class is counterbalanced by the aristocracy and that is why the government in England is dignified, attractive, and majestic, whereas the government in France is liberal, base, trivial, miserable, and shameful. . . .'[3]

At the end of 1847, after his return to Russia, Belinsky had time to reconsider his one-sided condemnation. The bourgeoisie, he wrote in the letter to Botkin quoted above, 'had its past, its historical moment of greatness, and rendered tremendous services to mankind'. 'States without a middle class are condemned to eternal nothingness.' 'I know that industry is the source of all evil, but I also know that it is the source of society's prosperity.' He thought that perhaps the ambiguity of the term was to blame for all the difficulties. 'Who is not a *bourgeois*? Probably only the *ouvrier* toiling by the sweat of his brow in someone else's field. All today's enemies of the bourgeoisie and defenders of the people are as much members of this class as were Robespierre and Saint-Just. Because of the want of precision and ambiguity of the term *bourgeoisie* Herzen's *Letters sont attaquables*.' 'It is not the bourgeoisie as a whole we should attack,' he concluded, 'but the big capitalists who must be fought as the plague or cholera of contemporary France.'[4]

[1] Belinsky, xii. 449.   [2] Ibid., p. 450.   [3] Ibid.,p. 451.
[4] Ibid., pp. 448–9, 453. Belinsky made similar though milder strictures in his

Although Belinsky hoped that this formula would make it possible to reconcile Herzen's standpoint with that of Botkin and Annenkov, no such simple compromise was of course possible. A more precise use of language would not have made the controversy less tempestuous, and Herzen, who regarded the 'petty capitalist' as 'the worst bourgeois of all,'[1] was hardly likely to be satisfied by the distinction between 'big capitalists' and 'the bourgeoisie as a whole'. The compromise Belinsky wished to effect was based on the illusion that the dispute was about the role of the middle class, whereas in fact it was about capitalism as an over-all social system and about the desirability of this system. There can be no doubt that by the end of 1847 Belinsky and Herzen held quite divergent views on this fundamental issue.

Belinsky's last word on the argument is to be found in the letter he sent to Annenkov in February 1848, a few days before his death from tuberculosis. Although he was already too sick to hold a pen and had to dictate the letter, it lacks none of his characteristic passionate involvement. The most interesting passage from this remarkable document deserves to be quoted in its entirety.

I am now reading Voltaire's stories and they constantly make me want to spit in the face of this idiot, this ass, this beast of a fellow, Louis Blanc. The only work of Rousseau's I have read is his *Confessions*, but judging by them and also by the religious veneration with which he is surrounded by these donkeys, I have taken a thorough dislike to him. He reminds me of Dostoevsky with his firm belief that he is envied and persecuted by the whole of mankind. Rousseau's life was repulsive, amoral. But what a noble character Voltaire had! What warm fellow feeling he showed for everything that was human and rational, how deeply he sympathized with the unhappiness of simple people! How much he did for humanity! It is true he sometimes calls the common people a *vil populace*, but that is because it is obscurantist, superstitious, fanatical, bloodthirsty, and likes tortures and executions. By the way, our croyant friend [i.e. Bakunin] and our Slavophiles did much to help me get rid of my mystical belief in the people. Where and when has

---

review of the *Letters from the Avenue Marigny* in the 'Review of Russian Literature for the Year 1847'. Belinsky, x. 353–4.

[1] These words were written in the autumn of 1848, although they express a point of view that was formed earlier. Herzen, vi. 60.

the people ever liberated itself? Everything has always been accomplished by individuals. I was an ass twice over when I called you a conservative in our arguments about the bourgeoisie. And you were a wise man. The entire future of France lies in the hands of the bourgeoisie, all progress depends on it alone, the people can only play a passive auxiliary role in historical events. When I said in Paris that Russia needs a new Peter the Great, our believing friend attacked this idea as a heresy and maintained that the people should manage its own affairs. What a naïve, arcadian idea! . . . Our believing friend also tried to convince me that God should preserve Russia from the bourgeoisie. And yet it has become obvious by now that the process of internal civic development in Russia will not start until our gentry has become transformed into a bourgeoisie. Poland is the best example of what happens to a state without a bourgeoisie in full enjoyment of all its rights. . . . Our believing friend and the Slavophiles have done me a great service. You must not be surprised by this juxtaposition: the best of the Slavophiles regard the people in the same light as our believing friend; they have absorbed these ideas from the socialists and in their articles quote George Sand and Louis Blanc.[1]

These words were written on 15 February (26 February by the New-Style calendar) when the February revolution had already broken out in Paris. It is difficult to say whether Belinsky knew of this. Bearing in mind his illness and the time it took for news from France to reach Russia, he was probably unaware of the outbreak of the revolution—at any rate he does not mention it in his letter. We know from other sources that the Westernizers welcomed the revolution as confirmation of their belief that the bourgeoisie was still capable of fighting for progress. Belinsky, who, in Herzen's phrase, died taking the glow of revolution for 'the rising dawn'[2] probably thought the same. No doubt he would have changed his mind if he had lived long enough to see the closing stages of the June days. This seems more than likely in view of the fact that his acceptance of the bourgeoisie had many features in common with his previous self-imposed reconciliation with reality. Belinsky 'accepted' the bourgeoisie as a historical necessity—not because he was really in sympathy with it, but because he could see no other force capable of struggling for universal 'super-bourgeois' values. In

---

[1] Belinsky, xii. 467–8.
[2] Herzen, *My Past and Thoughts*, ii. 140.

spite of the lip-service he paid to the workers, Botkin's support for the bourgeoisie was far more natural than the effort at self-persuasion made by 'Vissarion the Furious'.

There is no point, however, in speculating on the might-have-beens of history. In the present context it is important only to emphasize that Belinsky's attitude was determined by his Westernism, which in turn was shaped by its relationship to Slavophilism, its main negative frame of reference. It is significant that after supporting Herzen and Bakunin in the Paris discussions, Belinsky changed his mind when he returned home and was once more confronted by Russian problems, and by the day-to-day struggle against Slavophilism and the doctrine of Official Nationality. The ideas of the French Enlightenment became associated in his mind with the Petrine reforms, while the issue of people versus bourgeoisie became associated with that of people versus individuals or people versus 'society' (as the carrier of the 'principle of personality'). At the same time he identified the French socialists' attitude to the bourgeoisie and common people with the Slavophiles' idealization of the Russian people and their criticism of Western capitalism. It is important to stress that this association of ideas was by no means fortuitous but flowed from the very nature of Westernism as an anti-Slavophile ideological structure.

TWO UTOPIAS

It is time now to systematize the main argument of this chapter in order to bring out the essential nature of the conflict between Slavophilism and Westernism. A confrontation of this kind will not only show Slavophilism in relation to Westernism, but will also contribute to a more concrete interpretation of the latter by concentrating on the aspects which determined the Westernizers' negative attitude towards Slavophilism or—after 1842— were determined by this attitude. It is not my intention to recapitulate the main points arising in the polemics and discussions of the 1840s, since these were usually blurred by the intrusion of day-to-day problems that seemed important at the time, but add nothing to our understanding of the way in which the two ideologies stood in a meaningful relationship to each other. In any case, public polemics were relatively few as the Slavophiles had no regular journal of their own at the time and did not publish their most important work until the 1850s. The chief aim of this confrontation, therefore, is rather to bring out the basic pattern of the Slavophile/Westernizer controversy or, in other words, to construct an 'ideal model' which will highlight the most essential features of the two ideologies and make possible an objective assessment of their mutual interdependence.

Using this approach, the controversy dividing the two camps can be summed up under the following nine headings:

1. *The conception of personality.* In reply to the 'Western' ideal of the 'autonomous individual', the Slavophiles put forward their concept of the 'integral personality'. They regarded the principle of autonomy as the source of all evil and by autonomy meant not only the autonomy of the individual in relation to society, but also the autonomization of the separate spiritual faculties and the separate spheres of human activity. The autonomy of the individual, they argued, leads to the disintegration of society and condemns human beings to isolation and loneliness; the autonomy of the separate spiritual faculties (especially of reason) destroys faith and consequently disrupts the integral personality and brings about its fragmentation. Personal wholeness can only be achieved if the individual is in complete harmony with the community and ready to resign his autonomy in favour of the supra-individual faith uniting it. To the Westernizers, for whom *samobýtnaya, samozakonnaya lichnost'* was the ultimate goal of the historical process and the pivot on which their philosophical discussions revolved, this conception was something utterly alien. They too perceived the danger of disintegration (especially Herzen) but tried to resolve the problem without sacrificing their faith in the autonomy of the individual.

2. *Freedom.* By freedom the Westernizers meant freedom of the individual; to them this was something obvious and self-evident. The individual is free when he can emancipate himself from traditional routine, from 'ready-made solutions' and 'fixed patterns of behaviour'; when he can extend the range of his possible choices and the part played by conscious decision-making. To the Slavophiles, on the contrary, freedom was a function of communal life; the individual is free when he succeeds in *internalizing* and assimilating completely traditional

values and patterns of behaviour. Freedom conceived thus does not depend on autonomous acts (the Westernizing 'philosophy of action') but on the individual's spontaneous identification with the community (*sobornost'*). The maximization of choices, of situations in which the individual is forced to rely on his own judgement, was rejected by the Slavophiles as a negative value.

3. *Reflection.* The Westernizers thought of the rationalization and individuation of the consciousness achieved through the 'agony of reflection' as a necessary prerequisite of freedom. The Slavophile response to this was the idealization of non-reflective faith, the conviction that reflection is only a by-product of the 'false turning' chosen by Western civilizations. The feeling that an excess of reflection kills spontaneity and leads to the paralysis of the will was also shared by the Westernizers, but the conclusions they drew from this were quite different. The Slavophiles combated all forms of rationalism (i.e. any autonomous philosophy) whereas the Westernizers called for the 'transcendence' of reflection through exteriorization, through bridging the gap between philosophy and practical activity. To the Slavophiles spontaneity suffered as a result of the individual's separation from the church, which they conceived as a perfect social organism illuminated by grace; the Westernizers (or at least some of them) ascribed the pernicious results of reflection to separation from nature and turned their attention to Feuerbach's materialist philosophy with its rehabilitation of the 'natural immediacy' of human existence.

4. *Universalism.* To the Westernizers the rationalization of consciousness meant the universalization of the thought process and the overcoming of all particularism; they hoped that individuals and nations would become emancipated from 'natural determinations' and be imbued by the 'universally human element', by the universality of reason. The Slavophiles, on their part, either openly attacked universalism ('abstract humanity' as Khomyakov referred to it) or—which amounted to the same thing—opposed it with a Christian universalism which conveniently allowed them to identify authentic universal values with the Orthodox Church and humanity with the Russian people.

5. *Consciousness and action.* The Westernizers' 'philosophy of action' posited the transformation of reality in accordance with

the postulates of reason and conscious volition; the Slavophiles set out to demonstrate that it was disastrous to try and substitute the individual rational intellect for the irrational elemental force of history. According to the philosophy of action the individual expresses himself in conscious acts, whereas the Slavophiles held that the ideal personality can only be realized through the inner concentration of the spirit and the thorough assimilation of the 'truly Christian social principles' handed down by tradition.

6. *Historicism.* Two different ideal personalities were paralleled by two different conceptions of historicism. For the Westernizers the historical process meant the evolution of consciousness and the rationalization of social relations, whereas the Slavophiles regarded the essence of history as a divine mystery and shared the conservative romantics' dislike of all forms of historical rationalism. The Westernizers tried to overcome the 'abstract' and 'unhistorical' rationalism of the Enlightenment without rejecting rationalism as such, but by giving it a new 'historical' basis; the Slavophiles went much further in their rejection of the ideas of the Enlightenment and French Revolution, which they treated as a violation of true history. Under the influence of Left-Hegelianism the Westernizers admitted the possibility of sudden leaps in history (negation), while the Slavophiles enshrined uninterrupted historical continuity as an absolute good and condemned any sudden break with the past as a betrayal of 'historicity', conceived as an inner norm, a vital principle of growth of the given social organism.[1] The Slavophile/Westernizer controversy was, from this point of view, a dispute between conservative-romantic historicism and Hegelian historicism. It should be stressed, however, that historicism as such was not *necessarily* a component of either Westernism or Slavophilism. Both could be combined with different types of unhistorical thought or, to put it more precisely, the difficulties inherent in both types of historicism were at times 'transcended' by the abandonment of historicism in the last resort. Each type of historicism, however, had its corresponding unhistoricism: the Westernizers were partly attracted to the unhistorical ideals of the Enlightenment with

[1] On the two types of historicism see K. Mannheim, *Essays on the Sociology of Knowledge* (London 1959), p. 106.

their appeal to 'reason and human nature' (Belinsky was prone to this), but also to positivist unhistoricism (Maïkov). Among the Slavophiles unhistoricism took the form of the sentimental and moralistic utopia of Konstantin Aksakov, which absolutized the traditional values of the patriarchal past in order to set them up in opposition to the real historical process.

7. *State and Law.* To the Westernizers the progressive rationalization of social relations meant the replacement of immediate, emotional, and traditional bonds by juridical and political norms (Kavelin); according to this conception the centralized absolutist state had its definite place in historical development as a system that paved the way for the rule of law and therefore also for the emancipation of the individual. The Slavophiles agreed with this argument but drew entirely different conclusions from it; namely that juridical and political rationalization was the obserse side of the internal atomization of society. The social solidarity they idealized was the kind which binds the individual to the community without the interference of institutional forms—a solidarity based on a common faith, traditions, and customs. They held up the Russian village commune as an example of this kind of solidarity.

8. *Nationality.* The two sides also dffered in their attitudes to the 'folk' and 'folk' culture. Both Slavophiles and Westernizers regarded the common people as the mainstay of traditional— and irrational—values, and the educated classes as the main representatives of such 'universal' values as 'personality' and 'consciousness' (in the Westernizers' sense of the words). The conclusions they drew from this were of course entirely different: the Slavophiles called for a 'return to the people', while the Westernizers thought that the 'people' should be transformed into a 'nation', i.e. into a people 'raised to the level of consciousness' and 'individualized through thought'. This led to a number of other essential differences in the way the two sides understood Russian history and the Petrine reforms, in their interpretation of such concepts as 'nation' or 'nationality' in literature, and in their attitude towards 'folk' culture, etc.

9. *Capitalism.* The entire controversy between the Slavophiles and Westernizers was summed up, as it were, in their attitude to capitalism. It should be stressed that not all participants in the dispute were quite clear as to where the line of demarcation

ran. On the whole the Slavophiles showed more insight in this respect than their opponents. Their consistent attacks on capitalism from a conservative–romantic standpoint were based on the idealization of personal and social values rooted in a pre-capitalist epoch. For the Westernizers the main enemy was in fact the pre-capitalist system, i.e. feudalism in the broad Marxist sense of the word. They criticized both Russian feudalism and European capitalism from a 'super-bourgeois' position, i.e. from the point of view of sublimated liberal-democratic values which were, in fact, a by-product of early capitalism and the bourgeoisie's struggle against feudalism. The inner logic of the Slavophile analysis led to the outright rejection of the capitalist system, whereas Westernism as a thought structure implied the acceptance of bourgeois development. Anyone who was not prepared to accept this conclusion inevitably had to break with Westernism, as Herzen was to do.

An analysis of the essential content of Slavophilism and Westernism leads to the conclusion that the two systems were not so much political ideologies with concrete, limited, and attainable ends, as two types of *Weltanschauung*, two utopias, equally 'transcendent' in relation to existing social realities. They were doomed to remain at this pre-political stage because the Russia of Nicholas I allowed no outlet for political action. This utopian sublimation of values allowed the Slavophiles to criticize not just capitalism but also Western feudalism and the Russian serf system; the Westernizers, on the other hand, were able to attack capitalism as a system incompatible with the postulates of reason and the 'autonomous personality'. This utopian quality perhaps accounts for certain obscurities in the two thought structures, but it also resulted in a high degree of inner consistency. A concrete political situation is always less homogeneous than its utopian image and political practice demands compromises which are easily avoided in theory. That is why Westernism as a philosophical movement disintegrated as soon as its members were faced by the concrete reality of Western Europe, while the Slavophile utopia—born at a time when all political action was out of the question—did not survive the reforms of Alexander II.

Although both the Slavophilism and Westernism of the 1840s can be called 'utopias' they were not equally coherent and internally consistent systems of thought. The Westernism of the 1840s was not a homogeneous movement but rather a meeting-ground of potentially divergent trends, a common platform for all thinkers—both democrats, like Belinsky, and moderate liberals, like Kavelin—who believed that Russia could and should follow the general pattern of European development. It emerged as a definite movement in 1842, when Slavophilism became a serious 'negative frame of reference' for the Russian Left-Hegelians, and declined in 1848 after Belinsky's death and Herzen's conversion to 'Russian socialism'. Classical Slavophilism, on the other hand, existed as a coherent doctrine for at least twenty years (from about 1839 to 1861) and even during its decline preserved its characteristic thought style. Kireevsky, Khomyakov and Konstantin Aksakov all represented different versions of a *single Weltanschauung*, while for Belinsky, Herzen, and Granovsky Westernism was only *one aspect* of their total body of opinions—an aspect conditioned to a great extent by their common opposition to Slavophilism and the doctrine of Official Nationality.

The various themes selected for emphasis in this compara-tive analysis show to what extent one can speak of the 'negative parallelism' of the two ideological trends. It should be stressed that this selection by no means exhausts all aspects of Slavophilism and Westernism.

It should also be noted that although Westernism in its fully-fledged form was preceded by Slavophilism, its main pre-misses—and especially its concern for individual autonomy—were formulated independently, that is, not in response to the Slavophile challenge. In the formative stage of Westernism its main premisses were shaped as part of the negation of the 'formalistic' or romantic interpretation of Hegelianism. Never-theless, both the selection of certain aspects of Hegelianism and the rejection of others show clearly that Westernism was poten-tially anti-Slavophile from the very beginning; that it was pre-destined, as it were, to encounter Slavophilism and to engage in an ideological struggle with it over problems of mutual con-cern. This was partly because the representatives ov both trends shared a common 'space-time location' (to use Karl Mann-heim's term)[1] and also because they represented diametrically

[1] See Mannheim, 'The Problem of Generations' in *Essays on the Sociology of*

opposed viewpoints on issues concerning one generation in one country and one cultural milieu. This generation (the last before the Emancipation Act) brought up in the atmosphere of idealistic speculative philosophy, went through the bitter experience of being 'superfluous men', and, finally, has come to be known in the history of Russian literature and social thought as the 'men of the 1840s'. Looking back on this period from the perspective of later years Herzen thus described its 'dynamic-antinomic unity':[1] 'Yes, we were their opponents, but very strange ones. We had the same love, but not the same way of loving. . . . Like Janus, or the two-headed eagle, they and we looked in different directions while one heart throbbed within us.'[2]

It is of some interest to consider how far the Slavophile/Wester-nizer controversy had its analogies in Western European philosophy and social thought. In certain respects the stand-point of the Westernizers can be compared to the position of Western liberals and democrats in their polemics with the conservatives and in particular (as I have tried to show) to the standpoint of Hegel and the Left-wing Hegelians in their controversy with the conservative romanticists. It should be stressed, however, that the ideological situation in Russia in the 1840s had no counterpart in Western Europe, so that to concentrate on analogies while overlooking the specific character of Russian Westernism is to create a false impression. Strange as it may seem, the leading Westernizers were by no means ideally fitted for the task of opposing Slavophilism; this role would have been far better filled by representatives of various Western European intellectual trends: by bourgeois

---

Knowledge. From a Mannheimian point of view the Slavophiles and Westernizers represent two 'concrete groups' who express the world-view of two 'generation units' within one 'true generation'.

[1] Expression used by Mannheim.

[2] Herzen, *My Past and Thoughts*, ii. 302. The consciousness of being part of a specific generation was very strong in Herzen. From this point of view it is interesting to examine his adverse reaction to criticism of the 'superfluous men' (i.e. the generation of the 1840s as a whole) by the *raznotchintsȳ* of the 1860s, in particular Dobrolyubov (see 'Very Dangerous' and 'Lishnie lyudi i zhelcheviki', in vol. xlv of Herzen's collected works). It is equally significant that one of the 'superfluous men' he defended was Ivan Kireevsky. Herzen, xiv. 325.

democratic defenders of Enlightenment ideas, by the liberal economists, or by utilitarians like Jeremy Bentham. The Westernizing utopia reflected the weakness of the Russian bourgeoisie, the fact that in Russia the main exponent of progressive bourgeois thought was the intelligentsia of noble and (more rarely) non-noble origin, for whom capitalism was still something abstract. This is shown by the almost complete lack of interest in political economy, which was taken up only by minor figures such as Botkin and Maïkov. Belinsky and Herzen on the other hand showed no interest in such typical aspects of classical liberalism as the defence of free competition or bourgeois property rights. The sociological and economic implications of the emergence and decline of various forms of ownership, which were analysed in detail by Hegel and whose importance was clearly recognized by the Slavophiles, was only of marginal importance to Belinsky and Herzen and played no essential role in their thought structure. The analogy with Hegel on the issue of rationalism should not be exaggerated either; in the Westernizers' hierarchy of values individuality ranked above 'rationality' and not below it (the emphasis on the problem of rationalism in the present work is due to its important place in Slavophile doctrine). It is clear that the shared experience which affected the Westernizers most profoundly and helped to shape their *Weltanschauung*, was the painful as well as joyous process of the formation of the personality, its emancipation from 'natural determinations' by philosophy and literature, and its alienation from the immediate 'natural' environment.

The fact that Russian Westernism was an ideology of the intelligentsia, its far-reaching sublimation of liberal values, and —last but not least—the impossibility of any kind of political action, meant that the growing divergence between classical liberalism and bourgeois democracy in Western Europe was not visible in Russia and was reflected at most in abstract discussions on Jacobins and Girondists, the existence of God, etc. The role of Westernism as a platform uniting both potential liberals and potential radical democrats is therefore best illustrated by the term 'liberal-democratic utopia'.

In contradistinction to the Westernizing utopia, the utopia of the Slavophiles used as its raw material the concrete social existence and firmly rooted background of the hereditary Russian nobility. In their case, too, a sociological determined system of values became subject to sublimation—all the more easily since it was possible to reject all responsibility for government actions and to regard bureaucratic autocracy as the sole source of all obvious social evils. This is where we come up against the problem of 'Europeanization' which was of such paramount importance for the Slavophiles. It was discussed with great insight by Samarin in the passage on Slavophilism and European conservatism quoted in a previous chapter: 'In Europe both Toryism and Whiggism grew from the same *national* roots, developed in the same *national* environment. In Russia Whiggism was grafted on from outside. . . . Hence the struggle between Whiggism and Toryism in matters of faith, philosophy, and state administration is far more complicated here than in the West, for in Russia it also includes the struggle of *folkways* with a non-national abstract *civilization*.'[1]

It would be over-pedantic to try and correct Samarin's assertion that 'Russian Whiggism' was entirely foreign in origin; the important factor is that Europeanization existed both as a social reality and (even more) as a factor in the consciousness of both Slavophiles and Westernizers. It is true that the conservatives' appeal to the common people was not a specifically Russian phenomenon and that the enlightened classes in other countries could also be accused of cosmopolitanism ('Gallicization' in Germany corresponds to a certain limited extent to 'Europeanization' in Russia). Nevertheless it would appear that this 'folk' aspect of conservatism was stronger in Russia than elsewhere, something that was naturally reflected in the views on 'folk' and 'folk' culture held by the Westernizers.

To sum up, the classical Slavophilism of the 1840s was a strongly utopian variety of conservatism and its utopianism strongly emphasized the role of the peasantry. In fact, it was not so much an ideological defence of an existing tradition, as a utopian attempt to rehabilitate and revive a lost tradition. This utopian character—the outcome of social and political conditions in the Russia of Nicholas I—was responsible for the strength as well as the weakness of Slavophilism, its

[1] Samarin, *Sochineniya* (Moscow 1877), i. 402. This is a continuation of the sentence quoted on p. 229.

'noble-mindedness', which was recognized even by its opponents, its capacity for arousing the intellect and imagination, and at the same time its almost complete unsuitability as a programme for practical action.

PART FOUR

THE DISINTEGRATION
OF SLAVOPHILISM: DIFFERENT
CONTINUATIONS

10

Slavophilism in the 1860s

RUSSIA'S disastrous defeat in the Crimean War and the Emperor's death in circumstances that gave rise to suspicions of suicide, were regarded by both Westernizers and Slavophiles as a prelude to profound political and social changes. The new government realized that certain reforms, above all a solution to the peasant problem, were inevitable and indeed long overdue. Alexander II embarked on a course of partial concessions and a carefully sounded public opinion in order to find ways of introducing the most urgent reforms with the least detriment to the existing system. The period of great hopes and (to some extent) spontaneous civic activity that followed his accession to the throne became known as the 'thaw'.

The work of the universities [a Soviet historian has written about the beginning of this period] was somewhat less restricted, police supervision and censorship pressure weighed somewhat less heavily on writers and journalists, some of the most hated officials of the previous reign were removed (although the vast majority retained their posts), and a political amnesty was introduced, although this too was very limited in scope. Even men as loyal to the government as the Slavophiles were doubtful and asked anxiously: 'What will follow the *thaw*? Very good if it is to be spring and a fine summer, but if the thaw is only temporary, if afterwards everything is to be frostbound once more, life will be even more difficult to bear.'[1]

Nevertheless the end of the reign of Nicholas I also marked the beginning of the end for the Slavophile utopia. The new conditions created by the 'thaw' may not have brought about any basic changes in the country's authoritarian structure but they were responsible for profound changes in the general intellectual climate and could be said to have revolutionized social awareness. The most moderate and also most widespread

---

[1] *Istoriya russkoĭ literaturȳ* (Soviet Academy of Sciences, Moscow–Leningrad 1956), vol. viii, part 1, p. 14 (chapter written by S. M. Levin). The quotation after the colon is taken from V. S. Aksakova, *Dnevnik* (St. Petersburg 1913), p. 102.

aspect of these changes was the growing conviction that the public was competent to comment on political affairs and that public opinion should have a say in the reforms. The centre of gravity of discussions and public concern shifted to political and social issues of topical interest: philosophical enthusiasm yielded to an enthusiastic belief in science. The introspective outlook of the 'superfluous men', typical of both the utopias of the 1840s, and their far-reaching 'interiorization' of values could not survive in face of the general momentum towards 'realism', towards the implementation of ideals through practical activity in a concrete social setting. 'The age of the Onegins and Pechorins has gone', Herzen wrote in 1859. 'There are no *'superfluous men'* in Russia at the moment; on the contrary, this enormous land lacks hands for the plough. He who cannot now find a sphere of activity for himself cannot put the blame on others; he is truly a hollow man, empty-headed or indolent.'[1] *Mutatis mutandis*, the Slavophiles could have found these words an equally appropriate comment on their own utopianism. There was growing awareness that the time for all-embracing historiosophical structures was over, that in the new circumstances every ideology ought to manifest itself in a concrete, efficient, and practical programme of action. Under this insistence on action the Slavophile utopia too yielded to pragmatic considerations. Men with a gift for practical leadership such as Ivan Aksakov, Yuriï Samarin, A. I. Koshelëv, and Prince V. A. Cherkassky, now came to the fore. Among the older Slavophiles the 'realistic' Khomyakov adapted himself best to the new situation while the more consistent Slavophile 'romantics'—Ivan Kireevsky and Konstantin Aksakov—clung to their uncompromising utopianism. Kireevsky, who died on the threshold of the new epoch, never gave up his utopian belief that a return to lost traditions was a prerequisite of progress; Aksakov on the other hand fully accepted the abolition of serfdom and enfranchisement of the peasants, but remained fanatically faithful to his 'people's' utopia and judged all changes from his extreme point of view. This was clearly bound to lead to his increasing lack of orientation in the world of concrete political forces and his growing isolation in his own camp. In official circles his periodical *Hearsay* (*Molva*), founded

---

[1] Herzen, xiv. 119 ('Very Dangerous').

in 1857 and closed down for its 'political unreliability' after only a few months, gained Aksakov the reputation of a 'dangerous' man and among progressives that of a publicist who was not to be treated seriously.[1] The Slavophiles who were actively engaged in the emancipation reforms regarded him as a liability, an irresponsible man who (in Koshelëv's words) 'loses his temper and come out with all sorts of nonsensical statements'.[2]

The sad fate of the Slavophile utopia can be seen if we compare Konstantin Aksakov with Prince Vladimir Cherkassky, who aptly summed up his own attitude to Slavophile doctrine as a 'marriage of convenience'. 'Cherkassky', Koshelëv wrote in his memoirs, 'in no way considered Orthodox Christian teaching to be the foundation of our world-view, constantly attacked the village commune, and liked to make fun of the people—the idol worshipped, he said, by Khomyakov and K. Aksakov.[3]' Nevertheless Cherkassky was known as a Slavophile and indeed referred to himself as a member of the Slavophile movement: his position was determined not by his belief in Orthodoxy or the 'people's principle', but by a specific agrarian programme and model of political reforms that appealed to certain sections of the nobility. That such criteria could be decisive is eloquent evidence of the fact that the ideas defended by the Slavophiles in the great ideological debate of the 1840s had now receded into the background.

The main organ of the Slavophiles at this time was the quarterly *Russian Conversation* (*Russkaya Beseda*), published by Koshelëv from 1856 to 1860 (as a bimonthly from 1859). The Slavophiles did not find it easy to realize their old dream of having a regular journal of their own; first they had to secure the annulment of the special censorship restrictions imposed on the leading Slavophiles in connection with the *Moscow Miscellany* affair in 1852. The curator of the Moscow school district, Nazimov, had to try and persuade the minister of education, Norov, that the reputation of the Slavophiles as 'dangerous and harmful men, rather like Jacobins' was undeserved and that in reality they were 'utterly peaceful, devout family men, landowners who had not the slightest intention of disturbing the

---

[1] See Chernyshevsky, *Poln. sobr. soch.* (Moscow 1948), iv. 779.
[2] See Dement'ev, *Ocherki po istorii russkoĭ zhurnalistiki 1840–1850 gg*, p. 400.
[3] A. I. Koshelëv, *Zapiski (1812–1883)*, p. 84.

peace'.[1] After six months his petitions were crowned with success and in 1858 Koshelëv even gained permission to publish a special monthly supplement to the *Russkaya Beseda*, to be devoted entirely to the emancipation reforms and agricultural affairs. This supplement appeared for one year and was entitled *Good Husbandry (Selskoe Blagoustroĭstvo)*.

The Slavophiles' efforts to publish their own journal were greeted by Granovsky in characteristic fasion. In the previously quoted letter written to Kavelin on 2 October 1855, just before his death, he commented as follows:

I am overjoyed that they [the Slavophiles] have decided to publish a journal . . . I am glad, because their views ought to be demonstrated in full, ought to be seen in all their splendour. Then they will be forced in spite of themselves to remove the liberal embellishments by which they managed to delude little children. They will have to demonstrate the system's last word and this word is Orthodox patriarchy, not to be reconciled with any kind of progress.[2]

Nevertheless, Granovsky turned out to be mistaken. His reaction was typical of the Westernizers of the 1840s, for whom the outstanding aspect of Slavophilism was its undeniably conservative utopianism. The publication of their own journal during the 'thaw' did in fact induce the Slavophiles to sacrifice many 'embellishments' in favour of a practical interpretation of class interests. However, in keeping with the spirit of the time it was *conservative* embellishments that were rejected. In spite of Granovsky's predictions, the 'system's last word' (i.e. the Slavophiles' practical programme), turned out to be a specific variant of gentry liberalism rather than a defence of the *status quo*.

The transition from theory to 'practice' was a gradual process. In the first numbers of *Russian Conversation* the dominant themes were such typical issues of the 1840s as the crisis of European civilization or the need for a 'national' school of science. The controversies with the Westernizers were continued in an equally long-drawn-out polemic with the 'étatists', S. Solov'ëv and B. Chicherin, and in particular with the latter's

---

[1] Quoted from Dement'ev, op. cit., p. 359.
[2] Quoted from Vetrinsky (Cheshikhin), *T. N. Granovsky i ego vremya*, p. 364.

views on the origins of the village commune expounded in the *Russian Messenger* ((Russiĭ Vestnik),[1] the journal of the Moscow Westernizers. The Russian village commune, Chicherin argued, had nothing to do with the primitive kinship community. It arose in the sixteenth century and was not a product of the 'people' but of the centralized state, which was concerned to simplify the collection of taxes and to safeguard its fiscal requirements through the institution of 'collective liability' (*krugovaya poruka*). This thesis, which the Slavophiles found impossible to accept, initiated a long-drawn-out polemic between *Russian Conversation* and the *Russian Messenger*: according to Chernyshevsky's apt description, Chicherin persecuted the Slavophiles like a nightmare that could not be shaken off.[2] The controversy had its topical side, since the basic argument was about whether the village commune was to continue to function or to be abolished together with the institutions of serfdom and corvée; this aspect was lost, however, in long articles overloaded with historical facts which the average reader found hard to digest. The Slavophiles themselves soon became aware of this: as early as the end of 1856 Ivan Aksakov, the youngest of them, pointed out that their periodical 'did very little to meet contemporary needs' and that this was due to its extreme abstract character. Only Cherkassky's contributions on the peasant problem and the articles on railway developments aroused public interest. 'Slavophilism cannot become popular among our younger generation', Ivan Aksakov wrote in a letter on 9 October 1856. 'The demands for emancipation and for railways etc., etc., which now resound throughout Russia and merge into a nation-wide clamour, were originally formulated by the Westernizers and not by our side.'[3]

Russian Conversation was never widely read by the younger generation, even during the period when to all intents and purposes it was edited by Ivan Aksakov.[4] It must be admitted, however, that (in keeping with the views of the majority of contributors and the practical editor) efforts were made 'to do

---

[1] This polemic is discussed in Zavitnevich, *A. S. Khomyakov* (Kiev 1902), i. 285–331. Contemporary knowledge about the origins of the commune is discussed in J. Blum, *Lord and Peasant in Russia* (Princeton University Press 1961), chapter 24.
[2] Chernyshevsky, *Poln. sobr. soch.* iv. 731.
[3] Quoted from Dement'ev, op. cit., pp. 392–3.
[4] i.e. from the fourth number in 1858.

more to meet contemporary needs'. Orthodox *sobornost'* and ancient Russian 'spiritual wholeness' were outstripped by economic, social, and political issues. It was not the abstract nature of the subjects that was now responsible for the periodical's lack of popularity, but the fact that very concrete issues were treated from the point of view of the interests of an unpopular social class.

It is a matter of some interest that it was the ideological leader of the younger progressives, Nikolaï Chernyshevsky, who was most favourably disposed towards the Slavophile journal. In 1856 and 1857 he published a number of articles and press commentaries in the *Contemporary* (*Sovremennik*) in which he stressed the 'positive aspects' of Slavophilism and even went so far as to suggest that they appealed to him more than 'fossilized Westernism' (meaning the uncritical acceptance of Western European models). 'In Slavophilism'', Chernyshevsky wrote, 'there are healthy and valid elements deserving of support. And if it were necessary to make a choice of this kind, Slavophilism is better than that intellectual langour, that negation of contemporary convictions, which makes its appearance so frequently under the standard of loyalty to Western civilization.'[1]

Chernyshevsky's attitude was determined by his views on *laissez-faire* economics, which in the 1850s began to be identified with Westernism. He was on the whole reconciled to the fact that Russia was entering the phase of capitalist production, but anxious to avoid the negative results of uncontrolled development. Although the Slavophile philosophy and philosophy of history were for him nothing more than 'sterile dreams', he maintained that these could not obscure the basic content of Slavophilism, which had nothing to do with various conceptions of the 'relationship of nationality to the universally human element'.[2]

For Chernyshevsky the contribution of the Slavophiles was their criticism of capitalist Western Europe, the fact that they had drawn attention to the dangers and suffering involved in the proletarianization of the countryside and had propagated the preservation and strengthening of the village commune as

[1] Chernyshevsky, *Poln. sobr. soch.* iv. 760.
[2] Ibid., p. 724.

the best bulwark against ruinous economic individualism. The Slavophiles, he wrote,

read aright the meaning of the fate of the English and French farmers, and are anxious to ensure that we make good use of this lesson. They consider the communal utilization of the land at present in force in Russia as the most important guarantee, the essential precondition of the welfare of the agricultural class. In this respect they are greatly superior to many of the so-called Westernizers, who base their opinions on obsolete systems which are spiritually part of the bygone epoch, with its one-sided emphasis on the personal rights of each single individual, and who are prepared to inveigh thoughtlessly against these valuable old customs of ours on the grounds that they are incompatible with the postulates of systems that both science and the experience of the Western European nations have already proved to be invalid. All the theoretical errors made by the Slavophiles, and all their fantasies, are more than compensated for by their conviction that our village communes ought to remain unaffected by all changes in economic relations.[1]

Chernyshevsky's favourable view of the Slavophiles did not long survive and not simply because his praise was immediately countered by Koshelëv, who in his chilly reply asserted that the Russian village commune had nothing in common with 'Western associations', i.e. with socialism, whose influence he thought he could detect in Chernyshevsky's comments.[2] The factor that made any understanding or concerted action impossible was the Slavophile position on the land reform. During the preparations preceding the reform it became quite clear that the Slavophiles were defending the village commune from the point of view of the landowning interests and that they regarded it primarily as an institution that would put a brake on the peasants' social mobility (horizontal as well as vertical), would provide the landowners with a reserve of cheap and locally available labour, and would make possible the continued exercise of semi-feudal control. The Slavophiles were co-authors and defenders of the reform, whereas, once he had become disillusioned in the government measures, Chernyshevsky 'protested, execrated the Reform, wanted it to fail, wanted the government to get tied up in its equilibristics between the liberals and

---

[1] Ibid., p. 760.
[2] See Dement'ev, op. cit., p. 367.

the landlords, and wanted a crash to take place that would bring Russia on to the high road of open class struggle'.[1]

The very same reason that prevented an understanding between the Slavophiles and Chernyshevsky provided the basis for a lasting alliance between the Slavophile political leaders and their recent opponents, the liberal Westernizers. This process is best illustrated by the example of Kavelin, author of an anti-Slavophile synthesis of Russian history, whose position on the peasant question was identical with that of his Slavophile opponent, Samarin. 'In practical matters there are no differences between us', Samarin wrote to Kavelin in 1859.[2] This identity of views even extended to the issue of the village commune: in the 1860s Kavelin, who had once defended the 'principle of personality', came to believe that it was the Slavophiles rather than the Westernizers who were in the right on the commune controversy and that this was their great historical merit. Kavelin's motivation was not in the least influenced by the anti-capitalist utopias of Ivan Kireevsky or Konstantin Aksakov, but on the other hand fully accorded with the aims and programme of the Slavophiles' practical wing, men like Samarin, Koshelëv, and Cherkassky, who favoured capitalist development as long as it did not threaten the interests of the landowner. 'To begin with,' Kavelin wrote, 'let us put aside the Slavophile idyll of fraternity and love, said to be the basis of the communal disposal of the land and characteristic of the Russian people. In its present form the communal ownership of the land is a heavy yoke on the peasant's back, a chain which, together with the tax on "souls" and mutual guarantees, fetters him to the soil and deprives him of his liberty.'[3] Although he declared himself in favour of keeping and even strengthening this 'heavy yoke', Kavelin admitted that it had a deleterious effect on agricultural production. 'It is clear by now that communal ownership of the land does not favour agricultural progress nor does it stimulate the development of industry.'[4] For

[1] Lenin, *Collected Works* (Moscow–London, 1960–), i. 282.

[2] Quoted from S. S. Dmitriev, 'Slavyanofilÿ i slavyanofil'stvo' *Istorik-marksist* (1941), no. 1/89, p. 97.

[3] D. D. Kavelin, *Krest'yanskiĭ vopros*, *Sobr. soch.* ii. 461–5; see also N. A. Tsagolov, *Ocherki russkoĭ ekonomicheskoĭ mÿsli perioda padeniya krepostnogo prava* (Moscow 1956), pp. 333–42.

[4] Kavelin, *Sobr. soch.* ii. 281.

Kavelin the inestimable value of the village commune was its role as a 'talisman' offering protection against social upheavals and as an institution that would strengthen the position of the nobility in face of social change. In later years additional motives were fear of the social differentiation of the peasantry and of the emerging rural bourgeoisie, who represented a threat to the landed gentry.[1]

It could be argued that this parallel between Kavelin and the liberal Slavophiles is not entirely valid, since Kavelin's attitude to the village commune, as he himself emphasized, was not shared by the other liberal Westernizers of his day. In spite of this reservation it must be stated that during the preparations for the emancipation act the village commune was not a decisive issue, in spite of appearances to the contrary. Not only Kavelin but even Chicherin, the Slavophiles' 'nightmare', felt close to the Slavophile point of view, although the latter was an undeniable opponent of the village commune and a consistent supporter of a liberal (even a vulgar liberal) economic policy. In his memoirs Chicherin bestowed high praise on the Slavophiles' contribution to the emancipation act and reaffirmed his entire agreement with them on the 'essentials'. The best of the Slavophiles, Chicherin wrote, 'found it easy to agree with the Westernizers, for both sides were united by a common goal'. 'When the time was ripe for practical action the theoretical differences faded into the background and polemics died down.'[2]

This poses the question of whether the polemics of the 1840s were concerned with illusory issues and could be called a simple misunderstanding. Any such conclusion would surely be quite erroneous and would make it impossible to understand the ideological scene at the time. The anti-capitalist character of the Slavophile utopia was a fact as undeniable as the collaboration in a common cause of men as different as Granovsky and Belinsky, Kavelin and Herzen. Nostalgia for a lost tradition and the desire to revive it were quite as actual and grounded in the existing realities as the attempt to transplant new 'Western' values such as 'personality' and 'freedom'. New

---

[1] See Tsagolov, op. cit., p. 341.

[2] B. N. Chicherin, *Vospominaniya, Moskva sorokovykh godov* (Moscow 1929), pp. 225, 288. See also Tsagolov, op. cit., p. 283.

conditions, which forced the ideologists of both camps to make a brutally concrete choice, created a situation in which utopian visions were efficiently blocked by immediate class interests. If the two points of view were ultimately reconciled it was not because the utopias of the Slavophiles and liberal Westernizers shared some kind of latent 'essential content', but because both sides in fact betrayed their utopian ideals. The student of social thought cannot, however, afford to neglect utopias: as an important force in cultural formation they have an undeniable significance and tend to outlive the concrete social situation from which they originally sprang. As documentary evidence concerning historical figures and the social groups represented by them they are of no less importance than the acts of betrayal which follow them all too often.

The renunciation of the anti-capitalist utopia following the land reform and rapid expansion of capitalism in Russia resulted in the intellectual impoverishment of Slavophilism. Political developments, chief among them the appearance and quick growth of an organized revolutionary movement, were contributing factors.

The 'first revolutionary situation', as it came to be known, came about in Russia in the years 1859 to 1861 and reached its climax towards the end of 1861. There were several contributory factors, among them the revival of the national independence movement in Poland, the oppositional mood of part of the nobility, who sought to restrict autocracy by constitutional reforms, student protest against the reactionary measures of the ministry of education, and the unrest among both democratic elements and the conservative nobility, resentful of the fact that 'bureaucrats' had been entrusted with carrying out the reform. The most important elements, however, were the universal bitterness prevailing among the peasantry, and the illegal revolutionary movement. More than once the aid of the birch or the army was needed to persuade the peasants to accept the 'decree of 19 February'. Unrest was greatest in the Kazan province, where a peasant leader, Anton Petrov from the village of Bezdna, persuaded the local population that the decree had been forged by the nobility and that the 'true liberty' bestowed by the tsar on his people meant that the nobility was to relinquish all the arable land and retain only 'hills and pits, gullies and roads, sand and rushes, but not a twig of a forest'. The peasant demonstrations and the bloody repression that followed them helped to mobilize the democratic sections of the intelligentsia, as the large number of contemporary propaganda leaflets show. Shelgunov has called the years 1861 and 1862 the 'period of proclamations'; leaflets were handed out everywhere: in the street and in the theatre, slipped into coat-pockets or through doors. The first of these proclamations (so far not published) was Chernyshevsky's appeal, written in 'the famous town of Christiania', 'to the peasants of the landlords from one who desires their well-being, greetings'. This was quickly followed by three leaflets headed 'Great Russian' (*Velikoross*) (summer and autumn of 1861), N. V. Shelgunov's and M. I. Mikhailov's appeal 'To the Younger Generation' (autumn of 1861) outlining a programme for Russia's 'unique' non-capitalist economic development, and finally (in May 1862) P. G. Zaïchnevsky's 'Young Russia', which promised a revolution three times as bloody as the Jacobin, the wiping out of the entire ruling class, and the introduction of a 'social and democratic Russian republic'. The end of 1861 saw the emergence of the first all-Russian revolutionary organization 'Land and Freedom' (*Zemlya i Volya*). Its aims were to overthrow autocracy, hand over to the peasants all the land previously farmed by them, and convene a Land Assembly in order to work out a constitution and introduce representative government in Russia.

The 'revolutionary situation' did not become transformed into a revolution, for concerted action between the peasantry and the radical intelligentsia proved impossible: repression and arrests thinned the ranks of the revolutionaries and Chernyshevsky's imprisonment in 1862 deprived the democratic groups of an ideological leader who was universally respected. Moreover, the resurgence of conservative nationalist forces after the Polish uprising of 1863 led to the break-up and suppression of the Land and Freedom party, which was collaborating with the Polish rebels. In spite of these measures the government was not able to 'uproot' or even effectively impede the revolutionary movement. The outlook of the ideological heirs of the Slavophiles was profoundly affected by the upsurge of radical activity during the latter part of the nineteenth century, beginning with Karakozov's unsuccessful attempt on the tsar's life in 1866, followed by the Nechaev conspiracy in the late 1860s and early '70s, the Populist invasion of the countryside in 1874, the great political trials, and the foundation of a new 'Land and Freedom' organization in 1876, the Chigirin conspiracy of 1877, the foundation of the 'People's Will' (*Narodnaya Volya*) terrorist organization in 1879, and culminating in the assassination of Alexander II in 1881. Ideological divisions were now determined by attitudes taken to revolution: it was a further complication that the anti-capitalist utopia of a 'Russian', non-capitalist form of economic development based on the peasant commune was almost monopolized by the revolutionary Populists. On the other hand, the resurgence of nationalism after the Polish uprising, the renewed urgency of the Eastern question, and the colonization of Central Asia paved the way for the transformation of the conservative-romantic nationalism of the Slavophiles into a chauvinist nationalism that welcomed industrialization and urbanization if only as forces that would consolidate the political prestige of the empire and facilitate its expansion.

After the 'Great Reforms', therefore, conditions in Russia made it impossible for Slavophilism to continue to exist as a harmonious and homogeneous *Weltanschauung*. As early as 1872 Nikolaĭ Mikhailovsky commented perceptively:

A peevish patriotism, dreams of Russian hegemony over Slavdom or of the struggle of the Slavonic principle with the Romance and Teutonic principles are still possible today. But a homogeneous Slavophile view of the world is no longer possible. All that is possible are individual programmes in the Slavophile spirit, for instance a Slavophile political and economic programme. So far, however, from it being possible to unify or harmonize these programmes, each separate programme conceals insurmountable contradictions with a strong bias towards Westernism.[1]

The cessation—or gradual disappearance—of the Slavophile/ Westernizer controversy was also noted by the epigones of the Slavophile movement, although in their opinion this was not

[1] N. K. Mikhailovsky, 'Po povodu russkogo izdaniya knigi K. Marksa' in *Narodnicheskaya ekonomicheskaya literatura* (Moscow 1958), pp. 162–3.

due to the acceptance of capitalism as a social system by the Slavophiles but, on the contrary, to the widespread acceptance of Slavophile ideas. The following comment by Koshelëv is a characteristic expression of this point of view:

It is noteworthy that former pronouncements of ours which aroused the indignation and sneers of the Westernizers, have today become a universally held point of view. Who today does not support the maintenance of ties with the Slavs? Who today is opposed to research into ancient Russian monuments, folk customs, and other original aspects of our national existence? Who does not perceive that they have a profound meaning and great significance for our future? Who today denies the influence of the national element in science and art? Of course there are still issues—and very important ones—on which the so-called Slavophiles maintain a separate position and differ considerably from the so-called Westernizers; but the former controversy between them has died down and is a memory of the past rather than actual.[1]

It is perhaps better to refrain from commenting on these words, which utterly trivialize the controversies of the 1840s, and instead quote another viewpoint to complete the picture. The following passage is taken from an article by the ex-Slavophile (or rather former Slavophile sympathizer) E. Mamonov and was published in the *Russian Archives* of 1873, together with a detailed reply by Ivan Aksakov.

After the death of the Kireevsky brothers and of Khomyakov and Konstantin Aksakov, the most important Slavophile traditions became lost in the hands of those who followed them. They rejected the standpoint of their predecessors, became involved in difficulties, and thus this *truly libertarian* trend (*svobodneĭshee napravlenie*) became transformed into some sort of patriotic and orthodox doctrine which on the one hand aimed at universal Russification and on the other tried to convert everyone not just to the Orthodox Christianity of the people, but quite simply to a police religion taken over by Y. Samarin from the savage Latvians and Esthonians who have commercialized their religious conscience. Slavophilism lost its vitality and became a trivial, formal, and decrepit catechism of clerico-punitive maxims. Hence it was able to spread all over the Russian empire in the early 1860s, and to gain the approval of

---

[1] Koshelëv, *Zapiski*, pp. 77–8. An identical opinion was put forward by the Slavophile A. F. Hilferding in his foreword to Khomyakov's *Notes on Universal History*. See A. S. Khomyakov, vol. v.

mammas and generals everywhere, to draw into its fold all good little boys eager to get on in the world. Slavophiles shot up over night, like mushrooms, together with patriots of a very suspect kind. The Slavophile movement now met with the success from which Konstantin Aksakov had taken such pains to protect it.[1]

The three passages quoted above are not in fact contradictory, but reinforce and complement each other. By rejecting their own utopia in favour of a capitalist future, by actively collaborating in the government's reforms, the Slavophiles themselves helped to create objective preconditions for the inevitable disintegration of their *Weltanschauung*. On the other hand, Russia after the reforms provided fertile soil for the spread of appropriately modified and trivialized Slavophile ideas. In this two factors played a decisive role: first, the revolutionary movement and the consequent need for an ideological weapon to use against 'nihilism'; secondly, the Polish uprising of 1863, which stimulated a violent upsurge of Russian chauvinism. In the period of nationalism and reaction that followed, certain Slavophile ideas (vulgarized and deprived of their original anti-capitalist content) were absorbed and popularized as never before by the reactionary press and flavoured, as it were, the official cult of the Emperor and almost all variants of nationalism. Even autocracy changed its methods: although the 'triune' slogan in the reign of Nicholas included the word 'nationality', the Emperor had been a traditional ruler guided principally by state and dynastic considerations. He was opposed to Panslavism and disliked nationalistic excesses, expecially when these were directed against Germany. The next emperor, Alexander II, might be called a 'liberal' and a 'Westernizer', at least at the beginning of his reign. After his assassination the idea of a 'national' monarchy achieved its consummation—with his full beard and conscious assumption of a 'popular' and 'Orthodox' image Alexander III might be called a 'Slavophile' Emperor.

It is not the purpose of this book to make a detailed investigation of these changes, fascinating though they are. The infiltration of certain Slavophile ideas into the reactionary press and via the latter into the consciousness of entire sections of society, and also the degree to which they influenced govern-

---

[1] E. Mamonov, 'Slavyanofilȳ. Istoriko-kriticheskiǐ ocherk', *Russkiǐ Arkhiv*, xii (1873), 2489–90.

ment policy, are themes for a separate book that ought to be written by a professional historian. The aim of the present study is merely to distinguish between the main trends that were influenced by Slavophilism in its waning phase. These trends are of interest to the historian of ideas since their emergence involved the autonomization and modification of various aspects of Slavophile doctrine and thus, in retrospect, throws some light on the contradictions within it.

For the sake of greater clarity the heirs of Slavophilism might be called 'direct' or 'indirect', the determining factor being whether the given trend arose within Slavophilism (during the period of its disintegration) or only under the influence of the Slavophiles but essentially without their active, creative participation. This dividing line is merely conventional, of course, all the more so since these different trends did not on the whole appear separately but interlocked to varying degrees. Nevertheless, this division would seem to be justified as a necessary aid to an adequate typology. In any case, the term 'continuity' or 'heritage' is in itself a relative one. In order to avoid possible misunderstanding it is necessary to stress that the author has no intention of labelling all the thinkers discussed in the following chapters (Grigor'ev, Dostoevsky, or the young Solov'ëv, for instance) as nothing but 'indirect heirs' of Slavophilism. His aim is rather to trace the role various aspects of Slavophile doctrine played in their work and thus to examine Slavophilism from different perspectives, as a link in different developments. This necessitates a description of the most important outlets for Slavophile influence, including its influence on thinkers (such as Herzen) who continued *isolated Slavophile ideas* within the framework of an *entirely different Weltanschauung*. Hence. the purpose of the following chapters is to describe those leading trends in Russian social thought in the second half of the nineteenth century which stood in a meaningful relationship or were determined by their attitude to Slavophilism, took up issues central to Slavophilism, or were influenced by Slavophile doctrine and were at least partially in agreement with it.

From Utopia to Politics

AMONG the direct heirs of Slavophilism are to be found some
of the supporters of a trend that has come to be known as
'gentry liberalism'. In this context the term 'liberalism' does not
signify a specific social philosophy or style of thought opposed
to conservatism. Gentry liberalism was a concrete political trend
whose supporters were not united by a shared *Weltanschauung*
but by common practical aims dictated by the immediate (and
by no means 'sublimated') class interests of the nobility. Adherence to this trend was determined by such objective criteria as
attitudes to the revolution and agrarian question, and approval
of landowning (or 'Prussian') capitalism. This trend, which
must be called a political programme rather than a *Weltanschauung*, aimed at reconciling the role of the nobility with the
requirements of the new system but also at reconciling—as far
as possible—the new system with the needs of the nobility.[1]
Widely different trends, ranging from Westernism to Slavophilism and from a partial adaptation of bourgeois liberalism
to its negation, were used to justify this programme; a common
factor, however, even among extreme Westernizers, was a clear
rejection of Enlightenment provenance and of the radicalism
of the liberal utopia.

The epigones of Slavophilism were the chief ideologists of
Right-wing gentry liberalism. What distinguished them were
their attempts to preserve the village commune as an institution
blocking social differentiation, their nationalism and reliance
on absolutism, and their dislike and fear of any of the bolder
liberal measures attempted by the government. In this last

---

[1] The use of the term 'liberalism' in this context is, of course, inappropriate.
The term 'liberalism' should be used only for a specific political doctrine, and to
include among 'liberals' such convinced supporters of tsarist autocracy as Samarin
and Nikolaï Milyutin is highly misleading (because of his attitude to the emancipation reform Milyutin was even considered an 'extreme' liberal). The phrase 'gentry
liberalism' was however in common use during the period preceding the land
reform in Russia and has thus become a generally accepted historical label.

respect there was little unanimity: Samarin and Cherkassky combined liberalism in agrarian questions with a consistent hostility to constitutionalism; Koshelëv and (in the 1860s) Ivan Aksakov were moderates and while formally opposed to constitutionalism were in favour of restricting the domination of the bureaucracy, and called for an all-Russian Land Assembly which was, however, to be only an advisory body and have nothing in common with Western European parliamentarianism. This difference, to which only passing attention is drawn here, was already apparent during the preparations for the land reform and gradually deepened, so that it is possible to speak of the emergence of two trends *within* Slavophile 'liberalism'.

The ideology of these two trends—which might be called 'anti-constitutional' and 'semi-constitutional'—will be analysed through their main representatives, Samarin and Koshelëv. Their careers were almost completely parallel: in the 1840s both belonged to the Slavophile circle, and were distinguished by their 'practical' interests and active participation in public life; both took part in the preparations for the emancipation act; after the defeat of the Polish uprising both were sent on important government missions to Poland; and finally both were active in the *Zemstvos*. These similarities should not, however, conceal the differences between the two men which, as we shall try to show, can also be traced in the different periods of their activity.

Samarin's background was somewhat different from that of the other Slavophiles. His biographer, Baron B. E. Nolde, comments as follows: 'As if to contradict his entire career Samarin was born in St. Petersburg, in the specifically Petersburg milieu of the imperial court and aristocratic officialdom.'[1]

The opening words of this passage refer to the symbolic meaning that the Slavophiles attached to Russia's old and new capitals; in the next sentence Nolde emphasizes the fact that Samarin's father moved to Moscow in 1826, so that the future Slavophile thinker became a 'Muscovite' by the tender age of seven. The emphasis would seem to be incorrectly placed, however: Samarin's 'specifically Petersburgian' background was not contradicted but confirmed by his future career. He was

[1] B. E. Nolde, *Yury Samarin i ego vremya* (Paris 1926), p. 8.

undoubtedly the most 'Petersburgian' of the Slavophile ideologists and the ties linking him to the upper bureaucracy
turned out to be very strong. As a political thinker his contribution was to modify or reinterpret Slavophile doctrine for the use
of bureaucratic absolutism and to fuse the Slavophile variant
of gentry liberalism with a truly 'Petersburgian' bureaucratic conservatism.

There were two very important formative influences on
Samarin's thought: one of them was Lorenz von Stein's book
Socialism and Communism in Contemporary France (1842),[1] and the
other his participation in the special government mission (1845–
1848) set up to investigate social and communal relations in the
Baltic provinces. What impressed the young Samarin in the
work of the German conservative sociologist was not only the
subject-matter but also the underlying sociological premisses,
namely the radical opposition between 'society' and 'state' and
positive stress placed on the second term of the antithesis; the
assumption that the state was an arbiter standing above the
conflicts of individual, estate, and class particularism, the
guardian of a unity that was permanently threatened by the
lack of sufficient control over the particularist, centrifugal forces
of 'society'.[2] What he saw in Livonia, a country ruled by
German feudal barons, seemed to Samarin to substantiate
Stein's position. The proud independence of the Baltic barons,
their special privileges and carefully guarded freedoms, appeared to be a glaring example of relations typical of Western
feudalism but absolutely incompatible both with the traditions
of the Russian monarchy and with the general principles on
which states were founded.

The first prerequisite for the existence of a state [Samarin wrote on
his return from Riga] is the subordination of all particular rights
and interests—both those of local groups and those of estates—to
the interests of the whole, and the right of the supreme authorities,
whatever form they take, to decide irrevocably, without exception,
every issue where the general good is concerned, and to implement

---

[1] See B. E. Nolde, *Yuriĭ Samarin i ego vremya*, p. 34. In 1843 Samarin wrote a
lengthy article on this book (the article was unfortunately not finished and therefore never published).

[2] See the analysis of the sociological theories of Stein in H. Marcuse, *Reason and
Revolution. Hegel and the Rise of Social Theory* (The Humanities Press, New York
1954), pp. 374–88.

their decisions. If this right is relinquished or shared with anyone whatever, the authority of the state will inevitably be destroyed or duplicated.[1]

The fruits of Samarin's service as a member of the government commission in the Baltic provinces were a monograph entitled *A History of the Town of Riga* (published in 1852 as the first volume of the commission's reports) as well as the more important cycle *Letters from Riga* (1848). In view of the censorship the latter was not published but read by the author at private gatherings, distributed to leading government officials (among them N. A. Milyutin, P. D. Kiselev, and the Minister of Internal Affairs, L. A. Perovsky). The fact that the state that was to guard the 'general good' happened to be tsarist Russia, while the audacious barons were Germans, was not a matter of indifference to Samarin. In the *Letters from Riga* there is an insistent note of chauvinism strangely linked to an anti-aristocratic social demagogy. Samarin accused the administration—and thus the government of Nicholas I—of excessive tolerance for the privileges of the barons, of reluctance to carry through the total assimilation of the German minority, lack of care for the Latvian and Esthonian peasants exploited by the Germans, and, by default, neglect of the latter's Russification. It is hardly surprising that these statements aroused the anger of the Governor of Riga, Prince Suvorov. Samarin was arrested in March 1849 and after spending twelve days in the Peter and Paul Fortress was not released until the Tsar himself had delivered a reprimand. Samarin's conflict with Nicholas I was essentially a conflict between nationalist conservatism and traditional legitimist conservatism; in his audience with Samarin Nicholas told him:

You have stirred up the animosity of the Germans against the Russians, have set them against each other, whereas it is necessary to reconcile them; you attack whole estates who have given loyal service: beginning with Pahlen I could list up to a hundred and fifty generals. You want to turn Germans into Russians forcibly, by violence, sword in hand like a second Mohammed—but, just because we are Christians, we ought not to act in this fashion . . . Your attack was aimed directly at the government: what you really meant was that since the reign of the Emperor Peter we have been

[1] Quoted from Nolde, op. cit., p. 42.

surrounded by Germans and have ourselves become Germanicized. You must understand what you have done: you have mobilized public opinion against the government; this was leading to a repetition of the events of 14 December.[1]

His conversation with the Emperor naturally did nothing to make Samarin change his mind. His stay in the Baltic provinces strengthened his nationalism, his mistrust of all particularist and autonomous social forces, and his faith in the special mission of the centralized bureaucratic state. But it also convinced him of the need for emancipation, but accompanied by the right to own land, unlike the reforms introduced by the German nobility in the Baltic provinces in the years 1816–19.

Quite different influences shaped the intellectual evolution of Samarin's older friend, Alexander Koshelëv. As a former member of the Society of the Lovers of Wisdom Koshelëv was from the outset strongly influenced by Western European liberalism. He himself acknowledged his important debt to the Italian jurist and economist Pellegrino Rossi, whose lectures he attended in the early 1830s in Geneva, both at the university and as a member of a private group of eight Russians staying in Switzerland at that time. 'To Rossi', he wrote later, 'I owe the development of many new ideas and the firm consolidation of that *true liberalism* which, unfortunately, is so rare among us.'[2] The use of the term 'true liberalism' is quite characteristic of Koshelëv. The senior Slavophiles considered 'liberalism' to be almost synonymous with Westernism (Khomyakov referred to his political opinions as 'true conservatism'). This did not deter Koshelëv from stating in his memoirs that although Khomyakov had 'made no attempt to pass as a liberal' he was a man who was 'liberal' to the highest degree, both in his opinions and in his actions and that the Slavophiles in fact represented 'true liberalism', appropriate to Russian conditions and undefiled by the 'doctrinaire theories of the West'.[3] 'Who, if not we,' he asked, 'were more zealous supporters of emancipation, and moreover emancipation accompanied by as large an allocation of land as circumstances allowed? Who, if not we, turned out to be the most active participants in the *Zemstvos*? . . . It was we

---

[1] Quoted from Nolde, p. 48.
[2] Koshelëv, *Zapiski*, p. 39.
[3] See ibid., pp. 71–2, 39.

who turned out to be truly progressive liberals, and not those who called themselves by that name.'[1]

An analysis of Koshelëv's views makes it clear that his use of the word 'liberalism' was not fortuitous. Koshelëv was never an orthodox Slavophile and even during the reign of Nicholas combined Slavophile beliefs with quite unrelated ideas. This is illustrated by his report on the Great Exhibition, which he visited in 1852. Whereas Khomyakov had been enthusiastic about British Toryism, Koshelëv praised England for its industrial achievements and its intense agricultural cultivation. England's example, he wrote, had disproved the theories of Louis Blanc and other Frenchmen who demanded state intervention in the economic sphere.[2] This praise of the 'Manchester school' is far removed not only from classical Slavophilism but even from the Slavophilism of the second half of the century. Although they made practical concessions to capitalism, Samarin and Ivan Aksakov (and to a certain extent even Koshelëv himself in later years) retained their mistrust of bourgeois liberal economics, were in favour of protectionism, and, following F. List, of active state participation in economic development.

During the reign of Nicholas Koshelëv was, after Khomyakov, the most knowledgeable of the Slavophiles on agricultural matters and one of the most determined and active supporters of emancipation. In 1847, when he was Marshal of the Nobility in the province of Riazan, he sent a letter to the Minister of Internal Affairs urging the need for improvements in the conditions of the serfs. In an article published in the same year he tried to persuade the landed gentry that it would be in their own interest to switch to 'free' labour on their home farms: 'Only force of habit, only Eastern indolence (to refrain from using a stronger term) stops us from *emancipating ourselves* [*sic*!] from our serfs. We are almost all agreed that free labour is superior to serf labour, but though we know what is better we cling to the worse.'[3]

Among the Slavophiles Koshelëv did not stand alone on this issue and support for emancipation was not something specifically Slavophile. The superficiality and heterodoxy of Koshelëv's Slavophilism became apparent in the 1840s in his attitude

---

[1] Ibid., p. 78.   [2] See ibid., Appendix, p. 25.
[3] Ibid., Appendix, pp. 13–14.

to the village commune. In the chapter on Khomyakov mention was made of Koshelëv's lack of enthusiasm for the commune, which he supported by the typically liberal argument that it made progress in agriculture difficult if not impossible.[1] Khomyakov's arguments put forward in his exhaustive article in letter form, 'On the Russian Village Commune', did not convince the practical Koshelëv; his reply deserves a fuller analysis, as it reveals the radical doubts of an acknowledged Slavophile concerning the basic tenets of Slavophile doctrine.

Dismissing Khomyakov's statements on English and French agriculture, Koshelëv set out to prove that factors of paramount importance in agricultural development were the freedom of the peasantry, their right to own land, and a certain degree of decentralization which would allow provincial centres to develop independently. If the commune was retained, he argued, there would be no progress in Russian agriculture, even if the land was not redistributed more frequently than once every thirty years. The commune as it was now, he insisted, had little in common with the Slavophile ideal: 'Enthusiastic talk about the Russian village commune can only be pardoned in a Haxthausen, who has never been a permanent resident of Russia and does not even know Russian.'[2] Koshelëv wrote that he was at a loss to see what connection there was between the commune and the Orthodox Church, in what sense the Kremlin and the Kiev Cave Monastery could be called the 'roots of Russian life', and what kind of vital social principles could be derived from folk customs and folklore. To refuse to allow that Catholics or Protestants might have feelings of solidarity or community was not, he thought, a truly Christian sentiment; moreover, it was strange to claim a monopoly of brotherliness for the only nation in comporary Europe that imposed on its brothers the slavery of serfdom. Koshelëv's sharp formulations were not only directed against the applications of Slavophile doctrine, but to some extent represented an outright attack on the Slavophile hierarchy of values.

[1] See p. 231.
[2] Quoted from N. P. Kolupanov, *Biografiya A. I. Koshelova* (Moscow 1889–92), ii. 106–8, Appendix. The polemic between Koshelëv and Khomyakov is discussed in detail by P. K. Christoff, op. cit., pp. 222–32.

For you [he wrote to Khomyakov] the supreme expression of man is society and in a perfect society, therefore, the individual ought to to eliminated. For me society is an evil, but a necessary evil. Man has evolved from a state in which society did not exist and must one day return to that state. The more perfect the society, the more limited are its demands and the greater the freedom granted to the individual, the more unfettered the development of his power and capacities.[1]

It is difficult to see how a man who professed these opinions could be called a Slavophile. Probably the only explanation for Koshelëv's adherence to the Slavophile circle was that there were other links between its members than a shared *Weltanschauung* and that different individuals were motivated by different factors. Koshelëv was linked to the founders of Slavophile doctrine, in particular to Khomakov, by class background and ties of friendship; the Slavophile circle to him represented a group of wealthy and enlightened landowners who were moderately opposed to bureaucratic absolutism, faithful members of the Orthodox Church, critical of the West, but ready to apply its experiences and achievements to the modernization of Russian agriculture. These elements were enough to determine his position. In the new conditions following the 'thaw' Koshelëv, the energetic publisher of the journals *Russian Conversation* and *Good Husbandry*, therefore came to be regarded as one of the leading Slavophile politicians.

It should however be emphasized that in the 1850s Koshelëv no longer adhered to his earlier views on the village commune but, on the contrary, became one of its most zealous supporters. Towards the end of his life he even became convinced that the peasants' ties with the commune should be compulsory, that they should be as firmly attached to the soil as possible, and thus largely outside the scope of the new liberal reforms.

As N. Rubinstein has pointed out, the idea of a compulsory commune was a glaring contradiction and profanation of the moral ideal of K. Aksakov, whose utopian dream was of a community which would 'allow even war prisoners to belong to it if they so wished, to remain in it, be active within it, and live in it like brothers'. Koshelëv's plan (implemented by Alexander

[1] N. P. Kolupanov, op. cit.

III) turned the commune into an institution that converted even brothers into prisoners.[1]

The theoretical divergence between Samarin and Koshelëv— who represented two diametrically opposed deviations from classical Slavophilism, was reflected in their practical activity during the period of the Great Reforms. This was not immediately apparent: in their earliest pronouncements on the peasant question (1856–8) their agreement on fundamental issues was in fact more striking.

The Slavophiles' contribution to the land reform, their energetic campaign against open and concealed supporters of feudal relations and serf labour, came to be greatly idealized in later years. Even certain Marxist historians believed it possible to treat the Slavophiles as involuntary allies of Chernyshevsky and Herzen.[2] Any interpretation of this kind, however, is based on a complete misunderstanding: their sincere condemnation of the immorality of serfdom did not prevent the Slavophile leaders from assessing the reform from the point of view of the interests of the landed gentry. The long and carefully documented memoranda on the peasant question prepared by Samarin and Koshelëv show an admirable objectivity, detailed knowledge of the historical, economic, and juridical aspects of the problem, and not a trace of the utopianism against which Khomyakov had cautioned. Both of them defended the commune as an institution that would facilitate rural administration and control, guarantee the efficient collection of taxes and redemption payments, and provide the landowners with a locally available source of cheap labour. Both proposed a high redemption payment based not only on the value of the land but also on the peasants' feudal obligations to the landlords. Both were basically in favour of granting the peasants the whole

---

[1] See N. Rubinstein, 'Istoricheskaya teoriya slavyanofilov i eë klassovÿe korni', in *Russkaya istoricheskaya literatura v klassovom osveshchenii*, ed. by M. N. Pokrovsky (Moscow 1927), p. 106.

[2] See V. Stein, *Ocherki razvitiya russkoĭ obshchestvenno-ekonomicheskoĭ mÿsli XIX–XX vekov* (Leningrad 1948), pp. 12–13. Unlike Stein, who called the Slavophiles utopian socialists, the American scholar R. Wortman idealizes the liberalism of the Slavophile leaders and states: 'in their concrete notions of reform and their capacity to carry them out, the liberal Slavophiles far surpassed the Westernizers'. R. Wortman, 'Koshelëv, Samarin and Cherkassky, and the Fate of Liberal Slavophilism', *Slavic Review*, xxi. 2 (1962), 261.

of the land cultivated by them previously, but only because they quite correctly realized that existing allotments provided only the barest living and would not draw labour away from the manorial farm. Finally both thought that before the emancipation act came into force the landowners should be given the opportunity to conclude voluntary contracts with the peasants, within the framework of general provisions layed down by the government. Koshelëv, who placed special emphasis on this point, himself concluded a contract of this kind with his peasants, by which they received allotments of one desyatina, far smaller than the official land grant.

The land reform model proposed by Samarin and Koshelëv (and actually implemented by the government) was essentially a conscious adaptation of the Prussian model: with this in mind Samarin wrote a detailed monograph on the *Abolition of Serfdom and the Structure of Peasant and Landowner Relations in Prussia*.[1] Both men feared that social unrest might accompany the rapid and uncontrolled development of capitalism and thought that this danger could be removed or tempered by the institution of the commune and the active interference of a strong central government. The only difference of opinion between them before 1859 (the year that the Editorial Commissions were convened) concerned the period of 'transition'. Samarin was in favour of preserving labour obligations for ten or twelve years after emancipation, 'until a spontaneous balance is achieved between the supply and demand for free labour',[2] while Koshelev, who had more confidence in capitalism, urged that the new system be introduced at once and without any intervening stages.

A more serious difference between the two reformers was that they were divided on the question of working methods, and this influenced their entire subsequent careers. Both Samarin and Koshelëv belonged to provincial gentry committees (Samarin in Samara and Koshelëv in Riazan) and, characteristically, both preferred to be nominated by the government rather than elected, since this allowed them to be less dependent on the reactionary sentiments of the gentry. In spite of this, the analogy between the two men is not complete. Samarin and

[1] See Samarin, *Sochineniya* (Moscow 1878), ii. 191–401.
[2] Ibid. iii. 42. Quoted from N. A. Tsagolov, op. cit., p. 224.

Cherkassky, who supported a reform imposed 'from above', tried to persuade Koshelëv not to take part in the meetings of the Riazan deputies, but to act solely in his official capacity.[1] Koshelëv was by no means reluctant to make use of his official prerogatives, but rejected this advice since he felt that decisions of public concern ought only to be taken after consultation with representatives of the 'Land'. This difference of opinion became more pronounced after the establishment of the Editorial Commissions in 1859; Samarin and Cherkassky were nominated as members of the Commissions, whereas Koshelëv was overlooked, which naturally strengthened his dislike of 'bureaucracy'. Undue importance should not, however, be attached to this fact.[2] The political differences between Samarin and Koshelëv have far deeper roots: in his *Letters from Riga* the former showed that even in the 1840s he was already an apologist for a centralized and bureaucratic 'social monarchy', whereas the latter always tended towards anti-bureaucratic liberalism and in his memorial *On the State of Russian Finances*, submitted to the new emperor in 1855, proposed convening a 'Land' assembly.[3]

The first concrete conflict was not long in coming. Among the nobility, who were anxious about the future of their estates and offended by the bureaucratic manner in which the reform was being carried out, there were the beginnings of a movement for an oligarchic constitution, grouped largely around Senator Bezobrazov and his supporters. When deputies from provincial committees began to arrive in St. Petersburg in order to have their say in the work of the Editorial Commissions, Samarin's like-minded friend Nikolaï Milyutin, to all intents and purposes the leader of the Commission, sent a memorandum to the Emperor warning him that the nobility was scheming against both the 'people' and the state. As a result the Emperor gave instructions that the role of the gentry delegates be limited to

---

[1] See Koshelëv, *Zapiski*, p. 117.

[2] As Wortman does when he suggests that membership or failure to be nominated for the Editorial Committees had a decisive influence on the further careers of the Slavophile political leaders: 'Each figure had already fallen under the influence of a particular group: Koshelëv was becoming a part of the revivified forces of the gentry; Samarin and Cherkassky had become a part of a vigorous organ of the bureaucracy.' Wortman, op. cit., pp. 265–8.

[3] See Koshelëv, *Zapiski*, Appendix.

answering the commission's questions, and forbade them to hold official meetings or to put out any joint written petitions. These instructions aroused a wave of protests led, among others, by Koshelëv, and this in its turn prompted energetic counter-measures on the part of the 'bureaucracy', represented, among others, by Samarin and Cherkassky. It is hardly surprising that friendly relations between the leading Slavophile politicians cooled down considerably.[1]

The 'anti-bureaucratic' opposition included men of quite different political complexions, ranging from representatives of the oligarchical Right (M. Bezobrazov) to authentic liberals (A. M. Unkovsky and the Tver liberals).[2] Among them Koshelëv held an intermediate position; his political pro-gramme envisaged closer contacts between the Emperor and the 'people' (primarily the nobility) through the convention of a national 'Land' *Duma* which would act as an advisory body and both limit and counterbalance St. Petersburg officialdom. To the end of his life he adhered to these ideas, which he first expounded in two pamphlets published in Leipzig in 1862.[3] The time had come, he wrote, to prove by deeds that the nobility's dependence on officials had been abolished together with serfdom.[4] Russian history had proved that the principle of elected representation was perfectly reconcilable with auto-cracy. Bureaucracy was hated by all; the Emperor's goodwill did not bear fruit since the officials thwarted all his plans; it was they who violated legality, stifled freedom of speech and civic initiative; who distorted the land reform, and were the

---

[1] See Wortman, op. cit., pp. 266–77.

[2] The complexity of this period is illustrated by the fact that Chernyshevsky supported the demands of the Tver liberals. In his *Letters without an Address*, which were in fact addressed to the emperor, he wrote: 'Please do not ascribe this desire for general reforms at present cherished by the nobility to any specific motives or incentives connected with their social position. . . . In the plans dealing with the general legislative reforms, the reorganization of the administrative and legal system, and the introduction of freedom of speech, the nobility only represents all the other estates and does not come forward because it desires such changes more than any other estates but solely because under the present system it has an organization which allows it to express its wishes.' For Chernyshevsky demagogic reproaches that the demands of the liberals were only a mask for the selfish interests of the nobility were typical rather of bureaucrats such as Samarin and N. Milyutin.

[3] *Kakoĭ iskhod dlya Rossii iz nỹneshnego ee polozheniya?*; *Konstitutsiya, samodyerzhavie i zemskaya duma* (Leipzig 1862), Franz Wagner.

[4] See Koshelëv, *Kakoĭ iskhod . . .*, p. 19.

cause of the peasantry's mounting hostility towards the nobility (whose behaviour on the emancipation question Koshelëv called a model of patriotism).[1] The convention of a *Duma* would mean a return to ancient Russian traditions and not an artificial introduction of Western constitutionalism; Russia needed an autocratic tsar, for only he could ensure the balance of the interests of the various estates, since he himself stood above them.[2] On the issue of a 'constitution' Koshelëv wrote as follows:

If by this word we mean a system of government with a two-chamber parliament, an artificial balance of power, and a monarch who has been turned into a puppet, then we hope that a constitution of this kind will never be in force in Russia. At the same time we are utterly convinced that having learnt the country's true needs through the intermediary of the Land *Duma* the Emperor will—if not today then in due course—bestow on Russia legislation that will safeguard all the essential rights of man and citizen conquered in other countries by struggle and violence.[3]

This programme—which should be called semi-constitutional rather than constitutional—was decisively condemned by Samarin. As the ideologist of a social 'people's monarchy' the latter was seriously concerned lest Alexander II and the government make concessions to the mood of the nobility and lest 'Koshelëv's childish ideas' were put into practice.[4] In order to prevent such an outcome, Samarin undertook a campaign to activate and instruct the opponents of constitutionalism among the nobility. Among other things he composed an anti-constitutional manifesto (1862) which circulated in manuscript, since Ivan Aksakov, who sympathized with Koshelëv, could not make up his mind to print it in the Slavophile jounal *Day*.[5] The range of arguments put forward in the manifesto was very considerable and passed from a criticism of oligarchic tendencies and defence of the 'popular' nature of autocracy to threats

---

[1] See Koshelëv, *Kakoĭ iskhod*..., pp. 4–14; *Konstitutsiya, samoderzhavie* ..., pp. 41–5.
[2] See Koshelëv, *Konstitutsiya, samoderzhavie* . . ., p. 17. It is worth noting that his argument differed from those of the Slavophiles. For Koshelëv the need for autocratic government sprang from a flaw in the Russian national character, i.e. from the irrepressible 'tendency to licence', which required strong central government.
[3] Koshelëv, *Kakoĭ iskhod* . . ., p. 39.
[4] Samarin's letter to Cherkassky, 27 November 1862. Quoted from Nolde, op. cit., p. 178.   [5] Nolde, op. cit., pp. 176–7.

of an alliance between tsar and people directed against the nobility. 'A people's constitution', Samarin wrote, 'is still impossible here, and a constitution that would not be "popular", that is the rule of a minority not trusted by the majority, is a lie and a fraud.'[1] Torn from its context this quotation could have been endorsed by the ideologists of Populism, who postulated the primacy of 'social' over 'political' problems and sharply criticized the 'anti-popular' character of the constitutional programme. In Samarin's case, of course, the context makes it clear that in his criticism of constitutionalism he used the slogan of a 'people's constitution' only as a means of protecting the interests of the nobility as he saw them. Bureaucratic absolutism, Samarin argued, represented the only real guarantee of these interests, and the renunciation of their political pretensions in favour of tsarist absolutism was the price the nobility had to pay for the maintenance of its social position. In Samarin's view the Land *Duma* recommended by Koshelëv would become the scene of irresponsible pronouncements that would irritate both the Emperor and the people and lead to a direct alliance between them. In a letter to Cherkassky on 27 November 1862 Samarin was quite outspoken about his fears:

In the present circumstances [he wrote] the convention of a Land *Duma* would place an entire group of men who represent the essence of Russian education, the whole of educated Russia, between two fires; the impotence and isolation of this group would be utterly exposed and its idiotic ambitions would ensure an inevitable *rapprochement* between the ruler and the masses—a *rapprochement* at the expense of intermediate Russia [i.e. the nobility] and one that would favour arbitrary rule and ignorance. *Les suites peuvent être incalculables, et la leçon serait payée trop cher.*[2]

The document that best illustrates Samarin's political theories is probably his 'Letter to R. Fadeev' which, together with an article by F. Dmitriev, made up a volume entitled *Revolutionary Conservatism* published in 1875 in Berlin (in order to avoid censorship). The Letter polemicizes against the eminent Panslavist and conservative political leader General R. Fadeev, author of a book entitled *Russian Society: Present and Future*, which contained a programme for strengthening and providing

[1] Ibid., p. 178. [2] Ibid., pp. 178–9.

legal guarantees for the class privileges of the nobility, and attacked the 'bureaucratic' methods used to carry out the land reform. Samarin found Fadeev an eminently suitable opponent, since his ideas could be attacked on two fronts at once, both as too conservative and as too 'revolutionary'.

Fadeev's main argument was that every society owes its unity to a 'superior cultural group' that is an organic product of historical evolution. In Russia, as in the other countries of Europe, this section of society was the nobility; the bureaucratic reforms of the 1860s had weakened its position and helped to disintegrate it as a class, thus initiating a process of social atomization; the restoration of civic unity was therefore synonymous with the restoration of the nobility as the 'ruling estate'. According to Samarin, this diagnosis was based on the illusion that the Russian nobility could be compared to the Western European aristocracy. In fact, he maintained, it had always been an estate composed of 'men in service', and there was no point, therefore, in making a distinction between the nobility and the 'bureaucracy'—the Russian nobleman was the 'bureaucrat's' own brother, the same official after he had taken off his uniform and imagined himself to be a German *Junker* or an English *lord*.[1] True conservatism in Russia, Samarin insisted, was represented not by the nobility but by the common people; the 'anti-bureaucratic' pretensions of the nobility were therefore basically a form of 'revolutionism', and even akin to nihilism in their attempts to transplant Western models on to Russian soil and thus to destroy the historically conditioned social system.[2] Fadeev's attacks on bureaucracy, Samarin wrote, sprang from his conviction that the social substance could be forced into a ready-made mould borrowed from abroad, and was therefore itself the product of a bureaucratic and rationalistic rather than a conservative style of thought. 'Revolution', he wrote, 'is rationalism in action, or, in other words, a formally correct syllogism converted into a battering-ram and aimed at the freedom of the living social substance. Its first premiss is always an absolute dogma derived deductively or obtained by universalizing specific historical phenomena.'[3] This formula

---

[1] See Samarin and Dmitriev, *Revolyutsionnÿ konservatizm* (Berlin 1875), p. 49.
[2] See ibid., pp. 2–3.
[3] Ibid., p. 10.

was intended to prove that Fadeev's anti-bureaucratic conservatism was in fact 'revolutionism', since it was the so-called bureaucracy in Russia that represented 'vital traditions' and the 'freedom of the living social substance'.[1]

Samarin's more prosaic explanation of why the land reform had to be carried out 'bureaucratically' is equally revealing. The men who had drafted the emancipation act, he wrote, realized that it would disappoint the peasants. However, they faced the unembellished truth and did not try to console themselves with a fictitious picture of the nobility 'standing at the head of the common people and enjoying its confidence'. 'They knew', Samarin wrote in a direct appeal to Fadeev, 'that if the people perceived in the new statute the product of "its own organized moral and intellectual force", as you call the nobility, its disillusionment could assume a dangerous form and that a peaceful solution could only be relied on if the statute was accepted by the people as a direct expression of the Emperor's own thought and will, independent of any influence whatsoever on the part of the nobility.'[2] In similar fashion Samarin refuted Fadeev's reproach that the authors of the emancipation act had tried to reduce the nobility's influence on the peasantry. On the contrary, argued the 'incorrigible Slavophile' (as he called himself). The setting-up of the *Zemstvos* helped to consolidate the nobility's standing, since now the landowners would be able to bring their influence to bear on the peasants in their capacity as elected members of the *Zemstvos* rather than as representatives of the 'ruling estate'.[3]

This is indeed a far cry from the Slavophile utopia, from the 'love for the common people' and fanatical adherence to principles that had impressed Herzen so greatly in the Slavophiles—and also in Samarin—during the 1840s. The 'realistic'

---

[1] It is worth noting that in the 1850s, before the Editorial Committees started their work, Samarin's 'bureaucratic' sympathies were not quite so marked. In a note on the margin of de Tocqueville's *L'Ancien Régime et la révolution* he noted, in keeping with the views of the classical Slavophiles, his opposition to the 'autocracy of intellect and government' and drew a parallel between the 'tyranny of reason in the sphere of philosophy, faith, and conscience' and the 'tyranny of the central government in social life'. See Samarin, *Sochineniya*, i. 401–2. Samarin himself admitted that his ideas had undergone an evolution (see, e.g., *Revolyutsionnȳ konservatizm*, p. 30).

[2] Samarin and Dmitriev, *Revolyutsionnȳ Konservatizm*, p. 72.

[3] Ibid., pp. 27–8, 46.

transformation of Slavophilism destroyed the noble-mindedness and imaginative flights of the Slavophile utopia, but it cannot be denied that elements of classical Slavophile doctrine, torn from their context, continued to function in the ideologies of Samarin and Koshelëv, serving to mask or disguise the variously interpreted but altogether concrete class interests of the nobility. Samarin's apologia for a bureaucratic state had little in common with Konstantin Aksakov's conviction that statehood as such was a soulless mechanism, 'the principle of evil, of external constraint'; on the other hand it is true that the same Aksakov had also insisted that Russia had never had an aristocracy, that the Russian nobility was essentially an estate of 'servitors', that representatives of the 'Land' made no attempt to restrict the authority of the tsar and—unless invited to do so—did not interfere in political decisions. Koshelëv's flirtation with Western liberalism was clearly at odds with the spirit of the Slavophile utopia, but in support of his views he could point to the Slavophile critique of bureaucratic absolutism in the post-Petrine age, the ideal of a *rapprochement* between State and Land, the idealization of ancient Russian representative institutions and the demand for their restoration.

It is understandable that once Slavophilism was 'cleansed' of its utopian elements it made great headway among the gentry represented on the *Zemstvos*. In keeping with the spirit of the times, Koshelëv's version proved especially attractive since it provided an ideal ideological platform for the conservative liberals among the nobility, who were hostile to the bureaucracy, but reluctant to identify themselves with the outright demand for constitutional government. Among the most influential leaders of this group were Dmitry Shipov, for many years chairman of the Moscow *Zemstvo* (a position of symbolic significance from the point of view of Slavophile doctrine) and after 1905 one of the founders of the Octobrist party, and two younger Khomyakovs: Dmitry, an eminent lay leader in the Church, who propagated an 'independent' paternalist autocracy, and Nikolaï, the later Octobrist who was elected chairman of the third State *Duma* in 1907. The most outstanding politician of the three was undoubtedly Shipov,[1] whose 'Slavo-

---

[1] The ideas and activities of Shipov (until 1905) are discussed by G. Fischer, *Russian Liberalism. From Gentry to Intelligentsia* (Harvard University Press 1958).

philism' was largely confined to propagating the idea of a representative advisory body modelled on the ancient Russian Land Assemblies and to opposing 'Western' constitutional government as a potential breeding-ground of internecine power struggles. These notions, which satisfied neither the conservative liberals nor the consistent supporters of absolutism, formed the basis of the political programme set out in the collective memorial drafted by Shipov and presented by the provincial gentry marshals in 1905.[1]

Various aspects of this last stage in the evolution of Slavophilism as a political doctrine can here only be touched on in passing, since their closer analysis would require a detailed historical exposition outside the chronological or thematic scope of the present work. It is interesting, however, to quote the intelligent and malicious analysis of Shipov's programme made by P. N. Milyukov in his article 'A New Variant of Slayophile Political Doctrine'. The future leader of the Constitutional Democrats aptly pointed out that the anti-constitutional tirades of the epigones of Slavophilism were essentially a constitutional programme in disguise, although a programme that was exceptionally cowardly, anti-democratic, and openly prejudiced in favour of the gentry. In his concluding passage Milyukov wrote:

At last, it would appear, we begin to understand. And together with the dazzling new ideas and conjectures our brows clear: we begin to gaze earnestly at the mysterious, concentrated faces of the authors of the plan and say to them: give us your hands, friends, you belong to *our side*, you too are 'constitutionalists'.

But no! Wait a moment! You are constitutionalists, and so are we, but what have you done with our universal franchise and many other good things? I beg your pardon, gentlemen, whom are you trying to hoodwink? Those at the top or those below? Perhaps both at once? . . . No, you had better travel alone along that Byzantine road of yours and leave us to our Western European straightforwardness.[2]

An outline of the chief trends in Slavophile political thought of the second half of the century ought to include at least a

---

[1] Published in the journal *Law* (*Pravo*) (1905), no. 11.

[2] P. Milyukov, 'Novÿ variant slavyanofil'skoĭ politcheskoĭ doktriny̆', in *Russkoe*

short account of Samarin's and Koshelëv's position on the Polish question. This is important, if only because of the role they played in Congress Poland after the suppression of the 1863 uprising. Samarin was the source of ideological inspiration and close assistant of Nikolaï Milyutin, who was appointed state secretary in Poland by the Tsar from September 1863 to December 1866;[1] Koshelëv, at this time, was in charge of financial policies in Poland.

Samarin explained his point of view on the Polish question in a lengthy article entitled 'The Present-day Scope of the Polish Question' published in 1863 in the Slavophile periodical *Day*. According to Samarin the Polish question had three clearly distinct aspects, namely (1) the Polish nation, that is the Polish people who bore the stamp of an entirely distinct Slavonic nationality; (2) the Polish state, which had always been rapacious towards its neighbours; and (3) 'Polonism', a cultural force closely linked to Catholicism whose representatives were the Polish gentry and clergy. 'Polonism', Samarin argued, had transformed Poland into a 'sharp wedge driven by Latinism into the very heart of the Slavonic world with the aim of splitting it into fragments'.[2] It had been responsible for destroying the Slavonic village commune, had created a feudal aristocracy unknown in the other Slavonic nations, had turned the Polish state into an enemy of Slavdom and a faithful vassal of Europe. Poland had nevertheless remained a Slavonic nation and the 'Latin soul' of the nobility and clergy had not succeeded in killing the 'Slavonic soul' of the common people. Therefore, Samarin concluded, the Russian government ought to seek support among the people and declare uncompromising war on 'Polonism' in the name of 'Slavism'. The question of a possible re-emergence of the Polish state—within ethnic boundaries— would be tackled later. 'Poland's future, if she has a future, lies in the Slavonic world and in a harmonious coexistence with all nations, and not at the tail end of the Latin world.'[3]

Bogatstvo (1905), no. 4, p. 130. The programme of the Shipovites (and other neo-Slavophile groupings) is also analysed in M. D. Chadov, *Slavyanofilȳ i narodnoe predstavitel'stvo* (Kharkov 1906), chapter 5.

[1] On Samarin's influence on Milyutin see S. J. Zyzniewski, 'Milyutin and the Polish Question', in *Russian Thought and Politics, Harvard Slavic Studies*, vol. iv (1957).

[2] Samarin, *Sochineniya*, i. 333.

[3] Ibid., p. 342.

This diagnosis was responsible for Milyutin's policy of social demagogy with its artificial fanning of antagonism between the gentry and the peasantry, and for his campaign to restrict the influence and undermine the material base of Polish Catholicism. It explains his continual and finally successful attempts to persuade Russia to annul the concordat with the pope,[1] and finally, in spite of the lip-service paid to the Polish people's right to its own nationality, it provided a theoretical basis for such curious excesses of Russification as Prince Cherkassky's idea of replacing the Latin by the Cyrillic alphabet.[2] For the sake of historical accuracy it must be admitted that this 'Social Caesarism' policy did in fact benefit the Polish peasants. The land reform carried out in Congress Poland in accordance with a plan worked out by Milyutin, Samarin, and Cherkassky,[3] was far more advantageous to the peasants than its Russian counterpart. Polish peasants benefited from (proportionately) larger allotments, the immediate remission of all labour dues and debts, the right to customary easements, and, most important of all, the fact that no redemption payments were imposed.

In its practical consequences Koshelëv's standpoint on the Polish question differed somewhat from Samarin's. During his term of office as director (or, in other words, minister) of finance in Congress Poland Koshelëv came to the conclusion that the repressive measures undertaken after the uprising were being carried too far, that the total assimilation of Polish territory would be both easier and more effective if more 'liberal' methods were used. In particular he objected to Milyutin's policy towards the gentry. The Polish emancipation act, he wrote in his memoirs,

did not clash with my convictions, but knowing Prince Cherkassky and N. A. Milyutin, I feared lest the decree would not only be the last of the military acts aimed at suppressing the unrest in the Kingdom of Poland, but also the origin and source of other attempts to restrict and frustrate the nobility with whom I did not, of course,

---

[1] See Zyzniewski, op. cit., p. 247.

[2] See ibid., p. 246. In 1865 several school-books by S. P. Mikutsky and the Panslavist A. Hilferding were printed in Polish, but using the Cyrillic script. See M. Boro-Petrovich, op. cit., p. 167.

[3] The final version of the plan was the work of Samarin; see Zyzniewski, op. cit., p. 240; and A. Leroy-Beaulieu, *Un homme d'état russe* (Paris 1884), p. 224.

sympathize, but whom I considered to play an irreplaceable role in our day and age and for that reason at least to be deserving of a certain indulgence and protection.[1]

An even clearer and less veiled expression of this point of view is to be found in the special memorandum on the Polish question presented by Koshelëv to the Emperor in November 1866, after his resignation. 'We cannot concentrate all power in the hands of the peasants and rely solely on them,' Koshelëv wrote with instructive exaggeration; 'to do this would be to betray our entire traditions and change our entire system of government; one cannot conduct affairs in one part of the empire in a spirit of extreme democracy and in the rest uphold other and healthier principles.'[2] Or again: 'The introduction of a bureaucratic and ochlocratic system of this kind in one part of our state would have dire consequences in the others; it would mean infecting Russia with such a disease, injecting such venom into her healthy body, as would poison her own strength and prepare her downfall.'[3]

The differences that divided Koshelëv and Samarin on the Polish question were clearly related to their basic political conceptions. It is worth adding that neither of these conceptions in the long run satisfied the tsarist government which was ready to adopt a policy of 'social' absolutism in special circumstances, but preferred its traditional reliance on the propertied classes. After 1866, that is in the post-Milyutin era, the oppressive anti-Polish measures introduced in the 'Vistula provinces' were tempered neither by the more liberal administrative approach recommended by Koshelëv, nor by any kind of social reforms.

[1] Koshelëv, *Zapiski*, p. 143.   [2] Ibid., Appendix, p. 224.
[3] Ibid., p. 228.

12

From Slavophilism to Panslavism

In the domain of foreign policy the most important and also the most immediate successor to Slavophilism was Panslavism. The fact that it was in such close line of succession to Slavophilism and that its most influential leader was Ivan Aksakov, who thought of himself as loyally carrying out the testament of the earlier Slavophiles, has occasionally caused the two movements to be identified, to the detriment of a true understanding of either trend.

The relationship between Slavophilism and Panslavism is a complicated one and differs according to the particular thinker or period we are dealing with. From the point of view of the present study it is enough to distinguish between three main stages in the history of this relationship: the first includes almost the entire reign of Nicholas I, when Slavophilism appeared in its classical, utopian form; the second, intermediate stage covers the years 1853–61, from the events preceding the Crimean War to the death of Khomyakov and K. Aksakov; the third stage saw the rapid spread of Panslavist ideas and—Ivan Aksakov's convictions notwithstanding—their growing emancipation from Slavophile influence. The culminating point of this third stage—the time when Panslavism exerted its greatest influence on tsarist policy—came in the years immediately preceding the war with Turkey (1877–8) and Bulgarian independence.

During the first of these stages Slavophilism had little in common with Panslavism, whose theorist and propagator was Mikhail Pogodin, the leader of the nationalist faction among the proponents of Official Nationality. During the 1840s the only Slavophile to hold obvious pro-Slavonic sympathies bordering on Panslavism was Khomyakov. Originally even the term 'Slavophile' meant not so much a friend of the 'brother Slavs' as a man who upheld a 'pure Slavonic' as against a Westernized Russia. When he was arrested together with Samarin in 1849

Ivan Aksakov could in all good faith make the following statement to the police on the attitude of the Slavophiles towards
Panslavist trends:

We do not believe in Panslavism and consider it impossible:
(1) because unity of religion of the Slavic peoples would be indispensable for this, whereas the Catholicism of Bohemia and
Poland constitutes a hostile and alien element which is incompatible
with the element of Orthodoxy among the other Slavs; (2) all the
separate elements of the Slavic nationalities might be dissolved and
merged into a whole only in another mightier, more integrated,
more powerful element, that is the Russian; (3) the greater part of
these Slavic peoples are already infected by the influence of barren
Western liberalism which is contrary to the spirit of the Russian
people and which can never be grafted on to it. I admit that Russia
[*Rus'*] interests me much more than all the other Slavs, while my
brother Konstantin is even reproached for complete indifference
to all the Slavs except those of Russia, and then not all but particularly those of Great Russia.[1]

The deterioration in Russo–Turkish relations and the wave
of chauvinism that greeted Russian military intervention in
Moldavia and Wallachia brought about an entirely different
situation. Khomyakov was not alone in calling upon the
standards to fly and the trumpets to sound; a document preserved in the Moscow archives shows that Konstantin Aksakov
was also affected by the mood of the times and that it was he—
together with Khomyakov—who was the first to link Slavophile
ideas with a Panslavist political programme. Although in this
document—his memorial *On the Eastern Question* (6 February
1854)—Aksakov opposed the gentle and peaceful Slavonic
spirit (represented in its purest form by Russia) to predatory,
individualistic, and aggressive Europe, the memorial is by no
means an example of 'gentle' and 'peaceful' persuasion. Aksakov
stressed the need for a 'holy war' against Turkey's Western
allies, a war that would allow Russia to fulfil her 'Christian and
fraternal duty' of liberating all Slavs and all people of Orthodox
faith from the Turkish yoke. No more time should be lost, he
wrote, for the united power of Europe must be met by the
united power of Slavdom; 'doubt and hesitation are tantamount

[1] Quoted from Boro-Petrovich, *The Emergence of Russian Panslavism*, p. 41.

to lack of faith in God's aid and in ourselves'; if need be 'the whole of Russia will be transformed into a military camp'. This war of liberation, as Aksakov called it, which had been declared for the sake of 'moral principles', would bring Russia territorial advantages.

A new path to greatness and power thus opens up before Russia. . . . A great age is dawning, one of the greatest in world history—a lasting alliance of all Slavs under the supreme patronage of the Russian tsar. Moldavia and Wallachia, as regions inhabited by peoples without any individual significance, ought naturally to be incorporated into Russia. It is not likely, either, that anyone else will be able to keep possession of Constantinople. And since ignoble and ungrateful Austria opposes us, and has broken off all relations with Russia, she has released us from our obligations and untied our hands. There too [i.e. in Austria] Russia will fulfil her mission of liberating the ethnically homogeneous and largely Orthodox peoples; she will naturally incorporate her former province of Galicia and the whole Slavonic world will breathe more easily under the patronage of Russia once she finally fulfils her Christian and fraternal duty.[1]

This quotation contains the entire political programme of Panslavism in a nutshell. K. Aksakov's lengthy epistles to his parents, written during his travels abroad in 1860, prove that Panslavistic hopes were alive in him until the very end.[2]

A document of another kind, which shows the Slavophiles' attitude to Panslavism during this transitional period (1853–61) from a different angle, is the famous *Letter to the Serbs* (1860) written by Khomyakov and signed by the two Aksakov brothers, Koshelëv, Samarin, and several other Slavophiles and Slavophile sympathizers.[3] The *Letter* says nothing about a 'holy war' or a future Slavonic federation, or—God forbid—of Russian patronage over Slavdom: its advice is that of an experienced 'elder brother' given to a younger Slavonic nation that has only recently achieved independence. The *Letter to the Serbs* was an attempt to apply Slavophile doctrine to the situation of

---

[1] O vostochnom voprose, Tsentr. Gos. Lit. Arkhiv. (Moscow), fond 10, op. 1/219.

[2] See Tsentr. Gos. Lit. Arkhiv. (Moscow), fond 10, op. 1/26.

[3] Others who signed the *Letter to the Serbs* were M. Pogodin, I. Belyaev, N. Elagin, P. Bezsonov, P. Barten'ev, and F. Chizhov.

the Southern Slavs, an attempt to stimulate among them an intellectual movement close to the ideology of the authors of the *Letter*. It was therefore not so much an expression of Panslavism in the precise sense of the word (although the influence of Panslavism is not in doubt), as of Slavophilism in the literal, etymological sense of the word.

The greatest good fortune of the Serbs, maintained the authors of the long and rambling letter, was their Orthodox faith. This faith, however, was not merely a matter of religious rites, but must be raised to the rank of a social principle. The social expression of Orthodoxy was the commune and adherence to the decisions of the *mir* and this had been preserved only in the Orthodox lands. This communal principle implied the condemnation of glaring social inequality and of the cleavage between the upper classes and the people that was so typical of the Western nations and of Poland (whose downfall it had caused). Although many lessons could be learned from the West, there was no point in mere imitation as practised by the Russians, or rather by the 'enlightened layers of society' divorced from the people. The letter advised the Serbs to preserve their own strict customs, not to give up their national dress in order to please Europe, to maintain the purity of their native tongue, and to despise the whims of fashion; in a word, they should be themselves and not attempt to become Europeans, since a mania for all things European could mean the betrayal of true Slavdom, as the example of Poland had shown. Legal decisions should be based on the voice of conscience and not on formal prescriptions, and in all collective decisions the native Slavonic principle of unanimity should be applied or recourse should be taken to an acceptable arbiter. The government should be strong but must not restrict freedom of speech or the press. In fact, the *Letter* emphasized, Serbia had every chance of escaping the disease that had cost Russia so much and that had only recently begun to abate; her task was to seize this chance and provide the world with an example of a strong and happy Slavonic nation.

The 'new Moscow Gospel', as the *Letter* was described by the Serbian philologist and nationalist politician Djuro Daničić, did not on the whole inspire much enthusiasm among the Serbs. It had its supporters among the 'Russophils' but was strongly condemned by the progressive nationalist movements.[1] The eminent nationalist historian Stojan Novaković called the *Letter* an expression of Russia's aspiration to political hegemony over the Slavs and quoted the following passage from the programmatic leading article in I. Aksakov's paper *Day* in confirmation of his thesis: '*To liberate the Slavonic nations from material and spiritual oppression* and to bestow upon them *independent* spiritual and possibly *political* existence under the wing of the mighty Russian eagle—that is Russia's historical mission, moral privilege, and duty.'[2]

The periodical *Day* (*Den*) (1861–5), the first Panslavist journal in Russia with a large circulation, opens the third stage in the history of the transformation of Slavophilism into Panslavism, which witnessed the latter's emergence as a real political force. The leading figure during this time was Ivan Aksakov, who became chairman of the Slavophile Welfare Society in Moscow after Pogodin's death (i.e. after 1875). Under his leadership this Panslavist organization became extremely influential, especially during the Russo–Turkish war in 1877–8. It is safe to say that Ivan Aksakov was the best-known Slavophile in Russia as well as abroad and that from the 1860s to the 1880s the average educated Russian's knowledge of the senior Slavophiles came primarily from articles by Aksakov published in his journals *Day*, *Moscow* (*Moskva*) (1867–8), and *Russia* (*Ruś*) (1880–5). It is a measure of Aksakov's influence among the Southern Slavs that after Bulgaria achieved independence several electoral committees suggested him as a candidate for the throne.[3]

Unlike his brother, Ivan Aksakov was not an original mind and made no new contribution to Slavophile theory. In the 1840s and '50s he was the least 'orthodox' of the Slavophiles and the most susceptible to liberal and democratic ideas. 'A magnificent youth', Belinsky wrote in 1846. 'A Slavophile, who behaves as if he had never been a Slavophile.'[4] Aksakov's verses written in the 1840s had few specifically Slavophile characteristics: on the whole they tended to reflect the typical despondency and suffering of the 'superfluous men' and his verses on folk

---

[1] See Boro-Petrovich, op. cit., p. 101.   [2] *Den* (1861),no. 1.
[3] See Masaryk, op. cit. i. 289.
[4] Belinsky, xii. 296–7.

themes—which show his opposition to serfdom—are reminiscent of Nekrasov.[1] During the 'thaw' Koshelëv—himself hardly an orthodox Slavophile—rebuked Aksakov for his lack of reverence for the monarchy and Church, his excessive opposition to the government, and sympathy for Herzen's *Bell*.[2] It is even more of a paradox that as late as 1860—several months after he had taken over the editorship of the pro-Panslavist journal *Sail* . . . —which was closed down for its articles on freedom of speech and a critical attitude to the emancipation act—and immediately before becoming editor of the openly Panslavist *Day*, Aksakov still had doubts as to the feasability of Panslavist ideals and even wondered whether the Slavs under Austro-Hungarian rule were either desirous or capable of achieving independence.[3]

The year 1861 opened a new chapter in Aksakov's intellectual biography. The death of both his brother and of Khomyakov put an end to his vacillations and impelled him to assume the mantle of chief defender and dogmatic propagator of Slavophile doctrine; at the same time, under the impact of 'nihilism', his own political views grew more and more reactionary. A specific role in this process was played by the Polish uprising of 1863 and the terrorist activities of the People's Will organization which culminated in the assassination of Alexander II on 1 March 1881. Although at first Aksakov was not unsympathetic to the Polish demands for independence, after the outbreak of the uprising he became one of the leading organizers of the chauvinistic anti-Polish press campaign and for the rest of his life lost no opportunity of portraying Poles as 'renegades of Slavdom'. Under the impact of the revolutionary movement this one-time liberal—in the broadest meaning of the word— became bitterly hostile towards even the slightest manifestation of political liberalism, even to the extent of refusing to make a distinction between a 'liberal party' and an 'anti-Russian' party. Koshelëv, who during the 'thaw' had attempted to moderate Ivan Aksakov's liberal transports, towards the end of his life thus described his relationship with the latter:

[1] See Dement'ev and E. S. Kalmanovsky, 'Poeziya Ivana Aksakova' (Introduction to I. Aksakov), *Stikhotvoreniya i poemỹ* (Leningrad 1960).

[2] Dement'ev, *Ocherki* . . ., pp. 395–6.

[3] See K. Aksakov's account in a letter to his parents from Prague, 12 September 1860, Tsentr. Gos. Lit. Arkhiv. (Moscow), fond 10, op. 1/26.

In recent years, although we have maintained the most friendly personal relations, we have drawn far apart in our views, even on significant issues. He reproached me for deviating from Slavophilism and allowing myself to be influenced by my friends among the liberals; I reproached him for the loss of that animating spirit which had distinguished Khomyakov and made him great, and for clinging grimly to certain peculiarities and fortuitous attributes of Slavophilism which had some meaning once but have now lost it completely. . . . What I found particularly distasteful were Aksakov's outbursts against the liberals, against the juridical system, representative institutions, the new courts, etc. These pronouncements of his were openly aimed at us supporters of the new reforms and he thus stood, as it were, under the standard of Katkov.[1]

It is of course possible to find arguments in Aksakov's 'defence'. His personal honesty and high civic courage cannot be denied. He was capable of undertaking an energetic defence of freedom of conscience and freedom of speech and throughout his life clung to the belief that these were inborn rather than 'political' rights.[2] He stressed his independence, for instance by his sharp criticism of various government measures and his almost ostentatious conflicts with the censor; in 1873, when defending himself against the accusations of Mamonov quoted above, he pointed out not without a certain pride that all his periodicals so far—*Sail*, *Day*, *Moscow*, and *Moskvich*—had been closed down by the authorities.[3] All these facts do not, however, affect the over-all diagnosis that Ivan Aksakov represents a glaring example of the evolution of Slavophilism towards chauvinistic nationalism and extreme social and political reaction. His friendship with the reactionary Director General

[1] Koshelëv, *Zapiski*, pp. 249–50.

[2] This is shown by his letter to Pobedonostsev, 2 December 1870, in which he expresses his indignation at the Emperor's rejection of the address of the Moscow *Duma*: 'Is there no difference, then, between autocracy and oppression of the believer's conscience, opinion and words? Does it [the Russian autocracy] in fact deny all humanity, all dignity in its subjects and by turning them into dumb creatures demand from them one thing only, namely mindless obedience? . . . I confess that I thought otherwise: so too did those men who signed the Moscow address, but are they not now pouring ridicule on our Moscow idealism in Petersburg? . . . We are prepared to be obedient and we are obedient as no other nation in the world—but do not force us into lies, servility, and ignominy. Our social conscience aches from the unchanging falsehood and immorality of our situation, and the nagging need for truth is becoming more and more strongly felt.' Tsentr. Gos. Lit. Arkhiv. (Moscow), fond 10, op. 1/160.

[3] See *Russky Arkhiv* (1873), no. 12, p. 2529.

of the Holy Synod, Konstantin Pobedonostsev, his close relations with court circles, and the official condolences sent on his
death by Alexander III show how far he had travelled along
this road by the end of his life. While one ought not to overlook
the fact that in the last resort he did not identify himself
completely with the ultra-reactionary Pobedonostsev, this does
not affect the general trend of his political evolution.

A discussion of the ideological content of the seven volumes
of Ivan Aksakov's *Collected Works* would be out of place in the
present study. It is interesting to draw attention to what is
perhaps their most characteristic feature, namely Aksakov's
obstinate adherence to the 'letter' of Slavophilism, and almost
complete, though not conscious, sacrifice of the anti-capitalist
spirit of the Slavophile utopia. This too found symbolic expression in his presidency of one of the leading Moscow banks (the
Merchants' Mutual Credit Society) which he took on in 1874.
This does not mean that anti-capitalist elements simply disappeared without a trace: a more reasonable interpretation is that
they suffered a characteristic transformation into anti-Semitism
—the 'socialism of fools'[1]—which figured largely in Aksakov's
ideology after 1861 and clearly sets him apart from the earlier
Slavophiles.[2]

There would also seem to be little point in analysing the
contents of the first volume of Aksakov's *Works*, containing his
articles and pronouncements on the Slavonic question. All the
typical Panslavist stereotypes are to be found there—the antithesis of Slavdom and Europe, belligerent animosity towards
Austria, dismissal of the Poles as the traitors to Slavdom,
demands for the conquest of Constantinople and the establishment of a powerful federation of 'liberated' Slavs 'under the
wing of the Russian eagle'; what is missing however is an
original philosophy of history. One is forced to the conclusion
that whatever Aksakov may have intended, Panslavism played
a destructive role in relation to Slavophilism since it drew
attention away from its most meaningful aspects. Interest in
the Slavonic nations as carriers of superior moral principles

[1] An expression used by August Bebel.
[2] Among the epigones of Slavophilism the two open anti-Semites were I. Aksakov
and Y. Samarin. In classical Slavophilism anti-Semitism had no place. N. V.
Riasanovsky (op. cit., p. 115) writes: 'Anti-Semitism acquired a definite place in
the Slavophile ideology only after the death of the early Slavophiles.'

and above all of the 'community principle', and interest in
Slavonic lands as a possible testing-ground for the Slavophile
utopia (which still figures largely in the *Letter to the Serbs*),
gradually became narrowed down into speculations concerned
only with the interests of Russia as a great power. This point
of view, which attempted to reconcile the interests of the state
with Great Russian nationalism, brought Aksakov closer to the
'father of Panslavism' and first chairman of the Slavonic Welfare Society, Mikhail Pogodin. Like the latter, he too wanted to
see a 'national' government that would subordinate home
policies to Russian nationalism and foreign policies to Panslavism. Unlike Pogodin, however, he was able to be more open
about his aims and was not afraid to criticize the government
or to appeal directly to nationalistic circles. The most extreme
example of this was his speech to the Slavonic Society on
22 June 1878, in which he denounced Russian diplomats
('Petersburg diplomats' in his nomenclature) for their concessions at the Congress of Berlin and compared them to Nihilists
such as Vera Zasulich, who were 'devoid of all historical consciousness and all vital national feelings'.[1] Opinions of this kind
did not necessarily spring from Slavophile convictions. It is clear
that for all his subjective loyalty to family tradition, in Aksakov's
interpretation Slavophile doctrine had lost all independent
significance and had shrunk to little more than a stylistic
embellishment of chauvinistic nationalism.

Although Ivan Aksakov was the most active of the Panslavists
he was not their leading theorist, since pietism towards Slavophile doctrine prevented him from undertaking its revision and
reinterpretation. The first and probably unique systematic
exposition of Panslavism was Nikolaĭ Danilevsky's *Russia and
Europe* published in the periodical *Dawn* (*Zarya*) in 1869 and
reissued several times in subsequent years. The philosophical
interpretation of history expounded in this book will be discussed in another context; from the point of view of this chapter
it is interesting to examine to what extent Danilevsky's Panslavism was related to the ideas of the early Slavophiles.

---

[1] I. S. Aksakov, *Rech' proiznesennaya 22 iyunya 1878 v Moskovskom Slavyanskom
Blagotvoritel'nom Obchestve* (Berlin 1878), p. 21. For this speech Aksakov was
deprived of the right of residence in Moscow for several months.

Nikolaĭ Strakhov, an enthusiastic admirer of Danilevsky, wrote in his foreword to the third editon of *Russia and Europe* that the book could be 'called a complete catechism or codex of Slavophilism', and suggested that 'in days to come, Nikolaĭ Yakovlevich Danilevsky will perhaps be considered a Slavophile *par excellence*, the culminating point in the evolution of this trend, a writer who concentrated within himself the entire power of the Slavophile idea'. Elsewhere, however, Strakhov wrote that when he used the term Slavophilism what he had in mind was not the narrow historical sense of the word, but its 'abstract, universal, ideal' meaning: 'In actual fact this is not really Slavophilism but a separate doctrine expounded by Danilevsky, something that might be called "Danilevskyism" which contains Slavophilism but not the other way round.'[1] This reservation is certainly an important one: Danilevsky, a naturalist by profession and a former member of the Petrashevsky Circle, did not share Ivan Aksakov's scruples; he undertook a *conscious* selection and revision of Slavophile ideas, thus transforming them into components of an ideological structure differing from classical Slavophilism and constructed on different foundations.

In the first place Danilevsky—the theoretician of militant Panslavism—had to reject the Slavophile standpoint on statehood, since the vision of the conquest of Constantinople and the creation of a powerful economic and military federation of Slavonic nations led by Russia was clearly at odds with a doctrine that described Russians as a peace-loving Christian people who lived by the light of the 'inner truth' in small self-sufficient communes and regarded the state as a 'necessary evil'. In his assessment of the role of Peter the Great Danilevsky also laid stress on the political and military successes that helped to create a powerful empire rather than on the undignified 'aping' of Europe introduced by the reforms. The greatest changes are to be found in his interpretation of the historical mission of the Russian people: for the Slavophiles this mission had been the defence of the principles of 'true Christianity', social integrity, and spiritual wholeness, that is of certain universal ideals; for

<hr/>

[1] N. Y. Danilevsky, *Rossiya i Evropa. Vzglyad na kul'turnye i politcheskie otnosheniya slavyanskogo mira k germano-romanskomu*, 4th edn. (St. Petersburg 1889), iv, pp. xxiv–xxv.

Danilevsky the end that sanctified all the cruelties of Russian history was primarily the creation of a powerful state organism whose natural expansion would be subservient only to scientific evolutionary laws. Europe, he wrote indignantly, refused to recognize Russia's mission and assigned her merely a modest role in 'civilizing' Central Asia. A great nation could not be content with such a role; it was not for this that Russia had toiled in blood and sweat to build her state; she had not suffered serfdom and the Petrine Reforms merely in order to 'serve European civilization to five or six million uncouth louts from Kokand, Bukhara, and Khiva'.[1] Fortunately Russia's destiny was quite different; the Russian people, like the other Slavonic peoples, bore within it the germ of a new cultural and historic type of civilization which had nothing in common with the Germano-Romanic civilization of Europe. This new civilization would only come to flower with the conquest of Constantinople and its establishment as the capital of a Slavonic empire liberated and united by Russia. Therefore, Danilevsky argued, the 'concept of Slavdom' ought to be, after God, the supreme ideal of every Slav, an ideal standing 'higher than freedom, higher than learning, higher than education, higher than all worldly goods, for unless this ideal is realized all these are beyond our grasp'.[2]

According to Danilevsky, the Slavophiles had been mistaken in attributing an absolute and therefore universal value to 'Slavonic principles'. This was in effect the same mistake as that made by the Westernizers, who identified European civilization with a universal culture. Danilevsky denied the existence of universal values shared by the whole of mankind and instead suggested that humanity expresses itself solely in specific 'historico-cultural types' that cannot be compared but are simply different; to attempt to compare and evaluate them from the point of view of their supposedly universal significance is just as nonsensical, he argued, as to ask which concrete plant form— palm or cypress, oak or rose—better expresses the 'concept of plant'.[3] Since there can be no such thing as a universal mission,[4] the Slavs could not have been selected to fulfil such a mission,

[1] Ibid., pp. 62-3.
[3] See ibid., p. 121.
[2] Ibid., p. 133.
[4] See ibid.

nor could they—as a collective-body—represent 'true Christian principles' in their actions, since such principles only have validity in relation to individuals. The demand for the 'Christianization of politics', the 'mysticism and sentimentalism' of the period of the Holy Alliance, did not take into account the fact that only individuals are immortal and that self-sacrifice, the highest measure of Christian morality, can be demanded of them alone.

State and nation [Danilevsky wrote] are transitory phenomena existing in time alone and therefore the laws governing their activity, that is politics, can only be based on this temporal existence. This does not justify Machiavellism but only proves that everything must be measured by its own criteria, that every class of beings or phenomena is governed by its own laws. An eye for an eye and a tooth for a tooth, a severe law, the Benthamite principle of utilitarianism, of a properly conceived self-interest—that is the law governing foreign policy, the law of international relations; there is no room in it for love or self-sacrifice.[1]

In accordance with this 'law' Danilevsky called for the rejection of the surviving hold of legitimism on foreign policy and preached an openly cynical attitude to international alliances: 'We must abandon the notion of any kind of support for European interests, any kind of connection with this or that European political configuration; above all we must achieve complete freedom of manœuvre, the right to a potential alliance with any European state, regardless of what political principles it represents at any given moment, and on the sole condition that this alliance is in our interest.'[2]

A convenient amoral political programme of this kind was bound to be most welcome in nationalist circles. The term 'amoral' is not perhaps the most appropriate in this context: Danilevsky did not ignore moral criteria, but only selected a different concept—that of Slavdom rather than of Christianity—as the supreme moral frame of reference for Russia. From this 'Slavonic' standpoint it was easy for him to pronounce judgement on the 'Jesuitical gentry state of Poland', that 'Judas of Slavdom', which he compared to a hideous tarantula greedily devouring its eastern neighbour but unaware that its own body

---

[1] N. Y. Danilevsky, *Rossiya i Evropa*, pp. 31–2.
[2] Ibid., p. 488.

is being eaten by its western neighbours.[1] It was from this point of view, too, that he condemned imperial policy for its 'softness' towards Europe and accused the government of overlooking the interests of Russia and her Slavonic sister nations for the sake of currying favour with the West.[2] Even towards Poland, Danilevsky thought, the Russian government had shown an excess of truly gallant chivalry.[3]

On home policy Danilevsky's point of view largely coincided with Samarin's: both supported the notion of a 'social monarchy' that would stand above classes, both indulged in the same anti-aristocratic social demagogy, and defended Alexander II's 'Great Reforms'. On the latter issue, however, Danilevsky later changed his mind. In the original edition of *Russia and Europe* he defended the juridical reforms against the charge that they were 'aping Europe', insisted that specifically Western elements played an entirely secondary role in them, and quoted Khomyakov's defence of the jury system as a native Slavonic institution.[4] In the third posthumous edition, however, Nikolaï Strakhov included marginal notes made by Danilevsky (probably in 1880–1) in one of his own copies. 'What I wrote here is nothing but rubbish', Danilevsky commented on his previous statements. 'The reform had only just been introduced and people wanted to believe—and therefore did believe—that it would assume a sensible character; in actual fact it turned into a caricature of foreign ideas. If we had been more sober in our judgement we would and should have foreseen this.'[5] His previous comments on the jury system Danilevsky dismissed even more succinctly: 'As a legal form this is nonsense, appropriate for peoples with a primitive epic social system but not given the intricate political relations of a modern state.'[6]

These quotations show that, impelled by his dissatisfaction with the proceedings and verdicts of the great political trials

[1] See ibid., p. 33.

[2] See ibid., pp. 32–9.

[3] Danilevsky thought that in 1815 Alexander I should have demanded the Russian part of Galicia and left ethnic Poland to Austria and Prussia. He called the incorporation of Congress Poland into Russia a gesture due to the 'sentimental generosity' of the Emperor, who wished to restore Poland and thus to expiate his grandmother's guilt. See Danilevsky, op. cit., p. 33.

[4] Ibid., p. 300.

[5] Ibid., p. 300 n. 1.

[6] Ibid.

of the 1870s, Danilevsky moved closer to Katkov, the leading ideologist of the 'counter-reforms' of Alexander III. Katkov, it is worth adding, was also a militant Panslavist, although he could not lay claim to even partial Slavophile provenance. This fact provides additional support for the thesis that in its final stage Panslavism no longer had any need of this provenance.

13

Conservative Romanticism in the Second Half of the Nineteenth Century

DANILEVSKY owes his place in Russian intellectual history not only to his political doctrines but also to his theory of 'historico-cultural types', which cannot be regarded simply as a theoretical underpinning for Panslavism. In order fully to understand this theory, which might perhaps be said to derive from Slavophilism by an 'indirect' line of descent, it should be examined within the context of the evolution that took place in the romantic philosophy of history in Russia in the second half of the nineteenth century. From this point of view the ideas of the literary critic and romantic poet Apollon Grigor'ev are of particular interest.

Grigor'ev (1822–64), in the early 1850s one of the 'young editors of the *Muscovite* (*Moskvityanin*)',[1] and later the leading ideologist of the *pochvenniki*,[2] who were grouped around the journal *Time* (*Vremya*) edited by the Dostoevsky brothers, was not a member of the Slavophile circle but considered himself to be one of their disciples. His regard for Slavophile philosophy is shown by his sharp reply to Mikhail Dostoevsky, who asked him to refrain from calling Kireevsky and Khomyakov 'great thinkers', as this might expose their journal to ridicule in the eyes of progressive readers. Grigor'ev called this request a 'terrifying symptom', the worst possible testimony to the rationalistic 1860s.[3] Grigor'ev's own writings, however, contain a number of very critical comments on Slavophilism. Brought up in Zamoskvorech'e, a conservative old-style merchant suburb

---

[1] This was the name given to a number of writers grouped around A. N. Ostrovsky who wrote for the *Muscovite* in the early 1850s. The 'young editors' tried to change the character of Pogodin's journal, but were unable to overcome opposition to their plans and had to resign.

[2] From the word *pochva* meaning soil.

[3] See A. A. Grigor'ev, *Materialy dlya biografii*, ed. by Vl. Knazhnin (Petrograd 1917), p. 266.

of Moscow, the passionate and sensual 'last romantic' of the 1840s represented a strange cross between the 'open nature' of a robust Russian and the 'fractured soul' of the decadent aesthete. His impulsiveness and almost innate sense of 'homelessness', his disappointment in love and attacks of vague longing which found relief in crazy drinking bouts and revels with a guitar and gipsies, created around him a specific atmosphere quite unlike the Slavophiles' patriarchal traditionalism. It is interesting to note that Grigor'ev accused the Slavophiles of exaggerating the significance of the 'family principle' in Russian history and instead advanced the argument that Russians were far less concerned with the family than Western Europeans and had to be *forced* to adopt a settled way of life.[1] The Slavophiles, he wrote, had overlooked the essentially Schellingian dualism of the 'Russian principle',[2] which embraced not only strict *mores* and exact religious observation but also the unsubdued spontaneity of the 'open nature'—sinful but conscious of its sinfulness—portrayed in Ostrovsky's Lyubim Tortsov and in so many folk epic heroes.[3] By recognizing only the former aspect the Slavophiles, Grigor'ev thought, had committed the same error as the Old Believers, had lost their sense of the future, and had shown themselves incapable of understanding Schelling's profound notion that 'wild Bacchanalia' often heralded the appearance of a 'new God'.[4]

In March 1856, in reply to Koshelëv's invitation to contribute to the journal *Russian Conversation*,[5] Grigor'ev pointed out in a detailed letter that he was fully in agreement with the Slavophiles only in a 'negative sense': they had common dislikes, he wrote, but not common likes. He differed in his attitude to art and aesthetic values, for instance, to which, unlike the Slavophiles, he attached autonomous significance, and in his conception of nationality. The Slavophiles were enamoured of the ancient Boyar past[6] whereas he himself believed that vital national principles, the 'eternal essence of ancient Russia', had

---

[1] See the often quoted passage from Grigor'ev's poem 'Olimpiï Radin', *Izbrannie proizvedeniya* (Leningrad 1959), pp. 275–6.

[2] Grigor'ev, *Materialÿ* . . ., pp. 189, 198.

[3] See ibid., pp. 189, 198.

[4] Ibid., p. 183.

[5] See ibid., pp. 150–1.

[6] See ibid., p. 185.

been best preserved among social groups unaffected by serfdom and should therefore be sought among the conservative Moscow merchant class[1] rather than among the patriarchal peasantry. In view of these (and other less important) differences of opinion nothing came of the proposed collaboration with the Slavophiles. Grigor'ev's extravagant 'aestheticizing' romanticism was alien both to the Slavophile 'realists' and to the Slavophile 'utopians': from the point of view of their monistic, 'truly Christian' system of values they were bound to be suspicious of his rapturous delight in cultural pluralism, in the diversity of national cultures, in their 'scent' and 'colours', and of the aestheticism which affected even his conception of Orthodoxy. In this respect he was indeed much closer to Herder than to his Slavophile teachers.

Grigor'ev's philosophical views, like those of the Slavophiles, represented a variant of romantic irrationalism and were clearly influenced by Schelling's Philosophy of Revelation. In particular he opposed all rationalist 'theories' in the name of 'immediate', intuitive knowledge, and set 'life', 'organicity', and 'history' against 'theory' and 'logic'. His own philosophy he summed up in the following sentence: 'Not reason itself with its logical exigencies and the theories they give rise to, but reason and its logical exigencies plus life and its organic manifestations.'[2] The most dangerous theory, according to Grigor'ev, was the Hegelian philosophy of history. In his critique of Hegelianism he proposed to differentiate between what he called the 'sense of history' and the 'historical view', that is the theory—put forward by Belinsky among others—of infinite and universal progress.[3] In the name of the first (the 'sense of history') he dismissed the second (the 'historical view'), since he saw in it a mere 'theory', a new variant of the eighteenth-century point of view, with all its dogmatism and abstractness. The danger of this theory, he claimed, consists in its peculiar combination of fatalism and relativism, resulting in a moral indifferentism according to which neither individuals nor nations were responsible for their own lives, but were merely

---

[1] Ibid., pp. 151, 198.

[2] Grigor'ev, *Sochineniya* (St. Petersburg 1876), i. 624.

[3] See Grigor'ev's article 'Vzglyad na osnovȳ, znachenie i priëmȳ sovremennoĭ kritiki iskusstva' (1858), *Sochineniya*, vol. i.

instruments of the 'abstract spirit of mankind'. Hegel himself, he conceded, possessed the 'sense of history', but in his supporters it had disappeared altogether, so that they were left with nothing but a dogmatic teleological 'theory of history', an abstract model of development implying that the historical evolution of every nation must proceed according to the same rationally pre-established sequence of goals. This theory, like all varieties of rationalism, implied thus that it was possible to speak of an 'abstract spirit of mankind', a notion that Grigor'ev dismissed as illusory since in his view only concrete individualities—either individual human beings or collective individualities—could be said to possess reality.

In his critique of Hegelian 'instrumentalism' Grigor'ev used similar arguments to those put forward by Herzen and Belinsky—he attempted to demonstrate that personality cannot be reduced to the role of instrument of the *Weltgeist*. This similarity cannot be taken too far: Grigor'ev was essentially closer to the Polish philosophers who opposed panlogism and the autocracy of reason.[1] The thinkers of the philosophical Left in Russia set out to establish the autonomy of the individual and to free the latter from 'determination by natural forces'; Grigor'ev on the other hand was more interested in the originality, individuality, and unique (unrepeatable) typical features of individuals as representatives of this or that collective entity. Whereas Belinsky and Herzen valued in the individual personality the rational 'universally human' element, Grigor'ev valued it above all as an irrational 'uniqueness'. His conception of the nation, too, was intended to justify theories of a 'distinct' and specifically Russian evolutionary path. Herzen's identification of the personality with conscious and autonomous *activity* was also unacceptable to Grigor'ev, who thought that man's vocation is to listen to the irrational pulse of life, and not to seek conscious control over it. Life, he wrote, 'is directed by a creativity flowing from one source, by that vital focus of the supreme laws of life itself'.[2] The ultimate source of activity was God. Thus the 'sense of history' led Grigor'ev to discard the 'philosophy of action'.

Grigor'ev attributed the merit of transcending the 'historical

---

[1] Especially Libelt and Cieszkowski.
[2] Grigor'ev, *Sochineniya*, i. 205.

view' to the later Schelling, whose Philosophy of Revelation had once more endowed nations with a unique, irrational, exclusive personality unaffected by the so-called universal laws of human evolution. Nations, he wrote, are organisms each of which 'is locked up within itself, is governed by its own necessity, is permitted to live in its own way according to laws specific to itself, and need not serve as a transitional form for any other organism . . . several such *homogeneous* organisms, closely bound together by ties of cultural homogeneity, created the cycles of the ancient, medieval, and modern world'.[1]

This passage contains the essence of the notion later developed by Danilevsky in his theory of 'historico-cultural types'.[2] Elements of this theory can be found in Slavophile doctrine— for instance in the cyclical conception of historical time or in Khomyakov's critique of 'the mystical conception of a collective spirit of a collective mankind'—although they do not fit in with its Christian universalism.[3] In Grigor'ev's romantic aestheticism these elements were woven into a more consistent whole, although this entailed the sacrifice of the notion of a universal Church and the transformation of religion into one of the ingredients of a 'distinct' and 'exclusive' culture. Danilevsky's contribution was merely to elaborate the theory in various ways and—in the spirit of the times—to give it an underpinning of natural science.

Grigor'ev's dislike of Hegel's 'historical view' had its exact counterpart in Danilevsky's dislike of Darwinism.[4] For Schelling's Philosophy of Revelation Danilevsky substituted Cuvier's classification of species, and replaced the 'evolutionary' point of view by a morphological one. Aestheticism, or rather aesthetic criteria deriving beauty from the variety and distinctiveness of

[1] Ibid., pp. 209–10.

[2] In his *Natsional' nȳ vopros v Rossii* Solov'ëv stressed in particular that the theory of historico-cultural types was first put forward by the German historian Heinrich Rückert (1823–75). From the point of view of the present study Rückert's possible priority is of no consequence, since the *Weltanschauung* on which the theory was founded had much earlier roots. Both Rückert and Danilevsky essentially systematized a current conception which was very characteristic of romantic conservatism, aestheticism, and 'diversitarianism'. See A. O. Lovejoy, *The Great Chain of Being* (Harper Torchbooks, New York 1960), p. 294.

[3] See pp. 332–4.

[4] Danilevsky, op. cit., p. 87.

'types of organization' also figured largely in Danilevsky's doctrine. 'Beauty', he wrote, 'is the only spiritual aspect of matter and therefore the only connecting link between two basic principles of the universe. . . . The need for beauty is the sole spiritual need that matter alone can satisfy.' 'God desired to create beauty and therefore he created matter.'[1]

Cuvier's contribution, according to Danilevsky, was to differentiate between the 'evolutionary stage' of organisms and their 'types': 'These types are not evolutionary stages on the ladder of gradual perfectibility (stages that are, one might say, placed in a hierarchical order of subordination), but entirely different plans—plans without a common denominator—in which each entity evolves in a specific and distinct fashion towards the multiplicity and perfection of forms within its reach.'[2] Translated into historical terms this meant the elimination of one-directional universal progress. In place of abstract 'humanity' (a common denominator and a common measure of everything human) Danilevsky proposed the notion of 'all-humanity' (*vsechelovechestvo*), i.e. a plenitude and harmony arising out of cultural and national differences which could not be reduced to a common denominator or placed in an evolutionary line. Anticipating theories later worked out by Spengler and Arnold Toynbee,[3] Danilevsky divided mankind into 'historico-cultural types' comparable to different styles in architecture and painting;[4] progress was something that could only take place within the various types; the categories of organic growth, such as youth, maturity, and old age, could only be applied to historico-cultural types, and not to mankind as a whole.[5] In view of the multiplicity and variety of historical phenomena there was no point in attempting to formulate theories that claimed to embrace the whole of universal history; these were invariably based on the characteristic 'false perspective' of Europeocentrism—the unconscious identification of the history of mankind with the history of Europe.[6]

---

[1] Danilevsky op. cit., pp. xxx–xxxi.   [2] Ibid., p. 87.

[3] On Danilevsky's possible influence on Spengler, see P. Sorokin, *Social Philosophies of an Age of Crisis* (London 1952), p. 79; on the similarity (or differences) between the theories of Spengler and Tonybee see R. G. Collingwood, *The Idea of History* (Oxford University Press, New York 1957), pp. 181–3.

[4] See Danilevsky, op. cit., pp. 87–8.

[5] See ibid.   [6] See ibid., p. 85.

Danilevsky distinguished ten types of civilization in history: (1) Egyptian, (2) Chinese, (3) Assyro-Babylonian-Phoenician-Chaldean or Ancient Semitic, (4) Hindu, (5) Iranian, (6) Hebrew, (7) Ancient Greek, (8) Roman, (9) Neo-Semitic or Arabian, and (10) Germano-Romanic or European. From the point of view of their 'principles' these civilizations were 'incommensurable', but they could be compared from a formal point of view. There are 'mono-elemental' types, for instance, which could lay claim to achievements in one cultural sphere alone, and 'multi-elemental' types which could boast of cultural achievements in many spheres; some types were completely 'exclusive', whereas others were capable of assimilating 'cultural material' (but not 'principles'!) created by types coexisting with them or preceding them.[1] Cultural activity, in the broadest sense of the word, evolved in four principal spheres: (1) the religious sphere, (2) the cultural sphere, in the narrow sense of the word, i.e. science, art, and technology, (3) the political sphere, and (4) the social and economic sphere. Hebrew civilization was a mono-elemental religious type, ancient Greece represented the cultural (primarily artistic) type, and Rome was known for its political achievements; in contrast to the Chinese and Hindu civilizations each of these types was capable of assimilating the achievements of other cultures. European civilization was composed of two elements—political and cultural—and was capable of a far-reaching and creative assimilation.

Unlike the Slavophiles Danilevsky was not hostile to the Germano-Romanic 'principles' and did not judge European history by absolute aesthetic criteria. He regarded the European 'type' as one of the outstanding products of culture and history, perhaps the most outstanding so far, but at the same time he carried further the Slavophile diagnosis of the 'decay' and organic dissolution of Europe. European history, he thought, could be divided into three periods of peak achievement: the first was the thirteenth century, which saw the flowering of an aristocratic and theocratic culture. After intellectual liberation (in the fifteenth century) and the liberation of conscience (the Reformation) came the second period of achievement, the seventeenth century, which represented the creative apogee of

[1] See ibid., pp. 91–2.

European history. (This was the age, he thought, to which all European conservatives—with the exception of the Ultramontane Catholics, who wanted to go back even further—looked back with the greatest nostalgia.) Liberation from feudalism at the close of the eighteenth century ushered in the third and last period of achievement—the technical and industrial age. During this age (in 1848) new forces entered the historical arena, which, according to Danilevsky, desired the total liberation and total destruction of the old European culture. In a note added to a later edition of his book Danilevsky called the Paris Commune another and more terrifying embodiment of these forces: 'It was the beginning of the end.'[1]

Russia and the Slavonic nations were, however, exempted from this European decline. Russia, Danilevsky maintained, did not belong to Europe, whatever the Westernizers might cite to the contrary; best proof of this was that Europe herself did not think of her as 'one of us' and turned her back on her in hatred.[2] Positive evidence of Russia's distinctiveness was her solution to the peasant question, which entailed the distribution of land to the peasants but also the preservation of the village commune as a safeguard against proletarianization. By turning her back on Europe and shutting herself off from her, by conquering Constantinople and liberating and uniting her brother Slavs, Russia would create a new, eleventh type of culture. Danilevsky was sure that this would be the first 'tetra-elemental' type, since for the Slavs he claimed the ability to be active in all four spheres of culture, above all in the religious sphere (Orthodoxy) and the social and economic sphere (the agrarian solution).[3] Thanks to the Slavs' extra-subtle capacity for understanding other cultures and assimilating their achievements, the Slavonic 'type' was likely to be closest to the ideal of 'universal humanity'. For the time being, however, while this new type was in process of formation, Danilevsky thought that greater stress should be laid on individuality and distinctiveness

[1] See Danilevsky, op. cit., pp. 253–4.

[2] According to Danilevsky, hatred of Russia was the only bond uniting a divided Europe. 'In this respect clericalists join hands with liberals, Catholics with Protestants, conservatives with progressives, aristocrats with democrats, monarchists with anarchists, reds with whites, legitimists and Orleanists with Bonapartists.' Danilevsky, op. cit., p. 321.

[3] See ibid., pp. 516, 557.

than on the ideal of 'universal manhood' (in Herder's meaning of the term), which was fully attainable in God alone. Particularly in relations with Europe he recommended 'exclusivity and patriotic fanaticism' as an essential counterweight to European influence. In order to straighten the bent tree, he wrote, the utmost force must be used to pull it to the other side.[1]

It was thus that Danilevsky filled in the gaps in Panslavist policy with the elements of a Panslavist utopia. As we have already mentioned, it was characteristic of this utopia that it sanctioned and even postulated a brutal and utterly cynical 'realism' in the choice of means leading to the desired end. No doubt that is why in spite of its utopian elements Vladimir Solov'ëv called Danilevsky's doctrine a 'creeping' rather than a 'winged' theory.[2]

Both Grigor'ev and Danilevsky directly influenced the philosophy of Konstantin Leont'ev (1831–91), the most original individual personality among the extreme reactionaries of the reign of Alexander III. This ultra-conservative romantic was a figure as colourful as he was lonely; even in reactionary circles his ideas failed to call forth a response since they were too remote from any acceptable type of conservatism such as Katkov's.[3] Unlike the epigones of Slavophilism, Leont'ev cannot be called an ideologist of the 'Prussian' or any other road to capitalist development: he was an integral reactionary, the last uncompromising defender of Russian, Western European, or even Turkish feudalism.

The emotion that informs Leont'ev's entire work is a contemptuous hatred of 'bourgeois plebeianism', of the 'average man' and his philistine ideals of 'universal prosperity' and 'rational middle-class happiness'. After his death he was even referred to as the 'Russian Nietzsche'.[4] Aestheticism was an important component of this aversion to 'bourgeois values': even in his early youth Leont'ev disliked the railways, that

---

[1] See ibid., pp. 109, 468.

[2] See Solov'ëv, *Natsionalnyĭ vopros v Rossii*, 3rd edn. (St. Petersburg 1891), i. 112–13.

[3] Katkov refused to publish Leont'ev's *Byzantinism and Slavdom* in the *Russian Messenger*.

[4] See N. Berdyaev, *Konstantin Leont'ev. Ocherk iz istorii russkoĭ religioznoy mỹsli* (YMCA Press, Paris 1926), pp. 37–9.

symbol of bourgeois civilization, and condemned European dress, as 'unbearably commonplace' and devoid of the picturesque.[1] Man, he wrote, ought to model himself on nature, which 'adores multiplicity and magnificence of forms', whose inalienable attribute is beauty, systematically annihilated by universalizing tendencies. Beauty is revealed in clear-cut distinction, peculiarity, individuality, in a specific colouring; its prerequisite is differentiation and therefore inequality; by opposing harsh social differences in the name of the 'autonomous personality', liberal humanism and individualism 'destroyed the individuality of persons, provinces, and nations',[2] while all 'sentimentalism' or 'eudaemonism' prevented the emergence of powerful and splendid characters who were only formed by misfortunes and injustices.[3] If such liberal and egalitarian ideals as universal prosperity and the spread of middle-class values were to be implemented, mankind would be disgraced and history become meaningless. 'It is impossible', Leont'ev exclaimed, 'that mankind should become so disgustingly happy.'[4]

Is it not terrible, is it not humiliating to suppose that Moses climbed Mount Sinai, that the Hellenes built their enchanting citadels, that the Romans fought their Punic Wars, that the handsome Alexander crossed the Granicus in his plumed helmet and fought at Arbela, that the apostles proclaimed the word of God, that martyrs suffered, poets sang songs, painters painted, and knights glittered at tournaments—and all this so that the French, German, and Russian *bourgeois* in his ugly and ridiculous attire might enjoy the blessings of peace, 'individually' or 'collectively', on the ruins of past greatness? . . . One would have to blush for mankind if this shabby ideal of universal utility, of shallow, commonplace work and inglorious prosiness were to triumph for centuries.[5]

The same thoughts are developed in more detail in Leont'ev's chief work, *Byzantinism and Slavdom* (1875), which sets out the conclusions he drew from his nine years of diplomatic service in the Near East and his stay among Orthodox monks on Mount Athos. It has been aptly remarked that this book, which puts

---

[1] K. N. Leont'ev, *Sobranie sochineniĭ*, 9 vols. (St. Petersburg 1912–14), vii. 350.
[2] Ibid. v. 147.   [3] See Berdyaev, op. cit., p. 107.
[4] Leont'ev, *Sobr. soch.* vii. 469–70.
[5] Ibid. v. 426.

forward an original interpretation of the culture and evolution of social organisms, anticipates Spengler's theory of the transition from 'culture to civilization';[1] one might add that it also has certain features in common with contemporary criticism of mass culture.

Leont'ev suggests that not only biological evolution but also the evolution of artistic styles or whole social organisms passes through three fundamental stages. The starting-point is a period of simplicity, in which a primitive homogeneity prevails both in the whole and in its component parts. The transition to the second stage is a process of growing complexity in which both the whole and its component parts become individualized, but at the same time are welded together by the 'despotic unity of forms'; the climax of this second stage is a period of 'flourishing complexity', of maximum differentiation within the framework of a specific individualized morphological unit. From this moment evolution passes into disintegration and, through a secondary simplification, leads to a levelling fusion of the component elements and therefore a new monochromatic simplicity. This third stage—that of 'a levelling fusion and simplicity'— heralds the approaching death of the organism.

In his philosophy of history, Leont'ev made use of Danilevsky's theory of 'types', which he substituted for 'abstract humanity' as the protagonist in the process of evolution and disintegration. The history of Western Europe naturally provided a classic example of cultural decay that was both a lesson and warning to Russia. The climax of European progress was the period between the Renaissance and the eighteenth century; this was followed by the process of 'decay' which heralded the third stage, the disintegration of the differentiated morphological unity. During this stage everything became 'laxer and shallower'; while industry expanded and prosperity was on the increase, culture disintegrated because cultural individuality, its unique, unrepeatable style is possible only under an integrating 'despotism of form'; by this standard China and Turkey were more highly cultured than Belgium or Switzerland.[2]

---

[1] See Berdyaev, op. cit., pp. 95, 260. See also P. Sorokin: 'Indeed, in all its essential characteristics Spengler's work is a mere repetition of the social speculations of Leontieff and Danilevsky.' P. Sorokin, *Contemporary Sociological Theories* (Harper and Brothers, New York–London 1928), pp. 25–6, footnote 49.

[2] See Leont'ev, *Sobr. soch.* v. 147.

The main symptom of Europe's decay, according to Leont'ev, was the 'liberal and egalitarian process', which, he wrote,

is *the antithesis of the process of evolution.* In the process of evolution the inner idea firmly holds the social fabric in its organizing and despotic grip, and restricts its divergent and centrifugal tendencies. Progress, on the other hand, in its struggle against despotism—the despotism of estates, guilds, monasteries, and even fortunes—*is nothing other than a process of disintegration,* the process of that secondary simplification of the whole and levelling interfusion; this is a process which levels the morphological contours and destroys specific features organically (i.e. despotically) related to the given social body.[1]

From this theory Leont'ev drew special conclusions about the role of statesmen. Prior to the period of 'flourishing complexity', he suggested, right is on the side of the progressives who lead the nation from the stage of primitive simplicity towards differentiation and proliferation of forms. During the period of disintegration, however, right is on the side of the conservatives who try to hold back the process of atomization.[2] This was the situation not only in Europe but also in Russia, where the 'liberal and egalitarian process' had made headway after the death of Nicholas I. 'Russia must be frozen to save her from decay', was the thesis Leont'ev used to justify the ultra-reactionary programme put forward by Pobedonostsev.

Leont'ev agreed with Danilevsky that Russia, though exposed to the 'pestilent breath' of Europe, did not belong to the European 'type', but differed in his definition of the specific nature of 'Russianness'. Russia, he maintained, could not by any means be called a purely Slavonic country, since the originality of its culture was largely determined by its Asiatic elements.[3] Slavdom was something 'amorphous, spontaneous, unorganized',[4] whereas Russia was above all heir to the Byzantine civilization which Danilevsky, strangely enough, had overlooked in his theory of 'types'. From this Leont'ev concluded that the conquest of Constantinople would enable Russia to create a new cultural type that would not, however, be 'Slavonic' but 'neo-Byzantine'. Byzantinism, as embodied in Orthodoxy and autocracy, had been the 'disciplining principle' in

---

[1] See Leont'ev, *Sobr. soch.* v. pp. 198–9.   [2] See ibid., p. 208.
[3] See ibid. vii. 340.   [4] Ibid. v. 113.

Russian history. 'Slavism' as such did not exist, for without Byzantinism the Slavs were merely so much ethnographic material, extremely vulnerable to the disintegrating influence emanating from Europe;[1] if the southern Slavs had retained their originality it was only thanks to Turkey, who had 'frozen' their culture and fenced them off from liberal Europe.[2] During his stay in the Near East Leont'ev had fallen in love with Turkey and had, at the same time, come to hold the Slavs in thorough aversion. In particular he disliked the Bulgarians, in whom he claimed to see symptoms of a premature old age—the uninterrupted transition from the first to the third evolutionary stage, the immediate transformation of 'swineherds' into middle-class liberals.[3]

Leont'ev's harsh judgement of the Slavs was in part determined by his over-all attitude to nineteenth-century nationalism; he devoted a separate essay to this subject, with the revealing title *National Policy as an Instrument of World Revolution*. In it he put forward the view that nations are a creative force only when they represent a specific culture; 'naked' or purely 'tribal' nationalism is a force directed against culture and the state; by levelling internal differentiation it is, in fact, cosmopolitan; essentially it is merely a mask for liberal and egalitarian tendencies, a specific embodiment of the universal process of disintegration. To illustrate this thesis Leont'ev argued that under Turkish rule Greece had been an original country, whereas after gaining independence she had rapidly begun to lose her 'distinctiveness', thus disappointing the hopes of the Hellenists; the liberation of Italy and the unification of Germany proved equally disappointing;[4] nationalist movements among the Slavs were moving in the same direction: nationalist passions had caused the Bulgarians to quarrel with Orthodoxy as represented by the Greek metropolitan and to adopt a European constitution after gaining independence.[5] On the Slavonic

---

[1] See ibid., pp. 148–65.

[2] Danilevsky too wrote that 'the icy hand of the Turks' had protected the Southern Slavs against European influences. 'We see now that this icy hand was more useful to the Serbs than their liberation.' Danilevsky, op. cit., p. 345 and footnote.

[3] See Leont'ev, *Sobr. soch.* vii. 198, 518.

[4] See Leont'ev, *Natsional'naya politika kak orudie vsemirnoĭ revolyutsii* (Moscow 1889), pp. 8, 11, 13 (published under another title in vol vi of Leont'ev's *Works*).

[5] See ibid., pp. 46–7.

question Leont'ev tended to agree with Nicholas I rather than with Pogodin and the Panslavists. In his *Byzantinism and Slavdom* he argued that it was not the Slavs as such that were deserving of affection and support, but merely their originality;[1] in practice this meant that support should be granted not to the Slav nationalists but to the standardbearers of 'Byzantinism'—the Greek phanariots. This conclusion conflicted with the 'Slavonic' policies of the government of Alexander II and put a stop to Leont'ev's diplomatic career.

From having been Danilevsky's enthusiastic admirer and in a sense his disciple, Leont'ev came to repudiate Panslavism, the latter's brain-child. 'From now on', he wrote, 'we should regard Panslavism as something very dangerous if not downright fatal';[2] the 'younger brother' among the Slavs, who had been infected by the spirit of egalitarian liberalism, was in fact the worst enemy of the distinct Orthodox-Byzantine culture.[3] It was not by chance, Leont'ev wrote, that Panslavism had made headway in Russia at a time when liberal ideas were rapidly gaining ground, that is during the period of the 'Great Reforms' which had blurred the distinction between Russia and Europe in her decline.[4] This should not be taken to imply that Leont'ev was no longer interested in the conquest of Constantinople, but only that he was anxious for Russia to abandon the policy of 'liberating' her brother Slavs. Austria and Turkey, he felt, should long continue to rule over her Slavonic subjects, since the absence of political independence was the sole factor that induced them to cultivate their cultural distinctiveness.[5] In fact the Turkish and Austrian yokes should not be thrown off before Russia was mature enough for her mission and was herself able not only to liberate but also to direct the future of Slavdom.

Leont'ev was convinced that Constantinople would ultimately be conquered, but far from sure whether this was enough to allow Russia to create a new and original culture. She was a country that could hardly be called young, he wrote with regret;[6] although the policy of Alexander III was one

---

[1] See Leont'ev, *Sobr. soch.* v. 257.
[2] Leont'ev, *Natsional'naya politika* . . ., p. 44.
[3] See Leont'ev, *Sobr. soch.* v. 259.
[4] See Leont'ev, *Natsional'naya politika* . . ., p. 25.
[5] See ibid., p. 32; and *Sobr. soch.* v. 257-8.
[6] See Leont'ev, *Sobr. soch.* v. 258.

of 'salutary reaction' it was impossible to tell whether this would 'heal' Russian society, which since the 1860s had been profoundly affected by corrosive processes. Although the conquest of countries with an original Orthodox–Byzantine culture would strengthen Russian Byzantinism, Leont'ev deplored the fact that by gaining independence these countries were at the same time falling prey to the 'liberal and egalitarian' plague. Towards the end of his life, in the early 1890s, he finally lost his faith in Russia's capacity to create a distinct new cultural type. The future, he prophesied, belonged to socialism; perhaps, a Russian tsar would stand at the head of the socialist movement and would 'organize' and discipline it just as the Emperor Constantine had 'organized' Christianity; or perhaps, he wrote in another apocalyptic prophecy, a democratized and secularized Russia would become the land of anti-Christ.[1]

Throughout all his despairing doubts and catastrophic premonitions Leont'ev was consoled only by his conviction that the hated liberals would not triumph, that the new rulers who would emerge from the crisis of European and Russian culture would be neither 'liberal' nor 'mild'.[2] If further imitation of the sick West were to lead Russia to revolution, he wrote in 1880, this revolution would ultimately set up 'a regime whose strictness will surpass anything we have yet seen'.[3] European and Russian socialists, he wrote elsewhere, would not put up a memorial to the liberals:

They are right to despise them. . . . However hostile these people [the socialists] are to the actual conservatives and the forms and methods of their conservative activity, nevertheless all the essential aspects of conservative doctrines will prove useful to them. They will require terror, they will require discipline; traditions of humility, the habit of obedience, will be of use to them; nations who (let us suppose) have already managed successfully to reconstruct their economic life but have nevertheless failed to find satisfaction in earthly life, will blaze up with renewed enthusiasm for mystical doctrines.[4]

A cursory examination of Leont'ev's views suffices to show that he was not a Slavophile in either the historical or the

---

[1] Quoted from Berdyaev, op. cit., pp. 212, 217.
[2] See Leont'ev, *Sobr. soch.* vii. 213.   [3] Ibid., p. 205.   [4] Ibid., p. 217.

etymological meaning of the term. Among scholars opinions
are divided: earlier writers (P. Milyukov and S. Trubetskoĭ)[1]
called him a 'disillusioned Slovophile', the product of 'the disintegration of Slavophilism'; later however, under the influence
of Berdyaev's monograph, the prevailing point of view was that
Leont'ev's neo-Byzantinism was in no way related to Slavophile
doctrine and in fact represented its diametrical opposite. In
support of the former interpretation one may quote Leont'ev's
own reference to himself as a Slavophile; on the other hand it
must be noted that he also openly rejected classical Slavophilism
and frequently condemned it as an inconsistent doctrine that
served as a disguise for egalitarian and liberal trends. Leont'ev
considered himself to be truly indebted only to Grigor'ev and
Danilevsky, although the latter too he accused of holding many
'false and ill-considered' opinions. Kireevsky and Khomyakov
he tended to dismiss at times as mere precursors of Danilevsky.[2]

The meaningful relationship that undoubtedly exists between
Leont'ev and the Slavophiles is in no way invalidated by the
fact that in order to understand it one must first establish and
indeed highlight the *differences* dividing the author of *Byzantinism
and Slavdom* from both the classical Slavophiles and their
epigones. That both sides were clearly aware of these differences
is shown by Ivan Aksakov's dismissal of Leont'ev's views as a
'lascivious cult of the truncheon'.[3]

Two aspects of Leont'ev's philosophy of history have already
been touched upon, namely his attitude to the Slavs and his
'aestheticism'. As well as rejecting 'purely political Panslavism',
Leont'ev also sharply ridiculed such values traditionally
ascribed to the Slavs as 'mildness' and a 'peace-loving' nature.
In contrast to the Slavophiles, what he prized in the Russians—
from a purely 'tribal' point of view—was the infusion of Asiatic
('Turanian') blood and the 'Orthodox *intus-susceptio* of strong and
imperious German blood'.[4] Another Russian peculiarity, accor-

[1] See Milyukov, 'Razlozhenie slavyanofil'stva', in *Iz istorii russkoĭ intelligentsii*
(St. Petersburg 1902); and S. Trubetskoĭ, 'Razocharovannȳ slavyanofil', *Vestnik
Evropȳ* (1892), no. 10, *Sobr. soch.*, vol. i.
[2] See Leont'ev, *Sobr. soch.* vii. 216, 324. It is worth adding that elsewhere (vi.
335) Leont'ev admitted that in the 1860s he had been 'Khomyakov's disciple' and
that Slavophilism made a strong appeal to his 'Russian heart'.
[3] See M. D. Chadov, *Slavyanofily i narodne predstavitel'stvo* (Kharkov 1906), p. 45.
[4] Leont'ev, *Sobr. soch.* vii. 323.

ding to Leont'ev, was a proneness to brute force (*nasil'stvennost'*) which theoretically even Danilevsky had rejected and attributed to the 'European type' alone. This inclination gave rise to a love of armed conquest which the Russians shared with the ancient Romans, although the latter had made no attempt to conceal it and felt no 'false shame'.[1] On the issue of Russian 'family feeling' Leont'ev agreed with Grigor'ev and suggested that among the Great Russians the obverse of weak family ties was a deeply rooted monarchism.[2] Leont'ev's ideal tsar, however, was not a 'kind father' but a severe patriarch feared by his children; the Russian people, he claimed, likes severe generals and church dignitaries, for strict government is best suited to its 'Byzantine sentiments'.[3]

> Slavophilism [Leont'ev wrote] seemed to me to be too close to egalitarian liberalism to serve as a protective fence against the contemporary West. That is one thing; another aspect of this doctrine that aroused my mistrust was a certain one-sided moralism. This doctrine seemed to me unsatisfactory from the point of view of both state and aesthetics. On the issue of statehood Katkov was far more satisfactory. . . . As far as aesthetics are concerned, both in history and in life's external manifestation, I felt much closer to Herzen than to the true Slavophiles'[4]

This was a reference to Herzen's critique of the Western European bourgeoisie, in which aesthetic repulsion played an important role. Nevertheless Leont'ev's aestheticism would appear to belong rather to the conservative and romantic aestheticism of Grigor'ev and Danilevsky, which was closely related to their anti-universalism. Leont'ev best illustrates not only the anti-capitalist and anti-industrial edge of this aestheticism but also its basic immoralism—he boldly claimed that immoral acts and traits could be 'beautiful', that evil, in fact, was a necessary element in the aesthetics of multiplicity, colour, and force. This 'amoralism' contrasted strongly with Slavophile moralism and especially with Konstantin Aksakov's rejection of 'aesthetics'—the love of formal extravagance and delight in a 'fine gesture and pose'—as an expression of sinful pride characteristic of the West but alien to true 'Russian principles'. It is quite clear that the Slavophile vision of ancient Russia

---

[1] See ibid., pp. 320, 324.   [2] See ibid. v. 127–9.
[3] See ibid. vii. 180.   [4] Ibid. vi. 335–6.

with its 'harmony', homogeneous customs and morals, and the alleged absence of clearly demarcated class divisions, was the reverse of Leont'ev's aesthetic ideal. His vision of 'flourishing complexity' was more likely to be found in the West, with its government 'based on constraint', its division into conquerors and conquered, its splendid knighthood, and its Church ambitious for hegemony over the secular government. Unlike the Slavophiles Leont'ev admired 'ancient' Europe and ascribed Slavophile criticism of feudalism and the Western aristocracy to the influence of the 'new' and 'liberal' Europe. 'From this point of view', he wrote, 'I have always considered the Slavophiles to be men professing an utterly commmplace, European, and moderately liberal style of thought.'[1] This naturally affected their interpretation and judgement of the focal problems of Russian history. Leont'ev himself considered the cleavage between the nobility and the people which had so disturbed the Slavophiles to be a positive symptom:

Before Peter our society and *mores* showed greater homogeneity, a greater *similarity* of the component parts; the reign of Peter initiated a more distinct, more clear-cut social stratification, and gave rise to that diversity without which life cannot attain its full prime and there can be no creativity. It is a well-known fact that Peter further consolidated serfdom. . . . In the above sense Peter's despotism was progressive and aristocratic. Catherine's liberalism was definitely of a similar stamp. She led Russia to an age of full bloom and creativity. She increased inequality—that was her main contribution. She guarded serfdom (the integrity of the village commune, the communal ownership of the land), introduced it even in Little Russia, and on the other hand relieved the nobility by diminishing their sense of being 'servitors' and thereby strengthening such aristocratic features as family pride and a sense of personality; from the time of Catherine the nobility became somewhat more independent of the state but as in former days dominated and ruled over other classes. As an estate it became more distinct, clear-cut, and individualized, and entered the age when it gave birth to Derzhavin, Karamzin, Zhukovsky, Batyushkov, Pushkin, Gogol, and others.[2]

There is no need to enlarge on the essentially 'anti-Slavophile' nature of this conception, in which Leont'ev adapted his

---

[1] Leont'ev, *Sobr. soch.* vii. 431–2.　　　[2] Ibid. v. 133–4.

theory of three evolutionary stages to Russian history. It is worth adding however that he placed the reign of Nicholas I in the period of 'flourishing complexity' and thus interpreted the Emperor's mistrust and dislike of the Slavophiles: 'The Emperor Nicholas Pavlovich was right to be continuously suspicious that the golden caftan of their lofty "prophecies" concealed—from their own gaze—the narrow and ugly breeches of a vulgar European bourgeois.'[1]

On the political plane too Leont'ev's attitude to the aristocracy, to class division, and to the *class* privileges of the nobility, differed from that of the Slavophiles. He could not forgive the Slavophiles their collaboration in the liberal reforms of the 1860s and indignantly rejected as open concessions to egalitarianism the anti-aristocratic pronouncements of the epigones of Slavophilism (Y. Samarin and Ivan Aksakov), their constant reminders of the Russian nobility's origins as 'servitors' of the State. How consistent he was is shown by the fact that he rejected even the Slavophile-inspired 'democratic' policy of Russification: 'The Russification of the borderlands [i.e. the Baltic provinces and Poland]', he wrote, 'in fact means nothing other than their democratic Europeanization.'[2] The aristocratic traditions of the German barons and Polish gentry ought to be carefully protected by the tsars, especially at a time when 'nihilism' and other signs of 'decay' were spreading among the population of Russia: to persecute nobility and Jesuitism in Poland and support the Latvians and Esthonians at the expense of the Livonian and Courland barons was to aid the disintegrating force of egalitarianism and hasten the fatal process of homogenization. This is the explanation of his strange opinion about the Polish uprising of 1863; Leont'ev sympathized with it and regretted that after its defeat the victors were largely instrumental in speeding up the process of democratization.[3]

In his comments on the land reform, which are worth recalling here, Leont'ev also emphasized the twofold implications of the programme—what he called its liberal individualist (European) side and its communal-conservative (Russian) side.[4]

---

[1] Ibid. vii. 432.
[2] Ibid., p. 252.
[3] See Leont'ev, *Natsional'naya politika . . .*, p. 26 (*Sobr. soch.* vi. 170–1).
[4] See Leont'ev, *Sobr. soch.* vii. 322.

By confusing these two sides, and failing to differentiate between the 'beneficial effects of being chained to the soil' (i.e. the preservation and legal codification of the commune) and the risk of 'liberating the peasants from the rule of nobility', the Slavophiles and even Danilevsky and Katkov had, according to Leont'ev, fallen into the 'liberal trap'.

Last but not least, Leont'ev's conception of religion and therefore his interpretation of Orthodoxy differed radically from that of the Slavophiles. 'I realized', he wrote in his autobiography, 'that in matters concerning the state, in the purely political, and even (most surprisingly) in the religious sphere, I should never agree with the over-liberal views of the Moscow Slavophiles.'[1] The 'Russian Nietzsche' had a deep-seated aversion to moralizing and 'evangelical' Christianity and all attempts to 'humanize religion'; he was equally opposed to religious sentimentalism, to doctrines of love that overlooked fear (*timor Domini*), obedience, and authority. From this point of view Khomyakov's 'ecclesiastical democratism' and the Slavophile ideal of *sobornost'* were typical examples of a 'rosy' Christianity that was utterly alien to the authentic 'black' Christianity of the Orthodox monks on Mount Athos and the Optina cloister. For Leont'ev the 'ascetic and dogmatic Orthodox believer' was primarily distinguished by his 'Byzantine pessimism', his lack of faith in the possibility of harmony and universal brotherhood. Schopenhauer and Hartmann were thus perhaps closer to Christianity than the liberal socialist prophets of universal justice and welfare.[2] All great religions, Leont'ev argued, are 'doctrines of pessimism sanctioning suffering, wrongs, and the injustices of life on earth'.[3] He recalled with an almost sadistic approval that the New Testament not only failed to promise universal brotherhood, but also foretold a time when 'love will weaken' and the kingdom of the Anti-Christ will be established.[4]

It is hardly strange, therefore, that Leont'ev called 'Khomyakovian Orthodoxy' a species of 'nationalist Protestant heresy'. He was equally unconvinced by the Slavophile criticism of

---

[1] Leont'ev, *Moya literaturnaya sud'ba*, Literaturnoe nasledstvo (Moscow 1935) xxii–xxiv. 441.

[2] See Leont'ev, *Sobr. soch.* vii. 232–43.

[3] Ibid., p. 230.

[4] Leont'ev, *Vostok, Rossiya i slavyanstvo* (Moscow 1886), ii. 294.

Catholicism, although his views were undoubtedly influenced by the opinions of Khomyakov, for whom de Maistre's treatise *On the Pope* represented the purest distillation of the Catholic spirit. The difference was rather a matter of emphasis; Leont'ev approved of the dogma of papal infallibility since it pleased his aesthetic judgement. 'If I were in Rome,' he wrote in one of his letters, 'I should not hesitate to kiss not only the hand but also the slipper of Leo XIII. . . . Roman Catholicism suits my unabashed taste for despotism, my tendency to spiritual obedience, and attracts my heart and mind for many other reasons.'[1]

The above analysis would appear to support the thesis that there was no common ground between Leont'ev's theories and classical Slavophilism. Nevertheless there are in fact sound reasons for discussing his views in a chapter dealing with various neo-Slavophile trends. He himself, in an article on the epigones of Slavophilism, wrote: 'It is not enough *to continue* the work of the former Slavophiles; one must develop their doctrine while keeping faith with their central idea—the idea that we must *take heed not to become like the West*; the doctrine must be modified wherever it no longer makes sense.'[2]

The term 'modification' (*vidoizmenenie*) hardly seems in place here, since nothing is left to 'modify' where everything has been rejected—from the appraisal of ancient Russia and the Petrine reforms to the concept of *sobornost'* and the ideal of a free community of brothers. However, although the 'central idea' mentioned by Leont'ev is too vague to throw much light on his meaning, another statement of his, that 'true Slavophilism' really means 'love of culture', provides a more useful clue.[3] The word culture was used by Leont'ev in an anti-capitalist sense,[4] as the antithesis of 'liberal and egalitarian progress'. In noting

---

[1] See Berdyaev, op. cit., p. 245.

[2] Leont'ev, *Sobr. soch.* vii. 434.

[3] See ibid., vi. 189.

[4] In his letter cycle to Vl. Solov'ëv *On Political and Cultural Rationalism* Leont'ev, like the Slavophiles, treated capitalism as an inseparable aspect of the pernicious rationalization of social life and wrote: 'The rationalism of the exact sciences formed a natural alliance with the *rationalism of capital.*' Leont'ev, *Sobr. soch.* vi. 303.

This anti-capitalist sense given to the term *culture* was not only an isolated anticipation of the Spenglerian antithesis of 'culture' and 'civilization'. As R. Williams has shown in his *Culture and Society 1780–1950* (Columbia University Press, New York 1958), the word 'culture' was introduced into the English language by critics of capitalist industrialization and was associated with a critical attitude to external, mechanical 'civilization'.

that 'love of culture' was an important aspect of Slavophile doctrine Leont'ev showed that he understood the essentially anti-capitalist nature of Slavophile conservatism or, strictly speaking, of the Slavophile utopia.

It becomes clear at this point that the link between Leont'ev and the Slavophiles is that they in fact represent two diametrically opposed standpoints and at the same time two evolutionary stages within the framework of one ideology—the conservative romanticism of the Russian nobility. The conservative romanticism of the first half of the century found its fullest and most original expression in Slavophilism (in the 1840s it had a virtual monopoly). Leont'ev on the other hand was the most extreme— and isolated—representative of conservative romanticism during its decline, when attempts were made to restore feudalism. From the methodological point of view we are therefore fully justified in comparing Leont'ev with the Slavophiles and in discussing his views as a product of the disintegration of conservative romanticism in Russia. Each of the ideological structures thus compared forms a 'natural' frame of reference for the other.

An examination of the Slavophile utopia from the perspective of Leont'ev's ideas helps to bring out very strongly the specific nature of Slavophile conservatism discussed in earlier chapters. In contrast to Leont'ev, the Slavophile utopia represented a *populist* version of conservative romanticism which appeared at times to come close to 'Christian socialism' (although the dividing line was never crossed). We shall return to this question once more in later chapters.

14

The Return to the 'Soil'

In Russian conservatism Leont'ev stood alone, whereas the group of thinkers known as *pochvenniki* (from the Russian *pochva*, meaning 'soil') exerted considerable influence. The *pochvenniki*'s eagerness for the maximum 'democratization' of conservatism at times exceeded that of the Slavophiles (with the exception of Konstantin Aksakov); Apollon Grigor'ev, who had advanced the slogan 'democratism and immediacy'[1] as early as the reign of Nicholas I, accused the Slavophiles of adopting 'boyar manners' and 'Old-Believer attitudes' and maintained they had no right to wear the essentially *democratic* Russian national dress.[2]

The *pochvenniki* group—ideologists of a 'return to the soil'—was formally set up in the 1860s. Their press organ was the journal *Time* (*Vremya*) published by the Dostoevsky brothers from the beginning of 1861. The conciliatory spirit of their programme, which called for the reconciliation of the intelligentsia and the people, Westernism and Slavophilism, the West and Russia, seemed to contemporaries too eclectic and vague in its emphasis on compromise. In fact this ideology, as the following chapter sets out to show, possessed its own specific style and creative potential, shown by its role in the work of Dostoevsky. One of the leading *pochvenniki*—apart from Grigor'ev and Dostoevsky—was Nikolaĭ Strakhov,[3] but as he was somewhat less original than either, he may perhaps be omitted for the sake of brevity and the greater clarity of the over-all picture. Grigor'ev was discussed previously in connection with the theory of cultural types and the aesthetics of

---

[1] Grigor'ev, *Materialȳ dlya biografii*, p. 184.

[2] See ibid., p. 185.

[3] N. N. Strakhov (1828–96) was the most eclectic thinker among the *pochvenniki*: an admirer of Danilevsky, he was also influenced by Tolstoy (with whom he became friendly) and in philosophy he came close to Right Hegelianism. Strakhov's most important books are collections of his articles—*Mir kak tseloe, Bor'ba s Zapadom v russkoĭ literature*, and *Iz istorii literaturnogo nigilizma*.

diversity. In the present chapter his ideas will be examined
more from the point of view of their relationship to Dostoevsky.

Grigor'ev did not share the nostalgia for an imaginary ancient
Russia. For him the concept 'soil' meant 'native' and 'organic'
national principles evolving *here and now*. He differed from the
Slavophiles in his attitude to the philosophical searchings of
the Westernizers and to the problems of the 'superfluous men'.
He himself might be called a 'superfluous man' with Slavophile sympathies and there is a certain amount of truth in his
own comparison of himself to Turgenev's Rudin.[1] He was
attracted by the mysterious 'organic', 'plant-like' world of folklore, ancient Russian ikons, folk customs, and Orthodoxy
conceived as an 'elemental historical principle'.[2] However, he
was equally susceptible to the charm of contemporary literature, the poetry of 'reflection and consciousness', and the rebellious and individualistic poetry and prose of Lermontov.
For all his enthusiastic love of Russian writing, there were few
others as sensitive as he to the different 'colouring' and 'flavour'
of the works of foreign authors. For Grigor'ev a return to the
'soil' did not mean a rejection of 'Europeanism' (which he felt
had already become part of this 'soil') or the denial of the
'principle of personality'; in fact he considered 'uncompromising anti-individualism' to be the weak side of Slavophilism.[3]
In his view not only the 'meek type' (Pushkin's Belkin), but
also his opposite, the 'predatory' type (Pushkin's Aleko and
Lermontov's Pechorin), who represented individualism and
moral anxiety (*trevozhnoe nachalo*), had their roots in Russian
soil. An organic synthesis of respect for tradition and the 'personality' principle, of spontaneous, plant-like growth and
consciousness, of Slavophilism and Westernism was therefore
not inherently impossible. Such a synthesis, Grigor'ev thought,
had already taken place in the work of Pushkin and would
come about in society since great poets were always the most
perfect spiritual organs of their people and infallibly foreshadowed its future.

It is understandable that a man of Grigor'ev's personality
found it impossible to accept the enlightenment-styled rational-

---

[1] See Grigor'ev, *Materialy dlya biografii*, p. 255.
[2] See ibid., p. 247.   [3] See ibid., p. 215.

ism of Chernyshevsky and Dobrolyubov whom he accused of abstract 'theorizing'—of forcing the irrational richness of life into the Procrustean bed of logical categories and banal 'textbook rules'. From the point of view of this study it is particularly interesting to examine Grigor'ev's response to Dobrolyubov's article 'What is Oblomovism?' which sums up all the failings of the 'philosophical epoch' in the history of the Russian intelligentsia.

Dobrolyubov accused the 'idealists of the 1840s' (he excepted Belinsky and Herzen) of dandyism, empty phrasemongering, and an organic incapacity for action. At heart every one of the 'superfluous men', he insisted, was nothing more than an indolent Oblomov (from the well-known novel by Goncharov); their weakness of character stemmed directly from the feudal serf system which provided hot-house conditions for the privileged classes and thus perverted their characters. The 'superfluous men' were in fact a product of the very social realities they thought they were opposing. They fail to understand, Dobrolyubov wrote in another article,

the over-all significance of the milieu in which they move. But then how can they understand it, since they themselves are embedded in it; for though they may stretch upwards, their roots nevertheless cling to the soil. . . . What can be done about this? Turn the whole milieu upside-down? That would mean turning oneself upside-down too; Well, then, go on! Get into an empty box and try turning it upside-down with yourself inside it. What an effort is involved! On the other hand, if you approach from the side you can manage it with one push.[1]

Grigor'ev was prepared to admit that there was a connection between the psychological make-up of the 'superfluous men' and the enervating influence of serfdom described so vividly in Goncharov's *Oblomov*. However he drew quite different conclusions from this. To him the fact—insisted on by Dobrolyubov—that the 'superfluous men' were deeply rooted in the soil, was an argument in favour of their superiority to the 'rootless theoreticians'. The apathetic village Oblomovka became for him a symbol of the 'true mother' whom Dobrolyubov had bespattered with saliva like a mad dog.[2] The rule 'Love work

---

[1] M. Dobrolyubov, *Sobr. soch.* (Moscow 1950–2).
[2] See Grigor'ev, *Vospominaniya (i vospominaniya o nëm)*, p. 212.

and avoid indolence', he wrote, is entirely correct and praiseworthy in the abstract; however, as soon as we make use of it
in order to

dissect, as with a scalpel, what is called Oblomovka and Oblomovism, then, if we are living beings, organic products of soil and
nationality, Oblomovism, that poor wronged creature, makes its
voice heard in ourselves. It was the undoing of Zakhar [Oblomov's
servant] and his master, but on the other hand Lavretsky [a personage from Turgenev's *House of Gentlefolk*] bows down to it meekly and
finds in it new strength to love, live, and think. It took him a long
while to approach it, wandering like a hunter across field, swamp,
and mire; with an aching heart he saw and still sees its painful
sores and putrid wounds; but he can also see that it is an organic
part of his own being, that only rooted in Oblomovism can he avoid
an artificial life, a galvanic spasm; filled by this feeling he would
rather tumble into the extreme of submitting to it totally, than into
the opposite extreme of textbook rules.[1]

As the above passage shows, Grigor'ev (like Dobrolyubov,
though his conclusions were different) did not treat the 'superfluous men' as totally 'rootless'. This was a significant revision
of the Slavophile view, which did not pass unnoticed by contemporaries. Leont'ev, for instance, wrote:

I could see that the Slavophiles' attitude to Onegin, Rudin, and
other similar characters was cool and if they did not reprove their
ideals and way of life, as the nihilists did, it was solely because their
literary manners were more aristocratic, nobler, cleaner, and
simpler than the manners of the nihilists, whose strong point is
dirty-street-corner rhetoric. . . .
In the periodical *Time* I found just what I had hoped for: a
friendly attitude to our recent, admittedly *European*, but nevertheless sincere and fruitful disillusionment.[2]

This change in attitude to the 'superfluous men' also entailed a change in the scale of values. Like the Slavophiles,
Grigor'ev considered 'rootlessness' to be the greatest of all
evils, but he was not entirely happy with the ideal of total
adhesion to the soil: rootlessness, he thought, condemns men

---

[1] Grigor'ev, *Sochineniya*, i. 415.
[2] Geont'ev, 'Neskol'ko vospominaniĭ i mȳsleĭ o pokoĭnom A. Grigor'eve', in
A. Grigor'ev, *Vospominaniya* . . ., pp. 532–3.

to inner emptiness and sterility, while organic, plant-like rootedness in the soil prevents living on the level of 'consciousness'. Therefore he was especially attracted to 'superfluous men' who had repented, as it were, and had returned home after their 'wanderings'; unlike the Slavophiles he did not treat them as prodigal sons, but as men who had something new and valuable to contribute. He thus interpreted the ideological evolution of the most outstanding Russian writers, beginning with Pushkin and ending with Dostoevsky, as a process of 'striking roots', or a return to the native soil. Even the history of Russian literature as a whole he saw as a similar process whose last stage was represented by Koltsov, Ostrovsky, and Nekrasov—writers who had never torn themselves away from the soil and could in fact not have done so.[1] He accused the Slavophiles of utterly failing to understand Russian literature and called their ideology a one-sided (though organic) product of the Russian soil. It is characteristic that he felt Shchapov's 'Slavophile' Populism to be a fuller and more many sided expression of the 'people's principle'; Shchapov's historical research was for him the 'first provided concrete proof' of the rightness of his own thoughts on Russia.[2]

For Grigor'ev the ideal archetype of Russian national individuality, enriched by European elements, was Pushkin, a writer who had struck root in the soil 'without ceasing to be Aleko, Onegin, and Don Juan'.[3] 'I believe and know', he wrote, '. . . that only in Pushkin has there been a total and integral fusion of the elements of the powerful national spirit, that the strong one-sidedness of elements that are exclusively national, or, let us say, bound to the soil, as expressed in the work of Ostrovsky, ought to be balanced by a complex of other restless, uneasy (wandering, so to speak), but equally essential elements of the national spirit as expressed in the work of other writers.'[4] The national spirit expressed in Pushkin—a spirit two-sided, like everything that is vital, containing within itself both concentric and eccentric forces[5]—was held up by Grigor'ev as the 'new principle', the spirit of reconciliation and synthesis whose

[1] See Grigor'ev, 'Stikhotvoreniya N. Nekrasova', *Sobr. soch.*, ed. by V. Savodnik, 13th edn. (Moscow 1915), pp. 41–2.
[2] See Grigor'ev, *Materialy dlya biografii*, pp. 289–90.
[3] Ibid., p. 41.   [4] Ibid., p. 281.   [5] Ibid., pp. 188–9.

destiny it was to revive Russia and to breathe new life into the declining civilization of the West.[1]

In his articles for his periodical *Vremya* (in 1861) Fëdor Dostoevsky advanced similar ideas. Although calling for a return to the soil, he too defended the heritage of the uprooted 'men of the 1840s'[2] and wrote that Pushkin's work represented both the embodiment of the Russian national ideal, the real meaning of the 'St. Petersburg' epoch in Russian history, and at the same time the escape from European enslavement'.

The phenomenon of Pushkin [he wrote] is proof of the fact that the tree of our civilization has already matured enough to bear fruit, that the fruit is not rotten but splendid and golden. We owe to him our understanding that the Russian ideal is universal wholeness, universal reconciliation, and universal humanity. The Russian spirit and Russian intellect have not expressed themselves solely in Pushkin, but only in him have they been revealed in their full force, as a complete and absolute fact.[3]

There is one obvious connection between these ideas and Grigor'ev's views; their importance to Dostoevsky is shown by his famous *Address on Pushkin* (1880) published twenty years later. Although such ideas as 'synthesis' and 'reconciliation' were also to be found in Grigor'ev, Dostoevsky's special contribution was his emphasis on Russian universalism (in the sense of many-sidedness and ability to understand everything human.) 'We believe the Russian nation to be an unusual phenomenon in the history of mankind',[4] he wrote. Russians were people with an instinctive understanding for everything human, and entirely without that reserved 'exclusivity' which

---

[1] See Grigor'ev, *Materialÿ dlya biografii*, p. 201.

[2] In his article 'Literary Hysteria' (1861) Dostoevsky warmly defended the 'Westernizers who had been separated from the soil' against the attacks of Katkov's *Russian Messenger*. See K. Mochulsky, *Dostoevsky. Zhizn' i tvorchestvo* (Paris 1947), p. 184. Konstantin Aksakov's article on Russian literature, published posthumously in the first number of the journal *Day*, annoyed Dostoevsky by its lack of understanding for and condemnation of the literary tradition of the 'superfluous men'. 'No,' he wrote, 'you did not live with us, did not share our joys or our grief, you arrived here from the other side of the ocean.' F. M. Dostoevsky, *Polnoe Sobranie Sochinenii* (St. Petersburg 1895), xi. 158. Dostoevsky's indignation was shared by Grigor'ev (see *Vospominaniya (i vospominaniya o nëm)*, p. 363).

[3] Dostoevsky, *Poln. sobr. soch.* ix. 42.

[4] Ibid., p. 21.

Dostoevsky considered to be typical of the Western European nations.

The following interpretation of Dostoevsky's views requires a short comment on its scope and the author's intention. It is not my purpose to provide a total reconstruction of Dostoevsky's *Weltanschauung*, to analyse the 'philosophical sub-structure' of his works, or even to discuss the 'representation of reality' in his work as a whole, though this is indispensable to an understanding of the unconsciously accepted components of a writer's vision of the world. All I wish to do is to establish the relation between Slavophilism and Dostoevsky as an *ideologist of the pochvenniki group* by analysing and interpreting a complex of views with which the writer was in conscious sympathy and which he both discussed at length and attempted to popularize in his novels. An interpretation of this kind must in the first place concern itself with characteristic features of Dostoevsky's social utopia, namely the opposition he made between Russia and Europe, people and intelligentsia, 'Christ's truth' and individualistic 'licence'. For the purpose of this study it is desirable to concentrate on the first, positive member of the antithesis, namely on Dostoevsky's Orthodox-Christian utopia with its Slavophile overtones. This utopia, however, does not exhaust Dostoevsky's *Weltanschauung*, which can be interpreted as a product of the tension between the utopia and the ideas it opposes. This tension is not necessarily, as is often suggested, the product of contradictions between Dostoevsky the writer and Dostoevsky the thinker, but would seem rather to spring from a dialectical contradiction which manifested itself both in the writer's *Weltanschauung* and in his creative work.[1]

Dostoevsky's thought is both anthropocentric and antipsychological. Although his understanding of the human psyche was outstanding, his heroes are not mere psychological studies but embodiments of metaphysical ideas which have their own life and could not be explained on a merely psychological plane. The richness of his creative talent was the product of an unusually acute sensibility to the crisis of traditional

---

[1] This formulation comes from M. Gus, *Idei i obrazy F. M. Dostoevskogo* (Moscow 1962), p. 4. A detailed analysis of the philosophical problem of Dostoevsky's 'self-assertive' heroes will be found in Walicki, *Osobowość a historia* (chapter on 'Dostoevsky and the Idea of Freedom').

values (identified by him with Christianity) and to the absence of new 'unifying ideas'. While he was painfully aware of the disintegration of contemporary society, he clearly recognized the *historical* nature of this disintegration. 'Everyone for himself and only for himself, all relations for oneself alone', was how he described 'the fundamental idea of the bourgeoisie, which took the place of the previous social system at the end of last century; an idea which has become the chief idea of the present century all over Europe'.[1] 'The single unifying idea has been completely lost', says one of the leading characters in the *Adolescent* (1875), and another character, Vershilov, argues that during the decline of feudalism 'egoism has replaced the former union of ideas and everything has collapsed—only free individuals remain'.[2]

This diagnosis of bourgeois Western Europe took on a somewhat altered aspect when Dostoevsky came to deal with Russia; here in the foreground was the problem of the 'cleavage' between the Europeanized intelligentsia and the Orthodox people, or in other words, the 'uprootedness' that impelled the 'Russian Europeans' towards the tragic and fatal dialectics of unbridled licence.

Western Europe, according to Dostoevsky, had rejected the way of Christ, the God-man, and had instead chosen the way of the man-God, the deification of mortal man. This idea, which runs through *The Possessed*, *The Brothers Karamazov*, and *The Diary of a Writer*, was probably suggested to Dostoevsky by Feuerbach, to whose writings he was introduced in his youth as a member of the Petrashevsky Circle.[3] 'Anthropotheism is also a religion, only of another kind', wrote Speshnëv, another member of the circle and a friend of the young Dostoevsky. 'The adored subject is different, new, but not so the fact of

---

[1] Dostoevsky, *Poln. sobr. soch.* xi. 98. (It should be noted that this remark appears in a definitely anti-Semitic context.)

[2] *The Adolescent*, trans. by Andrew R. MacAndrew (Doubleday and Co., New York 1971), p. 65.

[3] See Walicki, *Osobowość a historia*, pp. 368–77. An additional (though indirect) confirmation of this thesis is provided by the young Solov'ëv's reflections on Feuerbach and Stirner in his *Crisis of Western Philosophy*. See below, p. 561, and also N. Strakhov's article on Feuerbach, *Bor'ba s Zapadom v russkoĭ literature* (St. Petersburg 1883), vol. ii. Both thinkers, who are close to Dostoevsky, and a product of the same intellectual tradition, regarded Feuerbach as the founder of a philosophy that deified man and thereby provided a justification for 'nihilism'.

adoration. Instead of a God-man we now have a man-God.'[1] The Dostoevsky of the 1860s and '70s would have agreed with this analysis, but would have drawn different conclusions from it. The religion of the man-God was to him a religion of self-willed individualism leading to murder, suicide, or despotism; the fate of his leading 'self-assertive' heroes is confined within the limits of this triad.[2]

The first variant—murder—is depicted most forcefully in *Crime and Punishment* with its 'pure' murder as an 'experiment'. Raskol'nikov kills his victim solely to find out if he is 'a louse like everyone else' or a free man, a Napoleon with the right to transgress against moral principles by virtue of the unrestrained and absolute autonomy of the self. Raskol'nikov's 'theory' was the Russian equivalent, as it were, of the ultra-individualistic philosophy of Stirner who wrote: 'My authority to commit murder derives from within myself, I have the right to kill if I do not forbid it myself, if I am not bound by the view that murder is an 'injustice'' and ''something'' impure''.[3] Raskol'-nikov's defeat was to be 'indirect proof' of the futility of this view: his experiment showed that man is not God, that he is not free to do as he likes, and that ethical norms cannot be ignored.

The second variant of absolute self-assertive individualism—the suicide experiment—is described in *The Possessed*. For Kirilov suicide is the only means of affirming his own freedom in a world devoid of God. 'If there's no God,' Kirilov reasons, 'then I'm God.'

If God exists, then the will is his and I can do nothing. If he doesn't exist then the will is mine and I must exercise my own will, my free will. . . . I can't imagine that there's not one person on our whole planet who, having put an end to God and believing in his own free will, will dare to exercise that will on the most important point. . . . I have an obligation to shoot myself because the supreme gesture of the free will is to kill oneself.[4]

By killing himself Kirilov wants to kill his fear of death and thus free mankind from God; in fact he merely achieves his own

[1] *Folisofskie i obshchestvenno-politicheskie proizvedeniya petrashevtsev* (Moscow 1953), p. 496.

[2] See Walicki, *Osobowość a historia*, pp. 377–416.

[3] M. Stirner, *Der Einzige und sein Eigentum* (Imperial Verlag, Berlin 1926), p. 221.

[4] *The Possessed*, trans. by Andrew MacAndrew (Signet Classic, New York 1962), p. 635.

annihilation. His death (by his own consent) is exploited by petty persons for their own shabby ends. Thus ends the second great experiment in the exercise of individualistic freedom.

In the sphere of social relations the final outcome of complete licence can only be despotism. Individualistic freedom leads to a 'lascivious' amd sadistic desire for power and is thus transformed into its opposite. 'I started out with the idea of unrestricted freedom,' says Shigalev in *The Possessed*, 'and I have arrived at unrestricted despotism. I must add, however, that any solution of the social problem other than mine is impossible.'[1] 'Shigalev's system' is a depressing vision of a society based on absolute obedience, absolute depersonalization. 'He offers as a final solution the division of mankind into two uneven categories. One-tenth will be granted individual freedom and full rights over the remaining nine-tenths who will lose their individuality and become something like a herd of cattle. . . . They will attain a state of primeval innocence, something akin to the original paradise on earth, although of course they will have to work.' The insistence on absolute equality among them does not even allow for inequality of talent: 'They cut out Cicero's tongue, gouge out Copernicus' eyes; they throw stones at Shakespeare—that's Shigalev's system for you! The slaves must be equal; without tyranny there has never yet been freedom or equality, but in the herd there is equality and that's what Shigalev teaches.'[2]

A modified and nobler version of 'Shigalev's system' is presented in the *Legend of the Grand Inquisitor* in book five of *The Brothers Karamazov*. The Grand Inquisitor exchanges freedom for bread, and takes away freedom in order to bestow happiness on his 'pitiful children'.[3] However, a prerequisite of this happiness is total and 'herd-like' depersonalization. The Inquisitor knows that men are weak and therefore lifts from them the burden of freedom, the burden of conscience and personal responsibility, replacing freedom by authority, and consenting unity, free unity, by unity based on compulsion. He transforms the Church into a state as a means of 'uniting all in one unanimous and harmonious ant-heap',[4] and when Christ descends

---

[1] *The Possessed*, trans. by Andrew MacAndrew pp. 384–5. [2] Ibid., p. 399.

[3] *The Brothers Karamazov*, trans. by Constance Garnett (Random House, New York 1933), p. 269. [4] Ibid., p. 267.

to earth in order to be among his people once more, wants him to be arrested and burnt as a heretic. Christ listens to his monologue in silence and then kisses him on the mouth as a sign of his forgiveness; the Inquisitor lets the Son of Man go but begs him never to return. In this confrontation of the Grand Inquisitor and the silent Christ, Dostoevsky wanted to show the moral victory of the God-man over the man-God.

The 'dialectic of licence' is closely bound up with Dostoevsky's philosophy of history, which shows obvious similarities with the Slavophile criticism of Western Europe. Like the Slavophiles Dostoevsky thought of the classical heritage as a source of evil that had distorted the Christian faith in the West. Pagan Rome had passed on to Catholicism the idea of the man-God (the Emperor, Apollo Belvedere) as well as the idea of unity based on compulsion (cf. similar views held by Kireevsky and Khomyakov).[1] The individual's protest against the Catholic 'unifying idea' led to social atomization and to the rule of the bourgeoisie whose philosophy is egoism and the law of the jungle. A new protest—this time against individualism and anarchy—gave birth to socialism, which Dostoevsky presented as a secularized form of the Catholic 'unity through compulsion'. Raskol'nikov's 'theory' was related—albeit only indirectly—with the selfish amoralism of the bourgeoisie (in his discussion with the capitalist Luzhin, Raskol'nikov argued that

---

[1] In his *Diary of a Writer* (1880) Dostoevsky wrote: 'Christian communes-churches arose, following which a new, hitherto unheard-of nation began to form itself—all-brotherly, all-humanitarian in the form of an Oecumenical Church. But it was subjected to persecution; its ideal was moulded underground, while on the earth's surface a huge edifice, an enormous ant-hill, was being erected—the ancient Roman Empire, which was also, as it were, an ideal and a solution of the moral aspirations of the ancient world; there arose the demigod; the Empire itself embodied the religious idea proving an outlet to all moral aspirations of the ancient world. The ant-hill, however, did not come to pass, having been undermined by the Church. A collision of two diametrically opposed ideas occurred: the man-God encountered the God-man, Apollo of Belvedere encountered Christ. A compromise took place: the Empire embraced Christianity, while the Church accepted the Roman law and the Roman state. A small part of the Church retired into the wilderness and continued there its original work: Christian communes again came into existence, and later monasteries. But these were merely tests, which continue even to our day. As we know, the remaining overwhelming portion of the Church subsequently split into two parts. In the Western part the state, at length, subdued the Church altogether. Papacy arose—a continuation of the ancient Roman Empire in a new incarnation.' *The Diary of a Writer*, trans. by Boris Brasol (George Brazillier, New York 1954), p. 1005.

from the point of view of the struggle for existence approved of by bourgeois economics murder can be a permissible act: 'Carry out logically the theory you were advocating just now, and it follows that people may be killed.')[1] The legend of the Grand Inquisitor and 'Shigalev's system' were intended to reveal the inadequacy of socialism.

The notion of an organic relationship between Catholicism and socialism, emphasized in the *Legend,* was one of Dostoevsky's favourite and almost obsessive theories. It first occurs in *The Idiot,* in Prince Myshkin's well-known monologue: 'For socialism too is an offspring of Catholicism and the essential Catholic idea. It too, like its brother atheism, springs from despair in opposition to Catholicism as a moral presence, to replace the lost moral power of religion, to quench the spiritual thirst of parched humanity, and to save it not through Christ but also through violence! This too is freedom through violence, this too is union through the sword and blood!'[2] Dostoevsky developed this notion in *The Diary of a Writer,* where he wrote: 'The present-day French socialism itself . . . is nothing but the truest and most direct continuation of the Catholic idea, its fullest, most final realization, its fatal consequence which has been evolved through centuries. French socialism is nothing else but a compulsory union of mankind—an idea which dates back to ancient Rome and which was fully conserved in Catholicism.'[3]

This analogy seems less curious if we remember that the Saint-Simonians in France advanced similar views on the connection between Catholicism and socialism, although in a positive sense, and that 'Saint-Simonian papism' was used as a frequent bogey in contemporary journalism. Dostoevsky's philosophy of history (at least as far as it dealt with the evolution of Western civilization) was in fact merely a specific modification of Slavophile doctrine. The notion that Catholicism was the heir of classical Rome, the formula 'unity through compulsion' (recalling Khomyakov's 'unity without freedom'), and the depiction of bourgeois social atomization (cf. Khomya-

---

[1] *Crime and Punishment,* trans. by Constance Garnett (Folio Society, London 1957), p. 127.

[2] *The Idiot,* trans. by Henry and Olga Carlisle (Signet Classic, New York 1969), pp. 561–2.

[3] *Diary of a Writer,* p. 563.

kov's 'freedom without unity') are all clearly influenced by Slavophilism. (In his definition of the Protestant 'idea' Khomyakov stressed that Protestantism had moved from the 'sphere of dogmatic religion' to 'philosophical thought' and the 'social sphere': 'The whole of the modern history of Europe belongs to Protestantism, even in countries which formally are Catholic.'[1]) The interpretation of socialism as the search for the lost 'unifying principle' and the desire to impose this principle on an atomized society also have their counterpart in Slavophile thought. Khomyakov wrote:

That is the meaning of the origin and decline of all systems of greater or lesser fame appearing under the banner of Owen or Saint-Simon and under the name of communism or socialism. All these systems, which appear to have been conjured up by the concrete symptoms of society's sickness and are apparently aimed at curing them, in actual fact spring from an internal sickness of the spirit and have tried to fill the void caused by the decline of faith and the illusion of faith that had existed before.[2]

Another variation on this theme is to be found in Grigor'ev's comments on a letter by George Sand, the favourite author of the young Dostoevsky. This letter, Grigor'ev wrote,

is a terrible exposure of an existence in which such notions as love and fraternity must be *invented*, in which the *universal* can only gain the submission of the particular, the individual, by compulsion and despotism, and—as compulsion—must arouse protest and resistance on the part of individuality; an exposure of an existence which—in a word—reveals two unavoidable extremes: the despotic absorption of personality by 'papism'—Roman papism or (basically it is all the same) Fourierist and Saint-Simonian popery—and the immoderate protest of the individual, a protest expressed in the doctrine of Max Stirner as a consistent deification of the individual.[3]

Like the Slavophiles, Dostoevsky contrasted the two forms of 'licence'—compulsion and individualistic protest against compulsion—with the ideal of an authentic fraternal community preserved in Orthodox and Russian folk traditions. In a community of this kind the individual is not set against the collective

---

[1] Khomyakov, i. 149–50. The Slavophiles' views on the connection between Protestantism and capitalist civilization anticipate in general outline Max Weber's well-known thesis.

[2] See p. 192.   [3] Grigor'ev, *Sochineniya* (St. Petersburg 1876), pp. 175–6.

but submits to it entirely, without demanding rights, setting conditions, or calculating profits; the collective, on the other hand, does not demand too great a sacrifice, but grants the individual freedom and safety guaranteed by fraternal love. A community of this kind cannot be *invented* or *manufactured*:

It must happen of itself. One must be instinctively drawn towards brotherhood, community, and harmony; one must be drawn despite the nation's age-old sufferings—despite the barbaric coarseness and ignorance rooted deeply in it, despite slavery since time immemorial, despite the invasions of foreigners. In short, the need for a brotherly community must be in the nature of the man; it must have been born with him, or else he must have assimilated the habit through the centuries.[1]

This conception of a 'brotherly community' was developed by Dostoevsky in his *Winter Notes on Summer Impressions* (1863)— a masterly series of essays describing his travels in Western Europe. At about the same time he published his short novel *Notes from the Underground* (1864) which portrays a man who has rejected all social bonds and any subordination of 'what is most precious and most important to us, namely our personality and our individuality'. The narrator is a 'man of the nineteenth century divorced from the people's principles'; he sets his own ego against the objective world and revolts against the fate of being merely a 'cog' in the social mechanism or 'the keys of a piano on which the laws of nature are indeed playing any tune they like'.[2] Dostoevsky's hero attempts to deny the entire moral order: 'Is the world to go to wrack and ruin or am I to have my cup of tea? Well, so far as I'm concerned, blow the world so long as I can have my cup of tea.'[3]

Up to this moment the *Notes from the Underground* are simply an illustration of the fatal consequences of licence. What complicates the interpretation of the novel is that the narrator at times voices the author's own thoughts. In his description of the Great Exhibition in *Winter Notes* Dostoevsky writes with obvious agitation of the 'might of Baal' and the 'Crystal

---

[1] *Winter Notes on Summer Impressions*, trans. by Richard Lee Renfield (Criterion Books, New York 1955), p. 112.

[2] *Notes from the Underground*, trans. by David Magarshak, *The Best Stories of Dostoevsky* (Random House, New York 1955), pp. 134, 136.

[3] Ibid., p. 232.

palace';[1] the narrator of *Notes from the Underground* describes an equally disturbing vision of the rationalized society of the future:

> Then . . . new economic relations will be established, relations all ready for use and calculated with mathematical exactitude, so that all sorts of problems will vanish in a twinkling simply because ready-made solutions will be provided for all of them. It is then that the Crystal Palace will be built. . . . But man is stupid, phenomenally stupid; I mean, he may not be really stupid, but on the other hand he is so ungrateful that you won't find anything like him in the whole wide world. I would not be at all surprised, for instance, if suddenly and without the slightest possible reason a gentleman of ignoble or rather reactionary and sardonic countenance were to arise amid all that coming reign of universal common sense and, gripping his sides firmly with his hands, were to say to us all, 'Well, gentlemen, what about giving all this common sense a great kick and letting it shiver in the dust before our feet simply to send all these logarithms to the devil so that we can again live according to our silly will?'[2]

The partial confusion between author and narrator has given rise to a number of erroneous interpretations; even today books are published stating that Dostoevsky 'reaffirms the absolute value and integrity of the single, separate individual'.[3] Nothing is further from the truth—it is clear that Dostoevsky approves not of the narrator's individualism, but only of his criticism of the rationalism of social bonds which is common to both Western capitalism and socialism. Man, for Dostoevsky, is not a rational being and cannot be at home in a rationalized society. In a society lacking authentic bonds, which cannot be based on calculating reason alone, the irrational protest of the 'underground man' is both justified and valid. In his original text Dostoevsky used this argument to prove the 'necessity for faith in Christ', but to his indignation the censors crossed out the passage concerned.[4] Nevertheless the author's intention is

---

[1] *Winter Notes on Summer Impressions*, p. 90.

[2] Ibid., p. 130.

[3] R. L. Jackson, *Dostoevsky's Underground Man in Russian Literature* (Mouton and Co., The Hague 1958), p. 14.

[4] In a letter to his brother Dostoevsky wrote: 'Those pigs of censors let pass all the places where I *pretended* to poke fun at everything and to blaspheme, and then

clear: the 'underground man' himself comments on his own standpoint:

All right, do it. Show me something more attractive. Give me another ideal. . . . Show me something better and I will follow you. . . . Well perhaps I'm afraid of this palace just because it is made of crystal and is forever indestructible and just because I shall not be able to stick my tongue out at it. . . . I know as well as twice-two that it is not the dark cellar that is better, but something else, something else altogether, something I long for but cannot find! To hell with the dark cellar.[1]

It is worth pointing out that Dostoevsky's attitude to the extreme and irrationalistic ultra-individualism of the 'underground man' exactly parallels Khomyakov's attitude to the irrationalist individualism of Stirner. He called Stirner's book a *valid* protest against rationalist civilization. Stirner's work, Khomyakov wrote,

has a historical significance that has been overlooked by the critics and quite clearly even more so by the author himself; it is significant as the fullest and final protest of the free spirit against all arbitrary bonds imposed from outside. It is the outcry of a soul that may perhaps be immoral but only because it has been deprived of all moral support; a soul that expresses ceaselessly though unconsciously its longing to be able to subordinate itself to a principle it would wish to realize and believe in and that rejects with indignation and hatred the daily practices of the Western 'systematizers' who have no faith but demand faith, who create arbitrary bonds and expect others to accept them meekly. Contemporary history is a living commentary on Max Stirner—a revolt of simple humanity against bookish sophistries that would deceive it with the phantoms of artificially manufactured spiritual principles, while the spiritual principles by which it was once truly guided no longer exist.[2]

In spite of his debt to the Slavophiles the sociological content of Dostoevsky's 'anti-Western' utopia differs considerably from that of the Slavophile utopia. Dostoevsky's advantage over the Slavophiles was that as an uprooted *déclassé* whose talent was

---

they crossed out the places where I used this to prove the need for faith in Christ.' Dostoevsky, *Pis'ma*, ed. by A. S. Dolinin (Moscow 1928), i. 353; see also *Sobr. soch.* iv. 596.

[1] *Notes from the Underground*, pp. 141, 143.
[2] Khomyakov, i. 150–1.

nurtured not in a 'nest of the gentry' but against the hectic background of a great city, he was able to examine the problem of the 'underground man' from the inside. It is no accident that the main setting of almost all his novels is St. Petersburg—a city of mists and white nights, a ghost-like city whose pulse beat to a faster tempo, a symbol of the forces that had swept in from the West and destroyed the peaceful life of 'holy Russia'.

Dostoevsky's utopia, like that of the Slavophiles, was essentially a conservative-romantic protest against capitalist civilization,[1] although unlike Slavophilism it was not a protest made from the standpoint of the pre-capitalist ruling class. This fact distinguished his world-view from the classical Slavophilism of the landowning nobility and at the same time allowed him to keep alive the anti-capitalist spirit of the Slavophile utopia in the second half of the nineteenth century. After the Great Reforms the anti-capitalist ideology of the gentry could only survive in an ultra-reactionary and anti-populist version (Leont'ev); 'the populism of the gentry' became an anachronism when the large landowners accepted capitalism and were only concerned to force through a specific mode of capitalist development. The new standard-bearers of anti-capitalist protest were now the petty bourgeois intelligentsia recruited from among the *déclassé* gentry and the *raznochintsȳ* (educated people of non-noble origin). The emancipation of the peasants, which put an end to the Slavophiles' anti-capitalist utopianism, drew the attention of progressive intellectuals to the contradictions inherent in the new economic relations and produced an outburst of petty-bourgeois criticism of capitalism. This criticism—which from an economic point of view was inevitably reactionary[2]—could be combined with a conservative or a revolutionary political ideology: Dostoevsky represented the first variant and the Populists the second. Another variant of tremendous sociological significance was Tolstoy's Christian anarchism—an anti-revolutionary ideology but one that was a

---

[1] See A. V. Lunacharsky, 'O "mnogogolost'nosti" Dostoevskogo', in *F. M. Dostoevsky v russkoĭ kritike* (Moscow 1956), p. 421.

[2] We must remember, however, that—as it was put by Lenin—the designation *reactionary* 'is not used to indicate a desire simply to restore medieval institutions, but the attempt to measure the new society with the old patriarchal yardstick, the desire to find a model in the old order and traditions, which are totally unsuited to the changed economic conditions' (Lenin, *Collected Works*, ii. 241).

direct reflection of the social *Weltanschauung* and (partially) of the interests of the exploited and ruined masses of the patriarchal peasantry. Although in many respects Tolstoy, the great heretic and uncompromising critic of all established authorities, was closer to Populism than Dostoevsky, the latter's social origins and experiences made him seem closer to the Populists than the aristocratic Tolstoy. In fact many Populist leaders considered Dostoevsky (of course, mistakenly) to be their ideological ally.[1] It was not by chance, Lunacharsky wrote, that Pobedonostsev and other 'highly placed patrons' 'never trusted him entirely and were always expecting him to provide an unpleasant surprise', and that 'the radical sections of society in his day sensed some affinity in him'.

Dostoevsky's social position made him a particularly acute observer of a characteristic problem of capitalism—the problem of uprooted individuals who were obsessed by an ambition that fed on the instability of the tottering social hierarchy. Dostoevsky's critical insight into bourgeois society is often more acute than that of the Slavophiles and is based on somewhat different assumptions. It is worth pointing out that the *Winter Notes* was inspired not so much by the Slavophiles as by Herzen.[2] Dostoevsky believed bourgeois freedom to be a purely negative quality and realized that the obverse of bourgeois individualism was the reification of inter-human relations, the power of money which 'eradicates all inequalities'[3] and therefore diminishes the personality. The following passage from the *Winter Notes* underlines this point: 'What is liberté? Freedom. What freedom? Equal freedom for each and all to do as they please within the limits of the law. When may a man do all he pleases? When he has a million. Does freedom give each man a million? No. What is the man without a million? The man without a million is not one who does all that he pleases, but rather one with whom one does all that one pleases.'[4]

The simplest way to become free, of course, is to make a million. This is the guiding 'idea' of the hero of *The Adolescent*.

---

[1] Much evidence of this was collected by A. S. Dolinin; see F. M. Dostoevsky, *Materialy i issledovaniya* (Leningrad 1935), pp. 52–3.

[2] During his visit to London Dostoevsky met Herzen and under his influence came to the conclusion that the 'bourgeois system' was the 'final form', the '*état adulte*', of Western civilization.

[3] *Winter Notes on Summer Impressions*, pp. 104–5.   [4] Ibid., p. 109.

So the whole point of my 'idea' is that money is the only road that can take a man to the *top*, the only force that can propel him there, even if he's a mediocrity. I, for instance, may not necessarily be a mediocrity, but when I look at my face in a mirror, I realize that my quite ordinary face is definitely a handicap. But if I were as rich as Rothschild, who would stop to look at my face? And if I just whistled, wouldn't thousands of women come rushing to offer me their charms? Indeed, I'm absolutely convinced that in the end they would sincerely think that I was the handsomest of men. I suppose I'm quite intelligent. But even if my brain power were ten times that of an average man, I am sure there'd always be someone around whose brain power was eleven times the average, and what would become of me then? But if I were Rothschild, that fellow with the brain to the eleventh power would be no rival to me, for they wouldn't even give him a chance to open his mouth when I was around. I may be witty, but if a Talleyrand or a Piron came along, my wit would appear dull in comparison with theirs. But if I were Rothschild, where would Piron or even Talleyrand be if they tried to outshine me? Money confers despotic power upon a man, but at the same time it is the greatest equalizer, that's where its main force lies: money eradicates all inequalities.[1]

It is interesting to compare this with an almost identical passage from *Economic and Philosophical Manuscripts from the year 1844* by the young Karl Marx:

That which exists for me through the medium of *money*, that which I can pay for (i.e. which money can buy), that *I am*, the possessor of the money. The properties of money are my own (the possessor's) properties and faculties. What I *am* and *can do* is, therefore, not at all determined by my individuality. I *am* ugly, but I can buy the most beautiful woman for myself. Consequently, I am not *ugly*, for the effect of ugliness, its power to repel, is annulled by money. As an individual I am *lame*, but money provides me with twenty-four legs. Therefore, I am not lame. I am a detestable, dishonourable, unscrupulous and stupid man, but money is honoured and so also its possessor. Money is the highest good, and so its possessor is good. Besides, money saves me the trouble of being dishonest; therefore I am presumed honest. I am *stupid*, but since money is *the real mind* of all things, how should its possessor be stupid? Moreover, he can buy talented people for himself, and is not he who has power over the talented more talented than they? I who can have, through the power of money, *everything* for which the human heart longs, do I

[1] *The Adolescent*, p. 90.

not possess all human abilities? Does not my money, therefore, transform all my incapacities into their opposites?[1]

These two passages again illustrate the interesting similarity, noted previously in this study, between conservative and socialist criticism of capitalism in nineteenth-century social thought. In the case of Marx this similarity is of course very limited in scope. In contradistinction to Marx, the Populists, who represented the Russian version of 'petty-bourgeois socialism', had adopted not only some of the critical weapons but also some of the positive content of conservative ideology, and especially its idealization of the pre-capitalist social structure. Little wonder, therefore, that in his article on *The Possessed* Nikolaï Mikhailovsky, the chief theorist of Populism, appealed to Dostoevsky to examine the Populist version of socialism more closely and to stop thinking of the revolutionaries as enemies of 'the people's truth': 'If you were not so fond of toying with the word "God", and if you were to examine more closely the socialism you despise, you would realize that it does not differ in certain particulars at least from the Russian people's truth.'[2] Instead of castigating men who are 'possessed' by the idea of serving the people, Mikhailovsky wrote, Dostoevsky ought to concentrate on another 'devil', namely the 'devil' of 'national wealth' (the Populist term for capitalism), which was by far 'the most widespread and more than anything else ignored the frontier between good and evil'. 'You should portray truly impenitent sinners, fanatic self-lovers, fanatics of intellect for intellect's sake, freedom for freedom's sake, wealth for wealth's sake.'[3]

The novel *The Adolescent* was in a way a reply to Mikhailovsky's appeal. Unlike Dostoevsky's other novels, it was published in the progressive journal *Notes of the Fatherland* (*Otechestvennÿe Zapiski*), at that time edited by Nikolaï Nekrasov, M. E. Shchedrin, and Mikhailovsky. Its warm reception by such Populist critics as Petr Tkachev and A. M. Skabichevsky did not however lead to a lasting *rapprochement*, since Dostoevsky's links with monarchist and conservative circles were too

[1] K. Marx, *Early Writings*, trans. and ed. by T. B. Bottomore (London 1963), p. 191.
[2] N. K. Mikhailovsky, *Sochineniya* (St. Petersburg 1896), i. 871.
[3] Ibid., p. 872.

close and his hatred of revolution too deeply rooted. And yet one cannot but recognize the truth of Lunacharsky's comment that Dostoevsky's idealization of Orthodoxy—his utopia of the 'church as a social idea'—was necessary to him partly because it allowed him not to 'sever entirely his inner bond with socialist truth while cursing materialistic socialism'.[1] It is significant that Dostoevsky did not even repudiate the label 'socialism': in the last number of *The Diary of a Writer* (January 1881) he used Herzen's term 'Russian socialism' to describe the ideals he attributed to the Russian people, 'the ideals of an earthly church, of universal brotherhood, and the unity of mankind'.[2]

The leitmotiv of Dostoevsky's Orthodox utopia—as indeed of the Slavophile utopia—is the idea of a return to the people, to 'the native soil'. 'Russia's salvation lies in the people', says the author's mouthpiece, the elder Zoshima. The messianistic note, the emphasis on the 'universal mission of the Russian nation', is much stronger in Dostoevsky than in the classical Slavophilism. In contrast to Danilevsky, who emphatically rejected the very idea of a universal mission, Dostoevsky believed that the conquest of Constantinople and the unification by Russia of all the Slavonic peoples would herald a new historical epoch in which Orthodox Russia would pronounce a 'new word' that would bring about the rebirth and salvation of mankind.

In his novels Dostoevsky's messianism appears in two versions. One of them is expressed by Shatov in *The Possessed*:

A people forms the body of its god. A nation is a nation only so long as it has its particular god and excludes as irreconcilable all other gods; so long as it believes that with the help of its gods it will conquer and destroy all other gods. . . . But there is only one truth and therefore only one people can possess it and, with it, the only true god, though other people may have their own particular gods and even great ones. Now the only god-bearing nation is the Russian nation.[3]

For Dostoevsky nation was a synonym for people. Again and again in his novels and journalism we find scathing criticism of

---

[1] *F. M. Dostoevsky v russkoĭ kritike*, p. 442.
[2] See *The Diary of a Writer*, p. 1029.   [3] *The Possessed*, p. 238.

the uprooted Russian intelligentsia whose atheism, he suggested, was a function of its divorce from the soil. 'You are
godless', Shatov says to Stavrogin, 'because you're the son of
the idle rich, the last of the idle rich. You've lost the ability to
distinguish between good and evil because you've lost touch
with the people of your own country. . . . Listen, Stavrogin,
find God through labour. That is the essence of everything.
Find God or you'll vanish without trace like a rotten fungus.
Find God through labour.' 'What sort of labour?' Stavrogin
asks. 'The work of a labourer, a peasant', is the reply.[1]

The extreme doctrine advanced by Shatov–Dostoevsky is
both nationalistic and anti-intellectual. It should be remembered however that *The Possessed* was written under the immediate impression of the Nechaev trial and is therefore a very
one-sided reflection of the author's outlook. A somewhat
different messianism, which does not reject 'alien gods' but
emphasizes Russia's mission in reconciling Europe and Russia,
the intelligentsia and the people—in fact a universal synthesis
—was advanced by Dostoevsky in his articles in *Vremya* even
in the early 1860s and later in his *Diary of a Writer*. 'Oh, do you
know, gentlemen,' he wrote in 1877, 'how dear this very
Europe, this "land of sacred miracles", how dear it is to us,
Slavophile dreamers,—according to you, haters of Europe! Do
you know how dear these "miracles" are to us; how we love
and revere with a stronger than brotherly feeling, those great
nations that inhabit her, everything great and the beautiful
which they have created!'[2] Europeanization had widened
Russia's horizons, and this should be appreciated by all. The
intelligentsia also had something of value to contribute:

We must bow before the people's truth and recognize it as such, we
must bow like prodigal children who, for two hundred years, have
been absent from home, but who nevertheless have returned
Russians . . . however, we must bow on one condition only, and
this—*sine qua non*: that the people accept from us those numerous
things which we have brought with us. Indeed, we cannot completely obliterate ourselves before the face of the people, or even—
before any truth of theirs, whatever it may be. Let what is our own
remain with us, and for nothing in the world shall we part with it,

---

[1] *The Possessed*, p. 242.
[2] *The Diary of a Writer*, p. 782.

not even—if it should come to this—for the happiness of the fusion with the people. In the reverse case, let us separate and let us both perish, apart.[1]

For Dostoevsky (as for Chaadaev) divorce from the soil and 'homelessness' were not just a misfortune, but also a chance to create a new 'universal man' free from the burden of the past and from national prejudices—a man who would 'bear the world's sufferings'. Dostoevsky agreed with Herzen that 'the thinking Russian is the most independent man in the world'.[2] The 'upper cultural layers of the Russian nation', says Vershilov in *The Adolescent*, 'have produced perhaps a thousand representatives (give or take a few) who are freer than any European, men whose fatherland is all mankind. No one can be freer and happier than a Russian wanderer belonging to the "chosen thousand"; I really mean that; it's not just a joke. Besides, I would never have exchanged that mental anguish for any other kind of happiness.'[3] Nevertheless, Dostoevsky called on these 'thousand wanderers' to return home. Only by submitting humbly to the 'people's truth', he thought, would they find peace and overcome the inner schism which—like the Slavophiles—he ascribed to their divorce from the soil. The scene in *The Adolescent* in which Vershilov breaks the ancient icon of the old pilgrim Makar has a symbolic significance. Vershilov undertook an *experiment*—he wanted to find out if he was right in believing that the icon would split into two ideally equal halves. His premonition proved correct: 'Vershilov turned towards me a flushed, almost purple face in which every feature shuddered. Please don't imagine this is a symbolic gesture, Sophia; it is not Makar's legacy that I have smashed— I just felt like smashing the icon, that's all. . . . But even so, I'll come back to you, to you, my last angel. Although if you insist, you may think it was symbolic. . . . In fact, I'm pretty sure it must have been.'[4]

The symbolism of this scene is obvious: the destruction of the people's (Orthodox Christian) heritage, inner schism, the announcement of the future return of the prodigal son through Sophia, a woman of the people. The marriage of Sophia and Vershilov is a symbol of future reconciliation, of the fusion of

[1] Ibid., p. 204.
[2] Herzen, vii. 332.
[3] *The Adolescent*, p. 490.
[4] Ibid., p. 526.

the lost intelligentsia and the people to whom it must some day return; for in spite of temptation (Sophia's seduction by Vershilov) the people has kept faith with its moral ideals and in its religion has preserved the pure undefiled image of Christ.

A lengthier treatment of the same theme, summing up two decades of reflection, is to be found in Dostoevsky's famous *Address on Pushkin* made at the unveiling of the Pushkin monument in Moscow (8 June 1880). In this speech Dostoevsky enlarged on Apollon Grigor'ev's favourite image of Pushkin as a synthetic expression of the Russian spirit, a 'prophetic' apparition who had shown the Russian nation its mission and its future.

In the character of Aleko, the hero of the poem *Gypsies*, and in Eugene Onegin, Dostoevsky suggested, Pushkin had been the first to portray 'a profound and purely Russian concept . . . the unhappy wanderer in his native land, the traditional Russian sufferer detached from the people who appeared in our society as a historical necessity'. For Dostoevsky the term 'wanderer' was an apt description of the entire Russian intelligentsia, both the 'superfluous men' of the 1840s and the Populists of the 1870s. 'These homeless vagrants', he continued, 'are wandering still and it seems it will be long before they disappear' . . .; they sought refuge in socialism, which did not exist in Aleko's times, and through it hoped to attain their goal of happiness for all mankind, for 'a Russian sufferer to find peace needs universal happiness—exactly this: nothing less will satisfy him—of course, as long as the proposition is confined to theory.'[1]

Before the wanderer can find peace, however, he must conquer his own soul and humble himself before 'the people's truth'. This 'Russian solution', which he claimed to find in Pushkin's poems, Dostoevsky summed up in the words 'humble thyself, proud man, and above all break thy pride';[2] Aleko failed to do this and therefore the gypsies asked him to leave. Onegin despised Tatiana—a meek girl inseparably bound to the soil—and when he humbled himself before her it was too late. The constant confrontation of the 'Russian wanderers' and the 'people's truth' in Pushkin's work proved to Dostoevsky the need for a 'return to the soil' and fusion with the people.

[1] *The Diary of a Writer*, p. 968.   [2] Ibid., p. 970.

At the same time he insisted that this return would not mean a rejection of universalist ideals; to prove this he cited Pushkin's unique 'universal susceptibility', his talent for becoming a Spaniard (*Don Juan*), an Arab (*Imitations of the Koran*), an Englishman (*A Feast during the Plague*), or an ancient Roman (*Egyptian Nights*)—while still remaining pre-eminently a national poet. In fact Dostoevsky insisted that this 'universal susceptibility' was a product of the Russian spirit which was one of 'all-human fellowship'; 'to become a genuine and complete Russian means . . . to become brother of all men, a *universal man*'. The division into Slavophiles and Westernizers he called a great, although historically inevitable misunderstanding. The impulse behind Peter's reforms was not mere utilitarianism but the desire to extend the frontiers of nationality to a genuine 'universal humanity'. 'If you analyse our history after Peter's reforms, you will find traces and indications of this idea . . . in the character of our intercourse with European nations, even in our state policies. For what else has Russia been doing in her policies, during these two centuries, but serving Europe much more than herself? I do not believe that this took place because of the mere want of aptitude on the part of our statesmen.'[1]

Oh the peoples of Europe [Dostoevsky exclaimed in euphoric vein] have no idea how dear they are to us! And later—in this I believe— we, well, not we but the Russians of the future, to the last man, will comprehend that to become a genuine Russian means to seek finally to reconcile all European controversies, to show the solution of European anguish in our all-human and all-unifying Russian soul, to embrace in it with brotherly love all our brothers, and finally, perhaps, to utter the ultimate word of great, universal harmony, of the fraternal accord of all nations abiding by the law of Christ's Gospel![2]

Before he delivered the *Address* Dostoevsky was seriously worried lest it be received coldly by his audience. To Pobedonostsev he wrote: 'I have prepared my Pushkin speech to express my (our, I venture to say) most extreme convictions

---

[1] In this formulation Dostoevsky took up Danilevsky's conception but at the same time polemicized with it (Danilevsky satirized Russian politicians who, he maintained, tried to curry favour with Europe at the expense of their native Russia).

[2] Dostoevsky, *Sobr. soch.* x. 458.

and therefore I do not exclude the possibility that it might arouse abusive criticism.'[1] His fears proved groundless. The *Address* was an unprecedented success; carried away by enthusiasm the crowd called the speaker 'our holy man, our prophet'; even Turgenev, who had been portrayed with some spite in *The Possessed*, embraced him, and members of the audience crowded round him to kiss his hands. The solemn moment of universal reconciliation between Slavophiles and Westernizers, conservatives and revolutionaries seemed already at hand. 'When at the end I proclaimed the idea of the universal unity of mankind,' Dostoevsky wrote to his wife, 'the audience fell into a frenzy; I can hardly tell you what a tumult, what a roar of approval broke out when I finished; people who did not know each other burst into tears, sobbed, fell into each others' arms, and swore that they would become better, that they would no longer hate but love each other.'[2]

Among those present was the Populist writer Gleb Uspensky; in his report of the address for the *Notes of the Fatherland* he wrote that it made a 'staggering impact' that was fully deserved, in spite of talk about 'a kind of *humility*', to which the audience paid no attention. After the text of the *Address* had appeared Uspensky felt it necessary to correct his report, to warn his readers that the impression made by the *Address* failed to reflect its 'real content' and that its success was largely based on a fallacy, since Pushkin's Tatiana, who rejected Onegin, the 'universal man', in order to remain faithful to her old general, was hardly a fit ideal for young progressives.[3]

Criticism from the conservative side came from Konstantin Leont'ev. He called Dostoevsky a heretic who wished to replace the teaching of the Church by 'rose-coloured Christianity', or, in other words, by the 'democratic egalitarianism' emanating from rotten Europe. The Gospels, Leont'ev wrote, promised neither universal brotherhood, nor harmony and concord, and for the Church the realization of such ideals would be the greatest misfortune.[4]

The enthusiasm aroused by the Address turned out to be

---

[1] Dostoevsky, *Pis'ma*, ed. by A. S. Dolinin (Moscow 1959), iv. 144.
[2] Ibid., p. 171.
[3] See *F. M. Dostoevsky v russkoï kritike*, pp. 233–41.
[4] Leont'ev, *Sobr. soch.* viii. 199–200.

short-lived; men who had embraced each other under its immediate impact soon decided, after some reflection, that the differences dividing them had not diminished by one iota. Only the epigones of Slavophilism continued to regard the *Address* with lasting and uncritical enthusiasm. Ivan Aksakov, as a Soviet critic has put it, accepted it 'as a party standard, as a declaration'.[1]

Ivan Aksakov's attitude was influenced first and foremost by his reverence for everything connected with the Slavophile utopia. The early Slavophiles, like the early German romantics,[2] had after all considered their country to be a *Menschheitsnation*: Khomyakov had written of the Slavonic capacity for understanding all that was human,[3] while Konstantin Aksakov had openly identified the Russian nation with humanity as such. Ivan Aksakov therefore saw Dostoevsky—a writer who had admitted to a 'utopian interpretation of history'[4] —as an heir to the true Slavophile lofty idealism, which had been corroded by the pressures of *Realpolitik*. Moreover, Dostoevsky's vision was quite acceptable, since it assumed that the fulfilment of Russia's universal mission depended on the realization of the political goal of Panslavism—namely the conquest of Constantinople and the unification of the Slavs. Many of Dostoevsky's own remarks encouraged others to include him among the Slavophiles; in the *Diary of a Writer* he frequently called himself a Slavophile and his comments on the founders of the Slavophile movement were always very favourable. For the sake of exactness it should be added, however, that in the early 1860s, when he wrote for *Vremya*, Dostoevsky's attitude to the Slavophiles was still very critical[5] and that even

[1] A. S. Dolinin, 'K istorii sozdaniya Bratev Karamazovykh', in *F. M. Dostoevsky. Materialy i issledovaniya* (Leningrad 1925), p. 55.

[2] See Guido de Ruggiero, *The History of European Liberalism*, trans. by R. G. Collingwood (Boston, Mass. 1959), p. 240.

[3] See Khomyakov, v. 108, 118.

[4] In his article 'The Utopian Interpretation of History' Dostoevsky wrote: 'If faith in the "new word" that Russia can pronounce to the world at the head of the united Orthodox nations is a "utopia" deserving nothing but ridicule, then I too should wish to be accounted one of these utopians, and take the entire ridicule upon myself.' *Poln. sobr. soch.* x. 229.

[5] In 1861 Dostoevsky wrote in an article: 'The Slavophiles are distinguished by a rare capacity for failing to recognize people belonging to their camp and a complete lack of understanding for contemporary reality.' *Poln. sobr. soch.* ix. 154.

when he was closest to them he never endorsed their views completely: 'In many respects I hold Slavophile convictions,' he wrote in 1877, 'even though I am not quite a Slavophile.'[1]

The difference between Dostoevsky and the Slavophiles is in fact a very basic one, although they were divided not so much by consciously understood and formulated convictions, as by their different social experiences. Both Dostoevsky and the Slavophiles shared a sense of deep crisis, of impending change, but Dostoevsky was able to give his subconscious premonitions a more profound expression, free from the archaic flavour and the 'Old-Boyar' features that clung to the writings of the Slavophiles. Dostoevsky's Orthodox people's utopia does not exhaust his entire *Weltanschauung*, if by *Weltanschauung* we understand a certain complex of *problems*, a way of looking at the world and of posing *questions*. The ambiguity and insecurity of his social position gave him a profound understanding of the demonic forces threatening the values defended by his utopia: the problems of the 'underground man', of Raskol'nikov and Ivan Karamazov, had been experienced by Dostoevsky himself —and were thus portrayed from the inside. That is why as a writer he has left behind him a powerful and penetrating vision of the fundamental conflicts and existentialist tensions of modern man, and why in the twentieth century his novels are admired more than ever although his social utopia may now be of little interest to his readers.

[1] *Diary of a Writer*, p. 779.

15

The Autonomization of Philosophical Romanticism: Vladimir Solov'ëv

TOWARDS the end of his life—at the time of *The Brothers Karamazov* and the *Address*—Dostoevsky came under the powerful spell of a young friend of his, the idealist philosopher Vladimir Solov'ëv. Alësha Karamazov is traditionally believed to have been modelled on Solov'ëv, and according to Dostoevsky's wife, Anna Grigorevna, Ivan Karamazov also has certain traits in common with him (this is substantiated by the similarity between Solov'ëv's philosophical theories and the theocratic utopia propagated by Ivan Karamazov).[1] Serge Hessen too made use of Solov'ëv's theories in his analysis of the philosophical substructure of *The Brothers Karamazov*.[2] There is no doubt, at any rate, that the friendship between Dostoevsky and Solov'ëv exerted a fruitful influence on both thinkers; Dostoevsky's importance for Solov'ëv is shown by the significant place the latter gave in his philosophy to the concept of 'Godmanhood', which figured so largely in *The Brothers Karamazov*.

Konstantin Leont'ev, the severe critic of Dostoevsky's 'rosy Christianity', also placed great hopes in Solov'ëv, whom he called a genius whose shoe-laces he was not fit to tie.[3] The epigones of classical Slavophilism, Yuriĭ Samarin and Ivan Aksakov, were also well disposed towards the young philosopher and expected great things of him. It is no exaggeration to say that in the 1870s Solov'ëv, the prophet of a 'free theocracy', aroused widespread interest and expectations among the 'philosophical Right' (to use a generalization)—that is among men who in one way or another still clung to the ideas first systematized in the 1840s in Slavophile doctrine.

[1] See K. Mochulsky, *Vladimir Solov'ëv. Zhizn' i uchenie* (Paris 1951), p. 80.
[2] See S. Hessen, 'Der Kampf der Utopie und der Autonomie des Guten in der Weltanschauung Dostoewskis und W. Solowjows', *Die Pädagogische Hochschule* (Baden 1929), no. 4.
[3] See Berdyaev, *Konstantin Leont'ev*, p. 155.

In Solov'ëv's early work Slavophile inspiration is particularly strong in his master's thesis on *The Crisis in Western Philosophy—Against Positivism* (1874). This thesis is basically a development and modification of the main argument of Ivan Kireevsky's dissertation *On the Necessity and Possibility of New Principles in Philosophy.*

Like Kireevsky, Solov'ëv defined the crisis of Western European philosophy as a crisis of rationalism—of all abstract and purely theoretical knowledge. Solov'ëv argued that in the development of human spirit philosophy expresses the stage of individualistic reflection, and as such forms an intermediate link between primitive religious unity and the future restoration of spiritual unity through the universal synthesis of science, philosophy, and religion. Philosophy, he wrote, 'is born when the people's faith ceased to be the faith of the individual thinking being and instead of a guiding-principle becomes merely a subject for speculation'.[1] The pluralism of philosophical systems was a product of the dissolution of primitive unity, the result of alienation and the self-affirmation of the individual ego. Western philosophy was born of the conflict of individual reason and faith (authority); its successive stages were the rationalization of faith (scholasticism), the total rejection of faith, and finally the total negation of all immediate knowledge, a conception that throws doubt on the substantiality of external world and implies the identity of being and thought (Hegel). Using this Slavophile framework (which he in fact often abandoned or obscured in his analysis of specific details), Solov'ëv advanced several notions of his own concerning nodal points in the dialectic of European thought, and devoted considerable attention to a number of systems, including those of Schopenhauer and Eduard von Hartmann. From the point of view of the present study the section of his thesis devoted to Hegel and post-Hegelian philosophy is of particular interest: in it Slavophile criticism of Hegelianism is organically fused with Dostoevsky's views on the destructive effects of the deification of man (the man-God).

Following Kireevsky and Khomyakov, Solov'ëv accused Hegel of depriving the thought process of its real substratum

---

[1] Vladimir Solov'ëv, *Sobranie sochineniĭ* (St. Petersburg, ed. Obshchestvennaya polza), i. 28.

and of identifying reality with the concept, the empty form.[1] By opposing Hegel's abstract panlogism, he argued, Feuerbach achieved a 'transition *ad hominem*'; he worshipped the real material thinking subject—the human being—and sanctified its autonomy and search for happiness. The formula 'man desires happiness' (the justification of socialism) gave rise logically to the formula 'I desire happiness' (the justification of the egoistic individualism expressed most fully in the philosophy of Max Stirner).[2] In this way philosophical rationalism led to anthropologism and this in turn to egoism. The negation of the objectivity of the universe (Hegel) turned into the negation of the objectivity of moral norms (Stirner). The deification of man did not, however, deliver him from suffering or death, which continued to be his inseparable companions throughout life (this awareness is to be found in Schopenhauer). Thus the only way to deliverance and the manifestation of one's self-affirmation is the act of suicide; this was understood by Hartmann, who deduced from it the idea of the collective suicide of mankind.[3]

Although for the young Solov'ëv Hartman's ideas were the most extreme illustration of the crisis of Western philosophy, they also paradoxically enough foreshadowed the third stage of the dialectical triad, namely the day when philosophy would fuse with religion and spiritual unity would be restored. Hartmann's 'philosophy of the unconscious' appeared to Solov'ëv to be a rehabilitation of the metaphysics rejected by the positivists, a return to the religious concept of 'universal unity'. Ascribing to Hartmann his own ideas (quite without justification) he proclaimed that the annihilation of the egoistic self-affirmation of individual entities at odds with one another would be followed not by the Buddhist *Nirvana*, but by the *apokatastasis ton panton*—the 'kingdom of spirits bound together by the universality of the absolute spirit'. Solov'ëv considered this notion to be the end-product of the entire evolution of Western philosophy (i.e. philosophy in general), amounting to a rediscovery of ancient truths preserved in the traditions of Eastern Christianity.

[1] In his description of Hegelian philosophy Solov'ëv referred to articles by Kireevsky and Khomyakov, as well as to an essay by N. G. published in *Russian Conversation* (1859), no. 3   [2] Solov'ëv, i. 118.   [3] See ibid., pp. 119–21.

It appears [the thesis concludes] that these inevitable results of the
Western philosophical evolution reconstitute in the form of *rational
cognition* those very truths which in the form of *faith and spiritual
contemplation* were part of the great theological doctrines of the East
(partly the ancient but above all the Christian East). This philosophy [i.e. that of Hartmann] thus seeks to combine the logical
perfection of *Western form with the rich content of Eastern contemplation.*
But basing itself on the data of positivist science, this philosophy
stretches out a hand to religion. The realization of this universal
synthesis of science, philosophy, and religion . . . ought to be the
supreme goal and end-product of the evolution of thought. The
achievement of this goal will mean the total reconstruction *of the
inner unity of the spiritual realm.*[1]

Parallels with Kireevsky (whose name was only once mentioned by Solov'ëv) are self-evident. In his study K. Mochulsky
sums them up as follows:

Solov'ëv has absorbed Kireevsky's view of the world *in toto*. His thesis
is not an independent piece of work: its basic concepts—the synthesis of philosophy and religion, the view of Western philosophy as the
evolution of rationalism, the idea of the integral unity of life, of
metaphysical cognition, the emphasis on the need to combine
Western philosophy with the speculative wisdom of the East—all
these were previously put forward by Kireevsky. His work too suggested to Solov'ëv the framework of his thesis, which starts with
criticism of scholasticism and proceeds via Descartes, Spinoza, and
Leibniz to Schelling and Hegel. The closing passage of the thesis is
a reasonably accurate repetition of the conclusions of Kireevsky's
third article ['On New Principles in Philosophy']. Solov'ëv's own
contribution is the unsatisfactory substitution of Hartmann for
Schelling; for Kireevsky the final evolution of Western philosophy
was Schelling's positive philosophy, whereas for Solov'ëv it was
reached in the doctrines of Hartmann; the former outlined a short
programme for a critique of rationalism, while the latter implemented
it with the force of his brilliant dialectic. He attempted to give his
work a more academic character suitable to a master's thesis, and
therefore removed all references to Russian messianism and opposed
Western thought not to Russian Orthodoxy but to the vague
'speculation of the East'.[2]

Although in principle this view is correct, it must be qualified
in one respect: the young Solov'ëv did not absorb Kireevsky's

---

[1] Solov'ev, i. 143–4.   [2] Mochulsky, *V. Solov'ëv . . .*, p. 54.

view of the world, but only the chief ideas contained in his philosophical programme. *The Crisis in Western Philosophy* is a more
purely speculative work than any of Kireevsky's articles, and
discusses neither the historical background that interested
Kireevsky (the Roman empire, European feudalism) nor
various forms of ownership or social bonds; the village commune or social relations in pre-Petrine Russia are not even
mentioned in passing. The notion of 'Orthodox thinking' has
been replaced by a vague generalization concerning the return
of philosophy to truths contained in the 'theological doctrines
of the East'—a generalization that appears at the end of the
book as a kind of *deus ex machina*. Solov'ëv adopted Kireevsky's
philosophical ideas but tore them from the total context of
Slavophile doctrine and by doing so set them up as autonomous
philosophical theory.

Shortly after presenting his thesis Solov'ëv came to know
Ivan Aksakov and Yuriĭ Samarin, and somewhat later Dostoevsky.[1] From them he took over a number of ideas current in their
circle, above all the belief in the historical destiny of the Russian
nation. The climax of Solov'ëv's specific version of Slavophilism came in 1877, the year of the Russo-Turkish war 'for
the liberation of the Slavs' which contributed largely to the
rise of 'Slavophile' nationalism. The outbreak of the war
stimulated Solov'ëv to give a public lecture under the title
'Three Forces'; in the same year Dostoevsky wrote in his *Diary
of a Writer* of the 'three ideas', his remarks being largely based
on the Slavophile conception of the Catholic, Protestant, and
Orthodox principles.[2]

In Solov'ëv's interpretation the actual carriers of the 'three
forces that govern the evolution of mankind from the dawn of
history'[3] are the 'three historical worlds' or rather three distinct
cultures represented by the Moslem East, Western civilization,
and Slavdom. The first represents a fossilized and despotic
unity precluding progress, individual independence, or the free
multiplicity of various life forms. In it all spheres of life are
subordinated to religion, which turns man into an inanimate

---

[1] Solov'ëv made Dostoevsky's acquaintance in 1873, but only became friendly
with him in 1877.

[2] See Dostoevsky, *The Diary of a Writer* (January 1877).

[3] Solov'ëv, i. 214.

tool of an 'inhuman God'.[1] The second force set against the 'inhuman God' the 'godless man'; its last word is 'universal egoism and anarchy, a multitude of separate entities unconnected by any kind of inner bonds',[2] the conflict of isolated 'life forms' and 'spheres of activity' at odds with one another, in short—'atomism in life, atomism in science, atomism in art'.[3] Neither of these forces can or indeed does occur in its 'pure' form—they are rather trends whose total and final realization would mean the annihilation of mankind. To prevent this is the mission of the third force, within whose capacity it is to achieve a synthesis of 'singularity' and 'multiplicity', to 'humanize' God and turn man towards God, to reconcile the West and East. This force can only draw its strength from divine revelation and its carrier can only be a nation that is able to mediate between the divine and human. Such an intermediary must be free from all one-sidedness and exclusivity: it must have unshaken faith in the divine, the ability to rise above its own particular interests, contempt for the things of this world, and the ability not to fritter away its energy in separate spheres of activity. These features, Solov'ëv concludes, 'are certainly typical of the tribal character of the Slavs and especially of the national character of the Russian people'.[4]

For the Slavophiles who, unlike Solov'ëv, insisted that the first two forces were both operating within the West, the equivalent of the Moslem East was Roman Catholicism ('unity without freedom'). This difference is of little importance, however, if we take into account the fact that they too considered the *last word* in European civilization to be not Catholicism but the Protestant principle of 'freedom without unity', which achieved its final embodiment in atheistic individualism, rationalism, and social atomization. At the same time it is worth noting that Khomyakov tried to draw parallels between Catholicism and Islam and even suggested that the caliphate had had a direct influence on the papacy.[5] It is clear that in spite of all differences, the young Solov'ëv's philosophy of history represented a variation on Slavophile themes.

Another essay characteristic of Slavophile influence is the *Philosophical Principles of Integral Knowledge* written in 1877, the

---

[1] Solov'ëv, i. 222.　　[2] Ibid., p. 214.　　[3] Ibid., p. 223.
[4] Ibid., p. 224.　　[5] See Khomyakov, vii. 77.

year of the lecture on the 'Three Forces'. The title itself harks back to the notion of 'wholeness' or 'integrity' expounded by Kireevsky. On the other hand, in this work Solov'ëv raised a number of ideas not to be found in Slavophile doctrine, for instance the notion that the collective subject of history was mankind, a 'real though collective organism'.[1] This conception involved the treatment of individual civilizations (for instance Western European civilization) as 'moments' in the over-all evolution of mankind which was the 'real individual being', Comte's 'Le Grand Être'.[2]

Solov'ëv argued that every development—not excepting the evolution of mankind—passes through three phases: a phase of primitive undifferentiated unity, a phase of differentiation during which the individual parts become separated, and a new phase of free unity in which differentiation is not destroyed but fused together by an inner organic bond. In the evolution of mankind the first phase—the phase of substantial monism— is represented by the Eastern world (including nineteenth-century Islam), and the second phase by Western European civilization. Both phases are necessary moments in the development cycle but in themselves are of unequal value—any kind of monism, Solov'ëv suggested, is superior to atomism: 'the first moment in the development cycle is superior to the second, taken in isolation, and the Moslem East is thus superior to Western civilization'.[3]

During the epoch of primitive 'substantial' unity the three spheres of human activity—the spheres of creativity, know-ledge, and social practice—were utterly subordinated to re-ligion. In the sphere of creativity technology (the first, material grade) became fused with art (the second, formal grade) and mysticism (the highest, absolute grade) in an undifferentiated and mystical creativity, or, in other words, a *theurgy*. In the sphere of knowledge positive science (the material grade) fused with abstract philosophy (the formal grade) and theology (the absolute grade) into an undifferentiated whole that might be called *theosophy*. In the sphere of social practice the economic

---

[1] Solov'ëv, i. 232.

[2] In a lecture on 'The Idea of Humanity in Auguste Comte' (delivered in 1898), Solov'ëv attempted to show that his 'Sophia' was identical with Comte's 'Le Grand Être'. See Mochulsky, op. cit., p. 104.

[3] Solov'ëv, i. 258.

society or Zemstvo (the material grade) fused with the state (the formal grade) and the Church (the absolute grade), thus creating a homogeneous and *theocratic* whole.[1] In the second development phase (represented by Western Europe) each of the grades within each sphere strove for autonomy and for mastery over the others. In the resulting struggle matter conquered spirit: in the social sphere Western civilization finally gave birth to economic socialism (the true scion of capitalism, as Solov'ëv called it),[2] in the sphere of knowledge to positivism, and in the sphere of creativity to utilitarian realism.[3] In accordance with the generally valid law of evolution, however, the first two phases must be followed by a third —that of *free unity*—in which the separate spheres or 'grades' of human creativity, knowledge, and social practice are once more united, but without losing their distinctness. In the three spheres of life this renewed unity expresses itself as a *free theurgy*, a *free theosophy*, and a *free theocracy*. 'In this way', Solov'ëv concluded, 'all spheres and grades of human existence become united in this third and final phase into an organic whole whose organs and members are based on trichotomy. The normal harmonious activity of all organs forms a new general sphere— the sphere of *integral life*. At the beginning its representative among mankind can only be the Russian nation.'[4]

After this introduction Solov'ëv proceeded to examine the idea of a 'free theosophy' or 'integral knowledge' in greater detail. He distinguished three types of philosophy—naturalism (empiricism), rationalism, and mysticism. Empiricism and rationalism arrive at the same final result by different paths, namely by denying the substantial reality of both the external world and the object of knowledge; the absurdity of this conclusion illustrates the bankruptcy of all 'scholastic' or theoretical philosophy. A superior type of cognition is mysticism, which bases itself on supernatural sources of knowledge and looks for 'vital and integral' truths that commit not only the intellect but also 'the will to goodness' and the 'sense of beauty'. Mysticism in itself cannot however be identified with the 'true philosophy', since the latter postulates the inner organic synthesis of all types of philosophical thought, analogous to the

---

[1] Solov'ëv, i. 243.   [2] See ibid., pp. 250–1.
[3] See ibid., p. 255.   [4] Ibid., p. 262.

synthesis of science, philosophy, and theology in a superior and free theosophical unity.[1] Summing up his reflections on the sources, method, and aims of 'integral knowledge' Solov'ëv wrote:

Free theosophy is knowledge whose subject is true being in its objective manifestations, whose aim is man's inner unification with true being, and whose materials are the facts of human experience in all its forms—that is above all mystical experience, followed by inner or psychic experience, and finally external or physical experience. Its basic form is intellectual insight or the intuitive perception of ideas, systematized with the aid of purely logical or abstract thought; its active source, or causative principle, is inspiration, that is the operation of higher ideal beings upon the human spirit.[2]

Solov'ëv's philosophical programme envisaged the elaboration of three main elements of his 'free theosophy'—'organic logic', 'organic metaphysics', and 'organic ethics'. *The Philosophical Principles of Integral Knowledge* break off at the section on 'organic logic'. By logic Solov'ëv meant the science of the absolute first principle or *Urprinzip*, or more accurately, the *logos* or first principle in its second phase of self-differentiation, corresponding to the second person of the Holy Trinity; the method of logic conceived thus is 'positive dialectics', fundamentally differing from Hegel's rationalist dialectics.[3] By means of 'positive dialectics' every item can be defined through its trichotomous relation to the absolute proto-principle: (1) in the substantial primary unity with the proto-principle, i.e. in pure potentiality or positive nothingness (in God the Father); (2) in self-differentiation, that is in the act of self-realization (in the *logos*, or the Son); (3) in free, that is mediated unity with the absolute first principle (in the Holy Spirit).[4] Differentiation between the separate logical categories (Solov'ëv intended to introduce twenty-seven such categories)[5] is only possible in the *logos* and is therefore relative, since the *logos* is by its very nature a relation. The three forms of this relation of absolute

[1] See ibid., p. 280.
[2] Ibid., p. 294.
[3] See ibid., pp. 314–15. This argument clearly betrays the influence of Khomyakov's critique of Hegel.
[4] See ibid., p. 346.
[5] See ibid., pp. 353–4.

first principle to everything and to itself are the concealed *logos*, the revealed *logos*, and the embodied or concrete *logos* (Christ).[1] These notions formed a connecting link, as it were, between Solov'ëv's 'logic' and the theme of 'Godmanhood' to which he devoted a series of public lectures in the following year (1878) and which aroused wide acclaim (they were attended by Dostoevsky among others).[2]

The Philosophical Principles of Integral Knowledge is undoubtedly one of Solov'ëv's most 'Slavophile' works, and at the same time his first attempt at evolving a philosophical system of his own. From the ideas he took over from the Slavophiles (chief among them Kireevsky's anti-rationalist doctrine of 'wholeness') Solov'ëv constructed a philosophical edifice in which Slavophile romanticism—torn from the context of Slavophile doctrine as a whole—became enshrined as pure philosophy, reminiscent of the elaborate systems of the philosophers of German romanticism (especially the late Schelling). Although Solov'ëv's view of Western Europe was influenced by the Slavophile philosophy of history, curiously enough his work shows no trace of such typically Slavophile conceptions of Russian history as the idealization of pre-Petrine Russia and of the peasant commune. He was certainly much closer to Ivan Kireevsky than to Konstantin Aksakov, whose Christianity, like Tolstoy's, was evangelical whereas Solov'ëv's was mystical. Where for Aksakov Christ was mainly a moral ideal, for Solov'ëv he was above all the *logos*, one of the aspects or 'moments' of Godhead.[3] Even by comparison with Kireevsky there is a considerable gap between Slavophile piety and Solov'ëv's attitude to religion. Kireevsky's mysticism was an effort of inner spiritual concentration far removed from the ecstatic and visionary states experienced by Solov'ëv. It belonged to the sphere of romantic traditionalism and is thus far more open to sociological interpretation than Solov'ëv's erotic mysticism and visions of 'eternal womanhood' ('Sophia', the world-soul).[4] Moreover, Solov'ëv's mysticism was ex-

---

[1] Solov'ev, p. 346.   [2] See Mochulsky, op. cit., p. 91.

[3] On the difference between 'evangelical Christianity' and 'mystical Christianity' as two ideal models of christological doctrines see L. Kolakowski, *Chrétiens sans église*, Paris 1969.

[4] 'Sophia' appeared to Solov'ëv three times; he described his visions in the poem 'Tri svidaniya'.

pressed in more speculative, philosophical, and heterodox terms, assimilated cabalistic Neoplatonic and Gnostic motifs, and continued to move away from Church doctrine.

A work that summed up and systematized the notions expounded by Solov'ëv in the 'preparatory' (Slavophile) stage of his intellectual evolution[1] was his doctoral dissertation entitled *A Critique of Abstract Principles* (1880). In this work, which contains a systematic exposition of epistemology and ethics, Solov'ëv reverts to the conception of a 'free theosophy' and 'free theocracy', although he substitutes the term 'all-unity' for 'wholeness'. What Solov'ëv called 'abstract principles' were various aspects of his 'all-unity' which, by separating from the whole and striving for autonomous existence, lost their true character, came into mutual conflict, and plunged humanity into a state of chaos.[2] In this situation it was the role of philosophy to strive to restore spiritual unity in the realm of knowledge as well as in society. In putting forward this programme Solov'ëv again made use of Slavophile ideas: his conception of faith as the foundation of all cognition was derived from Khomyakov's epistemology; his ideal of a 'free community' (*svobodnaya obshchinnost'*) founded on love and ruling out 'external authority' is a clearly recognizable version of the Slavophile ideal of *sobornost'*.[3]

For the purpose of this study there is little point in discussing the 'system' expounded in the *Critique of Abstract Principles* or in analysing its complex conceptual structure and its frequently irritating internal contradictions.[4] It is worth pointing out the

[1] In his monograph *Mirosozertsanie Vl. Solov'ëva*, 2 vols. (1913), E. N. Trubetskoï divides Solov'ëv's intellectual evolution into three periods: (1) the 'preparatory' period (until 1881); (2) the 'utopian' period (1882–90); and (3) the period of loss of faith in the possibility of the theocratic utopia. In this last period Solov'ëv transferred the idea of the unification of the churches outside historical time (*Tri razgovora, Povest'ob Antikhriste*). On this basis D. Stremooukhoff in *V. Soloviev et son œuvre messianique* (Strassbourg 1935), claimed that there was a fourth 'apocalyptic' period in Solov'ëv's philosophical evolution.

[2] See Solov'ëv, *Kritika otvlechennȳkh nachal* (Moscow 1880), p. vii.

[3] See ibid., p. xi.

[4] The most glaring contradiction in Solov'ëv's system was his eclectic attempt to reconcile the negation of the autonomy of ethics with the acceptance of the basic premisses of Kant's ethics, including the categorical imperative and the autonomy of the moral will. In *The Spirit of Russia*, ii. 256, Masaryk writes that in Solov'ëv's soul Plato struggled with Kant: 'Kant represents the self-sufficiency and independence of the individual critical understanding; Plato represents dependence upon the absolute, upon the revelation of the absolute, upon dogma, upon the church.'

ironical fact, however, that Solov'ëv, who rejected the idea of philosophy as an autonomous discipline, was Russia's first eminent professional philosopher and as such contributed to the autonomization of philosophy in his native country and to the separation of philosophical speculation from other spheres of human knowledge and activity. A comparison with the Slavophiles illustrates this particularly clearly. In Slavophile doctrine philosophy was a subordinate sphere, organically linked to certain social, historical, and economic views, and part of a specific set of religious and political convictions (the fact that this homogeneity was only entirely true of the Slavophile utopia and disintegrated in altered historical circumstances does not invalidate this statement). In the conception of the young Solov'ëv, Kireevsky's and Khomyakov's philosophical romanticism assumed an autonomous role, and, interestingly enough, became divorced from the socio-political ideology of the immediate followers of Slavophile thought.[1]

Solov'ëv finally broke with the Slavophiles in 1883 when he stopped publishing in Ivan Aksakov's journal *Rus'* and instead —to the indignation of his Right-wing friends—became a contributor to the liberal and Westernizing *European Messenger* (*Vestnik Evropy̆*). The immediate cause of the break was a change in Solov'ëv's attitude to Western civilization and philosophy and in particular his growing interest in Roman Catholicism. Even in his first university lecture (1880) he had advanced the view that Western philosophy—not only rationalist idealism but also materialism and naturalism—had also served the cause of Christianity by paving the way for the establishment of the kingdom of heaven on earth.[2] In three speeches dedicated to the memory of Dostoevsky (1881–3) Solov'ëv took up the idea of 'Godmanhood' and the universal reconciling mission of the Russian nation put forward in *The Brothers Karamazov* and the *Address*. The idea of the reconciliation of Catholicism and Orthodoxy—which was quite foreign to Dostoevsky—was the final conclusion with which Solov'ëv ended a series of seven articles entitled *The Great Dispute* published in Aksakov's *Rus'*

---

[1] The subsequent phases of Solov'ëv's philosophical evolution will be discussed only in so far as they have a bearing on his relation to Slavophilism.

[2] See Mochulsky, op. cit., p. 123.

(1881–3). In the first article of the series, in which official Orthodoxy was subjected to severe criticism, Solov'ëv still clung to the Slavophile view of Catholicism; in later articles, however, he abandoned this interpretation, declared his support for the Catholic principle of authority and spiritual discipline, and drew a clear distinction between Catholicism and 'papism'. In a personal letter to Aksakov he wrote:

It seems to me that you *only* see papism, whereas I see above all great and holy Rome, the eternal city, a fundamental and inseparable part of the universal Church. I believe in this Rome, I venerate it, adore it with all my heart, and with all the powers of my soul desire its regeneration for the sake of the unity and wholeness of the universal Church; let me be cursed as a patricide if ever I cast a word of condemnation at the sanctity of Rome.[1]

In the last article of *The Great Dispute* (entitled 'The General Foundations of the Unification of the Churches') Solov'ëv wrote that Christian policy must primarily be directed towards the restoration of church unity. Each of the two apostolic churches—Orthodoxy and Catholicism—was a universal Church, but only when united with the other and not when steeped in separatist isolationism and mutual hostility. The fusion of the two churches would mark the beginning of the universal unification of all Christian confessions in which the Protestant 'freedom principle' would also have a role to play. Thus would come about a freely realized spiritual unity, the essential precondition of the 'free theocracy'.

It is hardly surprising that Ivan Aksakov found difficulty in making up his mind to publish the last four articles of *The Great Dispute* in his journal. In fact they appeared in a cut version, accompanied by an editorial commentary and the author's replies printed alongside. A year later (in 1884) Aksakov himself was so irritated by Solov'ëv's deliberate anti-nationalism that he attacked him in a very sharp polemical article,[2] in which he wrote:

He who would claim to leap straight into universal brotherhood above the heads of his closest brethren is either a liar, or else a man

[1] Ibid., p. 143.
[2] The immediate reason for Aksakov's article ('Protiv natsional'nogo samoot-recheniya i panteisticheskikh tendentsiĭ, vȳskazavshikhsya v stat'yakh V. S. Solov'ëva') was Solov'ëv's article 'O narodnosti i narodnȳkh delakh Rossii' which

without feeling. . . . The fact that a Russian desires the unification of the Churches is praiseworthy, but in order to arrive at a correct understanding of this problem it is essential first to identify oneself with the spirit of one's own nation. Mr. Solov'ëv is not a universal man [*obshche-chelovek*] and therefore we must remind him of the words of Khomyakov: 'Only the life that does not separate itself from the life of the nation is granted true knowledge.'[1]

Solov'ëv's ecumenical speculations do not, however, explain his collaboration with the liberal positivists, men whose philosophical position must have been entirely alien to him. It is possible that in this instance he was influenced primarily by his desire to make clear his express disapproval of the reactionary nationalism of men like Pobedonostsev and Katkov. The reign of Alexander III was an era of rabid reaction in which no independent thinker could feel at ease. Solov'ëv himself was in fact one of the new era's first victims: his appeal to the new Emperor to pardon his father's assassins as an act of Christian mercy ended his academic career.[2] The emphasis on Russia's superiority to Europe, and the persecution of national and religious minorities were distasteful to the philosopher who had conceived 'Sophia'—the symbol of the universal world-soul or ideal humanity. All these factors combined to force Solov'ëv into taking a stand against the conservative ideologists of chauvinistic nationalism.

The articles Solov'ëv published in the liberal *European Messenger* between 1883 and 1891 became the nucleus of his book on *The National Problem in Russia*. In this he argued that, as a universal, supra-national religion, Christianity precludes all types of nationalism. Nations are organs of humanity destined to serve mankind instead of holding aloof for the sake of their particularist aims and material interests. Nationality should not be confused with nationalism, but bears the same relationship to it as 'personality' does to 'egoism'.[3] There is no

---

put forward the idea of 'national self-denial' in the name of all-humanitarian values. Solov'ëv cited the Petrine reforms as evidence of the fact that such an attitude distinguished the Russian people. The article was later included in Solov'ëv's book *Natsional'nȳ vopros v Rossii*.

[1] Mochulsky, op. cit., p. 145.
[2] Leo Tolstoy also made such an appeal.
[3] See Solov'ëv, *Natsional'nȳ vopros v Rossii* (St. Petersburg 1891), ii. 157.

sense in opposing Russia to Europe, since Russia is part of European civilization.[1] In the course of its history the Russian nation gave two outstanding examples of 'self-denial', of the ability to rise above its national 'exclusivity'; these were the 'calling of the Varangians' and the Petrine reforms.[2] For Solov'ëv this capacity for self-denial was an argument in favour of the conception of Russia as a nation with a universal mission, destined to serve the spiritual unification of mankind. 'By Russian nationality', he wrote, 'I do not mean an ethnic unit with its natural distinctive features or material interests, but a nation which senses that the universal cause of God stands above all distinct features and interests; a nation prepared to devote itself to this cause, a *theocratic* nation by destiny and duty.'[3]

Understandably enough one of the main targets of Solov'ëv's criticism was the theories of Danilevsky, whose political amoralism flatly contradicted Solov'ëv's own ideal of a 'Christianization' of politics. The theory of historico-cultural types ruled out the possibility of a spiritual reunification of mankind, made permanent the differences dividing nations, and contradicted one of Solov'ëv's favourite conceptions of humanity as a 'real collective organism'. As a 'systematized form of Russian nationalism' Slavophilism was not exempt from similar strictures, for although Solov'ëv recognized that classical Slavophilism differed from the chauvinism of the 1880s, he thought that they could be compared to two stages of the same development continuum; an entire article entitled 'Slavophilism and its Degeneration' was devoted to this very point.

In this article Solov'ëv argued that as an ideology Slavophilism was an artificial hybrid of European liberalism on the one hand and Muscovite 'archaeology' or the defence of the 'Asiatic caftan' on the other.[4] The Slavophiles condemned 'Russian sins' and called for the uprooting of evil from the Russian way of life, 'entirely as Europeans', drawing their inspiration from the general treasure-house of European ideas;[5] at the same time, however, they were nationalists who might talk of a 'universal Church' but really meant Russia, and turned religion into an 'attribute of nationality'.[6] Their

---

[1] See ibid. i. 141. [2] See ibid., pp. 25–46. [3] Ibid., p. 100
[4] Ibid. ii. 30–4. [5] Ibid., p. 32. [6] Ibid., p. 36.

criticism of the Western confessions was unjust and un-Christian, since it depended on the contrast between a *real* Catholicism and Protestantism with an *ideal* Orthodoxy that did not in fact exist.[1] The 'Nemesis of Slavophilism', Solov'ëv wrote, was Katkov;[2] he transformed the Slavophiles' idealistic nationalism into a brutal cult of force whose organized expression was the Russian state. He believed in the state with a truly Muslim fanaticism and in practice replaced Christianity with a form of 'rational and political Islamism'.[3] His contemporaries, the 'modern obscurantists' of the age of Alexander III, Solov'ëv dismissed as being at the level of 'zoological nationalism'.[4] The general conclusion of the article runs:

The cult of one's own nation as the chief carrier of the universal truth; followed by the cult of the nation as an elemental force not bound by the universal truth; and finally the cult of those one-sided national features and historical anomalies that divide our nation from the enlightened sections of mankind, i.e. the cult of the nation combined with an open denial of the very idea of universal truth— there you have the three consecutive phases of our nationalism, represented by the Slavophiles, Katkov, and the latest obscurantists. The first were unrealistic dreamers; the second was a realist with imagination; the third are realists without any imagination what-soever, but also entirely without shame.[5]

Solov'ëv drew practical conclusions from his condemnation of reactionary nationalism on religious and philosophical grounds and not only joined the liberal Westernizers in pro-tests against the persecution of the Jews and Russification of the Poles, but also showed considerable courage in his opposition to the policy of 'smothering and swallowing up', of strangling freedom of speech and conscience.[6] Nevertheless his position among his fellow publicists was somewhat peculiar, especially

---

[1] See Solov'ëv, *Natsional'nÿ vopros v Rossii*, ii. 41.

[2] Ibid., p. 80.

[3] Ibid., pp. 81–3.

[4] The only man named in this context was a certain Yarosh, author of an article 'Foreign and Russian critics of Russia' published in Katkov's *Russian Messenger* in January 1889; one of the things that shocked Solov'ëv in this article was the defence of Ivan the Terrible. This suggests that when Solov'ëv wrote of 'con-temporary obscurantists' he was thinking of Katkov's followers, although he tried to distinguish between the latter and Katkov himself. See ibid., p. 91.

[5] Ibid., p. 97.

[6] See ibid. i. 14.

when we consider that his closest collaboration with the liberals coincided with his greatest faith in theocratic utopianism. At the time that he was writing articles for the *European Messenger* he was also working on his *History and Future of Theocracy*, in which—in spite of his severe criticism of Slavophilism—he acknowledged the Slavophiles as his immediate precursors, involuntary prophets of 'free theocracy'. Solov'ëv's utopia, which looked forward to the unification of mankind under the spiritual authority of the pope and the secular authority of the Russian tsar, was certainly not a liberal utopia;[1] nor were his philosophical views in any way influenced by the positivism current among Russian liberals of his day. Although this was a cause of embarrassment to his colleagues on the *European Messenger*, Solov'ëv (in a letter to M. M. Stasulevich in 1888) dismissed their doubts without much ado.

In matters concerning Russian political and social life [he wrote] I have (in recent years) come to feel closest to the line represented by the *European Messenger* and I fail to understand why an intellectual difference of opinion concerning the supra-human sphere should prevent us from co-operating when our immediate aims are identical. On the contrary, experience has convinced me that metaphysical unanimity by no means facilitates co-operation if people desire different things.[2]

An excellent example of the difficulties Solov'ëv's contemporaries had when attempting to define his ideological position is the story of his relations with his ultra-reactionary admirer, Konstantin Leont'ev. Although Solov'ëv broke off relations with the epigones of Slavophilism, this did not involve a break with Leont'ev; in one of his articles attacking the nationalists and defending the priority of the 'ecclesiastical idea' over 'tribal and national aims', he referred to 'the work of the talented and original author of *Byzantinism and Slavdom*'.[3] Leont'ev considered Solov'ëv's collaboration with the liberals

---

[1] This caesaro-papist utopia was expounded in two books published in France (to avoid the censorship): *L'Idée russe* (Paris 1888) and *La Russie et l'église universelle* (Paris 1889). Pope Leo XIII called Solov'ëv's theories a beautiful idea that only a miracle could bring about: 'Bella idea! ma fuor d'un miracolo è cosa impossibile.' See Mochulsky, op. cit., p. 185. Solov'ëv also tried to convert the Croat bishop Strossmayer to his idea.

[2] Mochulsky, op. cit., p. 190.

[3] Solov'ëv, *Natsional'nȳ vopros v Rossii*, i. 32.

a painful misunderstanding but one he was inclined to forgive
in the name of the theocratic ideal; the attacks on Danilevsky
exasperated him, but at least he could console himself that they
were also directed at his pet enemy, 'naked' or 'tribal' nationalism. Moreover, he was personally in sympathy with Solov'ëv's
interest in Roman Catholicism and considered the reunification
of the Churches to be a noble idea, though, as an obedient son
of the Church, he declined to propagate it without the approval
of the Orthodox hierarchy.[1] It was not until Solov'ëv's article
'On the Decline of the Medieval World-View' (1891) that he
finally turned against him. Having convinced himself that
Solov'ëv's interpretation of Christianity was in the spirit of
'liberal and egalitarian progress', Leont'ev's admiration turned
to rancour; he denounced him as 'Satan', a scoundrel, and the
tool of the Antichrist, and in the last years of his life this hatred
became his overriding obsession.[2]

The attempt to define Solov'ëv's position on the variegated
map of Russian intellectual trends during the last quarter of
the nineteenth century encounters many difficulties, unlike
those involved in the interpretation of Slavophile doctrine. In
a sense one might say that Solov'ëv's philosophy belonged to a
no-man's-land—it was not an expression of any particular
ideology nor did it commit those who professed it to a lasting
alliance with any particular persons or trends. If Danilevsky's
doctrinè was (in Solov'ëv's words) 'creeping', then his own
conceptions were only too 'winged'. This description does not
of course remove the difficulties involved in an interpretation
of his work (something this study does not attempt to do), but
merely draws attention to an important aspect of the relations
between Solov'ëv's philosophy and Slavophile doctrine,
namely the problem of the transformation of a *relative* into an
absolute utopia.

Solov'ëv [wrote Mochulsky] did not have his roots in Russian
life; he lacked the strength and wholeness of the Slavophiles. He

---

[1] See Leont'ev's article 'Vladimir Solov'ov protiv Danilevskogo', *Sobr. soch.* vii;
especially pp. 285–90.
[2] Leont'ev thought that Solov'ëv should be banished and called on the clergy
to preach against him; see Mochulsky, op. cit., pp. 152–3, and Berdyaev, op. cit.,
pp. 156–7.

was not in any way a man of the 'soil', or steeped in the traditional way of life of gentry and peasants. In his perception of the world he was 'without family or tribe', a homeless wanderer, a somewhat abstract 'universal man'. His divorce from the soil, from organic elemental forces, surrounds his figure with an aura of spectrality, of immateriality, and weightlessness. He does not penetrate to the heart of reality but glides over its surface like a shadow. He is like someone 'not of this world'.[1]

These comments, formulated in the style of Dostoevsky, require a certain modification: the Slavophiles, who also belonged to the generation of 'superfluous men', were not wholly absorbed in the 'traditional way of life of gentry and peasants', otherwise they would hardly have called for a *return* to this tradition or have idealized it by contrast with existing social realities. This reservation does not, however, alter the fact that the utopianism of the Slavophiles differed essentially from Solov'ëv's utopianism. In a thoroughly sublimated and 'purified' fashion the Slavophile utopia drew its sustenance from a specific *social* mode of existence; Solov'ëv's utopia, on the other hand, was a speculative construct composed of heterogeneous elements and in sociological terms must be called 'unrepresentative'. It is possible to interpret the Slavophile utopia in terms of belonging to a specific class existing in a specific historical situation; a sociological interpretation of Solov'ëv's work, however, would seem to be possible only if we take as our starting-point not the notion of class *affiliation*, but of individual *alienation*, for which compensation is sought in dreams of an absolute and final unification of mankind. The Slavophile utopia could serve as the spring-board for an entirely 'realistic' political creed; Solov'ëv's theocratic utopia became transformed in the last years of his intellectual evolution into an apocalyptic vision and a mystical eschatology.

The 'starry' nature of Solov'ëv's utopia, its total divorce from the 'soil', makes it valueless as a document reflecting a certain historically shaped and objective (supra-individual) thought structure. This aspect, taken together with his ambition to create a philosophical system, determined Solov'ëv's role in the history of the reception of Slavophile ideas in Russia. The discovery of the Slavophiles *as philosophers*, the enormous

[1] Mochulsky, op. cit., p. 145.

influence of Slavophile ideas on Russian philosophy after 1905, was possible only thanks to Solov'ëv. His philosophical contribution allowed future generations to extract from Slavophile doctrine certain philosophical and religious ideas while ignoring not only their 'ancient Russian' utopia, which had lost its appeal in the twentieth century, but also the reactionary political views of the epigones of Slavophilism. Solov'ëv thus became a bridge, as it were, across which the liberal Russian intelligentsia were able to move from 'legal Marxism' to a Slavophile interpretation of Orthodoxy. At the turn of the nineteenth century a group of influential Russian intellectuals, the future authors of the almanac *Vekhi* (*Landmarks*), which proclaimed the abandonment of the revolutionary and materialist traditions of the Russian intelligentsia, underwent an intellectual evolution of this kind—from Marxism via Kantian ideas to Solov'ëv and from Solov'ëv to the Slavophiles.[1] One of the leaders of the group, Nikolaï Berdyaev, wrote thus about the Slavophiles:

Slavophilism was our first attempt at self-knowledge, our first independent ideology. Russia had been in existence for a thousand years, but Russian self-knowledge began at the moment that Ivan Kireevsky and Alexeï Khomyakov had the audacity to ask what Russia is, how to define her essential qualities, her destiny, and her place in the universe. . . . Problems raised by the Slavophiles and their religious solution are still relevant to us, but our generation is very different from the generation of the 1830s and '40s. They were idealists and romanticists, they were influenced by the idyllic and *Schönseeligheit*—whereas it has been our fate to become tragic realists. Our experience of the problem of East and West has been apocalyptic, and we connect it with eschatological premonitions and hopes. The Slavophiles . . . knew nothing of such fears, of this terror, or sense of tragedy; the ground did not tremble under their feet, nor did the earth burst into flames as it did under us.[2]

An analysis of the views of Berdyaev, Bulgakov, Frank, Gershenzon, and the other numerous representatives of the Solov'ëvian neo-Slavophile philosophical movement does not

---

[1] A vivid account of the philosophical path travelled at the turn of the nineteenth century by one of the co-authors of *Vekhi*, later the chief representative of the Khomyakovian and Solov'ëan school of theology, is to be found in S. Bulgakov, *Ot marksizma k idealizmu* (St. Petersburg 1904).

[2] Berdyaev, *A. S. Khomyakov* (Moscow 1912), pp. 2, 28.

fall within the scope of this book. However, in order to avoid misunderstandings, it should be emphasized that in contrast to Solov'ëv the ideas of these thinkers were not even figuratively speaking part of a 'no-man's-land'. They were a sociologically representative ideology, documentary evidence of the final stage in the bourgeois intelligentsia's—or strictly speaking its intellectual élite's—withdrawal towards conservative positions. Under the impact of the mass revolutionary movement they sought refuge in the élitist philosophy of the high priests of an autonomous culture, and—horror-struck—proclaimed the imminence of annihilation or mystical salvation. In the work of these thinkers religious, historiosophical, and epistemological ideas borrowed from Slavophilism were divorced (as in Solov'ëv's system) from the totality of Slavophile doctrine and thus took on a new ideological content and social function.

16

Slavophilism and Populism: Alexander Herzen's 'Russian Socialism'

In this final chapter one significant and controversial problem that remains to be discussed is the relation between the Slavophile and the Populist anti-capitalist utopias. This issue was touched upon in the chapters discussing the views of Konstantin Aksakov, Grigor'ev, and Dostoevsky.[1] The intellectual evolution of Alexander Herzen supplies material for a more detailed analysis, since Herzen might be called a natural link between the Slavophiles and Westernizers of the 1840s and the Populists of the 1860s and '70s.

Among the Westernizers of the 1840s Herzen was the only man who gave the issue of the village commune, raised by the Slavophiles, serious consideration. In this he was no doubt influenced by his utopian socialism, which played a more important role in his ideological evolution than in that of Belinsky, not to mention the other Westernizers. The idea of the commune reached Herzen not only via the Slavophiles but also via his conversations with Haxthausen and Mickiewicz's Paris lectures on Slavonic literature.[2] Herzen's chief informants, however, were the Slavophiles, and it is hardly strange, therefore, that his attitude to the peasant commune affected his attitude to Slavophilism as a whole, which he himself defined as an 'involuntary *juste milieu*'. To the Slavophiles, he wrote, 'I am a man of the West and to their enemies a man of the East.'[3]

Herzen's inner conflict is reflected in his *Diary*, which contains the following passage, dated 20 May 1843:

---

[1] See pp. 276–9, 535, 247–8, 550–1.

[2] 'Mickiewicz', wrote Herzen, 'is a Slavophile like Khomyakov and company, with this difference that he is a Pole and not a Muscovite, that he lives in Europe and not in Moscow, that he is not only concerned with Russia, but also with Czechs, Illyrians, etc. There is no doubt that Slavism has its true and beautiful side; this beautiful aspect of faith in the future is finest in the Poles.' Herzen, ii. 333.

[3] See the quotation on p. 437.

Our Slavophiles talk about the village commune principle, about the fact that we have no proletariat, about the periodic redistribution of arable land—all these are germs of something positive that is partially the result of backwardness. In the same way the property rights of the Bedouins lack the selfish character of European property rights; but on the other hand they [i.e. the Slavophiles] overlook the absolute lack of self-respect, the stupid endurance of all oppression, in a word, the impossibility of living in such conditions. Is it surprising that a sense of private property has not evolved among our peasantry if a peasant's land is not his own land, if even his wife, his daughter, or his son do not belong to him? What kind of property can a slave own? He is worse than a proletarian—he is a *res*, a tool for the cultivation of the land. His master cannot kill him just as in Peter's reign there were certain districts where he could not cut down oak-trees. Give the peasant legal rights and only then will he become a human being. Twelve million people *hors la loi. Carmen horrendum.*[1]

This is probably Herzen's most 'Western' comment on the commune; an entry made less than a year later, in February 1844, shows that he was impressed by Mickiewicz's description of the communal system of the Montenegrins:

The Montenegrins are an example of the furthest evolution of the Slavonic commune. In 1834 the Russian government tried to demoralize them, gave their ruler money, and tried to persuade him to introduce a senate, but nothing came of it; their system is totally democratic—unsophisticated in a patriarchal way, but energetic and strong. Europe is increasingly turning its attention to that mute world called Slavdom; it has many, many surprising things to show us.[2]

Herzen thought by then that the final word on the commune —and therefore by the same token on the historical role of Slavdom—should be left to history. In February 1844 he continues his reflections:

Did we have the right to decide that the future era whose standard proclaims not the individual but the community, not liberty but fraternity—and not an abstract fraternity but the organic distribution of labour—that this era does not belong to Europe? This is the crux of the matter. Will the Slavs, under the fruitful influence of Europe, realize her ideal and incorporate an aged Europe into their

---

[1] Herzen, ii. 288.   [2] Ibid., p. 335.

existence, or will Europe incorporate us into her rejuvenated course?
The Slavophiles make such decisions on the spot, as if the matter
had been settled long ago. It is true that there are certain indications, but the final decision is still far off.[1]

When he wrote these words Herzen could hardly have foreseen that he himself would consider the matter settled only a
few years later and settled, moreover, in line with the Slavophile point of view. The immediate cause of this change of
mind, which had after all been maturing gradually, was the
profound disillusionment—repulsion would not be too strong a
word—he experienced on his first contacts with bourgeois
Europe. In December 1847 he wrote in his *Letters from France
and Italy*: 'Long live the Russian village—it has a great future.'[2]
The events of 1848 reaffirmed Herzen in his pessimistic view of
Europe's future. It seemed to him that the failure of the
revolutions sealed the fate of Europe, that the bourgeoisie was
safely established for many years, and that even Western
socialists had become imbued by bourgeois traits and had
therefore failed to seize their great chance. This left Slavdom—
and above all Russia—as the last hope of mankind: Herzen
came to see Europe as the reincarnation of Rome in its decline,
the European socialists as the persecuted early Christians, and
the Slavs as the barbarians who were destined to destroy the
Roman empire and to make their own contribution to history
while at the same time being standard-bearers of Christian
ideals. This interpretation of history was contained in an
article entitled 'La Russie' (written in the form of an open
letter to Herwegh) which Herzen signed with the pseudonym
'Barbarian'. In an open letter to Mazzini (November 1849) he
tried to convince the Italian leader that Russia ought to conquer
Constantinople: 'The conquest of Constantinople would mark
the beginnings of a new Russia, the beginnings of a Slavonic
federation that would be both *democratic* and *social*.'[3]

Another consequence of Herzen's disillusionment with
Europe and European socialism was the intensification of
voluntaristic elements in his interpretation of history. When he
left Russia Herzen was still a Hegelian—albeit in a very broad
sense of the word; he may have attacked the submission of man

---

[1] Herzen, ii. 336.   [2] Ibid. v. 74.
[3] Ibid. vi. 230.

to the *Weltgeist*, and have put forward a voluntaristic and personalistic interpretation of Hegelianism, but he still retained his faith in the inevitable forward march of history and the rationality of the historical process as a whole. The triumph of the bourgeoisie in 1848—in fact the very existence of the bourgeoisie—undermined his optimism. The fact that the 'social religion' of the aristocracy had been replaced not by the noble faith of socialism but by the mundane and aesthetically repulsive world of shopkeepers seemed to him a glaring denial of historical reason.

History, Herzen came to believe at this time, is an eternal improvisation without an end in view and therefore every generation is an end in itself.[1] The laws of history are not governed by reason, since they are influenced not only by the intellect but also by chance and blind free will. That is why 'the submission of the individual to society, to the people, to humanity, to the Idea—is merely a continuation of human sacrifice, the immolation of the lamb to pacify God, the crucifixion of the innocent for the sake of the guilty'.[2] History makes no sense; like all existence it is both 'the means and the end, the cause and the effect', and if one looks for the final aim 'the purpose of everything living is—death'.[3] In history 'there are no frontiers, no itineraries', ordinary coincidences can interrupt its flow just as death interrupts human life: 'The death of one man is no less absurd than the end of the whole human race.'[4] Therefore, Herzen concluded, man should rely on himself and not on history. 'Man', he wrote, 'is freer than we are apt to think . . . We are standing on the edge of a precipice and we see it crumbling. Twilight descends and no guiding star appears in the sky. We shall find no haven but in ourselves, in the consciousness of our unlimited freedom, our autocratic independence.'[5]

These ideas were developed in Herzen's book *From the Other Shore* (1855). In his preface Herzen wrote that he dedicated the book to his son, since he had written nothing better so far and probably would not write anything better in future.[6] In many

---

[1] Herzen, *From the Other Shore*, trans. by Moura Budberg (Weidenfeld and Nicolson, London 1956), pp. 34, 36, 37.
[2] Ibid., pp. 134-5. [3] Ibid., p. 107. [4] Ibid., p. 40.
[5] Ibid., p. 128. [6] See ibid., p. 3.

respects he was undoubtedly right, since it would be difficult to find a more moving account of a crisis of belief. Today we would say that the theme of the book is the overthrow of all myths. 'Could you please explain to me', Herzen wrote, 'why belief in God is ridiculous and belief in humanity is not? Why belief in the kingdom of heaven is silly, but belief in utopias on earth is clever? Having discarded positive religion we have retained all the habits of religion, and having lost paradise in heaven, we believe in the coming paradise on earth and boast about it.'[1]

Herzen now argued that although history cannot be called 'rational' this does not mean it is at the mercy of the determinism of cause and effect. Only a moralist or sentimentalist would resent history, since whatever happens is clearly necessary. Necessity, on the other hand, should not be confused with 'rationality'; on the contrary, it is often 'unreasonable'. History is in the grip of blind *Naturgewalten* which are necessary in a causal sense, but do not imply any kind of teleological order. History 'rarely repeats herself, . . . she uses every chance, every coincidence, she knocks simultaneously at a thousand gates . . . who knows which may open?'[2] 'The *ultima ratio* of nature and history—of all forms of life—is the eternal restlessness of active tense matter striving for equilibrium only to lose it again.'[3] There is no justification for faith in a bright future guaranteed by the laws of history; to believe in inevitable historical progress is to believe in 'a Moloch who, . . . as a consolation to the exhausted, doomed multitudes crying *"morituri te salutant"*, give back only the mocking answer that after their death all will be beautiful on earth'.[4] Having posed the question what slogans and standards he should now support, Herzen declared simply that he was no longer looking for a standard but instead wished to get rid of the one he had.

Herzen's new philosophy of history rehabilitated Voltaire's individualistic scepticism.[5] His new advice was unambiguous: 'If only people wanted to save themselves instead of saving the world, to liberate themselves instead of liberating humanity, how much they would do for the salvation of the world and the liberation of humanity.'[6]

This pessimistic passage, however, was not Herzen's last

[1] Herzen, *From the Other Shore*, p. 120.   [2] Ibid., p. 34.
[3] Ibid., p. 107.   [4] Ibid., p. 36.   [5] Ibid., p. 139.   [6] Ibid., p. 128.

word. Although he now proclaimed the total destruction of all myths and 'faiths' he was already preparing to take up a new faith—faith in Russia and Slavdom, in 'Russian socialism' based on the village commune idealized by the Slavophiles. Although the foundations of 'Russian socialism' contradicted the extreme scepticism and pessimism of *From the Other Shore* and its clear message of non-commitment, this contradiction should be seen in dialectical terms. Herzen's pessimism was that of a Westernizer who had lost his faith in the future of Europe. In a discussion between a sceptical observer from 'outside' and a disillusioned but emotionally committed idealist, Herzen himself called his own despair 'the whim of a sulky lover'.[1] *Intellectually* he supported the sceptic, but in practice he adopted the position of the idealist whose loss of faith in Europe drove him to place his hopes elsewhere: 'I can see judgment, execution, death, but I can see neither resurrection nor mercy. *This part of the world* has done what it had to do; now its strength is exhausted; the people living in this zone have accomplished their mission, they grow dull, and backward. The stream of history has evidently found another bed—that is where I am going.'[2]

Herzen expounded his conception of 'Russian socialism' in a number of works intended primarily for the Western European reader—'La Russie' (1849), 'Lettre d'un russe à Mazzini' (1849), 'Du développement des idées révolutionnaires en Russie' (1850), 'Le Peuple russe et le socialisme' (Lettre à J. Michelet, 1851), 'To the Editors of the Polish Democrat' (1853, in Polish), 'La Russie et le vieux monde' (Lettres à W. Linton, 1854). In these letters he insisted that Russia was the land of the future and that Western European intellectuals should concentrate their attention on her, just as Tacitus had written his *Germania* when he foresaw the fall of Roman civilization. Although he agreed that Russia's most serious rival for the place vacated by the declining Western civilization was the United States, he dismissed the latter as the mere 'continuation of European development and nothing more', the final conclusion of the republican and philosophical ideas of Europe, 'a young country' but one that had no new 'principle' to contribute to the history of mankind.[3]

---

[1] Ibid., p. 77.   [2] Ibid., p. 78 (italics by A.W.).
[3] Herzen, xii. 136–9.

Herzen's new theory was underpinned by a philosophical and sociological interpretation of Russian history which, like the entire conception of 'Russian socialism', was an attempt at a synthesis of Slavophilism and Westernism, of the Slavophile 'people's principles' with the Westernizing 'idea of the personality'. Another important ingredient was Chaadaev's view of Russia as a country without history. Indeed Herzen's philosophy of history can safely be called an original fusion of elements taken from three philosophical interpretations of Russian history—that of Chaadaev, that of the Slavophiles, and that of the Westernizers of the 1840s (Belinsky, Granovsky, and Kavelin).

Russia's lack of history—the view he had adopted from Chaadaev—was not so much a disadvantage, Herzen suggested, as evidence of her superiority over the West. Russia lacked deeply rooted traditions which could be a source of social conservatism; Russian bureaucratic (non-national) despotism (a 'Napoleonic' despotism Herzen called it) had nothing in common with true conservatism, since it did not defend tradition but destroyed it.[1] On occasion Herzen derived this 'lack of history' from the 'negation of the past' forced through by Peter the Great, but more often he extended his thesis to include pre-Petrine Russia and maintained—like Chaadaev—that no Slavonic nation (with the exception of Poland) had ever been a 'historical' nation and that Slavdom belonged to the domain of geography rather than history.[2] Since the Russian past offered nothing worthy of attachment there was nothing to lose in a social upheaval (it is to be noted that Herzen left the commune outside history).[3] This argument led to the conclusion that socialism, 'the application of logic to statehood',[4] would meet no serious resistance in Russia. In fact, in a travesty of Marx's comment on the proletariat, one might say that in Herzen's view Russia was a proletarian among countries and had nothing to lose but its chains.

From the Slavophiles Herzen took over the view of the village commune as the embryonic stage of a new and higher

---

[1] See Herzen, vii. 290.
[2] See ibid., p. 16.
[3] See ibid., p. 15: 'Nous n'avons qu'à gagner, nous n'avons rien à perdre.'
[4] Ibid., p. 122.

form of society and the conviction that collectivism (which he called the 'socialist element' or even 'communism') was a national characteristic of the Russian people. 'Has not the socialism that divides Europe so deeply and so decisively into two hostile camps been recognized by the Slavophiles just as it has by us? It is a bridge on which we can join hands.'[1] Like the Slavophiles, Herzen stressed that the Russian people had not been affected by the legacy of Roman law and the individualistic view of property relations connected with it;[2] like them he valued the self-government principle of the communes and the unaffected spontaneity of relations between its members, which were not governed by contracts or codified laws.[3] Finally, like the Slavophiles, Herzen believed that the Orthodox faith in Russia was 'more faithful to the teaching of the Gospels than Catholicism',[4] that religious isolation had fortunately enabled the Russian people to avoid the demoralization of Catholicism and to remain apart from the 'sick' civilization of Europe.[5] Thanks to this isolation—that is thanks to Orthodoxy—the common people in Russia had been able to preserve its commune, which in turn had saved it from 'Mongolian barbarism' and the 'imperial civilization', had not given way under the pressure of the authorities, and had happily 'survived to see the emergence of socialism in Europe'.[6]

The Panslavist elements in Herzen's writings at this time, which so irritated Karl Marx and other West European socialists,[7] can also be traced to Slavophile influence. In the 1840s the Slavophiles were not yet Panslavists, although Khomyakov's philosophy of history struck a Panslavist note even then. Herzen's *Diary* (including the passages quoted above) leaves no doubt that Slavophile doctrine was partly

---

[1] Ibid., p. 118.

[2] See ibid. vii. 112, 351; vii. 319.

[3] See ibid. vii. 321, vi. 210.

[4] Ibid. vi. 174. It is worth recalling that for Herzen socialism was the 'fulfilment of Christianity' (see ibid. xii. 135).

[5] See ibid. vi. 175.

[6] Ibid. vii. 288.

[7] In the annexe to the first German edition of *Capital* Marx described Herzen as 'half a Russian but wholly a Muscovite', a man who prophesies that 'Europe needs rejuvenating with the help of the knout and a compulsory injection of Calmuck blood'. Quoted from *Perepiska K. Marksa i F. Engelsa s russkimi politicheskimi deyatelyami* (Moscow 1951), p. 293. In later editions of *Capital* these words were removed.

responsible for his belief in the 'new word' to be given to the world by the Slavonic peoples.

Towards the end of his article 'La Russie et le vieux monde' Herzen argued that by engaging in the war with Turkey Nicholas I was realizing 'the hidden aims of history':

> The hour of the Slavonic world has struck. The *Taborite*, the man of the village commune, is straightening his back. Is it socialism that has awakened him? Where will he plant his standard? Towards what centre of gravity will he be drawn?
>
> Neither Vienna, the German rococo city, not St. Petersburg, the new German city, nor Warsaw, a Catholic city, nor Moscow, an exclusively Russian city, can lay claim to be the capital of the united Slavs. This capital can only be Constantinople, the Rome of the Eastern Church, the main centre of the Graeco-Slavonic world, a city surrounded by Slavonic and Hellenic populations.
>
> The Teuto-Latin nations represent a continuation of the western empire; will the Slavonic world become a continuation of the eastern empire? I cannot tell, but Constantinople will surely slay St. Petersburg.[1]

These words were written in London on 20 February 1854 (8 February O.S.). At this very time (6–18 February) Konstantin Aksakov had just finished his memorial *On the Eastern Question*, in which he called for the conquest of Constantinople in the name of 'the people's principles' embodied by Russia and Slavdom.[2] Although the similarity of content and dates is by no means accidental, the fundamental difference should be noted that Aksakov's memorial marked the *beginnings* of Slavophile Panslavism, whereas Herzen's article was the *last* sign of his belief that the tsarist empire might be capable of realizing the 'hidden aims of history'.[3] After the Crimean War Slavophile Panslavism became transformed into chauvinist nationalism, whereas 'Russian socialism' became the ideology of the Populist agrarian revolution.

When we come to analyse further the historiosophical foundations on which Herzen's 'Russian socialism' is based, Westernizing elements are also seen to play an important part. If Russia was to seize its historical chance, Herzen's argument

---

[1] Herzen, xii. 165.   [2] See pp. 496–7.
[3] This expression was of course a clear contradiction of the philosophy of history underlying *From the Other Shore*, with its rejection of all providentialism.

ran, she needed an active force capable of awakening the 'Taborite' and of breathing new life into the static and patriarchal village commune. This force was the 'principle of individualism' embodied for the first time by Peter the Great, the 'revolutionary tsar who had denied tradition and nationality'.[1] This was a clear reference to Belinsky's view that the Petrine reforms had contributed a dynamic element to Russian reality and to Kavelin's interpretation of Peter's reforms as 'the first phase in the realization of the principle of personality in Russian history'.[2] Throughout the eighteenth century, Herzen argued, the tsarist system exerted a civilizing influence and encouraged the emancipation of the personality by creating à Europeanized upper layer of society which at first supported the government and later became hostile to it. The turning-point was the Decembrist rising: from that time on bureaucratic despotism in Russia became an unmistakably reactionary force. This meant that the new carrier of the 'personality principle' was the enlightened gentry and educated middle class,[3] with whom Herzen again identified the 'superfluous men'. 'To a greater or lesser degree,' he wrote, 'we are all Onegins, if we do not wish to be *officials* or *landowners*.'[4] The reason for this, he thought, was that since Peter's reign Russian education had been 'definitely universalistic in character'. 'Our upbringing is utterly remote from the milieu for which it is intended, and that constitutes its value. In Russia education uproots a young man from the immoral soil, humanizes him, transforms him into a civilized being, and places him in opposition to official Russia.'[5] The universality of his intellectual horizon, and his divorce from the soil, were responsible for the fact that 'the thinking Russian is the freest man in the world';[6] thanks to this freedom, which was the obverse of alienation, the Russian intelligentsia contained within itself 'the germ and intellectual centre of gravity of the future revolution'.

The future of Russia thus depended on whether it would prove possible to fuse the people's 'communism' with the 'personality principle' represented by the intelligentsia, or, in other

[1] Herzen, xii. 156. [2] See p. 407.
[3] See Herzen, vii. 297.
[4] Ibid., p. 74 (Herzen described Onegin as 'un homme superflu').
[5] Ibid. ii. 155.
[6] Ibid. vii. 332.

words, 'to preserve the commune' and at the same time to 'liberate the individual'.[1] In Herzen's eyes this amounted in fact to fusing native Russian principles with European achievements, with the liberty of the individual that was most strongly established in the Anglo-Saxon countries. 'The Anglo-Saxon nations', he wrote, 'have liberated the individual at the cost of his isolation, and by annihilating the community; the Russian nation has preserved the community principle but at the cost of the negation of individuality, of the total absorption of the individual human unit.'[2]

The motto of 'Russian socialism', which was to 'preserve the community while liberating the individual' was essentially a new formulation of Herzen's long-standing concern with the problem of achieving freedom without alienation, of reconciling a sense of autonomy with a sense of 'belonging'. Although it is important to emphasize this continuity, it should be noted that whereas in the 1840s Herzen postulated the reconciliation of the particular with the universal, of individualism with universalism, and of nature (the sphere of the particular) with logic (the sphere of impersonal universal laws), in the doctrine of Russian socialism individualism was treated not as the antithesis, but as the product of universalism. The chief goal now became the fusion of individualism (and universalism) with the ideal of community conceived as a bond with a concrete collective such as the Russian village commune. We may safely assume, however, that in both instances Herzen was concerned with satisfying the same psychological need.

Another similarity between Herzen's 'Russian socialism' and his earlier philosophical views is that both represent a revolt against a teleological conception of historical necessity, against the so-called 'objective laws of development' that force individuals and nations to move along a predestined path. In the 1840s this revolt was directed against the *supra-human* (and therefore *inhuman*) laws of the Hegelian *Weltgeist*, whereas later it was directed rather against the 'iron laws of political economy' which gave their stamp of approval to capitalism as a *necessary* phase of economic progress. The rational justification of this revolt was Herzen's argument that 'neither nature, nor history

---

[1] See Herzen, xii. 156: 'Conserver la commune et rendre l'individu libre'.
[2] Ibid.

is going in any particular direction and they are therefore ready to go anywhere they are told *provided it is possible*, in other words provided no obstacles stand in the way'.[1] Herzen's voluntaristic philosophy of history, with its stress on the conscious selection of goals and decisive action with a chosen end in view, was not, however, the only argument in favour of his 'Russian socialism'. The other constituent of the new doctrine was belief in Russia's 'distinctiveness' which ascribed a special virtue to Russia's 'separate' development and in particular to the institution of the village commune as an objective basis for a non-capitalist economic system. Both arguments were later taken over from Herzen by the theorists of Populism; the Populists' 'subjective sociology' stressed the role of consciousness and free will as opposed to 'historical necessity' (that is the necessity of passing through a capitalist phase), while the Populists' version of the doctrine of Russia's 'distinctiveness' was based on their conviction that in the objective conditions obtaining in Russia capitalism would be 'artificial' or even—in the long run—impossible. Populist economists in the 1870s and '80s (V. Flerovsky, V. Vorontsov, and N. Danielson) attempted to prove this thesis with the aid of a detailed analysis of the Russian economy.

Herzen's faith in Russia's 'distinctiveness', on the other hand, was supported largely by arguments of a historiosophical nature, which brought out clearly the connection between the Populist and Slavophile utopias. Herzen was conscious of his debt to the Slavophiles and retrospectively even idealized their role, especially after the death of the founders of the movement. In his 'Evolution of Revolutionary Ideas in Russia' (1850) his attitude to Slavophilism, was still fairly critical; although he accepted the Slavophiles as 'socialists' he discussed the controversies of the 1840s rather from the point of view of 'Belinsky and his friends'. His subsequent *rapprochement* with Slavophilism was influenced primarily by the liberal Westernizers' negative attitude to the village commune, which emerged in discussions on the projected land reforms. In his article 'Russian Germans and German Russians' (1859) Herzen did not hesitate to admit that he had changed his mind. 'We have become much closer to the Moscow Slavs', he wrote, 'than to all the species of

[1] Herzen, *My Past and Thoughts*, iv. 287.

Western Old Believers and Russian Germans.'[1] He was not put off by Koshelëv's emphatic statement made two years earlier (in 1857), in reply to a similar approach by Chernyshevsky, that the Slavophile view of the peasant commune had nothing in common with socialism.[2] In his lengthy and extraordinarily warm obituary notice on the death of Konstantin Aksakov, Herzen declared that 'the turning-point in Russian thought' began with the Slavophiles.[3] Under the immediate impression of Aksakov's posthumous *Comments* on the proposed land reforms, he even went so far as to suggest that their author 'would not have borne emancipation *by the birch* . . . he would have thrown himself into the ranks of the peasants'.[4] Even if we take into account that this comment concerned the most devoted utopian idealist among the Slavophiles it is, certainly, an indication of a far-going, idealization of Slavophilism. It is one of the ironies of history that the man who conceived the 'Russian socialist' utopia began to idealize the Slavophile utopia at the very moment that the Slavophiles themselves were about to abandon it.

Herzen's illusions about the Slavophiles were not dispelled until 1864, and then only partially. The circumstances and statements accompanying this event deserve a more detailed account as a most illuminating episode in the history of Russian social thought. In July 1864 Samarin, who was on a visit to England, expressed the wish to meet the editor of the *Bell*. This was just after the Polish uprising of 1863 which had brought about a final polarization of standpoints. (Herzen committed himself to support for the rebels while Samarin provided the ideological inspiration for the tsarist government's hate-

---

[1] Herzen, xiv. 160. Herzen even expressed the characteristic fear lest 'Western doctrinaire thinkers' (i.e. Chicherin, Babst, Vernadsky, and others) 'put the Emperor on a false track' (ibid., p. 185).

[2] See p. 465. Koshelëv rejected an 'alliance with the socialists', since he was afraid this might have an unfortunate influence on the government's attitude to the village commune; see N. P. Kolupanov, *Biografiya A. I. Koshelëva* (Moscow 1889–92), ii. 389. At the same time, however, he acknowledged the superiority of the socialists over the bourgeois liberals: 'The socialists' irrefutable merit is that they emphasize the lack of community spirit in European life'; 'Communism and socialism, temporarily defeated, are much stronger than their opponents.' Quoted from P. Sakulin, *Russkaya literatura i sotsializm*, 2nd ed. (Moscow 1924), part 1, p. 491.

[3] Herzen, xv. 9.

[4] Ibid., p. 120.

inspired campaign against Poland.) Herzen nevertheless was
not only delighted to agree to a meeting but even expressed the
conviction—in a letter to Samarin on 12 July 1864—that the
differences dividing them were essentially of minor importance:
'What are they concerned with? Orthodoxy? Let us leave what
is eternal to the other world. Sincere and holy love for the
Russian people, the Russian cause? In that sphere I yield
neither to you nor to all the Aksakovs.'[1]

The meeting took place, but even after the first seven-hour-
long discussion Herzen realized what he should have known
before, namely that Samarin was the 'Robespierre of the
monarchy'—an uncompromising and convinced opponent of
the political line of the *Bell*. The two following political discussions were even more heated and unpleasant. Nevertheless
Herzen did not agree with Samarin that their standpoints had
always been diametrically opposed. In his *Letters to an Opponent*
published six months later in the *Bell* he wrote as follows:

True enough, it would be difficult to imagine two men whose entire
moral make-up, and holiest of holies, whose ideals and searchings,
hopes and convictions are so utterly contrasted as yours and mine
. . . we belong to different worlds, different countries, and yet
nevertheless both you and I *serve the same cause*, are sincerely devoted
to it, and believe each other to be so.

By different roads we have arrived at *one point* which is a link
between us. I know that you will not admit it is possible to arrive
at the truth by different roads, but the facts are against you.[2]

So far from being sharply polemical in tone, the *Letters to an
Opponent* are pervaded by an elegiac melancholy. In them
Herzen once more looks back on his past, and once more
admits that he was mistaken in his earlier controversies with
the Slavophiles.[3] Only after his departure to the West, on the
ruins of the French Republic, had he come to advance ideas
that Khomyakov and the Kireevsky brothers had upheld in the
1840s;[4] this change of opinion, he admitted sadly, had not led
to a *rapprochement* with the Slavophiles, for they too had changed
their positions and had become 'defenders of German conceptions of the state';[5] moreover the Polish uprising was an insurmountable barrier between them. In conclusion he made a

[1] Ibid. xxvii. 390.   [2] Ibid. xvii. 275.   [3] See ibid., p. 274.
[4] See ibid., p. 279.   [5] Ibid., p. 276.

final appeal to the Slavophiles: 'Religion does not consist solely of *intolerance* and *persecution*. Why is that all you have taken from it?'[1]

The year 1864 opened a difficult period in Herzen's life for his support for the Poles cost him the enormous influence he had yielded in Russia until recently. He was rejected not only by old friends such as Turgenev and Kavelin, but also by Samarin, the representative of the idealized Slavophiles. At the same time the new young revolutionaries, especially the group known as the 'young *émigrés*', began to accuse him of vacillation, liberalism, and an aristocratic life-style.[2] These harsh accusations published in a pamphlet by A. Serno-Solov'ëvich, led to a complete break between them and Herzen. All these factors, taken in conjunction with the success of the labour movement in Western Europe, led Herzen to revise his views once more in the last year of his life, to abandon his 'Russian socialist utopia', and to put his hopes in the Socialist International (*Letters to an Old Friend*, 1869). Concretely this meant (1) a revival of Herzen's faith in Europe and a corresponding loss of faith in the idea of Russia's special mission; (2) the abandonment of his belief in the necessity and advisability of a great revolutionary cataclism in favour of a more gradual, evolutionary conception of progress; and (3) a partial return to an interpretation of history that laid stress on the necessity and inner 'logic' of the historical process.

It is one of the peculiar paradoxes of history that Herzen gave up his theory of 'Russian socialism' just as it was beginning to become influential in the Russian revolutionary movement. The year 1869, when, in Lenin's words, he 'turned his gaze to the International',[3] also saw the publication in Russia of Lavrov's *Historical Letters* and Mikhailovsky's *What is Progress?*, two works directly influenced by Herzen's ideas which were to mark the beginning of widespread interest in the anti-capitalist utopia of the Populists.

As has already been mentioned, Herzen's 'Russian socialism'

[1] Herzen, xvii. 296.

[2] See B. P. Koz'min, 'Gertsen, Ogarëov i "molodaya emigratsiya"', in *Iz istorii revolyutsionnoĭ mȳsli v Rossii* (Moscow 1961). The pamphlet by Serno-Solovovich, published in 1867, was entitled *Nashi domashnie dela*.

[3] See Lenin, *In Memory of Herzen* (*Collected Works*, xviii. 27).

represented a peculiar synthesis of the two utopias of the 1840s —the conservative utopia of the Slavophiles and the liberal 'super-bourgeois' utopia of the Westernizers. These mixed origins meant that 'Russian socialism' contained several heterogeneous and mutually exclusive elements. Herzen's comparison of Slavophilism and Westernism to the two faces of Janus has already been quoted a number of times in this book;[1] one might extend this comparison by pointing out that in conceiving the doctrine of 'Russian socialism' Herzen himself became transformed into a two-faced Janus and for that very reason became the spiritual father of Populism. After all, it was the Populists whom Lenin described as a 'Janus in matters of theory', looking with one face to the past and the other to the future'.[2]

Herzen's socialism, with its idealization of a pre-capitalist, natural economy of small producers suited the backward-looking Janus. Herzen's hatred of capitalism sprang in a large measure from a dislike of industrialization and urbanization as such. He gave vent to this dislike in such comments as 'the heyday of industry is over; like the era of aristocratic splendour it has outlived its day';[3] or in his description of great cities, like London, as 'absurdities', which ignored the absence of danger from feudal attacks and improvements in transport;[4] or in his insistence that Russia was the land of the future just because its relation to the West was that of a village to a town.[5] The evidently 'petty-bourgeois' nature of this kind of socialism was bound up with a hatred towards the petty bourgeoisie in capitalist societies and with an idealization of pre-capitalist social relations. In Herzen's eyes capitalism was a step backwards. 'The man of the future in Russia is the peasant',[6] he wrote, thus revealing his failure to understand that in spite of the survival of the commune the peasant economy after the reforms was 'just the ordinary petty-bourgeois mode of life'.[7] *Mutatis mutandis* (and taking into account the fact that Herzen was not an economist nor Sismondi a revolutionary)

[1] See pp. 20, 394, 452.   [2] Lenin, *Collected Works*, i. 503.
[3] Herzen, vi. 57.
[4] See ibid. xiv. 174.
[5] See ibid., pp. 172–3.
[6] Ibid. vii. 291.
[7] See Lenin, *Collected Works*, ii. 224.

one might apply to Herzen's socialism the phrase 'economic romanticism' Lenin used to describe Sismondi's ideas. These express a 'reactionary *petty bourgeois* point of view', Lenin wrote but emphasized that this must not be understood to mean that Sismondi defended the 'backward petty bourgeoisie'. 'Nowhere does Sismondi *defend them*; he wants to take the point of view of the labouring classes in general . . . his point of view is exactly the same as that of the modern Populists.' His theory was petty bourgeois because 'he does not understand the connection between petty commodity production (which he idealizes) and big capital (which he attacks)', because 'he *does not see* that his beloved small producer, the peasant, is in reality becoming a petty bourgeois.'[1]

It is worth recalling that in 1862 Ivan Turgenev, that uncompromising Westernizer, reproached Herzen with making a similar mistake. The Russian peasant, he wrote, has the makings of 'a bourgeois in a tanned sheepskin', much more repulsive than the Western European bourgeoisie criticized by Herzen.[2]

The doctrine of 'Russian socialism' enabled Herzen to combine a romantic and essentially conservative critique of capitalism with a belief in democracy and revolution, but at the same time created new difficulties which could only be apparently resolved, in the realm of pure theory. It is clear that the ideal of the autonomous personality, which Herzen upheld against the Slavophiles in the 1840s and against bourgeois Europe in the 1850s, was itself a product of capitalism and of European civilization (something that Herzen himself admitted), and could not be reconciled with pre-capitalist forms of production and social relations. This was responsible for a certain ambivalence in Herzen, particularly obvious after 1848. The man who (in *From the Other Shore*) passed judgement on the West from the point of view of the individual, conscious of 'his unlimited freedom, his autocratic independence', was not the same man who contrasted the Russian village commune with European capitalism and openly expressed his support for the Moscow Slavophiles.

---

[1] See Lenin, *Collected Works*, ii. 221.
[2] See *Pis'ma K. Dm. Kavelina i Iv. S. Turgeneva k Al. Iv. Gertsenu*, ed. by M. Dragomanov (Geneva 1892), pp. 160–2.

A similar ambivalence can easily be traced in the Populist theories of the 1870s and '80s.[1] According to the importance they ascribed to the 'individual' or to the 'people', they can be divided (on a purely conventional basis) into ideologies leaning more towards a 'Slavophile' or a 'Westernizing' point of view. At one pole there is Lavrov, with his theory of 'critically thinking individuals' and at the other such Right-wing Populists as Yuzov, who defended not only the 'interests' but also the 'opinions' of the people and criticized the intelligentsia in a truly Slavophile spirit. A most interesting example of the co-existence of both aspects of Populism is to be found in the ideas of Mikhailovsky. At the centre of Mikhailovsky's system of values was the autonomous individual on whose behalf he proclaimed 'a struggle for individuality' against all collective individualities ready to 'swallow up' the individual human being and against all 'objective laws of development' attempting to reduce it to a passive tool of history. At the same time Mikhailovsky went further than anyone else in his idealization of primitive communities, was delighted at all signs of a romantic idealization of the Middle Ages in the socialist movement, and was not afraid to declare in public that—as in the folk legend of a 'golden age'—his ideal was to be found in the past.[2]

Mikhailovsky was aware that his views were open to the charge of being mutually contradictory, and in his own defence argued that under capitalism the individual had far less autonomy than in the past and that bourgeois 'individualism' was in fact directed against the individual whom it subordinated to a 'system of maximum production'.[3] True individualism, according to this novel sociological theory, implies the

[1] This requires a certain qualification: In Herzen's world-view *personality*—the chief value of the liberal-democratic utopia of the 1840s—carried greater weight than it did in the world-view of the later ideologists of Populism. The Populists of the 1870s were ready to sacrifice the freedom of the individual for the sake of a solution to the 'social question'; with certain representatives of the Populist intelligentsia, and in particular with the 'conscience-stricken gentry' (which included Mikhailovsky) this took the form of a masochistic temporary 'abdication' of political freedom on the grounds that this was not desired or greatly needed by the people. For Herzen this attitude would have been inconceivable; he never gave up his conviction that 'the liberty of the individual is the greatest thing of all; it is on this and on this alone that the true will of the people can develop'. *From the Other Shore*, p. 12.

[2] See N. K. Mikhailovsky, *Poln. sobr. soch.* (St. Petersburg 1909), iii. 722; and *Sochineniya* (1896), i. 432–3.   [3] Mikhailovsky, *Sochineniya*, i. 430–45.

all-round development and self-sufficiency of the individual, and its independence of the social organism; as a system requiring a highly developed division of labour transforming the individual into the subordinate 'organ' of a powerful production apparatus, capitalism is therefore the greatest enemy of individuality. The most favourable conditions for the evolution of the personality are provided by a craftsmen's artel or a peasant commune founded on 'simple co-operation'. The peasant who, in a natural economy, is not dependent on the division of labour and can satisfy all his needs by himself, represents a higher 'type' of personality, more independent and many-sided, in spite of his low place on the ladder of economic development, and is therefore a natural ally of the intelligentsia in its 'struggle for individuality'. This theory precluded the synthesis of the 'communism' of the Russian peasant with the individualism of the Anglo-Saxon peoples; unlike Herzen Mikhailovsky accused the latter of exaggerated *anti-individualism* and insisted that so far from interfering with the flowering of the individual the village commune in fact helped to form a superior 'type of individuality'.

Thus Mikhailovsky's version of Populism represented a total acceptance of the pre-capitalist and pre-industrial type of society. It would however be rash to suggest that in this way the divided nature of Populism was overcome. A detailed analysis of Mikhailovsky's views (which cannot be undertaken here) would show that in his case too the petty-bourgeois socialism of the Populists was a doctrine combining conservatism with progressive ideas, and the idealization of the past with radical bourgeois democracy. In spite of Mikhailovsky's own protests, it is clear that in his case too the notion of 'personality', on whose behalf he opposed Russian capitalism, was ultimately a by-product of that very same capitalist evolution in Europe and Russia. It is this that Lenin had in mind when he wrote: 'When Mr. Mikhailovsky begins his 'sociology' with the 'individual' who protests against Russian capitalism as an accidental and temporary deviation from the right path, he defeats his own purpose because he does not realize that it was capitalism alone that created the conditions which made possible this protest of the individual.'[1]

[1] Lenin, *Collected Works*, i. 415.

No serious comparative study has so far dealt with the mutual relationship of the two main anti-capitalist utopias in Russia. No doubt this is due to the lack of evidence of any widespread Slavophile influence on the Populist leaders, and even more to the fact that the two groupings never engaged in any kind of joint political action. A different situation obtained in Germany, where anti-bourgeois alliances between the conservatives and the socialists were frequent in the 1860s, and social and economic doctrines combining conservative inspiration with a specific brand of 'socialism' flourished with an unusual vigour not found elsewhere.[1] The reasons for this difference, it would seem, are to be sought not so much in the ideology of the Russian Populists, as in the political conditions that made legal activities impossible for them and therefore forced them to concentrate on revolutionary struggle. The anti-liberal prejudice, characteristic of the majority of Populists, their view that constitutional and parliamentary forms of government were merely tools of the detested 'plutocracy',[2] was, of course, shared by the Slavophiles and their followers among the conservatives; however, the day-to-day political struggle convinced the Populists that their chief enemy was the tsarist system and that any kind of alliance with the defenders of autocracy was out of the question.

Another factor that prevented the infiltration of Slavophile ideas into Populism was a clearly defined difference in cultural traditions. The progressive Russian intelligentsia founded new traditions of its own, beginning with Belinsky and culminating in the rationalist atmosphere of the 1860s. Samarin once stated bitterly: 'For the generation educated by Belinsky, the *Annals of the Fatherland*, the *Contemporary*, etc., we and our milieu simply do not exist.'[3] The openly anti-scientific and religious form of the Slavophile utopia was bound to repel the 'thinking realists' who had been brought up on Chernyshevsky, Dobrolyubov, and Pisarev. The situation began to change in the 1870s, with the intelligentsia's abandonment of its one-sided faith in science

[1] See G. D. H. Cole, *A History of Socialist Thought* (London 1957), vol. ii: *Marxism and Anarchism 1850–1890*, chapters 2, 5, and 10.

[2] See G. Eliseev, 'Plutokratiya i eë osnovy' (1872), reprinted in *Narodnicheskaya ekonomicheskaya literatura* (Moscow 1958), pp. 125–60.

[3] Quoted from Dement'ev, *Ocherki po istorii rusoskoĭ zhurnalistiki 1840–1850*, p. 404.

(compromised by its connections with bourgeois apologists of capitalism), the renewed and more widespread interest in historical and ethical questions, and—above all—the unprecedented spread of the romantic idealization of the common people. This was noted by Mikhailovsky when he wrote (in 1877) of the new but *wasted* opportunities facing the Slavophiles (the 'true' Slavophiles, of course, and not the Panslavists).[1] However even when the slogan of 'merging with the people' was most influential, the classical Slavophiles' 'people's utopia' was not capable of interesting the Populist leaders to any extent. The economic writings of Karl Marlo (Winkelblech) and above all Rodbertus (German conservatives with 'socialist' leanings)[2] were widely read among the Populists, while Kireevsky and Khomyakov were not, and the main source of information about the Russian village commune continued to be the work of the Prussian conservative, Baron von Haxthausen.

The epigones of Slavophilism (as Mikhailovsky pointed out) also let slip the chance of arriving at an understanding with the Populists, and, on the contrary, moved even further away from the anti-capitalist spirit of the Slavophile utopia. Apart from the other reasons, this was a response not only to the revolutionary ideas and atheism of the majority of Populists but also (and above all) to the social character of the Populist movement. The English and German 'feudal socialists' could appeal to the industrial proletariat in the name of a common struggle against their common enemy—the bourgeoisie; this was possible because the proletariat in their countries saw its direct antagonist in the bourgeoisie, and not in the feudal aristocracy. The situation in Russia was quite different: in spite of its anti-capitalist ideology the Russian Populist movement was primarily an anti-feudal movement and as such it could not find supporters among the landowning nobility represented by Samarin, Koshelëv, and Ivan Aksakov.

Under the circumstances even more significance must be

[1] See Mikhailovsky, *Poln. sobr. soch.* iii. 856–7 (article on Danilevsky's *Russia and Europe*).

[2] Marlo was quoted as an authority by both Mikhailovsky and Eliseev (in the article 'Plutokratiya i eë osnovȳ'); Rodbertus exerted a considerable influence on the young Plekhanov, who published a lengthy essay on him in 1882. See Plekhanov, *Sochineniya*, i. 216–364.

attached to every piece of evidence showing that nevertheless certain Slavophile ideas penetrated Populist ideology and that some leading theorists of the Populist movement understood the anti-capitalist nature of the Slavophile utopia and were favourably disposed towards Slavophilism. Evidence of this kind to which attention has been drawn includes the undoubtedly Slavophile inspiration of the ideas of Shchapov and Eliseev, certain pronouncements made by Chernyshevsky, and the Populists' attitude to Dostoevsky. The most important historical argument, however, in favour of the thesis that Slavophilism stood in a 'meaningful relationship' to Populism is provided by the intellectual evolution of Alexander Herzen. The thinker who created the foundations of Populist doctrine was conscious of his debt to the Slavophiles. His theory of 'Russian socialism' formed a bridge linking the 'enlightened gentry' of the reign of Nicholas (which included both the Slavophiles and most of the Westernizers) with the non-noble intelligentsia of the second half of the century. For the historian of ideas it is an ideal laboratory example illustrating the connection between Populism and the Slavophile/Westernizer controversy of the 1840s.

Although a comparative study of Slavophilism or Populism and of similar trends in other countries does not fall within the scope of this book, it seems appropriate to point out the value of such a study not only for a better understanding of Russian intellectual history, but also for the general typology of anti-capitalist ideologies and their accompanying backward-looking utopias.[1] As an underdeveloped peasant country within the orbit of capitalist civilization, faced by the need to take certain basic decisions regarding its future, nineteenth-century Russia seems to provide particularly rich material for the researcher in this field.

---

[1] It might be said that the relation between the Populists and the Slavophiles recalls the relation between Cobbett and Burke; see R. Williams, *Culture and Society 1780–1950* (New York 1958), pp. 3–20.

Index